Innovative Practices

University of California, Berkeley

Englewood Cliffs, New Jersey

Library of Congress Cataloging in Publication Data

RUDDELL, ROBERT B
 Reading-language instruction: innovative practices.

 Includes bibliographies.
 1. Language arts. 2. Reading. I. Title.
LB1576.R78   372.6   72-12978
ISBN 0-13-753285-7

Reading-Language Instruction: Innovative Practices,
by Robert B. Ruddell

Copyright © 1974 by Prentice-Hall, Inc., Englewood Cliffs, N.J.

Printed in the United States of America
10   9   8   7   6   5   4   3   2   1

PRENTICE-HALL INTERNATIONAL, INC., *London*
PRENTICE-HALL OF AUSTRALIA, PTY. LTD., *Sydney*
PRENTICE-HALL OF CANADA, LTD., *Toronto*
PRENTICE-HALL OF INDIA PRIVATE LIMITED, *New Delhi*
PRENTICE-HALL OF JAPAN, INC., *Tokyo*

To Annette Arnold Ruddell,
Amy Rebecca Ruddell, and Robert Thomas Ruddell

Contents

8

SPEECH INTERACTION ROUTINES, WRITING CONVENTIONS, AND HANDWRITING: CLASSROOM DEVELOPMENT 239

9

NONSTANDARD DIALECTS AND SECOND LANGUAGE LEARNING: THE INSTRUCTIONAL PROGRAM 263

10

DECODING INSTRUCTION AND SPELLING STRATEGIES: UNDERSTANDING THE CODE 292

11

READING-LISTENING COMPREHENSION: LEVELS, SKILL COMPETENCIES, AND QUESTIONING STRATEGIES 361

16

TUTORS, TEACHING ASSISTANTS, AND PARENT EDUCATION:
A PROGRAM OF INVOLVEMENT   577

CRITERIA FOR EVALUATING READING SYSTEMS   621

AUTHOR INDEX   629

SUBJECT INDEX   634

Preface

This volume is designed specifically for the preservice and inservice classroom teacher who wishes to improve reading-language instruction. It incorporates the latest trends, research findings, and discipline-related knowledge into a communication framework which is the basis for instructional decision making in the classroom. Throughout the text a wide range of innovative practical ideas and experiences illustrate and model strategies for effective reading-language instruction. These ideas and experiences have been extensively field-tested in real classrooms.

The term *reading-language instruction* reflects the inseparable relationship between children's reading and language development. For example, emphasis on concept development through experiences in the home and early childhood education curriculum will directly enhance the child's reading and listening comprehension ability. His control and understanding of language will help him validate decoding through meaning in sentence and story contexts. Expressing his life experiences through oral and written language forms will help him develop an understanding of key components of story organization, which in turn will be of value in interpretative aspects of reading. Throughout this book the interrelated nature of communication skills instruction is emphasized.

The discussion has been organized to facilitate reader self-direction and instructional planning. Focusing questions at the beginning of each chapter are designed to help the reader establish a "set" for interaction with the discussion. These questions should also be valuable in initiating small-group discussions and idea exchange with fellow students.

Photographs and observational checklists throughout the book illustrate important concepts and encourage the reader to interact with the classroom environment. Direct involvement is critical to the development of teacher competencies for effective reading-language instruction. Use of the observational checklists will help the reader develop skill in evaluating the progress of individual children in the instructional setting. Charts and graphs illustrate classroom practices and summarize parts of the discussion.

It is of central importance that the discussion and the various instructional aids be used in conjunction with real children at a local school site. Only then can the reader derive the greatest value from the model teaching behavior and instructional strategies developed in the text.

A collection of readings entitled *Resources in Reading-Language Instruction* (Prentice-Hall, Inc., 1973) is also available for use with this volume. The chapters in the readings resource parallel the discussion in the text and serve four purposes: first, to illuminate issues and trends that directly affect the preservice and inservice professional development of teachers; second, to identify a knowledge base stemming from key disciplines and research having significant import to reading and language instruction; third, to derive from this knowledge base implications for classroom practice; and fourth, to present practical ideas for classroom instruction which relate directly to the discipline and research framework. The readings collection has potential value for graduate reading courses which follow the basic preservice preparation experience.

The book is organized to facilitate reader self-direction and instructional planning. In capsule form, the text is organized as follows:

Understanding of the role of the reading-language teacher, including background and applied knowledge, and understanding of and interaction with the child, parent, community, and school personnel (Chapter 1)

Integration of knowledge from reading-language-related disciplines into a communication framework for instructional decision making in the classroom (Chapter 2)

Development of an overview of our spoken and written language systems from their genesis to the present, with specific recommendations for introducing language concepts in the classroom (Chapter 3)

Summary of the development of children's language with implications for instructional practice (Chapter 4)

Critical overview of a wide range of reading-language programs with illustrations from currently used instructional programs (Chapter 5)

Formulation of instructional approaches to develop oral and written communication competencies and performances (description, narration, and exposition), using the child's experiential background as the basis of instruction (Chapters 6 and 7)

Development of both oral and written language interaction routines and handwriting with instructional approaches for the classroom (Chapter 8)

Description of nonstandard and second-language-related dialects of inner-city children (black, Chicano, and Chinese), with specific suggestions for developing appreciation of varied language forms and adding standard English to children's language repertoire (Chapter 9)

Formulation of decoding and spelling strategies based on recent linguistic and psychological knowledge, with suggestions for sequencing and developing the decoding program and the spelling program (Chapter 10)

Development of an innovative approach to comprehension and critical thinking instruction through comprehension levels, comprehension competencies, and questioning strategies (Chapter 11)

Discussion of approaches to developing independent reading in the content areas, with specific ideas for instruction in research and study skills (Chapter 12)

Examination of children's literature, emphasizing the importance of "literature plus response" to engage the reader actively and to develop positive and permanent reading attitudes and interests (Chapter 13)

Development of the concept of reading "miscue" analysis, emphasizing prevention of reading difficulties through careful observation and diagnosis of the child's reading-language performance and appropriate adjustment of instructional experiences (Chapter 14)

Contrast of group and individualized reading-language approaches, with recommendations for individualizing instruction through classroom organization, for example through learning centers (Chapter 15)

Plan of action to recruit, prepare, and use tutors, teaching assistants, and parents to help individualize reading-language instruction (Chapter 16)

Although many of the applied ideas used to illustrate key principles in this volume are drawn from the author's teaching and consulting experiences with children from kindergarten through the junior high grades, the opportunity to examine critically, refine, and expand these ideas was provided by a recent curriculum development project sponsored by the United States Office of Education. This $190,000 project, known as Project DELTA (Developing Excellence in Literacy Teaching Ability), focused on the development of preservice and inservice teacher competencies with the goal of improving reading-language instruction for children. As principal investigator and director of Project DELTA, the author worked directly with preservice and inservice teachers in designing and implementing an innovative reading-language curriculum. Various dimensions of the communication process were carefully examined, and ideas and experiences were formulated and applied in classroom practice, then evaluated on the basis of their success in direct classroom implementation. Project DELTA thus provided for field-testing a wide range of instructional experiences with elementary school youngsters, preservice teachers, and experienced inservice teachers.

The author expresses his appreciation to the children and teachers who participated in Project DELTA and to Herb Wong, principal of Washington Elementary School. He is also grateful to the Project DELTA staff who have contributed ideas and valuable reaction to the content of this volume, including Helen Bacon, Marilyn Hanf, Barbara Schmidt, Marilyn Williams, Arthur Williams, JoEllyn Taylor, and Kenneth Hoskisson.

Special acknowledgment and appreciation are given to Evelyn Jeanne Ahern, Eleanore K. Hartson, and JoEllyn Taylor, co-authors of *Resources*

Preface *in Reading-Language Instruction,* for their many ideas, suggestions, and reactions regarding the manuscript.

Recognition is also extended to Gloria Smallwood, Jim Richmond, Grover Mathewson, and Beverly Smith, graduate students in the Language and Reading Development Program, University of California, Berkeley, for their reactions and practical suggestions which have been incorporated in this volume.

Finally, the author is deeply grateful to his wife, Annette Ruddell, for the encouragement and support which made the completion of this work possible, and to his children, Amy and Robert, for providing him the opportunity to observe directly the development of the miraculous phenomenon of language.

1

Your Role as the Reading-Language Teacher in an Age of Change

Focusing Questions

1. What is the potential of the electronic revolution in facilitating the classroom teacher's attempt to individualize instruction? What cautions must he observe?
2. Why has the educational enterprise failed to achieve greater success in meeting the instructional needs of minority group youngsters?
3. What instructional value may be derived from the study of reading-language-related disciplines?
4. How can professional and community interaction help meet your children's instructional needs?
5. What are the instructional limitations of your school system and classroom? How might you overcome them?
6. What knowledge, skills, and attitudes does the classroom teacher need to develop an effective, individualized reading-language program?

At the Oakland Elementary school in Pittsburgh, some youngsters learn to use earphones before they can hold a pencil properly. Their school has none of the traditional classes or textbooks, they teach themselves with tape recorders, film and special work sheets. . . .

In Los Angeles, computer programs are being developed to help youngsters make more intelligent career choices.

Blind children may learn faster by listening to lessons in "compressed speech," which greatly speeds up the normal wordage rate.[1]

Technological changes such as these are already profoundly influencing the shape of American education, and according to language specialist Edmund Farrell there is more to come. By 1999, Farrell states:

Students will have improved printed materials of many types—paperbacks, short books with specific purposes, tutorial books, books that will send them

Your Role as the
Reading-Language
Teacher in an Age
of Change

to other experiences and resources and back to books again. Classrooms will have wall television screens on which can be projected both current events and life-like re-enactments of major scientific and cultural events. . . .

Through the computer, students will be able to retrieve data on demand from multimedia, multimode data banks; further, they will have access to computers through telephone lines in their homes. To lighten the teacher's load, the computer will compile students' records and provide continuous reports of students' progress.

. . . A conversationally interactive language, machine independent and available for execution of instructional programs on many computers, may eventually facilitate the use of computer-assisted instruction.[2]

How can products of the electronic revolution be used to individualize instruction and meet special learning needs? What cautions must be observed? *(Photo © 1972 Susan Ylvisaker/ Jeroboam)*

The classroom teacher has final responsibility for implementing curricula and assimilating new curricula and technological developments into the educational enterprise. He must deal not only with curriculum changes

Your Role as the
Reading-Language
Teacher in an Age
of Change

such as the "new English" and technological changes such as computer-assisted instruction; he must also be aware of the need for curriculum innovation to provide for such long-range possibilities as an automated twenty-hour work week.[3] Moreover, it is equally important that he be able to make these decisions for change from within the context of an essentially humanistic perspective. To quote Farrell again

> the electronic revolution must have the guidance of humanists if it is to be that which it can be, the instrumentality for releasing the creative potential of each individual, rather than an ingenious means of further degrading human life. The revolution will continue; what direction it takes depends in part upon the wisdom and participation brought to it by those of us who profess to teach English because we care about man.[4]

The central purpose of this text is to help you to become an effective reading-language teacher, but we shall also consider how to develop learning strategies and attitudes that will enhance critical life adjustment for a future time.

Free public education has made us a nation with one of the highest literacy rates and has been a major factor in the development of our standard of living. Yet one-fifth of our adult population failed to complete the eighth grade and one-seventh did not complete high school. About 15 percent of American adults read at the fourth-grade level or below, and another 25 percent are not up to sixth-grade standards. Inadequacies in oral and written expression are a major source of difficulty in the industrial world.[5]

Past reading-language programs and practices have not met the reading-language requirements of such minorities in our population as the black and Spanish-speaking ghetto children in cities like Los Angeles, Detroit, Chicago, and New York; the Appalachian white youngsters in rural and coal-depleted areas of Kentucky and West Virginia; and the Indian children on the desolate reservations of the Southwest. Nor have they proved adequate in developing the reading, oral, and writing skills of white middle-class children in the suburbs. We pay lip service to catchy phrases such as "the right to read" at the same time as we retain policies that have produced an adult population 40 percent of which have reached the reading-language achievement level of a twelve-year-old child, and then we are amazed that these individuals fail to meet the job requirements of a technological society.[6]

We must try to determine how the teacher in the classroom can raise the aspirations and achievement levels of children from conceptually different backgrounds, highly mobile families, and homes with pathetically little interest in the business of the school. We must assess the fit between the individual needs of pupils from various backgrounds and reading-language programs if we are to provide for the growing range of individual variation that must be accounted for if individual pupils are to achieve 3 functional, self-renewing levels of economic and social mobility. We must

How are instructional needs of children from various socioeconomic and ethnic backgrounds different? How are they similar?

(Photo © 1972 Susan Ylvisaker/ Jeroboam)

(Photo by Ernest Lowe)

(Photo by Ernest Lowe)

(Photo by Judith Borman Harding, BBM Associates)

Your Role as the
Reading-Language
Teacher in an Age
of Change

cut new instructional patterns if we are to be of real service to our children. We must ask how we can develop teaching effectiveness for reading-language skills across wide ability and achievement levels within classroom limitations that commonly include previously selected reading-language materials, established time schedules, and minimal instructional support from the overworked supervisor, curriculum director, or principal.

The components of an effective professional development program, whether preservice or inservice, may be viewed as an instructional troika:

1. "Who"—developing a clear understanding of the role of reading-language teacher
2. "Why"—building a background of discipline-derived concepts and understandings that will provide a basis for decision making in reading-language instruction
3. "How"—understanding reading-language methods and techniques and applying this knowledge to individual youngsters in classroom situations

The role of the reading-language teacher is introduced in this chapter and developed more fully throughout the text. The discipline-derived concepts are discussed specifically in Chapters 2 and 3 and woven into the remaining chapters as practical implications are derived from theory and research findings. This "why" component will anchor and enhance your decision-making ability in the classroom. As the late Professor David H. Russell stated, "Teaching is an art, and good teaching is a great art, but more and more it is an art influenced by scientific investigation."[7] The "how" components of reading-language instruction receive greatest attention in Chapters 5 through 16. By integrating the "who," "why," and "how" of reading-language instruction we can approach the optimal teaching level in this exciting art. It is extremely important that discussion of these basic components be reinforced with direct and vicarious classroom observation and participation. These experiences provide opportunity for you to interact with youngsters and become immersed in reading-language instruction as you exercise decision making with individual youngsters in simulated, and more importantly, real classrooms.

In the remainder of this chapter we shall deal with your role as the reading-language teacher and with curriculum guidelines and goals for the reading-language program.

YOUR ROLE AS THE READING-LANGUAGE TEACHER

The responsibilities of an effective reading-language teacher can be roughly categorized into three major areas (Figure 1-1). The first area, that of background knowledge and understanding, has to do with information

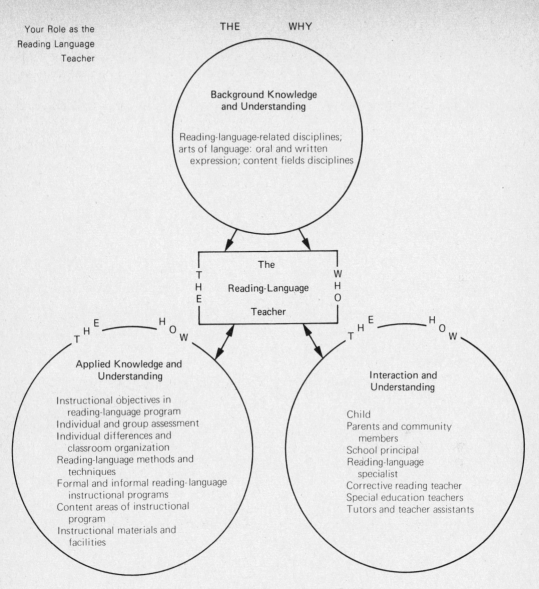

Figure 1-1. The Role of the Reading-Language Teacher

of great import in constructing and operating a curriculum in the class-room.

The next area, applied knowledge and understanding, comprises methods and procedures for meeting the needs of individual youngsters. The last area, interaction and understanding, provides for direct involvement in the instructional program as child, school, and community relationships are developed. As we examine each of these areas we should regularly inquire about important interrelationships among them.

7

Your Role as the
Reading-Language
Teacher in an Age
of Change

Background knowledge and understanding

To make decisions about the instructional program a teacher needs background knowledge and an understanding of the disciplines related to the reading-language curriculum. For example, we derive important learning principles and strategies from psychology. We know about the nature of the interaction among individuals, social institutions, and community groups from sociology, and about the structure and changing nature of language from linguistics. Psycholinguistics and sociolinguistics, two new fields of study formed by the fusion of disciplines, help us to understand how language is acquired and to appreciate dialectical variations in the language of various social groups.

As reading-language teachers we must be constantly concerned with the application of knowledge from other disciplines in our teaching. Most instructors in psychology, sociology, and linguistic courses are more concerned with discovering and transmitting a body of knowledge than with the application of this knowledge to the classroom. Fortunately, however, in recent years a number of scholars in language-related disciplines have devoted much attention to curriculum building at the elementary school level. Some of these scholars are psychologists Jerome Bruner, Robert Gagné, E. Paul Torrance, Martin V. Covington, and Richard S. Crutchfield; linguists Charles Fries, Henry Lee Smith, Jr., and David Reed; and sociolinguists Roger Shuy and William Labov.[8] The writings of these individuals help to identify the contributions of various disciplines to the reading-language curriculum, but it remains for the curriculum specialist and the reading-language teacher to translate concepts into practice and to test ideas in classroom settings.

Your understanding of the arts of language, including composition, language, and literature at various levels, and of disciplines in the content fields, such as science and mathematics, will help to assess the content validity of new materials and their potential value for the classroom.

Applied knowledge and understanding

As reading-language teacher you must be able to apply your background knowledge to children in order to teach them reading-language skills and to develop functional problem-solving strategies and positive attitudes toward the various forms of communication. To begin with, you must consider the instructional objectives you hope to achieve. These objectives may range from developing a spelling pattern generalization to using a complex level of comprehension such as inference of the main idea. To formulate such objectives you must first thoroughly understand the individual youngsters in your classroom and their instructional needs. Indeed, such an understanding is the basis of the design and organization of your reading-language instruction. (Because the process of developing reading-language skills, strategies, and attitudes is a long-term one, there must be some continuity, commonly based on grade level or cross-age groupings, in the progressive instructional units within your school. A common practice, usually initiated by the principal or curriculum consultant, is to have teacher groups within a school assume the responsibility for establishing long-term instructional goals.) When you establish instructional objectives you must take into account the materials you will use, your teaching strengths and interests, the facilities available, and, of greatest import, the characteristics of your pupils. Guidelines based on these considerations can serve as a general framework for building or modifying the instructional program. You will find it helpful in implementing such guidelines to establish sample instructional objectives together with evaluation techniques, in the form of teacher observations or oral and written responses to specific questions, for benchmarking progress. We shall have more to say about reading-language guidelines and goals later in this chapter.

The role of the successful reading-language teacher includes a wide range of instructional responsibilities. Which of these do you consider of highest priority? Of lowest priority?

Your instructional program must be designed to develop learning and problem-solving strategies that will enable individual youngsters to attack problems and reach solutions independently. These strategies must become functional over a wide range of tasks, from using decoding skills in attacking a new word to synthesizing various pieces of evidence in

Your Role as the
Reading-Language
Teacher in an Age
of Change

formulating possible solutions to an open-ended mystery story. Try to use a wide selection of children's literature to develop children's interests and attitudes toward reading.

Basic communication skills, learning strategies, and attitude development will be your major areas of instructional focus but your responsibilities may also include teaching science, mathematics, social studies, art, music, physical education, and other curriculum dimensions such as sex education, as required by the state or local school district. Your program will be most effective if you constantly look for ways of integrating the reading-language program with the subject matter content. This way you can provide valuable skill transfer for your pupils and at the same time reduce the preparation time you need to approach each skill and content area on a completely independent basis. For example, the problem-solving strategies employed in a mystery story—clearly defining the problem, searching for appropriate clues, and synthesizing data in formulating possible solutions—can also be applied to a science experiment on the water cycle.

Because of time pressures, administrative decisions, and inadequate professional preparation, many school systems rely heavily on publisher-produced materials (approximately 95 percent of the schools sampled in the Austin-Morrison study relied heavily on some form of basal reading programs).[9] Obviously the publishing industry has a major role in influencing the reading-language curriculum. Many of these programs were written by skilled reading-language specialists and competent classroom teachers and editors, but it is not unusual for new programs to be published with little or no field testing before release for classroom use. Select published programs with the utmost care. Following selection, your thorough understanding of a given reading-language program, combined with your background knowledge of the disciplines and modern techniques and methods of reading-language instruction, will enable you to adjust a particular program to the needs of individual children. You can perhaps use a published program to take care of one segment of your children's varied backgrounds, needs, and achievement levels—while other segments may require program development of your own design.

Child and professional interactions and understanding

A most important factor in your reading-language program is your personal understanding of the individual youngster. Your success in establishing rapport with your children will directly affect their achievements, attitudes, and interests in the reading-language program. This task is not extremely difficult in most cases, but with some children you will need patience, persistence, and understanding. Your classroom rapport must strike a balance between the "overprotective mother" and the "withdrawn school marm" if you are to establish a classroom environment that achieves the delicate balance between chaos and rigidity.

You must also consider the need for communication between classroom and community. You will have to interpret your reading-language curriculum to parents and to interested nonparent community leaders and groups. You already have an automatic communication line between classroom and parents through your pupils. Make every effort to encourage your youngsters to communicate with their parents about their learning activities. This may take the form of an end-of-day activity summary and a preview of tomorrow's activities, which serve to launch discussions between parent and child at home; or it may be in the form of the work that the child takes home for parent-child discussion. "Open house" and public school day are opportunities to invite the community into the classroom so that you may explain your curriculum, and parent-teacher conferences are also ways of enlisting parent support.

Give serious consideration to home visits early in the school year. (This practice, once common in rural schools, needs to be revived in our urban centers.) Such visits not only provide opportunities to interpret your program to seldom seen parents but can also provide insight into the child's and the parents' perceptions of you the teacher. You can also obtain information that is useful in understanding the child's reading-language progress. Such information may range from the discovery that the child has little opportunity to use English in the home because of a dominant second language or because of a low priority view of language use, to discovery that parental expectations are so great the child feels constantly defeated even though he is working at his highest potential.

Finally, you will need to communicate your instructional program to the professional staff of the school and on occasion to other teachers in the school district. This may be done through bulletin board displays demonstrating the nature of your curriculum by means of your children's achievements, through interschool teacher observations in your classroom, through visits from the principal and school district reading-language specialists, and the like. Inservice teacher workshops in reading-language instruction, normally held during the year, can provide for your own instructional growth, as well as that of other teachers, teacher assistants, and tutors, through the sharing of new ideas and instructional techniques.

Many school districts have a special services staff to aid your instructional program. Such a staff is commonly comprised of a school psychologist, to do special testing in the areas of intelligence and personality; an audiologist, to check for and work with hearing-deficient children; a sight conservation specialist, for the visually handicapped; and (of great importance to you) a corrective reading-language specialist, to work with pupils who are

11 deficient in reading-language skills, who have emotional or psychological

Your Role as the
Reading-Language
Teacher in an Age
of Change blocks to reading, or who have physiological impairments to reading. Such specialized professional support can help you improve your own teaching effectiveness and deal with the wide range of individual variations in your classroom.

CURRICULUM GUIDELINES AND GOALS

As you formulate or modify the reading-language program to provide for individual youngsters, you must consider an array of important child-centered factors:

1. What should be taught, or more properly, what should be learned?
2. How should learning experiences be organized for best results?
3. In what order should various elements of the curriculum be presented?
4. Through what teaching methods and techniques can the full possibilities of the curriculum be realized?
5. What instructional resources and materials are necessary to make optimum use of the curriculum?[10]

We shall offer answers to these questions in the remainder of the text, but in the final analysis, it is your responsibility to ask each question as you view the silhouette of each child in your classroom. Only then can you adequately determine and modify the content, continuity, unity, methods, and instructional resources you will need to teach individual youngsters. See Figure 1-2.

It is necessary to establish broad goals designed to develop basic communication skills, learning strategies, and language attitudes that lead to a high level of literacy for individual youngsters. Seven such goals follow.

1. The ability to communicate clearly in oral and written forms in a variety of social settings
2. The ability to understand and use oral and written language in both receptive and expressive forms
3. The ability to use comprehension and problem-solving strategies according to the purposes established in reading or listening situations
4. The ability to decode new words and to encode or spell words in a variety of reading and writing situations
5. The ability to use research and study skills to interpret content in subject matter areas
6. The ability to express, interpret, and enjoy creative thoughts
7. A sensitivity to and appreciation of language and literature in a variety of life situations

These seven goals embody a partial response to the first guideline question "What should be taught, or more properly, what should be learned?" Such broad goals, however, can only be realized in the classroom by placing them in operational forms for instruction as indicated in the last four guideline questions. The main body of this text is devoted to this purpose.

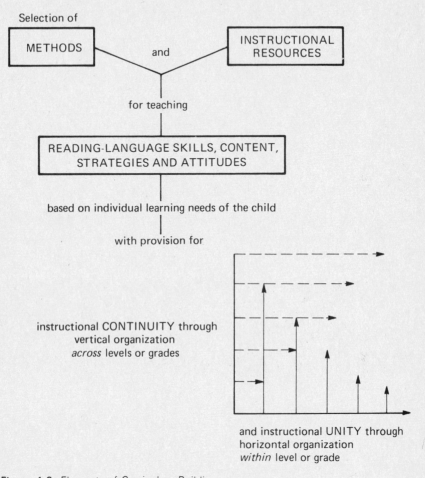

Figure 1-2. Elements of Curriculum Building

SUMMARY OF TEACHER-ORIENTED INSTRUCTIONAL GOALS

At this point we can identify several basic teacher-oriented instructional goals. To define your role as the reading-language teacher and identify critical areas of performance essential for effective teaching of reading-language skills, strategies, and attitudes, consider the following points:

13

1. Developing background knowledge of disciplines related to reading-language, oral and written arts of expression, and content fields disciplines

Your Role as the
Reading-Language
Teacher in an Age
of Change

✓ 2. Applying background knowledge to various components of the reading-language curriculum by
  A. Formulating instructional goals and objectives in the reading-language program
  B. Understanding and using publisher-produced instruments and developing your own observational and evaluational devices to assess and adjust to individuals and groups
  C. Interpreting assessment to adjust instructional objectives to individual achievement needs both vertically (across achievement levels) and horizontally (within an achievement level)
  D. Formulating and adjusting the reading-language instructional programs to meet pupil needs both in individual and group situations
  E. Understanding published and teacher-developed reading-language instructional programs
  F. Helping pupils relate skills, strategies, and attitudes in the reading-language program to the content areas of the curriculum

✓ 3. Developing and understanding interaction with children, parents, patrons, and professional staff by
  A. Relating to each pupil on a direct and personal basis
  B. Adjusting instructional programs to individual pupil needs with patience and persistence
  C. Communicating your instructional program to parents and community members
  D. Enlisting the aid of teaching assistants, tutors, parents, and community resources to enhance the instructional program at school and at home
  E. Using the specialized professional staff in the school district to meet the needs of special reading-language problems and disorders in your classroom

The remainder of this text will be devoted to ways of fulfilling these goals.

Footnotes

[1]"Research Boom in the Schools," *San Francisco Chronicle* (March 14, 1966). Reprinted by permission of the *San Francisco Chronicle.*

[2]Edmund J. Farrell, *Deciding the Future,* Research Report No. 12 (Urbana, Ill.: National Council of Teachers of English, 1971), pp. 124, 125.

[3]"Technology: The Cybernated Generation," *Time* (April 2, 1965), p. 87.

[4]Edmund J. Farrell, *English, Education, and the Electronic Revolution* (Champaign, Ill.: National Council of Teachers of English, 1967), p. 68.

[5]James R. Squire, "New Directions in Language Learning," *Elementary English,* 39 (October 1962), 535-44.

[6]Robert B. Ruddell and Arthur C. Williams, *A Research Investigation of a Literacy Teaching Model: Project DELTA,* U.S. Department of Health, Education, and Welfare, Office of Education, EPDA Project No. 005262 (1972), p. 2.

[7]David H. Russell, "Research: A Priority," *English Education Today* (Champaign, Ill.: National Council of Teachers of English, 1963), p. 31.

[8]Jerome S. Bruner, *The Process of Education* (Cambridge: Harvard University Press, 1960). Robert M. Gagné, *The Conditions of Learning* (New York: Holt, Rinehart and Winston, Inc.,

1965). E. Paul Torrance, "Motivating and Guiding Creative Reading," *How It Is Nowadays,* eds. Theodore Clymer and Robert B. Ruddell, Teacher's Edition (Boston: Ginn and Company, 1969), pp. 15-21. Martin V. Covington, Richard S. Crutchfield, and Lillian B. Davies, *The Productive Thinking Program* (Berkeley, Calif.: Brazelton Printing Company, 1966). Charles C. Fries, *Linguistics and Reading* (New York: Holt, Rinehart and Winston, 1963). Henry Lee Smith, Jr., *Linguistic Science and the Teaching of English* (Cambridge: Harvard University Press, 1956). David W. Reed, "A Theory of Language, Speech and Writing," *Linguistics and Reading,* Highlights of the Preconvention Institutes, Institute VI (Newark, Del.: International Reading Association, 1966), pp. 4-14, 15-25. Roger W. Shuy, "A Linguistic Background for Developing Beginning Reading Materials for Black Children," *Teaching Black Children To Read,* eds. Joan C. Baratz and Roger W. Shuy (Washington: Center for Applied Linguistics, 1969), pp. 117-37. William Labov, "Some Sources of Reading Problems for Negro Speakers of Nonstandard English," *New Directions in Elementary English,* ed. Alexander Frazier (Champaign, Ill.: National Council of Teachers of English, 1967), pp. 140-67.

[9]Mary C. Austin and Coleman Morrison, *The First R: The Harvard Report on Reading in Elementary Schools* (New York: The Macmillan Company, 1963).

[10]Hanna J. Hicks, *Administrative Leadership in the Elementary School* (New York: The Ronald Press Company, 1956).

2

A Communication Framework for the Reading-Language Teacher

Focusing Questions

1. How can reading-language-related disciplines be of value to decision making in your classroom?
2. What language concepts are basic to the communication process? How can they be integrated with and related to reading-language instruction in your classroom?
3. How can the communication framework be of value to you in formulating instructional objectives and in identifying reading-language difficulties of individual youngsters?
4. On the basis of the communication framework, what similarities are present in the processes of reading and listening? Speaking and writing? What differences?
5. Are there facets of the communication process which you feel are not accounted for in the communication framework? If so, can you incorporate them into the framework or relate them to your own framework?

Each hour of instructional time requires numerous instructional decisions, from altering the level of abstraction (as concepts in a space exploration story are introduced to an individual youngster) to encouraging the use of image-evoking vocabulary (in a composition lesson that recreates a school camping trip). In curriculum planning there may be time for careful lesson organization and development, but during actual instruction you must make decisions in a split second as you direct the learning activities of thirty-plus individuals. If these rapid-fire decisions are to be effective, it is essential that you achieve and fuse the first two teacher-oriented instructional goals identified in Chapter 1: that is, you must rapidly integrate your background knowledge of language and the way children learn (the instructional "why") with your applied classroom understandings (the instructional "how"). To do this it is of critical importance that you have a conceptual framework of the reading-language process that will enable you to identify the appropriate instructional experiences as quickly as you

16

recognize the specific improvements or difficulties of individual children
or instructional groups.

What instructional decisions would you anticipate in preparing for and developing
this story telling experience? *(Photo by Carole Graham, BBM Associates)*

We begin this chapter with a survey of language-related disciplines and
of basic instructional concepts derived from them. Then we integrate these
concepts into a communication framework that has proved a useful basis
for instructional decision making. Finally we briefly examine the act of
reading, using the framework to illustrate the various relationships. It is
important that you consistently try to relate the following discussion to
your own communication experiences with children.

IMPLICATIONS FROM THE DISCIPLINES: THE "WHY"

The most valuable bodies of knowledge for making decisions about reading-language instruction are linguistics (language description), psychology

(principles of learning), sociology (social group behavior and interaction), and interdisciplinary outgrowths such as sociolinguistics, psycholinguistics, and social psychology. (See Figure 2-1.)

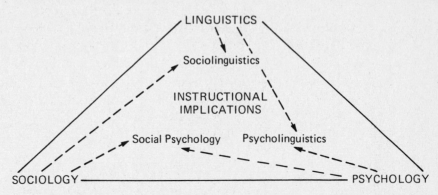

Figure 2-1. Reading-Language-Related Disciplines

Linguistics offers language description and generation as used in human interaction, together with the history and development of our language, its many varieties and variations. Psychology primarily offers information that helps to understand the learning experience as it applies to reading-language skills and processes. Sociology helps to understand group and individual behavior by localizing and examining the elements that can influence a child's interaction with his home environment, community groups, and the various individuals and groups in his school.

Sociolinguistics helps to understand language forms unique to various socio-ethnic groups. (In Chapter 9 we shall examine consistent language variations that can affect oral and written communications, together with our attitudes toward standard and nonstandard English forms used by our youngsters.) Social psychology provides insight into factors such as interests, attitudes, and values that influence personality development. This field is especially valuable for understanding the goals and drives of youngsters and the ways you can increase motivation in reading-language instruction. Psycholinguistics provides "a more realistic conception of what language is,"[1] by offering clues to the nature of language development and by examining the "psychological reality" of the linguist's units of analysis.[2] A major goal of the psycholinguist is to develop an explanation of how language is produced, and thus lead to an understanding of language performance. For our purposes this field can increase your understanding of language units related to comprehension and production of language in oral and written form.

A word of caution is in order at this point. Always be sure to think of
18 information and implications from the disciplines in terms of curriculum

development. The structure described by the language scholar, for example, may differ markedly from the optimal language structures your youngsters actually use in learning events. Always consider the "fit" between the concepts and principles of a given discipline and the reality of individual learning behavior in your classroom. As you consider the implications for practice of basic concepts from language-related disciplines, always evaluate these implications in terms of the actual classroom situation.

Be alert in your examination of the language-related disciplines for information that can enhance your own understanding and appreciation of language even though direct application may not be possible. For example, knowing the differences among Old English, Middle English, Early Modern English, and Modern English may help you to understand and appreciate the constantly changing nature of language, but it will probably be of minimal value in your first-grade program of reading instruction. On the other hand, the general notion of language change is of value in understanding language variation and the function of slang your youngsters use in particular social environments.

Study of the English language is not required in approximately 94 percent of the teacher education programs in the country,[3] even though 40 percent of elementary school classroom time is devoted to reading-language instruction.[4] It is vitally important that you the classroom teacher try to increase your understanding of language and language-related disciplines as a means of improving your instructional program.

CONCEPTS BASIC TO THE COMMUNICATION FRAMEWORK

The following concepts, derived from the previously identified disciplines, are essential to understanding the communication process and to planning and implementing your reading-language program.

Language: the sound system

What is a language? The answer to this seemingly simple question is central to any consideration of reading-language instruction. To begin to answer this question, let's examine and orally reproduce the following two sentences:

Es war spät, und die kleinen Vögel sangen.
'Twas brillig, and the slithy toves did gyre.

As you read these two sentences aloud you are undoubtedly aware of the use of a sound system; in fact you probably had difficulty with the sound system of the first sentence, because most English speakers are unfamiliar

19

not only with the sound system but also with the conventional meanings associated with the sounds of the German language.

The second sentence, from the poem "Jabberwocky," provides a familiar sound and grammatical system (word order, connecting words, inflectional endings) but the meaning is not very clear unless you have recently read or are familiar with Lewis Carroll. For all practical purposes we could arbitrarily assign the meanings of the words in the following English sentence to the "Jabberwocky" sentence:

It was late, and the little birds were singing.

This sentence is a literal translation of the German sentence, and its meaning of course differs from the meaning of the words from the Carroll poem. To speakers of English, who share a group of common experiences that are conceptualized and identified through specific word labels organized in familiar patterns, the meaning of the translation is immediately obvious.

From this brief illustration we can define a _language_ as _a system represented by sound symbols with conventional meanings shared by members of a linguistic group._ It is a system because there is an orderly and consistent method of organizing the sounds and sound patterns, and these sounds and sound patterns provide the basis for communication. These patterns of sound represent conventional meanings—of objects, actions, or states. We can readily see from our illustration that these meanings are arbitrary in nature: the small, warm-blooded flying vertebrates with feathers and wings are known as "die kleinen Vögel" in German, but as "the slithy toves" in "Jabberwocky." As members of the linguistic group known as English speakers we use a particular system of sounds with conventional meanings in order to communicate with each other about our feathered friends.

Almost all the scientific studies of the English language have taken place during the past 150 years. Earlier language scholars tried to fit the language into the grammatical mold of Latin, but nineteenth- and twentieth-century linguists have demonstrated that the sounds and patterns of English are different from Latin. The scientific study of language known as _linguistics_ is one of the most advanced disciplines in the social sciences, owing to the development of rigorous, objective and verifiable methods of language study.

Let's consider the components of "the system" of language. It would appear that we learn our sound system through various sound contrasts and independently of vocabulary items. The available research suggests that by the time the child is four to five years of age he has mastered the great majority of English sounds.[5] These sound units, or classes of sound, of a specific language such as English are called _phonemes._ More specifically, a _phoneme_ is the minimal sound unit for distinguishing meaning. For example, the spoken words _pin_ and _bin_ are distinguished by the initial consonant phonemes /p/ and /b/, while the spoken words _pin_ and _pan_ are distinguished by the medial vowel phonemes /i/ and /æ/.[6] The study of these minimal sound units is called *phonemics.*

It should be noted that the science of phonemics differs from that of phonetics. Phonemics is the study of sound units that distinguish meaning in *a specific language,* whereas phonetics is the study of speech sounds of *all languages.* The International Phonetic Alphabet (no longer widely used) was developed in the late 1800s to describe and differentiate a wide range of speech sounds in various languages, such as the different sound characteristics of the /p/ in the words /pin/ and /spin/. Place your hand a few inches from your mouth and pronounce the word *pin.* Note that a puff of air is emitted at the initial part of the word. Now pronounce *spin.* The puff of air is absent. This difference is characterized by two different sounds or *phones*—the first being the aspirated *p* and the second the unaspirated *p.*

As English speakers we "tune out" sound differences that don't make significant contrasts in our language, and so we group these two phones into one sound class, which we call the phoneme *p* or /p/. But if we were to learn to speak Korean or Hindi the difference between these two sounds of *p* would be important because they provide for meaning distinctions in words. (Of course the Korean or Hindu learning English would need to learn to disregard these sound distinctions.) Certain other phonemic distinctions will need to be developed, depending upon the variations in the languages. For example, the Spanish-speaking person has difficulty with the vowel contrasts that distinguish the words b*it* /i/ and b*eat* /iy/, b*et* /e/ and b*ait* /ey/, and initial consonant contrasts such as *s*ue /s/ and *z*oo /z/. The Navajo child has difficulty with initial consonant distinctions in words like *v*ote /v/ and *b*oat /b/, and *ch*ip /č/ and *g*yp /j/. Such difficulties are of course important to anyone who teaches English as a second language, and we shall devote further attention to this matter in Chapter 9.

English has approximately forty-four phonemes: twenty-one consonants, three semivowels, eight unglided vowels, four levels of stress, four levels of pitch, and four levels of juncture. *Consonants* are sounds characterized by complete or partial stoppage of the air stream, for example, pit /*p*it/, fit /*f*it/; variation in the use of the vocal cords as voiced or unvoiced, such as pit /*p*it/, bat /*b*at/; and variations in the type of obstruction presented by the tongue, lips, and teeth, for example, pit /*p*it/, kit /*k*it/. See Figure 2-2 for a complete list of the consonants and brief descriptions of their formation.

Those phonemes in the bottom row of Figure 2-2 differ from the others in that no air stoppage occurs. The phoneme /r/ is produced by a slight diversion of the air stream as the tongue curls toward the back of the mouth, as in rat /r*æ*t/. The phonemes /w/, /y/, and /h/ are known as *semivowels* because they are produced by using the vocal cords with no air stoppage. They may function in a simple role, yield /*y*/, or in a complex role with a vowel phoneme, ice /a*y*s/.

21

SOUND FORMATION

Air Passage	Vocal Cords Vibrate	Both Lips	Lower Lip and Upper Teeth	Tongue Tip and Upper Teeth	Tongue Tip Behind Upper Teeth	Front Tongue Near Front of Palate	Back of Tongue Near Soft Palate	Vocal Cords Only
Stopped Completely	no / yes	/p/ (pit) /b/ (bit)			/t/ (tip) /d/ (dip)		/k/ (kit) /g/ (go)	
Stopped Followed by Slow Release	no					/č/ (chip) /ǰ/ (jump)		
Released Through Narrow Opening	no / yes		/f/ (fan) /v/ (van)	/θ/ (thin) /d̵/ (then)	/s/ (sat) /z/ (zebra)	/š/ (ship) /ž/ (measure)		
Released Along Sides of Tongue	no				/l/ (led)			
Released Through Nose	yes	/m/ (man)			/n/ (nat)		/ŋ/ (ring)	
No Stoppage	yes	/w/ (wield)			/r/ (rat)	/y/ (yield)		/h/ (him)

Figure 2-2. Descriptions of Consonant and Semivowel Phonemes

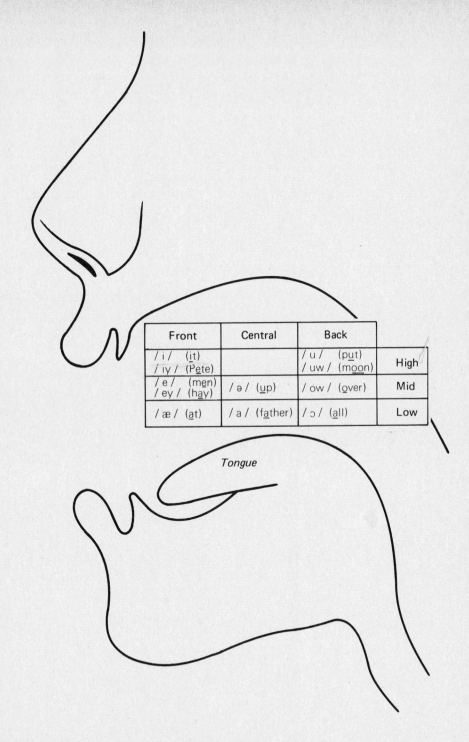

	Front	Central	Back	
	/ i / (it) / iy / (Pete)		/ u / (put) / uw / (moon)	High
	/ e / (men) / ey / (hay)	/ ə / (up)	/ ow / (over)	Mid
	/ æ / (at)	/ a / (father)	/ ɔ / (all)	Low

Tongue

23 **Figure 2-3**. Descriptions of Vowel Phonemes

Vowels are sounds characterized by use of the vocal cords and an absence of any obstruction in the air passage. These phonemes are influenced by the shape of the lips and by the relationship between the tongue and the palate. The tongue position is modified from front to back, it /it/, put /put/, and from high position to low position, it /it/, at /æt/. Descriptions of the formation of vowel sounds and their phonemic symbols are in Figure 2-3. The categories high, mid, and low refer to the position of the highest part of the tongue, while the categories front, central, and back refer to the tongue position in the mouth. As you pronounce the sample words that use each of the vowel phonemes, also note the rounded or stretched position of your lips.

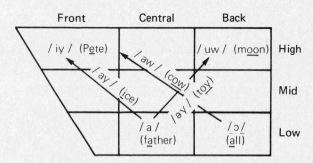

Figure 2-4. Vowels Produced by Glide

A number of vowel sounds are produced by gliding from one position to another. Examples of these are /ay/ *ice,* /aw/ *cow,* and /ɔy/ *toy,* as illustrated in Figure 2-4.

From this point we shall refer to those complex vowel sounds produced with two vowel sounds as *glided vowel sounds,* such as /ay/ in *ice.* These vowels are identical to the vowels traditionally called *long vowels* and *diphthongs.* The relatively simple vowel sounds produced with one vowel sound will be identified as *unglided vowel sounds,* such as /i/ in *it.* These vowel sounds have traditionally been called *short vowels.*

As previously indicated consonants and vowels are the *segmental phonemes,* but they are not the only components of our spoken language; there are also the *suprasegmentals*—pitch, stress, and juncture. *Pitch* is the relative height or frequency of your voice, relative to the rest of a word or sentence, as you pronounce a syllable. In some languages, such as Chinese, each word has its own pitch, which means that pitch provides an essential meaning for each word. In English pitch reflects the meaning we intend within a context:

Bobby is in the street.

and

Bobby is in the street?

24

Stress is the degree of loudness of a syllable in a sentence. We often also refer to stress as *accent*. Stress can also convey a particular meaning:

áddress—What is your áddress?

addréss—Will you addréss the letter?

How can this type of learning experience be used to emphasize the importance of pitch, stress, and juncture in oral communication? *(Photo © 1972 Susan Ylvisaker/ Jeroboam)*

The length or degree of pause between one segment of speech and the next is known as *juncture*. The influence of juncture on meaning is obvious in the following example:

/ays + kriym/ (ice cream)

/ay + skriym/ (I scream)

Your understanding of the English sound system will be of particular importance in teaching decoding skills and sentence meaning comprehension (Chapters 10 and 11). We shall return to other parts of this system after we have made a brief examination of our written system of language.

Language: the writing system

Our communication system makes provision for visual symbols to represent the basic vocal symbols of our spoken language. The minimal significant written unit in language is the *grapheme*. It is to writing what the phoneme is to speech. The letters of the alphabet (d - i - p /dip/), and in some instances combinations of these letters—digraphs (sh - i - p /šip/)—represent the sounds or phonemes of the spoken language to a high degree. Punctuation marks can convey the elements of pitch, stress, and juncture to some extent, such as the question mark in

John is h e r e ?

while numerals and arbitrary signs, such as H_2O, are used in specialized fields of study.

A major goal of your instructional program, previously identified in Chapter 1, is to develop the ability to decode or attack new words and to encode or spell words in a variety of reading and writing situations. One dimension of your curriculum will thus be to help children to understand the relationship between the writing system and the more familiar sound system. This relationship, illustrated in Figure 2-5, is commonly referred to as *phonic analysis* or *decoding*. For example, as the child looks at the printed letters k - i - t it will be necessary for him to learn to reproduce the oral equivalent /kit/.

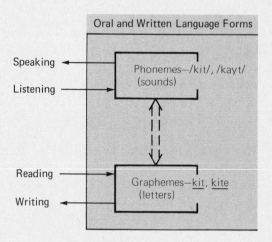

Figure 2-5. Letter–Sound Relationships

The relationship between the sound system and the writing system involves *encoding* or *spelling*. Should the child wish to represent the oral form /kit/ in written form he will need to formulate its graphic equivalent k - i - t. Figures 2-2, 2-3, and 2-4 show an initial inventory of consonant and vowel correspondences that the teacher will need to develop through reading and spelling instruction. The similarities and differences between the processes of decoding and encoding are dealt with in more detail in Chapter 10.

If we are to account for the nature of the English writing system, however, we need to know spelling units or letter patterns that allow us to predict sound correspondences beyond the simple grapheme-phoneme or letter-sound correspondences level. Consider the second example presented in Figure 2-5. The vowel graphemes in the word *kite* do not correspond directly with the vowel phonemes in /kayt/; but when you know the spelling pattern with a final *e* marker, you can produce the sound equivalent of the vowel grapheme *i* on a highly regular basis. The pattern prediction also applies to bit /bit/—bit*e* /bayt/, and bid /bid/—bid*e* /bayd/, and to other consistent correspondences such as, at /æt/—at*e* /eyt/, pet /pet/—Pet*e* /Piyt/, and us /əs/—us*e* /uws/. We shall briefly extend the concept of spelling-sound patterns and sound-spelling patterns in the following discussion and then develop it in greater detail in Chapter 10.

Meaningful language units

To this point our discussion has been mainly concerned with phonemes, units of language that distinguish meaning, and the ways these units are spoken and written. We shall now turn our attention to the meaning bearing units of the language.

Just as the atoms combine to form the elements of our periodic table, phonemes combine to form larger units—*morphemes*—of our language. A *morpheme* is a minimum meaningful unit of language; study of the ways these units function is known as *morphology*. Morphemes represent something in the real world or in the mind of the speaker or listener. The morpheme *boy,* for example, represents a young male human; *boys* is a complex form consisting of the lexical item *boy* and *-s,* the commonest form of the morpheme that represents the concept of more than one. From the latter example it is obvious that not every morpheme is a word, but simply that every morpheme communicates something meaningful to everyone who understands the language.

Morphemes are categorized in two classes—free and bound. A *free morpheme* is used independently in discourse—*boy, boil*—but a *bound morpheme* must be combined with a free morpheme—*-s, -ish, -ed,* and *-ing* in *boys, boyish, boiled,* and *boiling.*

A free morpheme can be further classified in at least two ways. (1) It can be classified on the basis of the bound morphemes or inflectional endings it can combine with. For example, *dog* belongs to a particular class because it can be inflected for the plural and the possessive, as in *dog, dogs, dog's, dogs'.* The word *brown* can take the suffix *-ish* to form *brownish,* but the word *cry* cannot, so the words must belong to separate classes. (2) It can 27 be classified on the basis of its position in a larger construction. For example, *adjectives* are words that can fill the blank in the sentence "Jack is the ____ boy."[7]

The bound morpheme can have a variety of forms to represent similar meanings. For example, *matches* /mæ čəz/ is the plural of *match* /mæč/, *dogs* /dɔgz/ the plural of *dog* /dɔg/, and *cats* /kæts/ the plural of *cat* /kæt/. In written language the plural forms can be signaled by *-es* or *-s* and in oral language by /əz/, /z/, or /s/. Many oral language forms are predictable on the basis of the sound environment. For example

/əz/ occurs after /s,z,š,ž,č, and j/, as in /mæčəz/

/z/ occurs after all other voiced sounds (vocal cords used), as in /dɔgz/,

and

/s/ occurs after all other voiceless sounds (vocal cords not used), as in /kæts/.

These examples suggest that there is a regular pattern in our sound system. An intermediate sound unit that can be predicted or determined by a *sound pattern* context is known as a *morphophoneme*.

Similarly, there are *letter patterns* or *spelling pattern units* in our writing system that provide consistent decoding clues to the sound equivalents. This unit may take the form of a letter or pattern marker that has no sound value itself but that preserves the word form and cues other sound values. The final *e* marker we have previously discussed (kit /kit/—kit*e* /kayt/) is such a unit. The unit may also be a relational unit that has a sound value and is essential to predict the sound value of other graphemes in a word. For example, if we consider the words extr*e*me and extr*e*mity from the standpoint of direct letter-sound correspondences, there appears to be little regularity in the second *e* grapheme of a given sound. But on a larger scale a very regular spelling pattern becomes immediately obvious. In the alterations extr*e*me, extr*emity;* obsc*e*ne, obsc*enity;* and ser*e*ne, ser*enity* we observe a consistent shift in the sound value (/iy/ to /i/) represented by the grapheme *e* with the addition of the suffix *-ity*.

The relationships between the various oral and written language forms discussed to this point are shown in Figure 2-6. As the figure illustrates, morphophonemes and letter patterns are the intermediate sound-spelling units between phoneme and grapheme units and those of the morpheme. The recent research on sound and spelling patterns by Richard Venezky, Ronald Wardhaugh, and David Reed will be of value to us in Chapter 10, when we consider decoding and encoding strategies.[8]

Patterns of language structure

The child's development of grammar, including morphology as just discussed, is more complex than his mastery of the sound system. One-word utterances—"telegraphic speech"—begin from twelve to eighteen months, and this expands to two-word utterances ("open door," "want Mommy") shortly thereafter.[9] By the time the child enters the first grade he possesses

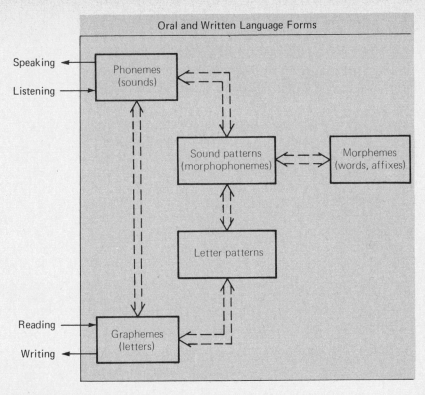

Figure 2-6. Letter-Sound, Pattern, and Word Relationships

a high degree of sophistication in his grammatical system. Let's look at the critical communication elements in this system.

Just as sounds and sound patterns combine in very regular ways to form morphemes, the morphemes in turn pattern themselves to form phrases and sentences. The patterning of words and word groups is known as *syntax.*

There are various ways to describe sentence elements and their relationships. The structural grammars of Charles Fries, Nelson Francis, and James Sledd[10] describe sentences in terms of patterns, such as:

     D   N   V D N
    The canary ate the cat.

    D = Determiner
    N = Noun
    V = Verb

Specific words, as previously discussed, are classified on the basis of their morphological characteristics or according to their function or position in a construction. For example, based on form a noun is a word that can be inflected for the plural and the possessive; taking position into consideration a noun is a word that can fill the slot in "The ____ was good."

This type of *structural* description offers a clear understanding of the relationships between words and word groups within the sentence. On an instructional level emphasis on an informal basis can highlight *relational meaning* in sentences. For example, the determiner *that* not only cues a noun that follows, it can also clarify or emphasize the semantic nature of the noun, as in *"That* dog was in our yard," as opposed to *"Some* dog was in our yard." Word substitutions that express key meaning relationships in sentences include:

phrase markers: Pete rode his new bike *to* the tree.
by the tree.
into the tree.

clause markers: We'll go skiing *if* the work is completed.
after the work is completed.
before the work is completed.

The contribution to meaning relationships through pattern expansion and elaboration is obvious in the following example:

The boy ran.
The boy ran *through the burning house.*
The boy ran through the burning house *quickly.*

Another view of language is offered by the generative transformational grammarian, whose viewpoint goes beyond the structural description of a sentence to make provision for predicting or generating sentences not observed. In transformational grammar the idea is to show the connection between related sentences rather than to describe them separately.[11] For example, from the sentence "The canary ate the cat," we can derive the following:

"The cat was eaten by the canary." (Passive)
"Did the cat eat the canary?" (Yes-No (Yes-No Question))
"Who ate the cat?" (Wh-Question)
"The canary didn't eat the cat." (Negative)
"The canary *did* eat the cat!" (Emphatic)

The above relationships would be expressed formally in terms of specific generalizations that rearrange, delete, or add structural elements to the base sentence "The canary ate the cat."

Discussions of transformational grammar came to view sentence production on two levels—surface structure and deep structure.[12] The *surface structure* level deals with oral and written language forms, including the phonological, graphological, and other "surface forms" of the sentence. This level would also include phonemes, graphemes, and sound and letter patterns. The *deep structure* contains rules that relate directly to the semantic content or meaning of a sentence. The relationship between the two levels is shown in the following illustration.

Deep structure: Use phrase structure rules to form

the canary (past marker) ate the cat (passive marker).

Use transformational rules to form

the cat was eaten by the canary.

Surface structure: Use phonological rules to form

/ ɖə kæt wəz iytən bay ɖə kənariy/

or graphological rules to write

the cat was eaten by the canary.

Obviously generative transformational grammar is a complex field of study. Those who wish to pursue it will find the texts by Owen Thomas, *Transformational Grammar and the Teacher of English,*[13] and Ronald Langacker, *Language and Its Structure,*[14] of value. We shall not consider the formal development of transformational grammar here; instead we shall identify relational meaning components in an informal fashion so as to enhance sentence meaning comprehension and sentence production in oral and written expression. Grammar is only an aid in identifying critical structural elements that contribute to meaning. Figure 2-7 incorporates syntax and relational meaning into the communication process. Recent work on generative transformational grammar also makes provisions for lexical items, which will be taken up in the following discussion.

Aspects of meaning

In our discussion of oral and written language forms to this point we have focused primarily on one type of meaning, *relational meaning*—the meaning carried by the structural components that underlie our system of language, or meaning relationships between free and bound morphemes, between and among word groups in sentences, and between and among sentences. We must also be concerned with *lexical meaning*— the conceptualization of experiences and the arbitrary labeling system that enables us to represent these experiences. We can consider this important language component from at least two perspectives—denotative meaning and connotative meaning. *Denotative meaning* may be thought of as a formalized type of meaning, as illustrated by the scientific description of *snow* as white, crystalline flakes of frozen water vapor. But we can also view *snow* from the standpoint of a *connotative meaning,* which is an associational type of meaning based on what snow connotes or brings to mind, such as cold, wet, white, flaky, even sleigh ride or cozy mountain cabin—depending on the experiences we associate with a winter environment.

In addition to relational and lexical meaning forms, we also utilize *nonlinguistic meaning* to enhance the communication process. For our immedi-

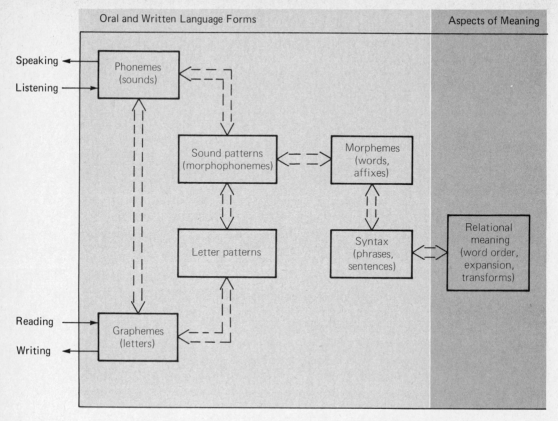

Figure 2-7. Oral and Written Language Forms and Relational Meaning

ate purposes this can take the form of body signals ranging from facial expression to hand gesture. Various signals and signs provide visually meaningful nonverbal clues to communication within a given culture.[15] As Dwight Bolinger emphasizes, various gestures used in communication are to some degree systematized and "cooperate with sound as part of a larger communicative act." He illustrates this by observing

In the following utterance,

You don't me a n it.

everything else can remain the same, yet with one's head held slightly forward, eyes widened, and mouth left open after the last word, the result is a question ("You surely don't mean it, do you?"), while with head erect, eyes not widened, and mouth closed afterward, it is a confident assertion. Facial gestures are sometimes the only way to tell a question from a statement.[16]

In this role-playing situation, what evidence suggests the value of nonverbal communication? Of verbal communication? How can this information help the classroom teacher? *(Photo by Mahon, Monkmeyer Press Photo Service)*

The study of this aspect of nonverbal communication, known as *kinesics,* must, along with various sign systems ($\langle s \rangle$ = curve ahead), be included in our study of the communication process.

Communication depends upon these various meaning forms. The child's conceptual development progresses rapidly from a relatively small number of words during the first and second years to many hundreds of words by the sixth year.[17] This growth derives from a wide range of experience and will continue throughout his lifespan.

How are his experience conceptualized and his concepts mobilized for use in reading-language experiences? Psychologists have provided only partial answers to these questions.

At least three levels seem to be involved in the conceptualization of experience and a fourth, more complex level is activated to use concepts. The first level is *sensation,* the stimulation offered in the child's environment, raw

information he is aware of through his senses of sound, touch, sight, taste, and smell. The child initially (birth to two years) relates to his environment through a sensori-motor means rather than via the symbolic language system. This level is basic to the first of five cumulative stages of cognitive development posited by the Swiss psychologist Jean Piaget.[18] More recent research suggests that a wide variety of sensation experiences during the early years of life is extremely important to later conceptual development.[19]

As the language-specific species, we move to organize various sensations in some manner. The process by which we act on the stimuli in our environment through selection is known as *perception.* We fuse sensations in some organized fashion that produces an awareness pattern. As we participate in a communication act we are constantly required to perceive and organize experiences through *auditory perception* and *visual perception* (including nonverbal stimuli). This requires that we select the pertinent stimulus or stimuli confronting us, based on our mental organization or strategy, and organize it in some fashion. For this we need a symbol-processing system that provides for the identification of relationships based on sensory input. Development of such a system is essential to Piaget's second developmental stage (age two to four)—that of preconceptual thought and early symbolic representation.

As the child grasps the organization of attributes through perception he comes to understand that these relationships can be symbolized in very specific ways—through word labels. As the Russian psychologist Lev Vygotsky has pointed out,[20] the preschool youngster explains the name of an object by its attributes. For example, a *cow* is called a *cow* because it has horns, and a *calf* is called a *calf* because its horns are still small, while a *dog* is called a *dog* because it is small and has no horns. The process of concept formation would thus appear initially to involve the development of categories that are then "tested" through examples and nonexamples in the child's environment.[21] This level of cognitive development corresponds roughly to the second and early part of the third intuitive thought stage (age four to seven) described by Piaget. The child learns to deal with the symbol system used in his language. He begins to conceptualize early levels of causality based for the most part on his perceptions, which may often lead to incorrect conclusions owing to the selection of irrelevant sensory stimuli. For example, he may conclude that a tall, narrow container holds more beads than a shallow container, even though he has observed the beads being transferred from one vessel into the other.

More formally, a *concept* may be thought of as a classification of objects or ideas based on common qualities the objects or ideas possess or fail to possess. Piaget[22] emphasizes that as cognitive activity takes place the individual must constantly assimilate the experience in his environment with his internal cognitive structures and accommodate or integrate the new experience with those previously conceptualized. Conceptual devel-

How would this experience lend itself to the effective development of new concepts? What new concepts would be most appropriate for the younger child? For the older child? *(Photo by Carole Graham, BBM Associates)*

opment during this fourth stage, known as concrete operations (age seven to eleven), allows the child to be less dependent upon his immediate perception of events as he relies more on logical thought.

In order for the child to be able to use and manipulate concepts in his environment, he needs to develop a method or methods to deal with specific problems. Such a method is known as a *cognitive strategy*. The

35 successful problem solver identifies the nature of the problem by isolating

a particular element or elements in it, relates appropriate knowledge to the problem, and formulates conclusions in acting to solve the problem.[23] Cognitive strategy is considered to be operationalized as a process of evaluating information, gathering data, building hypotheses, organizing and synthesizing data, and testing hypotheses. Additionally, the utilization of these factors must be guided by a constant awareness of the need to shift one's strategy to account for other approaches to problem solutions. This complex cognitive activity of problem solving corresponds to Piaget's fifth stage, that of formal operations.

Our understanding of the communication process must also account for the affective dimensions unique to the individual. Here we are concerned with *interests*, which direct our attention to particular activities or events in our environment;[24] *attitudes*, which are our learned, emotionally toned predispositions to react in certain ways toward persons, objects, and ideas;[25] and *values*, which may be categorized as our orientations toward the theoretical, aesthetic, economic, social, political, and religious, and which represent those basic ideas and commitments that are of greatest personal worth to us as individuals.[26]

The child's interests and attitudes are influenced for the most part by the adults around him. His first moral feelings probably take the form of "absolute prohibitions and prescriptions" based on parental dictates. These feelings based on adult evaluation of his actions are formulated during the preconceptual and intuitive thought periods. The child believes that his actions deserve punishment or praise depending on how they relate to the norms established in the home—without reference to "intentions or other mitigating circumstances." His attitudes continue to develop, and value groupings are formulated and ordered on the basis of relative priorities during the concrete operations stage. He comes to control his actions in relation to future needs (even though they are still somewhat immediate, such as completing today's homework assignment in anticipation of tomorrow's class needs and expectations). This is the development of *will*—a shift in attention from the influence of stimuli in the immediate environment to the dictates of future needs. His concept of moral rules is extended to include the value of game rules for the benefit of all participants rather than simply as prescriptive conventions. The adolescent continues to formulate his value system during the formal operations stage, but now he is influenced not only by highly esteemed individuals in the home but also by peer group ideals and values, and his motivation becomes increasingly subordinated to these values.[27]

The above components of personality development, which we will call *affective mobilizers*, become operational in the form of individual objectives and goals, which in turn relate directly to individual motivation as reflected in persistence and drive. This dynamic is supported by Dolores Durkin, who in her preschool reading research has found the preschool reader to be curious, serious, persistent, and able to concentrate.[28] Roy Kress, in a study of achieving and nonachieving elementary school readers, found the

former group to have more
more persistent in solving pr
phine Piekarz has found that the
more responses in interpreting a rea
which indicates greater involvement an
velopment of students thus deserves ca
language instruction.

At this point we need to conceptualize the relat
munication elements we have developed: auditory
ception, lexical meaning, nonlinguistic meaning, affe
cognitive strategies. It is important to realize that the an
and cognitive strategies at the bottom of the figure are act
behavior in all phases of the communication process. The mob
lish specific goals and motivation, while the strategies make pro
approaching a specific problem and working toward its solution. See
2-8.

Now we need to integrate the various aspects of meaning—lexical, relational, and nonlinguistic—in completing an act of communication. A number of people are trying to develop a semantic theory, but progress has been
understandably slow because of the extreme complexities involved in
relating lexical, relational, and nonlinguistic meaning components. Some
theorists have postulated that a semantic component in language serves to
assign meaning to each sentence through semantic markers.[31] For example,
semanticists have constructed semantic categories such as object-nonob-
ject, animate-inanimate, human-nonhuman, and male-female. A semantic
marker such as *male* represents the content of words like *man, boy,* or *father*
in contrast to words like *car, truth,* and *girl.*[32] In some respects this approach resembles the game of twenty questions—trying to narrow the
definition of the meaning under consideration. A sequence of such semantic markers constituting the dictionary would thus provide a semantic
reading and define the conceptual content of words. Then by using a set
of projection or interpretation rules, the lexical meanings would be integrated with the relational meanings to derive the sentence interpretation.
Postal, a psychologist, has noted that such characterizations will explain
semantic properties such as ambiguity (for example, I observed the ball),
paraphrase (John is a farmer; John is someone who farms), synonymy (not
living; dead) or anomaly (John married a potato pancake).

One difficulty, which is apparent in the discussion of sentence meaning,
is the ambiguity that results from the limitation of a one-sentence context.
To use an example from Katz and Fodor, the sentence "The bill is large"
can mean a sizable debt or the unusual size of a bird's beak.[33] Knowing
that the sentence is ambiguous is only a first step toward understanding
its meaning. The ambiguity can be resolved by a verbal context, such as
"Oh, I see you bought a new dress," or "My, what an unusual bird." It
can also be accounted for through a nonlinguistic meaning context if one
is purchasing clothing at a store or visiting a zoo. But developing general-

initiative in exhausting solutions and to be
...oblems under changing conditions.[29] Jose-
...high-level reader provides significantly
...ding passage than the inferior reader,
...d participation.[30] The affective de-
...reful consideration in reading-

...ionships among the com-
...perception, visual per-
...tive mobilizers, and
...ffective mobilizers
...ve in directing
...lizers estab-
...vision for
...Figure

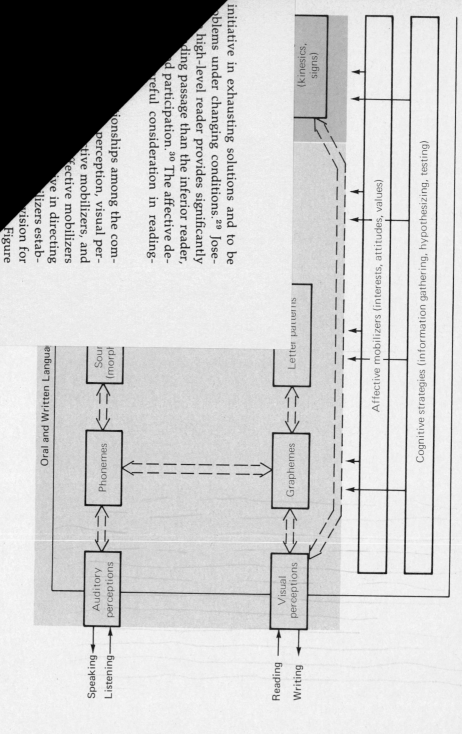

Figure 2-8. Oral and Written Language Forms and Aspects of Meaning

izations that define the larger verbal context and nonlinguistic meaning is an enormous task.

For our purposes we must add an interpretation component to the communication process that will utilize the lexical, relational, and nonlinguistic meanings. This interpretation process will vary according to the developmental level of the child. His ability to use concepts may range from his need to manipulate animate and inanimate objects at the concrete level (dog, chair), through a representational or functional level (a handkerchief is to blow your sneeze in), to a high degree of conceptual abstraction (honor, loyalty).[34] His interpretation ability will also be influenced by his ability to use and interpret figurative language forms like metaphors and hyperbole. This vital part of the communication process is at the extreme right of the communication model in Figure 2-9. We shall attend to the development of factual, interpretative, and applicative comprehension

What dimensions of the communication framework are critical for children's successful participation in this type of activity? *(Photo by David Strickler, Monkmeyer Press Photo Service)*

processes related to this area of the communication process in Chapter 11.

Memory and feedback. We need to know something about the function of memory and feedback if we are to account for the process of comprehending and generating language realistically. We can observe the use of short-term memory when we watch a child carry out a series of orally directed tasks, or when we attempt to take notes while listening to a fast-talking lecturer and find that we can only retain a few ideas during a short time sequence. Short-term memory is very limited: most of us can retain only five to nine items.[35] Short-term memory seems to be involved in processing not only words but also larger, more natural language "chunks" in the form of phrase units within sentences.

Long-term memory allows us to conceptualize and store lexical, relational, and nonlinguistic meanings, apparently on the basis of memory categories that serve to recall information economically several minutes or several years after an experience has been conceptualized.[36] This recall provides feedback for evaluating and reacting to events presented in running discourse, whether in the reading of a popular novel or in discussion about an Apollo moon landing.

Feedback is also necessary to evaluate decoding information obtained in the immediate written or oral context, and to evaluate the lexical and relational meanings which occur in immediate context. Feedback, as indicated by the lettered solid lines in Figure 2-9, originates at the semantic interpretation stage or, if this is insufficient, comes from the long-term memory.

USING THE COMMUNICATION MODEL

The communication model in Figure 2-9 may be arranged into five basic categories. The first, Oral and Written Language Forms, includes the phonological, graphological, morphological, and syntactical components. The second category, Aspects of Meaning, includes the meaning components—lexical, relational, and nonlinguistic. The third category, Interpretation, integrates the various meaning forms through factual, interpretive, and applicative processes. The fourth category, Memory and Feedback, provides for storing and transferring information from one part of the model to another to formulate and evaluate interpretations. The fifth category is Affective Mobilizers and Cognitive Strategies. These dual components interact with and serve to direct all dimensions of communication as the individual identifies specific goals and objectives and directs his thinking processes to achieve the established goals and objectives so as to culminate in the third category, interpretation. The process of communication becomes more meaningful when we follow the act of reading through the model. First read the following excerpt from a delightful story by

40 Russell Hoban. Then we shall use the communication model to focus on

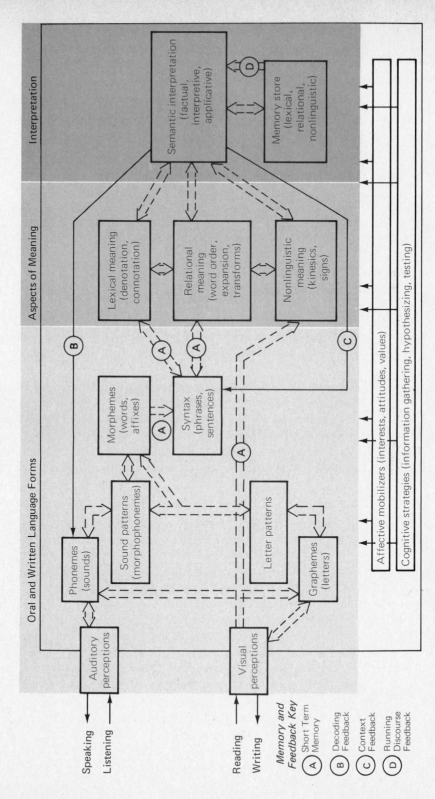

Figure 2-9. The Communication Framework

the processes of decoding and interpreting the italicized sentence from the standpoint of the early reader.

"That's funny," said Father. "I didn't make it. I wonder who did?"

"I did," said Charlie, waking up and coming out of the hollow tree. "That's my pond."

"That's your pond?" said Father.

"That's my pond," said Charlie.

"I thought you were a tramp," said Grandfather. "Tramps don't make ponds."

"Well," said Charlie, "sometimes I like to tramp around, and sometimes I like to make ponds."

"Any tramp that can make a pond like that is going to be some beaver one of these days," said Father.

"That's how it is now-a-days," said Grandfather. "You never know when a tramp will turn out to be a beaver."[37]

The printed page confronts the beginning reader with a representation of oral language—specifically, written language forms realized as letters, letter patterns, and punctuation symbols that provide intonation clues. A child's oral language system in most instances is highly developed in the form of sounds; sound pattern production; sentence production; lexical, relational, and nonlinguistic meaning; and, to some degree, interpretation. He has also developed certain specific interests, attitudes, and early values and he may have developed a strategy to approach decoding, meaning, and interpretative problems. As we examine the italicized sentence, be sure to relate the discussion to the communication model in Figure 2-9.

Oral and written language forms. An initial step in reading instruction is to help the child to perceive letters and letter patterns and to understand that these units represent his familiar sound system. You want him to be able to build letter-sound and letter pattern–sound pattern relationships within the context of the word (see dotted lines connecting these components in the model). In some instances you will focus on direct relationships between letter pattern sequence configurations and entire words or morphemes—commonly referred to as a sight vocabulary (see branched dotted line connecting the letter pattern and morpheme categories). Knowledge of root word and affix (prefixes and suffixes) boundaries can be a useful device for visual identification of letter units that are decodable on the basis of letter-sound and letter pattern–sound pattern clues. Feedback from interpretation of the previous context can provide valuable decoding clues by narrowing the possible words to be decoded (see feedback line for evaluating decoding information). Feedback information from the phrase and sentence structure can also help to limit the possible words for decoding based on intuitive word order and form class knowledge.

The following chart applies these various decoding strategies to our sample sentence as we assess the decoding information available, formulate decoding hypotheses about each word, and rapidly test the hypotheses through context in our attempt to decode the sentence.

"Well," said Charlie, "sometimes I like to tramp around, and sometimes I like to make ponds."

STRATEGY: ORAL AND WRITTEN LANGUAGE FORMS	SAMPLE WORDS
1. Letter-sound relationship consistent	Well - I - tramp - I - ponds
2. Letter pattern–sound pattern relationship consistent	*like* - *like* - *make*
3. Sight word	said - Charlie - to - to
4. Root word(s) and/or affix + 1, 2, or 3 above	some*time*s - sometimes - pond*s* - around
5. Root word and context	sometimes - ponds - around
6. Context, previous information	Charlie - tramp - ponds
7. Context, phrase, or sentence structure	said - to - tramp - and - to
8. Intonation clues	" " - , - . - capital letters
9. Nonlinguistic clues	illustrations in text

Obviously your instructional program will need provision for a variety of strategies in the decoding process to cover reading abilities as each child matures. As adult readers we rely heavily on letter pattern–sound pattern clues, a wide sight vocabulary, root words, and context clues.

Aspects of meaning. As a reader moves the sentence toward interpretation he begins to "chunk" the words into larger units or phrases that are so common in his developed oral language system. He does this by using the phrase and sentence component and by automatically assigning a temporary structure to the words and word groups—to be verified later by feedback information from the interpretation level (see feedback lines in model). He then processes the sentence through the various aspects of meaning. The lexical meaning component may be thought of as a "mental dictionary" of denotative and connotative meanings determined by the nature and variety of his experiences. The relational meaning component will account for such features as word order, function words, and subordination and will transform the sentence for integration at the interpretation level. Information of a nonlinguistic form, such as facial expression conveyed through a picture, is available through visual perception and will also be used at the interpretation level. The lexical, relational, and nonlinguistic meanings may interact before the final interpretation in order to define any of the three types of meaning more completely. Here is our

43

sample sentence again, to illustrate the meaning components that are essential to the final interpretation.

"Well," said Charlie, "sometimes I like to tramp around, and sometimes I like to make ponds."

STRATEGY: ASPECTS OF MEANING	WORDS AND WORD GROUPS
1. Lexical	*Charlie:* a little beaver, the main story character searching for his identity
	sometimes: at times or on occasion
	like: to enjoy or be fond of
	make: to build or construct
2. Relational	*Well:* an opener indicating that an explanation is to follow
	said: indicates Charlie is speaking
	I: refers to Charlie
	and: connects or relates the two sentence groups
3. Lexical and relational	*to tramp around:* wandering about on foot from one place to another
	to make: building or constructing
4. Lexical, relational, and nonverbal	*ponds:* more than one small body of standing water formed by the beaver dam (picture clues important here)

Interpretation. The final interpretation of the sentence takes place by integrating the lexical, relational, and nonlinguistic meanings. As previously noted, the reader's interpretation of the discourse will require that he account for previous information or events in the reading material. His interpretation will be greatly influenced by his level of conceptual maturity and his ability to handle concepts at the concrete, functional, and abstract levels. As we shall see in Chapter 11, his interpretive ability will be directly related to his thinking processes—using factual, interpretive, and applicative levels—and will be influenced by his understanding of special language devices such as metaphor, simile, irony, and hyperbole.

We shall now consider the base sentence interpretations and the final semantic interpretation of our sample sentence.

"Well," said Charlie, "sometimes I like to tramp around, and sometimes I like to make ponds."

BASE SENTENCE INTERPRETATION	SEMANTIC INTERPRETATION
Charlie tramps.	Factual Level
Charlie makes ponds.	Distinguishing details

BASE SENTENCE INTERPRETATION	SEMANTIC INTERPRETATION

Charlie likes tramping sometimes.
Charlie likes making ponds sometimes.
	Interpretive Level
	  Identifying details
	  Inferring cause-and-effect relationships

Charlie likes tramping sometimes, and Charlie likes building ponds sometimes.	Resulting in the interpretation that: Charlie the little beaver searching for his place in life enjoys wandering about from place to place on foot at times, and at other times he enjoys building beaver dams that form small bodies of standing water.

The semantic interpretation is then categorized, probably in a form more similar to the base sentence interpretation above, and retained in memory for immediate recall in evaluating running discourse or for later interpretive use.

Throughout the various stages of the communication process the reader will be directed by his affective mobilizers (see bottom of model). This direction may take the form of specific questions—for example, Why did Charlie think he wanted to become a tramp?—that help to identify specific content that can answer the question. On the other hand his attitude toward the topic or even toward the act of reading may be so potent in a positive or a negative sense as to impede his interpretation of the material or even to terminate his participation because of little motivation or drive. The cognitive strategies (see bottom of model) are likewise involved in all stages. These strategies not only provide an approach for achieving the established objective or objectives such as answering the question or questions Did Charlie's parents and grandparents change their attitude toward his activities? Why?; they also dictate a shift in approach should initial attempts prove fruitless.

We have moved from left to right through the communication model to examine the act of reading involving written and oral language forms, aspects of meaning, and interpretation. We would proceed through the model in the same direction if we wanted to examine the listening process, and in the reverse direction if we wanted to examine the process of writing or speaking.

This application of the communication model should demonstrate to you that the process of communication is indeed complex, and that morphological and syntactical language forms, meaning aspects, and interpretation are common to all types of communication, reading, writing, speech, and listening. The phonological language form and auditory perception are unique to speaking and listening, while the graphological system and visual perception are unique to reading and writing. The affective mobilizers and cognitive strategies apply to all components of the model. Thus similarities and differences in reading-language processing should become evident.

A more complete understanding of the communication process will enable you to do a better job of formulating instructional goals, building instructional objectives, and designing and implementing your reading-language instructional program. Knowing the various components of the communication process will provide you with a base for immediate and effective evaluation of reading-language achievement and a strategy for identifying difficulties that youngsters may have. We shall use this communication model often in Chapters 4 through 14 as we examine and develop instructional approaches to reading-language learning. In the next chapter we shall briefly consider the development of our oral and written language systems and derive seven classroom-related concepts of value in understanding and explaining the dynamics of language to youngsters.

Footnotes

[1]George A. Miller, "Some Preliminaries to Psycholinguistics," *American Psychologist,* 20 (1965), 15-20.

[2]Robert B. Ruddell, "Psycholinguistic Implications for a Systems of Communication Model," *Psycholinguistics and the Teaching of Reading* (April 1968), pp. 61-78.

[3]Committee on National Interest, *The National Interest and the Teaching of English* (Champaign, Ill.: National Council of Teachers of English, 1961).

[4]Committee on National Interest, *The National Interest and Continuing Education of Teachers of English* (Champaign, Ill.: National Council of Teachers of English, 1964).

[5]Susan Ervin-Tripp and Wick Miller, "Language Development," *Sixty-second Yearbook— NSSE* (Chicago: University of Chicago Press, 1963), pp. 108-43.

[6]The phonemic representation of a sound is shown by placing the phonemic symbol between two diagonal lines or bars.

[7]James Sledd, *A Short Introduction to English Grammar* (Chicago: Scott, Foresman and Company, 1959).

[8]Richard F. Venezky, "English Orthography: Its Graphic Structure and Its Relation to Sound," *Reading Research Quarterly,* 2 (Spring 1967), 75-106. Ronald Wardhaugh, *Reading: A Linguistic Perspective* (New York: Harcourt Brace Jovanovich, Inc., 1969), pp. 97-118. David W. Reed, "A Theory of Language, Speech and Writing," *Linguistics and Reading,* Highlights of the Preconvention Institutes (Newark, Del.: International Reading Association, 1966), pp. 4-25.

[9]Ervin-Tripp and Miller, "Language Development." Wick R. Miller and Susan Ervin, "The Development of Grammar in Child Language," *Monographs of the Society for Research in Child Development,* 19, No. 92 (1964), 9-34.

[10]Charles C. Fries, *The Structure of English* (New York: Harcourt Brace Jovanovich, Inc., 1952). Nelson W. Francis, *The Structure of American English* (New York: The Ronald Press Company, 1958). Sledd, *English Grammar.*

[11]Noam Chomsky, *Syntactic Structures* (The Hague: Mouton & Co., Publishers, 1957).

[12]J. A. Fodor and J. J. Katz, *The Structure of Language* (Englewood Cliffs, N.J.: Prentice-Hall, Inc., 1965). Jerrold J. Katz and Paul M. Postal, *An Integrated Theory of Linguistic Descriptions*

(Cambridge, Mass.: The M.I.T. Press, 1964), Research Monograph No. 26. Noam Chomsky, *Aspects of a Theory of Syntax* (Cambridge, Mass.: The M.I.T. Press, 1965).

[13](New York: Holt, Rinehart and Winston, 1965).

[14](New York: Harcourt Brace Jovanovich, Inc., 1968).

[15]Edward T. Hall, *The Silent Language* (New York: Doubleday & Company, Inc., 1959).

[16]Dwight Bolinger, *Aspects of Language* (New York: Harcourt Brace Jovanovich, Inc., 1968), pp. 14-15.

[17]Mary K. Smith, "Measurement of the Size of General English Vocabulary through the Elementary Grades and High School," *Genetic Psychology Monographs,* 24 (1941), 311-45. Medorah E. Smith, "An Investigation of the Development of the Sentence and the Extent of Vocabulary in Young Children," *Studies in Child Welfare,* 5 (Iowa City: State University of Iowa, 1926), No. 5, 28-71. Marie Lindsay, "A Descriptive Exploration of the Growth and Development of Spontaneous Oral Vocabulary of Elementary School Children" (unpublished doctoral dissertation, University of California, Berkeley, 1969).

[18]Jean Piaget, "The Genetic Approach to the Psychology of Thought," *Journal of Educational Psychology,* 52 (1961), 275-81. See also D. E. Berlyne, "Recent Developments in Piaget's Work," *British Journal of Educational Psychology,* 27 (1957), 1-12.

[19]Martin Deutsch, "The Disadvantaged Child and the Learning Process," *Education in Depressed Areas,* ed. A. Harry Passow (New York: Bureau of Publications, Teachers College, Columbia University, 1963), pp. 163-79.

[20]Lev S. Vygotsky, *Thought and Language* (Cambridge, Mass.: The M.I.T. Press, 1962).

[21]John B. Carroll, "Words, Meanings and Concepts," *Harvard Educational Review,* 34, No. 2 (Spring 1964), 178-202.

[22]Piaget, "The Genetic Approach to the Psychology of Thought."

[23]Karl C. Garrison, Albert J. Kingston, and Arthur S. McDonald, *Educational Psychology* (New York: Appleton-Century-Crofts, 1964). Benjamin S. Bloom and Lois J. Broder, "Problem-Solving Processes of College Students," *Supplementary Educational Monographs, No. 73* (Chicago: University of Chicago Press, 1950), pp. 1-31. Morris L. Bigge and Maurice P. Hunt, *Psychological Foundations of Education* (New York: Harper & Row, Publishers, 1962).

[24]John F. Travers, *Learning: Analysis and Application* (New York: David McKay Co., 1965), pp. 197-224.

[25]Herbert Klausmeier, *Learning and Human Abilities: Educational Psychology* (New York: Harper & Row, Publishers, 1961).

[26]W. F. Dukes, "Psychological Studies of Values," *Psychological Bulletin,* 52 (1955), 24-50.

[27]Berlyne, "Recent Developments in Piaget's Work."

[28]Dolores Durkin, "Children Who Learn To Read Before Grade One," *Reading Teacher,* 14 (1965), 112-17.

[29]Roy A. Kress, "An Investigation of the Relationship Between Concept Formation and Achievement in Reading" (unpublished doctoral dissertation, Temple University, 1955).

[30]Josephine A. Piekarz, "Getting Meaning from Reading," *Elementary School Journal,* 56 (1956), 303-9.

[31]J. J. Katz and J. A. Fodor, "The Structure of a Semantic Theory," *Language,* 39, No. 2 (1963), 170-210.

[32]Paul M. Postal, "Underlying and Superficial Linguistic Structure," *Harvard Educational Review,* 34 (1964), 246-66.

[33]Katz and Fodor, "The Structure of a Semantic Theory."

[34]H. Feifel and I. B. Lorge, "Qualitative Differences in the Vocabulary Responses of Children," *Journal of Educational Psychology,* 41 (January 1950), 1-18. David H. Russell, *The Dynamics of Reading,* ed. Robert B. Ruddell (Waltham, Mass.: Blaisdell Publishing Co., 1970).

[35]George A. Miller, "The Magical Number Seven, Plus or Minus Two," *Psychological Review,* 63 (1956), 81-97.

[36]Ulric Neisser, *Cognitive Psychology* (New York: Meredith Publishing Company, 1967).

[37]From *Charlie the Tramp* by Russell Hoban. Copyright © 1969 by Russell Hoban. Reprinted by permission of Four Winds Press.

3

The Dynamics of Language:
Classroom Concepts

Focusing Questions

1. What key factors have influenced the growth and development of the English language? What is the value of understanding these factors to classroom instruction?
2. What is the major difference between the modern study of language and that of the eighteenth century? Can this difference be related to your observation of language as used by children in your classroom?
3. How can an understanding of geographical and social language varieties be of value to reading-language instruction?
4. How has the English writing system developed? What are the implications of this development for reading and spelling instruction?
5. What significant concepts for classroom instruction can be derived from the study of language?

If we were to hear the speech of King Alfred (an English king in the ninth century) we would probably think we were hearing a foreign language. Likewise, we would have great difficulty understanding Chaucer's speech, and even Shakespeare's would sound strange. English is constantly undergoing change in phonology, morphology, syntax, and lexicon. We are rarely conscious of this change, except for slang and the appearance of new technical words, because the process is slow and gradual.

What does such a discussion have to do with reading-language instruction? Simply this: The way our language has developed has important implications for instruction. For example, we can understand the development of our lexical items or vocabulary more completely when we realize the ways English has obtained words from other languages through borrowing. We can also understand the reasons for a number of our so-called spelling "irregularities." Certainly an appreciation of language change and geographical and cultural variations will cause us to become more sensitive to geographical and nonstandard varieties of English and the use of slang

49

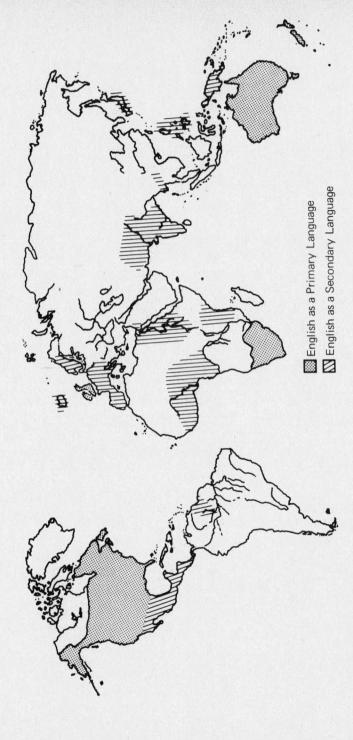

English as a Primary Language

English as a Secondary Language

Figure 3-1. World Use of English

for special purposes. (For example, "Bring your own *ax* man!" An *ax* is a guitar in the language of the jazz-rock world.)

Approximately 300 million of the world's population, about one in ten, use English as their primary language, and an additional 300-400 million understand and speak English to some degree, ranging from India and many other former British colonies to the Philippines (Figure 3-1). Thus one in every four persons uses English to some degree, which is astonishing when we consider that there are over 6,000 different languages in the world. English is the international language of aviation, spoken by pilots and control tower operators everywhere in the world. It is interesting that heavy equipment and other materials shipped from Russia to the Near East are stamped "Made In U.S.S.R."—in English.[1]

THE GENESIS OF ENGLISH

But what of the origin of this language, and what factors influenced its development? The earliest form of our language is thought to have been used by a small tribe of nomads who wandered through eastern Europe about 2500 B.C. These people divided into an eastern group and a western group, and these subdivided into several main language branches of the Indo-European language family.[2]

Our interest is in the *Western* group, which divided into Greek, Latin, Celtic, and *Germanic.* The latter group then subdivided into the East Germanic, which became Gothic, and the North Germanic, which produced Swedish, Danish, Norwegian, and Icelandic. The *West Germanic,* of greatest immediate interest to us, subdivided into High German, which later became modern German as we know it, and *Low German,* which developed into four languages, *English,* Dutch, Frisian, and Flemish.[3] The similarities among the following words reflect the "family" history of the languages. These family relationships are shown in Figure 3-2.

English	German	Dutch	Swedish	Danish
one	eins	een	en	een
two	zwei	twee	två	to
three	drei	drie	tre	tre
father	Vater	vader	fader	fader
mother	Mutter	moeder	moder	moder
brother	Bruder	broeder	brodoer	broder
sister	Schwester	zuster	syster	søster

Several thousand years after the origin of the small tribe of nomads, a descendant tribe known as the Celts crossed the channel from Europe to Britain with their meager possessions and settled on the island. About 55 B.C. the Romans, who had previously subdued France, conquered the island in order to obtain metal and food for the advancing edges of their civilization. Physical evidence of the Roman influence is still present in England in the form of ancient roads, walls, and baths, but there was little

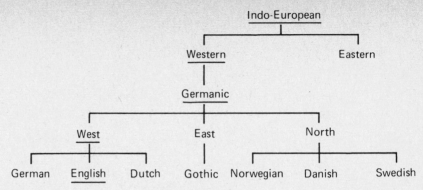

Figure 3-2. The Indo-European Language Tree

Roman influence on the language. Around 410 A.D. the Romans withdrew from the island in order to defend their tottering Italian homeland, leaving the island to the Romanized Celts.

With the withdrawal of the Roman armies the way was open for new invasions. Between 450 and 550 the Jutes, Angles, and Saxons migrated to Britain from Denmark and northern Germany, not without battle from the Celts. It was during this time that King Arthur lived (though he was probably not a king, as legend suggests, but a Romanized Celtic general who experienced some success against the Anglo-Saxons).

The language of the vanquished Romanized Celts had little influence on the Anglo-Saxon languages because there was little opportunity for interaction between speakers of the two language groups; the Anglo-Saxons regarded and treated the Celts as an inferior people.[4] The languages spoken by the Jutes, Saxons, and Angles were closely related, and they understood each other very well.

Old English

The period of the language now known as Old English extended from the earliest written documents, at the close of the seventh century, to about 1100 A.D. The Anglo-Saxon conversion to Christianity began toward the end of the sixth century, with the advent of Christian missionaries from Christianized countries and Rome into Britain. Saint Columba arrived from Christian Ireland in the second half of the sixth century and began to convert the native inhabitants. By the year 700 most Anglo-Saxons had become Christians.[5]

This conversion and related influences were of definite advantage to the inhabitants of Britain. One immediate result was the acquisition of an alphabet to record their own language. Although no manuscripts of their early writing have been found, manuscripts dating from about 1000 A.D.

contain work thought to have been written in the late seventh and early eighth centuries. During this time the English schools of writing were led by such authors as Caedmon, Bede, and the unknown author of Beowulf.[6]

The first large influx of foreign loanwords came into English during this period.[7] For example, the words *minister, candle, school,* and *silk* came from the Latin of the Church. The Danes and Norse invaded the island around 800 A.D., and by the tenth century they had integrated with the Anglo-Saxons. From the Danes English got such words as *egg, gift, sky, scant,* and *law.* The main body of Old English, however, remained predominantly West Germanic.

The lines below from *Beowulf,* the story of Beowulf, Grendel, and King Hrothgar, are a sample of Old English. They provide some feeling for the language, and despite the great difference between this language and present-day English we can recognize a few words, such as *what, we, day,* and *cyning* (king).

Beowulf, lines 1–11

Hwæt, wē Gār-Dena   in gēardagum,
What!   we of-Spear-Danes in yore-days

Þēodcyninga   þrym   gefrūnon,
of-folk-kings   prowess heard

hūȝā æ Þelingas ellen   fremedon!
how the princes   deeds-of-valor wrought

Oft Scyld Scēfing   sceaÞena   Þrēatum,
Oft Shield Sheaf-child of-enemies bands

monegum mǣgÞum meodosetla   oftēah,
from-many tribes   mead-benches tore

egsode   eorlas, syÞÞan ǣ rest wearÞ
terrified   earls   since   first   he-was

fēasceaft funden; hē Þæs   frōfre gebād;
wretched found   he for-that solace received

wēox under wolcnum weorÞmyndum Þāh,
grew under heavens honor   won

oÞ Þaet him ǣ ghwylc ymbsittendra
until   him everyone   of nearby peoples

ofer hronrāde   hȳran scolde,
over whale-road obey   had to

gomban gyldan; Þǣt wæs gōd cyning!
tribute   yield   he was good king

Old English was characterized by a relatively full inflectional system: three and four case endings for nouns and adjectives and fuller verbal endings than at any later time. The spelling system directly represented the sounds to a high degree. There were no silent syllables, and word order was not critical to meaning because the inflectional endings clarified relationships and meaning.

Middle English

In the year 1066 the military victory of William Duke of Normandy over Harold the Saxon in the Battle of Hastings initiated a chain of events that produced the greatest change in the English language up to that time.[8] Because the Normans spoke French, English was banned from the courts and in all polite and official usage; even so the Britons continued to use their own language. Great numbers of Normans came to the island, as rulers and landlords, but the movement was not a national migration as had been the case with the earlier invasions, so French, the language of the nobility, did not become the language of the people.[9]

After the conquest instruction in English practically ceased, partly because the English clergy, who had assumed the instructional role, were replaced with the Norman clerics. As a result illiteracy became more prevalent; English was neglected in writing and uncorrected by any sort of formal teaching.

Although sound changes had occurred in the language before the invasion, these tended to vary and change more rapidly afterwards than during any period before. It is possible that the conditions described above speeded this process. Many endings sounded alike after a time, and the result was less emphasis on case endings of nouns and adjectives and greater reliance on word order and structure words such as prepositions. The Middle English sentence fell increasingly into the word order of subject, predicate, complement that is basic to our language today.[10]

At the end of the twelfth century, England was a trilingual country: French for literary and courtly expression, Latin for the Church and legal purposes, and English for communication among the masses. A number of French words came into English during this period. When one spoke English, he often referred to French ideas, French customs, and French names. Words used in everyday activities included words related to government: *state, court, duke, duchess, chancellor, parliament, tax,* and *treaty;* words related to the Church: *pray, preach, religion, saint, trinity, clergy, sermon,* and *baptism;* words related to food: *beef, pork, veal, mutton, fruit,* and *cream;* words related to the household and learning: *chair, parlor, grammar,* and *study;* and words related to the military: *army, navy, soldier, troops, armor, enemy, march,* and *danger.*[11] It is important to note that most of the English function words such as prepositions, conjunctions, and auxiliaries—the glue that holds the sentence together—were not replaced by borrowings.

In 1204 another political event occurred that proved to be of importance to English: King John lost Normandy. Now the Norman nobility in England no longer had a "native homeland." The result was a new nationalism, the former Norman barons now considering themselves Englishmen, and English became the free tongue again. Otto Jespersen, a noted language historian, has emphasized that the heaviest influx of French vocabulary did not occur until this time.[12]

By the time of Edward I all Englishmen, regardless of descent, were united, and in 1362 the Chancellor opened Parliament with a speech in English.[13] English reappeared during the twelfth and thirteenth centuries as a written language. By the fourteenth century all important work was being translated into English, and very little was done in French.[14] The writings of Chaucer were the first to use many French and Latin words in common usage.

The following lines from *The Canterbury Tales*, relating the celebration of spring in England after the long winter, provide an interesting contrast between Middle English and Old English. Middle English made less use of case systems and inflections and relied more on word order and structure to express meaning.[15]

THE CANTERBURY TALES, lines 1–18

When that Aprill with his shoures soote
The droghte of *March*[16] hath *perced* to the roote,
And bathed every veyne in swich *licour*
of which *vertu engendred* is the *flour;*
Whan Zephirus eek with his sweete breeth
Inspired hath in every holt and heeth
The *tendre* croppes, and the yonge sonne
Hath in the Ram his halv[e] *cours* yronne,
And smale foweles maken *melodye,*
That slepen al the nyght with open ye
(So priketh hem *nature* in hir *corages*);
Thanne longen folk to goon on *pilgrimage*[s],
And *palmeres* for to seken *straunge* strondes,
To ferne halwes, kowthe in sondry londes;
And *specially* from every shires ende
Of Engelond to Caunterbury they wende,
The hooly blisful martir for to seke,
That hem hath holpen whan that they were seke.

Geoffrey Chaucer

The great influx of French words brought many new meanings to England, as well as equivalent labels (English: *cow, pig;* French: *beef, pork),*[17] especially after English was again accepted in all levels and classes.

Modern English

This period extends roughly from the seventeenth century to the present. Two major changes mark this period. The first is known as the great vowel shift, and the second involved the omission of certain vowel sounds in unstressed positions at the end of words.

The great vowel shift, which took place during the last of the fifteenth century and the sixteenth century, involved a systematic shift in pronunciation of the vowels.[18] An illustration is presented in the following:

	Middle English	Early Modern English	Modern English	
ride	/ridə/	/rəyd/	/rayd/	*ride*
but	/but/	/bət/	/bət/	*but*

In the first example *ride* was pronounced as the words *rid up* (omitting the last sound /p/) in Middle English, as a word that rhymes with the "Brooklyn pronunciation" of the word *bird* /bəyd/ in Early Modern English, and as the familiar pronunciation of the word *ride* /rayd/ in Modern English. The word *but* in Middle English was pronounced to rhyme with our modern pronunciation of the word *put* /put/; while in Early Modern and Modern English the word *but* is pronounced as /bət/.

The second major change was the complete elimination of certain vowel sounds in unstressed positions at the end of words. Dropping the ending schwa sound /ə/ produced certain grammatical changes. In Middle English, for example, this sound was used to distinguish adverbs, such as *slowe* /slawə/, from adjectives, such as *slow* /slaw/. It is thought that the loss of this distinctive ending for adverbs promoted the -*ly* ending that now distinguishes adverbs from adjectives in Modern English. Grammarians often insist on "Drive slow-*ly*" even though *slow,* following the ending loss, is a legitimate adverb derived from the Middle English *slowe.*[19]

At the time of the great vowel shift printers also began to standardize spelling. By the time they arrived at some conclusions many sound values had shifted, and as a result a number of sound-letter (phoneme-grapheme) correspondences were no longer regular. Discrepancies continued to arise because of letters inserted into words for etymological reasons. For example, the *b* in *doubt* was erroneously inserted in an attempt to account for The Latin derivative *debt.* Other problems arose by creating spelling through analogy: the *s* in *island* is there because of a decision to respell Middle English *iland* after the word *isle,* which was similar in meaning but unrelated in spelling.[20]

Printing, however, was one of the main reasons that London English was established as the standard literary language. William Caxton introduced printing into England in 1476, and from the beginning he used the then-current London language forms. His books and those of his successors

56

contributed to the adoption of London English as the prestige or standard dialect.[21] Many thousands of words came into the language during the Renaissance and were spread to the public by the printing presses. Latin and Greek were the main reservoirs when a new word was called for.

One of the greatest contributors to vocabulary was Shakespeare, whose writings are said to contain a vocabulary of about 21,000 words. The following sonnet from Shakespeare illustrates contrasts between Early Modern English and the Middle and Old English samples.

SONNET I

From fairest creatures we desire increase,
That thereby beauties Rose might never die,
But as the riper should by time decrease,
His tender heire might beare his memory:
But thou contracted to thine owne bright eyes,
Feed'st thy lights flame with selfe substantiall fewell,
Making a famine where aboundance lies,
Thy selfe thy foe, to thy sweet selfe too cruell:
Thou that art now the worlds fresh ornament,
And only herauld to the gaudy spring,
Within thine owne bud buriest thy content,
And tender chorle makst wast in niggarding:
    Pitty the world, or else this glutton be,
    To eate the worlds due, by the grave and thee.

William Shakespeare

By the end of the sixteenth century English was accepted as a language of serious scholarship.

During the seventeenth and eighteenth centuries a wave of reaction began to favor rigid standards for grammar and usage. This was a time of stylization and overrefinement in the arts, sciences, and society. The rich, educated, and status-sensitive considered themselves a great distance above the ordinary people, who they thought lived rather haphazardly, without learning, culture, or understanding. The concern for language standards resulted in part in Latin-based grammars. Such noted writers as Defoe, Addison, and Swift even advocated the establishment of an academy similar to those in France and Italy to issue final judgment on disputed questions of grammar and usage.[22] From the seventeenth century English was a battleground between the conflicting forces of the traditionalists and the innovators, the writers of grammars and the writers of literature, the philosophers of the language and the speakers of the language.

The practical need for a spelling standard and a pronunciation resource resulted in the first dictionary, published about 1600. It contained 2,500 words briefly defined. Samuel Johnson's *Dictionary of the English Language,* published in 1755 and revised in 1773, dominated the field in England for approximately one century. Even Dr. Johnson refused to mark the full pronunciation of words, because, as he said, "there was too much disagreement among the speakers."

From the seventeenth century to the present English was spread over the globe through the widespread colonization and commerce of the British Empire, to which it owes a great deal of its scope, as expressed in Charlton Laird's statement, "Trade followed the flag, linguistics followed trade, and the British flag during the last two centuries has been everywhere."[23]

English of course found its most fruitful soil in the Western Hemisphere, in the United States and Canada. At the time of the early English settlements in this country there was considerable variation (such variations are known as *dialects*) in the language used in England, which resulted in dialectal differences in the colonies along the eastern seaboard in what is now Massachusetts, Virginia, Maryland, and Rhode Island.[24] Because of geographical separation and poor transportation there was limited language interchange between the colonies and various dialectal forms were perpetuated that still exist today despite the effects of rapid forms of transportation and communication and the existence of a highly mobile population. This is most obvious in the eastern part of the United States, as indicated on the dialect map in Figure 3-3. Western expansion produced a great deal of dialect mixing, and as a consequence marked dialectal distinctions are not present in the West. (This has yet to be systematically investigated.)

The broad eastern dialect areas include the northern, midland, and southern areas. Dialectal variation may be considered from differences in *lexicon* (vocabulary), *grammar,* and *pronunciation.* For example, in the northern and midland areas the animal with a stripe down its back and at times of a putrid odor is known as a *skunk,* while in the South and parts of the Midland it is known as a *polecat.* In the northern area the utensil used to carry water or milk is known as a *pail,* but it is a *bucket* in the midland and southern areas. Grammatical variation is evident in the use of the past tense of the word *dive.* In the northern area the word commonly used is *dove,* while in the Midland and South it is *dived.* Pronunciation varieties are evident in pronunciation of the word *greasy,* which is pronounced /griysiy/ in the North and sections of the north Midland and /griyziy/ in the South. The words *Mary* (name of a girl), *marry* (to wed), and *merry* (happy) are pronounced with distinct differences in the Northern Proper region, but no distinction is made in the upper midwestern area.[25]

The significant point is that any one of these language varieties is as adequate and correct as another. Individuals reared in one section of the country simply use the language forms present in their environment. It is only necessary to reflect on the language used by Presidents Kennedy,

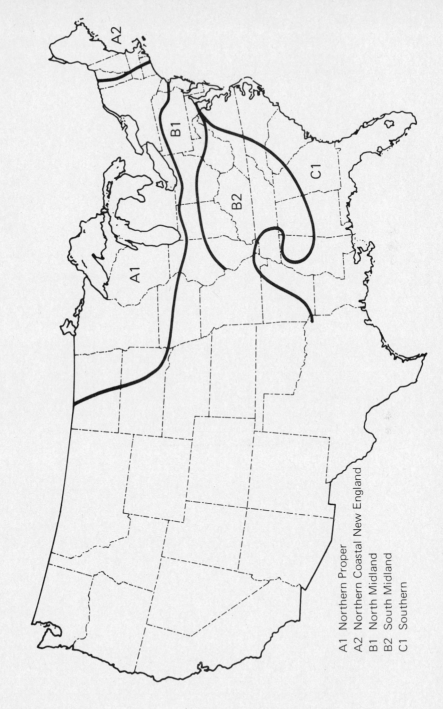

Figure 3-3. Geographical Language Variation in the United States

A1 Northern Proper
A2 Northern Coastal New England
B1 North Midland
B2 South Midland
C1 Southern

Johnson, and Nixon to observe distinctly different but acceptable varieties of our language. We shall pursue the implications of language variations from the standpoint of standard and nonstandard social varieties in Chapter 9.

From the time of the early settlements in this country the language contained a number of Indian loanwords, essentially from the Algonquian stock (which included Arapaho, Blackfoot, Cheyenne, Cree, Delaware, Fox, Micmac, Chippewa, and Penobscot tribes). These include *opossum, moose, skunk,* and *woodchuck* (creatures unique to the North American continent), vegetation names such as *hickory, pecan, squash,* and *persimmon,* and social custom and family member words such as *powwow, caucus, wampum, papoose,* and *squaw.*[26]

The language was a unifying element for immigrants from various countries who found some grasp of a second language essential for basic interaction. The immigrant populations also contributed new vocabulary to the language. From New Amsterdam came Dutch words *coleslaw, cookie, boss, dope, stoop* (porch), *sleigh, waffle,* and *Santa Claus.* From the Pennsylvania German came *fat-cakes* (doughnuts), *smearcase* (cottage cheese), *dunk* (to dip), *hex* (to cast a spell on), and possibly *applebutter.* By way of the Canadian border through French explorers the words *prairie, chowder, buccaneer, levee, voyager,* and possibly *gopher* entered the language. The words *mosquito* (little fly), *negro* (black, an adjective that was converted to a noun), *armada,* and *alligator* came into the language through Spanish. As the westward movement began more Spanish words came in as the interaction between the pioneers and Spanish-speaking people of the West and Southwest increased. These words included *burro, chili, pronto, patio, tornado,* and *cafeteria.*

Other borrowings thoroughly incorporated into the language include the African words *banjo, goober* (peanut), *chigger, hoodoo,* and *voodoo;* the Italian words *balcony, opera, piano, umbrella,* and *volcano;* the Persian words *caravan, khaki, shawl, sherbet, chess, lemon, turban,* and *borax;* the Greek words *acrobat, magic, barometer, elastic,* and *tactics;* and the Russian words *ruble, steppe,* and *vodka.*[27]

In our technological age we use combined borrowings to label new discoveries and inventions, as illustrated in the word *terramycin:* the first element is from Latin, and the second is from Greek. Other examples of combined forms from various sources include *astronaut, space docking, rapid transit, jumbojet, cinerama,* and *freeway.* We are constantly in the process of adding new vocabulary to our language.

Our language, derived from that of a small group of nomadic people in eastern Europe, is now one of the world's largest, most influential languages. During the past thousand years it has expanded through flexible absorption of vocabulary from many languages and through marked sound and grammatical changes. It is characterized by its extremely mixed vocabulary and by a simple inflection system that requires a relatively

What new concepts and word labels might be developed through this experience?
Has this vocabulary been borrowed, or created for a purpose unique to a highly
technical society? How could you find out? *(Photo by Bayer, Monkmeyer Press
Photo Service)*

fixed word order. Basic English has been offered to beginners through a
vocabulary of 850 words, which would seem to be adequate for basic
communication purposes. The advantages of English as a universal language appear to surpass those of Chinese and Russian by far,[28] but the
question of a universal language will have to be answered by future generations.

We shall now turn to the development of our writing system.

THE DEVELOPMENT OF WRITING

Our writing system is a most economical type of representation for our
language. The first writing system was of course pictographic: simple
drawings or pictures were used to represent events. Samples of pictographic writing on wood and rock have been calculated to be as old as
61 20,000 B.C.

A more advanced writing system is a logographic system, wherein every word has a separate symbol. Chinese, for example, has between 40,000 and 50,000 different characters. The dollar sign ($) and numerals (2, 8) are examples of word signs, but they can be represented in alphabetic form as well.

The syllabary writing system approaches our alphabetic system in economy. Japanese is such a system; it uses between seventy and eighty characters, each representing a syllable. These characters, used in combination with intonation pattern cues, provide for much greater economy than the logographic system.

Our advanced alphabetic system has not always been so efficient as it is now; it has in fact evolved through the writing systems just described to its present form. It is thought, however, that all writing systems derive from the Sumerian writing system developed in the Middle East about 3000 B.C. The Egyptian writing system, known as hieroglyphics (*hieros*, sacred, *glyphé*, carving), was developed under Sumerian influence. This system was a mixture of word writing and syllable writing. Ronald Langacker says of the evolution process:

> Word signs came to be used as syllabic signs by means of the rebus principle. For example, suppose word signs were available for *ray* and *sing*, but not for *racing*. The natural thing to do when the word *racing* was needed in a written message would be to represent it by combining the signs for *ray* and *sing*. When this system is followed consistently, the signs involved lose their status as word signs and take on purely phonetic significance. In this way a basically syllabic system can develop from a basically logographic one.[29]

The syllabic writing system of the Phoenicians developed from the Egyptian system. These people were seafaring traders, and it is thought that their form of writing was used along the western shores of the Aegean around the ninth century B.C. and was therefore the source of the Greek alphabet.[30]

Our principle of alphabetic writing was formulated by the Greeks, because of the difference between Greek and the Semitic languages. A writing system based on consonants alone was satisfactory and very economical for the Semitic languages, because vowels could be predicted from the patterning of the consonants, but Greek needed vowels in written communication to clarify meaning.[31] For example

> . . . the same sign for *ta* could also be used for *ti, te,* and *to.* Vowel signs were therefore added to the ambiguous syllabic signs to avoid confusion. Thus, if the sign for *ta* could also be used for *ti, te,* and *to,* one would add to it a sign for *a* to indicate that *ta* was meant. In effect then, *ta* was written *ta-a, ti* was written *ti-i,* and so on. When this device was used systematically, the original ambiguous syllabic signs came to be reinterpreted as signs for single consonants. The

sign for *ta,* when accompanied consistently by the *a* sign, was interpreted as standing for the single segment *t.*[32]

Our word alphabet was derived from the first two letters of the Greek alphabet—*aleph,* meaning *ox* in Hebrew, and *beth,* meaning *house.*

The Etruscans borrowed the alphabet from the Greeks, and the Romans borrowed it from the Etruscans for Latin. Latin was the scholarly language in the Middle Ages, and the monks who wrote in Latin developed new shapes for the letters, probably because of the need to write faster and to conserve space because of the scarcity of writing materials.

As indicated previously, Early Modern English scribes and orthographers effected a number of changes. One such change was an attempt to restore the Latin root by substituting *t* for *c* in such suffixes as *tion* and *tial* and thus producing *nation* and *essential* for Middle English *nacion* and *essenciall.* The letter *u* was often replaced with the letter *o* when in close context with the letters *m, n, u,* and *v.* This was a most logical step for creating legible manuscripts, because at the time there was no dot over the letter *i,* but the result was "irregularities" in words like *some, love,* and *ton.*[33]

Our present alphabet was developed with the invention of printing. Gutenberg's invention of a printing process using movable type around 1430 laid the foundation for widespread printing. Caxton began printing in London about 1476, and issued a first English edition of Chaucer in 1478. The first English printing press arrived in Massachusetts about twenty years after the landing of the Pilgrims, and the first English book published in this country was *The Whole Book of Psalmes Faithfully Translated into English Metre.*[34]

Source	Form	Representational System
Cave man	= ox	Pictographic
Sumerians and Egyptians		Word-syllabic
Phoenicians	(early form)	
	= aleph (later form)	Syllabic
Greeks	A = alpha	Alphabetic
Romans	A	
Monks	*a*	
Printing Press	a	

63   **Figure 3-4.** Development of Our Alphabet: The Letter *a*

Thus our alphabet has evolved (Figure 3-4) into an efficient system that represents over half a million words through twenty-six letters and a variety of letter patterns.

LANGUAGE CONCEPTS FOR THE CLASSROOM

As you develop a functional understanding of the origin of English and the ways it achieves its communicative function (Chapter 2), a wealth of ideas and implications becomes available for classroom application. You can draw numerous language concepts from the discussion in this chapter and from the communication model presented in Chapter 2. The following seven concepts relate directly to a classroom language skills program:

1. Language is a system actualized as sounds.
2. Pitch, stress, and juncture are important parts of the system.
3. The connection between a symbol and its meaning is arbitrary.
4. Lexical items and grammatical patterns convey meaning to those who know the code.
5. English has a characteristic group of grammatical patterns.
6. A language continually changes.
7. No language or dialect can be considered "better" or "worse" than any other.

As you interact with the following discussion try to extend these concepts through additional examples that are appropriate to youngsters at your level of interest. Many of the suggestions for application may be utilized at various levels by adjusting the degree of abstractness.

Language is a system actualized as sounds. Our reference to the sound system relates directly to the phonemes and the sound patterns in our language that distinguish meaning. You can build an awareness of our sound system by exploring the ways we produce various sounds and the roles played by our sound production apparatus. For example, if air does not escape from the lungs, can we speak? What happens if our vocal cords do not vibrate? (We whisper.) If our tongue does not move to help form sounds? Greater sensory awareness of sound production, like having children feel the vibration of their vocal cords by placing their fingers on their throats, can increase appreciation of our sound system.

As students develop a general awareness of the physiological apparatus involved in speech production you can examine specific sounds for production contrasts and their value in differentiating meaning. (See Figures 2-2 through 2-4 in Chapter 2 for descriptions of consonant and vowel production.) For example, the phonemes /m/ and /n/ can be prolonged indefinitely as air escapes through the nose to differentiate the words *mat* /mæt/ and *nat* /næt/. The value of these two sounds becomes obvious when children hold their noses and attempt to pronounce the words *mat* and *nat.* The phonemes /b/ and /p/ can be contrasted by noting that we use our vocal cords in combination with our lips to produce /b/, as in *bat* /bæt/, while we use only our lips to produce /p/, as in *pat* /pæt/.

You can also heighten awareness of our sound system through informal contrast with another language. This can be accomplished in a very effective and enjoyable way by listening to and learning several easy and delightful songs in a foreign language. "Silent Night" is readily available in many languages, and "Frère Jacques" in French and "The Happy Wanderer" and "Cradle Song" in German are appealing to children. You may wish to extend such an experience by focusing on the specific sounds in the words of a song that differ from English. For example, in "Silent Night" you can demonstrate that the German *ch* in *nacht* is pronounced using a sound similar to the /k/ phoneme in English but that it differs in that the air is released in a continuous stream similar to the way we produce the /h/ phoneme. Also, the German word *Knabe,* which has a sound sequence that does not occur in English, can be used to illustrate sound patterning that does not exist in our language. Once your students have discovered that other languages possess different sequences of sounds in their vocabularies, you may wish to use our sound system to explore English and non-English sound combinations. For example, is *nsasm* /nzəzm/ easier to pronounce than *ksikh* /ksikh/? (For some the last sound combination is very difficult to pronounce.)

Children also enjoy hearing simple familiar stories recorded or read in several languages. This is of value in increasing appreciation of other sound systems and is also relevant to the concept dealing with the arbitrary nature of language. *The Three Bears* and *Cinderella* work well because of the use of dialogue. This type of experience provides an excellent opportunity to capitalize on the abilities of children whose native language is other than English, or who speak a second language. Bilingual parents can also be very effective as community resource persons to present familiar stories in a second language.

Youngsters also enjoy building a repertoire of oral greetings in various languages. For example, *good morning* is *guten Morgen* in German, *buenos días* in Spanish, and *bonjour* in French. This type of experience involves a functional use of different sound systems and can be exciting for youngsters.

Some students fail to realize that sounds and letters are not synonymous, but that letters and letter patterns *represent* sounds and sound patterns. This confusion can be eliminated by examining different spellings that represent the same sound; for example, the sound /iy/ is represented by *ea* in *meat,* by *y* in *funny,* by *ee* in *see,* by *ie* in *believe,* by *e* in *me,* and by *i–e* in *elite.*

An understanding of the letter patterning and sound patterning of our language will lead to the clarification of the invalid statement that the English word fish /fiš/ can be spelled g-h-o-t-i. In this well-known example gh represents the /f/ sound in cough, *o* represents the /i/ sound

Cradle Song

WORDS BY KARL SIMROCK
MUSIC BY JOHANNES BRAHMS

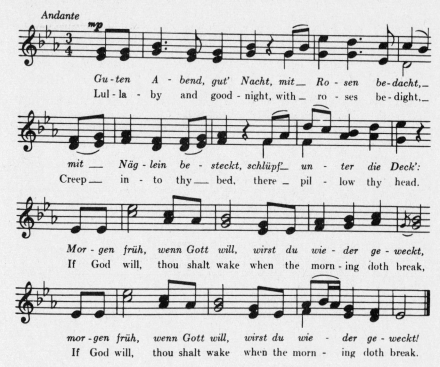

Andante

Gu - ten   A - bend, gut' Nacht, mit__ Ro - sen be - dacht,__
Lul - la - by   and   good - night, with__ ro - ses be - dight,__

mit __ Näg - lein be - steckt, schlüpf'__ un - ter die Deck':
Creep__   in - to thy__ bed, there __ pil - low thy head.

Mor - gen früh, wenn Gott will,   wirst du wie - der ge - weckt,
If   God will,   thou shalt wake when the morn - ing doth break,

mor - gen früh,   wenn Gott will,   wirst du wie - der ge - weckt!
If   God will,   thou shalt wake   when the morn - ing doth break.

From *Growing with Music* Related Arts Edition *by Harry R. Wilson, Walter Ehret, Alice
M. Knuth, Edward J. Herman, and Albert A. Renna © 1970 by Prentice-Hall, Inc., Englewood Cliffs, N.J. Reprinted by permission.*

in women, and *ti* represents the /š/ phoneme in the word nation. This
illustration does not represent our language in an accurate fashion because
of the regular sequence of phonemes: *gh* does not represent the /f/ phoneme in the initial position, nor does *ti* represent the /š/ phoneme in the
final position.

A useful technique for focusing attention on the sound-letter relationship
in our language is to present an interesting passage written in one of the
phonemic systems devised for English. This concept of a "new code" can
stimulate much enthusiasm for language study. For example, students
should be able to read part of the following passage without a complete
understanding of the symbols because the spellings are sufficiently like
conventional spellings.

ðə ˚'si ˈsɻpṇt

˚'si ˈsɻpṇts ar ˚'larj mə˚'rin ǽnəməlz əv ˈmost ən˚'yuẑuəl ˚'hæbəts ṇ
ə˚'pʊɻṇts | ðe ar ab'zɻvd ˚'onli ʌn ˚'worm ˚'wed̢ɻ | ˚'jenərli ʌn ˚'ɔgəst ɾ

66

sɛpˈˈtɛmbr̩ | wɛn ðe °ˈsəmtaˈmz °ˈraˈz tə ðə °ˈsrfəs °ˈloŋ ɪˈnəf tə gɛt ˈʌntə ðə
ˈpepr̩z ‖

The Sea Serpent

Sea serpents are large marine animals of most unusual habits and appearance.
They are observed only in warm weather, generally in August or September,
when they sometimes rise to the surface long enough to get into the papers.[35]

Pitch, stress, and juncture are important parts of the system. Children find great
pleasure in manipulating the elements of pitch (raising or lowering of the
voice), stress (loudness of voice), and juncture (pauses in speech) to derive
and alter meanings. You can highlight the important aspects of oral language by considering the meaning variations produced by pitch in the
simple sentence, "She ate it."

She ^{ate} it. (answer to "What did she do?")

She ^{ate it?} (question expressing surprise)

A third meaning can be produced by adding a stress variation:

She ate it. (answer to "Who ate it?")

The effect of juncture is realized in the following sentence, which can be
interpreted two ways:

It was a deep   blue sea.

It was a deep blue   sea.

By reading a brief passage from a story first with no intonation and then
with much expression you can extend appreciation of intonation patterns
further. Consider the following excerpt from *Three Billy Goats Gruff* (punctuation has been omitted to emphasize the point):

so one day they sent the youngest billy goat gruff over the bridge trip trap trip
trap went his hooves as he crossed the bridge who's that tripping over my bridge
shouted the troll in an angry voice it is only little billy goat gruff said the
youngest goat in a small voice for he was very frightened.

Contrast this version with an expressive reading of this:

So one day they sent the youngest Billy Goat Gruff over the bridge. Trip-Trap,
Trip-Trap *(softly),* went his hooves as he crossed the bridge.

"Who's that tripping over my bridge?" *(angrily)* shouted the Troll in an angry
voice.

"It is only Little Billy Goat Gruff," *(timidly)* said the youngest goat in a small
voice, for he was very frightened.

The importance of intonation to meaning is well communicated in Jonathan's variations on the refrain "There are no bears on Hemlock Mountain," as he tries to convince himself while crossing desolate Hemlock Mountain in the settling dusk with the borrowed pot.[36]

The effect of varied stress patterns plays an important role in determining vowel values in words. We shall develop this concept in detail in Chapter 10, but an example will illustrate the point here. The word *can* not only possess two different meanings in the following sentences, but the vowel has a different sound value under stress (in the first sentence) than when there is little stress (in the second sentence):

Bring the fruit can. /kæn/
I can run fast. /kən/

(Note the value of introducing words in a sentence context to develop appropriate stress and meaning values.)

As noted previously, children use normal intonation patterns without having to learn them formally, but they often have difficulty transferring this knowledge to oral reading. The relationship between oral language intonation and punctuation clues, although incomplete, should be emphasized in the classroom. Note for example that when a period is used a falling fading intonation pattern is present:

The canary
ate
the cat.

A question mark with the same sentence produces a rising intonation at the end of the sentence:

ate the cat?
The can^ary

An initial question marker, such as *what,* may produce a falling, fading intonation even though the sentence ends with a question mark:

What is the can
ary do.
ing?

A semicolon may produce a falling intonation:

The canary
walked; the cat ran.

while a comma may express a rising intonation:

After the meal,
the canary flew home.

These various graphic clues to intonation, and in turn to meaning, deserve instructional consideration in the reading-language skills program.

The connection between a symbol and its meaning is arbitrary. Within the classroom the arbitrary nature of language may be approached from a "productive thinking" standpoint. Encourage children to hypothesize
68 about factors affecting our control over language. For example, what type

of language or form of communication would be used by a boy or girl if he or she were reared on an island inhabited only by mute persons? This situation could be contrasted with language expectancy for a Chinese baby reared in an American, English-speaking family. In the latter case you might ask: Would we expect the child to speak Chinese, English with a Chinese "accent," or English? Why? With more advanced students you may wish to explore the hypothesis that language is a species-specific characteristic by examining animal "languages" (the ant, the bee, the dog, and various types of birds) and contrasting methods of communication with our own.

You may want to give some attention to the connection between the language of a particular people and their world view—that is, the ways they view and categorize their universe for comprehension purposes. Benjamin Lee Whorf has pointed out that the Hopi Indian world view, which does not include the notion of past, present, and future time, correlates with the lack of these tense markers in the grammar.[37] Many scholars question his viewpoint, but his conclusions support the hypothesis that the grammar of a language influences people's world view. In any respect it seems likely that cultural outlook and grammatical structure have been developed together throughout the generations.

At the higher grade levels a discussion of "phonetic symbolism" may prove to be of interest. For example you may ask, Do you think there is any relationship between the "length" of the vowel sound /i/ in the words *little* and *tip* and the meanings of these words? Very meager evidence is present of course to support the role of phonetic symbolism in word formation. Even onomatopoeic words appear to be arbitrary; for example, dogs say "bow-wow" in English, "how-how" in Arabic, and "wang-wang" in Chinese.

By initiating discussion with these kinds of illustrations you can move toward the conclusion that the symbols in a given language are unique to that language and have an arbitrary relationship to the referent or meaning, that sound sequences have meanings only by agreement among members of the same speech community. The children may wish to extend this concept of arbitrary relationships by generating and using nonsense words to refer to familiar objects: wug = boy; dap = girl. You might even develop a classroom language by switching the meaning of several pairs of English words and using the new arbitrary relationships in classroom communication for a short time. For example, "Open the desk!" could really mean "Open the door!"

Youngsters also find the collection of equivalent words from several languages highly motivating: *dog* is *Hund* in German, *perro* in Spanish, *asarii* in Comanche, and *sabaka* in Russian. A related activity, mentioned earlier, is the use of a storyteller relating a familiar tale in another language.

An introductory understanding of the arbitrariness of our grammatical patterns can be developed by noting the importance of word order to

69

How can experiences like this be used to illustrate the arbitrary nature of a language? What English equivalents can be used for the Spanish fiesta? *(Photo © 1972 Roger Lubin/Jeroboam)*

meaning in English sentences and comparing this with the word order in other languages. For example, in Latin *Homo equum mordet, Equum homo mordet,* or any other ordering of these words means *The man bites the horse.* However, when we alter the word order in English by interchanging *man* and *horse* we produce an entirely different meaning. An opportunity is present to help children understand that grammatical relationships in languages like Latin and German are signaled by inflectional endings but that word order, to a great extent, expresses such relationships in English.

Lexical items and grammatical patterns convey meaning to those who know the code. As we emphasized in Chapter 2, if children are to understand oral and written communication, they must understand the denotative and connotative meaning of individual words. They must also be aware of the meaning conveyed by structural signals such as intonation patterns, prefixes, suffixes, function words expressing relationships within the sentence, and word order.

Your children will be very much aware of the importance of vocabulary meaning to comprehension, particularly in the intermediate grades, when the content areas of the curriculum begin to be developed. The importance of lexicon can be easily demonstrated from your personal reading and literature program. A sentence from Ormondroyd's *David and the Phoenix* will serve as illustration: "The Feline's existence was terminated as a direct result of its inquisitiveness," which translates very simply as "Curiosity killed the cat"—provided we know the lexicon.

A novel approach that helps students become aware of the importance of lexical and relational meaning is the use of nonsense constructions. For example, in the sentence *The wug iggled a zig snorkily,* there is no lexical meaning, but the relational meaning is clearly present: something did something to something in a particular manner. We can tell that *wug* and *zig* are nouns, *iggled* is a verb, and *snorkily* is an adverb because of their positions in the sentence, the types of affixes they combine with, and the function words used with them *(the, a).* The works of Lewis Carroll and certain writings of Dr. Seuss can be used in the classroom to demonstrate relational as well as lexical meaning components of our language.

You can also pursue the ways different languages express relational meaning. English depends mainly on word order, but Latin signaled functional meaning primarily through inflectional endings. Let's take a closer look at *Homo mordet equum.* The *-o* stem of *homo* shows that it is the subject. The *-et* ending of *mordet* indicates that it is the third person singular form of a particular tense of a particular kind of verb. The *-um* ending of *equum* shows that it is the direct object. These three words can be arranged in any order and they will still say *The man bites the horse.* If the word order in English is changed, to *The horse bites the man,* and we want to say this in Latin, we must change the inflectional suffixes of the nouns to form *Hominem equus mordet.*

Again, using a speaker of a second language in the classroom or community is an excellent means of examining and contrasting relational meaning in his language with that of English. Through discussions such as those suggested above children can become aware of the importance not only of lexical meaning but of relational meaning as well.

English has a characteristic group of grammatical patterns. If we were merely to list words and the order of words in each sentence, we would have millions of word-sentence strings. But a sentence has structures within structures, and every sentence is generated from constructions that occur repeatedly. Viewed as a combination of these constructions, the number of sentence types is amazingly small. This systematic patterning accounts in part for the rapid development of children's language during the pre-school years.

You can approach this patterning systematically by building several basic sentence patterns and then expanding and transforming them in various ways. For example, by using word cards or word blocks with words belonging to a particular form class (part of speech) printed on each side of a given card or block, you can build several basic patterns:

1	2		
(noun)	(verb)		
George	rode.		

1	2		4
(noun)	(verb)	(noun marker)	(noun)
George	rode	the	bike.

By turning the word cards or rotating the blocks you can demonstrate the structure of a sentence through word substitution:

George	rode	the	bike.
Bill	drove	this	truck.

The sentence may then be expanded to produce:

George rode the bike around the house.

and transformed in a variety of ways:

George didn't ride the bike.
Did George ride the bike?
The bike was ridden by George.
George *did* ride the bike.

It is important that children understand the flexible nature of our language and the alternate ways in which ideas can be expressed. This approach suggests an informal exploration of the alternatives available in our language for communication purposes.

A language continually changes. In our early discussion of language change in this chapter there are a number of specific implications for the classroom. A dramatic demonstration of change from Old English through Modern English can be made with a recording that illustrates various periods of language development,[38] but be sure to point out that the various periods were not distinctly different at a given time; rather, that the changes occurred at a gradual pace to transform Old English forms into Middle English forms and in turn into Modern English. Emphasize also that widely used languages of today were derived from earlier common languages. For example, a detailed family tree of the Germanic and Italic languages (Figure 3-5) will prove to be of interest to your more advanced students.[39] A recording or reading of a sample of German will show children the sound resemblance of German to Old English, and the contrast of both to present-day English. The explanation for this is in the language tree: German and English both come from a common ancestor (and both have of course changed over the years). Encourage your students to hypothesize about factors that produce language change as well as those that inhibit language variation. Explanations may range from the influence of dialect mixing to migrations of people to geographical barriers that reduce interaction among people.

Following a general introduction to language change you can launch discussions on four types of changes: the sound system (phonology), word formation (morphology), grammatical variation (syntax), and meaning (semantics). The following ideas illustrate each of these areas and may be related to components of the communication model developed in Chapter 2.

We are aware that the sound system of English, the first area, has changed over several centuries. For example, in Old English the words *ether* and *either* would have sounded alike because the voiceless th / đ / and the voiced th /θ/ were not separate phonemes. Old English þ represented the voiceless phoneme /θ/, and the voiced sound / đ /, though in existence, did not provide for meaning differentiation when contrasted with /θ/. By the time of Middle English, however, these two sounds were separate phonemes and so distinguished the words *ether* and *either* in spoken language.

Sometimes a phoneme is added to a word: the Early Modern English word /vermin/ later became /varmint/. Sometimes a sound is lost: the Modern English word *knight* /niyt/ lost the initial sound /k/ in Middle English. This process accounts for a number of the spelling "irregularities" in our language, though from the standpoint of the writing system the *k* serves an important meaning function by visually distinguishing *knight* from *night.*

Language also changes in morphology, the second major area. We can form new words from the internal elements of our language. For example, an affix can be added to change the function or meaning of a word in a sentence, as in *wall-type telephone,* where *-type* is added. The extraction of the verb *enthuse* from the noun *enthusiasm* illustrates the type of change

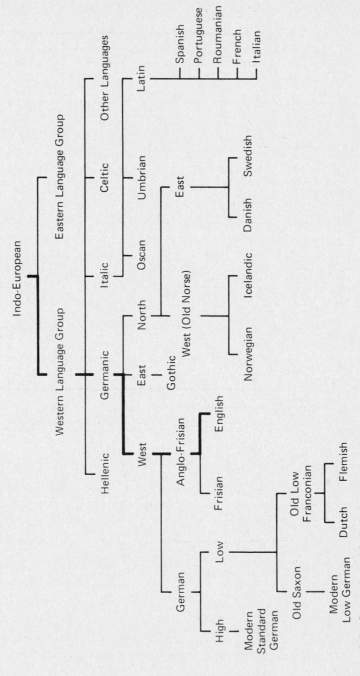

Figure 3-5. Germanic and Italic Languages

known as *back formation*—where a word is formed from, but looks as if it is the base of, another word. Another example is the formation of *pea* from *peas;* the singular form in Old English was *pise.* Occasionally a plus juncture or slight pause-break between words is misinterpreted: *an eut* became *a newt* (a small salamander), and *a nadder* became *an adder.* Repetitive formations such as *walkie-talkie* and *boogie-woogie* account for a few new forms. Such words as *motel, brunch,* and *smog* are formed by blending existing parts.[40]

We also derive vocabulary through borrowings. For example the word *astronaut* is derived from Greek; literally it means *star* (astro) *sailor* (naut). We also borrow words and shift their use to fit a new concept. The Germanic words *god, heaven,* and *hell* were adjusted to Christian concepts. Occasionally a foreign word is translated literally: our word *gospel* descended from Old English *godspell,* meaning *good news,* which is a literal translation of Greek *euangelion.*

Borrowed words can be assimilated quickly and used in the formation of other words, or restricted and thereby retain characteristics of the foreign pronunciation. For example, the Latin word *discus* has been borrowed into English four times: directly into Old English, producing *dish;* directly into Middle English, producing *disk;* through French into Middle English, producing *dais* (a slightly raised platform at one end of a classroom or banquet hall); and directly into Modern English, producing the athletic term *discus.*

An interesting discussion can be developed in the classroom by considering the reasoning behind the trade names of commercial products. Consider for example the names *Mustang, Maverick,* and *Roadrunner,* and the terms *Vel, Brillo,* and *Fab.* Could the auto names be related to the positive image projected by a particular animal? What relationship might exist between the latter products and the words *velvet, brilliant,* and *fabulous?* The use of metaphorical extension is obvious in such scientific terminology as sound *wave,* radiation *belt,* and solar *storm;* in marketing through Plymouth *Fury* and *Spring* cigarettes; and in slang forms such as LSD *trip.*[41] The power of language can begin to be appreciated through this type of discussion.

Syntax is the third area of change. Changes in word order are one example of this change. In its present form there are only a few verbs (modals) in our language, such as *can, may,* and *will,* that can precede the word *not: Bill can/not go. Bill will/not go.* We consider such forms as *Bill likes not steak* ungrammatical, but this was not the case earlier.[42] Changes in the selection of auxiliary verb forms have also occurred. In Old English it was quite acceptable to say, *He wæs cumen (He has come).* By Middle English the form could be used only with certain verbs (intransitive) of movement, as in *He is gone;* and by the eighteenth century the construction had almost entirely disappeared, except in frozen forms such as *He is risen.* At the intermediate grade level changes in the structure of the language can best

be approached by using literature such as Marguerite de Angeli's *The Door*

What resources are available in your classroom to encourage the young language sleuth? In your school library? *(Photo by Lew Merrim, Monkmeyer Press Photo Service)*

in the Wall for examples of older language forms cast in a story context using dialogue.[43]

The fourth type of change is in semantics. Students need to understand that words are not permanently bound to their meanings, that ideas, attitudes, beliefs, and events in our culture produce semantic change. The "real" meaning of a word is what a speaker means at a particular time, not its original meaning. Obviously a dictionary is authoritative only to the extent that it records and reflects meanings in a culture. This can be illustrated by the meaning of *squeal.* Its figurative impact has decreased, and now its common meaning is *to inform.*

Words can become narrower or more general in meaning. For example, the word *mete,* meaning *food* in Old English, is now *meat,* with the narrower meaning of *edible flesh.* Middle English *bridde,* meaning *young bird,* has become *bird,* with no specification for age. A word may take on a stronger meaning, as exemplified by the Germanic *kwalljan, to torment,* which became Old English *cwellan* meaning *to kill.* In turn *cwellan* has weakened in meaning to *quell (to subdue or quiet).* A word may also take on a pleasanter meaning, as in the case of Old English *styweard, swineherd,* which became Modern English *steward;* or a more derogatory meaning, such as *saelig,* meaning *blessed* in Old English but holding an entirely different meaning in our Modern English word *silly.*

76 Semantic change and vocabulary borrowings can provide exciting study.

A class can examine slang, words that have dropped out of the language or changed in meaning, new words that have been invented, and words borrowed from other languages. Slang is especially appropriate because changes often occur rapidly enough for the children to observe them personally. An awareness of the changing nature of our language can be extended by the young language sleuth to the daily skimming of newspapers and magazines to identify recently invented words and words borrowed from other languages in recent years.

No language or dialect can be considered "better" or "worse" than any other. The purpose of this concept is to help children develop an unbiased outlook toward languages and dialects that vary from their own. No language is "primitive," even though its speakers may live in a primitive fashion relative to our standards. The Aucas, a fierce head-hunting tribe in Ecuador, have a language the grammatical categories and phonological patterns of which are just as complicated as those of English. Their language does not have so many technical and scientific words as English because the Aucas do not have our technological innovations in their culture. Vocabulary is a basic index of the interests and needs of the people who speak the language. Languages have the facility to cope with new concepts, as shown by the vocabulary additions in our language during the past century; consider, for instance, the words that automobiles have brought into the language, ranging from *sparkplug* to *freeway.*

Your students will have a more positive attitude toward other languages if you provide an opportunity for them to learn about the adequacy of each language in expressing the concepts needed. The adaptation of vocabulary to the needs of a cultural group can be shown by the fact that Eskimos have a variety of words for snow, while English speakers generally (skiers excepted) have only one, and some languages in the tropics have none. An understanding of concept adaptation will be enhanced by the study of English words that have been borrowed, such as *coyote, mustang,* and *plaza* from Spanish; *chipmunk, moose,* and *sequoia* from Indian; *gopher, dime,* and *prairie* from French; *frankfurter* and *noodles* from German; *balcony* and *umbrella* from Italian; and *banjo* and *voodoo* from African languages; and by the examination of words and word groups that have been invented, ranging from *hippie* and *astrojet* to *flower power* and *space docking.*

You may also want the class to describe or draw an imaginary animal and then to invent a name for it, or vice versa. They may use existing morphemes or make up new names—for example, "What do you think a *zib* might look like? Use your imagination and draw a picture of it." Verbs can be treated in a similar way; one child may perform a certain action and the class may design a new label for it: "John *glings* very well, doesn't he?" This type of discussion can be extended into the social studies area by exploring the predicament the early settlers faced when they saw the American Indian's way of life—including new customs, animals, and vegetation—for the first time.

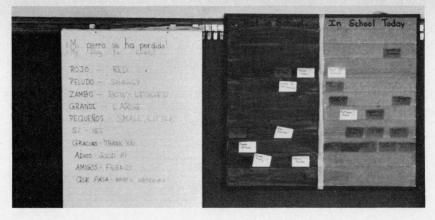

How can language study projects such as this help your students develop appreciation of other languages? Of other cultures?

The objective outlook toward language should also be related to geographical and social dialects. It is important to realize that when the speakers of a dialect use, or understand (and thereby in effect agree upon) a certain language form—whether in the sound, grammatical, or lexical systems— the form or forms are correct to them. Our previous discussion of graphical varieties of English and a brief sketch of the dialect map for the eastern United States will be of value in developing an appreciation of geographical language variations. A vocabulary chart such as the following will prove to be of interest when it is related to the dialect map.

Item	Northern	Midland	Southern	You
Paper container	bag	sack	sack	_____
Place for getting water	faucet	spigot spicket hydrant	spigot spicket hydrant	_____
Container	pail	bucket	bucket	
Frying pan	spider	skillet	skillet spider	
Animal with unusual odor	skunk	skunk polecat woods-pussy	polecat	_____
Insect with tiny phosphorescent light	firefly	lightning bug	lightning bug	
Cherry seed	pit stone	seed stone	seed stone	_____
To become ill	get sick	take sick	take sick	_____

78

You can also use poems, stories, plays, and songs with dialect variations. These might include passages from Shaw's *Pygmalion,* a recording of *My Fair Lady,* and tapes of American folk songs or recordings from various geographical regions of the United States and English-speaking countries (England or Australia). Several records are readily available for this purpose.[44] You should stress that every way of speaking English is a dialect, even though one may not be aware of his own "accent." Your classroom may contain children who speak a dialect different from yours and from that of the other children in the class. This direct language source could provide an excellent opportunity to demonstrate language diversity. The children should speculate on the relationship between geographical barriers and dialect boundaries as they examine the dialect map (Figure 3-3). For example, do you think there is any relationship between the Appalachian Mountain Range and the dialect boundary separating the Southern and South-Midland areas? Why?

Social varieties of language, generally subdivided by sociolinguists into standard and nonstandard English, also deserve special attention in the classroom. *Standard English* is a dialect(s) that has accepted status by the majority population and is imposed upon other varieties of English, largely owing to the social and political position of the people who use the dialect.[45] *Nonstandard English* consists of the varieties of English that deviate from the standard form(s). Variation in the sound system is exemplified by the simplification of certain consonant clusters—/st/ to /s/, /nd/ to /n/, and so forth. As a result the words *past* and *pass* are both pronounced *pass* /pæs/, and the words *mend* and *men* are pronounced *men* /men/. The most noticeable differences, however—and the differences the hypersensitive standard dialect speaker objects to most—are in grammatical variations, such as:

> The cat be walking on the table.

and

> Every day the boy be pulling a wagon.

Such variation in a grammatical system is highly consistent for the nonstandard English speaker. In the nonstandard language environment these forms are more appropriate in communication than the standard forms, *The cat is walking on the table,* and *Every day the boy is pulling a wagon.* The important point is to become aware of the regularity of nonstandard language forms in the language of your children. We shall consider your responsibility as a language skills teacher for developing a second dialect for nonstandard English speakers in Chapter 9. Our main focus will relate to the appropriateness of various language forms in various social environments.

You can help students understand the nature of language better by cultivating their awareness of other forms of communication, by contrasting language with nonlanguage forms such as art, noises, and gestures, and with language-based systems such as writing, Morse Code, Braille, and secret writing codes. Children enjoy inventing nonlanguage systems of communication using kinesics (facial expressions and gestures).

The final development and implementation of these language concepts will depend on your ability to utilize them in the classroom with specific adjustments for individual needs and interests. Requisites to the successful introduction of these basic ideas about language include an enthusiastic and objective outlook toward language and the development of individual backgrounds relative to the concepts identified. As a creative reading-language teacher you can successfully devise and explore many additional ways to introduce basic language concepts to your charges, so that your children will increase their understanding of the nature of language and the ways language is our primary communication system. The study of the nature of language through these basic concepts can be an exciting and highly motivating enterprise.

Footnotes

[1]Lincoln Barnett, "The English Language," *Life* (March 2, 1962), pp. 78–83.

[2]Paul Roberts, *Understanding English* (New York: Harper & Row, Publishers, 1958).

[3]Ibid. See also Stuart Robertson, *The Development of Modern English* (Englewood Cliffs, N.J.: Prentice-Hall, Inc., 1954).

[4]Roberts, *Understanding English.*

[5]Charlton Laird, *The Miracle of Language* (New York: World Publishing Company, 1953).

[6]Margaret Schlauch, *The Gift of Language* (New York: Dover Publications, Inc., 1955).

[7]William Benton, "English Language," *Encyclopaedia Britannica,* 14th ed. (Chicago: Encyclopaedia Britannica, Inc., 1959), Vol. VIII, 555–62.

[8]Thomas Pyles, *The Origins and Development of the English Language* (New York: Harcourt Brace Jovanovich, Inc., 1964).

[9]Robertson, *The Development of Modern English.*

[10]Roberts, *Understanding English;* and C. L. Wrenn, *The English Language* (New York: Barnes & Noble, Inc., 1952).

[11]Ronald W. Langacker, *Language and Its Structure* (New York: Harcourt Brace Jovanovich, Inc., 1968), p. 178.

[12]Otto Jespersen, *Growth and Structure of the English Language* (Garden City, N.Y.: Doubleday & Company, Inc., 1955).

[13]William H. Schofield, *English Literature* (New York: The Macmillan Company, 1921).

[14]Laird, *The Miracle of Language.*

[15]Roberts, *Understanding English.*

[16]French vocabulary is in italic.

[17]Pyles, *Origins of the English Language,* p. 335.

[18]David W. Reed, "The Great Vowel Shift," a summary of personal correspondence in Robert B. Ruddell, *Linguistics and Language Learning* (San Francisco: KQED, Channel 9, ITV, 1967).

[19]Ibid.

[20]C. L. Wrenn, *The English Language.*

[21]Benton, "English Language."

[22]Robert C. Pooley, *Teaching English Grammar* (New York: Appleton-Century-Crofts, 1957); and Schlauch, *The Gift of Language.*

[23]Laird, *The Miracle of Language,* p. 242.

[24]Roger W. Shuy, *Discovering American Dialects* (Champaign, Ill.: National Council of Teachers of English, 1967).

[25]Jean Malmstrom and Annabel Ashley, *Dialects—U.S.A.* (Champaign, Ill.: National Council of Teachers of English, 1963); and Roger W. Shuy, *Discovering American Dialects.*

[26]Pyles, *Origins of the English Language;* and Langacker, *Language and Its Structure.*

[27]Pyles, *Origins of the English Language.* Shuy, *Discovering American Dialects.* Albert C. Baugh, *A History of the English Language* (New York: Appleton-Century-Crofts, 1957).

[28]Schlauch, *The Gift of Language.*

[29]Langacker, *Language and Its Structure,* p. 65.

[30]I. J. Gelb, *A Study of Writing* (Chicago: University of Chicago Press, 1963).

[31]Dwight Bolinger, *Aspects of Language* (New York: Harcourt Brace Jovanovich, Inc., 1968).

[32]Langacker, *Language and Its Structure,* p. 66.

[33]Richard F. Venezky, "English Orthography: Its Graphic Structure and Its Relation to Sound," *Reading Research Quarterly,* 2 (Spring 1967), 84.

[34]David H. Russell, *Children Learn To Read* (Boston: Ginn and Company, 1962).

[35]Kenneth L. Pike, *Phonemics: A Technique for Reducing Language to Writing* (Ann Arbor: University of Michigan Press, 1947), p. 47.

[36]Alice Dalgliesh, *The Bears on Hemlock Mountain* (New York: Charles Scribner's Sons, 1952).

[37]Benjamin Lee Whorf, *Language, Thought and Reality* (Cambridge, Mass.: The M.I.T. Press, 1956).

[38]Evelyn Gott and Raven I. McDavid, Jr., *Our Changing Language* (New York: McGraw-Hill Book & Educational Services Group, 1965). A recording.

[39]Pyles, *Origins of the English Language,* p. 78.

[40]Morton W. Bloomfield and Leonard Newmark, *A Linguistic Introduction to the History of English* (New York: Alfred A. Knopf, Inc., 1963).

[41]Langacker, *Language and Its Structure,* pp. 182, 183.

[42]Ibid., p. 187.

[43]Marguerite de Angeli, *The Door in the Wall* (Garden City, N.Y.: Doubleday & Company, Inc., 1949).

[44]Gott and McDavid, *Our Changing Language;* and John T. Muri and Raven I. McDavid, Jr., *Americans Speaking* (Champaign, Ill.: National Council of Teachers of English, 1967).

[45]Edgar H. Sturtevant, *Linguistic Change* (Chicago: University of Chicago Press, 1961), p. 157.

4

Children's Language Development: Implications for Practice

Focusing Questions

1. What instructional implications can be developed from the study of children's language growth?
2. How does a child's language competency differ from his language performance?
3. What key factors appear to influence and enhance children's language development? How do these factors differ for children from varied socioeconomic and ethnic backgrounds?
4. What evidence supports the interrelated nature of reading-language skill development?
5. What are functional varieties of language? How can this concept help you meet the learning needs of youngsters in your classroom?

If you are to identify and account for individual variation in reading-language achievement it is paramount that you develop an understanding of the nature of children's language growth. It is also essential that you possess some understanding of nonstandard English and of the relationship between language achievement and important socio-ethnic variables. These things are the bases for formulating realistic achievement expectations for your youngsters.

In the following discussion we use the communication framework developed in Chapter 2 to contrast the child's language competence with his performance. Then we shall survey preschool and elementary school language development. Throughout the discussion the relationship between language growth and important socio-ethnic variables will be emphasized. We conclude this chapter by identifying implications that are directly related to reading-language instruction.

As you relate the following discussion to youngsters in your classroom it is important to distinguish between a youngster's language performance, which can be observed directly, and his competence, which is the knowledge that underlies his observable performance.[1] We can only infer an individual's underlying competencies from observations of his performance, but we must exercise great caution in our inference about an individual youngster's competence on the basis of his performance. As language specialist Kenneth Goodman has emphasized, an early reader who has just moved to the stage of effective silent reading with high comprehension of content may appear distracted and disrupted when he has to read orally in the classroom. Assuming the child's comprehension is of good quality, his "poor" oral reading performance may reflect a high degree of meaning competence rather than the lack of such competence.[2]

You must also examine language performance in oral and written forms in an objective fashion and avoid confusing language performance in a nonstandard dialect with lack of language competence. For instance, after reading *Charlie the Tramp* (see Chapter 2) you may ask a child "How do you think Charlie learned to build the beaver dam?" A performance response such as "Well, Charlie he watch his father build dat dam, and learn from him" indicates that the child possesses competence in understanding and responding to the question even though he uses nonstandard forms in his performance. You must thus probe various performance modes as you make inferences about specific learner competencies.

The student's spoken or written performance will be directly influenced by his knowledge of meanings (lexical, relational, nonlinguistic) and his ability to interpret these meanings through oral and written language. His listening and reading comprehension performance will be directly related to his ability to perceive oral and written language forms and his knowledge of various aspects of meaning, which in turn must be integrated as various meanings are interpreted in the comprehension process. Both in the role as speaker or writer and as listener or reader, he will use his affective mobilizers and cognitive strategies in establishing purposes and objectives in communication and in formulating problem-solving strategies in all dimensions of the communication process—thus directly influencing his reading-language performance.

In the classroom you use your communication competencies and performance abilities to interact with thirty or more youngsters whose competencies and performances are at various stages of development. Using the communication model from Chapter 2 we can identify in a simplified fashion the performances and underlying competencies[3] essential to the interaction process we call communication.

83

Children's
Language
Development:
Implications for
Practice

PERFORMANCE

COMPETENCE

Speaking or Writing

1. Thinking initiated by using *interpretation abilities* and directed by *affective mobilizers* and *cognitive strategies;* for example, a child's explanation reflects: ability to infer beyond information available; ability to apply information to a new situation.

   Knowledge of: strategies in identifying, organizing, interpreting, and applying information; objectives and motives based on interests, attitudes, and values.

2. *Aspects of meaning* make provision for using interpretation to formulate the specific ideas to be expressed; for example, a child's explanation reflects: ability to identify specific concepts discussed; ability to use key connecting words, such as *but* or *however;* ability to perceive meanings expressed through gesture or facial expression.

   Knowledge of: lexical meanings including denotative and connotative; relational meanings including word order, expansions, and transformations; and nonlinguistic meanings such as sign systems.

3. *Oral or written language forms* are used to present specific ideas through speech or writing; for example, a child's oral or written language reflects ability to produce: appropriate forms of intonation or punctuation; inflectional endings; word order.

   Knowledge of: syntactic forms, including phrases and sentences; morphemes, including words and affixes; sound patterns and sounds; written equivalents of sound system—letter patterns, letters, and punctuation in writing.

Listening or Reading

4. *Oral or written language forms* are perceived; for example, a child's listening or reading recall reflects perception of individual words, phrases, and sentences.

   Knowledge of: phonemes and sound patterns; graphemes and letter patterns; morphemes or words and affixes; and syntactic forms or phrases and sentences.

5. *Aspects of meaning* are used to formulate meaning of language forms; for example, a child's listening or reading comprehension reflects ability: to understand specific concepts discussed; to use key connecting words such as *but* or *however* in deriving sentence meaning; to integrate nonlinguistic signs to define lexical meaning more clearly.

   Knowledge of: lexical meanings; relational meanings; and nonlinguistic meaning components.

6. *Interpretation* provides for integration of meaning and is directed by *affective mobilizers* to identify purposes of communication and by *cognitive strategies* to gather and synthesize information leading to alternate understanding and explanations; for example, a child's comprehension reflects: ability to infer beyond information provided and to propose alternate conclusions; ability to apply information in a new situation.

Knowledge of: interpretation modes including factive, interpretative, and applied types; objectives and motives based on interests, attitudes, and values.

7. Individual verbal or nonverbal responses indicate that ideas are understood, misinterpreted, or not understood.

See competencies required for 1, 2, and 3.

Communication difficulties that result in misinterpretation or impeded understanding can occur at any point in the process. These can range from performance difficulties, such as inaccurate auditory perception of sounds or visual perception of letters, to competence difficulties, such as inadequate knowledge of word meanings and relationships. It is therefore important to know the performance and competence components essential to reading-language achievement. The child's language environment, including his instructional program, play a vital role in enhancing some aspects of language competence and performance leading to more effective communication through oral and written language.

PRESCHOOL AND ELEMENTARY SCHOOL LANGUAGE DEVELOPMENT

We know little about the exact nature of how the miraculous phenomenon of language is developed. Two recent theories that have received great acclaim hold (1) that in a more traditional sense language is acquired through an elaborate association and mediational learning process,[4] and (2) that language as the specific characteristic of humans develops as latent structures are "triggered" physiologically and influenced by the model language available to the child.[5] Convincing arguments have been posited for both points of view; however, it would seem plausible that both theories contribute to understanding language acquisition. If we assume that latent language structures are present and basic to the development of 85 grammatical competence and language performance,[6] it is also logical to

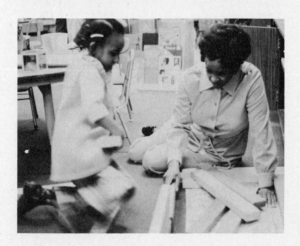

86   How would these experiences contribute to the children's language growth?

assume that value for the child stems from consistent social reinforcement and sentence expansion opportunities in refining and extending child grammar[7] as well as lexicon.[8] Our purpose, however, is not to review theories of language acquisition but to provide a brief overview of preschool and elementary school language development and to examine factors that are significantly related to children's language achievement.

Oral and written language forms

Phonological development. Various status studies have consistently shown that by the time the child enters the first grade he has a high degree of control over his phonological system,[9] that in fact by the time the child is four to five years of age he has mastered the great majority of English sounds.[10] This is indicated by his ability to use phonemes and intonation to discriminate various words and word groups; we know he can do this because we see he can comprehend specific oral directions and produce the great majority of speech sounds. Mildred Templin has studied the production of sounds at various ages and has found that most children can produce most sounds and sound patterns by age five or six. Figure 4-1 presents a summary of her findings.[11]

Templin noted that the initial cluster *hw,* the medial cluster *hw,* and the final clusters *lfth* and *tl* were produced correctly by only 25 percent of the pupils at eight years of age, but the difficulties with the *hw* clusters may be accounted for by dialectal variation. As would be expected, there is a close relationship between ability to produce sounds and ability to discriminate sounds auditorially.[12]

Wick Miller, a sociolinguist, has emphasized that the child's phonological system is acquired largely independent of vocabulary items.[13] The child seems to rely initially on sound contrasts between consonants and vowels, for example, p/p/ and a/a/. He may then contrast front and back consonants, for example, p/p/ and t/t/, followed by systematic contrasts such as voiced and voiceless consonants, for example, b/b/ and p/p/. By utilizing a comparatively small number of contrasts the child comes to learn most of the sounds in his language. It is thus obvious that the child's phonological system develops at a rapid pace during the preschool years and is for the most part highly functional by the time of his entrance into kindergarten or first grade.

We can draw several conclusions about phonological language development from this brief discussion:

1. The system is acquired by sound contrasts such as consonant-vowel, front and back consonants, and voiced-voiceless.
2. The complete vowel system is acquired before the complete consonant system.

Chronological Age	Sound Element

3	All vowels
	Consonants
	  Initial position - m, n, p, t, k, b, d, g, f, h, w
	  Medial position - m, n, p, k, b, d, g, f, h, w, ng
	  Final position - m, n, p, t, f, ng, ngk

3.5	Consonants
	  Initial position - y
	  Medial position - s, z, y
	  Final position - r, s, rk, ks, mp, pt, rm, mr, nr,
	                    pr, kr, br, dr, gr, sm

4	Consonants
	  Initial position - s, sh, j, r, l, pl, pr, tr, tw,
	                     kl, kr, kw, bl, br, dr, gl, sk, sm,
	                     sn, sp, st
	  Medial position - v, r, l
	  Final position - k, b, d, g, sh, lp, rt, ft, lt, fr,
	                    mpt, mps

4.5	Consonants
	  Initial position - ch, gr, fr
	  Medial position - sh, ch
	  Final position - ch, lf

5	Consonants
	  Initial position - fl, str
	  Medial position - j
	  Final position - rp, lb, rd, rf, rn, shr, mbr

6	Consonants
	  Initial position - th, v, th, skw
	  Medial position - t, th
	  Final position - th, v, l, lk, rb, rg, rth, nt, nd, ~~thr~~
	                    pl, kl, bl, gl, fl, sl, str, rst,
	                    ngkl, nggl, rj, ntth, rch

7	Consonants
	  Initial position - z, thr, shr, sl, sw, skr, spl, spr
	  Medial position - ~~th,~~ zh
	  Final position - ~~th,~~ z, ah, j, lz, zm, lth, sk, st,
	                    skr, kst, jd

8	Consonants
	  Initial position -
	  Medial position -
	  Final position - kt, tr, sp

Figure 4-1. Ages at Which 75 Percent of Subjects Produced Each Tested Sound Element Correctly. *(From Templin, Mildred C. Certain Language Skills in Children: Their Development and Interrelationships. Child Welfare Monograph #26. University of Minnesota Press, Minneapolis, © 1957, University of Minnesota.)*

3. The first consonant contrasts developed appear to be initial consonants.

4. Consonant clusters are developed later, by blending single consonants.

5. Most children will have developed most of the sound system by kindergarten or grade one, but some will not—so variation in ability to produce the complete sound repertoire should be anticipated.

The research discussed is for the most part based on the assumption that the child's language environment has consisted of standard English phonological forms. In Chapter 9 we shall examine phonological variations that are commonly and consistently used by nonstandard speakers of English.

Morphology and syntax development. The child's morphological and syntactical development is also well along by the time he enters primary school.[14] His fantastic progress in forming sentences has moved from single words midway through the second year to a high degree of control over his grammatical system by the fourth and fifth years.

The child's early sentence formation consists of such utterances as "Where go," "Where Mommie," "Want cookie," "No bib," "That doggie," "See bird," "See doggie," "See horsie." These types of utterances illustrate syntactic patterning in early language development consisting of pivot words *(that, where, want, see,)* and remainder words *(go, Mommie, cookie, bird).* The pivot words occur with high frequency, typically in the initial position; they correspond partially to adult word classes such as determiners *(that),* and adverbs *(where).* Verbs such as *want* and *see* may also serve as pivot words in the initial or final position. The remainder words occur with a comparatively low frequency and will later correspond to noun, verb, and adjective classes in adult language.[15]

Following the development of two-word utterances the child's "telegraphic speech" expands rapidly, and within one to two years his grammatical system has reached a high degree of complexity. He can now use modals *(shall, will),* prepositions, conjunctions, and inflectional morphemes such as the plural forms of nouns and tenses for verbs. He can also use grammatical operations that provide for questions, negatives, and infinitives.[16]

The learning process involved in this early language development seems to include some degree of imitation, but more importantly the ability to generalize. Susan Ervin-Tripp has noted, for example, that the child says "blocks," "toys," and "dogs" some weeks before he generalizes to regularize irregular forms such as *feet, men, sheep* by saying "foots," "mans," and "sheeps." She has also observed that the past tense develops in a similar yet different way. Irregular past tense forms such as *broke, came,* and *went* were used correctly the first times they were observed. This may be because of the high frequency of these verb forms; but it is interesting to note that when a child begins to use the past tenses of regular verbs, such as *walked* and *watched,* he overgeneralizes to the irregular verb forms and says a word like *breaked* rather than the correct form—*broke*—he had used before. The important inference here is that the child's ability to generalize and extend production of language forms is basic to language learning.[17] Imitating an appropriate adult model is important in language learning, but the child's ability to form generalizations about language patterning appears to be central. The fact that the child comprehends adult language utterances considerably before he can produce such utterances also lends support to the importance of internalized grammatical generalizations that are basic to comprehension and production.[18]

The control of morphology and syntactical patterning by the preschooler and primary grade child has been demonstrated in a variety of studies.[19] Such evidence indicates that by kindergarten or first grade the child is able to comprehend sentences and produce expanded and elaborated sentences through the use of movables (words, phrases, or clauses with no fixed position in the sentence, such as, The boy hit the ball *yesterday)* and transformed subordination elements (The man *next to you* is my teacher).

It is important to be aware, however, that according to research such as that by Carol Chomsky the developmental sequence in syntactical control extends well into the elementary grades.[20] Paula Menyuk has identified some sequential components in children's syntax that extend from nursery school into the first grade, and noted that even in the first grade some patterns, such as "if" and "so" clauses, perfects, and nominalizations, are still in the process of development.[21] Eric Lenneberg has discussed the difficulties mentally retarded children have with transformations in the passive voice,[22] and Mildred Templin has shown a definite relationship between sentence complexity and grade level.[23]

The research of Ruth Strickland examined the language development of school children in grades one through six. Using a special linguistic key designed to analyze patterns of syntax in children's oral language, she found that children at all grade levels could expand and elaborate their sentences through the use of movables and subordinating elements, that sentence complexity increased with grade level, and that the use of movables and patterns of subordination was related to the variables of intelligence, mental age, occupation status of parents, and parental education.[24]

Strickland's depth study of the relationship between children's oral language development and reading achievement at the sixth grade level revealed a significant relationship between oral reading interpretation and the use of movables and elements of subordination in oral language. Children who ranked high in silent reading comprehension and listening comprehension were found to make greater use of movables and subordination in their oral language than did children who ranked low.

The longitudinal study by Walter Loban and his colleagues extending from kindergarten through grade twelve is a major contribution to research on children's language development. This research revealed that throughout the elementary grades the average communication unit length—essentially the number of words in a word group possessing independent predication, such as "I know a boy with red hair"—increased progressively with each grade level, indicating a developmental sequence of complexity in sentence structure. Children who were high in general language ability at the kindergarten level, based on vocabulary scores and teacher ratings, were also high in reading ability. The opposite was true for those students who were low in general language ability. Loban noted that differences between the high and low groups increased from year to year and that language control increased much more rapidly for the high group. Additionally, the high group consistently demonstrated greater control over clauses and "movables within movables," such as

He went *back home* *yesterday,* *on a bus.*
M_1 M_2 M_3
(place)   (time)   (manner)

The low group used many more partial expressions or incomplete sentence patterns than the high group. During the early years of elementary school, the entire group and the high subgroup reduced the number and length of mazes (meaningless speech fragments):

(Our, uh) our dog (well he) got away.
(I'm goin') I'm goin' to build a flying saucer but I can't think how yet.

When the low subgroup was studied separately, however, during the elementary school years the average number of words in mazes increased.

Loban noted that the degree of subordination used in oral and written language was related to socioeconomic status. Boys in the low subgroup were more limited in their utilization of syntax than girls in the low subgroup, but boys in the high subgroup surpassed their opposite sex counterparts.

Loban concluded that speaking, reading, writing, and listening show a positive relationship, and that competence in the spoken language appeared to be a necessary base for competence in writing and in reading.[25]

The work of O'Donnell, Griffin, and Norris at kindergarten and grades one, two, three, four, and seven also supports the general notion of a developmental sequence of syntax acquisition in the elementary grades. These researchers observed that some transformations such as relative clause ("The man *who was wearing a coat*") were used much more frequently in kindergarten than in later grades while other items, like noun modification by a participle ("The man *wearing a coat*"), were more frequent in later grades. The researchers noted that such a developmental sequence appears logical from the standpoint of transformational grammar in that many of the later constructions are derived from more complex rules that delete certain sentence elements in consolidating several base sentences into one more complex, concise sentence construction. Sentence complexity, measured by the number of words in a T-unit of single independent predication[26] (including grammatically attached subordinate clauses), increased with grade level.

Also of interest in the O'Donnell, Griffin, and Norris research was the finding of distinct variation in the syntax of speech and writing in grades three, five, and seven. In the third grade oral expression was deemed superior to written expression in transformational complexity but in grades five and seven the reverse was true.[27]

The progressive development of oral language complexity identified in these studies is apparent in the increase in words per unit as indicated in Table 4-1 (constructed by John Carroll).[28]

Loban and O'Donnell both found a decrease in the length of meaningless speech fragments (mazes or garbles) for most children, which is a reflection of greater language control. An interesting exception, previously identified, is in Loban's research for those students classified as "low group." The number of speech fragments or mazes for this group increased. Table 4-1 also shows that Loban's "high group" uses more words per communication unit than the "low group," thus indicating more complex language maturity. Loban concluded that the "low group" said less and had more difficulty saying it than the "high group."[29]

The detailed research of Kellogg Hunt on the written expression of students at grades four, eight, and twelve and of mature adults revealed that the younger students produced shorter, less complex units of language, and that older students expanded their written language units, as revealed in longer T-units, by consolidating sentences into clauses, particularly in nominal structures. Superior adults were found to differ from the students at grade twelve primarily in the length of the clauses they used.[30]

Figure 4-2 summarizes the research of Loban, Hunt, and O'Donnell et al. on written expression, as reported by Carroll.[31] The increase in control of written expression is evident throughout the grades, as is the variation in written language control among "high," "central," and "low" groups.

An extensive study by Lester Harrell compared selected language variables in the speech and writing of children aged nine, eleven, thirteen, and fifteen, using a short movie as the speech and writing stimulus. He found that the length of the compositions and clauses used in oral and written expression increased with age, and that the older children used a larger percentage of subordinate clauses in both written and spoken composition. He also found that children used a larger percentage of subordinate clauses in writing than in speaking, that they used more adverb and adjective clauses in written compositions and more noun clauses in speaking. A larger percentage of adverb clauses, excepting those of time and cause, were used in the children's speech. The developmental increase of each language variable in relation to age was greater for written compositions than for oral. These findings, similar to those of the O'Donnell study, suggest that by the intermediate grades the child has some production

92

Table 4-1. Selected Data on Development of Speaking Skills[*]

Study / Measure	Approx. Age: 5 / Grade: K	6 / 1	7 / 2	8 / 3	9 / 4	10 / 5	11 / 6	12 / 7	13 / 8	14 / 9	15 / 10	16 / 11	17 / 12
Templin (1957) Words per Remark	5.7	6.6	7.3	7.6									
Strickland (1962) Mean Sentence Length (in Words)		11.04			13.04		13.58						
Loban (1967, Table 8) Words per Communication Unit													
Total Group:	5.13	6.06	6.46	6.91	7.68	7.89	8.37	9.10	9.43	9.47	9.58	10.82	11.09
High Group:	6.01	6.89	7.17	7.65	8.52	8.72	9.39	10.45	10.85	10.84	11.09	12.16	12.94
Low Group:	4.29	5.08	5.70	6.04	6.55	6.75	7.37	8.12	8.54	8.37	8.39	9.46	10.34
O'Donnell et al. (1967) Words per T-unit	7.07	7.97	8.33	8.73		8.90		9.80					
Loban (1966, Table 6) Words in Mazes as % of Total Words													
Total Group:	12.30	9.97	8.88	6.15	7.11	7.41	7.53	6.34	6.34	6.12			
High Group:	9.17	7.57	6.65	4.98	5.43	5.17	5.17	6.11	5.51	4.34			
Low Group:	11.92	15.51	10.49	10.62	9.74	9.27	9.49	10.95	9.83	8.85			
Loban (1967, Table 13) Words in Mazes as % of Total Words (with changed definition of "maze")													
Total Group:	7.94	7.08	6.48	5.95	6.82	6.99	7.14	7.06	6.84	6.19	6.48	6.55	7.04
High Group:	8.98	7.24	5.22	4.87	5.79	5.79	5.88	5.71	5.60	5.05	5.80	6.60	7.49
Low Group:	7.76	8.07	8.04	7.50	9.41	8.32	9.29	9.83	8.97	7.99	6.79	7.97	8.42
O'Donnell et al. (1967, computed from Tables 5 and 6) Garbles per 100 words	5.41	3.57	4.58	2.64		1.64		1.48					

[*]Reprinted by permission of Educational Testing Service and the National Council of Teachers of English.

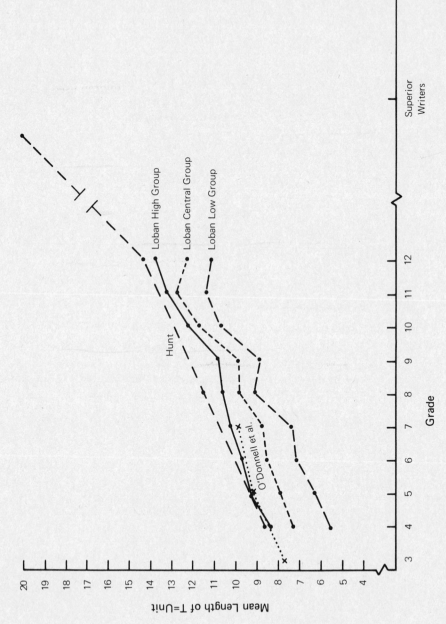

Figure 4-2.

control over stylistic variations that require more complex constructions in written expression.[32]

Research that contrasts the language development of children possessing hearing deficiency with that of normal children brings the relationship between oral language experiences and written language production into sharper focus. Heider and Heider secured written compositions based on a motion picture from a large number of deaf and normal children ranging in age from eleven to seventeen years and eight to fourteen years, respectively. Although the deaf children were three years older, their compositions resembled the less mature normal children. The deaf children used fewer words and clauses, while the normal children used more compound and complex sentences with a large number of words in coordinate and subordinate clauses, which indicates a more advanced development in language production.[33]

The written language of normal and defective hearing children has also been examined by Mildred Templin.[34] She found children with hearing deficiencies to use more words in their explanations of natural phenomena than hearing children of the same age, grade, and intelligence. She interpreted this to reflect less adequate control over vocabulary and perhaps syntax rather than to represent a more complex type of expression. The children with defective hearing apparently needed more words to express a concept because of low efficiency in expressing their ideas through elaborated sentences and more abstract vocabulary.

Both the Heider and Heider and the Templin studies point to a significant relationship between oral and written language development. The opportunity for oral language experience through hearing appears to have a direct influence on performance in written language.

We can draw several conclusions from this discussion of children's morphological and syntactical language development:

1. The child's grammatical system is influenced by the language in his environment, but his ability to generalize about his morphological and syntactical systems appears to be central to his rapid acquisition of language.
2. The sequence of morphological and syntactical development is from two-word utterances and "telegraphic" speech to control over modals, prepositions, conjunctions, inflectional endings such as the plural forms of nouns and tenses of verbs, and grammatical operations that provide for questions, negatives, and infinitives.
3. Although the child's morphological control is for the most part complete by first grade, his syntactical control in producing oral and written language using more complex subordination appears to continue to develop throughout the elementary school years. This suggests that classroom teachers should view the child's language from the standpoint of continuing maturation rather than from the standpoint of simply "refining" a language system which is completely developed.

4. The development of control over syntactical complexity in oral language and written language appears to be closely related.

Again, most of the research discussed would seem to assume standard English to be the language environment of the child. We shall consider morphological and syntactical forms unique to the nonstandard speaker in Chapter 9.

Aspects of meaning

Lexical meaning. As we observed in Chapter 2, the child's conceptual development makes rapid progress during the preschool years, and by his first year of school he has control over many hundreds of words. There is ample evidence to support the view that concepts develop along a continuum, from concrete, through semiconcrete or functional, to the abstract levels.[35] Russell and Saadeh contrasted conceptual responses at grades three, six, and nine on multiple-choice questions designed to measure various levels of abstraction. They concluded that third grade children favored "concrete" responses, while sixth grade and ninth grade children favored "functional" and "abstract" responses.[36] As Susan Ervin-Tripp has emphasized, a child's conceptual maturation moves from concrete referents to "hierarchies of superordinates which may have rather vague features (e.g., mammal, vertebrate) and they [adults] speak of nonvisible referents such as politics and energy."[37] The maturation levels parallel the development of Piaget's conceptual stages discussed in Chapter 2.[38]

Various background variables have been credited with enhancement of lexical aspects of language performance. Vera John and Leo Goldstein's verbal mediation research reveals that a child's verbal interactions with mature speakers provide important opportunities for testing tentative notions about word meanings.[39] Such opportunities appear to produce greater verbal control and enable the child to rely on words as mediators facilitating thought. Vygotsky has suggested that the availability of adults for dialogue with the child is very important to language acquisition.[40] This contention receives support from Edith Davis's early research, which revealed that only children developed language facility more rapidly than children with siblings, and that children with siblings developed language facility faster than twins.[41]

Esther Milner investigated the effect of factors in the home environment on language achievement by selecting high and low achievers in first grade reading and then exploring the children's use of language in the home through depth interviews. She found that the high-achieving children had an enriched verbal environment: there were more books available, and they were read to more often by highly esteemed adults. The high-scoring children also engaged in conversation with their parents more often than the low-scoring children. She noted further that in many of the home environments of low-scoring children there was little evidence of a posi-

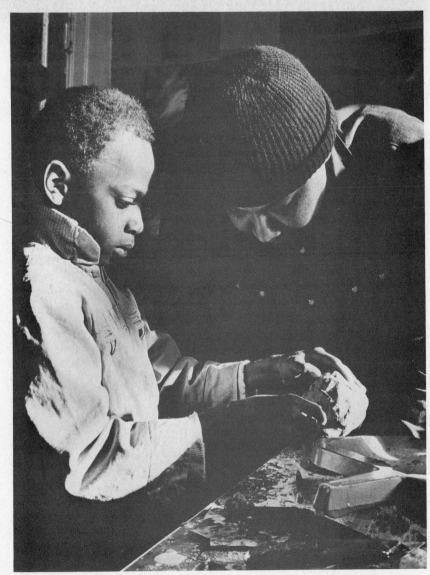

What aspects of this experience are important to the development of meaningful concepts? *(Photo by Earl Dotter, BBM Associates)*

tive family atmosphere, nor did the children have an adult relationship pattern established. There appeared to be little opportunity for these children to interact verbally with adults who possessed adequate speech patterns and who were of high personal value to the children.[42]

Relational meaning. The close relationship between language comprehension and relational meaning receives support from a variety of sources. The previously cited research of Fraser, Bellugi, and Brown supports the view that children must comprehend grammatical contrasts before they can produce such contrasts.[43] Strickland and Loban both report significant relationships between children's reading and listening comprehension achievement and their demonstrated use of movables and subordination in oral language.[44]

In his early study of mistakes in paragraph reading of sixth grade children, Thorndike noted that understanding a paragraph depends upon selecting the right elements and synthesizing them in the right relations.[45] The child's ability to comprehend material, whether written or spoken, seems to be a function of his ability to see the relationships among key elements in the sentence. Thus relating various subordinating elements to the central idea of the sentence is of basic importance for comprehending the discourse.

Using a "disarranged phrase test," Helen Gibbons studied the relationship between third grade children's ability to understand the structure of sentences and their reading achievement. She found a high correlation (.89) between ability to see relationships among parts of sentences and ability to understand the sentence, when intelligence was partialed out. She also found a significant correlation (.72) between ability to see relationships among parts of sentences and total reading achievement.[46]

MacKinnon's research underlines the importance of familiarity with syntactic patterning to reading achievement. In a detailed study of beginning readers he observed that children trying to decode unfamiliar reading materials attempted to substitute syntactic patterns they had previously read and were familiar with for unfamiliar patterns.[47]

In my own research I examined the effect on reading comprehension at the fourth grade level of written patterns of language structure that occur with high and low frequency in children's oral language. I controlled the vocabulary difficulty, sentence length, and subject content in a series of reading passages, then examined the relationship between reading comprehension and pattern complexity. I found reading comprehension scores on passages written with high-frequency patterns of language structure to be significantly higher than comprehension scores on passages written with low-frequency patterns of language structure.[48]

A child's understanding of sentence structure should enhance his ability to narrow alternate word meanings and thus contribute to comprehension. For example, the word *this* not only cues a noun that follows but may also clarify or emphasize the semantic nature of the noun (*This* red bike hit the boy versus *A* red bike hit the boy). Miller and Miller, Heise, and Lichten have demonstrated that words in context following a similar grammatical pattern are perceived more accurately than when they are in isolation.[49] Additional support for the importance of context in narrowing semantic possibilities is found in the research of Goodman. He has shown that although children may be unable to decode words in isolation, they deal successfully with the same words in a running context.[50] These findings indicate the importance of contextual associations that provide enough delimiting information that the child can determine the semantic role of a word and recognize and comprehend it in a sentence.

A longitudinal study I have recently completed shows that the sentence and paragraph meaning comprehension of first and second grade children can be significantly enhanced by emphasizing the meaning relationships among key structural elements within and between sentences.[51] The doctoral research of Ernest Baele, which was part of this study, indicated that by the end of third grade the children who had participated in the treatment stressing sentence subordination and the relationships among key structural elements were writing longer communication units with greater clausal complexity, which shows control over subordination and more complex constructions in the written language performance.[52] This research parallels to some degree the preschool oral language research of Courtney Cazden. Her work with two- and three-year-old children indicated that the use of full grammatical sentences in response to the children's verbal expression, and the expansion of their telegraphic speech to full adult grammatical sentences, resulted in improved performance on several measures of grammatical development when contrasted with a control group. The "richness of verbal stimulation" appeared to be very important in extending grammatical control.[53] These findings indicate that language comprehension and production can be enhanced in the preschool and early grades by placing emphasis on structural relationships that influence meaning within and between sentences.

We may summarize our discussion on aspects of meaning by identifying the following conclusions:

1. The child's conceptual development moves along a developmental continuum from a concrete, through a semiconcrete or functional, to an abstract level. You must be aware of the child's conceptual level when you introduce and develop lexical meanings in the classroom.
2. Relational meanings directly influence the child's comprehension performance. His comprehension ability and control over expressive forms can be enhanced in the instructional program through special emphasis on relational meaning knowledge. It is important not only to account for specific word knowledge in your instructional program, but also for knowledge of the ways words, phrases, and sentences interact to convey intended meanings.
3. The child's language competence and performance appear to be directly related to several variables: opportunity to use a wide range of language forms with a mature speaker; language interaction with a highly esteemed adult; the "richness of verbal stimulation" afforded by the language environment; a positive attitude toward language use; opportunities to explore alternate ways of expressing ideas in concise forms through various types of sentence subordination; and individual characteristics such as level of conceptual development.

A child's ability to use lexical and relational meanings to comprehend language develops rapidly during the preschool years. His development of interpretation or comprehension ability (including interpretive and applicative levels) is directly related to his intellectual maturation, as he moves through the concrete operations stage, and enters the formal operations stage, during the elementary school years. We shall examine the development of comprehension abilities in detail in Chapter 11, in the context of comprehension levels, skill competencies, and question strategies.

As we discussed in Chapter 2, the child's affective mobilizers enabling him to formulate specific communication objectives are critical to his language performance. These objectives are based on his interests, attitudes, and values and become operationalized as he interacts in oral or written communication settings. They directly influence his self-direction and motivation, as revealed in his persistence and drive.[54]

The importance of a cognitive strategy to concept building and utilization has been clearly demonstrated in the work of Bruner, Goodnow, and Austin.[55] A child must develop a symbol-processing system before he can conceptualize his experience. He must also be able to formulate alternate strategies for such things as decoding new words, and comprehending oral or written material by means of high-level comprehension skills. There is considerable research showing the relationship between language comprehension and ability to modify and reorganize previously formed concepts.[56]

In short, the child must develop interpretation abilities for a variety of communication situations. His affective mobilizers provide for self-directing behavior through personal and immediate communication objectives that lead to active participation, persistence, and drive; his cognitive strategy provides methods of organizing and assimilating data and of formulating and testing hypotheses.

Factors affecting interpretation

The child's comprehension abilities, including factual, interpretive, and applicative levels, will certainly be influenced by the previously discussed variations in relational and lexical meaning. An added concern in the classroom setting, however, must be that of accounting for functional varieties in the language. (By functional varieties we mean language styles used in various environments.) For our purposes these can be ranged along a continuum consisting of three levels—informal, formal, and literary.[57] If we place oral expression and written language forms on this continuum, we can examine the "fit" between these forms of communication for the standard and nonstandard speaker in the early grades.[58]

Table 4-2. Levels of Functional Variety in Oral and Written Language

Functional Variety Level	Oral Language	Written Language
Informal	Home and school language	Personal notes, letters to friends, unedited language experience stories
Formal	Classroom explanations, lectures, public speeches	School textbooks, edited language experience stories
Literary	Formal papers, speech as an art form	Literature as an art form, aesthetic dimensions of written language

It is immediately obvious that the first written material the child encounters in the instructional setting is in most cases at least one level above his informal, familiar oral language style. The speaker of nonstandard English must account not only for levels of functional variety in the standard dialect, but also for dialectal variation (Chapter 9). If he is from a language environment where there has been little opportunity to develop a shift in functional variety he is at a decided handicap when he approaches the printed page, which most likely is written on the formal level. For example, *hafta, gonna, hadda, oughta, hasta,* and *wanna* are quite appropriate in informal conversational settings for oral language, but in written language they are *have to, going to, had to, ought to, has to,* and *want to.*[59] The contractions *I'll, she'll, he'll,* and *they'll* are appropriate in informal oral language situations, but the textbook equivalents *I will, she will, he will,* and *they will* are on the formal level and for many children represent the first encounter with printed matter.

Speakers of standard and nonstandard forms must accommodate the functional variety shift between informal styles and formal literary styles. As Goodman has pointed out, certain oral language sequences that result from sound pattern rules cutting across morpheme boundaries in the flow of speech are so common that young speakers do not differentiate the individual components in the sequence, as in *going to (gonna), with them (with'm), with him (with'm), must have (must'v),* and *should have (should'v).*[60] Oral language at the informal level may use one unit that forms printed on the formal level show as two units. This variation must be taken into account in the instructional program.

Additional understanding of the relationship between the interpretation process and nonstandard (as well as standard) syntactical forms may be obtained in the work of Basil Bernstein, whose research supports the viewpoint that the "restricted" code associated with lower socioeconomic status and related language experiences is syntactically redundant and characterized by limited subordination.[61] The "elaborated" code appears

to make provision for developing meaningful explication of specific topics with strangers or new group members at the formal functional variety level. The contributions of syntactical factors to the "elaborated" code appear to be in terms of subordination and the expression of complex relationships in varied language environments. Although these dimensions can be handled in the restricted code, there appears to be a degree of economy in the utilization of the elaborated code with a majority population that does not employ the nonstandard language forms. The elaborated code is also expected to provide for easier transition from comprehension of informal oral language forms to comprehension of formal written language forms, particularly in terms of the greater subordination control required in the stylistic shift from an informal to a formal functional variety level.

In classroom instruction children are frequently required to provide information at the formal functional variety level. As Bernstein has emphasized, this means that a child from a low socioeconomic environment, one that uses a restricted code, has to produce language in situations which he is neither equipped nor oriented to handle. This may be due not only to the past discussion of certain syntactical factors (relational meaning), but also to his limited classroom-oriented lexical control and limited experience in shifting from an informal, intimate style developed to cope with immediate and concrete needs to a formal style characterized by abstractions with highly efficient explanatory power. It is essential that our language skills

How can this type of discussion provide for better understanding and use of functional varieties of language?

curriculum incorporate experiences designed to enhance the child's relational and lexical understandings and his ability to comprehend and utilize language forms at various functional variety levels. An added value should be expected from such development in the child's internal use of language to direct his own behavior.[62] This may take the form of greater effectiveness in noticing experiences, storing information by possessing adequate labels for concepts, provision for planning in a vicarious manner, explaining operations to himself, and relating experiences across time and space. Our instructional program must thus account for conceptual development, attitudes, and problem-solving strategies if the child is to benefit fully from learning opportunities. Instructional techniques related to this problem receive specific attention in Chapters 6 through 14.

IMPLICATIONS FOR THE READING-LANGUAGE PROGRAM

These discussions of language development, functional varieties of language, and related socio-ethnic variables show more clearly the complex nature of language learning. We shall use this information as the basis for generating instructional practices in Chapters 6 through 14, but it is important to summarize and focus our discussion at this point. The discussions in this chapter suggest at least five implications for reading-language instruction.

1. The child's language development is greatly influenced by two critical factors: (1) his ability to formulate and grasp generalizations about the system of language, and (2) the language model or models in his environmental setting. Although the early home environment plays a major role in a child's language development, the teacher's language and that of other children appears to exert a positive influence on language development in the classroom setting. There is evidence to indicate that the instructional program can enhance a child's oral and written expression and comprehension performance. Such devices as the tape recorder should be considered for individual or group listening activities as ways of presenting appropriate and contrasting language models to the children. Oral language enrichment activities such as role playing, story telling, and group discussions of direct experiences deserve strong emphasis, particularly with children from culturally different backgrounds.

2. Oral language development is an important requisite for written language development. Oral language activities such as reading literature to children, dramatic play, and dialogue, combined with extensive use of experience charts, can help children understand how intonation and punctuation may be used to convey meaning in oral and written expression, respectively. Such activities also provide excellent ways to show children how language provides for description and narration in developing story characters and story settings.

3. Listening and reading comprehension are closely interrelated and involve similar components. We must develop comprehension ability by carefully establishing purposes or objectives for listening and reading ranging from direct recall of details in a newspaper article to critical evaluation of a news story by contrasting story development and related information in two local papers with different editorial policies. The development of interpretation skills in your instructional program is essential if your youngsters are to obtain maximum benefit from the language environment that surrounds them.

 4. A wide range of language development should be expected in the elementary classroom. Your understanding of individual children will be more complete, and will enable you to plan a more adequate reading-language program, if you can account for the socio-ethnic variables that may have precipitated the range of individual language differences, variables such as the opportunity to use language in the home, the degree of language interaction between parent and child, the language model provided by the parent, the value the highly esteemed adult places on language development, and such individual characteristics as hearing acuity and intellectual development.

5. There must be consideration given to functional variety differences between the home and the school. Variations in informal and formal language settings may present interference problems for the child who is unfamiliar with the formal language variety common to school reading materials and other aspects of classroom communication. We shall offer specific instructional suggestions for the development of various functional variety levels in Chapters 6 through 9.

Careful provision must be made for the child's conceptual development in relation to his range of experiences. He needs a firm understanding of the concept he is attempting to comprehend or express if his communication attempt is to be successful. His elementary school language experiences must account for his concrete operation and early formal operation developmental stages.

Although researchers of children's language development have explored only a small segment of the vast cognitive-affective realm, a high degree of interrelatedness between oral and written language skill development is evident. The implementation of derived implications such as those identified above require an understanding of available reading-language programs and an awareness of ways we can use and adapt such programs as an instructional resource in our classrooms. We shall examine this aspect of reading-language instruction in the next chapter, on program characteristics and instructional implementation.

Footnotes

[1]Dan I. Slobin, *Psycholinguistics* (Glenview, Ill.: Scott, Foresman and Company, 1971), p. 6.

[2]Kenneth S. Goodman, "Behind the Eye: What Happens in Reading," *Reading, Process and Program* (Champaign, Ill.: National Council of Teachers of English, 1970), pp. 3–38.

[3]John C. Mellon, "Linguistics, Language Development, and the Concept of Language-Rich Classroom Environments" (unpublished paper presented at the National Council of Teachers of English Annual Convention, November 1970, Atlanta), pp. 5–14.

[4]B. F. Skinner, *Verbal Behavior* (New York: Appleton-Century-Crofts, 1957). Arthur W. Staats and Carolyn K. Staats, *Complex Human Behavior* (New York: Holt, Rinehart and Winston, Inc., 1964).

[5]Noam Chomsky, "Review of Skinner's Verbal Behavior," *Language,* XXXV (1959), 26–58. Eric Lenneberg, *Biological Foundations of Language* (New York: John Wiley & Sons, Inc., 1967).

[6]Philip B. Gough, "The Limitations of Imitation: The Problem of Language Acquisition," *New Directions in Elementary English,* ed. Alexander Frazier (Champaign, Ill.: National Council of Teachers of English, 1967).

[7]Courtney B. Cazden, "Environmental Assistance to the Child's Acquisition of Grammar" (unpublished doctoral dissertation, Harvard University, 1965).

[8]Vera P. John and Leo S. Goldstein, "The Social Context of Language Acquisition," *Merrill-Palmer Quarterly of Behavior and Development,* X, No. 3 (1964), 265–74.

[9]Dorothea A. McCarthy, "Language Development in Children," *Manual of Child Psychology,* ed. L. Carmichael (New York: John Wiley & Sons, Inc., 1954), pp. 492–630. Mildred Templin, *Certain Language Skills in Children,* University of Minnesota Institute of Child Welfare Monographs (Minneapolis: University of Minnesota Press, 1957).

[10]Susan M. Ervin and W. R. Miller, "Language Development," *Child Psychology,* Sixty-second Yearbook of the National Society for the Study of Education, ed. H. Stevenson (Chicago: University of Chicago Press, 1963), pp. 108–43.

[11]Templin, *Certain Language Skills in Children,* p. 51.

[12]Ibid., p. 124.

[13]Wick R. Miller, "Language Acquisition and Reading" (paper presented at the NCTE Institute on Oral Language and Reading, Charleston, W. Va., Spring 1967), p. 3.

[14]Jean Berko, "The Child's Learning of English Morphology," *Word,* XIV (1958), 140–77. Robert B. Ruddell and Barbara W. Graves, "Socio-Ethnic Status and the Language Achievement of First Grade Children," *Elementary English,* XLV (May 1967), 730–39.

[15]Ervin and Miller, "Language Development." Also Wick R. Miller and Susan Ervin, "The Development of Grammar in Child Language," *Monographs of the Society for Research in Child Development,* XIX, No. 92 (1964), 9–34.

[16]Miller, "Language Acquisition and Reading."

[17]Gough, "The Limitations of Imitation."

[18]Ibid. Colin Fraser, Ursula Bellugi, and Roger Brown, "Control of Grammar in Imitation, Comprehension, and Production," *Journal of Verbal Learning and Verbal Behavior,* II (August 1963), 121–35.

[19]Fraser, Bellugi, and Brown, "Control of Grammar." Roger Brown and Colin Fraser, "The Acquisition of Syntax," *The Acquisition of Language,* eds. U. Bellugi and R. W. Brown, Monographs of the Society for Research in Child Development, XXIX, No. 1 (1964), 43–79. Ruth G. Strickland, *The Language of Elementary School Children: Its Relationship to the Language of Reading Textbooks and the Quality of Reading of Selected Children,* Bulletin of the School of Education, XXXVIII, No. 4 (Bloomington: Indiana University Press, 1962). Walter D. Loban, *The Language of Elementary School Children* (Champaign, Ill.: National Council of Teachers of English, 1963). Ruddell and Graves, "Socio-Ethnic Status and Language Achievement." Roy C. O'Donnell, William J. Griffin, and Raymond C. Norris, *Syntax of Kindergarten and Elementary School Children: A Transformational Analysis* (Champaign, Ill.: National Council of Teachers of English, 1967).

[20]Carol Chomsky, *The Acquisition of Syntax in Children from 5 to 10* (Cambridge: The MIT Press, 1969).

[21]Paula Menyuk, "Syntactic Structures in the Language of Children," *Child Development,* XXXIV (June 1963), 407–22.

[22]Eric Lenneberg, "Speech as a Motor Skill with Special Reference to Nonaphasic Disorders," *Monographs of the Society for Research in Child Development,* XXIX (1964), 115–27.

[23]Templin, *Certain Language Skills in Children.*

[24]Strickland, *The Language of Elementary School Children.*

[25]Loban, *The Language of Elementary School Children.* See also Walter Loban, *Language Ability: Grades Seven, Eight, and Nine* (Washington, D.C.: Office of Education, 1966), Cooperative Research Monograph No. 18, OE-30018; and his *Language Ability: Grades Ten, Eleven, and Twelve* (University of California, Berkeley, 1967), Final USOE Cooperative Research Report, Project No. 2387.

[26]This unit of analysis was developed by Kellogg Hunt and is similar to Loban's communication unit.

[27]O'Donnell, Griffin, and Norris, *Syntax of Kindergarten and Elementary School Children.*

[28]John Carroll, "Development of Native Language Skills Beyond the Early Years," *Research Bulletin* (Princeton: Educational Testing Service, 1968), p. 58.

[29]Loban, *Language Ability: Grades Seven, Eight, and Nine* (1966). Loban, *Language Ability: Grades Ten, Eleven, and Twelve* (1967). O'Donnell, Griffin, and Norris, *Syntax of Kindergarten and Elementary School Children.*

[30]Kellogg W. Hunt, *Grammatical Structures Written at Three Grade Levels* (Champaign, Ill.: National Council of Teachers of English, 1965).

[31]Carroll, "Development of Native Language Skills," p. 74. Reprinted by permission of Educational Testing Service and the National Council of Teachers of English.

[32]Lester E. Harrell, "An Inter-Comparison of the Quality and Rate of the Development of the Oral and Written Language in Children," *Monographs of the Society for Research in Child Development,* XXII, No. 3 (1957).

[33]F. K. Heider and Grace M. Heider, "A Comparison of Sentence Structure of Deaf and Hearing Children," *Psychological Monographs,* LII (1940), 42–103.

[34]Mildred C. Templin, *The Development of Reasoning in Children with Normal and Defective Hearing* (Minneapolis: University of Minnesota Press, 1950).

[35]H. Feifel and I. B. Lorge, "Qualitative Differences in the Vocabulary Responses of Children," *Journal of Educational Psychology,* XLI (1950), 1–18.

[36]David H. Russell and I. Q. Saadeh, "Qualitative Levels in Children's Vocabularies," *Journal of Educational Psychology,* XLIII (1962), 170–74.

[37]Susan Ervin-Tripp, "Language Development," *Review of Child Development Research* (New York: Russell Sage Foundation, 1967), pp. 55–105.

[38]Jean Piaget, "The Genetic Approach to the Psychology of Thought," *Journal of Educational Psychology,* LII (1961), 275–81. D. E. Berlyne, "Recent Developments in Piaget's Work," *British Journal of Educational Psychology,* XXVII (1957), 1–12.

[39]John and Goldstein, "The Social Context of Language Acquisition."

[40]Lev S. Vygotsky, *Thought and Language* (Cambridge: The M.I.T. Press, 1962).

[41]Edith A. Davis, *The Development of Linguistic Skill in Twins, Singletons with Siblings, and Only Children from Ages Five to Ten Years* (Minneapolis: University of Minnesota Press, 1937).

[42]Esther Milner, "A Study of the Relationship Between Reading Readiness in Grade One School Children and Patterns of Parent-Child Interaction," *Sixty-second Yearbook—NSSE* (Chicago: University of Chicago Press, 1963), pp. 108–43.

[43]Fraser, Bellugi, and Brown, "Control of Grammar."

[44]Strickland, *The Language of Elementary School Children.* Loban, *The Language of Elementary School Children.*

[45]E. L. Thorndike, "Reading and Reasoning: A Study of Mistakes in Paragraph Reading," *Journal of Educational Psychology,* VIII (1917), 323–32.

[46]Helen D. Gibbons, "Reading and Sentence Elements," *Elementary English Review,* XVIII (February 1941), 42–46.

Implications
for the
Reading-Language
Program

[47] A. R. MacKinnon, *How Do Children Learn to Read* (Vancouver: The Clopp Clark Publishing Co., Ltd., 1959).

[48] Robert B. Ruddell, "Effect of the Similarity of Oral and Written Patterns of Language Structure on Reading Comprehension," *Elementary English,* XLII (April 1965), 403–10.

[49] G. A. Miller, "Some Psychological Studies of Grammar," *American Psychologist,* XVII (1962), 748–62. G. A. Miller, G. A. Heise, and W. Lichten, "The Intelligibility of Speech as a Function of the Context of the Test Material," *Journal of Experimental Psychology,* XLI (1951), 329–35.

[50] Kenneth S. Goodman, "A Linguistic Study of Cues and Miscues in Reading," *Elementary English,* XLII (1965), 639–43.

[51] Robert B. Ruddell, "Reading Instruction in First Grade with Varying Emphasis on the Regularity of Grapheme-Phoneme Correspondences and the Relation of Language Structure to Meaning," *The Reading Teacher,* XIX (May 1966), 653–60. Robert B. Ruddell, *Second and Third Year of a Longitudinal Study of Four Programs of Reading Instruction with Varying Emphasis on the Regularity of Grapheme-Phoneme Correspondences and the Relation of Language Structure to Meaning* (Washington: U.S. Department of Health, Education and Welfare, Office of Education, 1968), USOE Cooperative Research Projects Nos. 3099 and 78085.

[52] Ernest R. Baele, "The Effect of Primary Reading Programs Emphasizing Language Structure as Related to Meaning upon Children's Written Language Achievement at the Third Grade Level" (unpublished doctoral dissertation, University of California at Berkeley, 1968).

[53] Cazden, "Environmental Assistance to the Child's Acquisition of Grammar."

[54] Berlyne, "Recent Developments in Piaget's Work." Dolores Durkin, "Children Who Learn to Read Before Grade One," *Reading Teacher,* XIV (1965), 112–17.

[55] J. Bruner, J. Goodnow, and G. Austin, *A Study of Thinking* (New York: John Wiley & Sons, Inc., 1956).

[56] Harry Singer, "Conceptualization in Learning To Read," *New Frontiers in College-Adult Reading,* ed. G. B. Schick and M. M. May, Fifteenth Yearbook of the National Reading Conference (Milwaukee: National Reading Conference, 1966), pp. 116–32.

[57] Robert C. Pooley, *Teaching English Usage* (New York: Appleton-Century-Crofts, 1946).

[58] Robert B. Ruddell, "Language Acquisition and the Reading Process," in *Theoretical Models and Processes of Reading,* ed. Harry Singer and Robert B. Ruddell (Newark, Del.: International Reading Association, 1970), pp. 1–19.

[59] Marie R. Lindsay, "A Descriptive Exploration of the Growth and Development of Spontaneous Oral Vocabulary of Elementary School Children" (unpublished doctoral dissertation, University of California at Berkeley, 1969).

[60] Kenneth S. Goodman, "Words and Morphemes in Reading," *Psycholinguistics and the Teaching of Reading,* ed. K. Goodman and J. Fleming (Newark, Del.: International Reading Association, 1968), pp. 25–33.

[61] Basil Bernstein, "Social Structure, Language, and Learning," *Educational Research,* III (1961), 163–76. See also Bernstein, "Elaborated and Restricted Codes: A Note on Verbal Planning," *The Psychology of Language, Thought, and Instruction,* ed. John P. DeCecco (New York: Holt, Rinehart and Winston, Inc., 1967), pp. 101–3.

[62] A. R. Luria, "The Directive Function of Speech," *Word,* I, XV (1959a), 341–52; II, XV (1959b), 453–64.

5

An Introduction
to Reading-Language Programs

Focusing Questions

1. How does modern reading-language instruction differ from that of a century ago?
2. On the basis of the communication framework, how do modern reading programs differ in emphasis? What strengths and limitations result from these various emphases?
3. What key learning variables must be accounted for in successful reading-language instruction?
4. What teacher characteristics are essential for the successful development and implementation of the instructional program?
5. What criteria would you use in the examination and selection of a reading-language program or system? (See also the discussion of criteria in the Appendix.)

Our discussion to this point has been chiefly concerned with the "Who" of reading-language instruction—with your role as classroom teacher—and the "Why" of instruction—with background knowledge, including the nature of the reading-language process, language concepts, language development, and socio-ethnic variation in language. This knowledge is basic to the development of the reading-language curriculum and to the improvement of your instructional program, but if this background information is to be of value, it is essential that you know how to apply it in your instructional program. The remainder of this text will be devoted to this end.

We shall begin our discussion with a brief historical perspective of reading-language instruction. Our major focus, however, will be on developing an overview of reading-language programs within the framework of the communication model developed in Chapter 2. We shall identify seven instructional provisions that are essential for dealing with variation in your classroom, and we shall conclude with a discussion of four teacher competencies essential to successful classroom performance.

Although the most significant changes in reading-language instruction have occurred during the past half-century we will briefly chronicle the first 300 years of instruction in this country.

The content of reading material in the seventeenth century was heavily flavored with religion and patriotism. The primary reason for learning to read was to be able to pursue the Scriptures, according to the "Old Deluder Satan Law" passed in Massachusetts in 1647. The hornbook, a basic literary tool, was a paddle-shaped hardwood board covered by a thin sheet of transparent horn. It contained the alphabet and a few syllables, followed by the Lord's Prayer.

Figure 5-1. The hornbook.

The first school book, *The New England Primer*, published about 1690, consisted of a combined "religious manual, catechism, and speller."[1] Over three million copies of this text were printed. The approach to reading and spelling instruction using this "all-purpose" text consisted of a strong emphasis on letter name knowledge used to spell out words, followed by the attempt to pronounce them. Attention was also given to spelling (isolated syllables) and "sight word" vocabulary recognition. Oral reading, "spell-downs," and memorization of Biblical selections consumed a significant portion of the school day.

The classroom environment was comprised of the bare physical essentials common to a meeting hall. Rough backless benches were provided for the children while a rough plank served as the teacher's desk. Light and ventilation often originated from a log window formed by omitting a log, and a great stone fireplace gave the minimal heat necessary for survival.

Classroom procedures made little provision for individual differences, save for the few minutes given to recitation, and even this was largely the consequence of a shortage of books and writing materials. The teacher, usually a man, was a disciplinarian in the strict sense of the word. His preparation was minimal: the ability to read and write was the basic criterion. He was of course required to possess a high moral character.

Figure 5-2. *The New England Primer. Courtesy of Ginn and Company.*

The publication of Noah Webster's *The American Spelling Book* or *Blue-Back Speller* in 1783, with its emphases on establishing letter-sound relationships rather than on learning letter names only and isolated syllable pronunciation, was an advance in reading pedagogy. The content, historical selections designed to familiarize children with the Constitution and their

American (and to some degree their European) heritage, reflected the patriotism of the Revolutionary time. Moralistic selections were also included to enhance character and good citizenship. No provision was made for levels of difficulty or for learning differences in youngsters.

The instructional program of this period also stressed "articulation and pronunciation as a means of . . . bringing about greater unity in the American language,"[2] and the art of elocution, which was viewed as a necessity for a democratic form of government. Writing instruction dealt with how to use a quill pen, with little or no emphasis on composition.

McGuffey's graded readers, published in 1837 and destined to hold sway in American education for approximately forty years, were the first attempt to provide for difficulty levels in reading materials. The development of graded materials, which appeared in several reading programs in the 1800s, has been attributed to the influence of the German-Pestalozzian movement. Proponents of this movement called for the development of the mind through graded exercises "and the inclusion of material dealing with objects and experiences familiar to children."[3] McGuffey's program contained many more pictures than had earlier materials. In addition to the graded levels, and to the stress on phonics and syllables in isolation and in context, there was a repetition of new words as a means of developing a recognition vocabulary. The content continued to emphasize moralistic

LESSON XXVIII.

said	their	school	fa'ther	ev'er-y
roar	great	li'ons	slow'ly	look'ed
cross	chain	ca'ges	a-fraid'	pleas'ed
James	beasts	ma'ny	dan'ger	show'man
George	struck	ti'gers	walk'ed	play'mates

————◦◦:◦:◦◦————

THE WILD BEASTS

1. JAMES and George had been good boys at school, all the week.

2. They had been very kind and mild to their play-mates. So their father said he would take them to the show.

3. They saw at the show a great many wild beasts in cages.

4. Some of the beasts had a chain round one leg, made fast to a post.

5. There were lions, tigers, and a great many other beasts.

6. The boys walked round slowly, and looked at ev-er-y thing.

7. They felt a little afraid of some of the beasts.

8. But they were very much pleased with most that they saw.

9. The show-man went into the cage with the lion. The boys were then afraid.

10. But a man, who sat near them, told them there was no danger.

11. The show-man struck the lion with a large whip.

12. This made him roar very loud, and look cross, but he did not hurt the man.

13. James said, "I wish the man would come out. I do not like to see him there.

14. "The big lion might eat him up, and then I should be sorry "

15. James was a good boy, and did not like to see any one hurt.

EXERCISES.—Where did the father of James and George take them? Why? Ought not boys to be always kind? What is a show? Tell what the boys saw

Figure 5-3. *McGuffey's Second Eclectic Reader. Reprinted by permission of the American Book Company.*

and patriotic themes, but upper grade materials included literary selections and social science selections of educational and geographical nature. Oral reading and recitation of memorized passages were common components of the curriculum, and handwriting continued to take precedence over composition instruction.

Classroom organization of the mid-1800s attempted to account for individual variation through grades based on age categories. During the latter part of this century the one- and two-year normal schools provided impetus to teacher preparation. These institutions emphasized reading, writing, arithmetic, spelling, grammar, and the "science and art of teaching and classroom management."[4] Teacher preparation, however, focused for the most part on subject content, with little concern for innovative instructional methodology, so that instruction was based to a great extent on how the teacher remembered being taught. The early 1900s found women entering the teacher colleges and classrooms in prominent numbers.

Approximately 70 percent of the population at this time lived in rural settings.[5] As a result "school districts" were organized to provide a local school and a teacher. The one-room country school carried a large portion of the educational burden. In this setting the teacher assumed responsibility for the first six or eight grades. Urban schools were commonly three-

In what way would the instructional role of the teacher in the one-room country school (grades one through six) differ from the role of the teacher in today's classroom?

story buildings with four classrooms on the first two levels and a large assembly room on the third floor.[6] Desks now contained back supports and places for storage of children's materials, but they were screwed down to the oiled hardwood floors.

In the early part of the twentieth century the emphasis was on instructional evaluation through standardized tests. This assessment emphasis had some positive value, in that it provided an initial index of progress and demonstrated the need to provide for wide achievement variation among pupils; but its negative effects were that in some school systems administrative expectations placed extreme achievement pressures on teachers and youngsters.

The publishing industry continued to play an important instructional role, not only through publication of basal reading programs but also through development of supplementary reading materials. Emphasis was on broader reading content, including such areas as science, art, and economics. Handwriting retained its place in the classroom curriculum, but instruction now included a "composition" component, which consisted for the most part of the study of grammatical and usage rules.[7]

Teacher preparation became more extensive through the commonly accepted four-year teacher's colleges and university programs. New organizational plans were tried in the attempts to provide for individual pupil variations and interests. One such plan developed during the 1920s was the Dalton Plan, which was characterized by flexible grouping across grades through "subject laboratories" and by individual "contracts" established between pupil and teacher.

During the 1920s and 1930s emphasis was on "reading readiness." In part this took the form of teacher-pupil-derived experience charts that drew heavily on the pupil's background. The publishing industry produced the pre-primer, with the intent of providing an initial recognition vocabulary for the child. Phonics instruction, sound-letter relationships in the context of words, was still emphasized, but less so in the initial instruction than had been the case in previous periods. Teacher's manuals, containing detailed suggestions for introducing and developing word attack and comprehension activities based on the content of the child's reader, became commonplace at this time. Silent reading was particularly in vogue.

The concept of "language growth" emerged from a child-centered curriculum emphasis which was enhanced by the efforts of John Dewey and his followers.[8] The idea was to provide "enriched and direct experiences" through oral dramatization and creative writing in a content-oriented unit, which often related to the child's own experiences. Instruction in "correct usage" was still an important part of the curriculum. Spelling words were often derived from unit activities, although a spelling text was commonly used in classrooms.

World War II induction testing results and the apparent inability of service 113 personnel to follow detailed verbal instructions resulted in charges that the literacy level of America's youth was inadequate. Various literacy courses were offered by the armed services to raise performance levels. Remedial reading instruction began in the public schools during the late 1940s and has continued to the present time.

Basal reading programs of this period emphasized context clues and structural analysis in decoding new words. Initial instruction, however, emphasized the development of a sight vocabulary through frequent repetition of words in the story line. The readers also made provision for greater breadth in literary selections.

 During the 1950s and 1960s the role of the lay critic became more prominent, as exemplified by such works as Rudolph Flesch's *Why Johnny Can't Read* and Arthur Trace's *What Ivan Knows that Johnny Doesn't.*[9] Such criticism, which in the first case was based on misinterpretations of research findings, and in the second on faulty assumptions about children's reading,[10] may have produced some positive effects by causing professional educators to re-examine and tighten the rationale underlying reading-language instruction.

During the 1960s reading-language instruction felt the influence of the disciplines, particularly linguistics and psychology. This is evident in publisher-produced programs that placed specific controls on sound-letter correspondences and related syntactical patterning to comprehension. It is possible that this influence, combined with that of the lay critics, has led in part to earlier introduction of decoding skills and greater emphasis on vocabulary load and subject matter content in the primary grades. Although linguistically oriented (structural and transformational) grammars have replaced traditional grammar instruction in many classrooms, the development of oral and written expression still relies heavily on such activities as dramatization, role playing, oral reading by the teacher, and experience chart stories.

There is now a wide variety of materials available for the classroom, and special attention to children's literature has been facilitated by the availability of low-cost paperback tradebooks and easily accessible classroom and school library collections. Creators of basal reading and language programs have consciously tried to include quality literary selections for children, and some instructional programs also contain diagnostic tests to aid the teacher in evaluating progress.

The physical facilities of the modern classroom contrast sharply with those of the previous century. Most of today's classrooms are well lighted and ventilated with movable furniture to permit flexible grouping. Many teachers have tape recorders, record players, and filmstrip and 16 mm. projectors to play instructional tapes and records and to show films. But the visual aid that bridges the centuries and is common to all classrooms is still the chalkboard.

Professional preparation of teachers is now based on such practices as
fifth-year professional development programs and intern programs, both

of which parallel professional training in the medical profession. Federal and state financial support has enabled universities, colleges, and professional organizations to sponsor reading and language institutes to inform the classroom teacher and teachers of teachers of new reading-language-related information and practices. These efforts, however, have received little federal support in recent years, and much of the load remains for the inservice, experience-oriented teacher-training programs of the school district.

The learning needs characteristic of minority group children have received much more attention in recent years, in the form of studies of language and conceptual variation and attempts to sensitize teachers to their specific reading-language needs. There has also been development of problem-centered reading-language materials for these children that use high-interest, child-oriented experiences in story lines and pictures. Reading-language instruction for all minority group youngsters will require continued, extensive efforts on the part of researchers, people who prepare professional preparation programs, and classroom teachers if these children are to realize their full achievement potential.

What unique instructional needs should be anticipated for the minority group child? *(Photo © 1972 Susan Ylvisaker/Jeroboam)*

Federal agencies have sponsored research and development activities through universities and research and development centers to develop and field test instructional materials in school settings. Other researchers are examining the nature and process of reading-language learning, and there has been some success applying these research findings to reading-language curricula.

Key innovations in reading-language instruction during the past 350 years (most of which are comparatively recent) include the following:

1. Instructional aids: materials with carefully graded difficulty levels, detailed teacher manuals, supplementary reading-language materials, and audio-visual equipment and instructional materials
2. Evaluation and improvement of instruction through publisher-produced and teacher-made evaluation instruments
3. Development of a variety of decoding approaches including phonics, structural analysis, and context clues in the early primary grades
4. Development of an array of comprehension levels and skill competencies
5. Inclusion of quality literature and content to extend literary experiences and develop permanent reading interests
6. A shift from emphasis on subject matter to a child-centered, problem-centered curriculum with emphasis on utilizing the child's background problems and experiences as the basis for developing thinking strategies and oral and written expression
7. Teacher preparation based on language-related disciplines, innovative methodology, and direct experiences with youngsters through internship and student teaching roles
8. Inservice professional teacher development that introduces discipline-derived concepts and instructional methodology in institute and workshop seminars
9. Revision of classroom organization and instruction to provide for individual needs and variations—particularly those of minority group youngsters
10. Improvement of reading-language programs and professional preparation as outgrowths of the efforts of lay critics and vanguard professional educators
11. Creation of instructional methodology designed to develop the verbal potential of minority group children
12. Improvement of reading-language instruction through research and development activities

These innovations indeed represent progress in reading-language instruction; however, our instructional programs have far to go before there is the complete learning individualization that will develop the full potential of our youngsters. Now let's examine the characteristics of representative modern reading-language programs.

CHARACTERISTICS OF MODERN READING-LANGUAGE PROGRAMS

During the last decade a wide variety of reading-language programs has been developed, and teachers have used these programs in organizational plans ranging from totally individualized efforts to instruction of large members of youngsters. These programs can be roughly characterized on the basis of our communication model in the following ways:

1. Programs emphasizing control of grapheme-phoneme correspondences and letter-sound patterns for decoding and encoding
2. Programs emphasizing language structure (relational meaning) designed to enhance reading-listening comprehension and oral and written expression
3. Programs emphasizing conceptual (lexical meaning), interpretative (semantic interpretation), and problem-solving abilities (cognitive strategies) basic to reading-listening comprehension and oral and written expression
4. Programs emphasizing reading-language interests and attitudes (affective mobilizers)
5. Programs attempting to integrate the previous components in a systematic manner

The following are representative programs and sample pages that illustrate the range of programs available for classroom utilization.

Control of grapheme-phoneme correspondences and letter-sound patterns

Control of letter-sound correspondences and patterns has been attempted in two major ways. The first approach uses regular orthography but restricts the vocabulary: vocabulary with highly regular spelling-to-sound correspondences is developed first, followed by vocabulary with less predictable spelling correspondences. The second approach involves either a change in the orthography, as in the initial teaching alphabet devised by Sir James Pitman, or the use of regular orthography, with a color code system to key sound values in a consistent fashion.

REGULAR ORTHOGRAPHY

A systematic presentation of carefully controlled sound-letter correspondences based on regular English orthography has been utilized in reading programs produced by several publishers. One such program, the *Merrill Linguistic Readers*,[11] is produced by Merrill Publishing Company. This program initially develops letter name knowledge with primary emphasis on decoding skills. Sound-letter correspondences are carefully controlled: there are only unglided or short vowels with consistent graphic representation at the early levels (save for a few high frequency words, such as *the*). Minimal contrasts are emphasized as a sound-letter correspondence in a word is substituted for another to produce a new word, e.g., *p*ins, *b*ins. The program emphasizes the concept of spelling patterns such as consonant-vowel-consonant (*pin*) and consonant-vowel-consonant + e marker (*pine*).

117

● *Have the title read aloud. Be sure pupils understand that the pins in this story are repair parts for machinery.*

● *Guide the silent reading as necessary.*

A Pin for a Fan

How did Dad fix the broken fan?

Where did Dad keep pins?

Dad had pins in bins.

Why did Dad get a pin from a bin?

He had a pin for the fan.

How did he put it in the fan? (Remind pupils

He had to tap the pin *to hold markers below the second line of this sentence. Do this with*

into the fan. *the next sentence, also.)*

Where did Dad work?

Dad sat on a mat

to tap the pin.

What noise did Dad make?

He hit it — tap, tap, tap.

Did he fix the fan?

The fan ran.

● *Discuss the repair work that Dad did.*

● *Proceed to the oral reading, working toward normal intonation. When the fifth sentence is read aloud, tell pupils to pause for the dash. Have the entire story reread by several capable pupils.*

Figure 5-4. *From* Merrill Linguistic Readers, *Reader 2, by Charles C. Fries et al. Copyright 1966 by Charles E. Merrill Books, Inc.*

The limitation this imposes on vocabulary often produces stories of limited interest. No pictures are used in the child's text in order, according to the authors, to focus the child's attention on the decoding task, but there are pictures in the beginning workbook material in order to enhance the decoding exercises. The early material uses direct recall comprehension questions, mainly to evaluate the child's progress in decoding. The later levels involve some questions at the inference level.

Science Research Associates has produced the *SRA Basic Reading Series,*[12] which controls sound-letter correspondences to a high degree. The texts at the early levels contain words in sentence contexts but the story lines are severely restricted. The teacher's manual provides detailed suggestions for introducing vocabulary, but gives little emphasis to comprehension development. In later levels there is a range of selections from fairy tales to science-oriented content that have high interest potential.

McGraw-Hill Book Company has published a reading program, *Programmed Reading,*[13] that also conforms to the consistency principle. The unglided or short vowels and several consonant correspondences are introduced in the early stages, and glided or long vowels are gradually introduced as the program is developed. The system is presented in a programmed format that allows the pupil to check his response to an item immediately. The child is required to complete a given word by printing a letter in a response blank. Spelling ability is thus encouraged early in the program. Story illustrations are in cartoon form, and the same characters run throughout the program. The use of story characters throughout the series adds to the interest level of the story line, which otherwise closely resembles the two programs just discussed. The advanced story lines focus to a great extent on myths.

What are the advantages and disadvantages of self-directing reading materials?
(Photo © 1972 Susan Ylvisaker/Jeroboam)

The Linguistic-Science Readers[14] (Harper and Row) operate on the principle of consistent presentation of sound-letter correspondences at the early levels. The primer and first reader incorporate a concept the authors call the "graphonic base" (for example, *id:* d*id,* l*id,* r*id,* m*id*dle). One purpose of this "base" is to present a letter and sound pattern to the child without distorting letter-sound representations that may result when the child attempts to produce the sound represented by an isolated letter. The early part of this program deals exclusively with a story line and illustrations of animal characters, while the more advanced materials incorporate fanciful and imaginative stories.

Other programs based on the consistency principle and with regular orthography include Wayne State University Press materials, *Let's Read: A Linguistic Approach,*[15] and the *Miami Linguistic Readers*[16] published by D. C. Heath.

ALTERED ORTHOGRAPHY

The orthography has been changed by altering formation of the letter symbols or through a color code. The initial teaching alphabet (i/t/a) originally proposed by Sir James Pitman did not involve a change in method of reading instruction but dealt with a change in the printed medium presented to children. The forty-four letter characters (q and x were deleted and eighteen new characters were added) were designed to represent the consonants and the glided and unglided vowels of English.

The *Janet and John* series, the first English readers printed in i/t/a, and *The Downing Readers*[17] ally themselves closely with traditional basal reading programs in this country—in fact the former program is the English version of the *Alice and Jerry* series originally published in this country by Row Peterson. An eclectic approach relying on a sight vocabulary and phonic emphasis is present in both programs.

Once the initial teaching alphabet has been mastered, the children should be able to decode (pronounce) any material available in the medium. Research reports indicate that transfer to traditional symbols for reading purposes has produced very little difficulty. Since the children also learn to write with the new alphabet they must transfer to regular orthography in written form as well. This transfer is more difficult than the reading transfer and requires that the teacher demonstrate tolerance of the child's spelling forms until this transfer is complete.

A set of reading material has also been developed by ITA Publications. These materials, authored by Mazurkiewicz and Tanyzer,[18] place early emphasis on the development of alphabet knowledge, phonics, and writing. The authors have taken greater advantage of the possibilities of the new medium than earlier i/t/a programs by increasing the vocabulary load and using a greater variety of sentence patterns in the stories. Selections are used from *Humpty Dumpty Magazine,* which contains a number of high interest stories. Some selections from children's literature are now available in i/t/a, but the range and availability of such outside reading materials is not yet great.

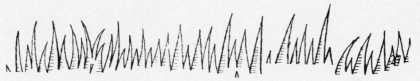

"his hous is tω littl.
his hous is not red.
a big den is best for a dienosaur
and the best big den is red."

Figure 5-5. *From Albert J. Mazurkiewicz and Harold J. Tanyzer,* Dinosaur Ben. *Reprinted by permission of ITA Publications.*

Words in Color, a program using a special color coding of letters, has been published by Learning Materials Incorporated.[19] The letter or letter group that represents a given phoneme has its own color assignment or color code. The glided or long *a* vowel sound, for example, is represented by the a in able, ai in mail, eigh in weigh, and ea in great, to mention four possibilities, and so all four are assigned a color, such as a shading of green. In all thirty-nine colors are used. Instruction depends heavily on the twenty-one wall charts containing color-coded letter combinations and colored chalk for presentation of color-coded correspondences. Fine color discrimination would seem essential for use of the materials; for example, ten shades of green are used. The reading material provided for the child is printed in black and white. The materials also make provision for "games of transformation" that encourage children to alter and create words by rearranging and expanding letters. The vocabulary in the reading material is systematically controlled: it moves from unglided (short vowel) correspondences into consonant correspondences to glided (long vowel) correspondences.

ADVANTAGES AND LIMITATIONS OF CONTROLLED CORRESPONDENCES

In summary, the control of sound-letter correspondences offers several advantages to the instructional program:

1. Systematic introduction of correspondences provides an understanding of sound-letter relationships by emphasizing that regularity is present to a degree in the English spelling system.
2. The emphasis on developing sound-letter correspondences can lead to early independence in decoding for some youngsters.

3. The introduction to the English spelling system can provide early spelling independence and a base for independent written expression.

Limitations of the control of sound-letter correspondences are:

1. The control of correspondences can result in a rigid, uninteresting story line.
2. The child may learn to view reading simply as the act of decoding with little concern for comprehension, appreciation, or enjoyment of reading, which in turn may reduce his desire to further his reading ability.
3. Programs that don't introduce spelling variations or "irregularities" may be preparing the child for a world of print that does not exist.

Programs based on language structure

Several recently developed programs have related the structural components of language to meaning by relying heavily on the oral language of children. This method directly or indirectly stresses the ways words relate to each other in conveying meaning, and does so by using the child's oral language as a basis. Encyclopaedia Britannica Press has published a program, *Language Experiences in Reading,* [20] that illustrates one form of this method. The philosophy of the approach is summarized as follows:

1. What he [the child] thinks about he can say.
2. What he says can be written (or dictated).
3. What has been written can be read.
4. He can read what he has written and what others have written for him to read.

Early interest in writing and reading is generated by the story line captured in the child's artistic expression. In the beginning stages of the language experience approach, the teacher may record the story using the child's oral language structures and vocabulary as the basis for the story material. In later stages the child develops his own story with the aid of the teacher and his individually developed spelling list.

Extensive individualized reading of trade books and basal readers available in the classroom is encouraged. Although word attack skills are a part of the program, they play a minor role. The teacher emphasizes correlation between sounds and letters as the child's individual spelling-writing list and story lines expand. The decoding aspect of the program has been observed to vary widely from teacher to teacher, depending in part on the teacher's own understanding of the decoding process. Some teachers develop and use their own word attack skills program in conjunction with the spelling-writing phase of the program, while others may rely heavily on an available reading program.

One major strength of this approach lies in its use of structural forms common to a child's oral language. Another is the high level of interest the child generates by creating, writing, and reading his own story line, but the teacher must be careful to see that the child develops systematic decoding skills.

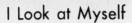

I Look at Myself   Name_____

See _____
    _____
                                                              1

                                                 Name _____

I Can Make Reading from Talk

Figure 5-6. *From Roach Van Allen,* Language Experiences in Reading *(1966).*
Reprinted by permission of Encyclopaedia Britannica Press, Inc., Chicago, Illinois
60611.

Program BUILD,[21] a primary grade reading-language program recently
published by Ginn and Company, utilizes patterns of language structure
that have been identified in children's oral language. One dimension of the
123 program emphasizes key structural language components used in convey-

ing meaning. The materials consist of student response booklets, a teacher's guide, word cards, and syntactic blocks containing words that belong to different form classes. In the early stages stress is on intonation patterns and meaning in oral language and on intonation and meaning relationships conveyed in written language through punctuation. The materials enable the child to manipulate the language by constructing his own sentences and stories with the syntactic blocks, by expanding base sentences into more complex constructions, by developing meaning relationships between and among words in sentences and between and among sentences, and by weaving broader ideas into the paragraph and story.

a. Word substitution in key positions in the sentence.

Example:

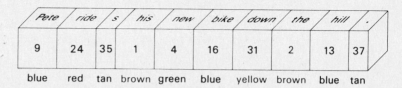

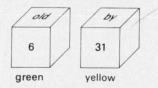

Figure 5-7. *From* Teachers' Guide, *of* Program BUILD: Basic Understandings in Language Development, *by Robert B. Ruddell, Barbara W. Graves, and Floyd W. Davis,* © Copyright, 1972, by Ginn and Company. Used with permission.

The pattern construction employs the principle of meaning contrast, and the student is constantly aware of meaning changes which result from new order arrangements and the addition and deletion of structural elements. Individual participation in sentence construction is a concrete kinesthetic experience designed to provide pupil interaction and motivation.

Sentence construction is related to an oral story context and designed to help the student understand how language is organized in a systematic manner. This understanding is extended through the three levels because of the color contrasts among the block patterns of the basic sentence structures. Levels I, II, and III place increasing emphasis on construction and comprehension of introductory, transitional, and concluding sentences. Throughout these three levels paragraph writing and comprehension of story development are developed. At first the student is introduced

My name is Tommy.

I am not very big.

But...

I am bigger
than a dog.

Figure 5-8. *From* Sounds of Numbers, *by Bill Martin, Jr., Holt, Rinehart and Winston, Inc., copyright © 1966. Used by permission.*

to paragraph and story writing through model paragraphs and stories, and then key characteristics of the model are identified. Then he uses the characteristics and guidelines to create his own paragraphs and stories. Although this program contains other dimensions, such as a word attack skills strand and a language strand, its uniqueness is its emphasis on structural elements related to meaning.

An innovative series of materials, *Sounds of Language Readers*,[22] published by Holt, Rinehart and Winston, approaches structure and meaning indirectly. This colorfully illustrated series uses varied print and graphic forms to show the word, phrase, and sentence pattern equivalents of oral language that contribute to the meaning. The program contains literary selections of good quality that appeal very much to children.

In the beginning the teacher reads a story and the children listen and follow the story development in their books. There is no systematic effort to develop decoding skills save for establishing a sight vocabulary. Suggestions are provided in the teacher's text for building comprehension and writing skills. This program is an excellent supplementary series for building positive attitudes toward reading and enjoyment of literature.

Scott, Foresman offers a set of plastic cubes stamped with words from specific form classes so that children can manipulate sentence elements.[23] A pamphlet provides general game suggestions for classroom use.

Chandler Publishing Company offers reading materials that attempt to present language structure similar to that used by children in conversational settings.[24] The authors control the vocabulary, but the structures utilized in story conversations appear to approximate those of children. Story lines are developed around topics of apparent interest to children (swings, bikes), and photographs accompany the story lines. More is said about this program in the next section of this chapter.

ADVANTAGES AND LIMITATIONS OF LANGUAGE STRUCTURE EMPHASIS

Programs that emphasize language structure offer several advantages:

1. The functions of word order, word substitution, sentence expansion, and intersentence relationships in developing the child's comprehension and oral language and writing abilities are clearly demonstrated.
2. The important relationship between oral and written language forms is developed to enhance listening and reading comprehension and expressive abilities.
3. The appreciation and enjoyment of language as used in a variety of oral and written situations (daily communication, children's literature) is developed.

126 But such approaches also have several important limitations:

1. The teacher must be aware of the range of comprehension and decoding skills essential to the development of a mature reader.
2. The teacher must be careful to provide an appraisal and evaluation component.
3. The teacher must account for a wide range of individual differences to develop and sustain interest and motivation.

All over the city, people read.

They read on streets and in stores.

They read in houses.

And they read in school.

All over the city, people read.

Figure 5-9. *From* People Read, *The Bank Street Readers, ed. Irma Simonton Black et al.* © *Copyright The Macmillan Company 1965 and used by permission.*

Conceptual, interpretative, and problem-solving development

Recent demands and pressures have caused a number of publishers to try to develop reading materials with particular concern for the experiential background of minority group students. Most of these efforts have only been partially successful (some of them have done no more than change skin tones and facial features in the pictures and photos of already existing programs), and much more will have to be done before the effort to provide reading materials designed for minority group experiences has real significance.

One reading series that obviously takes the minority group student into consideration is *The Bank Street Basal Reading Series*. [25] This program, published by Macmillan, incorporates oral language experiences related to story concepts in the first pre-primer. Most of the story settings are urban, and many involve problem situations designed to actively engage children. The illustrations identify racial groups in a variety of urban settings.

A detailed teacher guide contains suggestions for developing decoding and comprehension skills. The decoding method follows a traditional pattern —introducing consonants and delaying the development of vowel correspondences until grade two. A skills practice book is provided to reinforce the skills introduced, and diagnostic tests are provided to aid in evaluating individual pupil growth.

The Chandler Reading Program [26] is another serious attempt to provide reading-language experiences with a strong urban orientation. The early oral language experiences center around enlarged photographs and provide the concept development essential to the readiness and pre-primer reading experiences. Early paperback readers on such topics as *Swings, Bikes,* and the *Supermarket* utilize photographs and provide incentive to read about familiar experiences. The later hardback readers also contain urban-oriented story lines and photographs depicting children in interracial situations. The content stresses science, and social studies to a lesser extent. Starting with *Take a Big Look,* the books include folktales from various parts of the world.

The teacher's edition contains detailed suggestions for introducing and developing concepts and decoding and comprehension skills. Worksheets are available for reinforcing skills introduced in the teacher's guide. The pacing of the word attack skills is comparatively slow and there is heavy reliance on a sight vocabulary, but there is a planned reinforcement for recognition of the vocabulary.

An excellent supplementary set of materials is in the *Holt Urban Social Studies Series.* [27] This material provides interracial story lines and actual photographs of children in a wide variety of environments. The idea of developing more effective pupil identification with story characters through interracial, illustrated stories with urban themes seems to have potential.

"Good," said David. "Let's put it together.
First we have to slide the little stick
up to here on the big stick. Next we put
the paper on. There's a place on the sticks
for the string to go into. I'll hold the kite.
You put the string in the sticks right there."

"Is that all there is to it?" Tony asked.
"Just about. Now we have to use some
string and put it through the two holes
in the kite."

Figure 5-10. *From Laurence W. Carrillo et al.,* Chandler Reading Program, *1968.
Reprinted by permission of Materials for Today's Learning, Inc.*

Several supplementary programs are available for the express purpose of developing concepts, attitudes toward language, and interpretative and problem-solving abilities. *An Experience-Centered Language Program,* published by Franklin Publications, is one such program.[28] It develops concepts ranging from size and space relationships (smallest, middle sized, biggest; in front of, behind, under, inside) to concepts related to the home, family, and special feelings, and it does so with a multisensory approach. A central puppet character, Tim, is used to encourage and motivate the children to enter into active discussions of the concepts, through selections entitled, "Tim Thinks about Feelings," "Tim Dreams about Wishes," and the like.

There is a detailed teacher's manual, along with various materials. For example, one unit deals with concepts of texture, such as hard, soft, rough, smooth, heavy, light, and there are four blocks to provide appropriate tactile experiences: one block is smooth and light, while another is rough and heavy. Although many of the materials provided could be easily collected or constructed, the manual and detailed suggestions provide a systematic approach to concept building and language use that is an excellent base for more formal reading-language classroom experiences.

The Peabody Language Development Kits,[29] published by American Guidance Service, likewise provide for the development of concepts and higher thought processes. The program stresses auditory, visual, and tactual reception abilities; divergent, convergent, and associative thinking; and vocal and motor expression. The kits contain a detailed teacher's manual; vocabulary building cards; "Story" and "I Wonder" posters, designed to stimulate imaginations and develop continuity in story telling; puppets; stories and folktales on magnetic tape; a "teletalk" instrument, to stimulate oral language dialogue; and colored plastic chips to develop grouping and sequencing of colors. The program has considerable flexibility and can be used with children at various stages of conceptual development.

The Productive Thinking Program[30] provides for the development of interpretative and problem-solving abilities at the intermediate grade levels. This program offers a systematic approach in exploring various alternate solutions to mystery problems, such as "Jim Explores the Deserted House" presented in a comic strip format. As various clues are revealed the student is encouraged to record ideas at each step of the mystery and to reassess what he knows up to that point in the light of each new clue. Two characters, Jim and Lila, are present in each story, presumably for purposes of identification and motivation. An advisory character, Uncle John, guides Jim and Lila through questioning strategies at key points in each mystery. The program is a highly motivating approach to the development of divergent thinking and problem-solving abilities.

130

Here is an idea-tree showing all of Jim's ideas. As you know, he has already eliminated the possibility that it was a *real* ghost. But there are still three other general possibilities, and each of them leads to several particular ideas.

General Possibilities   **Particular Ideas**

REAL GHOST

FAKE GHOST
— to play joke on Jim
— to scare people away

SOMETHING MOVED THAT LOOKED LIKE A GHOST
— shadows of trees
— cobwebs
— bats flying
— cloud of dust
— torn wallpaper
— old sheet blowing in wind
— smoke

NOTHING THERE—JUST SEEMED TO BE
— darkness played tricks on Jim's eyes
— Jim just imagined it all

Figure 5-11. *From* The Productive Thinking Program *by Martin V. Covington et al. Copyright 1972 by Charles E. Merrill Publishing Co. Reprinted by permission of the publisher.*

ADVANTAGES AND LIMITATIONS OF CONCEPTUAL, INTERPRETATIVE, AND PROBLEM-SOLVING DEVELOPMENT

Specific advantages offered by such programs include:

1. Conceptual, interpretative, and problem-solving development in an environment that children are at least partially familiar with
2. Introduction and expansion of concepts related directly to children's homes and community problems and experiences
3. Photographs and illustrations depicting interracial and high interest situations that provide for identification with story characters
4. A systematic approach to concept development and interpretative and problem-solving abilities

Limitations in such programs include:

1. A special need to expand the literary experiences of children beyond those in the materials
2. A need for individual variation and pacing within the materials to account for differentiated progress
3. Provision for extending decoding skills and oral and written expression (especially in the supplementary programs)

Reading-language interests, attitudes, and values

One of the teacher's most difficult jobs centers about the development of children's positive interests and attitudes toward reading-language experiences.

This problem has been compounded by the lack of adequate literature and language resources in the elementary school setting and by a lack of understanding of the nature and value of literature to youngsters. As Virginia Reid, a children's literature specialist, has pointed out, children's literature

includes that prose and poetry which stimulate curiosity, stretch the imagination, and awaken a sense of wonder. It should extend children's horizons and should deepen their understanding of themselves and others. Literature for children should be words of substance and sincerity, and be told in effective and memorable language. [31]

The literary experience must be one that is meaningful to the child, because only through meaningful personal encounters with literature and language will he come to understand their value to him and thus develop positive and permanent interests and attitudes toward reading-language experiences.

As classroom teacher it is essential that you carefully individualize your instruction by supplementing the basal reading-language program (or programs) available in your classroom. Specific reading selections must be based on each child's interests, maturity, conceptual development, personal adjustment, and functioning reading achievement level. A vast reservoir exists in children's literature for providing opportunity for self-reflection and understanding (for example, de Angeli's *The Door in the Wall);* for developing greater empathy with difficulties encountered by others (Gates's *Blue Willow);* for broadening and extending meaningful concepts in subject areas (Averill's *Cartier Sails the St. Lawrence);* for vicarious adventures in other cultures that lead to better understanding of the world's people (DeJong's *The Wheel on the School);* and for pleasure and enjoyment from literary experiences (McCloskey's *Make Way for Ducklings).* Many of these values can be obtained through story telling and story reading by teacher and youngsters in the classroom. It is essential that you understand both children and children's literature on a friendly, personal basis to generate positive interests and attitudes toward literature.

One literature-centered program that deserves special mention is the one developed by classroom teachers and language, literature, and composition specialists at the English Curriculum Center at the University of Nebraska under the sponsorship of the U.S. Office of Education. The center's efforts have been directed toward "showing such literature as will make reading worth the effort, composition an exercise in the imitation of excellence, and language study more than a bore."[32] The seventy units, designed for kindergarten through grade six, are built around specific selections. The spirally arranged curriculum introduces concepts at a specified level and then returns to them at later levels with a higher degree of abstraction. The units are categorized according to what those at the center call "pseudo-genres": folktales, fanciful stories, animal stories, adventure stories, myth-fables, other lands and people, historical fiction, and biography.

The center units demonstrate how children's literature can be used to generate interest in language study. For example, awareness of how important intonation is to meaning is developed through Dalgliesh's *The Bears on Hemlock Mountain* by shifting the intonation pattern in the refrain, "There *are* no bears on Hemlock Mountain, no bears at all." The effect of provisional words on meaning is shown through Aunt Emma's cautious statement, "You know there *may* be bears on Hemlock Mountain!" and Jonathan's final statement, "There *are* bears on Hemlock Mountain." A story such as *Leif the Lucky,* by Ingri and Edgar D'Aulaire, is used to demonstrate the imagery created by figures of speech such as similes ("His eyes were as keen as the eyes of a snake and blue as steel," or "and he steered his ship so it wound its way over the waves like a serpent").

Another aspect of language developed in the units deals with word origins and the changing nature of our language. For example, through an examination of *The Merry Adventures of Robin Hood,* by Pyle, the ways that names came out of occupations or origins are established ("Midge the Miller," "David of Doncaster"). Understanding of language change is promoted by contrasting the dialogue in de Angeli's *Door in the Wall* with Modern

English: "Suddenly a voice rang out. 'Who goes there?' Robin stopped. ' 'Tis but I, Robin, . . .' " (p. 93) or " 'Aah,' he said. 'Art tha' but a shepherd boy, then?' he asked" (p. 94).

Another innovative program, *The World of Language,*[33] has recently been published by Follett Educational Corporation. This program, characterized as "an oral-language-based" English program, provides a rich literary experience for children in the form of poems, stories, and plays and introduces concepts ranging from rhyme and rhythm to imagery and mood through literary selections. The program generates considerable visual appeal through real-life photographs and art work depicting dynamic human interactions that are integrated with the selections. A basic strand running throughout the program deals with human relations, and there is considerable emphasis on positive attitudes toward self and others in a variety of social situations. The literary selections have been carefully chosen to achieve this end.

Emphasis is also given to the development and understanding of language concepts: different levels of usage, dialectal variation, slang, language change, codes, and nonverbal communication forms such as dance, photographs, art, and music. The result should be broader, more positive attitudes toward language and communication forms. There is some direct attention to grammatical concepts at the end of each level, but this is clearly not the major thrust. Various study skills, from map reading to photographic interpretation, are integrated throughout the series.

A teacher's manual incorporates the child's edition and includes instructional suggestions for enhancing the development of various selections. Key questions are suggested throughout the manual to aid in developing cognitive abilities and in evaluating the children's progress.

Other programs designed to build positive attitudes and interests toward reading-language experiences include two previously described programs —*Language Experiences in Reading* and *Program BUILD.*[34] The former program captures the immediate interests of the child and uses them as the base for reading-language instruction; the latter engages the child in the active manipulation of the structures of language in sentence, paragraph, and story construction and expands his understanding of levels of language usage, language codes, and the changing nature of our language.

ADVANTAGES AND LIMITATIONS OF READING-LANGUAGE INTERESTS, ATTITUDES, AND VALUES

The strengths of such programs are:

1. The child is actively engaged in literature and language study in highly motivating materials and situations.
2. High interest, motivation, and enjoyment of literature and language experiences should lead to permanent reading and language interests.

NAME

Break the Secret Code

Study the picture code below. Find out what it says. When you have decoded the message, do what it says.

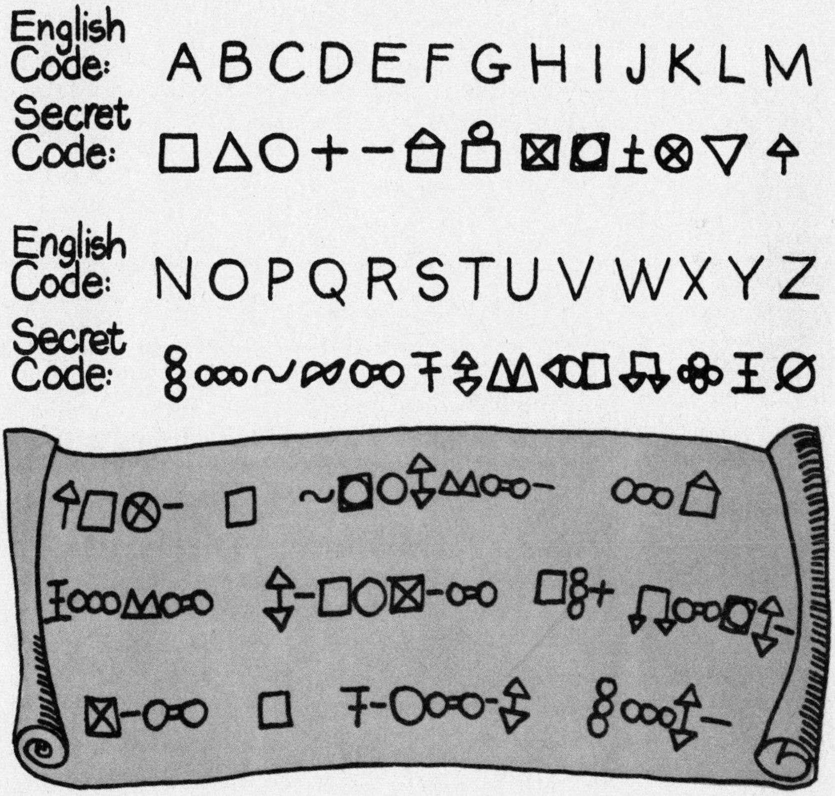

English Code: A B C D E F G H I J K L M

Secret Code: □ △ ○ + − ⌂ ⌂ ⊠ ⊡ ± ⊗ ▽ ⧫

English Code: N O P Q R S T U V W X Y Z

Secret Code: 8 ∞ ~ ⌀ ∞ ꝱ ⧫ ⋀ ◁ □ ꝱ ⊕ ⊥ Ø

Figure 5-12. *From* Building Up, *of* Program BUILD: Basic Understandings in Language Development, *by Robert B. Ruddell, Barbara W. Graves, and Floyd W. Davis,* © Copyright, 1972, by Ginn and Company. Used with permission.

135

3. An understanding of variations in language and literature relevant to daily life should provide for a broader tolerance of language variation and lead to a more complete understanding and appreciation of self and others.

Limitations of these programs are:

1. The teacher must be concerned with decoding abilities in order to produce independence in reading.
2. The teacher must serve as catalyst and resource in exposing the child to a broad overview of literary experiences through a range of children's literature.
3. The teacher must become highly familiar with children's literature and language concepts and children's interests as greater responsibility is assumed in developing the curriculum.

Integrated reading-language experiences

The successful reading-language instructional program incorporates these various approaches on the basis of the needs and interests of teacher and children. The following goals (outlined in Chapter 1) identify the important competencies the reading-language curriculum is to develop:

1. The ability to communicate clearly in oral and written forms in a variety of social settings
2. The ability to understand and use oral and written language in both receptive and expressive forms
3. The ability to use comprehension and problem-solving strategies in relation to the purpose established in reading and listening situations
4. The ability to decode new words and to encode or spell words as required in a variety of reading and writing situations
5. The ability to use research and study skills in interpreting content from subject areas
6. The ability to express, interpret, and enjoy thoughts in creative form
7. Sensitivity to and appreciation of language and literature as used in a variety of life situations

A number of publisher-produced programs try to achieve these goals by integrating various communication skills and by providing detailed suggestions for meeting individual differences.

Reading 360,[35] published by Ginn and Company, is a developmental reading series in thirteen levels for grades one through six. The initial levels approach aspects of language experience through the writing system and there is consistent emphasis on development of literal and particularly inferential comprehension skills. Divergent thinking is frequently encouraged through open-ended questions that are directly related to comprehension development. The decoding skills program uses a unique approach to word attack by encouraging children to utilize alternative approaches to analysis when blocked by an unknown word.

136

This program stresses literary understandings and enjoyment through attention to a story's plot, characterization, mood, and theme. The selections portray a range of social-moral values to help the youngster to understand his own values and to re-examine the ways he adjusts to problem situations. At Level 8, for example, most of the stories focus on a world of

What's a Folk Tale?

Storytelling is fun. Many, many years ago, when there were no television sets, movies, or books, even before men knew how to write, people loved to tell stories to each other. Grandparents told stories to parents. Parents told the same stories to their children. When the children grew up, they told the same stories to their children. And so it went, for many, many years, until these stories were finally written down. Many of these old stories are called folk tales.

Look at the pictures below. They are clues to some very old folk tales. Can you name the story?

What is alike about all these tales?
Which ones might have really happened?
Which ones have magic in them?
Is there something exciting in each one?
Who are the unpleasant characters?
What problem does the main character have?
How does each story end?

263

Figure 5-13. *From* Teachers' Edition of How It Is Nowadays, *by Theodore Clymer and Robert B. Ruddell, of the Reading 360 series,* © *Copyright, 1969, by Ginn and Company. Used with permission.*

change and the ways individuals adjust to change. Obvious concern has been given to literary quality. Beginning with Level 5 the final selection in each text is a full-length literary selection. There are numerous references to children's literature throughout to encourage the teacher to go beyond the selections provided.

Shadows tell us about the craters. They show that there are rings of mountains around these big holes. There are also mountains in the centers of some craters.

The moon shows us many "faces" as it rides along in the sky. It may be a thin crescent of light. It may look like a big letter D. The crescent, the letter D, and the full moon all reflect light from the sun.

Shadows have all kinds of stories to tell. There are old stories about Moon-Boy who lived on the moon. There are true stories which scientists are telling nowadays. There will be new stories that you can tell *after* you take a trip to see the shadows on the moon.

228

Figure 5-14. *From* Teachers' Edition of How It Is Nowadays, *by Theodore Clymer and Robert B. Ruddell, of the Reading 360 series, © Copyright, 1969, by Ginn and Company. Used with permission.*

Selections from content areas are included at the primary levels to develop the reading skills unique to content areas and necessary for the intermediate grades.

A detailed teacher's edition is provided with each level of the program, containing specific suggestions for developing each literary selection from the standpoint of motivation, vocabulary development, decoding and comprehension skills, and literary enjoyment and suggesting optional activities designed to provide for needs and variations of individual youngsters in the areas of decoding, comprehension, language, and creativity. It also provides evaluation activities at the completion of each unit within a given level and includes an informal reading inventory for each level, for purposes of pupil placement in individual or group instruction. Diagnostic information obtained from this inventory can be used to design the instructional program to meet individual differences. Achievement tests are also available for use at the completion of each level, and a skills handbook has been developed for each level that provides for continued development and reinforcement of the reading-language skills introduced in the program.

A number of other programs contain many of the same characteristics: *The Houghton Mifflin Readers, The Young America Basic Reading Program,* published by Lyons and Carnahan, *Scott, Foresman Reading Systems, The Harper and Row Basic Reading Program,* and the *Open Court Correlated Language Arts Program.*[36]

In order to achieve the seven goals outlined above it is essential that you the classroom teacher supplement and adjust your program or programs to the needs of individual youngsters in your classroom. One ever-present danger in using publisher-produced reading-language programs is the tendency to develop too great a dependence on the materials provided. This may take the form of limiting children in a particular grade to one level of an adopted text, of not giving adequate attention to outside literary experiences, or of stereotyping reading-language achievements within an established group. Ordinarily, such inappropriate teaching behavior is by no means entirely the fault of the published program (though sometimes part of the problem is at the administrative level where poor text selection and distribution practices may occur), but instead stems in large part from the performance of you, the classroom teacher. You can eliminate such teaching practices only by taking extra care to provide for individual differences in the classroom.

Professionally developed publisher-produced reading-language programs contain a number of values designed to achieve the goals outlined above:

1. Guided, systematic introduction and development of reading-language abilities and appreciations
2. Provision for continuous growth in basic reading-language skill areas within and across grade levels

3. Techniques for evaluating children's achievement growth and resource suggestions for enhancing this growth
4. Literary selections, skill sequencing, and instructional suggestions designed to help save teacher time (for other teaching responsibilities such as science, social studies, art, music, and the like)

But it is absolutely essential that you adjust any publisher-produced program to the needs, experiential backgrounds, concept development, and interests of individual youngsters. This immediately suggests the need for a collection of children's literary selections, the use of experience stories and charts which can involve the children's experiences in enhancing oral and written expression, and an in-depth understanding of the youngsters in your classroom.

CONCEPTS BASIC TO OPTIMAL INDIVIDUAL LEARNING EXPERIENCES

Our overview of reading-language programs clearly indicates the variety of instructional approaches present in a representative sample of instructional materials. It will thus be necessary for you to examine the instructional resources available in your classroom and ask how a program or programs may be expected to achieve the reading-language objectives you have established. Further, your provision for individual youngsters may require a methodological approach other than that present in the instructional program available to you. For example, you may find that the synthetic phonic approach used in the McGraw-Hill *Programmed Reading* is effective for building decoding skills for some students in your class but much less effective for others, in which case you may need to shift to an analytic-synthetic approach using the same materials, use one of the reading programs identified in the section on integrated reading-language experiences, or build word attack skills through an incidental synthetic or analytic teacher-developed program such as the language experience approach. This decision can be made only by you, the classroom teacher, and to make it you will need considerable familiarity with various types of instructional materials and, more important, an understanding of various approaches to reading-language instruction so that you can account for the individual learning differences in your classroom.

Thus provision for optimal learning conditions in the classroom must account for the "fit" between your proposed instructional program and your children's backgrounds: past learning experiences, conceptual development, learning strategies, interests, and motivations. Classroom learning experiences and opportunities must make provision for the following seven concepts if your efforts are to be successful.

First, you must determine each child's *readiness level,* by exploring his background of reading-language experiences and how he has fared with these experiences regardless of his grade placement. This will include an assessment of his functioning level of language maturity, including

140

conceptual development (lexical meaning), syntactical development (relational meaning), and affective development (attitude toward reading-language learning). His degree of control over the vocabulary and language forms that are unique and necessary to the classroom environment must receive special consideration.

Second, the child's *motivation* will be of basic importance to his success in the instructional setting. Try to consider this element from intrinsic and extrinsic perspectives. A child's ability to establish goals will vary, but it is extremely important if he is to derive functional pleasure and sense of accomplishment from his participation in direct or vicarious experiences, whether in the oral language activity of an interview or a role-playing situation or in listening to a poem or fairy tale reading. For some young-sters the development of interest and persistence can be enhanced by helping the child establish individual goals related to an activity and by providing consistent verbal encouragement. You must search constantly to identify the interests, attitudes, and values that youngsters bring to the

What learning factors will the teacher need to account for in successful reading-language instruction? *(Photo by Nancy Sue Graham, BBM Associates)*

classroom, and to use this information to develop persistence and drive in the learning activity.

Third, consider the *sequencing* and *pacing* of the concepts and skills you introduce and develop in the reading-language program. Some youngsters will require provision for the slow, careful development of concepts in a logical, step-by-step ordering, while others will have basic concepts established and can comprehend abstract relationships with little instructional development at a very rapid pace. These two factors can be adjusted only on the basis of the readiness level information you obtain at the outset of instruction.

Fourth, examine each child's *responses* within the instructional context carefully. As you observe the youngster's response you must evaluate it in terms of concept integration with previous background information and as it reflects the conceptual level of the child's thinking. Give particular concern to evidence indicating the child's success in accommodating and assimilating new concepts within his conceptual frame of reference. Your ability to utilize analytical, interpretative, and evaluative questions in a wide range of reading-language experiences will enhance such an assessment greatly.

Fifth, *reinforcement* and *feedback,* the consequences of the learner's activity, are of great importance to both the child and you, because of their ties to motivation and their influence on the child's persistence and success in learning experiences. You must constantly reflect on the types of feedback you provide. For example, if feedback is consistently positive, perhaps you need to raise the conceptual level of classroom questions and discussions, whereas if it is consistently negative, probably the conceptual level is inappropriately difficult. The child's negative responses, however, can provide a valuable contrast by identifying the unique characteristics (and those that fail to be unique) of a given concept that will eventually enhance understanding.

Sixth, *transfer,* the provision in the reading-language program for utilizing concept and skill development in a new learning situation, is of great import. Transfer occurs in part through the examination of similarities and differences among concepts across subject matter areas. A systematic approach to problem solving, for example, can be applied in the social science area through inferences about the rationale supporting the civil rights movement, and in the science area through the development of hypotheses about crater formations on the moon. Again, opportunity must be present for the child to accommodate and assimilate new concepts and skills into his present conceptual hierarchy.

Seventh, you need to give special concern to individual and group *social interaction* in classroom learning experiences. To do this, you must assess the individuals and status groups the individual children hold in high or low esteem because of attitudes in the home, the community, and at school. Knowledge about the child's attitudes toward interaction with these individuals and groups can provide information that can lead to more effective communication with the child. For example, you may find that a child has had little experience discussing ideas in family or peer group situations and so requires special encouragement to contribute to a group discussion. Other youngsters may have had little opportunity to assume responsibility of any kind at home and so will need help in establishing independent goals as they function in individual learning activities. Some youngsters may require special attention as they learn to contribute to a classroom climate that provides for freedom in discussions and at the same time to exercise restraint and responsibility not only in sharing ideas with others but also in attending to, examining, and respecting responsible ideas of others.

These seven factors are basic to any learning environment. They apply, of course, not only to reading-language instruction but to other areas of curricula as well. Outstanding teachers often account for them on an intuitive basis; however, a greater conceptual awareness of them should enable you to adjust reading-language instruction to meet the needs of individual youngsters more effectively. In fact, your success as an elementary teacher will be a direct function of your ability to account for these factors with your individual charges.

THE KEY TO SUCCESSFUL READING-LANGUAGE INSTRUCTION

In the final analysis the success of the reading-language program in achieving instructional objectives is a result of the ways you the classroom teacher develop and implement instruction. You are the professional who must assess your children's successes and difficulties and adjust your program accordingly. The following personal characteristics are essential to successful classroom instruction:

1. Flexibility and willingness to explore the effectiveness of your own ideas and those of others in a constructively critical way. Carefully consider your own instructional program and ask, "Why is my program successful with many of my children and less successful with others? What specific instructional knowledge, methods, and techniques contribute to this success or lack of success? How can I maintain the more effective techniques while replacing the less effective ones?"

2. Acute power to observe your children in various classroom reading-language learning experiences. Consider the following questions for a moment: "Do most of my children who excel in oral language also excel in reading and in written expression? If so, how might this be explained? What interrelationships exist among the various basic communication skills of reading, writing, speaking, and listening? How can my communication skills program be adjusted to maximize the transfer from one skill

143

area such as oral language to a second skill area such as reading? What specific language difficulty is my lowest achiever experiencing, and what specific step or steps can I take to help remedy this difficulty?"

3. Firm understanding of the reading-language program or programs available in your classroom. Ask yourself: "How are the word attack and comprehension skills sequenced? Why are they sequenced in this manner? Do I have diagnostic tests that provide clues to the progressive development of various communication skills? If not, what informal evaluation inventory could I devise to benchmark the progress of my youngsters? If so, how do I use information after I have it? Are special materials provided or can available materials be adapted for use in eliminating specific difficulties my children are experiencing? How can I supplement the publisher-produced program or programs provided to meet the needs of my youngsters?"

4. Continuous consideration of ways each child's aspiration level can be realistically raised. Consider your classroom for a moment, and ask: "How can I help insure that each child will achieve some degree of success each day, even if the success appears to be small? Do my children understand the significance of the activities we engage in each day? If not, why? How can I help each child establish realistic, achievable goals in his reading-language program?"

You must seek to foster these characteristics and to answer these and other questions throughout your professional career. In the following chapter we shall examine language as it reflects experience and consider detailed practical suggestions to enhance the child's expression through language based on encounter with his world.

Footnotes

[1] David H. Russell, *Children Learn to Read* (Boston: Ginn and Company, 1961), p. 61.

[2] Nila B. Smith, *American Reading Instruction* (Newark, Del.: The International Reading Association, 1965), p. 69.

[3] Ibid., p. 82.

[4] Robert W. Richey, *Planning for Teaching* (New York: McGraw-Hill Book Company, 1969).

[5] Theodore L. Reller and Edgar L. Morphet, *Comparative Educational Administration* (Englewood Cliffs, N.J.: Prentice-Hall, Inc., 1962), p. 166.

[6] Richey, *Planning for Teaching.*

[7] Wallace W. Douglas, "On Teaching the Process of Writing," in *New Directions in Elementary English,* ed. Alexander Frazier (Champaign, Ill.: National Council of Teachers of English, 1967), pp. 183–95.

[8] Muriel Crosby, *Curriculum Development for Elementary Schools in a Changing Society* (Boston: D. C. Heath & Company, 1964), p. 12.

[9] Rudolph Flesch, *Why Johnny Can't Read* (New York: Harper & Row, Publishers, 1955). Arthur Trace, *What Ivan Knows that Johnny Doesn't* (New York: Random House, Inc., 1961).

[10] John B. Carroll, "The Case of Dr. Flesch," *American Psychologist,* 11 (1956), 158–63, David H. Russell, "The Content of the Material," *The Dynamics of Reading,* ed. Robert B. Ruddell (Waltham, Mass.: Blaisdell Publishing Co., 1970).

[11]Charles C. Fries et al., *Merrill Linguistic Readers* (Columbus, O.: Charles E. Merrill Publishing Co., 1966).

[12]Donald E. Rasmussen and Lenine Goldberg, *SRA Basic Reading Series* (Chicago: Science Research Associates, Inc., 1965).

[13]Cynthia Dee Buchanan, *Programmed Reading* (New York: McGraw-Hill Book Company, Webster Division, 1964).

[14]Clara G. Stratemeyer and Henry Lee Smith, Jr., *The Linguistic-Science Readers* (Evanston, Ill.: Harper & Row, Publishers, 1963).

[15]Leonard Bloomfield and Clarence L. Barnhart, *Let's Read: A Linguistic Approach* (Detroit: Wayne State University Press, 1961).

[16]Ralph F. Robinett, *Miami Linguistic Readers* (Boston: D. C. Heath & Company, 1966).

[17]John A. Downing, *The Downing Readers* (London: Initial Teaching Publishing Co., Ltd., 1964).

[18]Albert J. Mazurkiewicz and Harold J. Tanyzer, *Early-to-Read ITA Program* (New York: ITA Publications, 1964).

[19]Caleb Gattengo, *Words in Color* (Chicago: Learning Materials, Inc., 1962).

[20]Roach Van Allen and Claryce Allen, *Language Experiences in Reading* (Chicago: Encyclopaedia Britannica Press, 1966).

[21]Robert B. Ruddell, Barbara W. Graves, and Floyd W. Davis, *Program BUILD: Basic Understandings in Language Development* (Boston: Ginn and Company, 1972).

[22]Bill Martin, Jr., *The Sounds of Language* (New York: Holt, Rinehart and Winston, Inc., 1967).

[23]Buela Stolpen, Priscilla Tyler, and Eleanor Pounds, *Linguistic Block Series* (Chicago: Scott, Foresman and Company, 1963).

[24]Lawrence W. Carrillo et al., *Chandler Reading Program* (San Francisco: Chandler Publishing Co., 1968).

[25]Irma S. Black, *The Bank Street Basal Reading Series* (New York: The Macmillan Company, 1966).

[26]Carrillo et al., *Chandler Reading Program*.

[27]Peter Buckley and Hortense Jones, *Holt Urban Social Studies Series* (New York: Holt, Rinehart and Winston, Inc., 1966).

[28]Ruth Montgomery Jackson, *An Experience-Centered Language Program* (Pasadena, Calif.: Franklin Publications, Inc., 1967).

[29]Lloyd M. Dunn and James O. Smith, *Peabody Language Development Kits* (Circle Pines, Minn.: American Guidance Service, Inc., 1969).

[30]Martin V. Covington, Richard S. Crutchfield, Lillian B. Davies, and Robert M. Olton, Jr., *The Productive Thinking Program* (Columbus, O.: Charles E. Merrill Publishing Co., 1972).

[31]Virginia Reid, in *The Dynamics of Reading,* ed. Robert B. Ruddell (Waltham, Mass.: Blaisdell Press, 1970), p. 233.

[32]Nebraska Curriculum Development Center, *A Curriculum for English: Introduction to the Elementary School Program K-6* (Lincoln: University of Nebraska, 1965), p. 2.

[33]Murial Crosby, *The World of Language* (Chicago: Follett Educational Corporation, 1970).

[34]Allen and Allen, *Language Experiences in Reading.* Ruddell, Graves, and Davis, *Program BUILD.*

[35]Theodore Clymer et al., *Reading 360* (Boston: Ginn and Company, 1970).

[36]William K. Durr et al., *The Houghton Mifflin Readers* (Boston: Houghton Mifflin Company, 1971). Leo Fay et al., *The Young America Basic Reading Program* (Chicago: Lyons and Carnahan, Educational Division, Meredith Corporation, 1972). Helen M. Robinson et al., *Scott, Foresman Reading Systems* (Glenview, Ill.: Scott, Foresman and Company, 1971). *The Harper and Row Basic Reading Program* (New York: Harper & Row, Publishers, 1966). *Open Court Correlated Language Arts Program* (La Salle, Ill., 1967).

6

Encounter to Expression: Language as Experience

Focusing Questions

1. What instructional goals are central to the development of the ability to communicate effectively?
2. How can a developmental view of language be of value in formulating communication skills instruction?
3. How can children's life experiences be used in language instruction?
4. What language features must be accounted for in the development of descriptive abilities? Narrative abilities? What instructional experiences can be used to develop these features?
5. How can oral and written expression be of value in developing reading-listening comprehension abilities?
6. How can children's progress in language development be evaluated?

The child's encounter with his environment during the preschool years offers a rich base for developing a wide range of understandings about his world. His control over language during this period develops rapidly (as described in Chapter 4) and enables him to represent his experiences in a symbolic fashion both internally and externally. His internal use of language lets him simulate experiences derived from his immediate environment and direct his activities. These will range from self-directed role playing as a family member (mother or father) to determining how a model airplane wing strut can be mounted. The external use of language lets him relate to others as he meets his own needs and becomes accountable to family members and his own peer group.

Even though the child's language maturity has developed at a phenomenal rate during the preschool years, further growth will take place throughout kindergarten and the elementary school years. A major function of the elementary school is to enhance this language growth. Many preservice

How can experiences like this develop children's oral expression?

and inservice teacher-training approaches have been tried to develop language instruction, including emphasis on usage and mechanics, lists of activities for language instruction, and traditional or modern grammar focusing on the formal mastery of sentence elements and forms, but these approaches have been of limited value because they have failed to consider a developmental growth pattern for the child based on his cognitive and language maturation.[1] It is essential that we use a child-centered approach, one that begins with the child's experience and internal use of language and moves via his descriptions, story forms, and explanations to organized language control that enables him to symbolize his observations and feelings. These expressive types of language involve considerable overlap of oral and written language. The child's description of his story characters is basic to his narrative, and both description and narration are essential to his explanation of yesterday's bicycle accident. Even though such overlap exists, it is useful to consider the nature of these types within a developmental sequence based on the child's language growth. The ideas in this chapter should help to develop the child's descriptive and narrative abilities and to promote cognition and language growth. The chapter also contains specific techniques for evaluating language growth.

It is important that this discussion account for the components of the language framework described in Chapter 2 and for the research discussed in Chapter 4. The framework should help you to organize and integrate the 147 theoretical and practical aspects of language instruction, and after this chapter you should be able to go beyond the suggestions presented here and tailor child-centered language activities to individual needs.

GOALS OF LANGUAGE INSTRUCTION

Our diverse population of children come from home situations that may include common denominators such as "Sesame Street," "Captain Kangaroo," and perhaps "The Electric Company," but that vary widely in provision for verbal stimulation and the opportunity to interact with others by means of language. As a result it is necessary to observe each child's oral language use carefully. His level of language control will be revealed in the vocabulary he uses in class discussions, his syntactical maturity in his sentence patterns and the subordination therein, his organizing and interpreting abilities in oral expression, and his attitudes toward participation in verbal tasks.[2] At the end of this chapter there is an oral language inventory that will be valuable in identifying specific areas of instructional need. Only when you have this information can you determine the essential instructional elements your language curriculum needs, which may range from developing a child's personal security and self-concept in using language to stimulating language-oriented experiences through verbal participation.

Language-oriented goals for the instructional program include development of

1. The ability to use clear communication in oral and written form in a variety of social settings
2. The ability to understand and use oral and written language in expressive form
3. The ability to express, interpret, and enjoy thought in creative form
4. Sensitivity to and appreciation of language as used in a variety of life situations

These goals are to guide the discussion that follows.

EXPERIENCING, OBSERVING, AND DESCRIBING

To develop observational and descriptive abilities the child must create or re-create mental images based on his experience and interaction with his environment. His success will be directly related to control over four key areas of the communication framework (discussed in Chapter 2): (1) *lexical meaning*, knowledge of vocabulary, particularly nouns, verbs, adjectives, and adverbs that develop and create particular symbolic associations and meanings; (2) *relational meaning*, the word order, sentence subordination, and sentence organization that support the imagery he is attempting to create or re-create; (3) *interpretation and problem solving*, including the abili-

148

ties to classify, categorize, and sequence ideas, to make comparisons and identify relationships, and to observe, gather, and synthesize information; and (4) *interests, attitudes, and values,* which control the selection and organization of ideas and content.

If we are to account for an instructional organization or language curriculum based on the child's world view in kindergarten and the early grades, we must provide numerous opportunities for him to use language in a variety of settings. The developmental sequence we shall use begins with experiencing through art and informal expression and progresses to extending and organizing oral and written description. The activities suggested here apply from kindergarten through the intermediate grades, though you should adapt and adjust them to the needs of your children. Specifically, the developmental, child-centered organization includes the following instructional dimensions:

1. Expressing experiences through pictorial and informal sharing
2. Sharing experiences orally with small groups through pictures or objects
3. Sharing description through pantomime
4. Comparing individual descriptions
5. Using immediate environment and creative impressions for written description
6. Extending and organizing oral and written description through image-evoking vocabulary, comparisons such as similes, sentence expansion and transformation, supporting of the paragraph or story idea, and awareness of the audience

To determine how to bring these topics to the classroom we shall examine each of them, along with practical examples and suggestions designed to aid their implementation.

Pictorial and informal sharing

An effective way to involve the child with language at a high level of interest is to encourage him to express his thought through art form— finger painting, brush painting, or a simple drawing—and then to provide him with an opportunity to share his creation with the teacher, the teacher's assistant, or even another pupil. The main objective at this point is to develop language fluency, to encourage the child to talk about his effort, to express himself orally.

The experiences described above can easily be followed by having the child suggest a caption for his creative work and then recording it. Such an approach helps the child realize that his ideas represented in pictorial form can also be represented through oral and written language. By displaying this work in a bulletin board space or in some other fashion, perhaps through a collection of the child's pictures, the teacher can enhance the child's self-concept by showing him that indeed his work is recognized and is of worth to others. The following specific activities will be of value in enhancing early descriptive abilities.

How can informal sharing experiences enhance descriptive language abilities?

My Picture Story

Encourage your children to relive home experiences by expressing them in a variety of art media. After a child has completed his art expression, encourage him to describe his experience verbally. This may be initiated by suggesting that he give his work a name.

The child may dictate the name or title to you or your assistant. Write the name on a piece of lined tagboard and staple it to the bottom of the child's art work. Titles may range from word groups to simple sentences: My Rabbit; Our House; The Three Bears, Papa Bear, Mama Bear, and Baby Bear; My Dog Spotty; Mommy Is Watering the Flowers.

My Favorite Animal

A field trip such as a visit to a nearby park, farm, or zoo provides many opportunities for description. On very large pieces of art paper have the children draw the animals they most enjoyed, then have them cut out their animals, describe the animal's size, color, shape, distinguishing features, and tell how they imagine the animal might feel to the touch. This phase of the project may begin with oral discussion, progress to the chalkboard (where the teacher records descriptive vocabulary), and culminate in a writing experience by the child himself.

The cut-out of a giraffe may have a description such as the following on its reverse side: "A giraffe is very tall. He is yellow with spots. He has a very long neck and skinny long legs."

A giraffe is very tall. He is yellow with spots. He has a long neck.

Pin the cut-out "Zoo" on your bulletin board entitled "Animals Are Different."

Listening and Learning

To acquaint children with the ways they find out about their world and to help them become conscious of their senses, plan a unit on the five senses. Activities that will provide an opportunity for describing are leisurely listening walks with your class around your school block, school yard, or a nearby park. When you return to class, encourage the children to identify the sounds they heard and what made the sound. Record this information on a chart for easy reference in discussing and summarizing the walk.

Touching and Telling

To provide experiences for the sense of touch and describing, have the children help in collecting simple objects such as sand paper, wax paper, cotton, buttons, rocks, bits of fabrics, and small pets (if they are permitted

Sounds we heard	What made the sound
buzzing	bee, saw, lawn mower
hammering	carpenter
barking	dogs
banging	gates, doors
chirping	birds

in the classroom). Place this collection in a special place in your classroom. Set out a colorfully decorated coffee can containing descriptive words such as: smooth, rough, slick, furry, fuzzy, cushiony, cold, wet, bumpy, shiny, clammy, sharp, and so on. Let a child draw a word and identify the items that would go with the word. For example, the word *rough* might be applied to sand paper, rocks, weeds, some fabrics and papers, broken tiles or pottery, and the like.

These activities are valuable in building concepts and word labels that relate directly to the child's experiences.

Sharing descriptions with small groups

As the children create their own art forms and describe them to you, these descriptions can also profitably be shared with a small group of youngsters. Encourage a natural progression from description of the art form to a brief narrative about the art form. This will come more easily for some children than for others, but the child's reliance on his picture should facilitate the entire process for all. (We shall discuss this progression to narrative in the next section.)

Children in small-group discussions should have the opportunity to ask questions leading to clarification of the description provided, questions on how the description might be improved or that lead to other children's similar experiences. Such a discussion is best carried out under teacher direction in order to encourage variety in vocabulary, particularly verbs and adjectives that lead to more vivid imagery. Critical remarks by a child's classmates should be turned to constructive suggestions that improve the description provided. You will need to handle this with care, and to see that the reasons for the criticism are clearly stipulated where possible.

Variety can be developed in the instructional program by using concrete objects, picture collections, and literature selections that are of high interest to the children. Such variety will enable the child to expand his descriptive vocabulary and ideas along a continuum from concrete to abstract representations, and the literary selections will provide valuable language models not only for vocabulary enrichment but also for display of varied and extended sentence structures. The following practical suggestions will be of value in this effort.

Geometric Fun

In kindergarten and the primary grades the child is exposed to simple mathematical concepts pertinent to his daily life. One of these concepts is awareness of geometric shapes.

Have the children trace and cut two or more large paper geometric shapes (circle, square, rectangle, triangle), then have the children assemble and paste these shapes on large white art paper to form simple, familiar objects. For example, a triangle and a circle form an ice cream cone, a square and a triangle form a house, a rectangle and two small circles form a car.

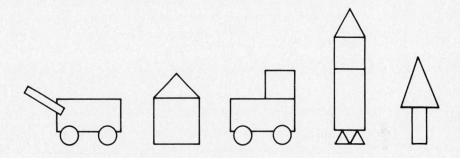

After the geometric pictures are completed, ask each child to describe his work to the rest of the class. The child's description should include what the object is, names of the geometric shapes, and what each shape represents. Such a description might sound like this:

This is an ice cream cone. A brown triangle is the cone. The red circle is the strawberry ice cream and the white circle is a scoop of vanilla.

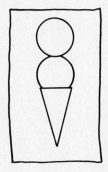

Other patterns and descriptions may be developed for a house, a Christmas tree, a rocket, a car, a train, and a snowman.

Comparison and classification of concrete items into living or nonliving things in the early grades help the child not only to understand scientific concepts but also to expand his descriptive vocabulary.

Make available, or have the children help collect, the following items: coins, nails, potted plants, foods, goldfish, glass of water, small caged animals like mice or hamsters, and any other items you can get. Construct a chart, based on a group discussion, listing information such as:

Living Things

Need air
Need food
Move
Grow
Reproduce their own kind

Have the children separate the living from the nonliving things on a large table by using the criteria on the chart. Then ask the children to select and describe one living and one nonliving thing. Descriptions can be shared as mysteries by having one child read a description and having others try to guess what is being described.

"I am a living furry creature. I have many little legs and the color of my coat will tell you what kind of winter we will have. Who am I?"

"I am thin, long, and hard. I have a flat head and a sharp tail. When I get hit on the head I hold things together. Who am I?"

Insect Description

The study of insects holds endless fascination for children of all ages, particularly boys. Children enjoy learning how to identify an insect by description and then classifying insects into their different groups. Plan such a research project with your class.

Encourage the children to look in their gardens, fields, woods, beaches, etc., for specimens that can be studied in detail under a magnifying glass or a microscope and made into a class collection.

From group discussion with the children develop a guide for presenting their insect reports to the group. These reports, accompanied by illustrations or specimens, should include descriptions of visual (color, size, shape), auditory (sounds produced), tactile (feel or touch), and olfactory (odor or smell) sensations to present important information about the insect.

154

```
┌─────────────────────────────────────────┐
│  Name of Insect: _____ │
│  Description: _____ │
│  _____ │
│  Where found: _____ │
│  _____ │
│  How it reproduces: _____ │
│  _____ │
│  How controlled: _____ │
│  _____ │
└─────────────────────────────────────────┘
```

Good Merchandising

For a social studies unit, a little classroom supermarket provides excellent opportunity for enriching the child's descriptive language experience.

Divide the children into small groups and have them prepare commercials to present to the class orally. Some sample ads might sound like this:

> "Wednesday's Special is energy-producing white rice at only 49¢ for the large 12 oz. box."

> "Gelatin is good for us because it contains a lot of body-building protein. Other foods in our store with lots of protein are fresh meat, poultry, fish, low-fat milk, and Grade A eggs. Keep your family strong and healthy. Buy some today."

> "Today's best buys at our store are blue-veined cheeses such as blue, gorgonzola, and Roquefort for your salads."

This description activity may be concluded with a contest to have the class or teacher select the best ads.

In the early grades the teacher will need to serve as recorder of ideas, using the chalkboard or newsprint to focus the descriptions and to help summarize ideas. Object and picture descriptions that have been discussed may also be used as stimuli to develop further artistic representations. Make provision for displaying the children's work on the bulletin board in the form of individual "books" constructed by each child. These can be labeled "My Story Book" and stored in each child's desk or in a central location for sharing with other children. A great deal of value can be obtained by teaming youngsters and asking them to share their experiences through each "My Story Book." Such a record of the child's efforts also enables him to note his own progress and to build self-confidence in his work.

Sharing description through pantomime

As children begin to formulate sensory descriptions from their experiences through vision, hearing, touch, taste, and smell, they find pantomime activities of great interest. The source of the pantomime idea may well be the artistic or verbal descriptions already discussed. Pantomime can precede artistic or verbal attempts at description, but it is also valuable after verbal activities, to stimulate a search for ways of expressing concepts through direct action.

How can pantomime and role playing facilitate the development of oral and written expression?

Showing Words Through Actions

From an informal discussion formulate a list of contrasting "expression words" such as joyful, playful, happy, sad, unhappy, and painful. Ask the children to show how the meanings of these words can be demonstrated through various facial expressions.

Extend this pantomime activity by establishing two characters who encounter each other for the first time. For example, one child may pantomime a curious baby brown bear while a second child pantomimes a frisky gray squirrel. What will happen on their first meeting? As the two children carry out their creative actions the other children should attempt to describe the actions taking place. You may culminate this activity by asking the children to indicate the word or words used to represent the actions.

Community Workers

In studying the interrelatedness of community life, how people work together to provide needed community services, children can express their ideas and concepts through pantomime. Ask each child to select a community helper and to think carefully about what this person does while he is working. Then have him pantomime the worker he has selected, and have the other children try to guess who the worker is. If the children are not able to guess the first time, the child who is pantomiming should repeat his performance with more clues to aid in identification of the worker he is portraying.

Examples:

    A policeman
        directs traffic
        writes traffic tickets
        helps find lost people
    A painter
        mixes paints
        climbs ladders
        brushes paint on
    A grocery cashier
        checks and weighs merchandise
        punches cash register
        gives change to customers
        bags groceries

Safety at School

There is a consistent need to develop awareness of safety practices on the school playground. Pantomime is an interesting and practical way to illustrate good safety habits.

Before you assign certain children to assume certain character roles and illustrate or formulate the important safety rules, ask questions such as these to stimulate thinking: What is the safest way to get a drink at the water fountain? Why? What is the safest way to get a turn on the swings? Why? There are many such questions, depending on the individual school situation.

Ask the children in a small group to determine how they will answer the safety questions through pantomime. Have them emphasize the key actions that characterize the answers. You can hold these activities in the actual outdoor setting or in the classroom. Discuss possible hazards or injuries that were avoided through good safety habits after each performance.

These skits may include

A group of children lining up in a single file and patiently waiting for their turn while the first child bends over the fountain for a drink.

Several children portraying unsafe methods or uses of playground equipment such as a baseball bat through gestures, then contrasting these with safe techniques.

Do You Read Me?

An interesting alternative to book reports is a pantomime skit. The class must set up certain rules in order that the children can easily guess the name of the book. For example, bonus points might be given for naming the author of the book. Game rules should also include stipulations that the book be well known, lend itself fairly easily to pantomime, and be portrayable within a short period of time. The librarian can be a resource in this endeavor. An advantage to this type of book reporting is that groups of children rather than just individual children can participate.

Two examples of book reporting through pantomime are:

In portraying *Runaway Ralph* a youngster might indicate through gestures the mouse's physical characteristics—whiskers, ears, and long tail—then imitate the mouse placing his helmet and goggles on his head, revving up his motorcycle, and riding down the road.[3]

Charlie, of *Charlie and the Chocolate Factory,* portrays that hungry look, finds the golden ticket in the gutter, tells his very old, feeble Uncle Joe about the ticket, and at the end goes up in the glass elevator to survey his newly acquired chocolate factory.[4]

The children in the audience should be encouraged to put into words the action that is being pantomimed.

As a pantomime takes place you the teacher may wish to make notes or descriptions related to the pantomime, such as summarizing a description of a character's actions or an event in the pantomime.

Comparing descriptions

As children improve their abilities to observe and to describe what they observe orally, encourage them to compare descriptions and identify qualities that build imagery. This leads directly to awareness of the need for adequate labels. It also provides opportunities to build word groups that provide clear, image-evoking descriptions. The following activities are designed to further these abilities.

What Did You See?

Select two teams of five children. Each team is to observe closely the activities and events that occurred on the playground during the same

158

recess period. Each team is then to write five image-evoking sentences describing activities they observed during recess. Some sentences may be like these:

A silvery bird, high above us, vanished into the cloud.

The mighty oak with limbs stretching toward the blue sky was still there.

Share the sentences with the rest of the class and contrast those that deal with the same subject. For example:

The clanging sound of metal rings meeting hurt our ears.

The metal rings banged together with a loud noise.

Which sentence do you like best? Why?

Comparing Smells

The following two poems deal with smells. Read them to the children. Contrast the imagery each poem presents. How do the "smells" differ in the two poems? Where are the different "smells" found? What words help you smell the "smells"?

SNIFF[5]

When school is out, we love to follow
our noses over hill and hollow,
smelling jewelweed and vetch,
sniffing fern and milkweed patch.

The airy fifth of our five senses
leads us under, over, fences.
We run like rabbits through bright hours
and poke our noses into flowers!

Frances M. Frost

SMELLS (JUNIOR)[6]

My Daddy smells like tobacco and books,
   Mother, like lavender and listerine;
Uncle John carries a whiff of cigars,
   Nannie smells starchy and soapy and clean.

Shandy, my dog, has a smell of his own
   (When he's been out in the rain he smells most);
But Katie, the cook is more splendid than all—
   She smells exactly like hot buttered toast!

                                                  Christopher Morley

Self-selected environment and creative impressions

The major value in letting the child select the stimulus for his oral or written impression lies in the interest or motivation this self-selection process produces. As teacher you will often need to help the child to select the environmental and creative impressions to describe. Display objects for possible description in the classroom so that the child can select an object, take it to his desk, and examine and describe it. You can stimulate memory impressions for descriptive purposes by asking a youngster to pretend he has changed his object into an imaginary animal and then to draw a picture of the animal and describe it. Small-group discussions, in which youngsters exchange ideas that will trigger new ideas of a highly creative nature, are also helpful.

Descriptions of real classroom animals or of the activities of family members will prove to be of high interest to many youngsters. At the early levels the written descriptions of some children can be exchanged with those of others for the purpose of using the descriptions as the bases for drawings. Descriptions and drawings can then be discussed to note how they match and fail to match, after which the written descriptions can be expanded into more complete "word pictures." A tape recorder will be of value should the children's efforts be exclusively oral. The descriptions can be listened to, discussed, and converted by the children into art, and followed up with discussions of the similarities and differences in the two forms.

The following are practical ideas for the development of written expression using self-selection in the environment and impressions from memory.

Odds and Ends Table

For purposes of stimulating children's creative impressions, collect a number of unusual objects, such as a piece of pipe, glass paperweight, nuts, bolts, screws, buttons, unusually shaped rocks, pieces of old costume jewelry, a small bottle containing rice or other seeds, or any other object that might be interesting to your children. Place a few of these objects on a separate table in the classroom. Change the objects on the table every week or so.

Have the children give that table a name. It might be called: The What Is It? Table, Odds and Ends Table, Mystery Objects, or something more original.

Place a tape recorder on the table. Have each child take a turn talking into the tape recorder to answer the following questions about one of the objects on the table: "What is it? What does it look like? Feel like? Sound like? Smell like? Taste like? Where did it come from? Whose is it? What could you do with it?"

The various descriptions may be contrasted several times each week (or at the conclusion of each day), with special attention paid to image-evoking words and word groups. These words and word groups may be recorded on newsprint and used as the basis for follow-up writing experiences.

Squiggles

Draw a short irregular curve, a long curving line, and a looping line on each piece of paper for the children. Have each child select one of the lines, make a picture out of it, and then describe the picture he has just drawn. Descriptions for pictures created from identical originals may then be contrasted, with special attention paid to the descriptive vocabulary.

 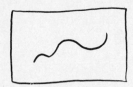 

Spill and Tell

Empty your desk of odds and ends—bent paper clips, extra rulers, old pens, an old calendar, and the like—into a large box or jar. Let a child spill the items on his desk, dice fashion, decide on a design or picture the objects form, and describe it to the group.

What's This?

In a large, deep box or ice cream carton place a number of tools—nails, screws, bolts, hammer, screw driver, t-level, etc.—from your garage or workshop. Have the children "fish" for one of these tools and describe the setting it has been in and could be found in, and its purpose.

Place the following *haiku* poems on the board or duplicate them for the children. Ask each child to read the poems and select one to use as a basis for a drawing, using any art form he desires. After each child has completed his drawing ask him to give a written or an oral reaction to the poem by describing his setting or place for the poem, the action, and his feelings about the poem.

> The moon in the water
> Turned a somersault
> And floated away.

Ryôta[7]

A drop of rain!
The frog wiped his forehead
With his wrist.

Issa[8]

Voices
Above the white clouds:
Skylarks.

Kyoroky[9]

"I've just come from a place
At the lake bottom"—that is the look
On the little duck's face.

Basho[10]

Throughout kindergarten and the early part of first grade it will of course be necessary for the teacher to record the children's oral descriptions. This provides for the early, very clear introduction of the concept that oral language can be represented in written form. This recording role will shift gradually to the children as they gain control over handwriting, develop spelling ability, and compile an individualized spelling dictionary.

You can effectively meet the constant need to spell words in the early grades by keeping cut lined paper at hand and quickly printing the word on the paper. The child can then use the word and file it alphabetically in his individualized spelling dictionary. A simple and effective way to formulate this dictionary is to use a small rectangular box, such as a cheese box, with alphabet dividers in the box. This dictionary should be stored at the child's desk so that he can readily refer to it whenever he needs to check a spelling. The major consideration is to ease the child's spelling burden so that he can focus on the ideas and thoughts he is attempting to express in written form. Accept frequent "phonetic spellings" in written form and correct them at a time other than when the child's ideas are being discussed.

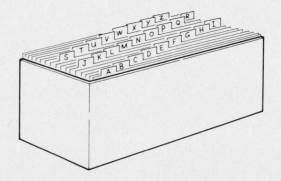

Extending and organizing description

The ideas presented to this point have been designed to stimulate and develop the child's interest in oral and written description along a developmental sequence. As the child gains confidence in his ability to use language in the classroom, it will be necessary to further extend and provide suggestions for organizing and developing descriptive expression. The following suggestions are organized according to areas identified early in this chapter and based on the language framework described in Chapter 2.

IMAGE-EVOKING VOCABULARY

The vocabulary that stimulates mental imagery is mainly nouns, verbs, adjectives, and adverbs that define the appearance or recreate the action in the description. These particular elements should be based on observed experiences, work with concrete objects, or pictorial forms such as illustrations, slides, photographs, or pictures from magazines. This allows the youngster to examine the event, object, or pictorial representation and generate his description from careful observations. Specific suggestions for building picture-evoking vocabulary follow.

Floating in the Blue

All children enjoy Winnie-the-Pooh's adventures. One of the most exciting and humorous is the one where Pooh holds onto a balloon to fool those suspicious bees high up in a tree. Read to the children the song Winnie sings while floating in the air:

> How sweet to be a Cloud
>   Floating in the Blue!
> Every little cloud
> Always sings aloud,
>
> How sweet to be a Cloud
>   Floating in the Blue!
> It makes him very proud
> To be a little cloud.*

After you read the poem, encourage the children to describe how it must feel to be a cloud floating in the air and the things to be seen from the cloud.

*From the book *Winnie the Pooh* by A. A. Milne. Decorations by E. H. Shepard. Copyright, 1926, by E. P. Dutton & Co., Inc. Renewal, 1954, by A. A. Milne. Published by E. P. Dutton & Co., Inc. and used by their permission and by permission of The Canadian Publishers, McClelland and Stewart Limited, Toronto.

A cloud floating in the air feels like
  a fluffy marshmallow
  a bird's feather
  a leaf sailing in the wind
  a drop of water gliding down my window
We can see
  a row of tiny houses
  a white beach that looks like a long curvy snake
  a twisting turning river
  an eagle so close I can touch it

Words and Words and Words

Primary children can easily learn the meaning of *noun* with pictures and words from newspapers or magazines. Place a large tagboard chart titled *Names, Places, Things* on your bulletin board. Have the children cut out nouns from newspapers or magazines and paste these on your chart. (Younger children may just wish to bring magazine pictures that illustrate their understanding of the concept of a noun.)

Another bulletin board word activity for primary children deals with verbs, adverbs, and adjectives.

Many Words for Happy

This is Happy

(picture of dog)

Happy can	*How can Happy do it?*	*Happy is*
jump	quickly	good
bark		brown
————	————	————
————	————	————
————	————	————

Have children add new words in their own writing whenever they think of them.

Word Cannisters

Paint or cover four coffee cans with colored construction paper, each a different color. Label each cannister "nouns," "adjectives," "verbs," or "adverbs." Keep small pieces of paper or tagboard near the cannisters for the children and encourage them to write at least one word for each cannister and drop these papers into the appropriate can. After you have collected a number of papers in each can, have the children draw out one or two words from each of the four cans. Write these words on the chalkboard, then have the children build a sentence from these words (verb endings or forms may need adjusting). The following are two sentences that might have been developed with this word game:

164

The cuddly, blue fish did swim slowly.

The wrinkled man sang angrily.

Some of these sentences may be very humorous, but that adds flavor and interest to the game. At times more than one noun, adjective, or adverb may have to be drawn to make the game more challenging.

COMPARISONS

The use of comparison—specifically, simile—with young children can lead to word pictures possessing high interest. The children should be encouraged to create descriptions by associating their specific topics of description with familiar mental images. It is important to relate to a child's background of experiences for specific comparisons. The following suggestions will prove to be of value in developing comparisons at the early levels.

Like a . . .

Place three simple pictures, of the sun, of storm clouds, and of a boy's angry face, on the board. Discuss these pictures' similarities. The children should conclude that the gloomy, angry countenance of the boy is similar to the storm clouds but not similar to the sunny radiance of the sun. You might say, "His face looked like a storm cloud." Make more comparisons with other sets of pictures, until you think the children are ready to deal with groups of words, then follow with the next activity on similes.

Similes

With masking tape attach a magazine picture of a pretty girl and a picture

165 of a rose to the chalkboard. Under these pictures write the sentence

She is like a rose.

Discuss why you made the comparison and explain that two things that are not alike but that are exactly compared are called similes.

Write this incomplete simile on the board:

Bill is brave as a _____.

Help the children make a comparison. They might suggest *lion,* but any animal that may be compared to Bill's bravery will be correct.

Before you encourage the children to work further on similes either individually or in groups, whether with magazine pictures or words, be certain to stress that they must be specific in their comparisons and that the words *like* or *as* are to be used in their similes.

The following are more incomplete similes to use in class.

My brother is as strong (weak) as an _____.
This candy is as hard as a _____.
The paste is thick like a _____.
Janet is pretty as a _____.
My sandwich is as dry as _____.
The rain is falling like _____.
The ice is slick as _____.

Encourage the children to use comparisons in their oral and written descriptions of animals and people, and in their observations of nature. We shall consider another form of comparison, that of metaphor, later.

EXPANDING AND TRANSFORMING SENTENCES

The sentence structure we shall talk about here is not that of formal grammar, but is instead based on an inductive approach designed to create awareness of the ways sentence development can contribute to description, so that youngsters can expand and combine sentences more effectively in order to sharpen meaning. The following suggestions will be helpful to this end.

Building Sentences

The purpose of language activity is to help children feel secure in manipulating sentences in ways that will result in more descriptive sentence development.

Help the children with the first set of sentences. Discuss how the sentence "Rico bats" is expanded to "Rico bats (the ball or the fly)." Let the children supply the remainder of the sentence.

1. Rico bats.
2. Rico bats (the) (ball).

3. Jackson bats (the) (ball).
4. Rico and Jackson (bat the ball).
5. (They) (bat the ball).

1. Regie likes baseball.
2. Bert likes baseball.
3. _____ and _____ like baseball.
4. _____ like baseball.

1. Rudi (hit) a homer.
2. Tony _____ a homer.
3. _____ and _____ hit a homer.
4. _____ hit a homer.

1. Sal helped Willie fix the bike.
2. Sal helped me fix the bike.
3. Sal helped _____ and _____ fix the bike.
4. Sal helped _____ fix the bike.

1. Lee saw Sonny (at school).
2. Lee saw Diego (at school).
3. Lee saw (Sonny) and (Diego) (at school).
4. Lee saw (them) (at school).
5. (He) saw (them) (at school).

1. Rose served (mother) pie.
2. Rose served (father) pie.
3. Rose served _____ and _____ pie.
4. Rose served _____ pie.
5. (She) served them pie and (ice cream or coffee).

Interest in this type of sentence activity can be greatly enhanced by printing the vocabulary on tagboard strips. The words can then be physically moved, substituted, and reordered as demanded by the meaning intended. For example:

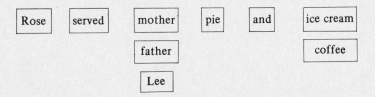

In working with sentence expansion and transformation, it is extremely important to develop the exercises at a concrete level. Whenever possible, word cards, word blocks, or phrase cards should be used so that the child can physically add, reorder, or delete elements in the sentence. This dimension of the instructional program helps the child become consciously aware of what he intuitively does with the language, and helps him develop effective control over sentence structure as conveyor of meaning.

Supporting dialogue or story idea

It is essential to develop the relationship between single descriptive sentences and the more complex thesis in a conversation, dialogue, or story. Sentence development should not be isolated from the broader descriptive context. Sentence isolation can be avoided by encouraging the child to work not only toward image-evoking description, but also toward use of such description in follow-up discussions and particularly in developing a descriptive paragraph which may be part of a story. The use of description in narration will be discussed in the next section of this chapter. Several suggestions for using sentence description to support dialogue or a story line are indicated below.

About the Wizard

Read the children the following paragraph from *The Wizard of Oz.*

> As they walked on, the green glow became brighter and brighter and it seemed that at last *they* were nearing the end of their *travels.* Yet it was afternoon before they came to the *great wall* that surrounded the *city.* It was high, and thick, and of a *bright green color.* [11]

Ask the children to guess the well-known story this selection comes from. Help them by rereading the paragraph and emphasizing the words in italic. Some children will have no difficulty figuring out that the descriptive paragraph gives an immediate summary of the plot of *The Wizard of Oz.* Before the correct answer is given, read the next paragraph aloud.

> In front of them, and at the end of the road of yellow brick, was a big gate, all studded with emeralds that glittered so in the sun that even the painted eyes of the Scarecrow were dazzled by their brilliancy.

The children should now have no difficulty identifying the story, through the clues of the yellow brick road, the emeralds, and the Scarecrow. Discuss the vocabulary and descriptive phrases that make it possible to immediately visualize the setting. What vocabulary could be substituted to create another mental image?

As a follow-up activity for writing descriptive supporting dialogue, have the children select one of the characters in *The Wizard of Oz,* such as Dorothy, Scarecrow, the Cowardly Lion, or the Tin Woodman. Ask them to write two sentences that this character might have spoken to the Wizard. In the first sentence the character should describe himself; in the second sentence he should describe what he needs from the Wizard.

Complete the project by having the children draw a picture of their story character talking to the Wizard of Oz.

Read the children the following paragraph from *Charlie the Tramp* (explain too that Charlie is a beaver).

Charlie heard the frogs and the crickets singing in the quiet of the night and he heard something else. He heard a trickling, tickling kind of a little song that had no words.[12]

Ask the children the following questions: "Did you like the paragraph? Does it make you want to hear more about what is happening? Does it make you wonder about the little song Charlie hears? What kinds of things could sing a trickling, tickling kind of wordless song?"

Some children may conclude that the song is the sound of water. If after the second reading, the children have no clue as to the mood and setting, continue reading with this paragraph.

He saw a little stream that sang as it ran in the moonlight, and he sat down and listened to the song again. But the sound of the trickling kept tickling Charlie, and he could not sit still.

Discuss this paragraph with the children. Then write the following sentences on the board.

He saw a little stream and heard the noise it made and he sat down.

He saw a little stream that sang as it ran in the moonlight and he sat down and listened to the song again. (Hoban)

Let the children decide why Hoban's sentence about Charlie is more than just an ordinary description. Discuss what words in the sentence add to the description and the mood of the story.

As a follow-up assignment, ask each child to write one sentence about an event that happened to him. Ask several children to tell briefly about the events that led up to their sentence. Discuss the sentences and encourage the group to suggest ways each sentence might be developed to create greater interest through imagery.

AWARENESS OF AUDIENCE

As a youngster's descriptive abilities develop he will need to become aware of the background and knowledge of his potential audience, at least informally. Classroom discussions, for example, should highlight description for an audience that is already fairly familiar with a given topic, in contrast to discussions before an audience that is encountering the topic for the first time. The following suggestions should help to create audience awareness.

Is This Me?

Ask the children to select one classmate to work with during this activity. The two, however, are not to collaborate in the actual writing; instead, each is to describe the other's physical characteristics and personality traits in a few brief paragraphs, and to include a drawing with his description.

169

After the descriptions and pictures are completed, have each pair exchange their work to read about themselves. The descriptions and pictures might also be read aloud and shared with the class.

As an added dimension to the activity, each child may wish to take his partner's description of him home and ask his mother, father, or other family members to guess who the description might fit.

Who Am I?

Children enjoy playing the guessing game "Who Am I?" Have a child describe a member of the class or a familiar object in the classroom to the teacher or his classmates. Some descriptions might be similar to these.

WHO AM I?

I am round.
I have a face.
I have two hands.
I have no body.
I make a ticking sound.

(clock)

WHO AM I?

I am a boy.
I am seven years old.
My hair is brown.
My eyes are brown.
My skin is black.
My brother's name is Roy.
I like cornchips and kickball.

(name of child)

WHO AM I?

I am a rectangle.
I am hard.
You can break me.
I help keep out the heat and cold.
You can see through me.

(window)

Permit at least three chances to guess the correct answer. Help guide each child to select those features of a person or object that will result in rapid recognition of his description.

After there have been several representative descriptions of objects and class members, launch a discussion on the likelihood that these descriptions would be recognized by children in another classroom. The object descriptions would of course be easier to recognize than the pupil descriptions because of the audience's familiarity with the objects. In this way the children can come to realize the importance of taking audience familiarity into account. You may encourage the children to explore changes in their descriptions that would help an outside audience recognize them, such as where they live, the name of their parents, and so on.

You should constantly be alert to ways of improving children's descriptive abilities. Point out the ways we symbolize our physical world through word labels and verbal description. Reserve a section of the classroom bulletin board for descriptive writing. Use children's literature, the school newspaper, and interesting classroom discussions to bring description to the attention of your youngsters. Vivid description is an extremely important aspect of expression, and an important base for the discussion that follows.

NARRATING

From an instructional standpoint narration should be developed simultaneously with descriptive abilities, since descriptive details are the building blocks of characterization, place settings, and story actions.[13] These elements are woven together according to the purpose of the speaker or writer. He may simply want to convey the events of a weekend vacation trip, or it may involve conscious plot development at a more advanced level. Instruction should point out organizational features of narration that establish characters, develop locations, establish time, and signal the actions and events of the plot. In the kindergarten and early grades emphasis should be on characters in simple settings, with straightforward events to relate the action. In the intermediate grades characterization, story setting, action, climax, and resolution will all become more complex.

As we did with description, we can identify elements from our language framework that are essential for narration. A number of these elements overlap with those of description, but some are unique to story development. These overlapping and unique elements are:

> *Lexical meaning,* vocabulary essential for description and narrative expression
> *Relational meaning* and understanding of sentence subordination and organization, transitional elements in story lines, written conventions that reflect narrative style
> *Interpretation and problem solving,* understanding of sequence, identification of relationships, causal relations; organizing of facts, events, and ideas; illustrations and examples; collection and synthesis of information to develop a story plot and alternate story endings
> *Interests, attitudes,* and *values* that provide for the selection of content

The steps in the instructional program for developing narration also follow a sequence that starts with informal sharing of personal experiences and concludes with a focus on specific aspects of narration. The following discussion will thus be developed around these topics:

1. Observing and relating through pictorial and oral expression
2. Sharing the story with a small group through pictures

3. Acting out through puppetry, creative dramatics, and role playing
4. Recording ideas through creative writing
5. Comparing individual story lines
6. Extending and organizing narration through
   characters
   setting
   story development (plot)
   vocabulary, sentence, sentence transition, and paragraph development
   audience consideration

Try to use what you know and have learned about description to help your children learn how to use descriptive imagery in their narrations.

Observing and relating: the pictorial narrative

The importance of the child's firsthand experience as the source for his picture narrative cannot be overemphasized. A brief story line is a natural outgrowth of a child's early descriptive art forms. Although the picture may not adequately portray the sequence of events in a story, it is very common to find that the simple illustration of a story character or story object will provide the basis for a series of story events. When the child is encouraged to pretend that the character portrayed by his art form is central to a story line, his imagination often becomes engaged to the extent that a series of interesting events will follow. Questions such as "Who is this? Where is this place? What other people might be involved in your story? What exciting thing could your character do? What could he do before this picture was drawn? After this picture was drawn? and Why do you like or dislike this character?" will stimulate the imagination.

The use of the child's own drawing or art form produces high motivation and interest, which provides for direct interaction with the story character or characters.

After the child has shared the brief picture narrative with his teacher or a classmate, he should create a caption for the picture. This caption, which can be printed at the bottom of the picture (in some cases this will have to be done by the teacher), reinforces the relationship between oral language and written expression.

The following specific ideas will help to develop the picture narrative.

Mr. Bogey's Terrible Trouble

The following story can be used to develop individual picture books. Read each part and ask the children to draw pictures to illustrate each of the three parts. The character and his problem are, of course, supplied, but each child solves the problem in his third picture.

1. Once upon a time there was a nice dog named Mr. Bogey. He had floppy ears, spots on his face and a tiny tail that always pointed to the sky.
2. One day Mr. Bogey went for a walk. He wanted to meet other friendly animals who would play with him. On the corner of Park and Green Streets

he met Shadow, a black cat. He had never seen a cat before. So Mr. Bogey
sniffed and barked at Shadow.

3. (Draw what happened to Mr. Bogey. Then tell your teacher or write what
happened in your picture that ended this story.)

After the three pictures are developed, read the first two parts again. Each
child can then complete the story by explaining his third picture in the
sequence. You may wish to record several of the story endings on newsprint and compare the conclusions for their creative and qualitative considerations. Titles may be developed for each picture or for the third picture
only. The three pictures can then be stapled together as the child's picture
book.

The Strange Monster

Here is a story for the child to listen to and then to illustrate. He is to
formulate his own conclusion. This story need not be completed in one
session. Have each child make a cover for his book, then send the book
home with the duplicated story attached to his book. Encourage his mother
or some other adult in the home to read and share the story with him, and
to discuss his picture conclusion.

1. Once upon a time there was a strange monster. He had lots of curly hair
and many legs. He lived in a cave.
2. One day the monster crawled out of his cave and went for a walk. He was
in a strange, wonderful place. It had lots of plants in many colors and a pond
with a weird, beautiful fish.
3. Suddenly he saw a huge building. It had lots of windows and a big point
on top. It was surrounded by lots of pretty flowers.
4. After the monster left the building, he met a _____
_____
_____ .

An organized picture file can be of great value for stimulating creative story
lines. Build a collection of pictures from magazines, publishers' brochures,
textbooks, and other sources, and organize them on the basis of concepts
that will be familiar to your youngsters. Such a picture file may consist of
individual pictures—that is, single pictures—or of a sequence—a series of
pictures that create the story visually. Single pictures that depict people of
various sizes in a variety of poses, dress, and actions can be of great value
in developing descriptive vocabulary. For example, by focusing on appearance, the size and dress may be considered; by focusing on facial expression, the happy, sad, or indifferent nature of the character can be discussed;
and by focusing on small groups of people, the relationship between character or characters and the action in the picture can be evaluated. In the
early grades a caption can be made up on the basis of a discussion of the
picture action. At the upper grades the same picture can serve as a stimulus
for a brief narrative.

The following specific ideas will be of value in developing the pictorial
narrative in the classroom.

Your Folder Stories

Staple interesting magazine pictures to the upper halves of the insides of
filing folders. Staple writing paper to the bottom halves. As the child tells
a brief narrative about the character(s) in the picture and what happened
to him (them), record his language on the writing paper (your assistant or
student tutor may help in this activity). Make several such folders for your
class. After each child has dictated his story to you, place the completed
story in a special place in the "library corner" in order to share it with other
children. Story sharing may take place orally with a small group of children
who have responded to the same picture. Older children can do this independently and then read and discuss the stories created for a specific
picture in a small-group activity.

Cartoon Yarns

The colorful Sunday comics are a fertile resource for matching narratives
through pictures that appeal to children. Cut out any simple comic strip.
Blank out the dialogue with masking tape and have the children insert
their own oral version of what happened. If you have two copies of the
same strip, let the child compare his story with that of the cartoonist.

A variation of this is to omit one panel in the strip and let the child supply
not only the missing segment of the story but the drawing or cartoon as
well.

A Special Day

Show the children a film such as "A Special Day" (Universal City, Calif.:
Universal Education and Visual Arts, 1966). In this brief film two children,
a dog, and the father of the girl meet on the beach. This meeting develops

into a special friendship, a special day. The film is touching and delightful, and will suggest to the children very special days of their own.

Have each child tell a story about his special day. Remind him to include answers to the following questions in his story. You may wish to record several of the stories on newsprint for discussion purposes.

Who had a special day?
What happened on that day?
Where did it happen?
When did it happen?
Why did it happen?

Sharing the story with a small group

After a child has developed his picture story or narrative and briefly discussed it with the teacher or another youngster, he should be provided with an opportunity for sharing the story with a small group or even with the class. Here the picture serves as a prop and provides some security for the child—particularly in providing cues for the narrative. Such an experience should include opportunity for the audience to ask questions about the picture in the story. The discussion may also trigger different characterizations or expanded characterization and possibly alternative endings.

The small group or class discussion will also give children a chance to observe quality examples of characterization, place location, story action, and climax. Value will be accrued by recording these examples on the chalkboard and emphasizing the key story elements. Specific examples for developing story sharing include:

The Three Bears

After reading "The Three Bears" to the class or small group ask the children to draw a picture of one happening in the story. Discuss the picture with the class. Ask the children to describe one picture that tells the beginning of the story (bears are walking in the forest, or Goldilocks enters the bears' home). Then have children draw one picture that tells the middle of the story (Goldilocks in the house eating, or testing food or furniture). Finally, let someone pick a picture that depicts the ending (Goldilocks waking to see the bears watching her, or running out of the house).

Ask a child to place the pictures in the right order, and record the child's story on tape. Other children may wish to provide special sound effects— the "crunch, crunch" of the bears' footsteps made by rubbing two pieces of sandpaper together, for example.

This activity, which can continue with other pictures, helps children develop the concept that a story has a beginning, middle, and ending.

You Are There

Display a photograph or drawing of a cactus. Ask your children to make believe they are standing in front of a real cactus, then have them write imaginary answers to these three questions:

1. Where are you?
2. What lives or grows near the cactus?
3. What can happen to the cactus?

After the children have answered these questions, have the group decide the kinds of stories that could take place in this setting. Then have the group make up a story orally. Start the story with a sentence such as, "The hungry little jackrabbit was looking for food." Have the children contribute narration that carries the action of the story to a logical conclusion. What, where, when, and why questions will be of value in stimulating discussion.

This activity may be used with action photographs or drawings, such as a boy crossing a busy city street, a deer running through the forest, etc. Magazine pictures from *Life* and newspaper pictures portraying human drama will prove to be especially valuable in motivating the children's narrative expression.

The Meanest Man in the World

Ask your children to think what "The Meanest Man in the World" might be like and then have them draw a picture of him. Have each child share his picture with the other children and tell why the man looks and is so mean. Some sample responses might be: "The meanest man in the world is ten feet tall and has very long arms and throws thumbtacks all over the highway so that automobiles will get flat tires," or "This must be the meanest guy in the world. He has small beady eyes and a long nose. His ears are so large that he can use them like wings. He flies down from building tops and trips children who are just coming out of the ice cream store holding their cones." Then ask the children to imagine that their "meanest man in the world" finally meets "the kindest man in the world." Ask them to write a short story about what happens when the two men meet.

This activity can be repeated with other characters like "The Happiest Boy in the World," "Two Unhappy Teen-agers," or "The Strongest Boy in Bay City."

Acting out

Acting out, or role playing, provides an opportunity for children to use language in a highly creative manner. This mode of expression will often free the inhibited child as he assumes the role, say, of a strong character. At the early level this can be done most simply by letting the child portray his own feelings through the use of puppets. Hand puppets are particularly effective in this regard. At later levels physical props will help the child portray a particular role himself. By using various hats, for example, the child can take on characteristics of a little old lady, or a sailor, or a tough guy more effectively.

Be sure to give careful consideration to the nature of the character a child is to portray; otherwise the experience can deteriorate into an awkward and embarrassing situation. Puppets automatically account in part for

What opportunity does this experience provide for the development of narrative expression? *(Photo by Hays, Monkmeyer Press Photo Service)*

visual appearance, but the child must also consider how to use actions and language to characterize. What actions and language, for example, suggest an aggressive character, a genteel and thoughtful character, a humorous person? What actions and language tell where the action is taking place, build excitement in a story to a high point, or bring a story to an end? These aspects of narration will, of course, need to be developed gradually; otherwise the child can be overwhelmed by the many aspects and components of his role in the narrative. As the child projects himself into the character with a rough story line in mind, he will find that his own background of experience will cause many of these elements to fall into place automatically.

Children's literature has an important place in this part of the language program. A particular story or event, such as Tigger visiting Pooh for breakfast, can serve as a ready model for the story line. A child can then proceed to re-create the story in his own language using puppets or a few props.

The following ideas suggest ways acting out can enhance language development.

New Fairy Tales

In order to develop a folk or fairy tale with ease, recall briefly the plots of some fairy tales such as "Cinderella" or "The Bremen Town Musicians" to show that folk or fairy tales have common plot patterns. The characteristics of a folk tale may be written on the chalkboard or discussed orally:

In most fairy tales

1. Animals and objects have human traits.
2. There are make-believe creatures such as elves, giants, fairies, and goblins.
3. Ordinary people have strange or unusual experiences.
4. The "bad" creature is usually punished or chased away forever.

The following three fairy tale characters may aid the children in telling their own fairy tales:

King Fonger is a kind man. He helps his people in almost every way. The people in his kingdom are well fed, happy, and handsome.

Prince Andrew is a spoiled young boy. He is also mean to his parents, servants, and friends. No one likes him and he makes his parents cry.

The ninety-year-old witch, named Gisella, plans to do something to help her king and queen change Prince Andrew.

Make stick masks of these and other characters. Let the children form
performing groups for their fairy tale. Give special attention to the language of each character.

Puppet Affair

Let children make their favorite TV character into a paper-bag puppet. Ask
them to think about the character's basic character traits. Batman, for

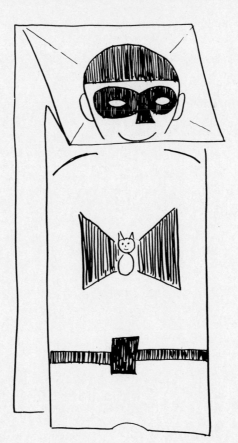

example, is brave, strong, and good. Explore with the children the kind of language he would use. A child might demonstrate with, "Robin, I know where that sly, low, miserable, vile Joker is. Get the batcar out and zowie! off we go to get him." After the discussion and demonstration the children may conclude that Batman's language and voice must portray a serious, forceful, direct, and self-confident character. Contrast Batman's language with another TV character such as Minnie Mouse, where a definite style shift is required. The children would conclude that Minnie Mouse is silly, giggly, helpless, squeaky-voiced, and so forth.

To add flavor and deeper understanding to the exercise, have the children use their puppets to portray characteristics that are the opposite of their TV character. This would make Batman cowardly, weak, and evil, and Minnie Mouse would be serious, independent, and mature.

Actor's Workshop

Ask the children to think about these characters and what they are doing.

1. A little boy walking up a flight of stairs
2. An angry motorist after an accident
3. A happy child who has just won a bicycle
4. You shopping in a department store with ten dollars in your pocket

Select a child to act out the first character and discuss the performance, then have the other three characters acted out and discussed.

Have the children form four committees, based on these four characters. Each may join the committee whose character appeals to him most. Give the children a limit of fifteen minutes to decide on a dramatization that tells about each character and what happened to him.

People Help People

This language activity goes well with a social studies unit on community workers. Briefly discuss or review the need for community helpers such as milkman, doctor, mailman, policeman, etc. Then pose this question as a beginning to extending the children's knowledge of characters through role playing:

"If mother left the coffee pot on the stove too long and it started a small fire, what would she do?"

Select a child to act out the role of the mother. She can select any other actors she may need, such as firemen or neighbors, to help her answer the question in dramatized format. Explore the language of the mother and the other actors. For example, Mother's language, in this emergency, must convey urgency, concern, anxiety, fear, and determination, while that of a fireman should convey calm, efficiency, and action.

180

Encourage the children to ask other questions regarding community helpers and continue to select as many children as possible to act out the actions of each helper.

Recording ideas through creative writing

It is common for children to have difficulty capturing their ideas in written form. This difficulty may be due in part to the emphasis placed on writing mechanics, correct spelling, neatness, and teacher-imposed style differences. In the early stages of written expression these aspects should receive minor emphasis; the major concern should be for the ideas to be expressed.

Early writing experiences grow best out of oral discussions, from story ideas suggested by the children. Devote special attention to youngsters who have difficulty expanding ideas. They may need small-group discussion of a particular topic, or individual help in deriving a story thread from their personal background of experience. Once the nub of an idea has been identified, it may be expanded by probing the who, where, when, what, and how of the story. Team children with similar abilities and interests and use such questions as story starters in a small-group discussion.

The following suggestions should help to stimulate creative writing of the narrative type.

Toothy Stories

Primary children love to speculate about the activities and characteristics of the "tooth fairy," since she affects them so personally. Encourage the children to write a story about their tooth fairy. In order to help them formulate their narrative, suggest that their story contain answers to the following questions:

Who is the Tooth Fairy?
What does she do?
How can she find your tooth?
What does she do with all the teeth she collects?

(Cut writing paper in the shape of a tooth.)

You Do the Rest

Here are the beginnings and endings of three stories. Have each child select one and complete the story.

Sadie was a kitten. Sometimes Sadie and Scratch _____
_____
_____
_____ .

That is why Sadie will never go near the pond again.

Snafu was a fine king but he always _____
_____
_____
_____.

Everyone in the kingdom, especially King Snafu, now whispers when someone is sleeping.

Plimpton had a problem. He had a nose that was ten inches long. Fortunately he_____
_____
_____
_____.

The shop was very successful.

After the stories have been completed, group the children on the basis of their story selection and have the children in each group share their versions. Emphasize the story logic that is required because of the preset beginnings and endings.

The Surprise

Help your children write their own family character books. The suggested pages will help them bring to the surface characteristics of people and places they know intimately.

Duplicate the pages and have the children complete them. The pages may be completed in several different writing sessions. Be sure to leave sufficient space for drawings. Staple the pages together and have the children create interesting construction paper book covers.

Pages 1 through 4 describe the child's family unit; pages 5 and 6 describe his home and play area. Now that the child has the story characters, he is to write on page 7 what happened when his uncle (or friend) _____ came to visit and brought _____.

page 1	page 2
Here I am. My name is _____. I like _____.	Here is my mother and/or father. They _____ _____.

```
                                            page 3

My brother's name is
_____.
He_____.
```

```
                                            page 4

My sister's name is
_____ .
She_____.
```

```
                                            page 5

Here is where we live.  My
bed is_____
_____.
```

```
                                            page 6

This is where I play.  You
can see_____
_____.
```

```
                                            page 7

My Uncle (or friend)_____
_____
came to visit us.  He_____
_____.
```

Tell It Like It Is

Have each child select and write about one of these story ideas.

1. You are a noodle in the bag on a shelf. A shopper has just picked the bag up and put it in her shopping cart. Tell how it feels to be in the bag, where you are going, and what happens to you.
2. You are a small plant beginning to grow. A gardener has just bought you in a nursery. Tell all about your trip, how you feel, and what happened to you.
3. You are a pet kangaroo named Sam. You like to see the sights in the city. Tell what happens to you on a city bus on your way to the zoo. What did your owner finally decide to do with you?
4. You are a turtle and the good fairy has just given you two wishes. Tell what you wished, how it felt, and what finally happened to you.

For Authors Only

Cut tagboard into large, playing-card size pieces of paper. You may need about fifty cards for the deck. On one side of the card write a story title from the following list of suggestions. You or the children may wish to illustrate the title on the reverse side of the card. To select a title for his story, a child may wish to shuffle the cards and draw one or several. After the stories are written, compare narratives with the same titles.

Here are some titles. You may wish to add your own favorite ones.

The Mouse that Roared
Sadie the Savage
The Millionaire Tramp
Fabulous Fanny
Mrs. Plimpton's Money Tree
Trouble in Twin Creeks
The Mystery of Baby Jane
A Visitor from Mars
The Case of the Purple Parrot
The Queen's Confession
Twelve Days till Christmas
The Secret Classroom
A Barrel of Laughs
Dudley Did It Again
Three Yellow Roses
Porky Won a Contest
A Special Day
Fonger Found Toad Eggs
Hair-Curling Events
Twenty Stout Men
A Dress for Debbie
The Happy Witch
Walter Found a Treasure
My Favorite Meal
The Drag Race Caper
How to Snag a Dragon
The Tale of the Wise Owl
The Charming Snake
Jungle Jamboree
The Lonely House
Breakfast with Polly Pig
Why Pigs Have Curly Tails
The Case of the Coughing Mouse

Comparing individual story lines

Once children have completed creative narratives, small group discussions will be of value in exploring factors that contribute to the interest of the story line. You will need to be readily available to react to questions and note the progress of the discussions. As previously suggested, you can use a newsprint chart to record key parts of the class discussion and make them available later so that the children can refer to their past oral and written experiences. This will provide for a range of factors that have contributed to the interest level: for example, initial sentences that interest the reader, phrases that contribute to imagery, and word groups expressing who, where, when, and what. In this manner the children's descriptive sense is developed and related to the organizational sequence of ideas in the story line.

Extending and organizing narration

Description is basic to narration, but other dimensions are also essential. The following discussion identifies other key elements to focus on in the elementary school instructional program.

CHARACTERS

Early attempts to describe characters will deal mostly with visual characteristics, but it is important for the child to highlight other dimensions to portray the interaction of the character with other people and things and to identify feelings and attitudes. Other descriptive elements are comparison with other well-known people or objects (for example using simile), statements of what the character is not like, conversations wherein other characters say what they think about the character in question, and the like. Specific suggestions for simple characterization include:

What Does Your Character Look Like?

Using similes will help children come to understand ways animals and people may be visualized by comparison. Have the children complete the following similes:

My dog has a face like a _____.
The dragon's _____ looked like a long winding fence.
Amy's face was as round as an _____.
Bob's feet were as big as _____.
The news photographer used his _____ like an eye.
The giant's _____ wrapped the man like a _____.
The thin, hungry boy looked like a _____.
He used his spoon like a _____.

After the children share their responses, encourage them to discuss the ways a simile can help build a reader's understanding of a story character; for example, How is a giant's hug like a blanket? Have the children search for similes in their classroom literature selections and create their own comparisons in their individual story development.

THE MONSTER

It's a shape.

It has a big, scary eye.

It has great big teeth.

It has big sharp teeth.

It's nose looks like a green spear.

Its horns can grow and grow and grow

until they reach the sky.

"They" can scratch you. They can kill you, too.

The arms are sharp, long and yellow.

The feet have shiny sharp claws.

The monster has a baby inside.

by Pam, Carl, Lalo, Wendy, Michelle, Patrick, John

John

What aspects of description are reflected in the children's "monster responses,"
which have been recorded by their teacher?

Mirror, Mirror on the Wall

Hang an inexpensive mirror on the creative writing bulletin board in your
classroom. Tape the following typewritten instructions on the bottom of
the mirror, and place a large envelope below for the written compositions.

The mirror on the wall needs this information about you. Write the answers on
a piece of paper and place it in the pocket below the mirror.

1. Who are you? (Name)
2. What do you look like?
3. What does your voice sound like?
4. How big are you?
5. How old are you?
6. What are you like?
7. Where do you live?
8. Why do some people like you?
9. Why do some people stay clear of you?
10. What do you like to do on Saturdays?

Who Said It?

Let the children select two of the five pieces of dialogue below and write
about the characters whose dialogue they have selected. Remind the children to explore the following points:

1. Who said it?
2. How does the character look?

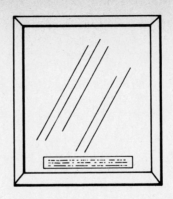

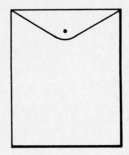

3. How might he act?
4. What does he do?
5. Why did he say it?

"There are too many dollars in this bundle."
"Look at that ladybug eating the green bug."
"Why did you turn left in this one-way street?"
"Twelve people went in but only eleven came out."
"I think that lemonade tasted strange."

Weepy Walter

Help children think and write about an interesting character by suggesting that they consider these questions about a boy named Weepy Walter. Let the children supply the answers to these questions either orally or in written form.

1. How old is he?
2. What does he look like?
3. Why does he weep?
4. When does he weep?
5. What does his family look and act like?

Now that the children have enough information about Weepy Walter, have them write a brief story about him. The children may wish to use a suggested topic, such as

Weepy Walter meets Happy Henry at Pine Valley Ranch.
Weepy Walter and Bozo the Clown star in the Bingling Brothers Circus.

The Emperor's New Clothes

Make available several copies of Hans Christian Andersen's *The Emperor's New Clothes*.[14] Have the children read it and verify the following six statements either in their own words or the author's words. Your discussion of the ways language conveys the meaning of the following words will be of great value in extending the children's expressive ability.

PROVE IT

1. The emperor is *vain*.
2. The emperor is *extravagant*.
3. The emperor is *remote* from his people.
4. The emperor is *gullible*.
5. The emperor is *stupid*.
6. The emperor felt *embarrassed*.

SETTING

To develop setting or location of a narrative, the child will need to project himself into the appropriate surroundings. This is extremely simple at the early grades, but in the upper elementary grades the story lines will need to account for such factors as time period and the location of the story ranging from the fairy tale opening "Once upon a time long ago in a land far away" to the re-creation of events the child participated in during a recent vacation: "During our Easter vacation last year we were driving east on Highway 80." It is very important that there be awareness of the relationships among setting, time, and plot.

TV Homework

Make the following homework assignment to give children more awareness of setting. Instruct them to watch two television shows in an evening, and then answer the following questions:

Name of the show: _____

1. Where did the story take place?
   (geographical location, climate, land, ocean,
   desert, forest, etc.)
2. When did the story take place?
   (year, season, time of day, modern times,
   ancient times, frontier days, etc.)
   (This question is not to be confused with the
   actual programming time of the TV show.)
3. Can you relate the characters to the
   setting and surroundings? For example:

Character	Setting	Surroundings
a cowboy	desert country badlands	horses, cattle, ranches, rustlers
a spaceman	moon, deep space, another planet	space ship, space suit, computers, robots, monsters
a sailor	ocean, storms	ships, diving equipment, fish

4. How would the story need to be different if it had been written one hundred years earlier? One hundred years later? Would the characters dress the same way? Would the setting be similar? Would the surroundings look different?

This same exercise can be used to contrast two literature selections.

What's in the News?

Clip a series of news items—pictures, story captions, and the news articles —from the daily newspaper. Paste each news story on a separate piece of tagboard. Below each news clipping print the questions

WHERE did it happen?
WHEN did it happen?
HOW did it happen?
WHO did it happen to?

Have the children write their answers on a separate sheet of paper. Permit other children to examine the answers for accuracy based on the news article, or provide for self-checking by placing the answers on the reverse side of each tagboard.

Where and When

Have the children read *Charlotte's Web.*[15] Encourage them to write detailed descriptions in their answers to the following questions about setting. Such answers must include reactions to: What did it look like there? What were some of the smells or sounds? The use of stimulating, sensory vocabulary is most desirable.

WHERE

1. Where does the story take place? (city, suburb, etc.)?
2. Where does Charlotte meet Wilbur after school each day?
3. Where does Templeton live?
4. Where is the county fair?

WHEN

1. When does Fern find Wilbur (season of the year)?
2. When does Charlotte spin her web?
3. When is Wilbur taken to the fair?
4. When did Charlotte's babies hatch?

After the children have responded to these questions discuss the importance of this information to the story.

PLOT

Plot is the relationship between the characters and events that leads to the climax and conclusion. Again the child is to be encouraged to use his imagination to project himself into the story to consider the characters in the time and setting and the experiences the characters might participate in. This type of thinking can be developed by reading part of a selection aloud, stopping just before the climax, and having the children account for the relationships between characters and events.

After you have considered the climax, take up the conclusion. This will require that the implications of story events and character or characters be carefully developed. Use small-group discussions to consider optional conclusions, which may range from a most logical outcome to a highly creative or novel ending.

The following suggestions will be of value in studying plot.

Monkey Business

Let the children find the high point or climax to a story such as *Caps for Sale.*[16] Read the story, but stop just before the climax (when the cap peddler becomes so angered by the monkeys imitating him and not returning his caps that he pulls off his cap and throws it on the ground). Now ask the children to decide how they would have gotten the monkeys to return the caps. They may develop a climax similar to that of the author (that the monkeys will imitate the peddler), but in any event discuss and explore all the possibilities, ideas, and optional high points the children propose. After your children have reacted to the story, complete the reading and compare the author's treatment of the story to their own.

Junior Editors

Duplicate and distribute to your class the following story (written by a nine-year-old girl).

The Four-Legged, One-Eyed Monster

Once upon a time this little girl was left on an island by herself. Her name was Katie.

Katie's family left her because they couldn't feed her.

One night as she was going to sleep something touched her. She jumped. She saw a one-eyed, four-legged creature. She thought she was dreaming but she wasn't.

All of a sudden he picked her up. She screamed with all her might. So he covered her mouth.

He took her to his cave and said, "I will keep you for my wife. So go and cook dinner while I fetch some milk. Do not try to get away. If you do, I will catch you and eat you."

So Katie stayed with him.

One day when he was sick, she got away. As she was running she remembered the matches in her pocket. She took them out and set the cave afire. The monster was gone.

So she built a house and stayed on the island until she woke up in her bed in her own room in Oakland.

Ask your children to discuss the following questions and attempt to relate the characters to the setting, develop the climax, and bring the story to a conclusion.

1. What other reason could the author have given for Katie's being stranded on the island?
2. How else could the author have got rid of the monster?
3. How else, other than waking up, could the story have ended? What other way can you get Katie off the island?

Something's Missing

Duplicate and distribute the following stories to your children. Encourage them to develop the crucial climaxes in the stories (point out that they will need to give careful attention to the beginning and conclusion of each story to make the climax both logical and exciting).

The two boys rode their bikes to the bank of the river. Today they were going to have fun fishing.

"What are you using for bait, David?" asked Paul.

"Jeff gave me some grasshoppers, but they are almost gone," said David.

"I think I will fish from that big rock," said Paul. He crawled out on the rock with his fishing pole.

"Look out!" called David.

_____

_____

_____

One thing that did cheer Paul up was that everyone in his family ate *his* fish for dinner that night.

Mrs. Rabbit and Mrs. Mole were having tea and cake one afternoon.

"What would you do, Mrs. Rabbit, if some strange animals came to your front door?"

"Why, Mrs. Mole, I would ask them to come in and have some tea and cake," said Mrs. Rabbit.

Just then Mrs. Mole looked out the front door and said, "My goodness, here come three very strange looking animals!"

_____

_____

Mrs. Rabbit became famous throughout the forest. She was so busy that she could no longer take the time to chat with her friend Mrs. Mole.

A Tale of Many Authors

Use the following procedure to develop "A Tale of Many Authors":

1. The first author (child) writes the beginning of the story. He introduces the character and setting. (Urge the children to write clearly so that succeeding authors will be able to work with the story.)
2. At this point have each child exchange his paper with another child.
3. The next author develops the problem to a climax that is consistent with the characterization and setting developed by the first author.
4. Stories are again exchanged.
5. The third author brings the story to a novel conclusion.
6. Have a story conference to compare and evaluate the development of the characters, the setting, the problem, the climax, and the conclusion of each story.
7. Based on the conference have a brief rewriting session. "Publish" the stories by duplicating them on ditto paper. You may wish to bind the stories and place them in the "library corner" for the enjoyment of other children, or to send them home for parent-child enjoyment.

VOCABULARY, SENTENCE, SENTENCE TRANSITION, AND PARAGRAPH DEVELOPMENT

Sentence development for narrative purposes will rely heavily on vocabulary that evokes vivid imagery. As previously mentioned (in "Descriptive Expression") such development depends on picture-evoking nouns that are described more completely through adjectives and placed in action through the selection of verbs and adverbs.

Sentences are the means of presenting the ideas that comprise characterization, setting, and plot. The child should try for sentence variety through various constructions and patterns. Often a number of short, simple sentences can be more effective if they are combined into a single, more elaborate sentence. On the other hand, the run-on sentence that many children use may contain an overload of information that several short, precise constructions would express more effectively.

No magic formula exists for the development of sentence structure in written expression, but generally speaking a variety of sentence forms tends to produce a higher interest level in early written expression. Give special attention to transitional sentences. The following exercises can be useful to develop vocabulary, sentence pattern variation, and transitional sentences.

Word Bank

Label with a red felt pen several large manila envelopes with the following categories: Mystery Words, Weather Words, Feeling Words, and Tasting Words. Pin these envelopes to a bulletin board entitled "Word Bank."

Make four small pieces of paper available to the children and ask them to write one word for each envelope on the slips of paper, then have each child "deposit" the slips of paper in the appropriate envelope.

Ask a child to read the words deposited in an envelope and have the class decide whether all the words belong in that "account." Those words not appropriate to the category are then reclassified.

Then ask each child to select one word from each envelope and develop a brief story using the words selected.

Word Bank

Weather Words	Mystery Words	Feeling Words	Tasting Words
sunny	dark	happy	sweet
foggy	scream	sad	sour
smoggy	clue	weeping	bitter
cold	hatchet	laughing	delicious
icy	ghost	frowning	spicy
chilly	chains	calm	chewy
gray	rattling	serene	hot
bright	creaky	nervous	mushy

The Noun Train Story

Write the following sentences on strips of lined tagboard and pin them to a bulletin board entitled "The Noun Train." (Make sure that you leave enough room for each blank so that a variety of answers can be inserted.) Give the children construction paper cut into the shape of box cars. On these train cars the children are to write a noun that can be used in the sentences. After the children write their words, have them pin their words to the bulletin board. Compare the various stories, noting meaning changes that result from various noun groups.

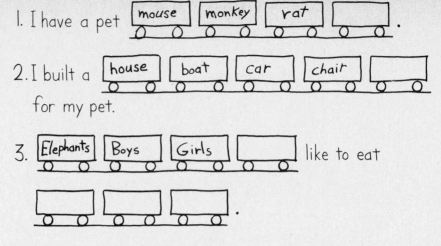

1. I have a pet mouse monkey rat ___ .

2. I built a house boat car chair ___ for my pet.

3. Elephants Boys Girls ___ like to eat ___ ___ ___ .

Adjectives

Complete the first sentence with a small group of children. They are to complete each sentence using their own adjectives.

1. I found my (blue)   sweater.
   (new)
   (torn)
   (pull-over)
   (ski)

2. His _____ camera is broken.
   _____
   _____
   _____
   _____

3. That _____ cake is good.
   _____
   _____
   _____
   _____

4. Our _____ car is in the garage.
   _____
   _____
   _____
   _____

5. I am very _____.
   _____
   _____
   _____

6. My mother is very _____.

                                                              _____
                                                              _____
                                                              _____
                                                              _____

   7. This car is _____.

                              _____
                              _____
                              _____
                  _____

Compare the adjectives in several of the sentences and encourage the children to note the range of possibilities for sentence development.

Vital Verbs

Here are two verb-supplying exercises children enjoy. Remind them that we want to create action for the people. You may start the discussion with an open sentence, such as

   I can _____.

and encourage the children to provide as many verbs as possible.

Continue with the following sentences.

   A top can (spin), (roll), (break).
   The big dog _____, _____, _____.
   Betty can _____ the cake.
   We can _____ in the park until it becomes dark.
   Tom will _____ the ball very hard.

Discuss the ways different verbs alter meaning.

Adverb Game

Write the beginning of a sentence on the chalkboard. Have the children provide an image-evoking adverb to complete the sentence.

Here are some sample sentences and answers.

   The man ran down the street _____.
                                       _____ (angrily)
                                      _____ (blissfully)
                                      _____ (carefully)
   He bit his tongue _____.
                                _____ (accidentally)
                                _____ (deeply)
                                _____ (severely)

My doctor cleaned the wound _____.
_____ (carefully)
_____ (slowly)
_____ (quickly)

She accepted the swimming trophy _____.

_____

_____

Father chewed the apple _____.

_____

_____

Note how the various adverbs alter, but refine, the meaning and imagery created in the sentence.

Stop Those Run-Away Sentences

Have the children cross out the connecting *ands* in the following sentences, and draw a "stop sign" (a hexagon with red crayon) after each sentence. Then have them rewrite the sentences with correct punctuation, omitting the "illegal" *ands.*

I rode my bike to the swimming pool   and it cost 25¢ to get into the pool and when I got there all of my friends had gone home.

We went to Bobbins Ice Cream Store   and I like the bubble gum flavor best of all   and my friend Jack ordered a strawberry ice cream sundae.

Compare each rewritten paragraph with the original noting the information and clarity in each.

Three Little Mice

Duplicate this little story of Fletcher, Bun Bun, and Mum, who are three little mice who decided to go to Australia. Focus the children's attention on how the use of the word *and* has resulted in very long run-on sentences. Explain to the children that each paragraph should be rewritten so that it contains more than one sentence.

One day a little mouse named Mum got up and he put on his clothes and ate a big breakfast and he went to visit his friends Fletcher and Bun Bun.

Fletcher and Bun Bun wanted to go on a long trip and they wanted Mum to go with them and they planned to fly to the large country of Australia to visit the kangaroos.

When they got there they liked what they saw and as they were playing in the green grass they saw kangaroos and they also saw a koala bear in the tree.

After each paragraph has been rewritten, compare the new versions of the story with the old.

Off to School

To help children in sentence expansion, duplicate or write the following sentences on the board. Encourage the children to expand each sentence to add more meaning to the story. (Keep in mind that the sentences are all related.)

Ann walked to school. $\longrightarrow$ Ann walked slowly up Park Street to her school.
Two boys were kicking cans. $\longrightarrow$ Two boys were kicking empty cans on the sidewalk.
Rosie was playing. $\longrightarrow$ _____.
The bell rang. $\longrightarrow$ _____.
The teacher is waving. $\longrightarrow$ _____.
We ate crackers and drank milk. $\longrightarrow$ _____

A Better Beginning

Duplicate or write on the board the following exercise for improving beginning sentences.

Read each paragraph carefully. Examine the beginning sentence in each paragraph. Write an improved beginning sentence under the paragraph that will tell more about the central character.

William is a boy. He opened one eye, then both eyes and sat up in bed. William stretched and yawned and then smiled to himself. It was a special day. He could hear his mother humming in the kitchen. Peggy, his younger sister, was giving orders to her favorite doll. Father's electric razor was buzzing softly in another part of the house.

Mr. Miller looked. Then he murmured the words, "More fire hydrants are coming." Then he looked at Mr. Wallace standing next to him. They both looked at the billboard again and at the barking puppy in front of it.

Jerry walked. He felt cold and tired. He had to protect himself from the cold, humid air. Everywhere he looked it was white. "When is this ordeal going to end?" he thought to himself. Finally, he touched the door and banged his fist against it.

The Missing Sentence

Duplicate or write on the board the following paragraphs. In each paragraph the beginning sentence is missing. Have the children write the beginning sentence. Encourage the children to consider reader interest and the sequence of events that follows the introductory sentence before they write anything.

197

_____. He looked around. There was nothing in the old, dark shack except some garden tools and three clay pots. Peter had just bent over to pick up one of the shovels when he heard a soft, moaning sound. He was so frightened that he could not move. Then, after a few seconds, he tried to jump toward the door, but something tripped him, and he landed on the moist rough wooden floor.

_____. It looked finished. The fort had all of the things they had planned. It had a door in the back and two peepholes in the side walls to watch out for enemies. The boys even had enough room for a broken old chair and a box for a table. Kevin put all of their important belongings in the box. The only thing that seemed to bother them was that there wasn't enough light in the fort.

The concept of the paragraph—as the major unit for themes or ideas and as a way of showing a shift in speakers or in supporting ideas—is important to narrative form. The use of indentation and quotation marks to set off the language spoken by the characters can be introduced and developed at a simple level to show a shift in speakers. The other concept—shift in supporting ideas—is more complex and so requires constant consideration in the instructional program. One way this can be done is by reading a literature model to the children and having them identify the idea shifts. Having the child proofread his own work can also focus on this idea; once he has expressed his ideas in the running narrative, he can proofread what he has written to see where paragraphing can help the reader comprehend the discussion better. The following exercises should help to develop understanding of the paragraph concept.

Talk Written Down

Read the first half of the following story to the class. Explain that you will read this part of the story again and that at the second reading the children are to raise their hand whenever they think an indentation is required to show that a different person is speaking. Then place the ending of the story on the chalkboard and have the children write the ending, indenting each paragraph in which a different person speaks.

Three boys named Will, Rob, and Slim were playing at the edge of a pond.

"Look at those frogs," said Will.

"Wow," said Rob, "I'd sure like to have a few of those."

"I'll show ya how to get them," chuckled Slim, and he grabbed a rock and started to hit a frog.

"Stop it," yelled Will. "Yea, stop it, Slim. I don't want them dead," Rob chimed in. Will gave Slim a little push. Slim landed in the pond. The boys laughed.

"Thanks a lot," growled Slim. "Help me out. I promise not to hurt the frogs. They might get me."

Duplicate this story. Direct the children to circle the sentences that have common ideas to form a paragraph. Then have the children rewrite the first paragraphs of the story on another piece of paper. Remind the children to indent the first sentence in each new paragraph.

Mr. Fox lived in the woods.

One morning when he got up, he was hungry.

He could not find a thing to eat.

Mr. Fox went out of his house.

He went for a walk in the woods.

Soon Mr. Fox saw a skunk.

He decided that skunks were not good to eat.

So he did not eat the skunk.

Mr. Fox came to a white house.

There he saw five small rabbits peeking out the window.

Rabbits are good to eat.

So the old fox went to the door and knocked.

No one answered.

Mr. Fox picked up a rock and threw it at the window.

As he was about to climb in, he heard a noise.

It was a dog and he was afraid of dogs.

So hungry Mr. Fox ran away.

This exercise can be used with any simple story. Prepare the story in block form, so as not to define the paragraphs, and let the children identify and reconstruct paragraphs representing common ideas in the story.

Two Wishes

Duplicate the following beginning paragraph and ask the children to complete the story by writing three paragraphs. The first two paragraphs must tell about a different wish, and the last should be used to conclude the story.

Once upon a time a poor man set out for the nearest village to find a job. The only thing he owned was a black, scrawny but lovable cat. Along the way he met an old woman. She, too, was hungry and she started to cry. The kind man felt so sorry for her that he offered to give her the only thing he owned. As he handed her the cat she spoke, "Dear, kind man, for being so good to me you shall have two wishes."

(Tell about the first wish) _____

_____

_____

_____ .

(Tell about the second wish.) _____

_____

_____

_____

(Story ending) _____

_____

Why I Want to Own a Chocolate Factory

Read *Charley and the Chocolate Factory* to the children, then discuss the book briefly, focusing on how Charley must have felt when he became the owner of the Willie Wonka Chocolate Factory.

Ask the children to write a short composition of several paragraphs entitled "Why I Want to Own Charley's Chocolate Factory."

Place the following paragraph guidelines on the chalkboard, and discuss each briefly.

Paragraph 1. The *introductory paragraph* tells about your ideas for using Charley's Chocolate Factory.

Paragraph 2. The *supporting paragraph* tells more about one or two of your ideas in greater detail.

Paragraph 3. The *concluding paragraph* may review the main idea or ideas of your story very briefly, or suggest what you now plan to do with the Chocolate Factory.

Ask several children to read their stories aloud to the class and compare their ideas.

AUDIENCE CONSIDERATION

As the young writer develops his narrative he will need to be aware of his potential readers. This is not of major consequence in the early writing experiences, but it is an awareness that should eventually be created. The child can be made vividly aware of the importance of his audience by exchanging stories with classroom partners and listening to their reactions on things like the use of vocabulary, character and location development, climax and conclusion. Afterward these ideas should be fed into a small-group or a class discussion so that both strong areas and areas needing additional effort can be identified. You should conclude this type of discussion by identifying key points of value to the entire class.

Ideas for developing an awareness of audience consideration include the following:

Who Is Your Reader?

This assignment is designed to create awareness of different audiences or potential readers. The writing experience may be developed in three different steps:

1. Write a news article for the class about an interesting experience such as a weekend camping trip.
2. Write a brief letter about the same experience to a close friend who was there.
3. Compare and contrast the article and the letter.

Then have a discussion based on questions like the following:

Is the article or the letter more detailed? Why?
Are the same experiences discussed? Why? or why not?
Is the same vocabulary used?
In what ways is the article similar to the letter?

What I Do after School

Ask each child to write two letters about his after-school activities on any given day. The first letter should be addressed to his mother or friend, the second to the principal of your school.

Before anyone does any writing, have the children consider the following questions:

Who needs more detailed information? Why?
Is there a difference in the use of vocabulary between a letter to a mother and one to a principal?
Are there differences in the formal or informal nature of the letters?

After the letters are written, have the children read some of their letters to the group to see whether the letters reflect an awareness of their intended readers.

EVALUATING EXPRESSIVE CONTROL

The evaluation of children's progress in oral and written expression is an ongoing process. Opportunities to observe children's description and narration extend from story-sharing time at the beginning of the school day to field trip experiences where careful observation and description are of great import. All are opportunities to benchmark children's performances.

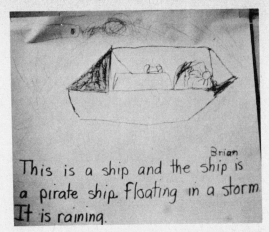

This is a ship and the ship is
a pirate ship floating in a storm.
It is raining.

Brian

I drawed a picture for my
mother and my sister, and I have
a Barbie doll and I have a Don.

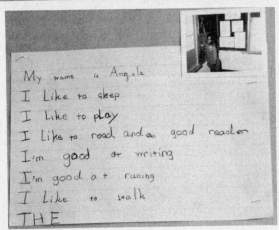

My name is Angela
I Like to sleep
I Like to play
I Like to read and a good reader
I'm good at writing
I'm good at runing
I Like to walk
THE

Speculate on the way in which these written experiences were developed. Use the Oral and Written Language Inventory below to evaluate the written expression of each child. According to your evaluation, what instructional recommendations seem appropriate?

Most teachers develop norms of expectation based on the child's experiential background, his language control at the beginning of the school year, and an estimate of his language potential. Because information available early in the year is limited, the teacher's estimates will be highly subjective. Only through continued encounter with the child in a wide range of language situations will her judgment be substantiated. The following checklist has been designed to relate the discussion in this chapter to evaluating language control.[17]

Teacher's record of oral and written language inventory

I. QUALITY OF EXPRESSION

When the child speaks or writes, what quality of ideas does he express?
Low   1   2   3   4   5   High

Is his topic *original* or stereotypic? Is his expression *imaginative* or dull? Does the child's language show a *sense of description,* or is his expression bland and factual? Does the child emotionally *involve* himself with the characters he is describing, or is he detached? Does his expression reflect a *curiosity* about the topic, or is the information stated without interest? Does the child use *relevant information,* or does he include much unnecessary or irrelevant material?

	Weak	Average	Strong
A. Originality	⎯⎯	⎯⎯	⎯⎯
B. Imagination	⎯⎯	⎯⎯	⎯⎯
C. Description	⎯⎯	⎯⎯	⎯⎯
D. Involvement	⎯⎯	⎯⎯	⎯⎯
E. Curiosity	⎯⎯	⎯⎯	⎯⎯
F. Relevant Info.	⎯⎯	⎯⎯	⎯⎯

II. ORGANIZATION OF EXPRESSION

When the child speaks or writes, does he express himself in a logical, organized manner?   Low   1   2   3   4   5   High

Does he properly *introduce* the topic, or does he just begin at any random place? Are his ideas *developed* and expanded, or does he jump from the beginning to the end without development? Is his communication satisfactorily *concluded,* or does it end abruptly? Does he organize his events in a logical, *sequential* order, or are the happenings mixed and disordered? Are the main ideas and minor details *related* together into a whole, or are they disconnected? Does he unite the parts of his story with *transitional phrases,* or does he isolate the major parts from each other? Does he show *sensitivity* to his audience (a listener or reader) by controlling his language so the audience understands what he is saying, or is he usually unconcerned or

unaware?

Encounter to		Weak	Average	Strong
Expression:	A. Introduction	_____	_____	_____
Language as	B. Development	_____	_____	_____
Experience	C. Conclusion	_____	_____	_____
	D. Sequencing	_____	_____	_____
	E. Relationships	_____	_____	_____
	F. Transitions	_____	_____	_____
	G. Audience	_____	_____	_____

III. QUALITY AND CONTROL OF LANGUAGE

Low 1 2 3 4 5 High

A. *Vocabulary.* When the child speaks or writes does he exhibit a large and varied *range of vocabulary,* or is his stock of words limited and narrow? Does he use vocabulary with *effective precision*—putting the right word in the right place—or does he use common, overused words that only approximate his meaning? Does his language reveal a *knowledge of concepts,* or does he appear to have a lack of experiences and concepts?

	Weak	Average	Strong
Range of vocabulary	_____	_____	_____
Effective precision	_____	_____	_____
Knowledge of concepts	_____	_____	_____

B. *Sentence Development.* Does the child use a *variety of sentence types* (declarative, interrogative, etc.) when he speaks or writes, or does he use mainly one type? Does he use a *range of the basic sentence patterns* (noun, verb: "Randolph ate"; noun, verb, object: "Tom hit the boy"), or does he restrict himself to one or two patterns? Does he arrange the words *within* a sentence in *many* interesting ways ("one day the dog found a bone"; "the dog found a bone one day"; "finding a bone one day the dog . . ."), or does he limit his ordering?

	Weak	Average	Strong
Variety of sentence types	_____	_____	_____
Range of sentence patterns	_____	_____	_____
Diversification of *inner* sentence style	_____	_____	_____

IV. FLUENCY OF LANGUAGE
Low 1 2 3 4 5 High

With regard to the *quantity* of language, does the child fail to express his thoughts because he says or writes too little, or does he possess a flexibility

of quantity—an ability to adjust the amount of language to be *appropriate*
to his purpose—or is he verbose—overtalking most of the time?

	Weak	Average	Strong
A. Quantity	_____	_____	_____
B. Appropriateness	_____	_____	_____

V. PERSONAL RESPONSE TO LANGUAGE

Low 1 2 3 4 5 High

Does the child find *pleasure* and enjoyment in speaking and writing, or does
he *dislike* speaking or writing?

	Weak	Average	Strong
Pleasure	_____	_____	_____

VI. TECHNICAL SKILLS IN ORAL EXPRESSION

Low 1 2 3 4 5 High

	Weak	Average	Strong
A. Articulation Does the child speak distinctly, or is he difficult to understand?	_____	_____	_____
B. Volume Is the child's volume appropriate for his purpose, or does he speak too softly or too loudly?	_____	_____	_____
C. Mazes (many) Is the child's speech fluent or is it filled with mazes? (In "The dog *w-w-wanted to get wanted to* wanted to see his master," the italic part is called a *maze*, a confusing tangle of words.)	_____	_____	_____
D. Inflection Does the child use inflection in speech to further the meaning and quality of his expression, or does he fail to adjust tone, pauses, pitch, and stress?	_____	_____	_____
E. Style Switch Can the child change or switch from one style of speaking or writing to another—from formal to informal to colloquial, or from nonstandard to standard English?	_____	_____	_____

205

VII. TECHNICAL SKILLS IN WRITTEN EXPRESSION

Low 1 2 3 4 5 High

	Weak	Average	Strong
A. Spelling Does the child spell words in the traditional (correct) way? Does he spell words "phonetically" but not the same as traditional orthography? Does he spell words not as they sound and not in the traditional manner?	___	___	___
B. Punctuation Does the child know and use accepted punctuation in his writing, or is his writing mainly without capitalization and punctuation?	___	___	___
C. Usage Does the child employ the standard usage, or does he vary from this ("he don't"; "I ain't got no money"; "them girls are hitting me"; "I seen him take the pencil")?	___	___	___
D. Style Switch Can the child change or switch from one style of writing to another—from formal to informal to colloquial, or from nonstandard to standard English?	___	___	___
E. Handwriting Is the child's handwriting legible or illegible?	___	___	___

Summary of classroom oral or written inventory: child's record

Name of Child _____ Date _____

Grade _____ Teacher _____

I. QUALITY OF EXPRESSION

General Score: Low 1 2 3 4 5 High

Specific Skills	Weak	Average	Strong
A. Originality	___	___	___
B. Imagination	___	___	___

IV. Fluency of Language

   C. Description   _____   _____   _____
   D. Involvement   _____   _____   _____
   E. Curiosity   _____   _____   _____
   F. Relevant Information   _____   _____   _____
   Comments

II. ORGANIZATION OF EXPRESSION

General Score: Low   1   2   3   4   5   High

Specific Skills	Weak	Average	Strong
A. Introduction	_____	_____	_____
B. Development	_____	_____	_____
C. Conclusion	_____	_____	_____
D. Sequencing	_____	_____	_____
E. Relationship	_____	_____	_____
F. Transitions	_____	_____	_____
G. Audience	_____	_____	_____

Comments

III. QUALITY AND CONTROL OF LANGUAGE

General Score: Low   1   2   3   4   5   High

Specific Skills	Weak	Average	Strong
A. Vocabulary			
Range	_____	_____	_____
Effective use	_____	_____	_____
Knowledge of concepts	_____	_____	_____
B. Sentence Development			
Variety of sentence types	_____	_____	_____
Range of sentence patterns	_____	_____	_____
Diversification of *inner* sentence style	_____	_____	_____

Comments

IV. FLUENCY OF LANGUAGE

General Score: Low   1   2   3   4   5   High

Specific Skills	Weak	Average	Strong
A. Quantity	_____	_____	_____
B. Appropriateness	_____	_____	_____

Comments

V. PERSONAL RESPONSE TO LANGUAGE

General Score: Low 1 2 3 4 5 High

Specific Skills	*Weak*	*Average*	*Strong*
A. Pleasure	___	___	___

Comments

VI. TECHNICAL SKILLS IN ORAL EXPRESSION

General Score: Low 1 2 3 4 5 High

Specific Skills	*Weak*	*Average*	*Strong*
A. Articulation	___	___	___
B. Volume	___	___	___
C. Mazes	___	___	___
D. Inflection	___	___	___
E. Style Switch	___	___	___

Comments

VII. TECHNICAL SKILLS IN WRITTEN EXPRESSION

General Score: Low 1 2 3 4 5 High

Specific Skills	*Weak*	*Average*	*Strong*
A. Spelling	___	___	___
B. Punctuation	___	___	___
C. Usage	___	___	___
D. Style Switch	___	___	___
E. Handwriting	___	___	___

Comments

This checklist will help you to observe each child's progress and to adjust and develop the language curriculum.

Footnotes

[1]Aaron Bar-Adon and Werner F. Leopold, *Child Language: A Book of Readings* (Englewood Cliffs, N.J.: Prentice-Hall, Inc., 1971). *Cognition and the Development of Language,* ed. John R. Hayes (New York: John Wiley & Sons, Inc., 1970). James Moffett, *Teaching the Universe of*

208

Discourse (Boston: Houghton Mifflin Company, 1968). Robert B. Ruddell and Arthur C. Williams, *A Research Investigation of a Literacy Teaching Model: Project DELTA,* U.S. Department of Health, Education, and Welfare, Office of Education, EDPA Project No. 005262 (1972).

[2]Paul S. Anderson, *Language Skills in Elementary Education* (New York: The Macmillan Company, 1972). Paul C. Burns, Betty L. Broman, and Alberta L. Lowe, *The Language Arts in Childhood Education* (Chicago: Rand McNally & Co., 1971). Harry A. Greene and Walter T. Petty, *Developing Language Skills in the Elementary Schools* (Boston: Allyn & Bacon, Inc., 1971). *Creative Experiences in Oral Language,* ed. Mabel Wright Henry (Champaign, Ill.: National Council of Teachers of English, 1967). Ruth G. Strickland, *The Language Arts in the Elementary School* (Lexington, Mass.: D. C. Heath & Company, 1969).

[3]Beverly Cleary, *Runaway Ralph* (New York: William Morrow & Co., Inc., 1970).

[4]Roald Dahl, *Charlie and the Chocolate Factory* (New York: Alfred A. Knopf, Inc., 1964).

[5]May Hill Arbuthnot, *Time for Poetry* (Glenview, Ill.: Scott, Foresman and Company, 1961). By permission of Lillian G. Stevens.

[6]From the book *The Rocking Horse* by Christopher Morley. Copyright 1919, renewal 1947 by Christopher Morley. Reprinted by permission of J. B. Lippincott Company.

[7]© Hallmark Cards, Inc. Reprinted by permission of Hokuseido Press, Tokyo, and Hallmark Cards, Inc.

[8]Originally published by the University of California Press; reprinted by permission of The Regents of the University of California.

[9]© Hallmark Cards, Inc. Reprinted by permission of Hokuseido Press, Tokyo, and Hallmark Cards, Inc.

[10]Reprinted by permission of Hokuseido Press, Tokyo.

[11]L. Frank Baum, *The Wizard of Oz* (London: J. M. Dent & Sons, Ltd., 1965), p. 61. Italics added.

[12]From *Charlie the Tramp* by Russell Hoban. Copyright © 1969 by Russell Hoban. Reprinted by permission of Four Winds Press.

[13]Alvina Treut Burrows, Doris C. Jackson, and Dorothy O. Saunders, *They All Want to Write* (New York: Holt, Rinehart and Winston, Inc., 1964). Ruth Kearney Carlson, *Writing Aids Through the Grades* (New York: Columbia University Press, 1970). Edward B. Jenkinson and Donald A. Seybold, *Writing as a Process of Discovery* (Bloomington, Ind.: Indiana University Press, 1970). Grace E. Wilson, *Composition Situations* (Champaign, Ill.: National Council of Teachers of English, 1966).

[14]Hans Christian Andersen, *The Emperor's New Clothes* (New York: Scholastic Book Services, 1968). Pictures by Virginia Lee Burton.

[15]E. B. White, *Charlotte's Web* (New York: Harper & Row, Publishers, 1952).

[16]Esphyr Slobodkina, *Caps for Sale* (New York: Scholastic Book Services, 1968).

[17]Ruddell and Williams, *A Research Investigation of a Literacy Teaching Model: Project DELTA.*

Additional References

CARLSON, RUTH KEARNEY, *Sparkling Words: Two Hundred Practical and Creative Writing Ideas* (Berkeley, Calif.: Wagner Printing Company, 1968).

EARLY, MARGARET, ed., *Language Face to Face* (Syracuse, N.Y.: Syracuse University Press, 1971).

FRAZIER, ALEXANDER, ed., *New Directions in Elementary English* (Champaign, Ill.: National Council of Teachers of English, 1967).

HAYES, JOHN R., ed., *Cognition and the Development of Language* (New York: John Wiley & Sons, Inc., 1970.)

HEILMAN, ARTHUR W., and ELIZABETH ANN HOLMES, *Smuggling Language into the Teaching of Reading* (Columbus, Ohio: Charles E. Merrill Publishing Co., 1972).

INDIANAPOLIS PUBLIC SCHOOLS, *The Oral-Aural-Visual Program for Teaching Language Arts: DAV Concepts Guide* (Indianapolis, Ind., 1967).

KINDER, ROBERT FARRAR, *Guidelines for Building English Language Arts Curriculums, K–12* (Hartford, Conn.: State Department of Education, 1969).

LAMB, POSE, *Linguistics in Proper Perspective* (Columbus, Ohio: Charles E. Merrill Publishing Co., 1967).

LEE, DORRIS M., and R. V. ALLEN, *Learning to Read Through Experience* (New York: Appleton-Century-Crofts, 1963).

McCULLOUGH, CONSTANCE M., *Handbook for Teaching the Language Arts* (San Francisco: Chandler Publishing Co., 1969).

MOFFETT, JAMES, *A Student-Centered Language Arts Curriculum, Grades K–6: A Handbook for Teachers* (Boston: Houghton Mifflin Company, 1968).

PETTY, WALTER T., and MARY E. BOWEN, *Slithery Snakes and Other Aids to Children's Writing* (New York: Appleton-Century-Crofts, 1967).

POSSIEN, WILMA M., *They All Need to Talk* (New York: Appleton-Century-Crofts, 1969).

PORTLAND PUBLIC SCHOOLS, *Language Arts Guide, K–8* (Portland, Ore., 1970).

SMITH, E. BROOKS, KENNETH S. GOODMAN, and ROBERT MERIDITH, *Language and Thinking in the Elementary School* (New York: Holt, Rinehart and Winston, Inc., 1970).

STAUFFER, RUSSELL G., *The Language-Experience Approach to the Teaching of Reading* (New. York: Harper & Row, Publishers, 1970).

TIEDT, IRIS M., and SIDNEY W. TIEDT, eds., *Readings on Contemporary English in the Elementary School* (Englewood Cliffs, N.J.: Prentice-Hall, Inc., 1967).

7

Observation to Exposition: Increasing Language Control

Focusing Questions

1. What features of language are critical to the development of expository ability? How are they similar to the features needed for description and narration? How do they differ?
2. How can the development of exposition be related to the content areas of the curriculum? What instructional experiences can provide for this?
3. How can expository instruction be used to develop reading-listening comprehension abilities?
4. How can expository expression be evaluated? What evaluative aspects are similar to those for description and narration? What expository features require special evaluative attention?

Exposition is one of the most common forms of discourse required of the student and the adult. The word *exposition* literally means to expose or explain a subject. Exposition explains through facts or ideas; it leads the listener or reader to understand the nature or use of a specific concept or idea.

In the elementary grades instruction about exposition is based mostly on direct observational experiences, but in upper grades it is also based on vicarious experiences such as books and film.[1] Specific areas of emphasis are explaining new information and events by means of comparative descriptions, establishing causal relationships, and developing logical organization. We have already considered several aspects of these in the previous chapter, but as is to be expected, there is overlap.

The child's success with expository expression is directly related to his control of the following areas of the communication framework (Chapter 2): lexical meaning, relational meaning, and interpretation and problem solving. These areas contribute to the task of exposition in the following

ways:

Lexical meaning (the child's vocabulary store) provides labels essential to re-creating personal observations.

Relational meaning (knowledge of the structural components that underlie our system of language) involves sentence organization and subordinating elements to provide clear descriptions and explanations.

Interpretation and problem-solving components essential to exposition include: the ability to sequence and identify relationships; the analytical and integrative abilities to organize facts, events, and ideas, and to provide illustrations and develop causal relations; the evaluation ability for making judgments; and the problem-solving ability that provides for information gathering, synthesis, and hypothesis building and testing.

Exposition differs from description and narration in the level of abstractions the child uses to assimilate, integrate, organize, and convey his understanding of facts, events, and ideas to others.[2]

We shall use a developmental instructional sequence similar to the one we used for description and narration as the guideline for discussing exposition. This sequence, which moves from observational experiences and expression to detailed organized explanation, includes the following instructional dimensions:

1. Observational experiences and expression through art forms and oral language
2. Sharing observations with small groups through demonstration and discussion
3. Organizing explanation for group writing experiences recorded by the teacher
4. Individual records of explanation
5. Extending and organizing explanation through
   Ordering ideas, collecting data, and using illustrations and examples
   Using facts, events, and ideas to make comparisons that establish relationships and lead to generalizations
   Developing objectivity, inferring beyond data, drawing conclusions, and predicting outcomes

We shall develop these steps for teaching exposition by using a variety of practical suggestions for classroom implementation.

OBSERVATIONAL EXPERIENCES AND EXPRESSION THROUGH ART FORMS AND ORAL LANGUAGE

The child's firsthand experiences provide a rich contextual resource for recording and explaining. These experiences range from the familiar, such as walking to and from school or watching mother mend or make a dress

212

How can discussions with community workers stimulate children's observational power and expressive ability? *(Photo by Mimi Forsyth, Monkmeyer Press Photo*

Service)

to the unusual, such as a carefully planned field trip or a science experiment. An effective way to involve the child in recording and explaining his experiences is through the medium of art and through oral language. A child's simple crayon drawing or tempera painting that reflects his observations will greatly facilitate his understanding and explanation of how a fish swims, or of the miraculous metamorphosis of a butterfly. Combining art with verbal explanation is a valuable way to develop exposition at all elementary grade levels.

To help the child sharpen his observation of specific experiences the following questions will be of value: What does it look like? Is it similar to anything that I know? What does it do? How does it work? How did it come to be this way? What is its use and importance? How can I explain or re-create this experience for others?

Opportunities to record and explain through art and oral language are unlimited in the elementary curriculum. Some of the ways this approach may be used are:

Explaining the duties of a student patrol
Explaining how cookies are made based on observations of mother's baking
Studying and explaining the rain cycle
Recording and explaining pints and quarts, after witnessing a mathematics demonstration on liquid measure
Recording and explaining the geographical characteristics of the United States and Canada

The following specific ideas on reporting observational experiences and expression indicate the value of art forms and oral language in the classroom.

AFTER A FIELD TRIP

Following a field trip (to a dairy, grocery store, zoo) pass out art paper and have each child draw one object or animal that interested him on the trip. While the work is in progress, circulate and encourage each child to re-live or explain to you what he is drawing, what it does, how it came to be this way, and how it is important to us. A primary youngster gave this explanation based on his art form of the walk-in refrigerator in the meat department of a supermarket:

This is the walk-in refrigerator at Varsity Market. They had big chunks of meat hanging down from big hooks. The cold room keeps the meat fresh. When the butcher needs to sell more meat he takes the meat down and cuts it up.

214   After a trip to a dairy a primary youngster made the following explanation:

This is Bossie and she's the mother cow. Her calf's name is Daisy. Bossie is a Jersey cow and gives lots of milk. Then it's pumped into clean pipes and put into bottles. Milk is good for people.

HOW A SEED GROWS

Encourage your children to participate in a science unit on seeds on an individual basis. Have them bring in clean plastic tumblers or jars and a small number of dried beans, such as pinto, navy, and lima. Supply small blotters for the tumblers and jars.

Place the seeds between the blotters and the outside surfaces of the container and then add a small amount of water. Have the children care for and observe their projects each day. Supply each child with a large piece of art paper on which to keep a record of the seed development and growth in art form. These papers may be folded and numbered to note the growth sequence as follows:

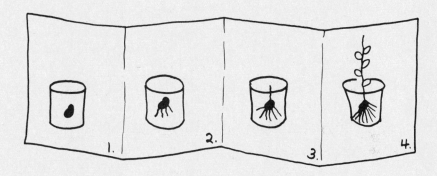

Since the seeds develop at different rates, encourage each child to explain his observations, referring to his art record as he converses with you.

MAKING CEMENT

In order for a child at the intermediate level to write an individual report, he often needs to begin by organizing and developing his thinking about the subject he has chosen to write about. An effective way for the child to think his subject through is to build or draw the object or the process in question and then discuss it with the teacher on an individual basis. This also gives the teacher an opportunity to determine his level of language maturity. The teacher may find it necessary to help him read a difficult passage in a resource book, order relevant facts, or understand the vocabulary applicable to the project or topic.

After researching the process of making Portland cement a child developed the following diagram:

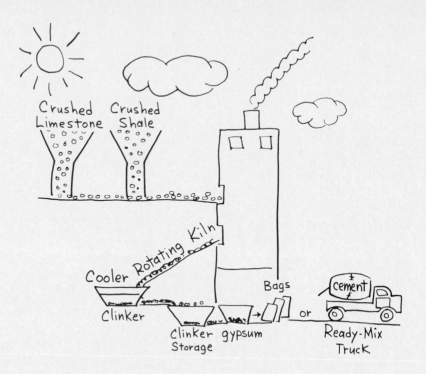

The student then used the diagram to explain the process to his teacher in this fashion:

> Crushed limestone and shale, which is hardened clay, are mixed together, and it's sent through several mills, kilns, and coolers. The main step is heating the rock in a rotating kiln and cooling it. This mixture is now called clinker. Clinker looks like small, hard, glass-like balls. Then it's ground into a fine powder and mixed with a small amount of gypsum. Mixing gypsum with the clinker helps control the rate of hardening. Finally, the Portland cement is put into heavy paper bags or mixed with water and sent out in ready-mix cement trucks. When the cement is poured and it becomes hard, it is called concrete.

Once the teacher feels the explanation is satisfactory, he can encourage the child to use his visual aid and present the oral explanation to a small group or the class.

SHARING OBSERVATIONS WITH SMALL GROUPS THROUGH DEMONSTRATION AND DISCUSSION

A natural progression for exposition is from art forms and oral language to sharing observations with a small group of peers. This sharing can be either extemporaneous or prepared and rehearsed, depending on the

Sharing
Observations with
Small Groups
Through
Demonstration and
Discussion

maturity of the child and the complexity of the subject or idea. Topics for sharing range from simple explanations, such as, for a new student, the physical lay-out of the school, to more theoretical material, such as the contributions of a specific ethnic group to the growth and culture of the United States.

Group expository experiences place different demands on the student than does individualized child-teacher sharing through art form and oral language. Sentence clarity and a precise vocabulary are important for clear explanations. The child must also structure or order his ideas and material in a logical sequence.

To support his explanation the child should establish and develop the relationships among specific details. Visual aids will serve an important role in this effort. In explanations of simple materials he can use art forms such as drawings or paintings, but for subjects with a higher degree of abstraction, he may require more sophisticated aids such as detailed mod-

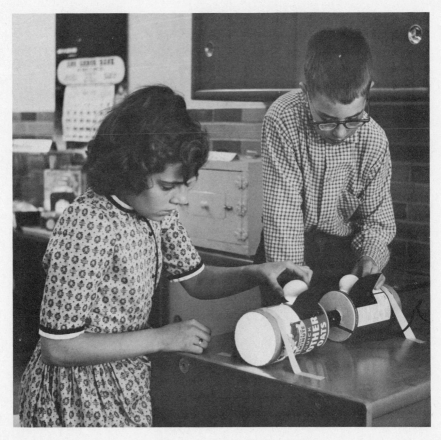

Of what value are visual aids in the development of language control? *(Photo by Hays, Monkmeyer Press Photo Service)*

els, diagrams on the chalkboard, transparencies projected with an overhead projector, photographs, books, tape recordings, or even films.

Presentations or demonstrations will come easily for some children, but for others they will be more difficult. The teacher may need to help with the organization of materials or ideas. Opportunity should be provided afterward for listeners to ask questions. Such discussion can often help the child reorganize his ideas, reinforce his understanding, and summarize his exposition. Questions and comments should be constructive and related to the explanation in such a way as to improve or clarify the exposition. Such group interaction may lead other children to contribute additional information. Such discussion is best carried out under teacher direction, to ensure objectivity and to develop concepts related to the topic so as to extend understandings.

The teacher should provide a display table and bulletin board space in the classroom where the child can place visual aids or other prepared materials for further inspection or perusal by the class.

Specific activities for developing exposition through small group sharing include the following.

HELPING NEW ARRIVALS KNOW THE SCHOOL

There is always a need, especially at the beginning of the school year, to acquaint new children with the school's physical lay-out. Student hosts and hostesses can provide valuable assistance in this respect.

Suggest that children who wish to help in this way draw a very simple map of the school on a large piece of poster paper or tagboard. This art project involves simple but important map skills. Then direct the children to develop a clear explanation of the map, and then to lead a small group of new arrivals through the school. Consider using a similar experience to orient new students who enter the school during the year.

This art and language activity can be particularly helpful in developing children's self-concept through the direct application of exposition in the familiar school setting.

A child's map of the school may look like the one on page 219.

DINOSAURS GALORE

Young children, particularly boys, are especially fond of small plastic models, like the dinosaurs often found in cereal boxes or for sale in variety stores. These models are a good place to begin an oral exposition on dinosaurs.

Help the children make a diorama setting for their collections. They will need small cardboard boxes, about the size of a shoe box, whose open side will face the viewer. They may also need poster paint or water colors for painting the backdrop, plastic or real greenery for "large" trees, small stones and pebbles, and small branches and twigs.

Make available a generous number of easy-to-read books on dinosaurs, and encourage the children to construct their diorama based on their reading about dinosaurs with the other youngsters. They may need special help with the pronunciation of dinosaur names. Some sample oral explanations are:

Dinosaurs lived 200 million years ago, during the Age of Reptiles.

This is David's Brontosaurus. He was sixty to seventy feet long. His head was very small. He lived in the swamps and ate plants.

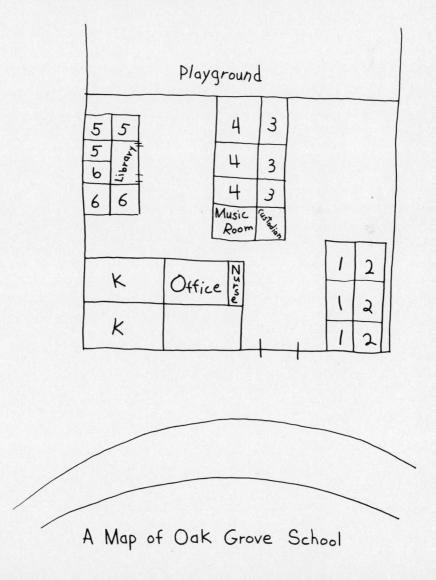

A Map of Oak Grove School

Tyrannosaurus Rex was the king of the meat eaters. His jaws and teeth were huge, but his front legs were small.

Here is Triceratops. He had three horns, which he used when fighting. He was the most fierce of the plant eaters.

A ROCK HOUND

Often a boy or girl returns from a family camping or vacation trip with numerous materials that can serve as motivation for an interesting and informative oral exposition. For example, the child who has collected colorful rocks or seashells on his trip should be given an opportunity to display his collection and to explain where and how he found them. He may also wish to label them.

A marvelous opportunity exists at the intermediate level for the child to focus his interest and knowledge so as to develop a specific, detailed understanding and exposition about just one rock or shell. Help the child find books and other resource materials containing detailed information about this rock. Once he has collected enough data, help him organize his presentation for the class. Suggest that his explanation answer the following questions: What is it? What does it look like? Where is it found? How was it formed? How old is it? What are its uses?

One such "rock hound" report on obsidian was as follows:

> This shiny, glassy black rock I am holding is obsidian. It is a natural glass, but it's stronger than window glass. As you can see, it has brownish-red and black streaks in it. Sometimes it is grayish and may have brighter color streaks of green, silver, or purple in it. The streaks are the lava that has started to crystallize into a fine-grained rock.
>
> Obsidian is an igneous rock, which means that it was formed many thousands of years ago in the United States when volcanoes were active. As the lava spilled out on the ground and hardened, obsidian and other rock were formed.
>
> The western United States volcanic belt, which extends down into Mexico, is where obsidian was formed and can now be found. I found this sample near Globe, Arizona. (Child pointed to map and indicated with a sweep of his hand the western region of the U.S. and the general location of Globe, Arizona.)
>
> When obsidian is compared to other rocks and minerals it is not considered very old.
>
> The American Indians and the Aztecs and Mayans of Mexico found obsidian valuable. They used the stone to make tools and decorative objects like jewelry. (A few samples of obsidian were passed around. Questions were asked and answered by our rock "authority.")

A FOLLOW-UP EXPERIENCE

The teacher encouraged the child who had been working on the art form
220 and oral language explanation of making cement to present his digested

material and data to a small group of the class. She used his original diagram to help him organize his presentation, and she helped him develop other visual aids to enhance the presentation. Together they developed the following sequence for the group presentation:

MAKING AND USING CEMENT

1. Introduction. Tell about how I became interested in cement when our patio was poured. (Show photo of patio and a piece of cement.)
2. Uses of Cement. (Show magazine pictures of buildings, bridges, streets, driveways, patios, etc.)
3. Making Cement. (Show pieces of limestone and clay and use the diagram to explain how cement is made.)
4. Closing. Suggest that everyone look for different uses of cement and think about how it's made when they see concrete or a cement truck. (Show toy ready-mix cement truck.)

Following the presentation, the children discussed the widespread use of cement in cities and the need to reserve space for planting trees and shrubs, carefully examined the materials used in presentation, and asked follow-up questions.[3]

ORGANIZING EXPLANATIONS FOR GROUP WRITING EXPERIENCES RECORDED BY THE TEACHER

The teacher can demonstrate the transition from oral to written exposition by recording information provided by the child or by the class discussion. Newsprint or chalkboard space should be available for this purpose. A group of children or the class may wish to dictate reports to the teacher on firsthand experiences based on data for social studies and science projects. An experiment on heat expansion or a field trip to the fire station are two such experiences a class can discuss and review as the teacher records. This type of recording will introduce children to techniques of organization in expository writing. The sequence of steps or events in the experiment or field trip can be represented through topic sentences that re-create the children's experience. These sentences can in turn be the starting point for paragraph development. The teacher can demonstrate how to develop a paragraph with supporting details from one topic sentence, and then have the children develop supporting details for one of the other topic sentences on the chalkboard.

In the upper elementary grades many of the expository writing experiences will of course be derived from content areas such as the social studies and science curricula. Here it is important for the teacher to engage the children in a discussion of the sequence of events and the logic of exposition. This can be illustrated by examining procedures in experiments or the succession of events in social science articles. Children soon learn that simple outlining can be very helpful preparation for individual written reports.

OUR TERRARIUM

After completing the planting of a terrarium, a third grade class dictated the following information about their experience to the teacher:

We planted a spiny wood fern, a maidenhair fern, a strawberry plant, and grape ivy in our terrarium.

The soil in the terrarium is very loose, soft, and moist.

A terrarium is like a little glass house. We have plants and rocks in it.

Eddie is going to bring a salamander to live in the terrarium. Mrs. Cutter asked some boys to bring earthworms to keep the soil loose.

The children discussed the sequence of sentences in this dictation and ordered them into paragraphs. The completed story was then rewritten on the chalkboard and recorded by the children on their paper. The children took final stories and drawings home to share with parents. The completed story looked like this:

Our Terrarium

A terrarium is like a little glass house. We have plants and rocks in it.

The soil in the terrarium is very loose, soft, and moist. We planted a spiny wood fern, a maidenhair fern, a strawberry plant, and grape ivy in our terrarium.

Mrs. Cutter asked some boys to bring earthworms to keep the soil loose. Eddie is going to bring a salamander to live in the terrarium.

OUR SOLAR SYSTEM

The study of the solar system in the intermediate grades provides an excellent opportunity for the development of cooperative group exposition. After the children have been exposed to and are thoroughly familiar with information about the sun and the planets through science resource books, films, and group discussions, ask them to give pertinent information about the sun and the planets and record this information on the chalkboard as it is provided. (Work on only a few members of the solar system at each dictating session.) Once you have several key sentences, ask a child to read the exposition. Following group discussion and revision, record the final version on a ditto master for duplication and distribution to the class.

In one class the children dictated the following facts about the sun:

The Sun

The sun keeps the earth from being cold, dark, and lifeless.

The sun is a star and is enormous. It is as big as a million earths.

The sun is very hot. No one could get near it.

222

There are many explosions on the sun. These look like spots and are called Sunspots.

The sun is 93 million miles from earth.

The teacher recorded the following exposition on another day:

Neptune and Uranus

Uranus was not discovered until 1781. It was named for the god of the heavens. People with very good eyesight can sometimes see Uranus without a telescope.

Uranus is the seventh planet from the sun. It is very cold on Uranus.

Neptune was discovered in 1884. It was named for the god of the sea. No one can see Neptune without a telescope.

Neptune is the eighth planet from the sun. The temperature on Neptune is very, very cold.

Have the children start with the sun and sequence the duplicated expositions in order of the planets in the solar system. Staple or bind the discussions in a construction paper cover to make reference books. Let those who wish illustrate their covers with their conceptions of our solar system.

INDIVIDUAL RECORDS OF EXPLANATION

The child's first attempt at written exposition may begin with a record of simple facts about the weather for a weather chart. Or it may be helping to prepare captions for bulletin board displays of skill or content areas such as reading, spelling, social studies, science, or health. From these he may be involved in joint ventures with the teacher to ease the transition from a group-dictated to an independent expository effort. For example, the teacher can start a list of events after a class experiment or visitation and then have the child complete the list independently.

To increase independence in written exposition at the primary level, use activities such as recording a list of the materials used in a science experiment, writing a concluding sentence about the findings of a science experiment, or explaining the need for certain foods in our diet. As teacher you must design many and varied writing experiences to provide ample opportunity for beginners to learn to recognize and include information vital to their exposition. The child must also learn how to plan and organize information in order to develop his exposition in clear fashion.

Because the child at the intermediate grade level has increased his control of reading and writing skills, many incorrectly assume that he is able to prepare an expository report on an assigned topic with little or no assistance from the teacher. Often the unfortunate result is that the child copies directly from a social studies or science text without understanding the content or developing an ability to explain the topic in his own language.

At the intermediate grade level, the teacher must continue to encourage the child to produce exposition related to content areas, and to reinforce and expand the expository skills learned in the earlier grades in both oral and written form. These expository skills, which overlap with the skills of description and narration, include such key elements as finding and describing facts supportive to the main thesis, time sequence, sentence-meaning clarity, paragraph development, and outlining.

For more advanced exposition the child must become aware of his potential audience, must view and present the facts and problems of his thesis with objectivity, and must explain his ideas in detail by utilizing comparison and establishing relationships through illustrations and examples that lead to and permit generalization.

How can the development of expository writing be enhanced through demonstrations such as this? *(Photo by Shackman, Monkmeyer Press Photo Service)*

These elements are basic to expository composition. They can be soundly promoted through various functional writing activities including letters, announcements, class books, individual books, illustrated displays, reports for science and social studies, review and criticism of children's books, explaining solutions in math, and describing processes in physical education, health, or science. The child who produces writing that is genuinely his own thereby enhances his self-concept and feeling of language control, and does so through experiences that are rewarding for both student and teacher. The following activities can help to develop the child's ability to write exposition.

USING AN OUTLINE

The brief outline that the child and the teacher developed for the oral report "Making and Using Cement" (see the section entitled "Sharing Observations with Small Groups Through Demonstration and Discussion") helped serve as a guideline in developing his written exposition. After the oral report some changes were effected (descriptions were extended and expanded and details explaining the process of cement-making were added), but the essential outline was retained. The report was enclosed in a gray construction paper booklet, which the youngster decorated by pasting a magazine picture collage of concrete structures and projects. Included in the report was a carefully drawn diagram of the cement process and other illustrative materials such as magazine pictures of cement trucks and a photograph of the child's newly poured backyard patio.

The following is the child's written exposition.

Making and Using Cement

Have you ever wondered how important cement is to you and me? Cement is a material used in the construction of buildings, highways, streets, driveways, bridges, and many other things. My backyard cement patio was just poured three weeks ago.

There are many steps in making cement. The main steps are mixing and grinding crushed limestone and clay to a very fine powder. This fine powder is then burned in a gigantic rotating kiln at a temperature of 2400° to 2800° F. The new material that comes out of the kiln is called clinker. Clinker looks like small, hard, glass-like balls, and it is also ground into a fine powder. Finally, the fine clinker is mixed with a small amount of gypsum to control the rate of hardening. When Portland cement is mixed with water it turns into a hard surface called concrete.

Portland cement is packaged either in heavy paper bags or is taken from the mill to the place where it is used by a rotating-drum cement truck already mixed with water.

Cement is very important to us.

Projects of this nature should be displayed in a special section of the classroom along with materials used in oral presentation (a piece of concrete, pictures showing the uses of concrete, and the like). The teacher should encourage the student to construct a self-assessment chart so he and others can follow his progress from the initial idea to the completion and display of his project.

CREATING TOPIC SENTENCES

Topic sentences contain key information. In some expository paragraphs topic sentences are brief overviews designed to arouse reader interest. The language activity below contains three paragraphs whose topic sentences have been omitted. Have the children read each paragraph carefully and create a topic sentence for it.

(Topic sentence: *"There are many kinds of postage stamps,"* or *"Postage stamps have an important story to tell."*) They are like a picture gallery in the history of our country. Some postage stamps have pictures of our important leaders. Other stamps show pictures of important places. Still others show important happenings like the Pony Express.

(_____).

A rural postman delivers mail by car. He is like a Post Office on wheels. When he sees a red flag up on a rural mailbox, he stops to pick up mail and packages. People who live in the country depend on the rural mailman.

(_____).

Man has learned to adjust to the forces of nature, or weather. He has learned to clothe his body. Man has built homes for protection. Man has built dams to control floods and irrigation canals to bring water to arid lands. Man has developed methods of weather forecasting, but he has not been able to control it.

After everyone has written topic sentences, discuss the appropriateness of each. Encourage the children to observe the type of information and the ways it relates to the content of the paragraph.

PLANNING A PARTY

There is a continual need to create opportunities for efforts in practical writing that requires organized outlining. One such activity can be related to various local, state, national, and religious holidays and the planning of classroom parties. Have the children meet in small groups to discuss the nature of the holiday. Then plan festive activities in relation to the holiday. (It may save time to organize the groups so that each develops one facet of the party, such as food, entertainment, decorations, serving, and clean-up.)

Suggest that each committee elect one member to act as secretary. Provide the "secretary" with sufficient paper for the committee's list of suggestions. After the suggestions have been recorded, have another member of the group read them aloud to the entire class and then discuss them. The revised suggestions should be organized in outline form on the chalkboard.

For a Halloween party one classroom recorded the final discussion in this fashion:

FOOD: MRS. OTT'S PARENT COMMITTEE

1. Witches Brew (Cherry soda with licorice bits)
2. Trick-or-treat sugar cookies
3. Halloween candy

SERVING

Placemats, napkins, cups—Cindy, Kim, Shirley
Serve food—David, Paul, Eric, Cynthia, Laura, Annie

DECORATIONS

Draw draperies—James
Hang skeletons around the room—Bill
Carve jack-o-lantern and light it—Bob and Hugh
Make cobwebs from string—Amy and Clara

ENTERTAINMENT

Play scary music—Andrew
Play haunted house record—Jo Ann
Play "Boilerburst" game—Alpha
Tell scary stories—Mr. Brownell

CLEAN-UP

1. Throw out placemats—Mary Ann
2. Throw out napkins and cups—LeRoy
3. Wash desks—Darcy
4. Empty waste baskets—John and Alan

THANK YOU

The thank-you letter is an important practical writing activity requiring the ability to reflect on and organize ideas to illustrate specific points of interest and to account for audience awareness. Opportunities for such letters present themselves after field trips, parties, visiting lecturers, visits from other children in the school, or exciting assemblies or musical programs.

In preparation for a thank-you note or letter encourage your children to identify some of the interesting highlights of the visit or program. Place these on the board and discuss each briefly. Do not let spelling be a limiting factor for the children. Spell difficult words on the chalkboard and circulate throughout the classroom jotting down words on pieces of notepaper for the children. Encourage the students to spell phonetically and help correct the words after the letters are written.

The following thank-you letters were written by second graders after a trip to a nearby supermarket. Note the individuality of style that makes them especially interesting.

Dear Mr. Hundley,

It was fun going on the tour inside the meat room, and in the freezer and then coming out. I like the machine that puts a stamp on the beef. I like that machine that crushes the cardboard. I especially like your wonderful store.

Your friend,
Alan

Dear Mister Hundley,

Thank you for showing us around personally. I loved it. And the part I liked best was when I went into that freezer. I nearly froze stiff. Thank you.

Love,
Brian

Dear Mr. Hundley,

Thank you for having us come to Alpha Beta Market. I especially liked the freezer because it's so cold. And on hot days it will cool you off. But there is only one thing wrong, on cold days you freeze to death! I hope you have a nice summer. You will probably spend it in the freezer! Have fun!

Your friend,
Karen

HISTORY AND THE CONTRIBUTIONS OF AMERICAN MINORITY GROUPS

Many intermediate classes study the historical development and contributions of minority groups. Once the children are deeply involved in the subject through reading, talking it through, listening, and illustrating facts, help them decide how they wish to summarize their study. Here, for example, is a brief list of the important milestones and personages in black history:

Black Americans
Harriet Tubman
Frederick Douglass and his Grandmother
George Washington Carver
Booker T. Washington
Why the Civil War Started
The Document Lincoln Made
The March on Washington
Black Americans Today
Malcolm X
Martin Luther King, Jr.
Julian Bond

Let the children dictate their ideas to you and record them on the chalkboard, then have each child write a brief exposition on a topic of interest to him. The following expositions on Harriet Tubman are by fourth graders.

Harriet Tubman

Harriet Tubman was a woman who freed many slaves. She took her family and relatives and even strangers.

She took them to a place called the Underground Railroad. It is not exactly a railroad, it is a group of houses with people called station masters. They take people and hide them in their attic or cellar until sunset. Then the slaves walk to the next station and so on.

Harriet Tubman

Harriet Tubman was born in 1820.

She helped free slaves. She used the Underground Railroad. She prayed and hid the slaves in the stinkiest swamps.

Lincoln made a document: all slaves were free.

The following expositions on black history are from a fourth grade class.

Frederick Douglass and Grandmother

One time when Frederick Douglass was little he talked to his grandmother. "Where is Mother?"

His grandmother said, "She was a slave. She cooked for Captain Aaron."

And one day grandmother was thinking and she took him to the park and she told him to play with the children and he started crying. But his grandmother was gone.

But when he was a man he was Lincoln's friend in the Civil War. He helped Lincoln fight for Black People's rights.

The Document Lincoln Made

Do you know that slavery lasted almost 250 years? But slavery is not allowed now. By December of that year the war ended. On April 1865 Lincoln said all the slaves were free, free at last, free. But slave owners did not pay attention to the Document and many slaves joined the North Army to fight for their rights.

The children may wish to illustrate parts of their written discussions. Duplicate the discussions so that you have several copies of each for the class; collect and bind these into a book entitled *Black Americans.* Add the collection to your classroom reference library and use it to stimulate small-group discussions on the contributions of American minority groups. Such activities should improve your youngsters' understanding of the struggles and contributions of a wide range of minorities in America.

EXTENDING AND ORGANIZING EXPOSITION

The ideas presented to this point have been designed to develop exposition in a sequence proceeding from oral to written forms by developing key expository elements throughout the elementary grades. As the child gains confidence in his ability to present ideas in the expository mode, it will be necessary to extend his ability to understand and perform idea organization and to use information to establish relationships, develop generalizations, draw objective conclusions, and predict outcomes based on available data. The following suggestions, based on the communication framework in Chapter 2, are organized along these lines.

Ordering ideas, collecting data, and using illustrations and examples

In exposition the organization of ideas determines the effectiveness of the communication. The writer has a choice of many arrangements, but he should be aware of several basic patterns so that he can select the organization best suited for his topic.

In a process composition, for example—in which the child needs to explain how a clock works, how paper is made, or how to prepare a wooden surface for painting—the child simply describes the sequence of steps or events that produces the desired understanding or result, but such a description will of course depend upon the writer's knowledge, ability, and experience if it is to be the most efficient and appropriate explanation sequence.

Social science compositions require a different kind of chronological order. An exposition of the history of California, for example, might develop along a sequence from the early California Indians to English and Spanish explorations to the mission period to the Spanish settlers (the rancho life) to the influx of Americans coming for gold to the changes in California occasioned by the stagecoach and the railroad and finally to the modern industrial and agricultural period.

Another pattern for expository development is to group items with similar characteristics. For example, in an expository composition about unusual animals (birds, reptiles, or fish), the creatures may be described and grouped on the basis of their classification in the discussion. In an exposition about well-known figures in black history, personages may be arranged according to their contributions in such fields as education, literature, law, science, agriculture, government, and so forth.

230 If the writer is using exposition to support a particular thesis or viewpoint,

it is important that he employ factual details and illustrations or examples to support the validity of the thesis statement. For example, if the thesis is the danger of drugs, specific facts about tobacco, alcohol, and hard drugs should be cited. For impact, the exposition should also include specific illustrations or accounts of individuals who have experienced physical or psychological harm from the misuse of such drugs.

The following examples further illustrate how idea organization, examples, and illustrations can be used in developing exposition in the classroom.

HOW DO YOU ORDER IDEAS?

For a process composition, one wherein the child explains how something works, have him order ideas or place explanations in proper sequence by jotting down words or phrases on the following blank form. The completed form illustrates its use:

TITLE: HOW THE FIRE DEPARTMENT
REACTS TO A FIRE

1. *(What happened first.)* Fire starts in a dept. store
2. *(What happened next.)* Automatic alarm goes off and someone also phones the fire dept.
3. *(Next.)* Fire dept. receives call and alarm
4. Two engines and two hook-and-ladders are sent out
5. Firemen put out fire and clean up
6. *(Last.)* Cause of fire is investigated

The completed form can be an outline or guideline for the final exposition, with each step a separate paragraph in the final essay.

SHUFFLING THE ORDER: USE YOUR PARTNER

Children may wish to write each paragraph of their expositions on separate sheets of paper, then shuffle and reshuffle them, then identify the sequence that best suits the topic. Papers are then numbered in order, proofread, and rewritten in final form. The same procedure can be used by having pairs of students read and organize each other's exposition and then having each discuss the logic of his organization.

PARAGRAPHING AND SEQUENCING

Use the following practice with any brief selection to help children organize and arrange material sequentially by paragraphs. First, the child reads the selection. Next, he circles the sentences that pertain to subheadings of the topic. Finally, he rewrites the exposition, with the paragraphs arranged in proper sequence.

In the following selection paragraphs about the planets are identified and sequenced on the basis of their distances from the sun.

The Planets

1. Mercury is brown and goes around in its orbit in eighty-eight days. It is very, very close to the sun.
4. Mars is red. It has canals and there may be life on Mars. It also has little green plants on it. Its polar cap gets smaller and bigger as the seasons go by.
5. Jupiter is the biggest planet in the solar system. It has poisonous gases.
6. Saturn is full of poisonous gases like Jupiter. It has colorful rings.
8. Neptune is the same color as Uranus but is smaller than Uranus.
2. Venus is the second planet in the solar system. It is also brown like Mercury.
3. Earth is blue and green. It is close to the sun and it has a shield so the sun's rays won't burn the earth.
7. Uranus is blue and green. Uranus is the seventh planet in the solar system.
9. Pluto is brown. It is bigger than Mercury. It takes about 248 earth years to go around in its orbit.

COLLECTING AND ORGANIZING DATA

An information outline can help children organize information obtained from direct observation, books, or the mass media. Important points to include in the exposition should be determined in class discussion.

The following are two such outlines. The first can be used by children studying the life of an animal or bird. The second is for studying the important facts about a country.

Name of animal: _____

1. Description: _____
   _____
2. Habitat: _____
   _____
3. Food: _____
   _____
4. Home and young: _____
   _____
5. Unusual qualities or features: _____
   _____

Name of Country: _____
Location: _____
Area: _____
Population: _____
Capital: _____
Largest cities: _____
Highest mountain peak: _____

Major rivers: _____

Major lakes:_____

Climate:_____

Flag:_____

Anthem:_____

Form of government:_____

Unit of currency:_____

Language:_____

Religions:_____

Chief crops:_____

Chief industries:_____

Major exports:_____

Major imports:_____

USING ILLUSTRATIONS AND EXAMPLES

One of the most effective ways to support a position or thesis statement is with illustrations and examples. Use this technique with your children by identifying a main idea or thesis statement from class discussion and encouraging them to develop supporting illustrations or examples of one paragraph each.

Getting along with relatives is sometimes difficult.

How not to grow tomatoes.

It takes much work to win a football (baseball) game.

Our classes should be smaller.

Why we need to control water pollution.

American minority groups have contributed much to America.

After each child has had sufficient time to develop his example, group the children on the basis of the statement selected. Have each example read to the group and then have children discuss the illustration and the ways it supports the statement.

Using facts, events, and ideas to make comparisons

Using comparison or contrast is another method of explaining and developing new concepts. Once he has developed new concepts and relationships, a writer may wish to compare them to concepts and relationships that are already familiar to the reader. For example, to explain the function of the human heart, one can note its similarity to a water pump; one can compare the eye to a camera. Other comparisons or contrasts may be those made across points of time: communication by television may be contrasted with radio of the 1920s, or with town criers of the Revolutionary period.

Contrasts and comparisons that explain ideas by reference to the existing knowledge of the child can establish effective relationships and thereby lead to important generalizations related to the topic being developed. The following activities will be of value in extending the child's expository control.

CAN YOU MAKE A COMPARISON?

An important technique for explaining ideas is that of comparison. Exercises such as the following may prove useful in developing an understanding of comparison. Place the words in the left column on the chalkboard and encourage the children to create comparative examples that would be useful in developing an understanding of each object, event, or person. Discuss and contrast the various examples provided.

Fuel oil: (coal, wood)
Bottle opener: (lever, crowbar)
Human heart:_____
Human eye:_____
Launching a space shot:_____
Willie Mays: (any athlete of like skill)
Joe Namath:_____
The Jackson Five: _____
Melting of polar ice cap: (defrosting refrigerator)

CAN YOU FIND AN EXAMPLE OF COMPARISON AND CONTRAST?

The writer who indicates similarities and differences can often clarify ideas for the reader.

A fourth grader's composition on zoo animals demonstrates the use of comparison to show similarities between the lion and the cat.

> Lions come from Africa. They make good zoo animals. The babies are called cubs and can be born in captivity. Lions are like cats. They belong to the cat family. Just like cats, they are meat eaters. Their teeth are very long and sharp for tearing the meat. They also like to hunt mostly at night. Their feet are cushioned and they have sharp claws that can be pulled in when they do not need them. Lions and cats have long whiskers. The lion cubs play just like kittens.

A science exposition about plants and animals illustrates the use of contrast.

> Plants and animals are living things. A few living things, like sponges, act like both animal and plant. You can tell the difference between living things and things that are not living, like rocks, metals, pencils by remembering what living things do.

Living things move. They breathe air and they grow. Plants and animals need food and sunshine. They reproduce their own kind. A rock, a car, or a book doesn't do any of these things.

Encourage your children to locate examples of comparison and contrast in their science or social studies materials. Discuss these examples in small groups, noting how the explanation is aided by contrast and comparison with familiar concepts.

CLEAR SENTENCES

Some carefully organized and fully documented expositions suffer from a lack of clarity, owing to the vague use of "thens," "whens," and "ands." The following exercise is designed to give children the opportunity to examine and rewrite a group of sentences in order to clarify the paragraph.

Duplicate each set of sentences or write them on the chalkboard. First, have a child read the sentences. Next, have the children examine the meaning of the sentences carefully. Discuss with the children which words can be omitted or which phrases condensed to tighten and clarify a group of sentences.

Sentences for revision:

Then the mother hummingbird sits on the eggs. The mother hummingbird lays two tiny white eggs in the nest. And the eggs are very small. And they are about the size of green peas. Then after two weeks the eggs hatch into tiny baby birds.

The sentences may be revised to read like this:

The mother hummingbird lays two tiny white eggs in the nest. The eggs are very small, about the size of green peas. After two weeks the eggs hatch into two tiny baby birds.

Other sentences for revision:

Then the kangaroo rat can jump far and fast with his long hind legs and large feet. And he can hop twenty feet a second. Then the kangaroo rat can change direction in mid-air.

Then some of the water goes back into air. Water comes and goes in a cycle. Then it falls in some form from the clouds. And much of it is used on earth.

After the class has rewritten the first set of sentences, encourage the children to rewrite the other paragraphs individually. Once the sentences have been rewritten, discuss and compare the different answers, highlighting varied and individual revisions that improve meaning and clarity.

Developing objectivity, inferring beyond data, drawing conclusions, predicting outcomes

It is important for the child to understand that in developing his exposition he may need to draw conclusions or predict outcomes beyond his research information. For example, in chronicling scientific experiments in the classroom the child may need to explain cause-and-effect relationships by inferring beyond the data presented. In the study of an Indian culture the child, like the archeologist, will need to use information based on the discovery of artifacts—tools, pottery, glass beads, clothing, food—to infer the nature of the Indian civilization.

To make inferences the child must be as objective as possible. For example, the concept of ecology is today an emotionally charged issue because of the growing sense of need for immediate action to preserve our environment, and it is possible that the child or exposition writer may incorrectly conclude that government agencies, industry, or scientists have made no positive attempts to rectify air pollution, when in fact consumer advocates, legislators, and university and industry researchers have been pressed into service. It would be necessary in such a composition for the child to list those advances in air pollution that have been made in the past few years as well as to identify those factors or contributors that require further correction and control.

Qualities of fair-mindedness that you should encourage are reporting all the facts completely, avoiding vague abstractions, and eliminating biased interpretations and judgment.

WHAT MIGHT HAVE HAPPENED?

This exercise is intended to give children an opportunity to understand that more than one conclusion can be drawn from the same data or observation, depending on the point of view.

Duplicate the example below and encourage your children to write their conclusions from the point of view of one of the persons indicated.

A man, approximately 6'1" in height, about fifty-five years of age, dressed in an expensive oxford gray suit, is found lying face down on the pavement on the corner of Kearny and Montgomery Streets, the financial center of San Francisco.

He does not seem to move. His complexion is pale and he is bleeding from the nose. Scattered about him are various-sized papers that have come from an open luggage-brown attaché case. A dark green hat lies near the attaché case.

Nearby, in front of the window of a travel agency office, stands a tall, aluminum ladder.

A crowd has gathered around the man and the following people give these explanations.

What might have happened from the point of view of

1. The secretary from the eleventh floor of the building
2. The window-washer
3. The paper vendor who stood on the corner diagonally across the street
4. The bus driver
5. The policeman
6. The doctor
7. The wife of the man

After the children have completed their answers, read several aloud and discuss them. The discussion should illustrate that various reasonable conclusions are possible, but the group may conclude that insufficient data were given to reach a valid conclusion. If this happens, encourage the children to formulate questions that would provide the information necessary to determine what happened.

FAMILY HISTORY

As an opportunity to gather and report data objectively, ask each child to investigate and describe the history of a family member. The following discussion is a factual description and background of a fifth grader's father:

> John Lazarus is my father. He is 5'10" tall and weighs 185 pounds. His complexion is dark and his hair is black. My father was born on January 24, 1930, in Fresno, California.
>
> His father, my grandfather, came from Armenia. So did his mother, Sophie. Grandfather was a farmer who raised grapes and cotton. My father did not like farming.
>
> He left Fresno after high school to go to the University of Arizona in Tucson. He graduated in June 1949. Father was expected to learn more about farming, but he became interested in engineering. He learned how roads, bridges, and large buildings are built. So, father became a civil engineer.
>
> In his last year at college he met a girl named Louise Smith. They married after his graduation, and Louise is now my mother. There are three children in my family.
>
> Father works as a civil engineer for the California Department of Highways.

This information may be shared in small groups as the children note similarities and differences in their family backgrounds.

EVALUATING EXPOSITORY EXPRESSION

The evaluation of children's oral and written explanations must take place throughout the school day both in informal and in formal instructional settings.[4] Attention must be given to many of the same elements identified at the conclusion of Chapter 6 in the "Oral and Written Language Inventory." Return to that inventory and carefully examine the discussion related to the following three dimensions: quality of expression, organization of expression, and quality and control of language (vocabulary and sentence development).

Give specific attention to the child's interpretive and problem-solving abilities, to the analytical and integrative abilities that are used to organize and synthesize information. Also give consideration to developmental differences in children's attempts to account for abstract concepts, explanations, and causal relationships in their expositions.

Expository control closely parallels the development of descriptive and narrative expression at early levels but will differ in the upper intermediate grades when more abstract exposition is attempted. The teacher must be constantly alert for opportunities to observe the child's progress and to help develop expository abilities in the content areas as well as in other activities throughout the school day.

Footnotes

[1]Ruth Kearney Carlson, *Writing Aids Through the Grades* (New York: Teachers College, Columbia University Press, 1970). Edward B. Jenkinson and Donald A. Seybold, *Writing as a Process of Discovery* (Bloomington: Indiana University Press, 1970). James Moffett, *A Student-Centered Language Arts Curriculum, Grades K–6: A Handbook for Teachers* (Boston, Mass.: Houghton Mifflin Company, 1968). Grace E. Wilson, *Composition Situations* (Champaign, Ill.: National Council of Teachers of English, 1966).

[2]Moffett, *A Student-Centered Language Arts Curriculum.*

[3]The later section in this chapter entitled "Individual Records of Explanation" contains a description of how the child made a final write-up of this learning and reporting experience.

[4]Paul S. Anderson, *Language Skills in Elementary Education* (New York: The Macmillan Company, 1972). Gertrude A. Boyd, *Teaching Communication Skills in the Elementary School* (New York: Van Nostrand Reinhold Company, 1970). Paul C. Burns, Betty L. Broman, and Alberta L. Lowe, *The Language Arts in Childhood Education* (Chicago: Rand McNally & Co., 1971). Moffett, *A Student-Centered Language Arts Curriculum.*

Additional References

PETTY, WALTER T., and MARY E. BOWEN, *Slithery Snakes and Other Aids to Children's Writing* (New York: Appleton-Century-Crofts, 1967).

TIEDT, IRIS M., and SIDNEY W. TIEDT, *Contemporary English in the Elementary School* (Englewood Cliffs, N.J.: Prentice-Hall, Inc., 1967).

8

Speech Interaction Routines, Writing Conventions, and Handwriting: Classroom Development

Focusing Questions

1. What speech interaction routines and writing conventions are especially important to the elementary school child?
2. How can meaningful social experiences be used to develop these routines and conventions?
3. How is a child's awareness of speech interaction routines and writing conventions related to his home environment?
4. What are the major goals of handwriting instruction? How can these goals be meaningfully effected in classroom instruction?
5. What sequence of instruction should be used in the transition from manuscript to cursive handwriting? What special provision in handwriting instruction is necessary for the left-handed child?

The instructional program must make provision for helping the child become aware of and gain control over language interaction routines that are important to communication in a range of social settings. These routines, common to oral language, vary according to the social setting.[1] Writing conventions, which parallel these oral routines to some degree, will be discussed later in this chapter,[2] as will the development of manuscript and cursive handwriting skills.

SPEECH INTERACTION ROUTINES

The understanding and control of speech interaction routines are important because they enable the child to enter into both novel and routine communication settings, to understand accepted procedures of introduction, to appreciate the rights of others in communication, to grasp basic 239 information in public announcements, to understand appropriate tele-

Speech Interaction
Routines, Writing
Conventions, and
Handwriting:
Classroom
Development

phone usage, and to request information in new settings.[3] The following routines should be made functional through oral language situations in the classroom.

Greetings and introductions. The use of appropriate greetings and introductions is basic to oral communication; nevertheless, not all children have an opportunity to establish these important speech interaction routines. The following classroom-oriented activities will develop this aspect of speech interaction.

GREETINGS

The use of a toy or teaching-aid clock will greatly facilitate this language activity. Ask one child to set the time of day and have two others decide on the proper greeting to be used at that time. The children can assign themselves characters familiar to them in daily life and roleplay using the greetings.

Place the following greetings on the chalkboard for children to refer to as they play this game:

Good morning	before lunch
Good afternoon	after lunch
Good evening	after dinner (depending on the dinner hour)
Good night	after dark
It's a nice day	any time during the day, assuming it is a nice day
Hi	any time to a good friend
Hello	any time to a good friend or a familiar adult
How do you do *or* It's nice to meet you	any time when introduced to a strange adult

SAYING HELLO

Children should understand when to use informal and formal greetings, and that pronouncing the person's name after the greeting adds personal appreciation to the greeting. Invite the children, through role playing, to respond with appropriate greetings as they pretend to meet the following people:

Friend	Hi, Hello
Teacher	Hello, Mrs. _____
	Good morning, Miss _____
	Good afternoon, Mr. _____

Service station man   Hello, Mr. _____

Good morning, Mr. _____

Good afternoon, Mr. _____

Doctor   Hello, Dr. _____

Mailman   Hello, Mr. _____

Hi, Mr. _____

Minister   How do you do, Reverend _____

Hello, Father _____

Hello, Rabbi _____

WHEN YOU MEET

This activity is designed to develop an understanding and awareness of the need for a proper response after an introduction to either a familiar or a strange adult. Ask the children, "Do you sometimes wonder how you should greet a grown-up, like your teacher, your principal, your neighbor, or your dentist, if you meet him on the way to school some morning?" Ask one child to roleplay himself and others to play the other adults, and have them develop the social occasion using the greetings. For example, the children might conclude that "Good morning" would be a good greeting before lunch, or that they can use the word "Hello" followed by the adult's name.

Ask the following questions: "Do you sometimes wonder what to say to an adult whom you do not know or whom you have never met; people like your father's boss, your mother's new friend, or the new minister? Make believe that you have just been introduced to one of these persons. What would you say?" Invite children to roleplay these scenes and use the various greetings. Children will soon need to contrast these responses with the responses they use with familiar adults, and they will soon realize that greetings used with new adult acquaintances, more formal in nature, may require such a response as "How do you do, Mr. _____." The shaking of hands between boys and men may be practiced. Girls should understand that the shaking of hands with either a man or a woman is optional.

INTRODUCTIONS

The idea to be developed in this activity is that there are many ways of introducing people properly and that knowing how to do it the right way expresses friendship and appreciation to the person being introduced.

Place these rules of introduction on the chalkboard:

Introduce the younger person to the older.
Introduce the male to the female.
Introduce the person of lower title to the person of higher title.

241

Speech Interaction
Routines, Writing
Conventions, and
Handwriting:
Classroom
Development

Invite a group of three children to demonstrate the proper introductions for the following situation:

You bring home two new school friends to meet your mother.

"Mother, these are my new friends. This is Dolores Santos and Tina Olivarez. Dolores and Tina, this is my mother."

Then divide your class into groups of three and have the children in each group take the role of one of the persons in each of the following situations:

When you bring home a new friend to meet your brother or sister.
When you introduce two of your friends who do not know each other. One is a boy, the other is a girl.
Mother and Father are visiting school. Introduce them to your teacher.

Understanding communication rights: listening and speaking. The instructional program should develop appreciation of communication rights, including the opportunity to share in discussion topics and to provide others with the courtesy of attention. Give attention to the child who monopolizes the conversation and shows little respect for the communication rights of other children in the discussion. The following instructional examples are ways to develop appreciation of communication rights.

ARE YOU REALLY LISTENING?

This activity is designed to help children become aware of the importance of listening attentively, thereby demonstrating appreciation and understanding of the rights of the speaker. Set up a tape recorder and invite three boys to discuss a topic such as the latest model cars one should collect, the outcome of a school football or kickball game, or whether it is better to own a certain baseball card or football card. Have another group discuss such topics as the best picnic they ever attended, their favorite food, or why they should help mother at home.

After the taping is over, ask all of the children to listen to the discussions. Suggest that the children (1) decide if everyone in the discussion group had a chance to finish his sentence or whether the speakers were interrupted, (2) listen for the person in the discussion group whose statements related to the previous speaker's comments to indicate that the responder was listening, and (3) listen for any person in the group who might have taken over the discussion and did not permit others to air their ideas.

If listening appreciation and courtesy were absent in the tape-recorded conversation, discuss this with the children. You may wish to have the same group of children record another topic demonstrating courteous listening skills.

How is appreciation of communication rights important in this type of setting?
(Photo by Hays, Monkmeyer Press Photo Service)

WHAT WOULD YOU DO?

The role-playing experiences that are suggested in this oral language activity will help develop understanding of the need for listening courteously. In both informal and formal social situations, an individual should consider how to extricate himself in a polite way from the conversational setting if the speaker is showing little consideration for him.

Ask the children if they have ever talked to another person who talks continuously and demands that his or her directions be followed. Read the following dialogue between two children to your class:

243

Speech Interaction
Routines, Writing
Conventions, and
Handwriting:
Classroom
Development

Mary (to Sherri): Say, let's play school. I'll bring my teen-age doll and clothes and you bring all of your dolls over to my house after school today.

Sherri: But . . .

Mary: Then we'll set up all of my little chairs, set the dolls in the chairs, and, you know, use the old workbooks we have and teach the dolls to spell. I'm going to read them a story, too. You'll need to bring some pencils and crayons, too.

Sherri: But, I—I don't know if . . .

Mary: After we finish playing school, we'll ask Cynthia to play jacks with us. And . . .

Open the discussion by asking the children to react to Mary's statements and to imagine Sherri's feeling throughout the conversation. The children may conclude that Mary showed lack of consideration for Sherri by not permitting her to express her ideas and feelings about the proposed play activity, and may even deduce that Sherri needs to get her mother's permission for these arrangements.

Other situations for role playing that may help children understand the role of courteous and appreciative listening follow:

1. Four children are talking about their pets but do not let one of the group say anything.
2. An older sister is yelling at a younger sister about eating too many cookies.
3. A grandfather tells his grandson about a certain battle in which he participated. The child has heard the same story many times before.
4. A neighbor politely asks a young boy not to walk through his flower bed.

Public announcements: basic information. Children need to be aware of some of the informational items that are essential to public announcements. For example, if there is a meeting to occur later in the week they will need to know the time, location, meeting content, and the individuals or group responsible for the meeting. The relationship between intonation and meaning also affects the clarity of announcements. In many elementary schools the public address system can provide real experience in developing and making public announcements. Other direct experiences are announcement opportunities at various school-oriented functions such as "pot luck" dinners, back-to-school and open-house nights, and other special events.

Telephone usage. The telephone is a vital instrument in the operation of our daily lives. Instruction in telephone usage should include how to answer the telephone, how to take messages, and how to record message information with sufficient detail to enable a call to be returned. Role playing can be of great value in developing telephone usage skills, as the following
examples illustrate.

WHO IS CALLING, PLEASE?

This oral language activity is designed to help children understand the proper use of a telephone: how to answer properly, take messages, and accurately convey information to the caller. It requires one or two toy telephones or a free-loan demonstration kit from your local telephone company containing interesting telephone usage information for elementary school children, two real telephones, and a device that simulates the ringing sound, the dial tone, and busy signals to teach children to understand and differentiate the most common telephone signals.

After you have set your stage with either the toy phones or the demonstrator kit, invite a group of children to demonstrate telephone usage for the class. Help the group that is role playing demonstrate good usage of the instrument, and encourage good voice intonation and volume, and good telephone courtesy. Permit sufficient practice so that all the children have the opportunity to use these instruments at least once and preferably many times.

What telephone courtesies and guidelines do you consider important for classroom development? How can an activity like this help develop them? *(Photo by Irene B. Bayer, Monkmeyer Press Photo Service)*

Speech Interaction
Routines, Writing
Conventions, and
Handwriting:
Classroom
Development

Listed below are a number of problem situations involving incoming and outgoing telephone calls that will help the role playing.

RING, RING, RING

Invite the children to roleplay by verbalizing dialogues and situations such as the following.

Setting the scene: The Miller family is watching television. The telephone rings. Father asks Diane to answer it.

Diane: Hello. This is Diane Miller.

Voice: Is Mr. Miller there?

Diane: (What will Diane say next?)

Setting the scene: The Hopkins family is eating dinner. The telephone rings. Mother answers the phone.

Mother: Hello. This is Mrs. Hopkins.

Voice: I'm calling about the United Crusade Fund.

Mother: (What will she say next? The assumption here is that she will ask to return the call after dinner, but the children may have a satisfactory alternate response.)

Setting the scene: Toni and Justin are doing their homework. Mother and Father are at a church meeting. The telephone rings.

Toni: Hello. Toni Walters speaking.

Voice: May I speak to Mr. Walters, please?

Toni: (What will Toni say next?)

TELEPHONE GUIDELINES

To help children roleplay the preceding activities, make two charts like the following and place them near the telephones. One chart gives guidelines for outgoing calls, the other for incoming calls.

WHEN YOU MAKE A CALL

1. Dial correctly.
2. Allow time for the person to answer (ten rings).
3. Tell who you are.
4. Leave a message if the person you want is not there.
5. Don't go on and on and on. (Don't hog the phone.)

WHEN THE TELEPHONE RINGS

1. Answer promptly.
2. Tell who you are in a slow, clear, loud voice.

3. Speak into the transmitter.
4. Do not yell.
5. If the call is for someone else, tell the caller to wait and then go for that person.
6. If the call is for someone who is not at home, carefully write the message down.

Telephone problem situations the children can roleplay follow, but before long children will wish to use their imaginations to make up other social and business situations requiring the use of the telephone.

OUTGOING CALLS

1. When you can't remember the exact homework and you call a friend on the telephone
2. When you need to know what time your grandmother's plane will arrive
3. When you find a stray, injured animal in your backyard that needs special medical help
4. When you wish to find the owner of a stray white kitten
5. When your mother discovers that there is smoke and fire in your garage
6. When you need to know the correct time

INCOMING CALLS

1. A woman wishes to speak to your mother
2. A man wishes to speak to your older brother, who is in the backyard playing basketball
3. A friend is calling you to ask you over to play with him
4. An adult is phoning your mother, who is at the grocery store and will be right back
5. A neighbor calls your mother for help because her clothes washer overflowed
6. A classmate phones you to invite you to a birthday party

Requesting information in new situations. Here the child must interact with other individuals on first contact to obtain specific information ranging from directions to get to a particular address to finding out where to find a particular book in the library. The crucial thing is for children to realize the need to ask clear questions and to provide sufficient information to obtain the requested information.

WHICH WAY IS IT TO . . .

Asking for information such as the location of a book or directions to a certain place is frequently difficult for some children. This oral language activity, with guidelines for role playing and discussion, has been designed to illustrate informational-type questions necessary to obtain help and information from an adult and to build the child's self-confidence for this type of interaction.

247

Speech Interaction
Routines, Writing
Conventions, and
Handwriting:
Classroom
Development

Ask the children if they have ever stopped a grown-up to ask for directions or information in a department store, grocery store, library, neighborhood, and the like. Invite them to participate in acting out the following problem situations. After each enactment, briefly discuss whether the child in the conversation asked clear questions and gave enough information to obtain the desired help or information.

Situation: A child needs directions in finding a book about horses in the school or public library and approaches the librarian behind the counter. Some of the conversation might sound like this:

Child: Would you please help me?

Librarian: If I can, I'll be glad to.

Child: I'm looking for an interesting book.

Librarian: What do you like to read about?

Child: I like horses. (Horses are my favorite.)

Librarian: I like to read about horses, too. Come with me and I'll show you how you can find books about horses.

The roleplaying may be extended by having the librarian show the child the way to the library catalogues, look for the drawer containing those topics beginning with "H," find the card in the file, and then look for the books in the stacks on domestic animals, specifically horses (636.1). The librarian might then suggest that the child browse in that area, whereupon the child thanks the librarian.

Other role-playing situations are

1. Asking for directions to the nearest variety store
2. Seeking help from a grocery clerk in locating a package of spaghetti
3. Requesting the location of a movie theater from a policeman

INFORMATION NEEDED

An example of a child needing to interact with other individuals on first contact by communicating specific information to that person is in a store, when the child wishes to select a gift for a special occasion, such as Mother's Day. Promote a discussion of experiences on such occasions. Discuss guidelines, such as the following, that serve to identify information necessary to bring the matter to a satisfactory conclusion.

1. How much can you afford to spend?
2. What type of gift would Mother like?
3. What kinds of things does Mother already have?
4. If size is important (such as stockings), what is the exact size?
5. Would you like the purchase to be gift-wrapped?

Conclude this discussion by taperecording and comparing two role-playing situations. The first is to be between a well-informed boy or girl selecting a present for a parent or friend and the "salesperson." The second situation is to be between a poorly informed boy or girl and the same "salesperson." The recordings should not only reveal the importance of information in the selection of a gift but also demonstrate the importance of being able to ask the right question.

These routines will be developed in many home situations, but there

How can this type of experience develop ability to request information in a new setting? What preplanning in the classroom can facilitate this effort? *(Photo by Hays, Monkmeyer Press Photo Service)*

should be reinforcement of these for children who have previously been introduced to them. For youngsters who have little chance at home to develop these routines, this experience will substantially improve their communication effectiveness.

WRITING CONVENTIONS

A variety of written language conventions can be identified that parallel to some degree the oral language routines discussed above.[4] Just as a number of the oral language routines reflect concern for and appreciation of the listener, the written language forms demonstrate appreciation for the reader. The following written language routines deserve special consideration in the instructional program.

Following consistent and accepted letter-writing practices. This includes letter openings and closings—capitalization, use of comma, proper name, and punctuation. As previously discussed, paragraphing is of distinct value in identifying idea shifts.

A FRIENDLY LETTER

A large, colorful chart such as the following, which shows the correct format of a friendly letter, is always helpful to children. It is especially helpful to show punctuation marks in a bright color.

Date   April 4, 1973

Greeting   Dear Charlie,

Body   We sure miss you. Our class went on a field trip to the
                       planetarium. It was fun.
                            Get well soon and come back to school.

Closing   Your friend,

Signature   Jerry

AN INVITATION

Occasions such as class performances, Public Schools Week, Open House, birthday parties, Christmas plays, Halloween parade, and the like are good opportunities for letter writing. Encourage the children to word their own letters of invitation, but remind them of the information that must be incorporated by putting the following reminders on the chalkboard.

Be sure to tell

1. The *month* of the year
2. The *day* of the week
3. The *time* of day

4. The *type* of event
5. The *place* of the event

The following are letters of invitation from a second grader and a fifth grader:

November 10, 1972

Dear Parents,

    Please come to see our play on Wednesday, November 23 at two o'clock. Our class will act out the story of Thanksgiving in our room. We will also have good things to eat.

The Second Grade, Room 104

November 5, 1972

Dear Parents,

    You are invited to attend the premier of an original movie made by our fifth grade class. The film, called "Who Is Sylvia?," will be shown in Room 304, Tuesday, November 14.

    Please come.

Mrs. Turner's Fifth Grade

If the writing is of a personal nature, that is, if the writer is trying to capture ideas for himself, usage, spelling, and handwriting may be of a highly informal nature. If, however, the writer is expressing ideas that are to be read by others, such as in a business letter requesting information or in a personal note to a friend, it is important that he realize and accept the responsibility for clarity of expression, and legibility, and correct spelling. This, in effect, says to the reader, "My main purpose in writing to you is to communicate certain ideas, and I do not want you to be distracted by incorrect spelling or the need to spend time in deciphering my handwriting."

TWO LETTERS

The following two letters, written by the same primary child, illustrate the effect of assumed information on the spelling and usage of a second grader in a personal and a business letter. The personal letter, to the grandmother, is a less exacting sample of letter writing, in contrast to the letter to the radio station, which was written with great care and detail. Given the different requirements, both letters are quite acceptable.

Date	July 28, 1973
Greeting	Dear grandmother,
Body	I got your dollar and spent it. David lost a tooth and got money to. I need 1943, 1941 and 1939 pennies.
Closing	Love,
Signature	Paul

251

Speech Interaction
Routines, Writing
Conventions, and
Handwriting:
Classroom
Development

Heading *(return* *address,* *date)*		444 Cutting Blvd. Berkeley, Calif. 94707 June 21, 1972

Inside address   Mr. David Hammerhill
(name, title,   KKHI Radio Station
address)   St. Francis Hotel
                    San Francisco, Calif. 94108

Greeting   Dear Mr. Hammerhill:

Body   I listen to your Saturday morning program every week. You said that you will play what people ask for. I like the music from the movie "2001 Space Odessy." Please play it.

Closing   Your friend,
Signature   Paul Johnson

The next exercise provides guidelines for proofreading and experience in developing letter-writing form.

PROOFREADING A LETTER

Duplicate or write on the chalkboard the following guidelines and letter. Have the children proofread the letter, circle all errors, then rewrite it in correct form.

1. Proofread your letter form: date, greeting, margin, indentation, and closing.
2. Proofread your sentences for clarity.
3. Proofread your punctuation.
4. Proofread your spelling.

April 7 1973

Dear parents, our school is holding. open house on april 14. we have a greet dell to show you. in our classrooms we want to show you some of the wok we have done this yeer. in our multi-prupose room you will also see science experments. visit our school library also and see the winning art projects. please plan to come. you will enjoy it. Your sun, Mike.

Notes and letters for different social situations. Routines of this nature range from personal thank-you notes to friends to a business letter expressing appreciation of services performed by a company or requesting information. The important point here is to help the child understand how to determine which form is appropriate for such correspondence. As previously discussed, this should include an understanding of the appropriate heading, indentation, punctuation, and conclusion.

PERSONAL OR BUSINESS

Children should understand that there are many occasions for letter writing, each requiring a different approach or a different form, of either a personal or a business nature.

To help children classify which events call for either a personal or a business letter, write the following phrases on the chalkboard, then briefly discuss the type of letter and the possible contents of each. Ask the children to write either P (personal letter) or B (business letter) after each phrase.

An ill friend (P)
A reply to a department store (B)
Inviting a boy to a party (P)
Thanking Grandmother for her gift (P)
To the mayor of your city (B)
To the president of the Rotary Club (B)
To the Department of Motor Vehicles (B)
To the telephone company (B)
To a company asking for a job (B)
To a friend who has moved away (P)

TAKE A LETTER!

Ask the child to dictate two brief letters into a tape or cassette recorder, the first letter from group A and the second from group B or group C.

GROUP A

1. A letter to a relative such as your aunt, uncle, grandmother, or grandfather
2. A letter to a close friend in your class

GROUP B

1. A letter to your teacher
2. A letter to the principal of your school

GROUP C

1. A letter to your favorite TV star
2. A letter to the mayor of your city
3. A letter to the president of the United States

Transcribe each dictation in double- or triple-spaced form. Discuss each letter with the child, noting how the content and ideas expressed vary. Encourage the child to identify the changes and additions necessary to develop the ideas in each letter. Note the difference in informal and formal form appropriate for each letter. After the child has revised and rewritten the letters, they may be shared with the class and mailed.

SINCERELY YOURS

The following language activity is designed to help children understand the type of note or letter that is appropriate for various social situations. The children are to draw a line from the social situation in the left column to the type of note or letter to be used as listed in the right column.

Speech Interaction
Routines, Writing
Conventions, and
Handwriting:
Classroom
Development

WHICH FORM WOULD YOU USE?

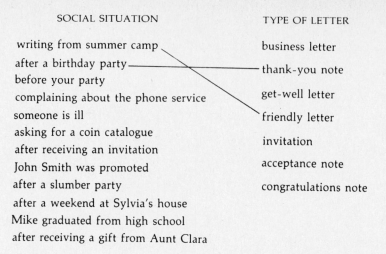

SOCIAL SITUATION	TYPE OF LETTER
writing from summer camp	business letter
after a birthday party	thank-you note
before your party	
complaining about the phone service	get-well letter
someone is ill	friendly letter
asking for a coin catalogue	invitation
after receiving an invitation	
John Smith was promoted	acceptance note
after a slumber party	congratulations note
after a weekend at Sylvia's house	
Mike graduated from high school	
after receiving a gift from Aunt Clara	

Preparation of school and community announcements. Opportunity should be provided in school to prepare posters or charts containing information related to school meetings or social events. These can range from an announcement of the Halloween parade to parent invitations for the Christmas play. As was the case with oral announcements, such written announcements must account for the important characteristics: time, place, nature of the activity, and individuals or group responsible. This type of written language routine can be effectively related to the art program by preparing and decorating posters. Of course legibility should be a prime concern in developing such posters and charts.

POSTERS

Children thoroughly enjoy preparation for school events. PTA or parent club functions such as book fairs, carnivals, or other fund-raising events provide a good opportunity for children to write and draw posters. Since such posters are designed not only to inform but also to generate interest in the school and community, the children must realize the importance of their art work and written language in attracting attention.

Posters can be drawn in any art medium, but the drawing should be simple in design and large and legible. Wording should be confined to supplying the needed data: what, when, where, and who. The poster, on page 255 prepared by a first grade class, fits all the important requirements of an interesting poster.

Handwriting legibility. Written language forms to be read by others should be legible enough that the reader does not have to struggle to read the message. It is important, however, to realize that this dimension of writing can be overstressed. The primary goal should be to ask "What is the idea being communicated?" not "Is every letter perfectly formed?" Nevertheless, the youngster should feel the responsibility to write legibly.

254 As was the case in requesting information in oral language, clarity of

thought in requesting information in written language is extremely important. Again the value of proofreading should be stressed. The child should
accept the responsibility of expressing his ideas clearly. This responsibility
can be taught in part by pairing youngsters in the classroom and asking
each to read the other's work. Small-group discussions can serve to identify problems in clarity, and you should make instructional provision for
such problems through appropriate written language experiences.

HANDWRITING INSTRUCTION

At early levels the teacher plays a major role as recorder for the child, but
eventually the child must develop the handwriting skill he needs to
achieve independence in written expression. The symbolization of thought
has progressed from oral language and representation in the child's art
forms to the teacher's role as recorder through written symbolization. It is
of great importance that positive attitudes be developed toward symbolization of experience in written form, so that the child can realize his need
to symbolize his thoughts in written form for others to read. Just as he
learned to express himself through oral language and early drawings he
now must learn the importance of expressing his thoughts in the written
symbol system. For many children interest will grow from watching the
teacher write stories on the board or on newsprint. Other youngsters will
255　find the written code curiously interesting and will try to refine their

Speech Interaction
Routines, Writing
Conventions, and
Handwriting:
Classroom
Development

eye-hand motor control. But some children will be quite content to let the teacher do the writing. They will require constant encouragement to develop handwriting forms. Your program in handwriting will need to account for a wide spectrum of learning needs and motivational levels.

The major goals in informal and formal handwriting instruction are:

1. To represent meaningful ideas in a form that can be read by others or by one's self at a later time
2. To develop fluency in producing legible written forms so as to inhibit thought as little as possible
3. To develop varied speeds and legibilities to cover purposes ranging from personal to public writing, and from note taking to research reports

The child's first important experience with handwriting is printing his own name. This may consist of tracing or copying his name from a master name card printed by the teacher and attached to the child's desk. Early experience in manuscript writing will be based on "circle" and "stick" forms, most of which resemble the printed forms the child encounters in his reading material.

Instruction in handwriting should attempt to capitalize on the child's interests and experiences. Too often the teacher overemphasizes neatness and precision of letter formation and fails to be concerned enough with what is being communicated. This misplaced emphasis often produces reluctant handwriters who are more concerned with letter formation than with idea formation. It is easy for the teacher to fall into the least-effort practice of red-penciling handwriting efforts and written mechanics and not attending also to the organization and development of the child's ideas. The era of precise script and highly decorative letter formation as the hallmark of the literate person is past. Now we must emphasize first the ideas to be expressed and second the form of this expression. Informal dimensions of the handwriting program beyond the child's own name should include

Labeling familiar objects in the room (sink, piano, chalkboard, rocking chair, desk, and so forth)
Labeling child-selected pictures from magazines or newspapers (bicycle, truck, spaceship, train)
Picture titles for child's art work (My Kitten, My House)
Story titles for child's art work (Our Zoo Visit, The Trip to the Pumpkin Patch)
Sentence description for child's self-selected pictures or for his art work

Writing numerals should also follow a functional approach, through such activities as writing birthday dates, telephone numbers, and addresses, and numbering pictures in a story sequence. Be sure to give attention to spacing between words and in dates or number sequences. A helpful suggestion for early manuscript printing is to space the width of one finger between words and commas, and the width of two fingers after periods or between sentences.

The child will need teacher aid and direction to record his labels or titles
in manuscript form. You can do this by preparing several stacks of rectan-

gular pieces of lined writing paper (3" X 5") and having these in convenient places in the room. After recording the lable or title on the paper, the child can take it to his seat and reproduce it by himself, using the lined paper. If each child has alphabet dividers in a cheese box "Word Bank," he can file the teacher's copy in his "bank" for future reference. As he gains handwriting control, you should extend the informal meaning approach to handwriting suggested here to include thank-you notes, letters, science record-keeping, and stories, to mention but a few functional and meaningful experiences.

Handwriting instruction of a formal nature should also provide a meaningful dimension for the child. Handwriting practice programs should be applied directly to classroom activities. The handwriting experiences of kindergarten and first grade children should be on lined chalkboards or newsprint, so as to allow for limited small-muscle control. As the child's eye-hand motor control develops, wide lined paper can be introduced. In early encounters with such paper, the top half of the page should be blank (for pictures) and the bottom half should be lined heavily with three-fourths to one-inch lines, with each line divided in half by light or dotted lines. The heavy lines make provision for capital letters, while the light or dotted lines provide guides for lower-case letter formation.

Some children will be better off with large, soft-lead beginner's pencils until they develop more precise muscular control. Another valuable aid is a large permanent alphabet and samples of numerals zero through nine. These letters and numerals should be large and easily visible to all children.

One manuscript alphabet is presented in Figure 8-1. Note that the sequence of letter part production is indicated by numeral while the direction of letter formation is shown by arrow. The letter formation begins at the top of the letter and generally moves from left to right, with letters formed from straight lines, circles, and circle and line segments. The capital and tall letters are two spaces high and of equal height, while the small letters are one space high.

Letters formed by a circle and line segment are a, b, d, g, o, p, and q; those made of line segments only are i, k, l, t, v, w, x, y, and z; those constructed from parts of circles and line segments are c, e, f, h, j, m, n, r, s, and u. Recent research indicates that the most difficult lower-case letters for the first grade child, in order of difficulty, are q, g, p, y, j, and m. The easiest letters are l, o, and h. These findings support the logical expectation of letter confusability based on similarity of letter forms, and also relate to frequency of letter use.[5]

The transition from manuscript to cursive writing occurs in many school settings during the third grade. Although heated debate has been carried out regarding the need for change from manuscript to cursive writing, the accepted rationale for the change is based on three points. (1) Cursive writing leads to greater writing ease and fluency. (2) Parents and the business community traditionally expect "longhand" to be part of the

Speech Interaction
Routines, Writing
Conventions, and
Handwriting:
Classroom
Development

school's literacy program. (3) Teachers beyond the primary grades antici-pate that the child can use cursive writing that conforms with their own written forms. Some school systems have recently provided the child with the option of continuing manuscript or developing cursive writing, but most systems still introduce cursive forms late in the second grade or early in the third grade. There is little hard evidence to support the value of cursive writing, but (2) and (3) above will undoubtedly extend the pres-ence of cursive writing in the school curriculum for years to come.

Figure 8-1. *From* Better Handwriting for You, *Book 1, by J. Kendrick Noble. Copyright © 1972, 1966 by Noble and Noble, Publishers, Inc. Reprinted by per-mission of Noble and Noble, Publishers, Inc.*

During the transition from manuscript to cursive writing the teacher should continue to rely heavily on functional utilization of writing, to emphasize what the child has to say rather than the specific writing form used. There are several benchmarks in the child's progress through the transition stage. First, the child should have fluent control of the manu-script forms, because many of these forms transfer directly to cursive writing. Second, he should demonstrate ability to read the cursive forms the teacher develops gradually through directions on the chalkboard and in other written forms about the classroom. Third, he should be motivated to develop cursive writing. For some children this will develop from teacher and parent modeling, from trying to develop the "grown-up" form of handwriting, starting with their own names and progressing to individ-ual captions and story lines. For others this form of handwriting will seem to be of little importance. For these children the teacher would do well to spend time on more significant aspects of reading-language instruction and postpone cursive instruction until a later, more appropriate time.

The cursive instructional program should focus first on letter forms that are similar in both writing systems and then move to differences between the two systems. The following points will be helpful in this effort.

1. The small letters a, c, d, g, h, i, j, l, m, n, o, p, q, t, u, x, and y are very similar in both forms, as are the capital letters B, C, K, L, O, P, R, and U. These letters and their similarities should be emphasized first.

Figure 8-2. *From Better Handwriting for You, Book 3, by J. Kendrick Noble. Copyright © 1962, 1966 by Noble and Noble, Publishers, Inc. Reprinted by permission of Noble and Noble, Publishers, Inc.*

2. The letters of each word are connected, and most programs recommend that the pencil remain on the page until the word is completed. Thus the letters t, i, and j are finalized after the completion of the final letter of the word.
3. Special attention will be required for the letters b, e, f, k, r, s, v, w, and z, which do not follow the manuscript forms.
4. Capital letters are important, but because the child will use the lower-case letters over 95 percent of the time he should spend more time practicing lower-case letters.
5. The cursive forms have slant, which aids in controlling and connecting letters. The slanted-letter formations are produced in part by placing the paper at an angle in front of the child. (Notice that this is in contrast to manuscript writing, which is characterized by vertical letter formation and vertical paper placement.)

Early instruction in cursive writing should provide for clear comparison of the cursive and manuscript forms using letters with similar visual forms.[6]

259

Speech Interaction
Routines, Writing
Conventions, and
Handwriting:
Classroom
Development

Use the chalkboard often during the initial transitional stage. Also use lined paper with light and heavy alternating lines one-half inch in width for short and tall letter formation. As eye-hand motor control develops, reduce these to one-half inch and three-eights of an inch. Each child should use a soft lead (No. 2) pencil of comfortable length (at least five or six inches).

The children should be encouraged to produce large letters in the early stages to counteract the common letter "tightening" effect that novice cursive writers tend to experience. Spacing between words in cursive writing is provided by end strokes on words, and this one factor will greatly improve legibility. Anderson identifies the letter demons as *a* that looks like *o, u,* or *ci; l* that becomes *li; d* that looks like *cl; e* that looks like *i* or the reverse; *m* and *n* that appear like *w* and *u; t* that looks like *l* or *i;* and *r* that appears to be *e* or *n.*[7] These conclusions on letter demons correspond closely with Newland's early study, which identified the four error types leading to most illegibility: (1) failure to close letters; (2) closing looped strokes; (3) looping nonlooped strokes; and (4) straight-up rather than rounded strokes.[8] Practice on individual letter formation will be necessary to account for these problems in legibility. The writing program should be individualized to the degree that specific problems are identified through learner feedback that leads to correction. Many children will move easily from the manuscript to legible cursive forms; those who do so should be moved rapidly through the cursive instruction program. Lock-step total class instruction should be avoided at all costs. The major goals should be legible, fluent writing, not overly perfected forms that greatly reduce motivation to express ideas in written form.

Approximately 10 percent of the youngsters in the elementary school are left handed. The handwriting difficulties of these youngsters stem largely from a world designed for right-handedness, from handwriting instruction to the construction of school seating equipment. The research by Enstrom on left-handed writing offers several important suggestions for instruction. One of the most crucial findings suggests that the writing paper should be rotated clockwise about thirty degrees for the left-handed writer, so that the right bottom corner of the paper points toward the vertical centerline of the body. The pencil should be placed so that the blunt end points over the left shoulder. Elbows should remain close to the body. Provision for

more easily observing writing production by the left-handed child can be made by encouraging him to grasp the writing point of the pencil at least one and one-fourth inches further back than the right-handed child. Also, he should be seated at a comparatively low desk so that he can see the point of letter formation by looking directly over his hand.[9] The teacher should anticipate variation in cursive letter slant for the left-handed writer; vertical and left-slanted strokes will be common for some children. Some left-handed writers should continue manuscript writing during the elementary years should great difficulty develop in mastering cursive forms.

After competency has been developed in children's manuscript and cursive forms, skill maintenance opportunities should be provided through functional and meaningful activities. Manuscript forms will be used in content areas through labeling of charts, graphs, and maps, and through construction of school posters. Cursive forms will be common to personal letters and invitations, letters requesting information and materials, and research reports. Again legibility and fluency are the prime handwriting goals to enable the child to express his thoughts and ideas in written form.

Footnotes

[1]Basil Bernstein, "Social Class, Linguistic Codes, and Grammatical Elements," *Language and Speech,* 5:221–40 (1962). John L. Fischer, "Social Influence on the Choice of a Linguistic Variant," *Word,* 14:47–56 (1959). Paul V. Gump, Phill Schoggen, and Fritz Redl, "The Behavior of the Same Child in Different Milieus," *The Stream of Behavior,* ed. R. G. Barker (New York: Appleton-Century-Crofts, 1963). Dell Hymes, "The Ethnography of Speaking," *Anthropology and Human Behavior,* eds. T. Gladwin and W. Sturtevant (Washington, D. C.: Anthropological Society of Washington, 1962), pp. 15–53. William Labov, "The Logic of Nonstandard Dialect," *20th Annual Round Table, Monograph Series on Languages and Linguistics,* ed. James E. Alatis (Washington, D. C.: Georgetown University Press, 1970), pp. 1–43.

[2]Paul S. Anderson, *Language Skills in Elementary Education* (New York: The Macmillan Company, 1972). Paul C. Burns, Betty L. Broman, and Alberta L. Lowe, *The Language Arts in Childhood Education* (Chicago: Rand McNally & Co., 1971). James Moffett, *A Student-Centered Language Arts Curriculum, Grades K–6: A Handbook for Teachers* (Boston: Houghton Mifflin Company, 1968). Ruth G. Strickland, *The Language Arts in the Elementary School* (Lexington, Mass.: D. C. Heath & Company, 1969).

[3]Strickland, *The Language Arts in the Elementary School.* Susan Ervin-Tripp, "An Analysis of the Interaction of Language, Topic, and Listener," *American Anthropologist,* 66, 2 (December 1964), 86–102.

[4]Anderson, *Language Skills in Elementary Education.* Harry A. Greene and Walter T. Petty, *Developing Language Skills in the Elementary Schools* (Boston: Allyn & Bacon, Inc., 1971). Moffett, *A Student-Centered Language Arts Curriculum.* Strickland, *The Language Arts in the Elementary School.* Iris M. Tiedt and Sidney W. Tiedt, *Contemporary English in the Elementary School* (Englewood Cliffs, N. J.: Prentice-Hall, Inc., 1967).

[5]Edward R. Lewis and Hilda P. Lewis, "Which Manuscript Letters Are Hard for First Graders," *Elementary English* (December 1964), 41:855–58.

[6]Anderson, *Language Skills in Elementary Education,* p. 188.

[7]Ibid.

[8]T. Ernest Newland, "An Analytical Study of the Development of Illegibilities in Handwriting from Lower Grades to Adulthood," *Journal of Education Research* (December 1932), 26:-249–58.

Speech Interaction
Routines, Writing
Conventions, and
Handwriting:
Classroom
Development

[9]Eric A. Enstrom, "The Extent of the Use of the Left Hand in Handwriting and Determination of the Relative Efficiency of the Various Hand–Wrist–Arm–Paper Adjustments," *Dissertation Abstracts,* 27, No. 5 (University of Michigan, 1957).

Additional References

CRUIKSHANK, DONALD R., *The Language of Children* (Columbus, Ohio: The Ohio State University Press, 1971).

ENSTROM, E. A., and DORIS C. ENSTROM, "But I Can't Read His Writing," *Grade Teacher* (January 1966).

JOOS, MARTIN, *The Five Clocks,* Supplement to the International Journal of American Linguistics, 28, Part V (1962).

HENRY, MABEL WRIGHT, ed., *Creative Experiences in Oral Language* (Champaign, Ill.: National Council of Teachers of English, 1967).

KINDER, ROBERT F., *Guidelines for Building English Language Arts Curriculums, K–12* (Hartford, Conn.: State Department of Education, 1969).

NEW YORK BOARD OF EDUCATION, *Nonstandard Dialect* (Champaign, Ill.: National Council of Teachers of English, 1968).

NOBLE, J. KENDRICK, *Better Handwriting for You* (New York: Noble and Noble Publishers, Inc., 1967).

ROSENHAUS, MAX, "You Can Teach Manuscript Writing with Six Rules," *Readings in the Language Arts,* eds. Verna D. Anderson et al. (New York: The Macmillan Company, 1966), pp. 167–71.

ZANER-BLOSER METHOD (Columbus, Ohio: Zaner-Bloser Company, 1965).

9

Nonstandard Dialects and Second Language Learning: The Instructional Program

Focusing Questions

1. How does a standard English dialect differ from a nonstandard or variant dialect? From a second language?
2. What communication skills should have highest priority for children using a nonstandard or variant dialect? A second language?
3. How is language stereotype related to economic and social mobility for individuals who speak a nonstandard dialect? What is your attitude toward nonstandard language forms? After interacting with the contents of this chapter, examine your attitude again. Has it been modified? If so, how do you now view variant language forms?
4. What specific variations in phonological, morphological, syntactical, and lexical forms are typical of nonstandard-speaking black children? Chicano children? Chinese-American children?
5. How are second-dialect and second-language learning similar? How are they different?
6. What instructional procedures are effective in second dialect and second language learning?
7. What implications for reading and spelling instruction can be derived from your study of nonstandard dialects? (Also see the discussion in Chapter 10.)

The minority group youngster who speaks a nonstandard or variant dialect is a major instructional concern for many teachers. The youngster whose native language is not English presents a unique problem in the instructional setting. Youngsters from several major minority groups may be expected to use nonstandard English and second language forms. These include

Black children in the ghetto urban centers and rural South
Chicano (Americans of Mexican descent) and Puerto Rican youngsters from Spanish-speaking homes
Chinese youngsters in major urban centers from Chinese-speaking homes

Only in recent years has research been conducted on the nature of variant dialects spoken by minority groups. Many language-related studies have

Nonstandard
Dialects and
Second Language
Learning: The
Instructional
Program

been made in the past on preschool and elementary school children reared in language environments where only standard English was spoken. Standard English, remember, is the dialect accepted by the majority because of the social and political position of the people who speak it. Geographical variations, however, are present in the accepted dialect (see Chapter 3), to such an extent that one could view standard English as a variety of dialects. A nonstandard, or variant, dialect contains consistent, and regular deviations from standard English dialect forms in the language of a specific group of speakers. Unfortunately, owing to limited information the public regards nonstandard dialects as "poor or sloppy English" and has come to use such dialects as class markers for "uneducated persons of low social status." William Labov, a sociolinguist, says that an individual using nonstandard speech forms 20 or 30 percent of the time will be heard as using these forms all of the time.[1] Variant dialect patterns used in the northern urban areas by blacks who have recently migrated from the South and by Appalachian whites serve as speech stereotypes.[2] A similar stereotype problem exists for many Chicano and Puerto Rican youngsters from Spanish-speaking homes. It is important that we understand something about the relationship between standard English and nonstandard English and second language forms.

The classroom teacher must develop sensitivities to the cultural values of the students he teaches. As Miles Zintz states:

> Too many teachers are inadequately prepared to understand or accept these dissimilar cultural values. Teachers come from homes where the drive for success and achievement has been internalized early, where "work for work's sake" is rewarded, and where time and energy are spent building for the future. Many children come to the classroom with a set of values and background of experience radically different from that of the average American child. To teach these children successfully, the teacher must be cognizant of these differences and must above all else seek to understand without disparagement those ideas, values, and practices different from his own.[3]

A child's feelings, attitudes, and emotional responses must be understood within his cultural frame of reference.[4]

I again emphasize that a nonstandard speech performance does not signal the absence of language competence, but simply indicates that the speaker has learned his language in an environment that uses this language system for communication purposes. Chicano, Puerto Rican, and Chinese youngsters can, however, present a different problem, resulting from conflict points between English and Spanish or Chinese. In this chapter we shall consider instructional priorities for minority group speakers and conflict points for nonstandard dialect and second language speakers, shall contrast second dialect instruction with second language instruction, and shall provide instructional suggestions for developing bidialectal speakers in the classroom.

Nonstandard
Dialects and
Second Language
Learning: The
Instructional
Program

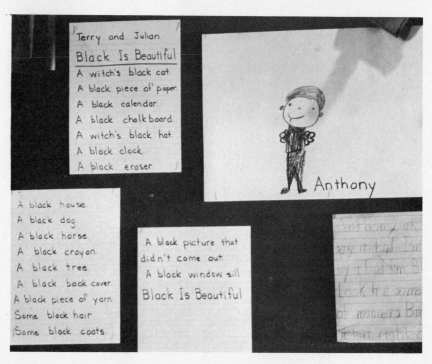

Terry and Julian
Black Is Beautiful
A witch's black cat.
A black piece of paper.
A black calendar.
A black chalkboard.
A witch's black hat.
A black clock.
A black eraser.

A black house.
A black dog.
A black horse.
A black crayon.
A black tree.
A black book cover.
A black piece of yarn.
Some black hair.
Some black coats.

A black picture that
didn't come out.
A black window sill
Black Is Beautiful

Anthony

What role does an understanding of cultural values play in developing the reading-
265 language program?

In the classroom we are immediately concerned with developing a variety of communication skills. It is thus essential that we determine communication priorities to meet the instructional needs of nonstandard and second language speakers. Labov has identified the following eight problem areas in order of priority:[5]

1. The ability to understand spoken English (of the teacher)
2. The ability to read and comprehend
3. The ability to communicate (to the teacher) in spoken English
4. The ability to communicate in writing
5. The ability to write in standard English grammar
6. The ability to spell correctly
7. The ability to use standard English grammar in speaking
8. The ability to speak with a prestige pattern of pronunciation (and to avoid stigmatized forms)

Labov cautions that should the teacher have difficulty understanding a child's oral or written language, he should attend first to these two areas.

From an instructional standpoint we are concerned with language deviations that interfere with the child's ability to comprehend oral and written language and to communicate with the teacher in spoken form. Recent research suggests that there is little comprehension interference for the nonstandard-speaking black child as a consequence of conflict points in the sound and grammatical systems of standard and nonstandard English,[6] provided that there is sufficient context to resolve such meaning problems as those resulting from nonstandard English homophones—for example, initial consonant substitution causes the nonstandard-speaking black child to pronounce the words *stream* and *scream* as *scream*.[7]

The teacher, however, can have difficulty comprehending nonstandard forms. A publication by the New York Board of Education points out that though a single nonstandard feature may not interfere with communication a combination of nonstandard elements can. For example

Standard: She is wild.
Nonstandard: She wow.

Four different rules of the nonstandard dialect are operating here:

The linking verb is deleted.
The consonant cluster -*ld* is simplified with loss of final -*d*.
The final -*l* which results is not vocalized.
The diphthong *i* is simplified by a loss of the glide.

The intricate operation of nonstandard rules will often make it difficult for the standard speaker to trace the original intention of the nonstandard speaker.[8]

Such potential interference problems make it clear why teachers should understand the regular and consistent nature of nonstandard dialects.

Other comprehension interference results from conflict points between

English and other languages. A teacher should make a special effort to understand deviations between English and the language the child has learned at home. Later we shall identify several important variations in the sound and grammatical systems of English and Spanish and of English and Chinese.

The instructional program must also reflect concern for the relationship between language stereotypes in our society and the economic and social mobility of students who speak a nonstandard dialect or a language other than English. The educational program should provide the option for students to acquire standard language forms for use in various social environments. One would hope that the society might shift its attitude, but since this is not likely to occur in the foreseeable future the student should understand the nature of language stereotype and the importance of becoming bidialectal.[9] Just as we violate no law or moral principal if we wear (or fail to wear) a hat at all times, neither do we violate a law or moral principal if we use nonstandard English forms; but we must recognize that if we always wear our hat or use a nonstandard dialect (or for that matter a standard dialect) at all times, certain social and economic doors will be closed to us. The dominant population has altered attitudes to accept wider variation in social behavior, but one's language forms still critically affect his economic opportunities, higher education experiences, and social mobility.[10]

CONFLICT POINTS BETWEEN STANDARD AND NONSTANDARD DIALECTS

The following discussion highlights key conflict points between Standard English and the nonstandard dialects of black speakers. Some children will use these nonstandard features more than others, depending upon their language experiences. This discussion is not intended to be a complete inventory of conflict points. The purpose is to create an awareness and appreciation of the consistency and regularity in nonstandard language deviations by examining variations which we may expect to encounter in the elementary classroom.[11] Understanding and being able to recognize these variations will enable you to distinguish between "errors" and consistent language behavior.

Phonological and morphological variations

Variations in the sound system of nonstandard English present two types of problems. The first is the formation of homophones produced by alternating or absent phonemes, and the second consists of sound variations that affect the child's grammatical forms (relational meaning) and in some cases sentence meaning.

The first of the lists that follow contains homophone formations for the nonstandard black speaker that result from alternating phonemes, while the second contains variations that result from the absence or simplification of phonemes.[12]

267

Nonstandard
Dialects and
Second Language
Learning: The
Instructional
Program

Position	Standard Form	Nonstandard Form	To the Standard English Speaker ____ sounds like ____	
Initial	/str/	/skr/	stream	scream
			strap	scrap
Initial	/šr/	/sr/	shrimp	srimp
Initial	/d̶/	/d/	this	dis
			that	dat
Initial	/θr/	/tr/	three	tree
			thrust	trust
Final	/θ/	/f/	Ruth	roof
Final	/d̶/	/v/	bathe	bave
Final	/nt/	/n/	meant	men
			bent	Ben
Final	/ŋ/	/n/	sing	sin
Final	/sks/	/səs/	masks	masses
Before nasals	/i/	/e/	pin	pen
			since	cents
Before /r or l/	/ih/	/eh/	beer	bear
			peel	pail
Before /r/	/uh/	/oh/	poor	pour
Before /l/	/oy/	/ɔh/	boil	ball
			oil	all
Any	/ay/	/ah/	find	fond
			time	Tom
Any	/aw/	/ah/	found	fond

Position	Standard Form	Nonstandard Form	To the Standard English Speaker ____ sounds like ____	
Final, or before consonants	/l/	absent	tool	too
			toll	toe
			fault	fought
			help	hep
Final or Medial	/r/	absent	four	foe
			guard	God
			Carol	Cal
			carried	cade
Final	/d/	absent	road	row
Final	/g/	absent	log	law
Final	/k/	absent	back	baa
Final	/t/	absent	boot	boo
Final	/dnt/	/tn/	didn't	dit'n
			shouldn't	shut'n
Final	/skt/	/ks/	asked	axed
Final	/sts/	/s/	fists	fis

268

Your awareness of these variations can help you with problems ranging from misinterpreting the child's oral language and oral reading performance to understanding spelling difficulties, and locating words in the dictionary.

The phonological variations that affect the grammatical system frequently involve simplification of final consonant clusters ending with /t,d,z/ and /s/ (/l/ excepted). They include the following:[13]

Position	Standard Form	Nonstandard Form		To the Standard English Speaker _____ sounds like _____		Grammatical Consequence
Final	/ft/	/f/		laughed	laugh	Past tense
			also	tuft	tough	not signaled
Final	/md/	/m/		aimed	aim	Past tense
						not signaled
Final	/nd/	/n/		fined	fine	Past tense
			also	wind	wine	not signaled
Final	/st/	/s/		passed	pass	Past tense
			also	past	pass	not signaled
Final	/zd/	/z/		buzzed	buzz	Past tense
				raised	raise	not signaled
Final	/l/	absent		you'll	you	Future tense
				they'll	they	not signaled
				he'll	he	
				she'll	she	
Final	/dz/	/d/		loads	load	Agreement not signaled
Final	/lz/	/l/		holes	hole	Agreement
		also	/z/	holes	hose	not signaled
Final	/mz/	/m/		comes	come	Agreement
		also	/z/	comes	cuz	not signaled
Final	/nz/	/n/		runs	run	Agreement
		also	/z/	runs	ruz	not signaled
Final	/ts/	/t/		hits	hit	Agreement
		also	/s/	hits	his	not signaled
Final	/ks/	/k/		knocks	knock	Agreement
		also	/s/	knocks	knock	not signaled

The effects of nonstandard forms on verb tense and subject-predicate agreement are clearly illustrated in the consistent deviations that have been identified. Their effects on morphological signaling are developed in the following discussion.

Morphological and syntactical forms

269 The largest number of grammatical deviations occur with verb usage, but there are also other form and pattern deviations.[14]

Nonstandard
Dialects and
Second Language
Learning: The
Instructional
Program

DESCRIPTION	EXAMPLE
A. Use of verb forms	
1. Copula omitted, as in	He tired. You playing here. He running away.
2. Standard use of copula for greater emphasis, as in	He *is* tired. You *are* playing.
3. Use of *be* in place of other verb forms (may indicate extended time), as in	They always *be* messing around. Most of the time he *be* in the house.
4. Standard use of *be* verb forms in tag question sentence or response, as in	He ain't tired, *is* he? Yes he *is.*
5. Subject-predicate agreement	
a. Use of substitute *be* verb forms, as in	I *is* going. There *was* two boys. You *is* too much.
b. Third person singular in present tense, absence or alternate use of -s form, as in	My mother *look* at television a lot. He *know* it. or We *likes* to ride our bikes. They *runs* down the street. or Somebody get *hurts.*
6. Past tense forms	
a. Absence of regular verb ending -ed	He *pick* me. He *turn* around.
b. Use of *ain't* to signal past tense with verbs not changed in past tense, as in	He *ain't* see me yesterday. I *ain't* see it.
c. Use of *ain't* in place of *doesn't, don't, hasn't,* etc., and at the front of questions and declaratives with strong effect, as in	*Ain't* he finish? *Ain't* nobody see it; *ain't* nobody hear it.
7. Absence of future tense marker *will* or contraction *'ll,* as in	She be comin' home. He hit you tomorrow.
8. Alternate use of irregular verbs, as in	They *rided* their bicycles. I would've *took* him.
B. Use of noun forms	
1. Plural overgeneralization, as in	mens, peoples, teeths, mices
2. Absence of plural form cued by preceding word, as in	two dog, several cat

270

DESCRIPTION	EXAMPLE
3. Absence of possessive markers with nouns, as in	That's *Roy* girl. *Calvin* old *man* car.
4. Omission of indefinite article *a* with nouns which have plural forms (count nouns), and addition of it to nouns without plural forms (mass nouns), as in	Give me chair. Give me a cash.

C. Use of pronoun forms

1. Substitution of *they* for *their* and *you* for *your,* as in	*They* eyes are brown. You brought it on *you* own self.
2. Substitution of *them* for *those* and use of *here* with *this,* as in	I have one of *them* hoops. This *here* book.
3. Substitution of *which* for *who* and in some cases the connector *and,* as in	Bill, *which* is six, is my brother. They were good, *which* we all was good.

D. Adjectives and adverbs

1. Use of *more* with adjectives in comparative form using *-er,* or use of equative construction without a change in adjective, as in	He is *more* taller than you. That girl is *more pretty* than the other one.
2. Omission of *-ly* ending common to adverbs, as in	She treated him cruel.
3. Alternate placement of adverbs such as *mostly,* as in	That's what *mostly* we call 'em. This is a crazy world we *absolutely* livin' in.
4. Substitution of *it* for *there,* as in	*It* was one on the table this mornin'.

E. Sentence patterns

1. Inversion of question forms, as in	He fixes that?
2. Omission of *do* forms in questions, as in	How he fix that? How it taste?
3. Redundant pattern elements	
a. Use of *at* in "where" questions, as in	Where you *at?* Where he work *at?*
b. Double negatives—use of a negative with each indefinite pronoun or adverb, as in	Nobody don't know. I ain't never had no trouble wit' none of them.
c. Doubling of forms, as in	My brother he going. I didn't play with only but Wayne and Tyrone.

Nonstandard
Dialects and
Second Language
Learning: The
Instructional
Program

Aspects of meaning

Many of these nonstandard forms, such as redundant pattern elements, should not interfere with the child's comprehension (even though his teacher may view the redundant *at* and double negatives with disdain). Other nonstandard forms, however, such as the omission of past tense markers, may impede comprehension, as illustrated in this test sentence created by Labov:[15]

When I passed by, I read the posters.

The pronunciation of *read* to reflect past tense is cued by the suffix *-ed* in *passed* and emphasizes the importance of this tense marker to accurate sentence meaning. We might also expect the child speaking a nonstandard dialect characterized by the absence of possessive forms, future and past tense markers, or alternate placement of adverbs to experience comprehension interference when he first has to cope with such markers and placement in standard forms of oral or written language. But if you understand the nonstandard forms the child uses you can focus initially on the ones that relate to comprehension, which is the first priority, rather than on the child's ability to produce standard English forms, which is a later priority option, especially in the kindergarten and early primary grades. You will also appreciate the child's oral reading performance in dialect as correct for his nonstandard dialect: the l-lessness, for example, that affects future forms, so that *you'll* becomes *you*, *he'll* becomes *he*, and *they'll* becomes *they*. Thus, the child who reads "He will go" as "He go" is correctly translating the sentence in his dialect. According to Shuy the ghetto child reads the written sentence "John asked *if* Mary *wore* a coat" as "John asked *did* Mary *wear* a coat."[16] In this instance the substitution of *did* for *if* and *wear* for *wore* is not an error in terms of the child's dialect. If, however, the child read "John asked Mary if did she wear a coat" or "John asked Mary if she wear a coat" or some other alteration that varies from nonstandard forms, it would indicate a reading difficulty. Consistent performance indicates that the child possesses a high degree of language competence in the same manner as the standard speaker of English.

You must pay attention to the nonstandard speaker's lexical meanings as well as to his use of equivalent labels. Certainly vocabulary is a critical factor in listening and reading comprehension. According to Metfessel's findings, second grade children from "concept-deprived" backgrounds have a comprehension vocabulary only one-third the size of those of their age-equivalent peers.[17] We must anticipate and account for a wide range of lexical control—particularly as related to the lexicon of instruction.

Always be careful to probe when a child possesses a meaning but lacks a label that enables him to use the meaning efficiently. Explore the possibility of equivalent labels. This problem is illustrated by equivalent labels such as *chunk* (to throw), *nohow* (at all, with not) and *whup* (spank).

Phonological variation that results in the production of nonstandard related homophones must also be considered. Research indicates that nonstandard homophones (for example, *holes, hose*—l-lessness) present more comprehension difficulties in the early primary grades than in the upper intermediate grades.[18] This was attributed to the ability of older children to use clues in the context to identify the meanings of words in question. It was also found, as would be expected, that contextual meaning clues in the immediate sentence were of value in clarifying meaning at all levels: "There is the *hole*," "There are three *holes*." Without additional meaning clues, homophones presented difficulty for children in the early grades: "Here is the *road*" was interpreted as "Here is the *row*." We shall give special attention to this later in the chapter.

ENGLISH AND SECOND LANGUAGE CONFLICT POINTS

Our major urban centers have large percentages of minority children, many of whom come from homes where Spanish and Chinese are spoken.[19] Additionally, in rural areas, especially in the Southwest, Spanish is commonly used in the home environment. Some of these children are bilingual, others have but limited control of English.[20] First we shall identify conflict points between English and language forms used by Chicano and Puerto Rican youngsters, then we shall identify conflict points between English and Chinese. Again the inventory is not intended to be complete; rather the purpose is to create an awareness of language differences so that you can understand them and appreciate their origin and so avoid viewing the child's language control from a negative perspective.

English and Spanish variations

The following are some of the differences between the English and Spanish sound systems.[21]

English Form	Spanish Equivalent	For the Spanish-English pronunciation of: _____ the child may say _____ or To the English speaker _____ sounds like _____	
/i/	/iy/	bit	beet
		pit	peat
/æ/	/e/ or /a/	bat	bet
		hat	hot

English Form	Spanish Equivalent	To the English speaker ___ sounds like ___	
/ə/	/e/ or /a/	but	bet
		fun	fawn
		shut	shot
/ey/	/e/	late	let
		mate	met
/u/	/uw/	full	fool
/b/	/p/	bar	par
		cab	cap
/b/ (between vowels)	/v/ [β]	babies	bavies
/v/	/b/ [b]	vote	boat
/š/	/č/	shoe	chew
/g/	/k/	goat	coat
		dug	duck
/ǰ/	/č/	jump	chump
	/y/		yump
/m/ (final)	/n/	comb	cone
		dime	dine
/θ/ (voiceless)	/s, t, or f/	thank	sank
		path	pass
/đ/ (voiced)	/d/	this	dis
		though	dough
/w/	/gw/	way	guay
/z/	/s/	zoo	sue
		buzz	bus
/ž/	/č/	measure	meachure
	/š/		meashure

The following grammatical variations provide some insight into conflict points between English and Spanish.[22]

DESCRIPTION	EXAMPLE	
	English Speaker	*Spanish-English Speaker*
A. Use of verb forms		
1. Subject-predicate agreement	The cars run.	The cars runs.
	The car runs.	The car run.
2. Tense	Joe said that he was ready.	Joe said that he is ready.
	I needed help yesterday.	I need help yesterday.
3. Use of *be*	I am five years old.	I have five years.
4. Negative	Joe isn't here.	Joe is no here.
	He didn't go home.	He no go home, *or*
		He didn't went home.
	Don't come.	No come.

274

DESCRIPTION	EXAMPLE	
	English Speaker	*Spanish-English Speaker*

B. Use of noun and determiner forms

  1. Plural form — The two cars are big. — The two car are big.

  2. Omission of determiner with noun in certain contexts — He is a farmer. — He is farmer.

C. Use of pronoun forms

  1. Omission in question — Is he a farmer? — Is farmer?

  2. Omission in statement — It is ready. — Is ready.

D. Use of adjectives

  1. Order — The red cap is pretty. — The cap red is pretty.

  2. Ending — The red caps are fine. — The caps red are fine.

  3. Comparison — It is bigger. / It's bigger. — Is more big.

      It is the biggest. / It's the biggest. — Is most big.

Here is a brief summary of the English and Spanish variations for the sound and grammatical systems.

1. Certain vowel sounds will be difficult for the Spanish-speaking child: /i/ bit; /æ/ bat; /ə/ but; and /u/ full.

2. English relies on voiced (vocal cords vibrate) and voiceless (vocal cords do not vibrate) sounds to establish meaning contrasts, but Spanish does not: bit-pit; buzz-bus.

3. The Spanish speaker does not use these sounds in his language: /v/ vote; /đ/ then; /z/ zoo, /ž/ measure; /ĵ/ jump. Often the speaker will replace these sounds with sounds he perceives to closely resemble them, or with sounds that frequently occur in similar positions in Spanish.

4. Words that end in /r/ plus the consonants /d,t,l,p/ and /s/ are pronounced without the final consonant: card-car, cart-car.

5. In Spanish the blend of /s/ and the consonant sounds /t,p,k,f,m,n,l/ does not occur, nor does any Spanish word begin with the /s/ + consonant sound. A vowel sound precedes the /s/, and the consonant that follows begins the second syllable of the word. Thus the child has the problem not only of starting the word with the /s/, but also of pronouncing two consonants *(star* may thus become *estar* and pronounced *es-tar)*. The final consonant clusters /sp/ *wasp,* /sk/ *disk,* and /st/ *last* also present problems in consonant pronunciation.

6. Grammatical differences between the two systems may include the following: agreement, verb tense, use of negative forms, omission of noun determiner in certain contexts, use of pronoun forms, order of adjectives, and comparison.

Nonstandard
Dialects and
Second Language
Learning: The
Instructional
Program

The summary serves only as an introduction to variations for English and Spanish-English speakers. Refer for additional discussion of these contrasts to the footnotes cited at the end of this chapter. Because of differences in Spanish-English dialects you will have to be alert to variations in the children's speech patterns and adjust the instructional program accordingly.

English and Chinese variations

The basic differences between English and Chinese are such that a Chinese student learning English must learn not only different sound and intonation systems but also a different set of language structures. There are many dialects of Chinese, but Mandarin, the national dialect, is spoken by approximately 70 percent of the Chinese people. Another major dialect is Cantonese, which is spoken by most children who come to the United States from Hong Kong, Kowloon, or Macao. There are even dialects within Cantonese. The Cantonese dialect known as the third, or "city," dialect, is the one we shall discuss here.

Tone level has important significance in distinguishing meaning of individual words in Chinese, but our discussion will contrast the Chinese sound system (vowels and consonants) and the grammatical system with English. As was the case with the Spanish and English contrasts, the Chinese and English language variations result from absence, substitution, or simplification of sound system components.[23]

		For the Chinese-English pronunciation of _____ *the child may say* _____	
		or	
English Form	*Chinese Equivalent*	*To the English speaker* _____ *sounds like* _____	
/iy/	/i/	beat	bit
/ey/	/e/ or /æ/	bait	bet or bat
	/ə/	came	come
/uw/	/u/	Luke	look
/b/	/p/ (final, unreleased)	rib	rip
/g/	/k/ (final, unreleased)	rig	rik
/d/	/t/ (final, unreleased)	rid	rit
/z/	/s/ (initial)	zoo	sue
/v/	/f/ (final)	have	half
	/w/ (initial)	vast	wast
/zh/	/s/	leisure	leaser
/θ/	/t/	thank	tank
	/s/	thank	sank
/đ/	/d/	that	dat
/š/	/s/	she	see
/č/	/č/ (final)	church	churchi

	English Form	Chinese Equivalent	To the English speaker _____ sounds like _____	
	/ǰ/	/ǰ/ (final)	judge	judgi
	/n/	/l/	need	lead
			good night	good light
	/r/	/l/	rice	lice
			read	lead
			radio	ladio
	/w/	/v/	will	vill

From these conflict points it becomes obvious that many English vowels either do not exist in Chinese or are sufficiently different to produce interference problems, and that many of the ending consonant sounds in English are not present in Chinese. This makes inflectional endings that signal agreement and tense a special problem.

Variations in the two grammatical systems follow:[24]

DESCRIPTION	EXAMPLE	
	English	*Chinese*
A. Use of verb forms		
1. Subject-predicate agreement	He lives in San Francisco.	He live in San Francisco.
2. Tense	I am working. You are talking. I had just finished watering the lawn.	I right at work. You right at talk. I just water finish lawn.
3. Use of *be*	He is sick.	He sick.
4. *Be* substitution	I was here yesterday.	I at here yesterday.
5. Negative	I cannot go.	I no can go.
B. Use of noun form		
1. Plural form	Many houses are beautiful.	Many house beautiful.
2. Omission of article with noun	George is the president.	George president.
C. Use of pronoun forms: no shift in person	You have known him a long time.	You know he long time.
D. Preposition omitted	I live in San Francisco.	I live San Francisco.
E. Connector omitted (conjunction)	You and I are alike.	You I alike.
F. Question form: word order	Are you going home? Will you come to my house for dinner?	You go home? You tonight come I of home dinner?

Nonstandard
Dialects and
Second Language
Learning: The
Instructional
Program

A brief summary of conflict points in the English and Chinese languages follows:

1. English has many more vowels than Chinese, for example /ay/ buy; /aw/ bough; /ɔ/ bought. There is specific difficulty with production of certain vowels such as the front vowels, /iy/ beat, /ey/ bait. This results in homophones for a significant number of English words: beat–bit, Luke–look, bait–bet.
2. A number of English consonant sounds are not in Chinese: /θ/ thank; / đ/ that; /š/ she; /n/ need; and /r/ rice.
3. Many English words end in consonants, but in Chinese many of the consonants are not used in final positions; for example, /f/ is used only initially in Chinese, and so the student has difficulty producing it in a final position. Often an extra syllable will be made of the final /f/: *day off* becomes *day offu*.
4. Consonant clusters are nonexistent in Cantonese. Those which occur at the ends of words present difficulty in forming plurals and past tenses using /s,t,d,z/: cap-caps, laugh-laughed, wish-wished, dog-dogs.
5. Most grammatical relationships are indicated by word order and auxiliary words: "He gave me two books" becomes "Yesterday he give I two book."
6. Numerical designations or auxiliary words are used to indicate plural forms in Chinese: "two books" is "two book."
7. A time word or phrase indicates the tense of a verb. An action verb followed by the auxiliary word *jaw* indicates past or completed tense: "He go jaw" means "He went."
8. Several English word classes—articles, prepositions, and some conjunctions—are reduced or absent in Chinese.
9. The question form in Chinese does not invert the noun and verb forms. Instead the order is similar to the statement form but the "empty" words *ma* or *la* are added to the end. For example, "Are you an American?" is "You are American *ma?*" in Chinese.
10. A subject and a predicate are not required in Chinese when the context is sufficient for understanding. For example, "It rains" may be represented as "Drop rain" in Chinese, while "The mountain is big" may be stated as "Mountain big" in Chinese.
11. Tone or pitch in Chinese distinguishes word meanings, but in English pitch combines with intonation to convey sentence meaning.

Extensive study of English and Chinese language contrasts will be essential if the teacher is to understand the complete range of conflict points thoroughly, but this brief summary should enable the English-speaking classroom teacher to understand a number of basic difficulties encountered by Chinese-speaking youngsters.

SECOND DIALECT AND SECOND LANGUAGE INSTRUCTION

In recent years new approaches to foreign language teaching have been carefully examined for clues to help teach standard English as a second dialect. A number of similarities have been identified—and a number of cautions. Virginia Allen has set forth five similarities between second dialect and second language instruction:

1. Both foreign-language programs and second-dialect programs are based on a contrastive analysis of the target language (or dialect) and the students' home language (or dialect). And the "target" chosen for analysis is not the literary form of the language, nor the idealized language prescribed by the older grammar textbooks, but rather the "language of educated ease."

2. Both foreign-language programs and second-dialect programs view the target language and the students' home language as equally valid systems of communication in their own respective orbits. The target language is not considered "better"; the students' vernacular is not considered "faulty."

3. Both programs tend to be structure-centered. That is, major attention is given to the grammatical structure of the target language or dialect, not to the vocabulary.

4. In both second-dialect classes and foreign-language classes, the linguistic system of the target is presented to the student in a series of small steps, each step rising out of the one before.

5. Both programs emphasize habit-formation. Success is measured in terms of the students' oral fluency in handling the language patterns that are habitual among native speakers of the target language or dialect. Achievement is *not* measured by the students' ability to recite rules or definitions, or to diagram sentences, or to label parts of speech.[25]

There are also similarities in the techniques of instruction. For example, mimicry, repetition, and substitution can be effective to help pupils listen to model patterns, respond to the patterns by repeating them or answering a question, and replace words in the pattern with those of their own choosing.[26]

It is important to realize, however, that a second dialect is not a foreign language. This should be readily apparent if you reflect on the continuum ranging from the nonstandard English of black youngsters to the Spanish and Chinese languages. The interference points are much more pronounced in the different languages than in the nonstandard dialects. As Kenneth Johnson has emphasized, this marked difference itself presents a major problem in the classroom, because teachers who work with children who speak only a foreign language tend to be much more empathetic with their language problems than with those of children who speak a nonstandard dialect of English.[27] The lack of empathy is often because the teacher doesn't understand the nature of the nonstandard dialect, which is characterized as a "poor" or "bad" form of English. It is thus of paramount importance that teachers understand the highly regular and consistent nature of nonstandard dialects and the systematic ways they differ from standard English.

Another major difference between second dialect and second language instruction relates directly to student motivation. Most nonstandard speakers are already bidialectal in that they can comprehend standard English forms and successfully communicate with those who use them.

Aural-Oral Development Steps

1. Pupils listen as teacher models pattern or asks for a response.

2. Class responds.

3. Groups respond.

4. Individuals respond.

5. Individuals converse with teacher guidance.

6. Individuals converse independently.

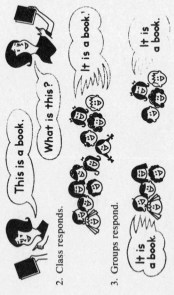

Helpful Teaching Procedures

Speak at a normal rate of speed and with proper intonation.

Use gestures and actions to help pupils understand.

Clarify concepts through the use of realia,[2] posters, display cards, pictures, puppets, and other visuals.

Encourage individual reactions.

Figure 9-1. *From* English Around the World, Level 1 Guidebook *by William F. Marquardt, Jean H. Miller and Eleanore Hosman. Copyright © 1970 by Scott, Foresman and Company. Reprinted by permission of the publisher.*

"Why, then," they ask, "should I learn a second dialect?" Motivation is very different for the foreign language speaker who is only beginning to comprehend and produce a few English sentences. As Allen points out, "There is value in an old pedagogical precept: Never start a drill until the need for that drill has been demonstrated. As far as second dialect teaching is concerned, it is not enough for the need to be perceived by the teacher; it must be perceived by the individual student himself."[28]

Johnson recommends that black students not be taught a standard dialect until adolescence because motivation is much greater then.[29] He states that during the ages of twelve to eighteen years the student

> becomes aware of differences in the kinds of English spoken by different groups. Also, during this period, children become aware of the social significance of the differences between varieties of English spoken. They realize that standard English has more prestige than other varieties of English, and they recognize that standard English is the language to be used in certain kinds of situations. Further, during the secondary grades, disadvantaged black children can be shown the need for learning standard English. Specifically, they can be helped to understand that standard English is the dialect for further education, and that it is the dialect which can broaden vocational opportunities. The recognition of these factors is necessary before these students can be motivated to learn standard English.[30]

RECOMMENDATIONS FOR THE INSTRUCTIONAL PROGRAM

Many teachers worry about a child's nonstandard language largely because they feel there is something inferior about it. This chapter should help you to identify consistencies in the language systems of nonstandard speakers, and to adjust your attitude toward language variation as a consequence.

In previous chapters we emphasized the symbolic nature of oral and written language, and recommended using art forms with oral and written language as an initial step in facilitating the child's ability to symbolize his experience. It is important that early stages of instruction make provision for the child to use his familiar dialect, which is his most fluent form of oral and written expression. At this stage nonstandard dialect should be accepted in oral expression as readily as standard dialect. Written expression of the nonstandard speaker, through language experience charts, should use regular orthography in recording the spelling of the child's oral language forms, but grammatical variation in the initial phases of instruction should be recorded as expressed by the child—in nonstandard form. A gradual transition to standard English in written expression should follow. Even when the teacher and other children in the class use a standard dialect, nonstandard language should be recognized as a highly regular and effective communication system, and the child should be encouraged to use it in his oral expression. You the teacher will need to examine your attitudes toward nonstandard English forms carefully if you are to carry out these recommendations effectively in the early grades.

281

Nonstandard
Dialects and
Second Language
Learning: The
Instructional
Program

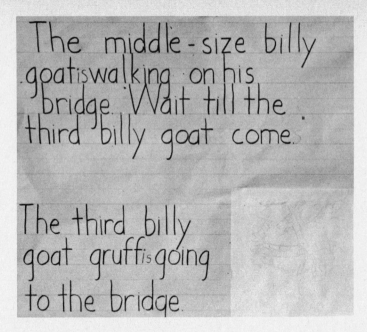

The middle-size billy goat is walking on his bridge. Wait till the third billy goat come.

The third billy goat gruff is going to the bridge.

What nonstandard language forms are apparent here? As the classroom teacher, how would you react to the use of these forms?

As the classroom teacher you have an important responsibility to develop your students' appreciation of language variation. You also have a responsibility to develop fluency and language control appropriate for various social situations. The specifics of these responsibilities are contained in the linguistic goals established by the New York City Board of Education as the basis for the oral language program for nonstandard English speakers:

Phase One. To show that, despite the existence of many dialects in the United States and the striking differences among some of them, every individual who wishes to should have the right and the opportunity to acquire a variety of standard English for the broader access to community life and the surer chance of economic success that it will give him.

Phase Two. To understand that there is an appropriate spoken language determined by circumstances and suitable to the place, time, and people involved.

Phase Three. To acquire ease in the use of standard English by learning effective listening skills and appropriate articulation and pronunciation.[31]

Activities that provide opportunities to acquire a form of standard English (Phase One) include the following:[32]

1. Compare the regional dialects in the United States.
   a. Use a regional dialect map (Chapter 3) to discuss the major dialects in the United States.

b. Play a tape recording and listen for differences in the dialects of well-known Americans such as John F. Kennedy, Lyndon B. Johnson, Richard M. Nixon, and Martin Luther King, Jr.

c. Listen to television personalities who have distinctive dialects, such as Flip Wilson, Alan King, Andy Griffith, Tennessee Ernie Ford, and Joey Bishop. Discuss the regions represented by these dialects and attempt to imitate the voices of these personalities to develop an understanding of the varied forms.

d. Observe dialects within your classroom and within your school; tape record these dialects and attempt to identify characteristics that will enable you to place them regionally.

2. Compare local standard and local nonstandard dialects.

   a. Observe differences in standard and nonstandard forms within the classroom by having students who use varied forms retell a story or news article in the standard and nonstandard forms. Tape record the various forms for class observation of pronunciation, syntax, and vocabulary.

   b. Using data such as those collected in the example above develop a chart showing standard and nonstandard equivalents (see standard and nonstandard language contrasts presented earlier in this chapter).

   c. Tape one-minute extemporaneous speeches of recommendation on topics such as "The Student of the Year Award," or "The Athlete of the Year Award." Listen carefully to each presentation for standard and nonstandard variations in pronunciation, syntax, and vocabulary. Imagine that each speech is to be made as part of a presentation of the award before a large school and community audience. Consider what changes would be appropriate in each presentation.

3. Acquire the ability to use the standard dialect.

   a. Use repetition and substitution drills to work on variations. Using familiar sentence structures, present the sentence that is to be immediately repeated by the students, such as the use of the verb *to be* in present tense:

   > John's in the lunch room.
   > He's in the lunch room.
   > Mary's in the lunch room.
   > She's in the lunch room.

   b. Use replacement drills to work on variations. Identify the replacement items the students are to use and write them on the chalkboard, for example, *he, hits, throws.* After you present a sentence, point to one of the words and have the students replace the equivalent form class in the sentence.

   > *Teacher:* Mike hits the ball. (Teacher points to *throws*)
   > *Students:* Mike throws the ball.
   > *Teacher:* Mike throws the ball. (Teacher points to *he*)
   > *Students:* He throws the ball.

   c. Use conversion drills to work on transformations. After you use patterns in repetition, substitution, and replacement drills, present a sentence the students are to transform. For example, question transformation:

Nonstandard
Dialects and
Second Language
Learning: The
Instructional
Program

Teacher: We play in the band.

Students: Do we play in the band?

d. Use cued-answer drills to establish contrasts. Use questions that require specific individual or group responses:

Teacher: Is Jim on the playground?

Students: Yes, he's here.

Teacher: What is Mary doing?

Students: Mary is reading the magazine.

e. Use dialogues that contain contrasts to be established. Establish the situation in the dialogue and read it with normal intonation patterns and gestures. Then present each line and have the students repeat it. Divide the students into two groups and rehearse and memorize the dialogue. Then present it to the class using props or aids to add realism and motivation to the presentation. The dialogue may be developed to account for a wide range of standard and nonstandard variations.

Activities designed to promote understanding of the appropriateness of language forms in various social settings (Phase Two) include the following.[33]

1. Develop the understanding that varied social situations require different functional varieties of language.
   a. Search magazines for pictures showing forms of dress appropriate for different occasions—a football game, a job interview, or a church event such as a wedding. Discuss the appropriateness of dress in the pictures selected. Have the class imagine a wardrobe switch: the football attire is worn to the wedding and the wedding attire is worn to the football game. Encourage the class to discuss language appropriateness at each of the social occasions identified with questions like, How would the vocabulary used in conversation differ?
   b. Engage the students in various role-playing situations requiring different variants of language. For example, playing ball in the school yard, delivering a message to the principal, going through an interview for a paper delivery route, serving as school guide for a visiting group of parents, making a presentation to the students in your school during an assembly. A detailed classroom experience valuable in establishing the relationship between "character role" and language follows:

   Collect many different hats or headdresses—used hats, "homemade" hats, or costume models from a variety store—as props for children playing different roles and expressing themselves in the language appropriate to that role and setting.

   Encourage groups of two or three children to select hats. You may, for example, establish three characters such as a radio reporter, a grandmother, and a fireman. As soon as the characters are selected and established, encourage the children to develop a very simple plot in order to give the conversation a frame of reference and direction. A sample plot for these characters might be as follows:

A fire has broken out in a three-story house. It is four o'clock in the morning. The radio reporter is interviewing the upset grandmother and a fireman as the fire is in progress.

Explain to the "actors" that they are to speak in the language that best represents the characters they are portraying.

Tape the impromptu conversation, then replay it and discuss the language forms that each character used. Stress the appropriate language form for the character and setting portrayed, noting variations in intonation, pronunciation, syntax, and vocabulary.

c. Invite several individuals from local businesses and representatives from community action groups to join members of the class in a panel discussion related to language use in business and in community development.

Activities designed to foster ease in the use of standard English forms (Phase Three) include the following:[34]

1. Provide opportunities to develop discrimination between standard and nonstandard English forms.
   a. Listen to recordings of comedians (Nipsey Russell, Myron Cohen, Godfrey Cambridge, Red Foxx) who use varied dialects and note variations in pronunciation, syntax, and vocabulary.
   b. Read poetry by authors who use standard and nonstandard dialects, e.g., Langston Hughes, James Weldon Johnson, Gwendolyn Brooks, and Oscar Brown. Identify specific differences between the two language forms and speculate on the reason the author used a particular form for a particular work.
2. Provide practice situations for articulation of specific sounds. Select a specific sound and use it in a variety of meaningful practice situations, like /s/ or /z/ or /əz/ used to form the plurals of "cats," "dogs," and "glasses"; /s/ or /z/ to form third person singular, present tense, for example, "I sing folk songs" versus "She sings folk songs," or "I look good" versus "It looks good." (See previous discussion for variations in the sound systems of standard and nonstandard English.)
3. Use repetition, substitution, replacement, transformation, cued-answer, and dialogue practice exercises to reinforce standard English forms. These exercises should use topics that have high student interest.

Student motivation is of primary importance in language activities designed to develop a second dialect. Johnson points out that motivation in pattern practice exercises can be increased by sharply reducing the time between the teacher's stimulus sentence and the student's response.[35] This suggests that drills and exercises should move at a much faster pace for the student speaking a nonstandard dialect than for the student speaking a foreign language, but it is important to emphasize that *the purpose here is to develop bidialectal language control, not to eliminate nonstandard language forms.*

Special attention should also be given to standard use of English spelling. In a detailed analysis of the spelling performance of black children who speak a nonstandard dialect, I identified two specific dialect-related prob-

Nonstandard
Dialects and
Second Language
Learning: The
Instructional
Program

lems.[36] The first was simplification of final consonant clusters: *told* was spelled *towd,* indicating simplification of *ld* to *d.* The second was hypercorrection: *foe* was spelled *for* or *four* or *fore.* In this case the phonetic [w] was replaced with *r,* perhaps because the child assumed from previous encounters with standard English spelling that the grapheme *r* should be used to represent the phonetic [w]. Homophones resulting from nonstandard language simplifications have already been identified. This problem is somewhat similar to that encountered by the standard speaker with words like *week* and *weak* or *bear* and *bare,* but the homophone problem is much more extensive for the nonstandard speaker.

It is very important that the teacher use meaningful contexts in spelling and writing activities in order to avoid the meaning problems that can result when homophones are used in isolation or in limited contexts. Awareness of the need for such contexts should help the teacher prevent homophone confusion directly related to a nonstandard dialect. The difficulty discussed above stemming from hypercorrection can be overcome in part as the child comes to understand the specific meaning of the word in question, the difference in the standard and nonstandard sound systems, and has sufficient opportunity to develop spelling correspondences through writing.

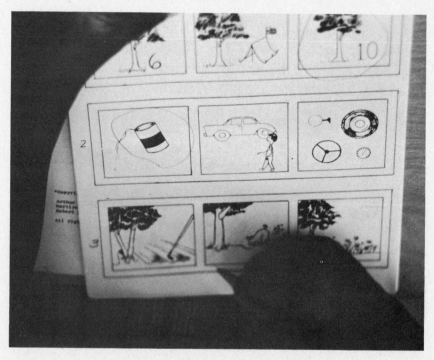

When the teacher said, "Circle the picture which shows the tent under the tree," why did this student circle the illustration showing the number ten under the tree?

Most homophone comprehension problems can be avoided by providing meaningful context. In the classroom, meaning should be established through pictures and running discourse. The following examples illustrate how to use such contexts.

HOMOPHONE PICTURE CARDS

Cut tagboard into 3" X 9" strips. (You may wish to make several sets of cards for your class.) Have the children help in the writing and drawing process. Write each of the following words clearly with either black crayon or felt pen on one side of a card. On the reverse side have the children draw a simple picture or sketch that conveys the meaning of the word.

Here is a beginning list for your word cards:

tent	ten
road	row
holes	hose
wild	wide
tool	two
log	law

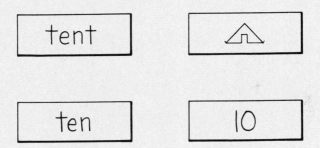

After the children have completed the cards, use them with the following activities.

SENTENCES FOR THE HOMOPHONE PICTURE CARDS

Read one pair of the following sentences at a time and instruct the child to find the cards that correctly complete the meaning of the sentences. Substitute other sentences to add variety to the exercise. These sentences may later be written on tagboard strips for use with the homophone picture cards as an individualized activity.

1. We will sleep in a (tent) .
2. I have (ten) fingers.

1. The (road) is bumpy.
2. Let's (row) down the river.

Nonstandard
Dialects and
Second Language
Learning: The
Instructional
Program

1. They are digging (holes) in the ground.
2. Water goes through a (hose) .

1. The tiger is a (wild) animal.
2. The river is very (wide) .

1. A hammer is a useful (tool) .
2. He has (two) hands.

1. The rabbit sat on the (log) .
2. There is a (law) against speeding.

FINISHING STORIES WITH HOMOPHONE PICTURE CARDS

Duplicate and read the following short stories aloud. The children are to use their homophone picture cards to find the proper words for completing the story. Some words are used more than once in each story. Ask the children to write the appropriate words in the blanks as you read the story aloud.

Following this activity the children may wish to compose their own stories based on their card words.

Two boys rode on their bikes down the _____ toward the bay. At the water's edge they saw _____ men getting into a _____ boat. The boat was _____ enough to hold all of the men, but it started sinking. It was a _____ sight! Do you think that _____ could have made the boat sink?

Roy needed to make _____ dollars to go to a Boy Scout camp and sleep in a _____ overnight. The money would help pay for the _____ and another camping _____. So, he found a way to do it.

Down the _____ from his house was a fallen _____. It was not against the _____ to chop the log into firewood. He chopped the firewood, sold it to a neighbor, and off to camp he went.

Although specific exercises have not been presented for developing English as a second language, many of the instructional suggestions for establishing a second dialect can be applied directly to teaching English as a second language. You will find the references cited in footnotes 19, 21, 25, and 26 of value in this effort.

In conclusion, as classroom teacher you must understand the nature of nonstandard language forms in order to comprehend oral language and oral reading performances. The use of a nonstandard dialect in language performance must not be equated with the absence of language competence.[37]

The instructional program should make provision at the upper intermediate and later grade levels for developing standard phonological and grammatical forms for the nonstandard speaker. There should also be instructional provision for children who enter school with language backgrounds other than English. Variations between English and the second
288 language must be understood so that conflict points can be dealt with.

Urban centers and rural areas of the Southwest should teach English as a second language to meet the needs of Americans of Mexican descent, Puerto Rican children, American Indian children, and Chinese children.

The understandings and instructional provisions outlined in this chapter are of vital importance to establishing children's self-concepts as language users and to building effective communication skills in the classroom. The option for the speaker of nonstandard English to establish a standard English dialect, and programs that teach English as a second language for speakers of other languages, are necessary if we are to maximize every child's opportunity for economic and social mobility.

Footnotes

[1]William Labov, "Some Sources of Reading Problems for Negro Speakers of Nonstandard English," *New Directions in Elementary English,* ed. Alexander Frazier (Champaign, Ill.: National Council of Teachers of English, 1967), p. 143.

[2]Ibid.; William A. Stewart, "Language and Communication Problems in Southern Appalachia," a paper prepared for the Appalachian Regional Educational Laboratory, Charleston, West Virginia, 1967; William A. Stewart, "Language Teaching Problems in Appalachia," in *The Florida FL Reporter,* eds. Alfred C. Aarons, Barbara Y. Gordon, and William A. Stewart, VII, No. 1 (Spring/Summer 1969), 58–59, 161.

[3]Miles V. Zintz, *The Reading Process* (Dubuque, Iowa: William C. Brown Company, Publishers, 1970), p. 326.

[4]Jack D. Forbes, *Mexican-Americans, A Handbook for Educators* (Berkeley: Far West Laboratory for Educational Research and Development, 1970). Robert W. Young, "A Glimpse of the Navajo Language," unpublished manuscript, Albuquerque Area Office, Bureau of Indian Affairs.

[5]Labov, "Some Sources of Reading Problems for Negro Speakers of Nonstandard English."

[6]Ruddell and Williams, *A Research Investigation of a Literacy Teaching Model: Project DELTA.* EPDA Project No. 005262 (U.S. Department of Health, Education, and Welfare, Office of Education, 1972). Rebecca Mammon, "The Effect of Nonstandard Speech on the Sentence Comprehension of Second and Fifth Grade Negro Children" (unpublished master's thesis, University of California, Berkeley, 1969).

[7]Ruddell and Williams, *A Research Investigation of a Literacy Teaching Model.*

[8]New York Board of Education, *Nonstandard Dialect* (Champaign, Ill.: National Council of Teachers of English, 1968), p. 15. Material adapted from *Nonstandard Dialect* with permission of the Board of Education of the City of New York.

[9]Kenneth R. Johnson, "When Should Standard English Be Taught to Speakers of Nonstandard Negro Dialect?" *Language Learning,* XX, No. 1 (1969), 19–30.

[10]Ibid. Thomas J. Creswell, "The Twenty Billion Dollar Misunderstanding," *Social Dialects and Language Learning,* ed. Roger W. Shuy (Champaign, Ill.: National Council of Teachers of English, 1964), pp. 69–73. William Labov, "Stages in the Acquisition of Standard English," *Social Dialects and Language Learning,* pp. 77–103. Lee A. Pederson, "Nonstandard Negro Speech in Chicago," *Nonstandard Speech and the Teaching of English,* ed. William A. Stewart (Washington: Center for Applied Linguistics, 1964), pp. 16–23.

[11]Kenneth R. Johnson, "Teachers' Attitude Toward the Nonstandard Negro Dialect—Let's Change It," *Elementary English,* 48:176–84 (February 1971).

[12]Labov, "Some Sources of Reading Problems for Negro Speakers of Nonstandard English." *Nonstandard Speech and the Teaching of English,* ed. Stewart. New York Board of Education, *Nonstandard Dialect. Social Dialects and Language Learning,* ed. Shuy.

[13]Labov, "Some Sources of Reading Problems for Negro Speakers of Nonstandard English."

Nonstandard
Dialects and
Second Language
Learning: The
Instructional
Program

[14]New York Board of Education, *Nonstandard Dialect*. Labov, "Some Sources of Reading Problems for Negro Speakers of Nonstandard English." Walter Loban, *Problems in Oral English* (Champaign, Ill.: National Council of Teachers of English, 1966).

[15]Labov, "Some Sources of Reading Problems for Negro Speakers of Nonstandard English," p. 161.

[16]Roger W. Shuy, "Some Language and Cultural Differences in a Theory of Reading," *Psycholinguistics and the Teaching of Reading,* ed. K. Goodman and J. Fleming (Newark, Del.: International Reading Association, 1968), pp. 34–47.

[17]Newton S. Metfessel, *The Disadvantaged Child,* eds. J. L. Frost and G. R. Hawkes (Boston: Houghton Mifflin Company, 1966).

[18]Ruddell and Williams, *A Research Investigation of a Literacy Teaching Model.* Mammon, "The Effect of Nonstandard Speech on Sentence Comprehension."

[19]San Francisco Unified School District, "Problems in Teaching English to Chinese-Speaking Students" (unpublished manuscript, Workshop in English, E-4, Summer 1969). Zintz, *The Reading Process.* Forbes, *Mexican-Americans.*

[20]Constance M. McCullough, *Handbook for Teaching the Language Arts* (San Francisco: Chandler Publishing Co., 1969), pp. 8–12.

[21]Leonard Olguin, *Shuck Loves Chirley* (Huntington Beach, Calif.: Golden West Publishing House, 1969). McCullough, *Handbook for Teaching the Language Arts.* Robert P. Stockwell and J. Donald Bowen, *The Sounds of English and Spanish* (Chicago: The University of Chicago Press, 1966). Eric H. Kadler, *Linguistics and Teaching Foreign Languages* (New York: Van Nostrand Reinhold Company, 1970). Sarita G. Schotta, *Teaching English as a Second Language* (Davis: University of California Publications in English, 1966). The discussion is based in part on personal communication with Eduardo Hernandez, of the Language-Behavior Research Laboratory, University of California, Berkeley.

[22]Ibid.

[23]San Francisco Unified School District, "Problems in Teaching English to Chinese-Speaking Students." McCullough, *Handbook for Teaching the Language Arts.* Marion L. Wong, "A Brief Comparative Study of the English and Chinese Languages in Relation to Teaching English as a Second Language and the Reading Curriculum" (unpublished manuscript, University of California, School of Education, Winter Quarter 1968). This discussion is based in part on personal communication with Anne Terrell, of the Chinatown–North Beach English Language Center, 550 Montgomery Street, 10th Floor, San Francisco, California. See Anne Terrell, C. Allen Tucker, and Mary Wong, *Elementary Oral English for Speakers of Cantonese: Teacher's Guide for Pronunciation Practice* (San Francisco: Chinatown–North Beach Community English Language Center, 1971).

[24]Ibid.

[25]Reprinted from "A Second Dialect Is Not a Foreign Language," by Virginia Allen, in *Linguistics and the Teaching of Standard English to Speakers of Other Languages or Dialects,* edited by James E. Alatis, © 1969, Georgetown University Press, Washington, D.C., pages 189–95.

[26]William F. Marquardt, Jean H. Miller, and Eleanore Hosman, *English Around the World, Level 1 Guidebook* (Glenview, Ill.: Scott, Foresman and Company, 1970), p. 71.

[27]Kenneth R. Johnson, "Pedagogical Problems of Using Second Language Techniques for Teaching Standard English to Speakers of Nonstandard Negro Dialect," *The Florida FL Reporter,* VII, No. 1 (Spring/Summer 1969), 78–80, 154.

[28]Allen, "A Second Dialect Is Not a Foreign Language," p. 191.

[29]Johnson, "When Should Standard English Be Taught to Speakers of Nonstandard Negro Dialect?"

[30]Ibid., p. 28.

[31]New York Board of Education, *Nonstandard Dialect.*

[32]Ibid.

Finishing Stories
with Homophone
Picture Cards

[33]Ibid.

[34]Ibid.

[35]Johnson, "Pedagogical Problems of Using Second Language Techniques."

[36]Ruddell and Williams, *A Research Investigation of a Literacy Teaching Model.*

[37]Yetta M. Goodman, "Qualitative Reading Miscue Analysis for Teacher Training," *Language and Learning to Read,* eds. Richard E. Hodges and E. Hugh Rudorf (Boston: Houghton Mifflin Company, 1972), pp. 160–66. Roger W. Shuy, "Speech Differences and Teaching Strategies: How Different Is Enough?" *Language and Learning to Read,* pp. 55–72.

10

Decoding Instruction and Spelling Strategies: Understanding the Code

Focusing Questions

1. What decoding and meaning strategies are critical to the development of independent word analysis abilities?
2. What prereading behaviors must be developed in the decoding program? How can they be assessed?
3. What is a *set for diversity?* Why is this an important concept for the beginning as well as the mature reader?
4. How can the following decoding strategies be introduced and developed in the instructional program: letter-sound correspondences, spelling pattern–sound pattern correspondences, graphemic base units, syllable units, context clues, rapid recognition vocabulary?
5. How are decoding and spelling instruction similar? How do they differ?
6. What spelling strategies are basic to the instructional program? How can they be implemented in the classroom?
7. How can a child's progress in decoding and spelling instruction be evaluated? (See also discussion in Chapter 14)

The mature reader has developed a high degree of decoding fluency through hours of encounter with the printed page. Most literate adults cannot recall how they mastered the decoding or word analysis process. It is important to have some empathy with the beginning reader as he approaches the printed page. Even though the mature reader already possesses decoding strategies, a few moments with a new writing code can serve to heighten one's awareness of the complex nature of the decoding process. This becomes immediately obvious if you try to use the new alphabet in Figure 10-1 to decode the caption under Hank Ketcham's cartoon.

A basic objective of the instructional program is to develop a relationship between the child's sound system and the writing system. Your application

New Alphabet

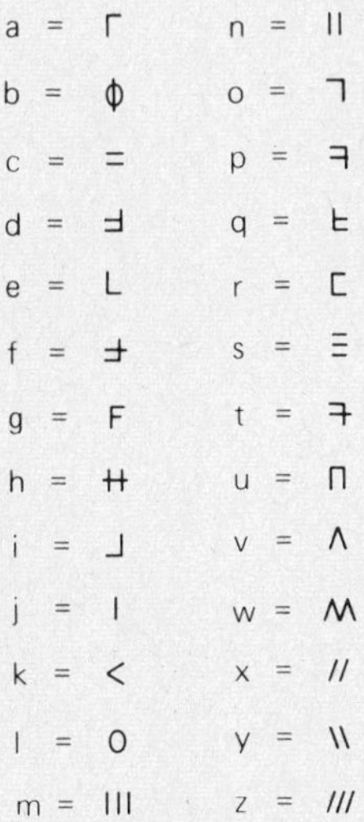

a = Γ		n = ‖
b = φ		o = ⌐
c = =		p = ⊣
d = ⊐		q = ⊢
e = ∟		r = ⊏
f = ⊹		s = ⧦
g = ⊦		t = ⊤
h = ⊪		u = ⊓
i = ⌐		v = ∧
j =			w = Μ
k = <		x = //
l = O		y = \\
m = ‖‖		z = ///

Dennis the Menace

By HANK KETCHAM

"⊪∟'∟ ⊏∟OLL⊣.... ⌐ ⌐⊓∟⊤ Μ⊏‖⊣ ⊤⌐ ∟LL
⊪⌐Μ ⊤⊪⌐∟ ∟⊏⊤⊏\\ =⌐‖‖L∟ ⌐⌐⊤."

Figure 10-1. *Cartoon reprinted by permission of Publishers-Hall Syndicate.*

of the writing code and of your highly developed individual communication abilities enabled you to comprehend the Ketcham cartoon. A child's decoding skills can be developed most effectively by using meaningful and interesting materials that are within his conceptual and experiential range.

The communication model in Chapter 2 identified several basic decoding and meaning strategies used by readers at various levels:

1. Letter-sound or grapheme-phoneme relationships, mat /mæt/
2. Letter pattern–sound pattern or spelling-sound correspondences, such as the final *e* in m*a*te /meyt/, and letter pattern suffix clusters that influence vowel values, as in s*a*ne /ey/–s*a*nity /æ/ and extr*e*me /iy/–extr*e*mity /i/
3. Rapid recognition vocabulary using word part or word configuration for identification, as in *Dennis*
4. Structural word bases identified by one of the above strategies and knowledge of word affixes, mat*s* /mæts/

293

5. Context, previous story information or immediate phrase or sentence information, as in "Dennis used the *bat* to keep the large hungry dog from *eating* his freshly caught *fish*."
6. Nonlinguistic clues provided in illustrations

Can you infer the strategy or strategies this youngster is using to decode the story?

The reader must develop a decoding competence that will enable him to use writing-sound units and meaning clues. As we noted in Chapter 5, children develop effective decoding skills through a wide range of instructional programs. Given the complex nature of the decoding process, it is surprising that approximately two children in every hundred have developed initial decoding competency before entering school.[1]

As you might expect, there is some similarity between the decoding process and spelling competence. Both depend on understanding how oral language forms are represented in writing. Just as the child comes to understand that the letters and letter patterns in *mat* and *mate* represent /mæt/ and /meyt/, he must also grasp an understanding of the reverse relationship. There are of course basic differences in the decoding and spelling processes: the former eventually becomes a rapid recognition process relying heavily on key visual elements and meaning clues, whereas the latter consistently requires the individual to completely re-create the written representation of the sound and sound patterns and use meaning clues to differentiate homophones like /beyr/ (bear or bare). Be alert, however, to key similarities in the two processes, particularly those that relate to decoding letter pattern–sound pattern relationships and syllabication instruction, because you can develop some degree of transfer from one process to the other in the instructional program.

Your knowledge of the way our writing system represents our sound system is a necessary but not a sufficient condition for effective decoding and spelling instruction; you must also understand certain instructional techniques. In the discussion that follows we shall first identify various decoding strategies and generalizations defining the relationship between our writing and sound systems; second, we shall suggest instructional techniques for developing these strategies and generalizations; third, we shall offer parallel strategies for spelling instruction; and finally, we shall briefly identify evaluation procedures for decoding and spelling instruction (evaluation procedures are treated in depth in Chapter 14).

DECODING STRATEGIES: TEACHER BACKGROUND

Prereading requisites

Competence in associating the written language units with their oral counterparts to obtain meaning depends on a variety of factors, including the child's recognition of distinctive auditory and visual language features. These features range from sounds and sound patterns to letters and letter patterns in the context of words, phrases, and sentences. In order, however, to use the "content" or knowledge strategies basic to effective decoding, the child must also develop perceptual strategies for word analysis. He must be efficient in recognizing and comparing letters and letter units, producing their oral counterparts and testing meanings within the context of the sentence or story. He must be efficient in systematic scanning as his eyes move from left to right in the search for familiar written language units within words displayed on the page and separated by blank spaces.[2]

The child's strategy must also include the ability to "decenter" perception in order to free his search from the "insistent features" of a word and locate the pertinent decoding unit or units.[3] This is particularly important for dealing with letters and letter patterns that represent more than one sound or sound pattern. In addition, if the child is to be effective in analyzing words and synthesizing or blending letter-sound relationships, his cognitive strategies must be sufficiently developed to account for the process of reversibility and reorganization as viewed by Piaget.[4] (There is further discussion on the development of these perceptual strategies later in this chapter, in the section on prereading activities.)

You should be cognizant of developmental stages in the decoding process. Singer's research, for example, supports the idea that as the reader becomes more mature in his ability to decode the printed page he tends to reorganize and shift strategies to use more efficient decoding units, which results in more proficient decoding performance.[5] As we previously mentioned, this reorganization may directly relate to the child's cognitive development as Piaget has posited in his theory of intellectual growth.

Gibson has emphasized that the teacher should also be concerned with the nature of children's motivation as decoding strategies are developed. Stimulating the child's natural curiosity and interest in securing information about his environment is viewed as critical to intrinsic motivation. The school environment and instruction should thus be designed to build on the child's "active urge to seek information" and to prevent the confusion and failure that blunt the child's curiosity and information search.[6]

If the child's active information search is to be fully utilized in the decoding program, the teacher must clearly understand various "content" strategies for decoding, that is, decoding units and patterns, and the instructional techniques for developing these strategies. The following discussion develops an overview of knowledge-based decoding strategies and then offers instructional techniques designed to enhance classroom development of the strategies. The sequence of decoding strategies will vary according to the reading program, whether publisher-produced or teacher-developed, but the discussion should serve as foundation for effective utilization of any program.

Letter-sound or grapheme-phoneme relationships

Understanding the strengths and limitations of letter-sound relationships is basic to understanding the decoding process. Approach letter-sound correspondences by considering their contexts within words. As later discussion makes clear, the isolation of consonant and vowel sounds results in distorted sound values, which can produce confusion and inhibit the child's understanding of decoding strategies.

The consonant correspondences of English are fairly consistent, however letters such as *c, g, s,* and *z* represent more than one sound: *c*an /k/, *c*enter /s/; *g*o /g/, *g*entle /j/; *s*in /s/, *s*ure /š/; and Zen /z/, a*z*ure /ž/. Consonant digraphs (literally, two graphs or letters), also characteristic of English spelling, represent single consonant phonemes or sounds: *ch*in /č/, *ph*oto /f/, *gn*aw /n/. Some diagraphs represent more than one sound: *th*in / θ /, *th*en / đ /; *ch*in /č/, *ch*asm /k/. Most of these variations will cause little difficulty if they are used in the context of meaningful vocabulary because the variable sounds are highly predictable on the basis of the sound or letter pattern context. Table 10-1 summarizes consonant correspondences found in initial, medial, and final positions in vocabulary.[7]

Vowel correspondences in English are more complex than consonant correspondences. As noted in Table 10-2 the vowel letters and vowel digraphs represent more than one vowel sound: b*i*t /i/, b*i*te /ay/; st*ei*n /ay/, re*cei*pt /iy/. Again, however, it is extremely important to understand that many of the correspondences are predictable from letter pattern context (b*i*t /i/, b*i*te /ay/) or affix pattern context (s*a*ne /ey/, s*a*nity /æ/). In a later

Table 10-1. Consonant Correspondences in Various Positions

Sound or Phoneme	Letter Label	Position		
		Initial	Medial	Final
/b/	b	bat	tuba	cab
/k/	c	can		
	k	kitten	baker	break
	ck		packer	sack
	ch	chasm		
	qu	quick	liquor	opaque
/s/	s	sit		
	ss		passer	pass
	c	city	racer	
	ps	psalm		
/č/	ch	chip	catcher	rich
	c	cello		
/d/	d	doll	soda	mad
/f/	f	fit	heifer	life
	ff		baffle	cuff
	ph	photo	siphon	
	gh			rough
/g/	g	get	tiger	rag
	gh	ghetto		
	gg		bigger	
/j/	g	gym		rage
	j	jump		
	dg		ledger	badge
/h/	h	house	ahead	
	wh	who		
/l/	l	lake	sailor	metal
	ll		filling	hall
/m/	m	man	tamer	ham
	mb		comber	tomb
	mm		summer	
/ŋ/	n	night	finer	hen
	nn		sinner	
	gn	gnaw		
	kn	knit		
/n/	ng		singer	sing
	n		drink	
/p/	p	picnic	piper	drip
	pp		supper	
/r/	r	rain	bearer	car
	rr		hurry	burr
	wr	wreck		
	rh	rhetoric		
/š/	sh	ship	smasher	lash
	s	sure		
	ci		specious	
	ce		ocean	
	ss		passion	
	ti		nation	
/t/	t	teacher	meter	hit
	tt		sitter	
	pt			receipt

Sound or Phoneme	Letter Label	Initial	Medial	Final
	bt		debtor	debt
/θ/	th	thin	ether	path
/ᵭ/	th	then	either	bathe
/v/	v	voice	mover	wave
/w/	w	work	shower	cow
/ks/	x			box
/y/	y	yard	Sawyer	say
/z/	z	zoo	blazer	
	s		loser	dogs
	zz		nozzle	jazz
/ž/	z		azure	
	s		measure	
	si		delusion	

section of this discussion we deal specifically with the predictability of spelling-sound correspondences within the contexts of words.

As we discussed in Chapter 2, vowels can generally be classified into two major groups: (1) unglided vowels or short vowel sounds that involve little or no glide or shift of the tongue in production, and (2) glided vowels or long vowels that require some degree of glide in production. Included in the glided category is the more traditional category of "diphthong." The unglided, or short, and glided, or long, vowel sounds are of course represented by the letter or letter combinations of *a, e, i, o, u, y,* and *w.*

Table 10-2. Vowel Correspondences

Sound Label	Vowel	Letter Label	Example
Unglided or short	/ae/	a	at
		au	laugh
Glided or long	/ey/	a.e	lane, ate
		ai	bait
		ea	break
		ei	rein
Unglided or short	/e/	e	men
		ea	head
		eo	leopard
		ai	said
		ie	friend
Glided or long	/iy/	e.e	Pete
		e	be
		ea	beat
		ee	beet
		ei	receive
		ie	belief
Unglided or short	/i/	i	bit
		ui	build
		y	hymn
		u	busy

Sound Label	Vowel	Letter Label	Example
Glided or long	/ay/	i.e	bite
		uy	buy
		ie	flies
		ai	aisle
Unglided or short	/a/	o	hot
Glided or long	/ow/	o.e	home
		oa	boat
		ow	show
		o	go
		ew	sew
Unglided or short	/ə/	u	bus
		oo	blood
		ou	enough
Glided or long	/yuw/	u.e	mule
		ew	few
Unglided or short	/u/	oo	good
		u	put
		ew	flew
		ui	fruit
Unglided or short	/ɔ/	a	talk
		au	Paul
		o	dog
		aw	law
Glided or diphthong	/aw/	ow	drown
		ou	loud
Glided or diphthong	/ɔy/	oy	toy
		oi	coin
Note: an unglided or short vowel followed by -r is sometimes referred to as an r-controlled vowel	/ar/, /er/ /ir/, /ɔr/ /ur/, /yur/ /ər/	ar, ea ea, oa oo, u.e e	cart, pear ear, oar poor, pure her

A major concern for teachers who wish to develop their own decoding program or to revise a publisher-designed program to meet classroom needs more effectively is how to determine the introductory sequence for consonant and vowel correspondences. The research literature offers a number of helpful suggestions. Coleman has suggested that *continuants* (consonants produced by the constant release of air—for example /s/ as in *s*ip) are easier to blend with other sounds than are consonants produced by stopping the air flow (/t/ as in *t*ip).[8] He feels that these consonants (such as /s/, sat; /f/, fan; /v/, van; and /m/, man) represent those which are highly "learnable" and should be among the early consonant correspondences introduced.[9] The rationale for introducing early consonants also needs to account for instructional utility, as related to development of vocabulary for meaningful sentences and frequency and familiarity in the child's language.

Authoritative opinion in the past has suggested that easily confused graphemes such as *p* and *g* and *b* and *d* should not be taught in close proximity, but recent research suggests that sequencing such consonants in close proximity can have instructional value.[10] Seeing such letters in contrastive pairs can help the child to focus on the distinctive features of the two letters in a word context and thus reduce the confusion that often results when such letters are developed in isolation.

In the past many basal readers have delayed teaching vowel correspondences until late in second grade materials, largely because of the belief that most consonants should be sequenced into the program first because of their regularity and the low priority of vowels in decoding. Such a viewpoint fails to account for the regularity of vowel correspondences in a letter pattern–sound pattern context and the importance of vowels in independent decoding. Most youngsters clearly articulate vowels by age three or four[11] and encounter vowels in their initial rapid recognition vocabulary. Early introduction of vowel correspondences expedites the development of independent decoding ability and understanding how the writing system represents oral language.

A partial rationale for sequencing vowel correspondences at the introductory stage may be obtained in the research on acoustical values for vowels which are dependent on the position in the syllable which they occupy. The work of Fairbanks[12] for example indicates that the vowels in the following words differ distinctly as to decibel level: cap /æ/ (4.5); talk /ɔ/ (3.8); shop /a/ (3.7); choke /ow/ (3.0); check /e/ (2.2); coop /yu/ (1.9); cup /ə/ (1.1); cheek /iy/ (1.0); cook /u/ (0.3); and pit /i/ (0.0). These findings suggest that vowels with higher intensity levels should be easier for children to identify in sound contexts, which is potentially a basis for establishing a sequence for developing letter-sound correspondences. This suggestion receives wide observational support from teachers who indicate that the vowel correspondence in *cap* /æ/ is much easier to develop than the vowel correspondence in *pit* /i/.

Some reading programs designated as "linguistic" use a simple sequence method of presenting vowel sounds (nap, lap, map /æ/), but there is evidence that teaching children to expect one-to-one sound-letter correspondence may inhibit the child's ability to transfer his decoding knowledge to letter-sound correspondences that do not fit this regular pattern.[13] This finding would suggest that children should be introduced to variable correspondences such as tap /æ/ and tape /ey/, rip /i/ and ripe /ay/ early in the instructional program. These variable letter-sound correspondences should be designed to establish a "set for diversity" as the child begins to anticipate "optional" sound correspondences for vowel letters within letter patterns.

Children appear to use a definite order strategy in decoding words. They first examine the initial letter or letters, then the final letter or letters, then middle letters, and finally the word shape as word identification cues.[14]

This strategy reinforces the importance of developing sound-letter correspondences the child can use in independent word recognition instead of emphasizing a rapid recognition vocabulary.

Understanding the nature of letter-sound correspondences and the related findings above should help you design or adjust the instructional program. Obviously, however, the instructional program must include decoding strategies that go beyond letter-sound correspondences. Spelling-sound units and letter pattern–sound pattern correspondences account for increased regularity in the English spelling-sound system.

Spelling pattern–sound pattern correspondences

As previously observed, the relationship between single letter and sound correspondences is highly regular for consonants but greatly varied for vowels. The vowel letters *a, e, i, o, u,* and *y* occur in various positions in words and represent a wide range of vowel sounds.[15] To account for greater regularity in letter-sound correspondences it is essential to utilize letter pattern–sound pattern correspondences that provide for consistencies in the writing-sound system. These patterns are based for the most part on letter pattern–sound pattern environments and on root word and affix structures (morphemes) of words. Although there will still be exceptions, most are historically based variations. The basis for the analysis is the *morphophoneme,* an intermediate sound unit predictable by deriving the sound pattern context from letter patterns. For purposes of our discussion we shall think of this relationship as spelling pattern–sound pattern correspondences.

Venezky's work has resulted in the identification of major predictable patterns for unglided or short vowels and glided or long vowels. A summary of these patterns, based on the letter pattern–sound pattern environment, follows.

1. A vowel letter represents a glided or long vowel sound when it is followed by a consonant unit and another vowel unit, which may include final *e: c*a*nine, m*e*dian, p*i*lot, v*o*gue, d*u*bious.
2. A vowel letter represents a glided or long vowel sound when it is followed by a consonant unit, which in turn is followed by *l* or *r* and another vowel unit, including final *e: l*a*dle, z*e*bra, m*i*crobe, n*o*ble, l*u*cre.
3. A vowel letter represents an unglided or short vowel sound when it is followed by a compound consonant unit such as *dg* /dj/ or *x* /ks/: b*a*dge, *e*xit, ch*i*cken, p*o*cket, l*u*xury.
4. A vowel letter represents an unglided or short vowel sound when it is followed by a cluster of consonant units, such as *dd* or *stl:* s*a*ddle, ant*e*nna, ep*i*stle, c*o*gnate, s*u*pper.
5. A vowel letter represents an unglided or short vowel sound when it is followed by a final consonant unit or units ending the word: s*a*t, *e*bb, h*i*tch, s*o*d, r*u*g.

Among a number of exceptions, Venezky notes two important subpatterns:

6. When the vowel letter is followed by a consonant and a final *e* it represents the glided or long vowel sound: b*a*ke, dec*a*de, f*i*ve, pr*i*ze, c*u*be, m*u*le, acc*e*de, ser*e*ne, c*o*ve, j*o*ke. This also holds for patterns where the vowel is followed by a consonant and *le:* c*y*cle; a consonant and *re:* medi*o*cre; or *ste:* ch*a*ste. The generalization also holds for polysyllabic words, even when the vowel before the final *e* is not stressed: micr*o*be, dec*a*de, sched*u*le, vol*u*me, plac*a*te.

7. When the vowel letter is followed by double or geminate consonants it represents the unglided or short vowel sound: *a*bbess, f*a*llacy, r*a*ttle, app*e*llate, dil*e*mma, m*e*ssage, art*i*llery, cr*i*bbage, w*i*llow, acc*o*mmodate, comm*e*rce, s*o*nnet, b*u*tton, p*u*ddle, t*u*nnel.

In addition to the letter pattern–sound pattern environment, predictable vowel values can also be based on the morphemic structure of words. For example, on the basis of the first generalization above, the initial vowel in the word *sanity* would represent a glided or long sound rather than an unglided or short sound. But on the basis of the sequence s*a*ne—s*a*n*i*ty, hum*a*ne—hum*a*n*i*ty, urb*a*ne—urb*a*n*i*ty another regular feature, based on the suffix *-ity,* becomes obvious. This generalization also holds for vowel letters *e, i, o,* and *u* (though the latter vowel is used infrequently). Examples of this alternation follow.

Vowel Letter	Glided or Long	Unglided or Short
e	extreme	extremity
	obscene	obscenity
	serene	serenity
	supreme	supremity
i	asinine	asininity
	divine	divinity
	malign	malignity
	senile	senility
o	frivolous	frivolity
	mediocre	mediocrity
	precocious	precocity
	verbose	verbosity
u	assume	assumption
	conduce	conduction
	presume	presumption
	reduce	reduction

Other common alternations include the suffix *-ic,* as in st*a*te—st*a*tic, m*e*ter—m*e*tric, paral*y*ze—paral*y*tic, ph*o*ne—ph*o*nic; and *-ion,* as in conc*e*de—conc*e*ssion, dec*i*de—dec*i*sion, red*u*ce—red*u*ction.

This discussion has focused on vowel spellings represented by single or primary vowel letters. Venezky observes that vowel spellings represented by two or secondary vowel letters occur less frequently and usually represent a limited number of vowel-sound correspondences. In addition, the letter pattern–sound pattern correspondences for secondary vowels tend not to vary with different stress patterns, as illustrated by contrasting the secondary vowel correspondences in n*eu*tral—n*eu*trality, c*au*se—c*au*sation with the primary vowel correspondences in m*e*lody—m*e*lodious, c*o*ne—c*o*nic.

Secondary spellings also differ from primary on the basis of historical perspective. Primary spellings are present in the oldest English records and have been subject to the sound changes that occurred during the transition from Old English to the present (see discussion in Chapter 3); the secondary vowel spellings came into English during the late Middle English period and so have experienced fewer sound changes.

A final clue to understanding the letter pattern–sound pattern relationships is found in the distinction between patterns based on the spelling system and those based on phonological habits. For example, the spelling generalization that the consonant letter *c* represents /s/ when followed by *e, i,* or *y* (as in city /sitiy/) and otherwise represents /k/ (as in cat /kat/) may be of value in the instructional program. On the other hand, the generalization that the final consonant *s* is pronounced as /z/ following voiced sounds (as in dogs /z/), as /əz/ (as in buzzes /əz/) after /s, z, š, ž, č, ǰ/, and as /s/ (hops /s/) in all other contexts is based on the sound system. For this reason the native speaker of English will automatically produce the latter changes, and so there is little need to be concerned with those in the instructional program.

The syllable: graphemic bases and syllable units

The decoding value of syllabication lies mainly in the visual identification of pronounceable units that can then be tested for meaning as the reader uses letter-sound correspondences, letter pattern–sound pattern correspondences, and context clues. It is not unusual to find reading instructional programs of the past that rely heavily on the dictionary approach to syllabication for decoding purposes. In some instances this required that the reader know how to pronounce the word before he could decode it, which resulted in substantial confusion for many children.

As Groff points out in his discussion of the syllable, English may be termed a "stress-timed language,"[16] therefore it is relatively easy to identify the number of syllables in a given word; it is more difficult, however, to establish syllable boundaries. "The syllable presents a problem similar to that of a cartographer deciding exactly how much of the valley between two hills belongs to each hill."[17]

The internal structure of the syllable is constituted by a major element or nucleus, usually a vowel. The sound features contrasted in a syllable are usually a vowel and consonant, which results in greater prominence for one part of the syllable. This contrast normally produces a "crest" effect for part of the syllable. The sounds (usually consonants) that precede and follow the vowel normally have less acoustical energy and are analogous to the sloping sides of a valley. The intonation pattern (pitch, stress, and juncture—see Chapters 2 and 3) within the word and sentence context will determine the degree of acoustical energy used in syllable production. This characteristic of English intonation may produce a pattern of stressed-unstressed syllables that results in the schwa sound /ə/. For example in the sentences "The fruit *can* /kæn/ is on the shelf," "I can /kən/ run fast," a different intonation pattern produces an obvious difference in vowel values.

Certain glided vowels can form syllables in themselves because of the peak resulting from concentration of acoustical energy. Certain consonant phonemes with vowel characteristics can also form syllables in certain sound pattern contexts—for example the syllabic consonants /l/, /m/, and /n/ in the words little, rhythm, and botany. Most such syllabic consonants occur when two successive and easily linked consonants occur in adjacent syllables and have almost identical points of articulation as is the case with /t/ and /l/ in the word little.[18]

GRAPHEMIC BASES: SPELLING-SOUND UNITS

What application can we make of this information on the syllable? The highly predictable acoustical energy given to vowel sounds provides a direct and predictable clue to visual segmentation of letter patterns in words for decoding instruction. These letter-sound units, which have been identified as *graphemic bases,*[19] consist of the following letter sequences:

1. Vowel letter(s) followed by a consonant: -at /æt/ in bat; -oat /owt/ in boat
2. Vowel letter(s) followed by a consonant cluster: -and /ænd/ in sand; -ound /ownd/ in pound
3. Vowel letter(s) followed by a consonant or consonant cluster and a final *e:* -ate /eyt/ in bate
4. Vowel letter(s) followed by a consonant or consonant cluster and a vowel letter: -unny /əniy/ in funny

The graphemic base closely approximates Jones's definition of a closed syllable or graphoneme, which she defines as a unit "which begins with a vowel and ends with a consonant, semivowel, or 'silent e'."[20]

This spelling-sound unit provides the early reader with a letter sequence that he can easily identify visually, avoids the sound distortion that results from pronunciation of individual sound-letter correspondences in isolation, and allows for application of letter-sound correspondence knowledge through blending. There is research that supports the notion that the highly predictable nature of the graphonic base unit greatly facilitates the decoding process.[21] Skailand found that children taught by a spelling

pattern approach of this type were significantly more effective in identifying words and syllables than were children taught by a single letter-sound or whole word approach.[22] Gibson et al. concluded that some children may come to use such units automatically in the decoding process,[23] but specific instruction in the visual recognition and utilization of larger letter units will facilitate the decoding abilities of many children.

Jones's analysis of a random sample of 1,432 words from the *Thorndike-Barnhart Beginning Dictionary* (Scott, Foresman, and Company, 1964) revealed that over 90 percent of the syllable units followed the vowel-consonant and vowel-consonant-final *e* pattern.[24] The utility of this unit for decoding instruction is thus obvious. As the reader gains control over the decoding system the graphonic base provides a rapid recognition spelling-sound unit that greatly enhances his decoding ability.

SYLLABLE UNITS

The concept of syllable we gave earlier in this section provides for an understanding of written language units that represent oral language equivalents. The visual identification of specific letter sequences for pronunciation purposes can greatly facilitate the decoding process. Specific generalizations, which will be developed from an instructional standpoint later in this chapter, account for four types of visual segmentation:

1. Identification of compound words
2. Identification of prefixes, suffixes, graphemic bases, and "root" words
3. Identification of consonant clusters and of consonant digraphs that serve to suggest word segmentation for pronounceable parts; the use of stress or accent in pronouncing multisyllabic words
4. Identification of consonant and vowel segmentation points that lead to pronounceable parts and to the understanding of stress in syllable pronunciation

Syllabication generalizations must always account for meaning in the sentence and story context. Instruction in this aspect of decoding must be adjusted to cognitive operations of the child. An abstract generalization will be of little value to the child unless he clearly understands its formulation and application. For this reason syllable generalizations can be most effectively developed by inducing them from familiar vocabulary and then applying them to decodable words already in the child's familiar oral language vocabulary.

Context clues

Context clues are valuable in the decoding process as meaning clues to narrow the limits for decoding new words and to test the meaningfulness of the word or words identified through letter-sound and letter pattern–

sound pattern relationships. For example, in the sentence "The small puppy wagged its tail," the child may have difficulty in decoding the word *small*. From the sentence context he may quickly conclude that the word could be *little, tiny,* or *small*. His recognition of the initial consonant cluster *sm* or the graphemic base *all* will immediately suggest that the word is *small*. The combined use of contextual knowledge and knowledge of the relationship between the writing and sound systems should be consistently emphasized. As the child matures in his decoding he will increasingly use context as a major device for decoding and understanding new vocabulary.

Context clues may be considered in four categories: nonlinguistic clues, lexical clues, relational clues, and interpretive clues. Nonlinguistic clues derive mostly from pictures that accompany the story and suggest the nature of the action. Lexical clues result from the meaningful content immediately surrounding the word in question. Relational clues stem from syntactical relationships in the sentence. Interpretive clues result from the child's awareness of story organization which lets him use contextual information to bridge sentences and paragraphs in the reading material. Suggestions for developing context clues occur later in this chapter.

Rapid recognition vocabulary

A number of words should be developed as rapid recognition vocabulary, because of the inconsistent nature of their writing-sound relationships, of their high utility in the reading process, or both. Many of the high-frequency words in English that develop relational meaning are highly irregular spelling-sound forms. Fortunately these words are not large in number, but they are used with great frequency.

A recent study by Johnson of the high-frequency words in two vocabulary studies identifies frequently used words that require particular attention.[25] The more recent of the two studies, conducted by Kucera and Francis, is based on an analysis of present-day American English.[26] Representative of the 220 words of greatest frequency are *the, of, and, to, a, in, that, is, was, he, for, it, with,* and *as.*

The second study was the one published in the early 1940s by Dolch.[27] This 220-word list is a combined list derived from *The Child Study Committee of the International Kindergarten Union's Vocabulary List* (1929), *The Gates Primary Word List* (1926), and *The Wheeler-Howell First Grade Vocabulary List* (1929). The Kucera-Francis list and the Dolch list have 138 words in common, which shows their importance to communication and stability over time.

The eighty-two Dolch words not on the Kucera-Francis list may in part be unique to early reading materials and children's language—words like *am, ask, ate, black, blue, yellow, buy, drink, eat, laugh, ran,* and *saw.* It is clear that many of the words from the Kucera-Francis list and the Dolch list are the structure or function words that are of critical importance to relational meaning, words that are the "glue" of our language. Because these words often fail to fit regular letter-sound and letter pattern–sound pattern correspondences, they must be established as rapid recognition vocabulary. The Kucera-Francis list and the Dolch words not found on this list are presented later in this chapter.

Another type of vocabulary that presents difficulty from the standpoint of English spelling-sound regularity is vocabulary borrowed from other languages, words like *sequoia, kayak, caribou, bureau, frijole,* and *pueblo.* There is a list of such words, including their origin, later in this chapter. Vocabulary of foreign origin can best be learned through dictionary use. A few of these words follow English spelling patterns to some degree, but many spelling-sound inconsistencies are present.

STRATEGIES FOR PREREADING INSTRUCTION

These decoding units and strategies provide the basis for the instructional program, but the teacher should anticipate a wide range of competence in children's prereading abilities, and should understand specific instructional techniques in order to develop the decoding program.

Readiness has been defined by Ausubel as "the adequacy of existing capacity in relation to the demands of a given learning task."[28] The child's success in developing early decoding ability will depend to a great extent on his level of prereading readiness. Major factors affecting his readiness include his language development, cognitive and affective development, and perceptual development (visual and auditory). Physiological factors such as visual and hearing acuity (discussed in Chapter 14) are also important.

Language development

The discussion of children's language development in Chapter 4 indicated that most children at the kindergarten and first grade levels have achieved a high degree of control over lexical and relational meaning, but that they may have difficulty with more complex grammatical forms. The listening and speaking vocabularies of children are of great value in the early stages of reading instruction.

The teacher's greatest concern must be language differences between home and school. It is very important that language labels and concepts unique to the instructional setting be clearly established. These include things like direction labels (left, right, top, bottom), ordering labels (first, second, third), and color labels (red, green, yellow, black, orange, blue).

You must also attend to instructional language varieties that differ from those used in the home. For example, printed language forms such as *I will, they will,* and *going to* differ from the familiar oral language units *I'll, they'll* and *gonna.* You can develop such variations effectively through a language experience approach to early reading by recording the child's oral language that serves to develop transition from an informal language style to a formal style encounter with printed materials.

If you understand the nonstandard language variations discussed in Chapter 9 you can determine when the child is experiencing difficulty in early reading and when his oral reading miscues directly reflect his highly consistent language forms (also see Chapter 14 for discussion of reading miscues). By utilizing the language forms the child brings to the classroom you can effectively improve the child's self-concept as a language user and relate this directly to reading instruction through language experience charts.[29] It is most important that the child's language facility and vocabulary be accepted as worthwhile in a meaningful way. Except for some degree of homophone and grammatical interference points (see Chapter 9) the child's language forms should not interfere with his early decoding instruction. You must not insist, however, that each word be enunciated according to a standard English norm. A language-based approach will enable the child to develop letter-sound and letter pattern–sound pattern correspondences appropriate to his dialect. Concern, however, will need to be given to the new labels and concepts developed in the reading material (see Chapter 11). This is important not only for minority group children but for all youngsters.

Cognitive and affective development

The act of decoding requires that the child perceive, match, sort, and reorganize language units. As we discussed earlier in this chapter and in Chapter 2, cognitive strategies must be developed to process symbols and conceptualize experience.[30] The child must be effective in drawing decoding inferences from sentence context and in shifting to new decoding sets when one decoding approach fails.[31] To do this his cognitive development must be at a level that enables him to use reversible operations and to reorganize decoding units in ways that lead to independent word analysis.[32]

Although various methodological problems can be identified in the early reading research dealing with optimal ages for the initiation of reading instruction, there is an interesting repetitive finding. Several research studies indicate that the best time to initiate decoding instruction is between the mental ages of six and seven.[33] This period corresponds with the development of the concrete operation stage and the corresponding mental processes defined by Piaget.[34] These mental operations appear to be necessary for analysis, reorganization, and synthesis of decoding units, except for decoding emphasis on sight vocabulary, which suggests that if children are to use spelling-sound units for decoding effectively, their cognitive development must have reached a level that provides for the necessary mental operations.

The research of Durkin clearly indicates that some children have already mastered basic decoding concepts by the time they begin the first grade.[35] Although the cognitive operations of these children appear to span a wide range as suggested by their mental age, most were found to be above average in mental maturation. Durkin did not explore the specifics of the children's cognitive development, but one might speculate that these early readers possessed some degree of control over such operations as reversibility.

The instructional program must account for individual levels of cognition by adjusting the degree of abstraction necessary for successful encounter with the writing system. Some children will require that the teacher, teaching assistant, or tutor record their personal experiences in print as the means of developing the basic concept that writing represents speech. Emphasis on sound-letter correspondences may best be introduced by using familiar concrete objects with initial sounds that correspond with three-dimensional manipulative letters that can be used to build familiar words, while with more advanced youngsters you can emphasize spelling pattern–sound pattern correspondences using familiar vocabulary. The specific instructional techniques discussed later in this chapter represent varying degrees of abstraction.

The child's inherent desire to learn should be a focal point in decoding instruction. Learning to read should be enjoyable to the child, not an onerous task undertaken because of intense pressure from teacher or parent. As Gibson observes, "Reading should be a consummatory activity that functions as its own incentive and reward because of the appeal of the information to be picked up. . . . Reduction of uncertainty is a potent internal reinforcer. Finding an answer to a practical question can do this.[36] As the individual confronts the reading task, his motivation as reflected in persistence and drive is extremely important. This viewpoint is supported by Durkin's findings that the preschool reader is a child who is serious and persistent, possesses the ability to concentrate, and is curious.[37] Many of the reading-language activities discussed so far have been designed to develop a high degree of motivation and interest in reading-language learning. The instructional suggestions that follow have this concern uppermost in mind.

Many factors influence cognitive and affective development, such as the degree of language interaction between parent and child, the value placed in the home on the importance of reading and language activities, experiences related to cognitive development, and the rate of individual maturation. The teacher's understanding of a child's level of cognitive and affective growth can be of great value in developing an instructional program that assures a successful initial encounter with reading.

Perceptual development

Prereading visual discrimination and auditory perception abilities are critical to early reading success. Basic to this development, however, as it relates to decoding instruction is the child's understanding of the representational nature of pictures and writing. An understanding of the way oral language is represented can be developed through activities such as the following:

1. Use illustrations and photographs as the basis for oral language discussions followed by the development of written labels for key persons, animals, or objects in the pictures.
2. Print the name of each child on tagboard and place it on his desk. After he recognizes his own name he can contrast it with other children's names.
3. Label objects in the classroom with word cards: chair, door, piano, chalkboard, and desk. Once children have some degree of familiarity with the representations for these familiar objects one group of children can remove the labels and another group can attempt to replace them in the appropriate locations.
4. Have children complete a drawing of a family member or favorite animal, then label the child's picture and display it on a bulletin board.

Such activities help the child grasp the understanding that our oral language can be represented by pictures and print.

Other activities may be related to "body talk," to the ways we express feelings through gestures. Pictures in magazines that illustrate concepts such as happy, sad, anger, love, and fear may be identified. Following a discussion of these illustrations the children may wish to enact such feelings using body gestures. The pictures may then be labeled and displayed in the classroom.

As the concept of picture and writing symbolization is developed, activities should be introduced for the purpose of developing visual discrimination. In the initial stage this may take the form of visual discrimination and matching of animals and objects. Finer discrimination can be developed by moving to geometric shapes, which may vary first in size, then in color, and at a more advanced stage in both size and color. Television programs such as "Sesame Street" and "Misterogers" provide for discrimination of geometric shapes and should serve to facilitate this aspect of visual discrimination. Some children may be well beyond this stage of perceptual

development.

For purposes of decoding, however, visual discrimination must be developed to a new level in that the child must be effective in discriminating between graphemes, some of which are very similar. Pick's research has indicated that presentation of letter pairs in the following order may prove useful in instruction:[38]

b-d, p-q	Differ in left-right orientation
n-w, n-u, m-w	Differ in top-bottom orientation
b-p, d-g	Differ in direction of extension
i-j, q-a, d-a, g-a, n-h	Differ in presence of extension
U-V, P-F, u-v	Differ in line-curve

Pick found that if these letter groups were presented in contrasting form children were more effective in their visual discrimination of them because they could recognize the relevant contrasting features.

Although letter name knowledge may prove useful in communicating about letter forms, it is not essential to letter discrimination. The visual features of letters are the most important factor in this early aspect of decoding. Introductory work in developing visual discrimination should

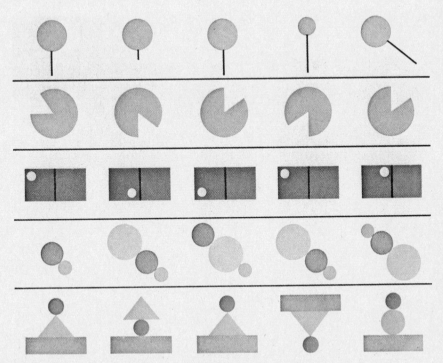

Figure 10-2. Visual Matching. *From Eldonna L. Evertts, Lyman C. Hunt, and Bernard J. Weiss,* About Me, *Teacher's Edition,* © *1973 by Holt, Rinehart and Winston, Inc.*

utilize concrete sensory activities and meaningful context as often as possible. The following examples illustrate this emphasis.

1. Cut out the specific letter or letters to be emphasized from heavy cardboard (¼ inch). Display the letter or letters under a picture that can be represented by a word that uses the letter(s) in the initial position, such as a three-dimensional *b* under the picture of a boat or book. Encourage the child to examine the letter, talk about the letter and picture, and identify other words beginning with the same sound—box, boy.

2. Prepare three letters, two of which are alike (b, b, l), as described above. Display two contrasting letters, *b* and *l*, before the child or children. Identify several words beginning with these letters by using pictures. Print the label under each picture based on the class discussion—ball, box, lion, lamp. Have the children match each cardboard letter with the beginning letter of the appropriate word representing the picture. Finally, display the three letters before the children and encourage them to identify which two letters are alike or "which one doesn't belong." In the discussion they should identify how the letters *b* and *l* are different in shape by noting the curved part of *b* as contrasted with *l.* Such an activity may be concluded by asking the children to draw pictures that represent words starting with each letter. Then you may print the picture word underneath the picture, contrasting the initial letters for each word picture. Give the child a chance to examine and match the three-dimensional letters with the initial letters for his word picture.

Other letter discrimination tasks may involve letter-matching games. For example, tagboard cards can be prepared with printed letters and a small picture representing the initial letter sound pasted in the upper lefthand corner. Children in teams of two can then draw letter cards from the card deck and match them with letters placed on the chalkboard or on a letter chart. A word that contains the letter should then be identified.

Initial instruction in letter discrimination may emphasize letters that are distinctly different visually, such as *b* and *l* as illustrated above. After the concept of letter discrimination based on shape has been introduced, develop the potentially confusable letter pairs identified by Pick by noting the different line orientations, such as the top and bottom extensions in *b* and *p.*

The next level of visual discrimination may consist of reinforcing letter discrimination by a tactile-kinesthetic approach. This may involve tracing the letter, as in Figure 10-3.

As the child develops visual discrimination skill he should have opportunities to identify specific graphemes in word contexts. For example, ask him to select from a series of word-picture cards—saw, goat, seal, cane, socks —those words that have the same initial letters. Similar activities can be developed for medial and final consonant letters and for vowel letters.

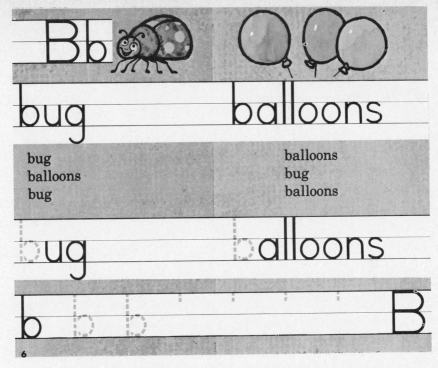

Figure 10-3. *From Leo Fay,* ABC and Me, © *Lyons & Carnahan. Reprinted by permission of Lyons & Carnahan.*

Practice in left-to-right sequencing requires constant attention in various activities. Two such exercises are shown in Figure 10-4.

The teacher should also develop the idea of left-to-right sequencing when he arranges material on the chalkboard, sequences material on the bulletin board, or displays pictures for story-telling purposes.

It should be emphasized that these instructional illustrations develop visual discrimination within a meaningful context. The primary emphasis on meaning has been at the word level, though the oral context used to discuss the words also incorporates sentence meaning. This instructional approach provides not only for introduction of a new visual discrimination concept based on the child's vocabulary knowledge but also for early association between the letter discrimination practice and the sound correspondences using familiar oral vocabulary.

The auditory discrimination abilities of many children will be well developed upon entrance to the school setting. Some children, however, will experience difficulty in discriminating sound contrasts when sounds are presented in isolation, as is the case in some instructional programs. Exercises used for auditory perception development should never contain sound units of less than a syllable; otherwise the sound values will be distorted and will result in confusion when the child attempts to apply sound discrimination knowledge to decoding tasks.

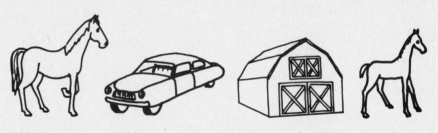

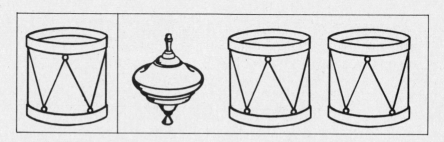

Figure 10-4. Gross Discrimination: Left-to-Right Progression. (Top) Have the pupils place their index fingers on the dot and trace the dashed line before discussing which two pictures are alike. (Bottom) Color the pictures in the row that are like the first picture. Begin the row at the left. *Bottom from* Phonics Workbook, *Book A, by Elwell, Murray, and Kucia. Copyright 1970 by Modern Curriculum Press and reprinted with their permission.*

Auditory discrimination begins during the child's early years. His familiarity with sound discrimination, however, has normally consisted of comprehending words within a sentence context, so when the decoding program requires him to focus on minimal contrasts in words such as *bat* and *pat,* some degree of confusion may result.

Exercises designed to focus attention on specific units of auditory discrimination should use vocabulary the child is familiar with. The criterion of meaning is also essential in auditory discrimination tasks. Activities such as the following develop auditory discrimination.

1. Identify a word that contains the initial sound to be emphasized, for example the initial consonant in *rope*. Ask the children to clap their hands when they hear a word that begins with the same sound. Pronounce words such as *rabbit, road, car, ring, home,* and *rain,* and note the children's responses.

2. Similar exercises may be carried out using rhyming endings, with the children identifying ending sounds that are alike: "Which words have ending sounds like *cot?*" (hot, cap, pot, cot, kit, nod). Exercises such as this provide the auditory base for later instruction dealing with vowel correspondences and graphemic bases. Literature experiences using rhyme (see Chapter 13) are also highly appropriate for developing auditory discrimination of ending sounds.

3. Following emphasis on auditory perception based on words, focus attention on picture representations with a similar purpose (Figure 10-5).

Figure 10-5. Auditory Discrimination: Rhyming Words; Cognitive Development: Association. From *Eldonna L. Evertts, Lyman C. Hunt, and Bernard J. Weiss,* About Me, *Teacher's Edition,* © *1973 by Holt, Rinehart and Winston, Inc.*

The exercises pictured in Figure 10-6 illustrate those used to develop auditory discrimination. Direct attention to the first picture. Have the picture on the left identified. Have pupils listen as you say the word *map,* noting its beginning sound. Have pupils listen and note the beginning sound of the name of each picture on the right of the line as it is identified. Then have a pupil give the name of the picture on the right of the line that begins with the same sound as the name of the picture on the left of the line.

Figure 10-6. Auditory Discrimination (*m*). *Reprinted from* On Our Way to Read *by Byron H. Van Roekel, Copyright* © *1966 Harper & Row, Publishers, Inc.*

Have the pupils look at the three pictures in the left-hand box of Figure 10-7. Ask a pupil to identify the picture in the circle (box). Have another pupil identify the two pictures under the picture in the circle (fox, deer).

Have pupils listen as you say box-deer-fox. Then have a pupil identify the two words that sounded almost alike.

Figure 10-7. Auditory Perception (Rhyming Words). *Reprinted from* On Our Way to Read *by Byron H. Van Roekel, Copyright © 1966 Harper & Row, Publishers, Inc.*

It is important to keep in mind that the children require different degrees of emphasis in developing auditory perception and visual discrimination abilities. In past instructional programs these two abilities have been separated so as to develop each skill. As the child develops ability in letter discrimination and auditory perception, stress the relationship of these two abilities directly through the development of letter-sound relationships within a meaningful word context, as illustrated in Figure 10-8. The exercises in Figure 10-9 and Figure 10-10 illustrate development of initial

Figure 10-8. Auditory Discrimination: Phoneme-Grapheme Correspondence /m/ m. From Eldonna L. Evertts, Lyman C. Hunt, and Bernard J. Weiss, Hear, See, Say! © 1973 by Holt, Rinehart and Winston, Inc.

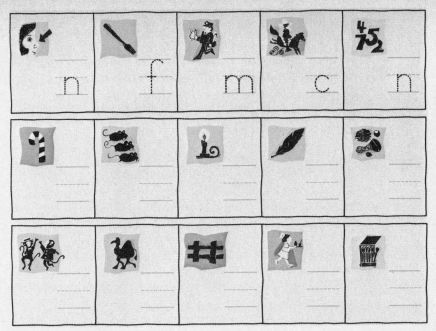

Figure 10-9. Visual-Auditory-Kinesthetic Reinforcement of Initial Consonants: n, f, m, c. *From* My Sound and Word Book, *by Theodore Clymer and Thomas C. Barrett, of the Reading 360 series.* © *Copyright, 1969, by Ginn and Company. Used with permission.*

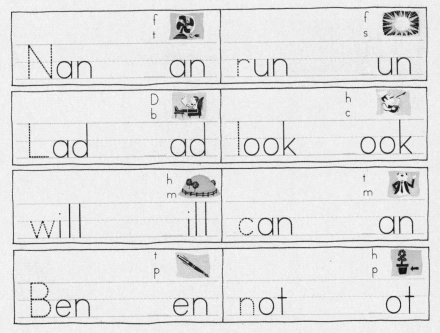

Figure 10-10. Substitution of Initial Consonants to Complete Words. *From* My Sound and Word Book, *by Theodore Clymer and Thomas C. Barrett, of the Reading 360 series.* © *Copyright, 1969, by Ginn and Company. Used with permission.*

consonants with in a meaningful picture and word context. These exercises also provide for a tactile-kinesthetic reinforcement, because the child writes the initial consonant to complete the word and sentence context. Vowel correspondences require similar attention. There are specific suggestions for the development of letter-sound and letter pattern–sound pattern units in the next section.

Evaluation of prereading competence

The evaluation of prereading ability is often based on reading readiness instruments. Because of the widespread practice of basing school entrance on chronological age there is a wide range of prereading readiness levels in the kindergarten or first grade classroom. Standardized readiness tests administered early in the first grade have been shown to correlate from .40 to approximately .60 with reading achievement at the end of the first grade.[39] The magnitude of these correlations indicates that at best readiness tests account for approximately one-third of the variance in reading achievement. This limited information, however, may be of some interpretive value to the classroom teacher. These instruments commonly evaluate the student's word knowledge, recognition of letter forms, word matching, shape completion, perception of beginning sounds, perception of ending sounds, listening comprehension (usually based on sentence context), letter name knowledge, and number knowledge. Some instruments make provision for drawing a human figure, in a draw-a-man test. The following list summarizes the nature of representative readiness instruments.

Clymer-Barrett Prereading Battery	Evaluates reading letters, word matching, discrimination of beginning and ending sounds, form completion, and sentence copying. Checklist of readiness behaviors provided. Group administered, thirty to ninety minutes (Personnel Press).
Harrison-Stroud Reading Readiness Profiles	Evaluates visual discrimination, use of context, context and auditory clues, auditory discrimination, and using symbols. Group administered, seventy-five minutes (Houghton Mifflin Company).
Lee-Clark Reading Readiness Test	Evaluates discrimination of letters, picture selection based on verbal description, discrimination of printed word forms. Group administered, fifteen minutes (California Test Bureau).

Metropolitan Readiness Test	Evaluates word meaning, listening in sentence context, matching letters and forms, alphabet knowledge, numbers and draw-a-man test. Group administered, sixty minutes (Harcourt Brace Jovanovich, Inc.).
Murphy-Durrell Diagnostic Reading Readiness Test	Evaluates auditory discrimination, visual discrimination, letter name knowledge, and learning rate. Group administered (Harcourt Brace Jovanovich, Inc.).

The most effective use of reading readiness test information is for instructional interpretation purposes rather than for predictive purposes.[40] Readiness instruments that have been developed to accompany reading programs may be more appropriate for instruction because the information measured is often directly related to the reading skills to be developed. In any case you should use such readiness information as but one source of information in meeting the instructional needs of children.

Although group mental maturity tests have been widely used in the past to assess the "intellectual potential" of the early reader, this practice may be seriously questioned. A major problem resides in the test-taking behavior required of young children and in possible cultural bias.[41] In addition, the substantial correlation between group mental maturity and group readiness tests makes little provision for additional information that may contribute to the design of the instructional program.

Teacher observation of classroom prereading performance is the most valid way of determining reading readiness.[42] Consideration of the following factors will be of substantial value in identifying the child's prereading readiness:

1. Comprehends oral language in simple story-reading or story-telling situations
2. Possesses adequate control and organization over oral language in retelling a simple story or personal experience
3. Understands labels essential to following directions
4. Demonstrates ability to use simple inference for story conclusions
5. Exhibits auditory perception development in identifying and producing words with similar beginning sounds and rhyming endings
6. Demonstrates visual discrimination ability by matching identical letters representing initial, medial, and final letters in familiar words
7. Exhibits sensory-motor control in simple line drawings of people or geometric forms or in writing his own name
8. Demonstrates an attention span adequate to participate in a given activity for five to ten minutes

9. Shows curiosity and interest in picture story books, pictures that accompany a story line, and in the way pictures or print represent oral language

10. Demonstrates persistence in completing simple tasks and can work cooperatively in small-group situations with other children

By combining information sources and relying heavily on direct classroom observations, you can most effectively determine the nature of the child's prereading readiness and construct an instructional program based on the individual readiness needs of specific youngsters.

INSTRUCTIONAL STRATEGIES FOR DECODING

Decoding ability should be developed from the earliest levels in the context of pronounceable, meaningful language units, that is, in the context of the syllable, word, and sentence. This approach enables the child to discover the way written language units represent oral language and to arrive at generalizations about the nature of this relationship. There will be times, however, when deductive development of letter-sound or letter pattern–sound pattern relationships will be appropriate, depending on the child's developmental level and the nature of the learning task. The following suggestions illustrate the way to develop decoding strategies in the classroom. Examine them with an eye toward application to individual youngsters. Most reading systems provide a decoding sequence in the instructional program, but if you should wish to adjust the sequence to meet the needs of individual youngsters more effectively or to design the instructional program within the classroom, the following techniques will be of value. These strategies can be used in conjunction with one another, and it is not necessary, for example, to develop letter-sound correspondences entirely before emphasizing graphemic bases.

Developing letter-sound or grapheme-phoneme correspondences

Instruction in developing letter-sound correspondences can be effectively initiated by using a small number of rapid recognition words developed from a familiar vocabulary and sentence context. The first correspondences will in many cases be consonants in the initial position in words, followed by the same consonants in final position, and consonant substitution in initial and final position. Early vowel correspondences will often be unglided or short vowel correspondences, followed by the glided or long vowel equivalents, with opportunity to contrast the unglided and glided vowel correspondences in letter pattern–sound pattern relationships.

Several teaching procedures should be kept clearly in mind:

1. Letter-sound correspondences should be developed in context through techniques such as minimal contrasts (bin, fin), not by isolating letters and sounds.

2. Children should understand that the "letters and letter patterns stand for or represent sounds and sound patterns," not that "letters make sounds."

3. Variations in dialect will result in different sound equivalents for letter-sound correspondences. This should not be cause for concern because the child will develop letter-sound and letter pattern–sound pattern equivalents based on his dialect. The option, of course, is to add a standard English dialect to the child's language repertoire before you initiate decoding instruction (see instruction priorities discussed in Chapter 9).

4. Build letter-sound correspondences through the use of reading that results in high interest reinforcement over a substantial period of time.

5. Use the following sequence as often as possible in developing letter-sound correspondences: introduce correspondence in known vocabulary context; develop visual association in letter context; provide a range of examples of a letter-sound correspondence in the same position in words; contrast a letter-sound correspondence with other correspondence in the same position; encourage children to provide examples of letter-sound correspondence in words they know and to use these words in sentence context.

Instructional techniques for developing letter-sound correspondences include the following.

INTRODUCTION OF LETTER-SOUND CORRESPONDENCE

A word card and a picture representing the word are displayed, for example, *ball*. The word is read, if necessary with your assistance, and used in oral context by discussing the type of ball and the child's experience with the ball represented by the picture. Picture cards (which may be prepared from magazines) representing objects with the initial consonant /b/ are also displayed. The child is encouraged to identify each word and to listen for the initial sound in each picture word—*boy, boat, book,* etc. As the words are identified you should write each word on the board and encourage the children to think of other words that begin with the same consonant sound.

You should then pronounce several words with the initial consonant /b/ and contrast initial consonants such as /p/ in *pin, pig, pitcher,* etc. Encourage the children to identify from the contrasting initial sounds the words that begin the same as the initial sound in *ball* /b/. Several of these words should also be added to the list on the chalkboard, contrasting the letter-sound correspondence in *ball* /b/ with the correspondence in *pin* /p/. Encourage the children to provide additional examples of words beginning with the same initial letter-sound correspondence.

After several consonant correspondences have been introduced, tagboard cards with the printed letters may be prepared. These cards should then be placed in the pocket chart or displayed on the table in front of the children. Then you can pronounce several words that contain the initial consonant sound and ask the children to identify the letter that represents that sound. This same reinforcement activity can be used with final consonants, vowel correspondences, and more advanced decoding skills.

DEVELOPING SUBSTITUTION USING CONTEXT

Prepare a series of sentences with vocabulary containing the consonant correspondence to be emphasized. Change the word containing the correspondence by substituting another consonant correspondence in the initial part of the word. The children are to read each sentence, examine the altered word below the sentence blank for information on possible words, and think of a word that will complete the sentence context. They should understand that the appropriate word can be identified by changing the initial consonant letter. For example:

1. The ＿＿ will eat the food.
   (fan)

2. The girls were playing ＿＿
   (rag).

3. The boy has a ＿＿ ball.
   (fig)

4. The paper was very ＿＿
   (shin).

Additional opportunity to generalize correspondences to new letter-sound contexts must be provided. The following exercises illustrate such generalization.

The exercise in Figure 10-12 *incorporates* the use of sentence context to aid in development of the correspondences.

Vowel correspondences can be developed in a similar fashion. For example, the glided or long vowel sound in the word *he* /iy/ can be introduced by placing words such as *me, he,* and *we* on the chalkboard or on newsprint (for later reference). Read the words aloud and encourage the children to note the similarity in the sounds. Emphasize the representation by the letter *e* of the vowel sound at the end of each word. After using these words in context, other vocabulary with the glided vowel /iy/ in the final position—bee, tree, knee, see—should be identified by you or the children. The letter representation of *e* as in *me* and *ee* as in *tree* for the ending vowel sound should be noted. Development of the vowel correspondence in *tree* will make provision for consideration of the glided or long vowel sound in words like jeep, seed, week, and weed.

Initial consonant substitution for these words is another way of emphasizing the glided vowel sound and makes direct provision for developing a letter pattern–sound pattern unit or graphemic base *-eep*. By using several bases such as *-eep, -eed,* and *-eek* and by substituting initial consonants, children can generate the following words:

-eep	-eed	-eek
jeep	seed	week
deep	feed	seek
weep	weed	peek

m   n

su___   ___ouse

trai___   ___urse

broo___   ___est

dru___   ___oon

Figure 10-11. Phonemic analysis: Correspondences /m/*m*, /n/*n* in Initial and Final Position. *From* Skills Handbook for A Duck Is a Duck and Helicopters and Gingerbread, *by Theodore Clymer and Billie Parr, of the Reading 360 series,* © *Copyright, 1969, by Ginn and Company. Used with permission.*

Figure 10-12. Substitution of Initial Consonants to Complete Words and Sentences. *From* My Sound and Word Book, *by Theodore Clymer and Thomas C. Barrett, of the Reading 360 series,* © *Copyright, 1969, by Ginn and Company. Used with permission.*

Introduction of the unglided or short vowel correspondences may precede or follow the development of glided or long vowel correspondences. The value of introducing letters and letter patterns that represent glided and unglided vowels in close proximity lies in establishing a "set for diversity" with children. Such a set will encourage them to reach the understanding that a given letter can represent several vowel values depending on the letter and sound context.

The procedure for introducing unglided or short vowel sounds may follow that already described. If you initially present words containing the unglided vowel correspondence, the child comes to understand the stable vowel value represented by the letter, for example, *fed, red, bed.* Then you can change the final consonant to develop several endings: *-ed, -et,* and *-en.* The children can then use these units with initial consonant substitution to create a group of similar words for each ending:

-ed	-et	-en
bed	pet	hen
red	net	men
fed	get	den

324 Once you have established the unglided or short vowel correspondence

/e/ as in *fed* and the glided or long vowel correspondence /iy/ as in *feed*, then you can introduce the "set for diversity" concept by contrasting correspondences, initially by observing sound values associated with letters in familiar word groups such as the following:

fed	feed
bet	beet
Ned	need
pep	peep
step	steep
slept	sleep

There is a wide range of reinforcement activities for further developing letter-sound contrasts. For example, words such as those above can be printed on three-by-five-inch tagboard cards, the cards can be shuffled, and the child matches the word pairs that represent the unglided and glided vowel values, such as *fed, feed.* Then he can use the vocabulary in sentence context: "José took the feed to the barn and fed the tiny kitten."

The following are game activities to reinforce letter-sound correspondences.

1. Develop a set of tagboard word cards containing the following words:

hid	hide	bet	beet
rid	ride	pep	peep
dim	dime	step	steep
Tim	time	Ned	need

The children stand in a circle with one player in the middle. The cards are distributed to the circle players. The teacher or another child with a master list of words pronounces a word representing an unglided (or glided) vowel sound, for example, *hid.* The child who has the card with *hid* is to exchange places with the child who has the word card with *hide,* the glided vowel equivalent. The latter player must of course recognize that he has the "matching" word to complete the exchange. The child in the center will attempt to slip into one of the vacated places in the circle before the two players can exchange places. The child without a space becomes the next center player.

2. Develop two sets of tagboard cards. On the first set print words with the vowel graphemes *a, e, i, o,* and *u* that represent the unglided or short vowel values, for example, *bat, pet, pig, pot,* and *nut.* Place a rectangle around each word. On the second deck also print words with vowel letters representing unglided vowels.

bag	led	pig	dog	cut
man	let	bid	fog	but

Shuffle both decks together and distribute the cards to a small group. The player to the right of the dealer places a card with a rectangle around it on the table if he has one. If he does not, the play passes to the next person until a word with a rectangle is played. Each player tries to play on the vowel correspondence represented by the word in the rectangle. When all words have been played on a particular correspondence the next word with a rectangle must be played. Players continue to play until all cards are down. The person who plays out his hand first wins the game.

Instructional exercises to introduce consonant clusters follow much the same pattern as identified for consonant and vowel correspondences. The child, for example, may have already learned a word like *frog* or *from* in his rapid recognition vocabulary which contains the cluster *fr.* These words would initially be printed on the chalkboard or newsprint. Focus attention on the similarity in the initial part of the two words. Other words with the same initial sound (free, freeze) would then be developed by the group within a meaningful context. Now the consonant cluster can be contrasted with other clusters, like tree and breeze, to observe the distinct sound and visual differences. As previously indicated, once a correspondence has been introduced, it is necessary that the learning be reinforced by using the correspondence in various decoding activities, especially in sentence and story context.

Developing spelling pattern–sound pattern correspondences

On the basis of the research discussed earlier in this chapter, a series of spelling pattern–sound pattern generalizations were identified. The main value of larger decoding units is in greater predictability of sound correspondences from the spelling or letter patterns. The following generalizations, ordered here from simple to complex, were noted for unglided or short vowels:

1. A vowel letter represents an unglided or short vowel sound when it is followed by a final consonant unit or units: sat, fat; ebb, set; bit, hitch; sod, cot; rug, putt.
2. A vowel letter represents an unglided or short vowel sound when it is followed by a compound consonant unit such as -*dg* /dj/ or -x /ks/: b*a*dge, *e*xit, ch*i*cken, p*o*cket, l*u*xury.
3. A vowel letter represents an unglided or short vowel sound when it is followed by a cluster of consonant units such as *dd* or *stl*: s*a*ddle, ant*e*nna, ep*i*stle, c*o*gnate, s*u*pper.
4. When a vowel letter is followed by double or geminate consonants, it represents the unglided or short vowel sound: *a*bbess, dil*e*mma, art*i*llery, c*o*mmerce, t*u*nnel.
5. Vowel letters that precede suffixes such as -*ity,* -*ic,* and -*ion* represent unglided or short vowel sounds: s*a*nity, st*a*tic, extr*e*mity, m*e*tric, con-c*e*ssion.

326

Generalizations for glided or long vowels represented by specific vowel letter patterns include:

1. When the vowel letter is followed by a consonant and a final *e,* it represents the glided or long vowel sound: b*a*ke, f*i*ve, m*u*le, ser*e*ne, c*o*ve. This generalization is probably one of the most familiar to teachers. The following related generalizations are also valuable in establishing letter pattern–sound pattern correspondences. When the vowel letter is followed in turn by a consonant and *le,* a consonant and *re,* or by *ste,* it represents the glided or long vowel value: c*y*cle, medi*o*cre, ch*a*ste. The final *e* pattern also applies to polysyllabic words, even when the previous vowel is not stressed: micr*o*be, dec*a*de, sched*u*le.

2. A vowel letter represents a glided or long vowel sound when it is followed by a consonant unit and another vowel unit, which may include a final *e*: c*a*nine, m*e*dian.

3. A vowel letter represents a glided or long vowel sound when it is followed by a consonant unit, which in turn is followed by *l* or *r* and another vowel unit, including final *e*: l*a*dle, m*i*crobe.

4. The vowel letters *oi* and *oy* are highly consistent in representing the glided vowel sound /əy/ in s*oi*l, n*oi*se, b*oy*, and t*oy*. The vowel letters *ou* and *ow* are consistent to a high degree in representing the glided vowel sound /aw/ in *ou*t, sh*ou*t, c*ow*, and h*ow*.

5. The following vowel letter clusters (secondary vowel letters) representing glided or long vowel sounds illustrate those having some degree of predictability: *ai* in m*ai*n: *ea* in tr*ea*t; *ee* in s*ee*d; *oa* in b*oa*t; *oo* in b*oo*ster.

6. When a vowel letter (or vowel letters) occurs as the last unit of a syllable and is preceded by a consonant unit, the letter (or letters) will often represent the glided vowel sound: sh*e,* tr*ee,* cr*y,* funn*y,* d*i*ner, d*o*main, n*o*tation.

Although spelling-sound generalizations for consonant correspondences are highly predictable, consonant digraphs representing consonant sounds need special attention. These include *ch* as in chin, catcher, catch; *ch* representing a different consonant sound, as in chasm; *gh* as in ghetto; *ph* as in photo; *th* as in thin, ether, path; *th* representing a different consonant sound, as in then, either, bathe; *ps* as in psalm; *sh* as in shin, smasher, lash; *kn* as in knit; *gn* as in gnaw; *rh* as in rhetoric; and *wh* as in who.

An illustration of a highly predictable consonant letter pattern generalization follows. The consonant letter *c* represents /s/ when followed by *e, i,* or *y* (ice, city, cyst), and /k/ in other letter pattern contexts (can, cut, come). A similar generalization applies to the letter *g.* The letter *g* represents /j̈/ when followed by letters *e, i,* or *y* (gem, gin, gipsy), and /g/ otherwise (gun, go, got).

The inductive-deductive development of these generalizations should follow the instructional pattern previously described, by introducing the patterns in vocabulary known to the child. Focus attention on the letter pattern context and the regular representation of the sound correspondence. The child should identify examples of the generalization. Finally,

What vowel generalizations are being developed? What instructional strategies
is the teacher using?

328

a contrasting spelling pattern should be noted as the child develops a "set for diversity" and optional decoding generalizations that will enable him to decode the word. The following exercises illustrate the application of this instructional sequence by focusing on the first letter pattern–sound pattern generalization for glided or long vowels and the first generalization for unglided or short vowels as described above.

Place two groups of words containing vowel letters representing a glided vowel with a final *e* marker on the board (kite, bite, site; mate, rate, hate). These words should be in the children's oral language repertoire and may already be present in their rapid recognition vocabulary. After you read the words and briefly discuss each meaning, encourage the children to use the words in a sentence. Then ask them to examine the words carefully for similarities in the sequence of letters. The obvious similarity is that all of these words end with the consonant letter *t* and the letter *e*. Then encourage the children to pronounce each word and note the words that have similar vowel sounds: kite, bite, site and mate, rate, hate. Based on the child's earlier knowledge of letter-sound correspondences these vowel sounds can be identified as glided or long vowel sounds. The relationship between the final *e* letter pattern and the vowel sound should then be established. This may be facilitated with other words with the *e* marker, words like Pete, note, cute, etc. Encourage the children to identify additional words that have the final *e* marker and that rhyme with the words on the board. It may then be concluded that when the vowel letter in a word is followed by a consonant and a final *e* the vowel letter will represent the glided or long vowel sound.

This lesson can be extended at a later point to develop the corresponding unglided or short vowel generalization. The two initial word lists can be contrasted with corresponding words without a final *e* marker:

kite	kit	mate	mat
bite	bit	rate	rat
site	sit	hate	hat

As the corresponding words for each set are read, the children should contrast the sound values of each word: kite, kit; bite, bit; site, sit, etc. On the basis of earlier knowledge of letter-sound correspondences they should easily note that the second set of words contains an unglided or short vowel sound. By focusing attention on the letter similarities in kit, bit, sit and mat, rat, and hat, they can conclude that in each word ending the vowel letter and a consonant are alike for each set of words, and that the vowel letter represents an unglided or short vowel sound. The two letter patterns should then be contrasted visually so that the children note the presence of the final *e* in the first set of words and its absence in the second set. It can then be concluded that a vowel letter represents an unglided or short vowel sound when it is followed by a consonant that ends the word.

This type of exercise serves to establish the "set for diversity" as the children develop optional expectations for letter-sound correspondences by using knowledge of letter pattern–sound pattern correspondences. The activity should again be followed by application of the generalizations as children are provided with the opportunity to read material containing vocabulary with these patterns.

The second glided or long vowel generalization described above can be developed at a more advanced level by grouping familiar vocabulary that contain letter patterns with a vowel followed by a consonant unit and another vowel unit, as in canine, dated, ladle; derail, median, zebra; pilot, digest, microbe. The letter pattern and sound pattern correspondence for each set of words should be carefully observed so that the children note similarities such as that a vowel letter followed by a consonant and another vowel unit (which may include a final e) represents the glided vowel sound. This generalization can then be effectively contrasted with the second, third, fourth, and fifth unglided or short vowel generalizations stated above.

The third glided vowel generalization—a vowel letter followed by a consonant unit which in turn is followed by l or r and another vowel unit (which may include final e)—should be considered in the same manner: ladle, zebra, microbe, noble, lucre. The generalization should be developed as previously illustrated with consideration of additional words derived by the children and used in available reading material.

These two glided or long vowel generalizations may be effectively contrasted with the second, third, fourth, and fifth unglided vowel generalizations described above. This is illustrated in the following words using one of the glided vowel generalizations and the four unglided vowel generalizations.

Glided or Long Vowel Pattern	Unglided or Short Vowel Pattern			
Pattern 2 -V + C + V-	Pattern 2 -V + Compound C-	Pattern 3 -V + C cluster-	Pattern 4 -V + double C-	Pattern 5 -V + C + ity, + ic, + ion-
canine	badge	saddle	abbess	sanity
dated	exit	antenna	dilemma	static
ladle	chicken	epistle	artillery	metric
pilot	pocket	cognate	commerce	concession
dubious	luxury	supper	tunnel	decision

Such contrast provides for development of the child's "set" for optional expectancies. For example, the letter pattern in the word *sanity*, which occurs under unglided vowel pattern 5, could be analyzed to fit the glided letter pattern 2. By testing the pronunciation of the word in sentence context, however, and by noting the suffix *ity*, the child can examine the optional pronunciations and select the appropriate decoding strategy. The additional glided or long vowel generalizations should be developed through similar instructional procedures. The child's letter pattern–sound pattern knowledge also has direct application in the next section of our discussion.

Developing syllable generalizations

The ability to use visual clues for identifying pronounceable units in words is a major goal in decoding instruction, because it enables the child to utilize his knowledge of letter-sound and letter pattern–sound pattern correspondences.

IDENTIFYING GRAPHEMIC BASE UNITS

The graphemic base provides one approach to visual identification of pronounceable units. As previously discussed, this base consists of the following letter sequence variations:

1. Vowel letter(s) + consonant: for example, *at*—bat, pat, boat, catalogue
2. Vowel letter(s) + consonant cluster: *and*—sand; *ound*—pound
3. Vowel letter(s) + consonant (or C cluster) + final *e*: *ate*—bate; *edge*—ledge
4. Vowel letter(s) + consonant or C cluster + vowel letter: *ogy*—fogy; *unny*—funny

In early reading instruction the graphemic base unit aids the decoding process by providing a rapid recognition letter sequence with stable sound values even in isolation. As the child identifies this unit in monosyllabic words he will need to identify the initial consonant and blend it with the unit for word identification. This decoded word will of course need to be tested for meaning within the context of the sentence. Instruction using the graphemic base is present at the early stages of decoding instruction whenever the child substitutes initial consonants with a rhyming ending. For example, place the words *fall, ball,* and *hall* on the chalkboard or newsprint. Following a discussion of these words in sentence context encourage the children to identify the letter sequence that is similar in all the words. After the graphemic base *all* has been underlined or circled additional words should be added by substituting initial consonants or initial consonant clusters: *call, stall, small,* etc. The children can use these words to develop their own rhyming sentences, which can be shared with the class.

As instruction proceeds the children will become familiar with additional initial consonant correspondences and graphemic bases that can be combined to form a wide range of new words. The following exercise provides a context for meaning clues facilitating the use of graphemic base *ight*.

Place the words *sight* and *bright* on the chalkboard. Ask the children to identify the letter sequence that is similar in both words—the graphemic base *ight.* Using the initial consonants *f, l,* and *n* and the consonant blends *fr* and *fl,* encourage the children to develop additional words for the following contexts:

The dog looked at the large bear in ____.
The animals joined each other to ____ the bear during the ____.
But the bear left the forest before day ____.

Two additional graphemic base exercises follow.

Explain to the children that there is a friendly creature in the woods that likes *akes.* Encourage them to imagine what kind of *akes* the creature might like. Write the words *lakes* and *cakes* on the chalkboard and indicate that the creature already has these two *akes.* After the children have discussed what this imaginary creature might be like, ask them to draw a picture of the creature and his two *akes,* then have them identify three more *akes* that the creature might like and draw these *akes* beside the creature. All of the new words are then labeled and the children share their pictures and words with the class.

Draw a spider web on a large piece of tagboard. Then place initial consonant and consonant clusters (*b, d, f, m, bl, st*) in various parts of the spider web. Write graphemic bases on the lefthand edges of three-by-five-inch tagboard cards. The game is played by placing the "spider web" on the table and distributing the cards to each child. If the child can match a graphemic base with an initial consonant in the spider web to make a word he has "found a fly." If he can decode the word using the consonant and graphemic base he "catches the fly" and scores one point.

The graphemic base can be used for effective decoding at a more advanced level by identifying decodable units in multisyllabic words. The letter pattern–sound pattern vowel generalizations discussed in the previous section will prove to be of substantial value in this effort after the decodable letter pattern unit has been visually identified. The following discussion deals with specific generalizations that further facilitate the use of letter-sound and letter pattern–sound pattern units.

IDENTIFYING SYLLABLE UNITS

Syllable generalizations can be developed most effectively by using the inductive-deductive approach described earlier. This instruction can effectively be initiated by using words in the children's rapid recognition vocabularies and encouraging them to search for visual units that will be effective in decoding new vocabulary. The generalization derived from this search should be utilized to identify additional words for application and followed by consideration of exceptions to the generalization. Opportunity must then be provided to apply the generalization in sentence and story context. The major value of syllabication generalizations of course will reside in decoding words of more than one syllable.

Shuy has developed a series of syllable generalizations based on the relationship between written and oral language units.[43] These rules utilize
visual clues to identify pronounceable units in decoding instruction. In
decoding unfamiliar words the first rule is applied. If it does not result in
a meaningful pronunciation based on sentence context, the second, third,
and fourth rules are used successively in the decoding effort.

Rule 1. First see if a word is a compound word, one made up of two or more
words you know or can easily decode (playmate = play + mate). If it is, read
its parts. Try saying it with the stress on the first part: PLAYmate. It must make
sense in the sentence you are reading.

Rule 2. Then look for prefixes, such as *de,* and suffixes, such as *ly,* and other
word endings you know, such as *ed.* Look for any larger word parts you know,
such as *ible.* If there are any, divide the word by removing that part and
decoding the rest (the "root" word) as usual. Try putting the stress on the
"root." Remember that some word endings like *ed* don't always form a separate
syllable (as in stopped).

Rule 3. Look in the middle of the word for a consonant cluster, such as the *sk*
in basket, or a consonant diagraph, such as the *sh* in bushel or the *ll* in bellow. (A
syllable that includes a doubled consonant letter is usually a stressed syllable.)

A. If you find a cluster of two consonant letters, such as the *sk* in basket, divide
the word into parts between the two letters of the cluster (bas/ket). If the
cluster is made up of three consonant letters, such as the *nkl* in twinkle,
divide after the second of the three consonant letters (twink/le). (For the
purpose of end-of-line word division in writing, some pupils may have
learned to divide words ending in *le* after the first of the three consonant
letters (han/dle). If these pupils find Rule 3 confusing, permit them to divide
words for decoding as they would for writing.)

B. If you find a consonant digraph, such as the *sh* in bushel, or the *ll* in bellow,
divide after the digraph. The spelling pattern of the first syllable will probably be CVC [consonant-vowel-consonant] or some variation of this pattern
(bas = CVC; twink = CCVCC), so try decoding this syllable with an unglided [short] vowel sound. Try putting the stress on the first syllable; vowel
letters in the syllables other than the stressed syllable will often stand for
the unglided vowel sound /ə/.

Rule 4. If there is no cluster of consonant letters in the middle of the word
(lizard), try the following steps. Divide the word after the consonant that
follows the first vowel letter (liz/ard) and decode the VC- or CVC-pattern
syllable as a word in this pattern is decoded—by giving the vowel an unglided
[short] sound. Give stress to this syllable. Vowel letters in other syllables will
usually stand for the unglided vowel sound /ə/. If this strategy does not result
in a word you know, try dividing after the first vowel letter (the *i* in tiger) or
after the first vowel digraph (the *ai* in raisin), and decode the first syllable as
a CV-pattern word is decoded—by giving the vowel a glided [long] sound. Give
stress to this syllable. Vowel letters in the other syllables will usually stand for
333   the unglided vowel sound /ə/.

The development of the first generalization for compound words will rely heavily on rapid recognition vocabulary the children have used often. For example, words such as *fireman, sidewalk, anyone, classroom* can be placed on the chalkboard and the children search for similarities in the word group. After they conclude that there are two known words in each of the words they should be introduced to the term *compound word,* noting that this label refers to a word made up of two or more words.

Emphasis on forming compound words should also be present in the instructional program. The following exercise illustrates this emphasis. Place the following words on the chalkboard:

some	to	_____
police	thing	_____
in	man	_____

Have the children match a word in the first column with a word in the second column to make a compound word, then use it in a sentence.

Just as a "set for diversity" was developed in instruction related to sound–letter and letter pattern–sound pattern correspondences, a similar "set" must be developed in compound word instruction, otherwise the search for "little words" in "big words" can lead to erroneous expectations. If you use words like *station, shopping,* and *somewhere,* the children can search for known words and test the value of these words in context. Emphasize the obvious point that identification of the words *at* in station, *pin* in shopping, and *me* and *her* in somewhere leads to inappropriate pronunciation clues, and that decoding these words requires a shift to alternate letter pattern–sound pattern correspondences.

The second generalization, using prefixes, suffixes, and roots, provides an important visual identification clue to segment new words for pronunciation. The following exercises are of value in developing this generalization. (There is a detailed discussion of prefix, suffix, and root related meaning in Chapter 11.)

Write the words *away* and *along* on the chalkboard. Decode these words, then discuss their meaning, and encourage the children to think of other words with the same prefix. Write these words on the chalkboard. Have the children listen to the words as you pronounce them, note which part of each word is pronounced with greatest volume or stress, and underline this part of the word. Observe that words that begin with a prefix such as *a* are usually pronounced with greater stress on the last part of the word. Note that separating the prefix from the rest of the word identifies pronounceable units (a-way, a-long), and that the prefix often represents the unglided or short vowel sound /ə/. This discussion can be followed by an exercise such as the following:

Divide the following words into parts, underline the stressed part, then use each word in the sentences below.

about _____ across _____ alone _____
apart _____ ashamed _____ above _____

1. We were _____ to leave.
2. There were clouds _____ us.
3. We took the puzzle _____.
4. Jim lives _____ from me.
5. She was _____ of the old clothes.
6. I walked home _____ after school.

Instruction in the use of suffixes can be developed by using words such as walking, working, going, eating, and playing, and noting the similarity in the word part *ing* and the remaining root word. Place such words on the chalkboard or newsprint, then cover the suffix to aid identification of the familiar root word. The graphemic base knowledge, which has been previously discussed, should also be utilized where possible in decoding suffix units.

You can also design suffix wheels to reinforce understanding of this syllabication concept by fastening tagboard circles of different size together with a paper rivet. Print the root word (jump, open, etc.) on the edge of the inner circle, and print appropriate suffixes *s, ed, ing* on the outer circle. Two children can play. The first spins the top circle and reads the word that is formed; the other uses this word in a sentence. This same activity can be prepared for use with prefixes (a-bout, a-bove, a-lone) and contractions (can-'t, did-n't, etc.).

The third generalization relies heavily on the children's knowledge of consonant cluster letters that represent more than one sound (*sk,* basket; *mbl,* grumble) and on consonant digraphs that represent one sound (*sh,* bushel; *ll,* bellow). In the case of two-letter consonant clusters, the pronounceable unit is identified by dividing the word between the two consonants—bas/ket. A three-consonant cluster is divided after the second consonant—grumb/le. Consonant diagraphs of course represent one consonant sound, and so the syllable division occurs after the digraph (bush-/el, bell/ow). The exercises in Figure 10-13 are designed to develop recognition and use of consonant digraphs.

Emphasis on identification of consonant clusters and sentence context is found in Figure 10-14.

The child's knowledge of letter pattern–sound pattern units will be of value in identifying pronounceable units on the basis of consonant cluster and consonant digraph segmentation. For example, in decoding the units in bas/ket, the first unglided or short vowel generalization applies—that is, a vowel letter represents an unglided or short vowel sound when it is followed by a final consonant unit, bas/ket = /bæs - kət/. In addition the first pronounceable unit, or syllable, will often be stressed, while the last unit will be unstressed and may represent the unglided vowel sound /ə/.

335

Look for two letters together that stand for one sound and circle them.

rocket	thin	bulldog
sorrow	chase	hammer
knife	hiccup	share

Read the word at the beginning of each row. Circle the two letters which together stand for one sound. Then underline all the words in the row with the two letters that stand for that sound. The first one is done for you.

1. (ch)ase	orchard	Peacham	crack
2. pussy	goodness	busy	mistress
3. muttered	rattlesnake	scatter	finally
4. prickly	price	Speck	rocket
5. cinnamon	command	winner	roadrunner
6. faithful	paint	breath	thumb
7. Spanish	sure	shook	eyelash
8. either	feather	those	trade

In each underlined word, circle the two consonant letters which together stand for one sound.

1. Farmer Brown carried a sack of corn.

2. Jim Hines works Thursdays at the Ice Cream Shop.

3. Just then Sally appeared at the window.

4. The two girls played together with the puppy.

Figure 10-13. Phonemic and Structural Analysis: Consonant Digraphs; Syllabication Rule 3. *From* Teachers' Edition of the Skills Handbook for How It Is Nowadays, *by Theodore Clymer and Robert B. Ruddell, of the Reading 360 series,* © Copyright, 1969, by Ginn and Company. Used with permission.

Underline the cluster of consonant letters in each word below.

sweet   border   raft   sender   sprain   skill   free

basket   street   best   green   fender   price   glass

Write the clusters of consonant letters in the cluster of grapes.
Do not write any cluster of letters more than once.

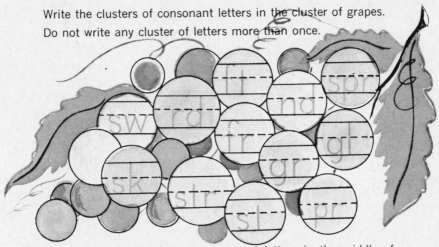

Draw a line between the two consonant letters in the middle of
each word in the boxes below. Choose the word from each box to
complete each sentence and circle it.

> entire
> enter

1. The teacher told us to do the _ _ _ _ page.

> temper
> tender

2. The lion took _ _ _ _ care of her cubs.

> murmur
> mongoose

3. The children began to _ _ _ _ to each other.

> expert
> excite

4. He asked an _ _ _ _ for advice.

Figure 10-14. Phonemic and Structural Analysis: Consonant Clusters; Syllabication Rule 3. *From* Teachers' Edition of the Skills Handbook for How It Is Nowadays,
by Theodore Clymer and Robert B. Ruddell, of the Reading 360 series, © *Copy-*
right, 1969, by Ginn and Company. Used by permission.

The exercises in Figures 10-15 and 10-16 further illustrate the third generalization.

Look for the cluster of consonant letters in the middle of the word and draw a line between the two letters. Write the two parts of the word on the line. Say the word and circle the loud part.

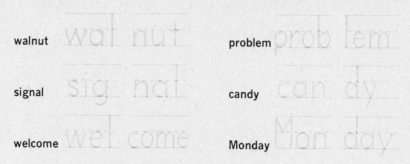

walnut   wal nut   problem   prob lem

signal   sig nal   candy   can dy

welcome   wel come   Monday   Mon day

Read the two parts of each word. Then write the two parts as a word on the line where it belongs. Circle the two consonant letters in the middle of the word that stand for two different sounds.

tin sel   whis per   sham poo   prac tice   mus tard

1. We hung gold _tinsel_ on the tree.

2. Do you like _mustard_ on your hot dog?

3. If you _practice_, you can learn to do anything well.

4. Everyone spoke in a _whisper_.

5. Sometimes _shampoo_ gets in my eyes when Mom washes my hair.

Figure 10-15. Structural Analysis: Syllabication Rule 3—Medial Consonant Clusters. *From* Teachers' Edition of Skills Handbook for How It is Nowadays, *by Theodore Clymer and Robert B. Ruddell, of the Reading 360 series, © Copyright, 1969, by Ginn and Company. Used with permission.*

Circle the two consonant letters which together stand for one sound.

barrel gallop pickle puppet bushel

Find the two parts in each word below by drawing a slash <u>after</u> the two consonant letters which together stand for one sound.

1. collect   3. lesson   5. parrot
2. bottom   4. hammer   6. chuckle

Now match each word above with its meaning. Write the matching number on the line in front of the meaning.

__5__ a big colorful bird   __1__ gather; bring together

__3__ something learned   __4__ a tool

__6__ a soft, quiet laugh   __2__ the lowest part or place

Make a slash in each word after the two letters which together stand for one sound. Then write the number for the word which belongs on the line.

1. knuckle   2. shallow   3. rather

I would __3__ go on a picnic than stay home.

Jim's baby brother plays in _____ water.

Bob scraped a _____ on the screen door.

Figure 10-16.Structural Analysis: Syllabication Rule 3—Medial Consonant Digraphs. *From* Teachers' Edition of Skills Handbook for How It Is Nowadays, *by Theodore Clymer and Robert B. Ruddell, of the Reading 360 series,* © *Copyright, 1969, by Ginn and Company. Used with permission.*

The fourth segmentation generalization applies to multisyllabic words with single consonant letters in medial positions. This principle has two options, placing the consonant in the first pronounceable unit (liz/ard), or placing it in the last pronounceable unit (ti/ger, rai/sin). Again, letter pattern–sound pattern generalization knowledge will assist in pronunciation. For example, when a vowel letter (or vowel letters) occurs as the last unit of a syllable and is preceded by a consonant unit, the letter(s) often represents the glided vowel sound, as in di/ner, do/main. Greatest stress is often placed on the first syllable, while little stress on the remaining syllables may result in an unglided vowel sound /ə/.

The fourth syllable generalization can readily be developed by utilizing several of the techniques discussed earlier. For example, known words (*lizard, desert, medal*) may be presented on the chalkboard or newsprint to develop the first option above. Following pronunciation, the segmentation generalization may be developed. Other words that follow this pattern should be identified and used in context by the children.

A "set for diversity" can easily be developed by using the second option presented for this generalization—that is, by presenting words such as *diner, lady, meadow*—which are segmented by placing the medial consonant in the last unit of the word. This "set" again emphasizes the importance of using alternate strategies for decoding new words.

You should use activities that provide reinforcement in blending syllable units and that can then be tested for meaning in context. One such activity with high motivation follows.

Cut four-by-eight-inch cards from tagboard and print two-syllable words containing a single medial consonant on each: *lizard, diner, tiger,* etc. Cut each word card between the appropriate letters to form pronounceable units: liz/ard, di/ner, etc. Place the two parts of each word card in an envelope, then divide the children into two teams and provide each child with a separate envelope. On a given signal the first member of each team opens his envelope, arranges the syllables, pronounces the word, and uses it in sentence context. The second member follows, and so on. The first team to correctly recombine, pronounce, and use the word in context wins. This activity can be used effectively with words containing more than two syllables. The vocabulary on the cards should be familiar to the children and perhaps selected directly from their reading material.

It will help many children if you have a brief statement about each syllable for display on newsprint or tagboard in a convenient location in the room. The following summary statement may serve this purpose.

To locate and test letter units for pronunciation in new words use the following clues:

1. Look for compound words.
2. Look for prefixes, suffixes, and root words.

3. Look for medial consonant clusters or consonant digraphs.
4. Look for a single medial consonant letter and test its location.
5. Use sentence and story contexts to test your pronunciation.

It is of course important that the child develop dictionary skills as an aid to decoding unknown words and developing knowledge of word meanings. Chapter 12 contains detailed instructions on dictionary and independent research skills.

Developing context clues

Context provides an important decoding resource from two perspectives: (1) as a test of the appropriateness of the word decoded by the child, and (2) as a source of decoding information the child can use in combination with his knowledge of writing-sound correspondences to decode unknown words.

The meaning test of appropriateness relies heavily on the child's language development, specifically his lexical and relational meaning store. It is of critical importance that reading material be selected taking these two factors into consideration so that the child can effectively use context as a check for decoding new vocabulary. This means that the teacher must have a clear understanding of the child's level of lexical and relational meaning development and that he know the story content well in order to develop concepts and labels that may present difficulty for the child.

Specific decoding information for use in decoding unknown words includes:

> Nonlinguistic clues (picture content)
> Lexical clues (word and sentence meaning clues)
> Relational clues (word order clues in sentence)
> Interpretation clues (meaning clues derived from previous sentences and story organization and development)

The child must use this information in coordination with his knowledge of letter-sound and letter pattern–sound pattern correspondences. Context will prove to be very limiting for independent decoding if it is relied on as the major decoding procedure. As a supplementary decoding technique the child must consistently pose several questions regarding the contextual information.

> Does the word the context suggests agree with the available pictures? With the semantic meaning of the sentence? With the meaning of the story?
> Does the word fit the sentence context from a word order or relational meaning standpoint?
> Does the tentative identification of the word check with letter-sound and letter pattern–sound pattern correspondence clues?

341

These questions will confirm or reject the tentative identification of a word based on context clues.

Nonlinguistic clues based on pictures or photographs can be of substantial value in developing concepts and labels essential for understanding the story. Most reading systems contain such clues from the prereading stage. Often large illustrations and photographs serve as a focal point in establishing concepts and related labels introduced in the story line. There is of course danger in the child's using picture context clues to the extent that he comes to rely so heavily on them that he fails to develop an understanding of decoding units.

By combining picture clues with sentence context and letter-sound correspondence knowledge, such as initial consonant identification, the child comes to realize the value of various types of decoding information. This combined approach is illustrated in the following exercise (assume picture is available):

1. Lad is a d__ __ .
2. The boy threw the ball h__ __ __ into the air.
3. Wilt dribbled the ball down the floor and ran into another player. The r__ __ __ __ __ __ blew his whistle.

Lexical and relational meaning clues both provide information that limits the range of words that can be used in context,[44] as noted in the following sentences.

1. The little _____ ran into the barn.
2. The _____ sank one of our ships.

In the first sentence the possibilities, based largely on relational meaning (word order and word class), might include calf, cow, kitten, while the second list might include torpedo, submarine, airplane, etc. The addition of lexical meaning serves to narrow the possibilities further.

1. The little _____, which was three days old, ran into the barn.
2. The deep-running _____ sank one of our ships.

Sufficient interpretation clues may be available from previous story information to limit context further and identify the specific word—calf or kitten in the first sentence, torpedo or submarine in the second. If not the reader must utilize his knowledge of decoding generalizations to identify the word. The initial consonant may be sufficient for this purpose.

1. The little c__ __ __ , which was three days old, ran into the barn.
2. The deep-running s__ __ __ __ __ __ __ __ sank one of our ships.

The sentences above illustrate the importance and some of the limitations of context clues as aids to decoding. The teacher must provide balance in decoding instruction to assure that the child develops a range of decoding abilities that lead to independence in word identification.

Other exercises illustrating the development of context clues follow.

1. Design several sentences that can be segmented into separate sentence units. Separate the sentence parts into two columns. On the basis of context the children are to identify the original sentence by drawing a line to connect the two parts.

Mike plays	a dog house
Joan likes to ride	with his pet squirrel.
Bob built	her new bicycle.

2. Select a group of sentences from reading materials and delete several letters in key words, or key words themselves (both lexical and relational). On the basis of context the children are to attempt to identify the words with missing letters, or the missing words.

The p____ drew their covered wagons into a large ____ for protection at night.
Both ____ stepped onto the moon's ____.
The huge tractor rig crashed th____ the divider wall and ____ the building.
The s____ caught the wind and the crew cheered as the ____ sped ____ the finish line.

3. Select several sentences from the children's reading material. Delete a key word in the sentence and leave a blank space. Provide the key word with another word in a multiple choice item. Based on the context the children are to circle the appropriate word.

Herb's <u>respectability</u> is to clean out the garage.
   responsibility
Peg lost her footing and fell <u>upward</u> into the water.
          backward
The <u>politician</u> told the boys where to find the racing book.
   librarian

There are many opportunities to use context throughout the reading activities of the day. By combining this meaning aspect of decoding with knowledge of the relationship between the writing and sound system the child can become highly effective in evaluating the appropriateness of words he decodes and thereby improve his decoding ability. Additional emphasis will be given to the use of context in Chapter 11.

Developing rapid recognition vocabulary

A comparatively small number of words occur with extremely high frequency in our language. Many of these words are those that unite vocabulary into highly regular sentence structure patterns. The reader must develop these words, many of which do not follow regular spelling patterns, as a rapid recognition vocabulary.

The following 220 words are the words of greatest frequency in the Kucera-Francis study of present-day American English.[45]

1. the	45. when	89. many
2. of	46. who	90. before
3. and	47. will	91. must
4. to	48. more	92. through
5. a	49. no	93. back
6. in	50. if	94. years
7. that	51. out	95. where
8. is	52. so	96. much
9. was	53. said	97. your
10. he	54. what	98. way
11. for	55. up	99. well
12. it	56. its	100. down
13. with	57. about	101. should
14. as	58. into	102. because
15. his	59. than	103. each
16. on	60. them	104. just
17. be	61. can	105. those
18. at	62. only	106. people
19. by	63. other	107. Mr.
20. I	64. new	108. how
21. this	65. some	109. too
22. had	66. could	110. little
23. not	67. time	111. state
24. are	68. these	112. good
25. but	69. two	113. very
26. from	70. may	114. make
27. or	71. then	115. world
28. have	72. do	116. still
29. an	73. first	117. own
30. they	74. any	118. see
31. which	75. my	119. men
32. one	76. now	120. work
33. you	77. such	121. long
34. were	78. like	122. get
35. her	79. our	123. here
36. all	80. over	124. between
37. she	81. man	125. both
38. there	82. me	126. life
39. would	83. even	127. being
40. their	84. most	128. under
41. we	85. made	129. never
42. him	86. after	130. day
43. been	87. also	131. same
44. has	88. did	132. another

133. know	163. home	192. less
134. while	164. small	193. public
135. last	165. found	194. put
136. might	166. Mrs.	195. thing
137. us	167. thought	196. almost
138. great	168. went	197. hand
139. old	169. say	198. enough
140. year	170. part	199. far
141. off	171. once	200. took
142. come	172. general	201. head
143. since	173. high	202. yet
144. against	174. upon	203. government
145. go	175. school	204. system
146. came	176. every	205. better
147. right	177. don't	206. set
148. used	178. does	207. told
149. take	179. got	208. nothing
150. three	180. united	209. night
151. states	181. left	210. end
152. himself	182. number	211. why
153. few	183. course	212. called
154. house	184. war	213. didn't
155. use	185. until	214. eyes
156. during	186. always	215. find
157. without	187. away	216. going
158. again	188. something	217. look
159. place	189. fact	218. asked
160. American	190. though	219. later
161. around	191. water	220. knew
162. however		

The eighty-two words from the Dolch Word List not found in the Kucera-Francis list are presented below.[46]

1. am	18. drink	35. hot
2. ask	19. eat	36. hurt
3. ate	20. eight	37. jump
4. best	21. fall	38. keep
5. big	22. fast	39. kind
6. black	23. five	40. laugh
7. blue	24. fly	41. let
8. bring	25. four	42. light
9. brown	26. full	43. live
10. buy	27. funny	44. myself
11. call	28. gave	45. open
12. carry	29. give	46. pick
13. clean	30. goes	47. play
14. cold	31. green	48. please
15. cut	32. grow	49. pretty
16. done	33. help	50. pull
17. draw	34. hold	51. ran

52. read	63. six	73. try
53. red	64. sleep	74. walk
54. ride	65. soon	75. want
55. round	66. start	76. warm
56. run	67. stop	77. wash
57. saw	68. tell	78. white
58. seven	69. ten	79. wish
59. shall	70. thank	80. write
60. show	71. today	81. yellow
61. sing	72. together	82. yes
62. sit		

These eighty-two words deserve careful consideration in that the source of the words may be more representative of words used by young children than some vocabulary on the Kucera-Francis list. Nevertheless many of the words of both lists are critical to a rapid recognition vocabulary and in turn to reading fluency.

Activities for developing rapid recognition vocabulary should always account for meaning through a picture context, written sentence context, or oral language context. Such activities include the following:

1. Cut pictures from magazines that represent vocabulary of high frequency: form classes, such as nouns (eyes, people); verbs (jump, eat, drink); and adjectives (little, blue, yellow). Paste the pictures in a large circle on tagboard. Attach a tagboard pointer in the center of the circle with a paper rivet. Prepare a set of tagboard word cards with the words representing the pictures. Each player spins the pointer and notes the word represented by the picture. He then sorts through the word cards, locates the word that matches the picture, and uses the word in a sentence.

2. Use illustrations or large pictures that represent a variety of high-frequency words for development. Prepare sentences on tagboard to match the action in the picture, for example

The boy threw the ball.

It crashed through the window.

The angry man is talking to the boy.

3. A variation of this exercise is to cut the tagboard sentences apart and provide a deck of word cards for each sentence.

The child builds a sentence to represent the action in the picture.

4. Prepare a set of word cards by printing each word in large letters on five-by-eight-inch tagboard. Paste a small picture as a clue to the word meaning on the opposite side of the card. Use the word cards as flash cards by exposing each word for a few seconds, then do a meaning check with

the picture on the reverse side. Or the child can pronounce the word using the picture clue reference and then trace the word with the index and middle finger to provide a tactile-kinesthetic reinforcement.

5. Prepare a paper tachistoscope (see Chapter 14) with words for rapid exposure. Two children may be teamed. One child flashes the word, the other child pronounces it, and then the first child uses it in a sentence. A game variation of this activity, known as "Fishing," may be developed by preparing individual word cards and placing a paper clip on each. The word cards are placed in a container and the child is provided with a "fishing pole"—a short stick with an attached string and magnet. The child "fishes" a word out of the container and reads it within a few seconds. If the child has difficulty reading the word the card is turned over and the picture clue is used, but the "fish" must be thrown back. A new word card is drawn from the container until the child is successful. This activity can be used with a small group of children. Each correctly pronounced word scores one point.

What is the value of word games like this one? What are their limitations? *(Photo by Hays, Monkmeyer Press Photo Service)*

Vocabulary of foreign origin is another area of concern. Because many of these words do not follow English spelling-sound patterns they produce some degree of difficulty in decoding. Vocabulary of this type (including language source and general topic) includes the following.

Language Source	Plants and Animals	Food	Culture	Miscellaneous
American Indian	sequoia catawba cayuse	supawn pemmican	manitou kayak	chautauqua
French	caribou	brioche a la mode parfait sazarac	bureau bateau pirogue	Cajun charivari rotisserie
Spanish	mesquite marijuana mosquito palomino	frijol tequila enchilada	sombrero serape lariat pueblo	coquina hombre savvy
German		blutwurst schnitzel zwieback	pinochle rathskeller turnverein	katzenjammer phooey spiel
Italian		spaghetti ravioli	duet opera piano virtuoso	granite balcony
Persian	lilac lemon	sherbet	caravan khaki borax	paradise check
Greek			acrobat barometer catastrophe	tactics tantalize elastic
Russian		vodka	ruble droshky	steppe

Words of this type are used less frequently and therefore are not so essential to the child's rapid recognition vocabulary as the Kucera-Francis and Dolch words, but they still need to be decoded. Development of most of this type of vocabulary will take place in the context of stories or reading of factual social science materials. While certain regular patterns can be identified (for example, in Spanish *qu* usually represents /k/ as in mesquite and mosquito), the use of the dictionary for identification of pronunciation is the most effective independent decoding resource. Chapter 12 contains a detailed discussion of dictionary skills development.

DEVELOPING SPELLING STRATEGIES

To spell a child must understand the way the writing system represents oral language forms. In contrast to reading, the child must re-create spelling units to represent sound units rather than produce sound units represented by written language forms. The intent of this discussion is not to develop detailed instructional techniques for spelling instruction, but instead to identify similarities and differences in the decoding and spelling processes that lead to spelling strategies and maximum transfer from decoding to spelling, and to recommend specific guidelines as a basis for developing spelling abilities.

Decoding and spelling instruction: similarities and differences

Our discussion of decoding instruction based on the communication model identified six instructional components for decoding instruction.

1. Perceptual development, auditory and visual
2. Letter-sound correspondences
3. Letter pattern–sound pattern correspondences
4. Syllabication units, graphemic bases and visual segmentation of words into pronounceable units
5. Context clues
6. Rapid recognition vocabulary

A parallel for each of these can be identified for spelling. As Hildreth has emphasized, the spelling process requires that the child clearly distinguish sounds and words, develop visual impressions of word forms, distinguish similar words visually, match sound elements to the graphic symbols representing them in words that are phonetically consistent, pronounce words accurately, and use syllabication.[47] We can clearly identify the nature of the spelling and decoding similarities and differences by considering the instructional components and related examples.

Perceptual development

Initial prereading and prespelling readiness are closely parallel processes. In both cases emphasis is on developing auditory perception so that the child can distinguish between words with minimal sound contrasts (/mit/, /bit/). Visual discrimination is also critical to both processes; the child learns to differentiate symbols so as to distinguish between words (mit, bit).

The spelling readiness program requires an additional component—that of eye-hand motor control in printing letters. This haptic or tactile-kinesthetic dimension of spelling can of course be used in the decoding process for reinforcing letter-sound correspondences. In spelling and in decoding tracing a word unit and the entire word facilitates development of visual memory of the word, and leads to rapid recognition of decoding units and to visual identification and feedback for re-creating letter sequences in spelling. In the early stages of spelling instruction, however, the essential

process of written letter identification *and* formation is one basic difference in the two processes. Nevertheless, a great deal of similarity is evident in developing early auditory perception and visual discrimination.

Letter-sound correspondences

To the extent that letters represent sound values in a consistent manner there is similarity between decoding and spelling at this level. A detailed study of simple grapheme-phoneme correspondences by Hanna and his colleagues revealed that in more than 17,000 words the great majority of consonants had single spellings that were used at least 80 percent of the time.[48] For example, the following consonant letter-sound correspondences were consistent over 90 percent of the time: /b/, big, tab; /d/, dig, mad; /l/, lake, help; /m/, man, ham: /n/, now, can; /p/, pill, stop; /r/, run, car; /t/, tin, pot. Only a few vowels, however, had this degree of regularity. Vowel letter-sound correspondences that were consistent at least 90 percent of the time included / æ /, at, can; /e/, ebb, pen; /ɔ/, on, top; / ə /, us, cup.[49]

These findings of course directly suggest that consonant correspondences are highly predictable while vowel correspondences considered as single units are to a great extent unpredictable. This problem, however, is present not only in spelling but in the decoding process as well. As we pointed out earlier, for greater predictability letter-sound correspondences must be considered in the context of larger letter-sound units. Obviously the same is true for sound-letter correspondences.

Letter pattern–sound pattern correspondences

Our previous discussions of pattern generalizations were based on letter patterns and predictable sound values for these patterns, particularly as related to vowels. With spelling, however, we are concerned with predicting spelling patterns from sound patterns. The letter combinations that represent sounds and function as spelling units are identified in Table 10-3.[50]

Table 10-3. The Major Spelling Units

Consonant Units				Vowel Units		
Simple			Complex	Primary	Compound	
b	k	s	ck	a	ai/ay	oa
c	l	sh	dg	e	au/aw	oe
ch	m	t	tch	i	ea	oi/oy
d	n	th	x	o	ee	oo
f	p	u		u	ei/ey	ou/ow
g	ph	v		y	eu/ew	ue
gh	q	w			ie	ui
h	r	wh				
j	rh	y				
		z				

The complex consonant spelling units represent two sounds, for example x (/ks/) in bo*x*, or they may be viewed as replacements for doubled consonants, for example dg (/ǰ/) in e*dg*e, ck (/k/) in lo*ck*, or tch (/č/) in ha*tch*. The vowel spelling units consisting of primary (single) and compound (two-letter) units clearly represent greater variation than do the consonant units.

Some degree of predictability of letter pattern sequences from sound values can be illustrated with the following generalization: "A glided or long vowel sound can be represented by a single vowel letter followed by a simple consonant unit and a final *e* letter," for example, /beyk/ = bake, /bey θ / = bathe. (Note that this generalization is the spelling equivalent to the first glided vowel generalization—that when a vowel letter is followed by a consonant and a final *e* it represents the glided or long vowel sound.) Glided or long vowel sounds, however, cannot be represented by a single vowel letter when the letter occurs before complex consonant units such as *ck, dg, tch,* and *x* (see table 10-3 for contrasting simple consonant units—*b, th,* etc.—and complex consonant units—*ck, dg*).

It is important that the child understand that some letters are used as markers to indicate spelling-sound relationships while others preserve letter or word patterns. For example,

> Final *e* is a marker in mate since it indicates the long pronunciation of *a*. It is a dual marker in *rage,* indicating the pronunciations of both *a* and *g* (compare *rag*). In love, *e* preserves a pattern which forbids *v* to occur in final position; in *mouse, house,* and *moose,* it indicates that the *s* is not a morphemic unit; that is, it is not a plural or third singular indicator. In *guide* and *guest, u* is a marker, showing the /g/ pronunciation of *g*. All of these patterns relate as much to spelling as to reading.[51]

Most of the spelling-sound generalizations discussed under decoding instruction have some degree of application for spelling instruction, especially the single vowel letter (primary vowel) generalizations.

Syllabication units

The accurate spelling of polysyllabic words can be greatly facilitated by an understanding of syllabication units. The clues for identification of syllable segments of course differ from those of the decoding process, where letter sequences offer a visual indication for a syllable. The speller must rely on auditory discrimination of sound values (each syllable contains a vowel or vowel-like sound) and his knowledge of word building (prefixes, suffixes, and compound word forms) in order to identify syllables.

The identification of the syllable unit coupled with an understanding of sound pattern–letter pattern correspondences can lead to greater predictability of sound-letter correspondences. Hanna, Hodges, and Hanna illustrate this point in Table 10-4.* The effect of stress on the predictability of sound-letter correspondences is demonstrated in Table 10-5.* It seems clear that much greater regularity can be achieved in representing the sound in written form by accounting for position and stress factors. The same is obviously true in spelling-sound correspondences, as the discussion on decoding instruction demonstrated.

Table 10-4. Effect of Position on Sound-Letter Correspondences

Sound	Position in Syllable and Most Common Spelling	Percentage of Use	Example
/ey/	Final position, a	81.0	fa vor
/iy/	Final position, e	90.6	le gal
/i/	Medial position, i	82.6	big
/ow/	Final position, o	92.0	no tice
/uw/	Final position, u	88.5	cu bic
/f/	Initial position, f	84.7	fan
/k/	Initial position, k c	87.7	coin
/ŋ/	Medial position, n	96.3	sink
/s/	Medial position, s	96.9	best

Table 10-5. Effect of Stress on Sound-Letter Correspondences

Sound	Conditions for Predicting Letter	Percentage of Use	Example
/č/	Initial position of primary-stressed syllable, ch	97	char´coal
/ǰ/	Initial position of unstressed syllable, g	82	co´gent
/š/	Initial position of unstressed syllable, t	84	frac´tion
/yuw/	Initial position of primary-stressed syllable, y	98	yes´ter day
/yuw/	Initial position of unstressed syllable, i	86	on´ion

The identification of word or morpheme boundaries is an excellent auditory clue to syllable segmentation for spelling. This applies readily to compound words (/fut bɔl/ = foot + ball), to prefixes (/diy sayd/ = de + cide), and to suffixes (/strik ən/ = strick + en). You will of course need to give special attention to generalizations for the written representation of root words used with suffixes, such as that with the *ing* of *racing, tracing,* the final *e* is dropped before adding the *ing.* One can accomplish this by forming the word racing from *race* + *ing* or, by reversing the process, from racing to form the root *race* and the suffix *ing,* and noting the change in

*Paul R. Hanna, Richard E. Hodges, Jean S. Hanna: *Spelling: Structure and Strategies.* Houghton Mifflin Company, 1971. Reprinted by permission of the publisher.

the root word. Similar treatment must be given words such as *rubbing* and *running,* the base words of which end in consonants preceded by unglided or short vowel sounds. Sound and sound clusters represented by digraphs and letter clusters and with distinctly different sound-letter representations require special attention and some degree of parallel decoding instruction—for example, the digraph *ch,* /čip/ = chip as compared to the cluster *s k;* /b æs kət/ = basket.

There are of course a number of high-frequency words that contain sounds, particularly vowels, with little predictability: /ow/ as in sew and dough, /ay/ as in fight and night. Other sound-letter correspondences, found in homophones, depend on context for identification, but present problems: /beyr/ = bare and bear, /piyr/ = peer and pier. In addition there are words of foreign origin that are pronounced as they are in the original language: /parfey/ = parfait, /lariət/ = lariat. These words will require emphasis on visual memory and utilization of dictionary skills (Chapter 12) for accurate spelling.

Context clues

In spelling instruction as in decoding instruction you must emphasize meaningful vocabulary and the development of new concepts and labels. A meaning emphasis in spelling instruction helps establish purpose and motivation for the child, which leads to more effective development of spelling generalizations and ability.

Certain sound-letter correspondences, those found in homophones but represented by different letters in written form, can only be determined through meaningful context, as illustrated by the following examples: /miyt/ = meet or meat, /wiyk/ = week or weak, /biyt/ = beet or beat, /beyt/ = bait or bate, /beyr/ = bear or bare. Context must clearly differentiate the meaning of such words for the child to establish the appropriate written representation.

The child who speaks a variant or nonstandard dialect will have many more homophones in his oral language than will the child who speaks a standard English dialect (see Chapter 9). The nonstandard-speaking black child, for example, may pronounce the words ten and tent as /ten/, the words hoe and hole as /how/ and the words win and wind as /win/. In *Project DELTA* we identified two areas of dialect-related spelling difficulty: (1) simplification of final consonant clusters as noted above (for example, *told* was spelled *towd*), and (2) hypercorrection (for example, *foe* /fow/ was spelled *for, four,* or *fore*).[52] Hypercorrection may be a result of the child's previous encounters with standard English spelling and the development of expectancies based on the teacher's standard English dialect.

Spelling instruction must account for dialect differences, especially for homophones present in the oral language of nonstandard or variant dialect speakers. The teacher must carefully establish the concept represented by a specific word label. Classroom exercises using spelling dictation should use vocabulary in a context that is meaningful to the child to aid in development of sound-letter correspondences. Carefully examine Chapter 9 to understand and anticipate dialect-related spelling problems more effectively.

Rapid recognition vocabulary

The emphasis in decoding and spelling instruction on rapid recognition vocabulary centers about development of a visual memory of words. The speller must re-create the word completely, whereas the reader produces an oral equivalent. The difference requires greater emphasis on *haptics* (sensory input using touch and kinesthetics). As Hanna, Hodges, and Hanna indicate:

> In writing a word, we call into play, in addition to aural-oral and visual cues, the sense of touch and the motor mechanisms (the muscles of the hand and arm that guide the act of writing). Haptical memory is fundamental to the mastery of activities such as typing and the reading of Braille. And although spelling ability normally is not so expressly dependent upon haptical experiences, sensorimotor impressions created by the writing of graphemes are relayed to our brain as a third kind of memory, a haptical record that—*in combination* with oral and auditory and visual recollections of words—aids in the multisensory-multimotor act of spelling.

> What has been described here may be characterized as the development of a "cognitive map" of spelling, a map that in construction involves the use of sense impressions stored in the brain: memories of sounds, visual forms, and the "feel" of words as they are written. In combination with the motor activities of speaking and writing, these multisensory-multimotor experiences form for most learners the basis of the act of spelling, although their relative importance varies with the individual.[53]

This statement reveals the importance of tactile-kinesthetic experiences in spelling and suggests a range of activities that include writing a word, tracing a word with the index and middle fingers, pronouncing it as the tracing occurs, and attempting to visualize it afterward.

Guidelines for a spelling program

Most teachers rely heavily on one of two approaches to spelling. The first is the publisher-produced spelling series. Past programs emphasized rote memory or presented a rigid sequence of vocabulary based on word frequency counts. Such programs ignored important linguistic and psychological principles. More recently authors of spelling programs have used these principles in program design. The second approach consists of informal spelling instruction based almost entirely on the child's oral language forms and written language demands. This approach of course places the major responsibility for instruction on the teacher and requires that he sequence his program within a developmental framework determined by the child's needs. These two approaches should be combined. A well-planned, well-developed spelling program can provide a frame of reference for classroom instruction, while the unique spelling needs of each child can best be met through a language-based approach such as that described in Chapters 6 and 7.

Regardless of your approach, there are a number of spelling instruction guidelines, developed by Hanna, Hodges, and Hanna, that can provide a basis for spelling instruction within the framework of various approaches. They are

1. The instructional program should make provision for developing the child's auditory perception and "pacing his maturing articulatory mechanisms, since these are the means which enable him to hear and say all the words that are necessary for communication in his language community."

2. The pupil should be helped to identify speech sounds in initial, medial, and final positions in monosyllabic words, and later in polysyllabic words.

3. After learning to identify speech sounds in various positions in words, the child learns how these sounds are represented in written form. "He is shown what alphabetic letters are most frequently used to represent certain phonemes whose spellings are highly predictable (most of the consonant phonemes and several short-vowel phonemes)."

4. After the child develops a basic knowledge of how to represent his speech in written form, the instructional program should help him "to observe simple but powerful principles that govern the most consistent" sound-letter correspondences.

5. The child should learn "to observe and formulate the principles which govern the less predictably spelled short-vowel phonemes and the long-vowel phonemes. The pupil also develops his word-building ability by (a) compounding new words out of known words (football from *foot* + *ball*), and (b) adding prefixes and suffixes to known words (*re* + *do* + *ing* = redoing)."

6. At the upper primary levels, the child "may be introduced to contextual (syntactic and meaning) cues that will help him to spell homonyms." The study of phonological and morphological factors related to spelling is continued "and through a systematic spiraling program involving these three components—phonological, morphological, and contextual—he develops a cognitive map that helps him master the spelling of the great preponderance of words in his aural-oral vocabulary, leaving only a fraction that must be learned by rote."

7. At the middle levels, the child should learn "something of the history of American-English orthography" and develop "knowledge of uses of the dictionary to reinforce and extend his cognitive map of our writing system." (See Chapters 3 and 12 for discussion of these two instructional areas.)[54]

EVALUATING DECODING AND SPELLING PROGRESS

The evaluation of progress in decoding and spelling achievement must be considered part of the instructional sequence rather than a formal assessment made at the beginning and end of the year. Ongoing evaluation of the child's decoding and spelling performance provides direct evidence of the strengths and weaknesses of the instructional program as well as the learning needs of each child. Such information is of a qualitative nature and requires that the teacher examine the nature of the decoding and spelling responses in order to design the next instructional experience. Standardized decoding and spelling achievement tests fail to yield this information; at best they provide a ranking of children as to raw score and "grade equivalent," information the teacher has already obtained from his observation of the children's performance.

Chapter 14 is devoted exclusively to evaluation and interpretation of reading-language miscues, but the following checklist will help you identify decoding and spelling areas that require special attention.

Skill Area	Decoding Miscue	Spelling Miscue	Word Example	Inference for Instruction
A. Perceptual Development 1. Auditory				
2. Visual				
B. Sound-symbol and Pattern Relationships 1. Consonants (identification, pattern based) 2. Consonant clusters 3. Consonant digraphs				
4. Vowels (identification, pattern based) 5. Vowel clusters 6. Vowel digraphs				
C. Syllabication units 1. Graphemic bases				
2. Compound words 3. Root words				
4. Prefixes 5. Suffixes				
6. Inflectional endings 7. Syllables				
8. Contractions				
9. Stress				
10. Environment 11. Position				

Skill Area	Decoding Miscue	Spelling Miscue	Word Example	Inference for Instruction
D. Context Clues 1. Picture clues 2. Grammatical clues (relational meaning) 3. Lexical clues (semantic meaning) 4. Organizational clues				
E. Rapid-recognition Vocabulary				

F. Summary of interpretation and instructional recommendations:
   1. Individual

   2. Group

Make notations on the checklist during instruction of individuals or small groups (use each child's initials to indicate miscues) for later analysis and to develop instructional inferences. As you develop experience using the checklist it can become a valuable aid for identifying instructional progress and designing the instructional program. Undoubtedly you will add areas that directly reflect the nature of the instructional program, such as dictionary skills. A decoding and spelling program based on individual needs is a crucial step in helping each child to acquire independent literacy skills.

Footnotes

[1]Dolores Durkin, "Children Who Learn to Read Before Grade One," *The Reading Teacher*, 14 (1961), 163–66. Dolores Durkin, "The Achievement of Preschool Readers: Two Longitudinal Studies," *Reading Research Quarterly*, 1 (Summer 1966), 5–36.

[2]Eleanor J. Gibson, "A Working Paper Summarizing Theory-Based Research on Reading and Its Implications for Instruction" (mimeographed manuscript, Cornell University, 1970).

[3]D. Elkind, "Piaget's Theory of Perceptual Development: Its Application to Reading and Special Education," *Journal of Special Education*, 1 (1967), 357–61.

[4]D. E. Berlyne, "Recent Developments in Piaget's Work," *British Journal of Educational Psychology*, 27 (1957), 1–12.

[5]Harry Singer, "Theoretical Models of Reading: Implications for Teaching and Research," *Theoretical Models and Processes of Reading*, Harry Singer and Robert B. Ruddell, eds. (Newark, Del.: International Reading Association, 1970), pp. 147–82.

[6]Gibson, "Theory-Based Research on Reading," p. 18.

[7]Ronald Wardhaugh, *Reading: A Linguistic Perspective* (New York: Harcourt Brace Jovanovich, Inc., 1969).

[8]See Chapter 2 for descriptions of consonant production.

[9]E. B. Coleman, *Collecting a Data Base for an Educational Technology*, Parts I and III (El Paso, Tex.: University of Texas, 1967).

[10]Eleanor J. Gibson, "Learning to Read," *Theoretical Models and Processes of Reading*, Singer and Ruddell, eds.

[11]Mildred C. Templin, *Certain Language Skills in Children* (Minneapolis: University of Minnesota Press, 1957).

[12]Grant Fairbanks, *Experimental Phonetics: Selected Articles* (Urbana: University of Illinois Press, 1966).

[13]Harry Levin, *A Basic Research Program on Reading* (Cooperative Research Project No. 639, Cornell University, 1963).

[14]B. Marchbanks and H. Levin, "Cues by Which Children Recognize Words," *Journal of Educational Psychology,* 56 (1965), 57–61.

[15]Richard Venezky, "English Orthography: Its Graphical Structure and Its Relation to Sound," *Reading Research Quarterly,* 2 (1967), 75–106.

[16]Patrick Groff, *The Syllable: Its Nature and Pedagogical Usefulness* (Portland, Ore.: Northwest Regional Educational Laboratory, 1971).

[17]Ibid., p. 28.

[18]Ralph R. Leutenegger, *The Sounds of American English* (Glenview, Ill.: Scott, Foresman and Company, 1963).

[19]Theodore Clymer and Robert B. Ruddell, *How It Is Nowadays,* teacher's ed., Reading 360 (Boston: Ginn and Company, 1973).

[20]Virginia W. Jones, *Decoding and Learning to Read* (Portland, Ore.: Northwest Regional Educational Laboratory, 1970).

[21]E. J. Gibson, A. Pick, H. Osser, and M. Hammond, "The Role of Grapheme-Phoneme Correspondence in the Perception of Words," *American Journal of Psychology,* 75 (1962), 554–70.

[22]Dawn B. Skailand, "A Comparison of Four Language Units in Teaching Beginning Reading" (unpublished doctoral dissertation, University of California, Berkeley, 1970).

[23]Gibson et al., "The Role of Grapheme-Phoneme Correspondence."

[24]Virginia Jones, *Occurrence of Graphonemes in the Vocabulary of Elementary School Children* (Portland, Ore.: Northwest Regional Educational Laboratory, 1969).

[25]Dale Johnson, "The Dolch List Reexamined," *The Reading Teacher,* 24 (February 1971), 449–57.

[26]H. Kucera and W. N. Francis, *Computational Analysis of Present-Day American English* (Providence, R. I.: Brown University Press, 1967).

[27]E. W. Dolch, *Teaching Primary Reading* (Champaign, Ill.: Garrard Publishing Co., 1941), pp. 196–215.

[28]David P. Ausubel, "Human Growth and Development," *Teachers College Record,* 60 (1959).

[29]Far West Laboratory for Educational Research and Development, *Teaching Reading as Decoding,* Minicourse 18 (1971). Robert B. Ruddell and Arthur C. Williams, *A Research Investigation of a Literacy Teaching Model: Project DELTA.* EPDA Project No. 005262 (U.S. Department of Health, Education and Welfare, Office of Education; 1972).

[30]J. Bruner, J. Goodnow, and G. Austin, *A Study of Thinking* (New York: John Wiley & Sons, Inc., 1956).

[31]R. A. Kress, "An Investigation of the Relationship Between Concept Formation and Achievement in Reading" (unpublished doctoral dissertation, Temple University, 1955). Harry Singer, "Conceptualization in Learning to Read," *New Frontiers in College and Adult Reading,* G. B. Schick and M. M. May, eds. (Milwaukee: The Fifteenth Yearbook of the National Reading Conference, 1966), pp. 116–22.

[32]Elkind, "Piaget's Theory of Perceptual Development."

[33]Arthur Gates, "The Necessary Mental Age for Beginning Reading," *Elementary School Journal,* 37 (1937), 497–508. Arthur Gates and David Russell, "The Effects of Delaying Beginning Reading a Half Year in the Case of Underprivileged Pupils with IQs of 75–95," *Journal of Educational Research,* 32 (1929), 321–28. Mabel V. Morphett and Carleton Washburne, "When Should Children Begin to Read?" *Elementary School Journal,* 31 (1931), 496–503.

[34]Jean Piaget, "The Genetic Approach to the Psychology of Thought," *Journal of Educational Psychology,* 52 (1961) 275–81.

Evaluating Decoding and Spelling Progress

[35]Durkin, "The Achievement of Preschool Readers."

[36]Gibson, "Theory-Based Research on Reading."

[37]Durkin, "Children Who Learn to Read Before Grade One."

[38]A. D. Pick, "Improvement of Visual and Tactual Form Discrimination," *Journal of Experimental Psychology,* 69 (1965), 331–39.

[39]N. Bremmer, "Do Readiness Tests Predict Success in Reading?" *Elementary School Journal,* 59 (4) (1959), 222–24. Blythe C. Mitchell, "The Metropolitan Readiness Tests as Predictors of First Grade Achievement," *Educational and Psychological Measurement,* 22 (Winter 1962), 765–72.

[40]Roger Farr, *Reading: What Can Be Measured?* (Newark, Del.: International Reading Association, 1969), p. 168.

[41]Problems associated with test-taking behavior are discussed in detail in Chapter 14.

[42]Farr, *Reading.* Elizabeth Zaruba, "Objective and Subjective Evaluation at Grade One," *Reading Teacher,* 22 (October 1968), 50–54.

[43]Roger W. Shuy, "Some Relationships of Linguistics to the Reading Process," in *Teachers' Edition of How It Is Nowadays,* by Theodore Clymer and Robert B. Ruddell, of the Reading 360 series, © Copyright, 1973, by Ginn and Company. Used with permission.

[44]Kenneth A. Goodman, "Analysis of Oral Reading Miscues: Applied Psycholinguistics," *Reading Research Quarterly,* 5 (1) (Fall 1969), 9–30.

[45]Kucera and Francis, *Computational Analysis of Present-Day American English.* From Dale Johnson, "The Dolch List Reexamined," in *The Reading Teacher* (February 1971), pp. 449–57. Reprinted with permission of Dale Johnson and the International Reading Association.

[46]From Dale Johnson, "The Dolch List Reexamined," in *The Reading Teacher* (February 1971), pp. 449–57. Reprinted with permission of Dale Johnson and the International Reading Association.

[47]Gertrude Hildreth, *Teaching Spelling: A Guide to Basic Principles and Practices* (New York: Holt, Rinehart and Winston, Inc., 1955).

[48]Paul R. Hanna, Jean S. Hanna, Richard E. Hodges, and Erwin H. Rudorf, Jr., *Phoneme-Grapheme Correspondences as Cues to Spelling Improvement.* OE-32008 (Washington: U. S. Department of Health, Education, and Welfare, 1966).

[49]Paul R. Hanna, Richard E. Hodges, and Jean S. Hanna, *Spelling: Structure and Strategies* (Boston: Houghton Mifflin Company, 1971).

[50]Richard L. Venezky, *Linguistics and Spelling* (Working Paper No. 15, Wisconsin Research and Development Center for Cognitive Learning, Madison, Wis., University of Wisconsin, 1969), p. 7. Reprinted by permission of the Board of Regents of the University of Wisconsin System.

[51]Venezky, *Linguistics and Spelling,* p. 8.

[52]Ruddell and Williams, *Project DELTA.*

[53]Hanna et al., *Spelling,* p. 104.

[54]Ibid., pp. 115–17.

Additional References

ANDERSON, PAUL S., *Language Skills in Elementary Education* (New York: The Macmillan Company, 1972).

APPLEGATE, MAUREE, *Easy in English* (New York: Harper & Row, Publishers, 1960), p. 470.

ATKINSON, RICHARD C., and DUNCAN N. HANSEN, "Computer-Assisted Instruction in Initial Reading: The Stanford Project," *Reading Research Quarterly,* II (1) (Fall 1966), 5–26.

BERKO, JEAN, "The Child's Learning of English Morphology," *Psycholinguistics,* ed. Sal Saporta (New York: Holt, Rinehart and Winston, Inc., 1961), pp. 359–75.

BISHOP, C. H., "Transfer Effects of Word and Letter Training in Reading," *Journal of Verbal Learning and Verbal Behavior,* 3 (1964), 215–21.

BLOOMFIELD, LEONARD, "Linguistics and Reading," *The Elementary English Review,* 19 (April 1942), 125–30, and (May 1942), 183–86.

BREZINSKI, JOSEPH E., "When Should Phonics Instruction Begin?" *Teaching Word Recognition Skills* (Newark, Del.: International Reading Association, 1971), pp. 60–64.

BURMEISTER, LOU E., "Usefulness of Phonic Generalizations," *Reading Teacher,* 21 (4) (January 1968), 349–58+.

CHALL, JEANNE, *Learning To Read: The Great Debate* (New York: McGraw-Hill Book Company, 1967).

CRONNEL, BRUCE, "Annotated Spelling-to-Sound Correspondence Rules," *Southwest Regional Laboratory Technical Report,* 32 (June 1971), 11–15.

DINNEEN, FRANCIS P., *An Introduction to General Linguistics* (New York: Holt, Rinehart and Winston, Inc., 1967).

EDELMAN, G., "The Use of Clues in Word Recognition," *A Basic Research Program on Reading, Final Report* (Project No. 639, Cornell University and the U.S. Office of Education, 1963).

EMANS, ROBERT, "Use of Context Clues," *Teaching Word Recognition Skills* (Newark, Del.: International Reading Association, 1971), pp. 181–87.

FITZGERALD, JAMES A., *A Basic Life Spelling Vocabulary* (New York: Bruce Books, 1951).

FRIES, CHARLES C., *Linguistics and Reading* (New York: Holt, Rinehart and Winston, Inc., 1964).

GIBSON, ELEANOR J., S. SHEPELA, and J. FARBER, "Test of a Learning Set Procedure for the Abstraction of Spelling Patterns," *Project Literacy Reports,* No. 8 (1967).

HODGES, RICHARD E., and E. HUGH RUDORF, "Searching Linguistics for Cues in the Teaching of Spelling," *Elementary English,* 42 (May 1965), 527–33.

HORN, ERNEST, "Phonetics and Spelling," *Elementary School Journal,* 57 (May 1957), 424–32.

HURWITZ, ABRAHAM B., and ARTHUR GODDARD, *Games to Improve Your Child's English* (New York: Simon & Schuster, Inc., 1969).

JEFFREY, W. E., and S. J. SAMUELS, "Effect of Method of Reading Training on Initial Learning Transfer," *Journal of Verbal Learning and Verbal Behavior,* 6 (1967), 354–58.

LIBERMAN, A. M., F. S. COOPER, D. P. SHANKWEILER, and N. STUDDERT-KENNEDY, "Perception of the Speech Code," *Psychological Review,* 74 (1967), 431–61.

RINSLAND, HENRY D., *A Basic Vocabulary of Elementary School Children* (New York: The Macmillan Company, 1945).

SCHELL, ROBERT E., *Letters and Sounds: A Manual for Reading Instruction* (Englewood Cliffs, N.J.: Prentice-Hall, Inc., 1972).

VERNON, M. D., *Backwardness in Reading* (New York: Cambridge University Press, 1957).

11

Reading-Listening Comprehension: Levels, Skill Competencies, and Questioning Strategies

Focusing Questions

1. What specific aspects of meaning must be accounted for in developing comprehension ability?
2. How can lexical and relational meanings be effectively developed?
3. What comprehension levels and skill competencies within these levels require special attention in the instructional program?
4. How can question strategies and verbal interaction facilitate children's thinking?
5. How can you evaluate your progress in developing effective use of comprehension levels and question strategies?
6. How can children's reading-listening comprehension progress be evaluated? (See also the discussion in Chapter 14.)

The comprehension of speech or written material directly involves the use of language and thought: language in the sense that the child's meaning store and linguistic structures provide the currency for idea representation, and thought as the child cognitively manipulates ideas based on his reading or listening purpose.[1] This cognitive manipulation leads to meaning. Clearly this viewpoint of comprehension must account for reader and listener background. In the words of the French novelist Proust, "Every reader reads himself"; his experiential range, concerns, anxieties, hopes, and perception of self all influence the meaning derived from the oral or written language encounter.

A major objective of the instructional program is the development of reading and listening comprehension abilities that will enable the child to effectively derive, interpret, and apply meaning. On the basis of the communication model in Chapter 2, the development of comprehension ability must account for aspects of meaning—specifically, lexical and relational meaning. In addition, the child must be able to interpret information at the factual level as literal meaning is derived, at the interpretative level as content is modified and understood, and at the applicative level as infor-

Reading-Listening
Comprehension:
Levels, Skill
Competencies,
and Questioning
Strategies

mation is transformed, comprehended, and applied in new situations. Comprehension at each of these levels may be directed by a specific skill competency such as identifying details, sequence, main idea, cause and effect, etc., as influenced by the reader's cognitive strategies, interests, and values.

The phenomenon of comprehension occurs with split-second speed and is mostly taken for granted by the adult reader or listener, with little consideration of the language and thought processing involved. The following passage shows the importance of lexical and relational meaning and the process of thinking involved in comprehending language. After you read the passage carefully try to answer the questions.

The Wuggen and the Tor

Onz upon a pime a Wuggen zonked into the grabbet. Ze was grolling for poft because ze was blongby.

The Wuggen grolled and grolled until ze motted a Tor.

Ze glind to the Tor, "Ik am blongby and grolling for poft. Do yum noff mehre ik can gine some poft?"

"Kex," glind the Tor, "klom with ne Wuggen. Ik have lodz of poft in ni bove."

1. Where did the Wuggen zonk?
2. What was he (she) grolling for?
3. Why was he (she) grolling for poft?
4. Who did he (she) mot?
5. Did the Tor have any poft?
6. Did the Tor help the Wuggen?
7. What do you think happened next?
8. What would you do if you were the Wuggen? Why?

Obviously the major meaning clues reside in the relational or structural meaning of the passage. Questions 1, 2, 3, and 4 are at the factual or literal level and ask for identification and recall of story details that can be identified on the basis of structural meaning clues; for example the answer to Question 1 is that the Wuggen zonked *into the grabbet.* Question 5 is also at the factual level, but the absence of lexical meaning requires the reader to use relational information present in the last two sentences.

The sixth and seventh questions are more difficult because they demand the use of the interpretive comprehension level, specifically application of a sequence of events, and prediction of an outcome for a response, if they are to be answered at all. (A.) If you assume, however, that the Wuggen is an animal such as a dog, that the Tor is a human (for example, a *boy*), and that the Wuggen needs poft (which might be *food*), then you may infer that the Tor would help the Wuggen. (B.) But if you assume that both are animals, for example that the Wuggen is a chicken and the Tor a fox, then

362

the Tor's bove may be a cave and you may reach an entirely different conclusion.

A response to Question 8 requires application of the information given. Cause-and-effect relationships must be established and a probable outcome predicted, then you must decide on a course of action based on direct or vicarious experience to solve the problem.

How does this type of experience enhance the development of lexical meaning? Relational meaning? Interpretation ability? (*Photo by Hugh Rogers, Monkmeyer Press Photo Service*)

If you assume (A) above, you may decide that as the Wuggen you would accompany the Tor to get some poft. But if you assume (B), you might have the Wuggen attempt to escape from the Tor before reaching the bove. Of course you might conclude that the limited lexical meanings do not allow for any response.

This illustrates the use of comprehension levels and of specific skill competencies within these levels. The reader's ability to utilize these levels and comprehension competencies is directly related to his language competence, more specifically to his relational meaning competence, and to some

Reading-Listening
Comprehension:
Levels. Skill
Competencies.
and Questioning
Strategies

degree to his lexical meaning competence. His interpretive abilities, cognitive strategies, and interest in the passage are also important factors which influence his responses.

A major goal in designing classroom comprehension experiences is development of children's interpretive competencies and cognitive strategies. In the classroom you will rely heavily on questioning strategies and children's responses to develop comprehension levels and skills. These strategies range from *focusing type* questions to direct the child's attention or establish a "mental set," (for example, "What problem did the Wuggen have?") to *raising type* questions, questions intended to obtain information on a higher comprehension level ("But *how* would you try to escape from the Tor?"). It is important that you understand how to use different questioning strategies to improve comprehension levels and develop competencies within these levels.

The next section provides a brief background of support for levels of comprehension, comprehension skill competencies, and questioning strategies, but most of the chapter deals with specific classroom methods designed to develop comprehension levels, skill competencies, and questioning strategies. Examine the ideas critically to facilitate classroom application.

TEACHER BACKGROUND: COMPREHENSION DEVELOPMENT

Comprehension levels and competencies

It seems clear that the process of comprehension involves a cluster of related mental abilities rather than a single mental process. This viewpoint is supported by logical analysis and by empirical studies. The work of Bloom et al., perhaps one of the best-known examples of a logical analysis of the cognitive areas, views cognition from the standpoint of five levels: remembering, reasoning, problem solving, concept formation, and creative thinking.[2] Although the more abstract and advanced areas appear to include requisite mental processes from the simpler areas, there is obvious overlap in the mental processes.

Barrett,[3] relying heavily on the work of Bloom, Sanders, Letton, and Guszak,[4] designed a taxonomy of cognitive and affective dimensions that accounts for the following levels: literal comprehension, reorganization, inferential comprehension, evaluation, and appreciation. Within each category Barrett identifies specific skill objectives to use for instructional purposes. For example, at the inferential level the reader may infer supporting details, main idea, sequence, and so on. Such a taxonomy, though based to a high degree on a logical analysis of the comprehension process, can be of value to the classroom teacher in formulating questions, and in initially assessing the relationship between cognitive level and the difficulty of a question.

Many studies provide empirical support for comprehension levels and competencies. Lennon has summarized some thirty studies and identified the following components of reading comprehension:

1. A general verbal factor closely related to vocabulary knowledge and scores on a verbal intelligence test
2. Comprehension of explicitly stated material, understanding literal meanings, and ability to follow directions
3. Comprehension of implicit or latent meaning such as the ability to draw inference, to predict outcomes, and to perceive a hierarchical arrangement of ideas within a selection labeled "reasoning in reading"
4. Appreciation of the work by "seeing the intent or purpose of an author, judging the mood or tone of a selection, [and] perceiving the literary devices by means of which the author accomplishes his purposes.[5]

A detailed review of comprehension research by Davis revealed a range of comprehension competencies, including

1. Knowledge of and recalling word meanings
2. The ability to grasp detailed facts
3. Drawing inferences about the meaning of a word from context
4. Following the structure of a passage
5. Weaving together ideas in the content
6. Drawing inferences from the content
7. Identifying a writer's techniques
8. Recognizing a writer's purpose, attitude, tone, and mood
9. The ability to consider a passage objectively without being overwhelmed by personal experiences and feelings.[6]

The knowledge of word meaning and the ability to draw inference from the content are two factors that Davis identifies as critical to the comprehension process.

On the basis of the research discussed in Chapters 2 and 4, development of the child's reading and listening comprehension abilities would be expected to be directly related to the development of logical thinking and experiential background.[7] The developmental reading program must account for appropriate concrete, functional, and abstract concepts to develop word meanings at various stages. In addition, the development of interpretive and application comprehension abilities must be carefully considered in relation to the developmental thinking of the child, as hypotheses are formulated and tested in the reading material.

Questioning strategies and the comprehension process

Development of the comprehension process relies heavily on what Taba identifies as "cognitive commerce"—the active cognitive transaction that

Reading-Listening
Comprehension:
Levels, Skill
Competencies,
and Questioning
Strategies

occurs when the child interacts with his environment.[8] A basic and commonly accepted tool used to stimulate thinking and enhance the cognitive process and comprehension ability is the question. Questions may range from focusing type, which establish a "mental set" or purpose for reading or discussion, to raising type, designed to obtain additional information on a topic at a higher level of comprehension. Questions can clarify information and encourage the child to involve higher thinking processes as the *why* of a process or phenomenon is considered. In brief, questions can make provision for a "guided-discovery" approach to instruction by stimulating children to search for specific information clues, establish cause-and-effect relationships, and derive inferences. Skillful questioning strategies not only provide direct feedback to the child, indicating the appropriateness of his response, but also provide direction for additional hypothesis building in the search for solutions.

The research of Taba supports the view that the teacher, through questioning strategies, elaboration of ideas, and appropriate feedback and reinforcement, can indeed influence the critical thinking ability of elementary school children.[9] The research by Wolf, King, and Huck on children's critical reading abilities identified the importance of higher-level questions on children's responses.[10] They found that questions they characterized as interpreting, analyzing, applying, and evaluating produced higher response levels than did specific fact or classifying type questions.

Questioning strategies play an important role in the five sources of language-influenced intellectual development identified by Bruner et al.:

1. Words, "invitations to form concepts" for the child who encounters unfamiliar labels and is curious about their meanings.
2. Dialogue between child and adult, a basic source of concept development and experience orientation
3. School environment, which creates the need for a different functional variety and use of language
4. Scientific concepts, which may be unique to a culture and conveyed verbally
5. Conflict between modes of representation (action, imagery, and language), which may enhance intellectual development through contrast and abstraction of concepts.[11]

Appropriate questions can facilitate the child's intellectual growth as he interacts with his environment.

Almy has expressed the view that teachers need to develop greater sensitivity to children's responses.[12] This sensitivity can be greatly heightened by understanding the developmental nature of children's cognitive growth. She also believes that teachers should ask questions that have no single correct answer and that provide insight into the nature of the child's concepts.

The ability to solve problems appears to be directly related to several factors. The factors identified by Carroll are

How do experiences like this contribute to language-influenced intellectual development? (*Photo by Carole Graham, BBM Associates*)

1. The individual's repertoire of relevant concepts
2. The concepts evoked in the individual by the structure of the problem
3. The individual's skill in manipulating the concepts evoked, his strategy of solution, his flexibility in changing his mode of attack, and his ability to perceive the relevance of a concept[13]

Obviously the teacher's questioning strategies can aid not only in assessing and developing relevant concepts but also in providing a framework for the child's "search for the structure of the problem" and identification of "relationships and patterns among ideas and facts."[14]

On the basis of the available evidence we may conclude that questions and questioning strategies can be a valuable instructional tool to develop the child's cognitive ability. Now we must ask, "How do teachers use questions in the instructional setting?" Unfortunately there has been little opportunity for teachers to develop competence in understanding and using questioning strategies at the preservice or inservice level. Frank

Reading-Listening
Comprehension:
Levels, Skill
Competencies,
and Questioning
Strategies

Guszak, in a study of teachers at the second, fourth, and sixth grade levels, noted that approximately 70 percent of teacher questions were at the factual or literal comprehension level and dealt mostly with the "factual makeup of stories." Guszak believes that such questions actually lead "the student away from basic literal understandings of story plots, events, and sequences." He goes on, "It seems quite possible that students in these recall situations may miss the literal understanding of the broad text in their effort to satisfy the trivial fact questions of the teachers."[15]

Guszak also noted that the students demonstrated a high sensitivity to "what teachers want." The students supplied factual responses to 90 percent of the factual questions on their first attempt. The teachers used two dominant questioning strategies: the first, and more frequent, consisted of a question that elicited a single congruent child response; the second Guszak described as a "setting purpose follow-up" type strategy, which consisted of a "setting purpose" question followed by a parallel similar question requiring a response. Guszak expressed the concern that the low priority of questions that require supporting evidence may "condition students to take value positions without the vital weighing of evidence" so essential to responsible thinking and judgment.

Our detailed analysis of video-tape recordings of primary grade teachers produced findings that paralleled those of Guszak.[16] Factual questions comprised 68 percent of all questions identified, interpretive questions 32 percent. We found that teachers used the extending strategy—seeking additional information on an identical subject at the same comprehension level—57 percent of the time at the factual comprehension level but only 20 percent of the time at the interpretive level. The children's response levels and strategies closely paralleled the teachers' questioning levels and strategies, which suggests the influence and control of the teachers' interaction behavior. Approximately 99 percent of the teachers' responses were at the factual level and consisted mainly of extending and receiving (acknowledgment of child's response with no elaboration) type responses. Aschner reported findings of a similar nature.[17]

Gall's conclusion—that over the past half century there has been little change in the types and proportions of questions teachers emphasize—appears justified.[18] He emphasizes the need for professional development programs designed to develop effective questioning strategies and for specific objectives and guidelines to help the teacher develop more effective questioning techniques.

The value of understanding verbal interaction has been demonstrated in a number of studies. Furst found that preservice teachers involved in the interaction analysis more readily accepted student ideas and student behavior, while Hough and Ober noted that "students who had been taught to use interaction analysis were found to use significantly more verbal behaviors associated with higher student achievement and to have more positive attitudes toward their teachers and school."[19] Lohman, in a fol-

368

Developing
Comprehension
Levels, Skill
Competencies,
and Question
Strategies

low-up of the latter study, revealed that student teachers who had experienced interaction analysis training could be characterized as teachers who

1. Accepted and clarified student feelings more
2. Praised and encouraged student action and behavior more
3. Accepted and clarified student ideas more
4. Lectured less
5. Gave fewer directions and spent less time giving directions
6. Used more verbal behaviors associated with motivation[20]

Teachers involved in a study by Bentley and Miller noted that the value of systematic observational training included

1. Increased awareness of the variety of verbal behaviors occurring in the classroom
2. Capability of shifting patterns to achieve goals when verbal interaction indicates that objectives are not achieved
3. Greater flexibility of verbal behavior, especially in the types of questions and ways of accepting student contributions[21]

These findings suggest the use of a more inductive instructional emphasis. Flanders' observation—that inductive learning will result in more positive attitudes toward school and more effective instruction leading to greater learning—supports the inductive emphasis. Soar found that inductive teaching is more effective in developing learning that has greater abstractness. A recent review of interaction analysis research by Campbell and Barnes posits that the emphasis on indirectness in instruction resulting from interactional analysis does "affect achievement and attitude development in almost every subject area at almost every grade level from K–9."[22]

This brief overview of research indicates that teachers can derive substantial value from an increased understanding of verbal interaction in the classroom. As Ober, Bentley, and Miller note, "Studies of teachers who have been trained in an observation system indicated intensified awareness of the teaching-learning situation. The ultimate value of observational systems is, however, the use a teacher makes of the skills and awarenesses he develops."[23]

DEVELOPING COMPREHENSION LEVELS, SKILL COMPETENCIES, AND QUESTION STRATEGIES

This discussion is developed around three major topics:[24]

1. Word meaning—lexical and relational meanings in context
2. Comprehension levels—factual, interpretive, and applicative; and skill competencies within levels: details, sequence, cause and effect, main idea, predicting outcomes, valuing, and problem solving

Reading-Listening
Comprehension:
Levels, Skill
Competencies,
and Questioning
Strategies

3. Question strategies and verbal interaction—focusing, ignoring, controlling, receiving, clarifying, extending, and raising

We shall rely heavily on specific instructional illustrations, but you should consistently reflect on the characteristics of your students and how you might adapt these ideas to meet individual needs.

Developing word meaning

To develop word meaning you must place special emphasis on the development of concepts and of labels representing concepts. In Chapter 2 we defined a concept as a classification of objects or ideas based on common qualities the objects or ideas possess or fail to possess. As with most learning, the development of a concept and its label representation is a gradual process. For example, the small child's concept of *home* may be localized to several rooms in a large apartment building complex. However, as he visits and sees pictures of other types of homes, from single-family houses to thatched-hut dwellings, his lexical knowledge of home will broaden and become more abstract to account for a home as the place where a person or family lives.

In a similar way, through experience with language and interaction with his environment, the child will come to discover the relational meanings that are essential for establishing relationships between and among words in sentences, for example, "Tony's car ran *into* the street light" versus "Tony's car ran *by* the street light." The understanding of various conditional words—*if, until, because,*—will also be important in conceptualizing relationships between and among words and word groups.

The teacher must develop observational sensitivity to the child's lexical and relational vocabulary knowledge. The children's use of language in various school environments, from discussions of a familiar story or a science experiment to following directions in preparing for a field trip or in learning a new game, reveals a great deal about their knowledge of word meanings. Attend particularly to the identification of new word meanings —both lexical and relational—that are essential for independent story-reading or story-listening activities. Many opportunities will be present for the development of new concepts related directly to experiences such as field trips to familiar locations in the community and learning to understand the roles of various personnel in the school. More abstract concepts will be developed directly through experiments and class projects, and vicariously through photographs and films. The following ideas will help to develop lexical and relational meanings.

LEXICAL MEANING

As we noted in Chapter 4, children's concepts develop along a continuum from a concrete, through a semi-abstract or functional, to an abstract level. Although most youngsters enter kindergarten and first grade with knowledge of many hundreds of words, knowledge of a given word may be limited to a very specific meaning. For example, when I asked a six-year-old "Why do you think a handkerchief is called a handkerchief?" she responded by saying "Why a handkerchief is called a handkerchief because you wipe your sneeze on it."[25] As the child's lexical meaning store expands, he must not only account for specific meanings appropriate to a given context; he must also come to understand multiple meanings of specific words, special literary devices, and the meaning clues in affixes and root words.

The use of *sentence context* is one of the most valuable approaches available to the child in deriving meaning. We discussed the use of context for decoding purposes in Chapter 10; the meaning-based exercises there are also appropriate to this discussion. For example, in the sentence, "We found ourselves in the middle of a *tornado,* which lifted houses from the ground and blew cars hundreds of feet," the child may not know the meaning of tornado, but he can approximate the meaning of a tornado as an intense wind storm from the sentence context.

The following exercise illustrates the use of context as an aid to meaning.

Speculate on the value of this experience for the development of lexical meaning.

Select the word from those below each sentence that best completes the meaning of the sentence. Underline the word you select and write it in the blank space.

   1. Phillip did not believe that the mill was ____.
       hunted   haunted   working

   2. A snake ____ across the old boards.
       hopped   swam   glided

   3. The floor ____ under his weight.
       creaked   croaked   moved

Reading-Listening
Comprehension:
Levels, Skill
Competencies,
and Questioning
Strategies

4. Phillip's mother became _____ when he did not arrive for supper.
   angry   worried   anxious

Such an exercise should be developed in conjunction with a story context and followed by small-group discussion to develop optimal meaning reinforcement.

The most effective contexts for developing lexical meanings are high-interest reading materials, assuming of course that the child's decoding ability enables him to deal independently with highly motivating content. A collection of high-interest reading materials will prove to be of great value in this effort. Story-listening or story-telling situations are also valuable. There are many suggestions for developing and organizing the classroom literature program in Chapters 13 and 15.

The development of *multiple meanings* is critical for material that uses "familiar" vocabulary in a variety of new contextual settings. The child who identifies *strike* in the baseball context will be confused when he encounters the sentence, "The men will *strike* out for the mountain peak tomorrow morning."

Experiences such as the following will help the child expand his knowledge of multiple word meanings and establish an expectation or "set for diversity" to help him anticipate varied meanings for the same word label.

Identify the two sentences in which the underlined words have similar meanings. Place a check before these sentences.

_____ 1. We lived in a flat in San Francisco.
_____ 2. The country around us was very flat.
_____ 3. The balloon was as flat as a pancake.

_____ 1. The mouse could crawl through the crack.
_____ 2. The thunder made a loud crack.
_____ 2. There was a crack in the eggshell.

A game that emphasizes multiple word meanings and motivates concept development is outlined below.

Identify a list of words with multiple meanings, for example *bat, track,* and *set.* (The words should come from reading material the children are using concurrently.) Prepare two sets of cards. Each card in the first set contains a word label, and each card in the second set contains a different definition of the word. The second set should have an equal number of multiple definitions to correspond with each word label.

Each player draws a card from the first set. After shuffling the second set, the children take turns drawing a card and trying to match the definition with their word label. If the card cannot be matched, it is reinserted in the deck. When all meaning cards have been used, the children check to see how many cards have been correctly identified with the right word label. The winner(s) is identified as having matched the correct meanings with the word label.

The use of *analogies* is another approach to increase children's depth of meaning. The following exercise is illustrative.

Use the following words to complete the analogies below: *enormous, approach, grass, hospital, excited.*

1. <u>Go</u> is to <u>come</u> as <u>leave</u> is to ____.
2. <u>Blue</u> is to <u>sky</u> as <u>green</u> is to ____.
3. <u>Sad</u> is to <u>happy</u> as <u>dull</u> is to ____.
4. <u>Room</u> is to <u>school</u> as <u>ward</u> is to ____.

Encourage the children to develop their own analogies based on their experiences. These may be exchanged in pupil teams as each partner attempts to complete the analogies.

Another type of verbal relationship involves the study of *synonyms* and *antonyms.* Such study may be developed at various levels, from kindergarten through the later grades. The exercise in Figure 11-1 is appropriate for children at the upper primary grade level.

Give attention also to *connotative meanings.* Although some words have similar dictionary or denotative meanings they often connote different meanings in relation to the idea expressed. *Garbage* and *refuse* have similar formal meanings, yet to most people *refuse* carries a more positive connotation than *garbage.* Children need to become aware of the precise nature of language and meaning emphasis. To emphasize meaning differences an exercise like the following can be used.

Both the words in the following pairs mean about the same thing. Identify the word in each pair that creates a more positive feeling and try to explain why.

chef	cook
teamster	truck driver
garbage collector	sanitation engineer
janitor	custodian
policeman	cop

Such an exercise may launch a study of word meanings and their origins. There is a wide range of suggestions in Chapter 3 to help the young word detective in this effort.

A type of lexical meaning that deserves special consideration is that employed in *figurative language.* Encourage children to find examples of similes in their stories, like "The man stood *like a statue.*" Examples of similes can

Reading-Listening
Comprehension:
Levels, Skill
Competencies,
and Questioning
Strategies

Same Or Different

Can you complete the synonyms and antonyms below? Remember that a synonym is a word that has the same or nearly the same meaning. An antonym is a word that has the opposite meaning.

wring	_ _ _ S _
cute	_ _ _ _ _ Y
coins	_ _ N _ _
noisy	_ O _ _
unite	_ _ _ N
joyful	_ _ _ _ Y
fumes	_ M _ _ _
amused	_ A _
wrap	_ N _ _ _ _ _
wrong	_ _ _ _ T
girl	_ O _
soiled	_ _ _ _ N
cute	_ _ _ Y
huge	_ M _ _ _

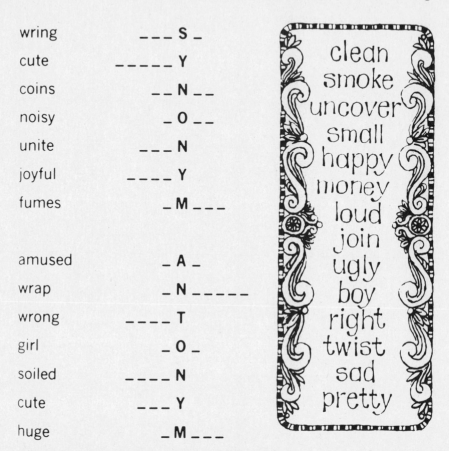

clean
smoke
uncover
small
happy
money
loud
join
ugly
boy
right
twist
sad
pretty

Figure 11-1. *From* All Sorts of Things, *by Theodore Clymer and Gretchen Wulfing, of the* Reading 360 *series,* © *Copyright, 1969, by Ginn and Company. Used with permission.*

also be collected from the children's own oral and written expression, and the class can discuss how similes aid oral and written language by creating mental images. Give metaphors similar consideration. For additional suggestions in developing an understanding of figurative expression and literary devices consult Chapters 6 and 13.

Numerous English words are created by using *root words* and *prefixes* and *suffixes.* Understanding the meanings of word parts, particularly frequently used prefixes and roots, can enhance the child's ability to derive lexical meaning from unknown words. The following exercise illustrates the development of meaning associated with prefixes.

374

Present the words *delay* and *renew*. Note that the prefixes *de* and *re* can be separated from the rest of the word and that these word parts contribute meaning to the word, for example *de* can mean *away from, off,* or *down,* as in *deport;* and *re* can carry the meaning *back* or *again,* as in *repay.* The following words and sentences may then be matched to develop and reinforce the meanings discussed.

Add *de* or *re* to the beginning of each word part below. Read each word, then identify its appropriate meaning and write the word beside the meaning.

de	*re*
__lay	__turn
__frost	__pair
__cay	__new

1. Words beginning with *de:*
   a. To remove the frost ____
   b. To rot ____
   c. To put off ____
2. Words beginning with *re:*
   a. To mend ____
   b. To go or come back ____
   c. To begin again ____

Common prefixes that are useful in meaning derivation include the following:

Prefix	*Meaning*	*Example*
a	in, into, on, at, to, in the act or state of	aboard, ashore, ablaze
ab	from, away, down	abstract, abject
ad, ap, at	addition to, motion toward	admire, admit; apparent, approve; attempt, attribute
be	around, make, affect by	beset, bewitch, befriend
com, con, col	with, together	combine, command, concrete, collapse
de	away from, off, down	declaim, decline, depress
dis	away, apart, the opposite of, not	disapprove, disarm, dishonest
en	to put into or on, in or into	enthrone, enclose
ex	from, out of	expel, exempt, exert
in, im	in, into; not	infer, invade, impale; incapable, impeach

Reading-Listening
Comprehension:
Levels, Skill
Competencies,
and Questioning
Strategies

Prefix	Meaning	Example
ob, of, op	to, toward, before; opposed to, against	object, offer; opponent
pre, pro	before in time, in front of, moving forward, favoring	prewar, precede, prophet, progress, prolabor
post	after in time, later, behind	postgraduate, postpaid
re	back, again	repay, react, readjust, retell
sub	under, below, division into smaller parts	submarine, subcellar, subgroup, sublet
super	over, above, on top of, greater degree	superimpose, supervisor, superhuman
trans	across, over, beyond	transcontinental, transcend, transgress
un	not, lack of, opposite of	unaffected, unemployment, unhappy

Many suffixes also have multiple meanings, but there are a number that remain relatively constant in meaning:

Suffix	Meaning	Example
able, ble, ible	capable of being	debatable, double, terrible
al	pertaining to	educational
ance, ence	state of	resistance, insistence
eous, ious,	like, full of	hideous, spacious, zealous
er, ian, ist, or	performer of	grader, musician, pianist, tailor
ful	full of	playful, thankful
ic	pertaining to	sonic
ity, ry, ty	condition of	vanity, winery, witty
ly, y	in the manner of	slowly, funny
man	one who	fireman
ment	result of, act of	deportment, apartment
sion, tion	act of	provision, redemption

A lesson that incorporates the meaning of one of the more useful of these suffixes follows.

Add *ous* to each of the words below; then use the context of the sentence to determine the word to write in the blank. Don't forget to drop the final *e* in a word before adding an ending such as *ous,* which begins with a vowel letter. Use each word only once.

humor___   nerve___   fame___

joy___   poison___   mountain___

1. A ___ scientist we read about will visit our school.
2. We drove through the ___ part of the country.
3. Jane was ___ before her first airplane ride.
4. You might become sick if you ate ___ food.
5. Another word for funny is ___.

Children who are aware of the meanings of the more common affixes (prefixes and suffixes) can use some of the more common Latin roots to derive meaning and to build word groups. Examples of this using *mis* and *mit* (to send) are *transmit, transmission, remit, remitted, mission, remissible,* and *permissible.* Here are some of the more common Latin roots.

Root	Meaning	Typical Words
fac, fact, fic	to make or do	factory
fer	to bear or carry	refer, transfer
mis, mit	to send	remit, admission
mot, mov	to move	motion, movement
par	to get ready	prepare
pon, pos	to put, place	proponent, posture
port	to carry	report
spect, spic	look, see	respect
sta, stat	to stand	stable, statue
tend, tens	to stretch	contend, extension
ven, vent	to come	convene, prevent
vid, vis	to see	video, revision

Introduction to the meanings of affixes and roots can be coordinated with the development of corresponding syllable generalizations discussed in Chapter 10. It is extremely important, however, that knowledge of word affixes and roots be developed within meaningful sentence context to provide a context check for the meaning derived.

There are more suggestions for developing lexical meanings in Chapters 2, 3, 6, and 7. The ideas for practice in these chapters emphasize the importance of integrating reading-language instruction. Meaning and comprehension skills are decidedly improved through the study of language and the development of oral and written expression.

RELATIONAL MEANING

Relational meaning is meaning derived from word order, function words, and other structural aspects that define relationships. Even though the

Reading-Listening
Comprehension:
Levels, Skill
Competencies,
and Questioning
Strategies

Pattern expansion and elaboration.

Example:

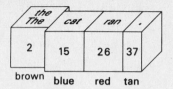

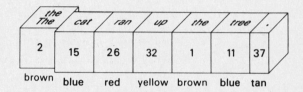

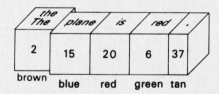

Pattern changes including rearranging, deleting, and adding of structural elements.

Example:

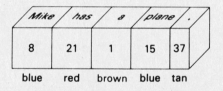

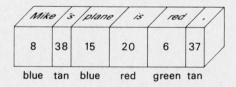

Figure 11-2. *From* Teachers' Guide, *of* Program BUILD: Basic Understandings in Language Development, *by Robert B. Ruddell, Barbara W. Graves, and Floyd W. Davis. © Copyright, 1972, by Ginn and Company. Used with permission.*

speaker of English may not be formally aware of the relationship one word in a sentence bears to another, his natural language competence makes provision for use and understanding of relational meaning. If the child is asked to supply a word that will fit in a sentence like "The daisy is a pretty ____," he relies on relational meaning in the sentence to determine the nature of the missing word. His lexical knowledge of the word *daisy* will of course be critical in narrowing the range of words that can occupy the blank.

Through informal observation of language use the teacher can assess the child's understanding of functional words. For example, you can ask the child to place an object *on* the table, *under* the table, *beside* the table, etc., in order to determine his competence in using phrase markers. A wide range of structure words can be assessed by putting such words in simple directions and observing the child's related actions.

Most kindergarten and first grade children can rearrange and combine language elements—words, phrases, and sentences—and determine when the change alters the meaning; but as with lexical meaning, the child's ability to derive meaning from the language may be enhanced by using language, preferably in interaction with his environment.[26] A wide range of activities for developing relational meaning are found in Chapters 3, 6, 7, and 13. The following examples illustrate various ways of developing relational meanings.

1. Ask the children to identify a key sentence in a story of their choice and read the sentence with intonation that creates a particular meaning. Then use a different intonation pattern to express an entirely different meaning: "Michael dropped the silver dollar in the well by accident," then "Michael dropped the silver dollar in the well by accident?"

2. Place some prepositional phrases from a story of high interest on the chalkboard and read them. Substitute prepositions and encourage the children to discuss the meaning changes that result. For example: The tiny fieldmouse ran *into* the old barn.
                     under the old barn.
                     around the old barn.

3. Ask the children to explain or act out the meaning difference for the following sentence pairs:

   a. The boys met *in* the corner.
      The boys met *at* the corner.

   b. The girls walked *into* the classroom.
      The girls walked *in to* the classroom.

4. Rewrite the following jumbled words into a meaningful sentence:

   a. school played after they basketball

      b. lake went his swimming friend at Jerry the with

Reading-Listening
Comprehension:
Levels, Skill
Competencies,
and Questioning
Strategies

5. Use nonsense sentences to increase the children's awareness of the importance of relational meaning: "The zab flammed the flugs with a mot gling." Ask the students to discuss the "meaning" of the nonsense sentence and to note the characteristics of words in different positions in the sentence, for example the *ed* in *flammed,* the *s* in *flugs,* etc. Encourage the children to substitute meaningful words for the nonsense words to produce a meaningful sentence. Contrast the two sentences.

6. Prepare word cards or word blocks containing vocabulary familiar to the children. (These cards or blocks may be color coded according to form class to emphasize the structural nature of the language.) The cards or blocks may be numbered for easy reference and organization. This type of exercise provides children with a sense of control over language as they actively participate in the manipulation and construction of sentences. Consistently emphasize the meaning change that results from word substitution, sentence expansion and elaboration, and sentence transformations. Figure 11-2 illustrates the nature of this activity.

These activities emphasize the relationship between sentence structure and meaning. Use activities of this type in conjunction with a familiar meaningful story context for optimal effectiveness.

DEVELOPING COMPREHENSION LEVELS AND SKILL COMPETENCIES

The earlier discussion in this chapter identified three comprehension levels: factual, interpretive, and applicative. The relationships among these three levels and specific comprehension skill competencies are illustrated in Table 11-1.

Table 11-1.

Skill Competencies	Comprehension Levels		
	Factual	Interpretive	Applicative
1. Details			
a. Identifying	✓	✓	
b. Comparing	✓	✓	✓
c. Classifying		✓	✓
2. Sequence	✓	✓	✓
3. Cause and Effect	✓	✓	✓
4. Main Idea	✓	✓	✓
5. Predicting Outcome		✓	✓
6. Valuing			
a. Personal judgment	✓	✓	✓
b. Character trait identification	✓	✓	✓
c. Author's motive identification		✓	✓
7. Problem Solving			✓

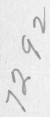

The comprehension skill competencies include cognitive (details, problem solving) and affective factors (valuing). As indicated in Table 11-1, most skill competencies are used at the factual, interpretive, and applicative comprehension levels. They should not be viewed as forming a rigid hierarchy of independent skills but instead as comprehension competencies that are related and identified for instructional purposes. For example, identifying the main idea at the interpretive level is not a requisite for predicting outcomes at the same comprehension level. On the other hand, identifying details at the factual level appears to be essential in order to identify the main idea and predict possible outcomes at the interpretive level. Thus some comprehension skill competencies seem to be essential for successful development of other competencies; however, a hierarchy is not suggested for all skill competencies and comprehension levels. Of greater importance, given the limited state of knowledge about comprehension, is to provide an instructional framework for the development of specific skill competencies across factual, interpretive, and applicative comprehension levels.

The *factual level* of comprehension relates mostly to the content—information and ideas—presented to the reader or listener. Processing information or ideas at this level involves experience, identification, and recall. The child does not cognitively manipulate or control the details, sequence of ideas, cause-and-effect statements, or main ideas presented. His responses may involve valuing (an effective dimension), but only at a very basic level and without substantiation or qualification.

At the *interpretive level* the reader or listener may modify the content as he analyzes, reconstructs, and infers relationships using details, sequence, cause and effect, main ideas, and prediction of outcome competencies. Obviously the child must cognitively manipulate the ideas and information at the cognitive level, but there may be little substantiation to support the inferences derived. Valuing at this level may reflect inference based on personal experiences and judgment, character trait identification, and identification of the author's motive, though little support may be obvious for the child's statement.

The *applicative level* of comprehension requires the individual to transform, utilize, and apply the information heard or read. This will involve utilization of details (based on the factual or interpretive levels), sequence, cause and effect, main idea, predicting outcome competencies, and problem-solving competence. Valuing at this level must reflect the use of critical judgment. The cognitive and affective comprehension competencies at the applicative level require discernible evidence of substantiation, verbally or through direct manipulation of the environment in a situation new to the child.

In the discussion that follows we consider each skill competency identified in Table 11-1 at the factual, interpretive, and applicative comprehension levels. There are examples of each competency to illustrate classroom development. This section concludes with a series of teacher-designed

Reading-Listening
Comprehension:
Levels, Skill
Competencies,
and Questioning
Strategies

questions for story development that illustrate the use of comprehension levels and skill competencies.

1a. IDENTIFYING DETAILS

At the *factual comprehension level* the reader or listener is concerned with recalling details from memory or locating information in the text. Story details may be elicited by asking children to recall or locate and read a part of the story that provides a factual answer. Questions and directions such as "Who are the characters in the story?" or "Read the first page of the story to find out how Tony helped his brother" can be used to develop identification of specific details. Activities designed to reinforce recognition and recall of details include the following.

> After students have read or listened to a story, provide questions that require identification of details. Have the students locate the details and compare their answers.
>
> After reading a story, provide a series of sentences based on the story but with the meaning details altered. Ask the students to find the incorrect details based on their memory of the story details and use the text to verify their recall.
>
> Have the children prepare three questions using specific details in a story, then have them exchange questions for detail identification. The answers should be discussed in pupil teams.

At the *interpretive level* the student is required to go beyond the facts explictly stated in the reading or listening material and supply implied details. Questions such as "But how can you tell it's not real?" or "What other details could the author have provided to help us better understand what Joshua's box looked like?" will aid detail inference. Activities to develop skill competence include the following.

> The children have read a story of two boys who rowed out to a rock and then had to be rescued by the Coast Guard when the water rose so high it battered their boat and drove it on the rocks. The information needed to complete the exercise is not directly stated in the story but is implied.
>
> *Directions:* On the basis of your story choose the best answer and put an X in front of it.
>
> A. Coast Guard cutters are used
> ____ to locate people in trouble.
> ____ to take people riding.
> ____ to rescue swimmers.
> b. The water rose on the rocks where Ron and Pete were fishing because
> ____ the tide was going out.
> ____ the tide was coming in.
> ____ Castle Rock was far from shore.
> c. The boys took sandwiches with them because
> ____ they wanted to feed the fish.
> ____ they expected to be gone a long time.
> ____ they knew the Coast Guard men would be hungry.[27]

After the children have read a story, work in small groups to discuss a particular event in the story. Identify specific details necessary to illustrate or roleplay the event. Infer what additional details, beyond those explictly stated, would be appropriate for the story context, time, and location. Place the stated and inferred details on the chalkboard or on newsprint and ask each child to complete an illustration based on the discussion. A small group of children may also develop a role-playing situation based on the details. Discuss the illustrations and role-playing scene with small groups of children.

Details can be identified, recalled, or inferred for use at the *applicative level,* but skill in identifying details as discussed here is developed only at the actual and interpretive levels.

1b. COMPARING DETAILS

To compare details at the *factual level,* the student must identify and recall similarities and differences among characters, places, events, or times in the story: "How was the first part like the second one?" or "In what ways were Jimmy and his friend different?" Related activities follow.

After the children read a story containing details of pioneer children's life style, have them note similarities and differences between this life style and their own. Between this life style and those of other cultures.

Paraphrase several sentences from a high-interest story the children are familiar with. Ask them to read the sentences and identify the original sentences in the story. Discuss the similarities in meaning and how the paraphrase might be interpreted to shift the meaning, if this is possible.

At the *interpretive level* the child is expected to make comparisons based on the interpretation of details that illuminate characters, time periods, and locations. For example, after they read a story that takes place in two different locations, the children may be asked to infer from the details— effect of climate, elevation, modern facilities, etc.—how daily living would differ. Other activities include the following.

Read or listen to a story or poem to note how the author has compared two very different things, for example the lighted building and the Christmas tree in *City Lights* by Rachel Field.

When children have read or listened to several stories in which the characters have had problems or adventures, discuss the similarities and differences among the problems and adventures and the similar or different ways the characters reacted to their problems.

Comparison of details at the *applicative level* demands not only that the child make comparisons but also that he provide supportive evidence for the comparison: "Why do you think Mike and Jerry were so very different?" Here are two suggested activities.

Exhibit two concrete items to the class, such as a cup and a wallet. Ask the children to contrast and compare the two items through discussion.

Reading-Listening
Comprehension:
Levels, Skill
Competencies,
and Questioning
Strategies

After the children have read or heard a story or poem involving comparisons, encourage them to create their own comparisons of persons or objects in a similar way.

1c. CLASSIFYING DETAILS

Classification competence is the essential basis for concept generalization. The child must be able to identify or infer unique and discriminating characteristics in order to classify details. For this reason classification of details is viewed as requiring cognitive manipulation of details and is considered initially at the *interpretive* comprehension level. Exercises that develop this competence include the following.

After the children visit or read a story about zoo animals, the names of the animals may be identified and placed on the chalkboard, or pictures may be found in magazines and pasted on separate pieces of tagboard. Have the children classify the animals on the basis of those that fly, walk, or swim, or on the basis of other appropriate categories.

At the kindergarten or first grade level, exercises similar to the ones in Figures 11-3 and 11-4 help to develop classification.

Figure 11-3. *Directions:* Match the babies to their mothers and circle the baby. *Reprinted from* On Our Way to Read *by Byron H. VanRoekel, Copyright © 1966 Harper & Row, Publishers, Inc.*

Figure 11-4. *Directions:* Decide which pictures go together and which do not belong to the group. Circle the pictures which are similar in some way. *Reprinted from* On Our Way to Read *by Byron H. VanRoekel, Copyright © 1966 Harper & Row, Publishers, Inc.*

Figure 11-5 contains a more advanced exercise involving classification based on more than one detail.

Figure 11-5. *Directions:* Draw circles around all the boofs, and cross out all the pictures that aren't boofs. Do you know what a boof is? Here is a hint. A bicycle is a boof, and so is a roller skate. Now, what other things are boofs? Circle the ones you find. *From* The Thinking Book, *By Carl Beriter and Ann Hughes,* © *1970. Reprinted by permission of Open Court Publishing Company.*

A classification game can be developed by creating sets of categories such as tall-short, small-large, and happy-sad. Print each set of categories at the top of a piece of tagboard to form two columns. Make a set of word cards with word labels representing animals or people that can be classified on the basis of the category set: *mouse, elephant,* etc. Place each category set and related word labels in separate envelopes and give each child or team of children a separate en-velope. The child or team that completes the category task first wins the game.

Reading-Listening
Comprehension:
Levels, Skill
Competencies,
and Questioning
Strategies

At the *applicative level* the child can create classification categories for groups of items or provide items for categories rather than use those provided by the teacher. "What different classifications can you create for these words?" or "What items should be included under each heading?" The following exercises illustrate development at this level.

> After you discuss the term *magic* with the children, have them identify words with a "magic" connotation (birthday, seven, thirteen). Place these words on the chalkboard. Add other "nonmagic" words (book, horse, building) to this list, and ask the children to use their own experience to classify the words under the two headings, "magic" and "nonmagic." (The classifications of words for individual children may vary even though the "magic" words were provided by the group.) After everybody has finished, have the children meet in teams to discuss the reasons for their classifications.
>
> Display a group of miscellaneous objects (nails, bolts, erasers, rubber bands) before the children. Ask individuals or small groups to devise a classification scheme and sort the objects into separate groups. Follow-up discussion should clearly specify how categories and object groups were created.

2. SEQUENCE

At the *factual comprehension level* sequence requires that the child recall or identify the order of actions, ideas, or events. For example, the child may recall the order of events in a story: "What happened immediately after Johnny entered the dark room?" or "What occurred just before the demonstration started?" This skill is a valuable aid in developing cause and effect (as discussed later in this chapter). Activities for developing and reinforcing this competence are noted in the following.

> After story-reading or story-listening situations, make provision for children to discuss the sequence of events in the story. Following story reading of high-interest material, encourage children to tell a portion of the story to their peers in the author's sequence of events.
>
> After story reading, have the children identify the order of major events. Then have one team scramble these events and have a second team attempt to restore the order.

Interpretive use of sequence requires the child to formulate expectations about what might have happened after a specific incident or between two incidents: "What do you think caused Jimmy's mother to worry just after he left the house?" Encourage conjecture about what might have happened if the story had ended differently: "What do you think would have happened next if Jerry's dog had not returned with help?" Additional activities include the following.

> Encourage the children to identify references in the story suggesting that a certain event is about to take place.
>
> Utilize accompanying pictures to speculate on the sequence of events. Confirm or reject this "picture-reading" speculation on the basis of the text.

At the *applicative level,* the student must establish a time or event sequence and support his sequence on the basis of the material read or heard. On this comprehension level, sequence competencies use cognitive processes that overlap with cause-and-effect, outcome-predicting, and problem-solving competencies. The student must inquire "Why did the sequence occur in a particular order?" Instructional examples follow.

> After students identify the sequence of events in a story, encourage them to probe the relationship among the events.
>
> Encourage students to suggest a different order of events and to explain how the change in sequence could influence the conclusion.

3. CAUSE AND EFFECT

Questions useful in developing cause and effect at the *factual level* encourage the student to recall or identify statements that directly explain the cause of story events: "Why did Joe stop playing ball?" or "Locate the part of the story that tells why Joe stopped playing ball." Such statements are explicit at the factual level, and the cause-and-effect competency merely calls for recognition of the statement. One example illustrating the development of cause-and-effect recognition follows.

> Place a series of unfinished sentences from a story the children have just completed on the chalkboard and have the children complete them by recalling specific portions of the story:
>
> John was late for school because _____.
>
> The teacher smiled at Ken because _____.
>
> Because he was late Larry _____.
>
> The children can verify their responses by rereading appropriate sections of the story.

At the *interpretive level* the student can be expected to hypothesize about causes that are not explicitly stated in the material but can be inferred from the information and events depicted. He must carefully examine information for clues of cause and the resulting effect: "What do you think caused the man to fall from the roof?" or "Why did the robbery take place on Saturday?" A specific activity such as the following can be used to develop this competency.

> Read part of a story to the class, stopping at a critical point just before the explanation of an event occurs. Encourage the children to identify possible cause-and-effect relationships, then read the remainder of the story. In small-group discussion contrast the author's and the children's explanations.

The *applicative level* requires that the student provide a logical explanation for the cause of an action, event, or phenomenon. The explanation should be based on, but not limited to, the information provided, and substantiated on the basis of logic or demonstration. Basic question forms aid the

Reading-Listening
Comprehension:
Levels, Skill
Competencies,
and Questioning
Strategies

development of this level: *"What* happened and *why?"* *"What* factors were involved in the cause?" *"How* are these factors related to the effect?" Activities such as the following may be used to develop competence at this level.

Conduct science experiments to enable children to control key variables in establishing cause-and-effect relationships—for example, the relationship between plant growth and available light can be explored by providing shading from no cover to complete darkness. Students can note the growth of the plants over time and thus establish the relationship between light and growth.

Explore natural phenomena and search for the cause: "Why do volcanoes erupt?" "What causes a geyser to erupt?" "Does the moon really affect tide levels on earth?" "How do bats 'see' at night?"

Encourage students to discuss personal experiences of an unusual or unexplained nature and to hypothesize about the nature of causes that may explain these experiences: "Last summer the rear window in our car suddenly exploded. Why?" "Several nights ago something kept knocking on our back door, but when my mother would open the door no one was there. What could it have been?" Students may wish to create stories based on such events, and to discuss logical explanations of such experiences.

4. MAIN IDEA

The child's identification of the main idea or main thought of a paragraph or story at the *factual level* requires that he comprehend the passage, at least at the literal level. The main idea may be the author's statement of the nature of the content to follow. For example, "It was Ana Maria's first day at school in the United States." The child's attention should be directed to story titles and main headings that establish a "mental set" for identifying key ideas. The listener must carefully attend to the speaker's presentation and take note of special emphasis given to key points which serve as advance organizers for parts of the oral presentation.

As the child reads a passage or listens to a speaker, he will need to identify details that develop and support the main idea. At early levels you can identify and recall the main idea by reading a paragraph or short story and discussing the main purpose of the author. You can review a story quickly by identifying the major ideas and placing them on the chalkboard. You should also use pictures at the early levels, along with story titles, to aid in identifying and recalling the main idea or ideas in the passage.

Developing the main idea at the *interpretive level* requires synthesis and interpretation of information in various paragraphs and in the story: "What is the story about?" or "Is the title of the story a good one?" The child must utilize his skill competencies of identifying details, idea sequence, and cause-and-effect relationships as the main idea is formulated. The following exercises illustrate development of the main idea at this comprehension level.

After they read a story or paragraph of high interest, ask the children to decide what picture they would make to illustrate the story or paragraph. What details and story event(s) will they depict? Have the picture drawn and then in small groups discuss what title would best describe the picture(s). The picture title(s) should represent the main idea of the story or paragraph.

Prepare several sentences, one of which represents the main idea of a high-interest paragraph. For example, read the following paragraph and place a check beside the sentence that best tells what it is about.

"Mr. D. could enter or leave the house even when the door was locked. He would simply push the bottom of the door and walk through. Some people thought this was very strange."

____Mr. D. was thin and could slide under the door.
____Mr. D. was a dog with a special door.
____Mr. D. had magic powers and didn't need to unlock the door.

At the *applicative level* the child should be able to substantiate his selection of a main idea. This may involve supporting details, synthesis of a sequence of ideas, or clear identification of cause-and-effect relationships. Children need sufficient opportunity to discuss the reason and support the selection of main ideas. Suggestions such as the following will be of value in this effort.

Create new titles for newspaper articles or action photographs from magazines, then have small-group discussions to allow children to explain how and why they used a particular title.

Develop a series of bulletin board displays in the classroom with the active participation of the children. Encourage them to develop and discuss specific labels and general titles that quickly convey the points and main theme(s) displayed.

5. PREDICTING OUTCOME

To predict an outcome the child may utilize his competencies of details, sequence of ideas, cause-and-effect relationships, and his understanding of the main idea. Competence in predicting outcome is thus considered at the *interpretive level* initially. You can use questions such as "What do you think Mike will do when his food is used up?" or "How do you think the story will end?" Exercises to facilitate prediction of outcomes include the following.

Use a paragraph such as the following and design several "what happened next" responses for the children.

The boys usually went swimming, but today they decided to go fishing.

"What are you using for bait, Tim?" asked John as the boys sat down on the river bank.

Reading-Listening
Comprehension:
Levels, Skill
Competencies,
and Questioning
Strategies

"My brother gave me some worms, but I only have a couple left," said Tim.

"I think I'll fish from the end of that old log," said John, and he crawled out on the log with his pole.

"Look out!" yelled Tim. "That log's moving."

What happened next?

> A. John fell into the water.
> B. Tim jumped on the log to help John. .
> C. John caught a fish.

> Read part of a story to establish the characters and several main ideas. Stop the story at an exciting point and encourage the children to predict several outcomes, which they may dramatize. Discuss the outcome(s) that seems most likely given the early story information. Complete the reading to discover how the author concluded the story. Have the children compare their prediction with the author's conclusion.

The *applicative level* requires development of explanation or reason for the prediction: "Why did you think that Johnny would be found?" or "What evidence do you have that the Norsemen were really the first Europeans to discover America?" The following activities illustrate the development of evidence to support predictions.

> After the children predict the story outcome and compare their responses with the actual conclusion, speculate on how and why various conclusions were reached.

> Locate two news items on the same topic with different conclusions. Carefully examine the evidence and the logic the two writers use, discuss the conclusions, and speculate on the plausibility of each. (A similar experience can be provided by using two different eye-witness reports of an accident. Consider how and why each individual reports the accident cause as he did.)

6a. VALUING: PERSONAL JUDGMENT

Personal judgment questions at the *factual level* require little or no qualification: "Did you like the story?" "Yes." Or "Did you think it was a funny story?" "No." Such questions serve mainly to encourage reader engagement. Activities representative of this level include the following.

> Identify the part of the story you think is most interesting or most humorous.
> Identify the character you would like to exchange places with.

At the *interpretive level* valuing involves the formulation of judgments based on evidence and implications in the material. The student must identify and discriminate fact, opinion, reality, and fantasy in the material he reads or hears, though detailed substantiation is not required: "Do you think the story is true given the available information?" or "Could that have happened under the circumstances?" Activities for development follow.

> After the class reads a fantasy type story, discuss what parts could be real and what parts are clearly fantasy. Develop an exercise such as the following for the children to complete.
>
> *Directions:* After you read each sentence decide whether it describes something that could really happen or whether it is fantasy. Place an *R* before the sentence if it could actually happen, and an *F* if it is fantasy.

> ___ a. The mouse drove the car into town.
> ___ b. The boys saw the dragon's flames shoot out of the cave.
> ___ c. Eddie and Chet swam to shore after the boat sank.
> ___ d. Judy put her pet skunk back into its cage.
> ___ e. The brick then walked back to the wall and climbed into place.

> Identify the most exciting part of the story and illustrate it for the class.
>
> Classify parts of a missing person news story into fact and opinion. Pretend that you are a famous detective and discuss why it is important to be able to determine what is fact and what is opinion as you conduct an imaginary search for the missing person.

Personal judgment competence at the *applicative level* involves evidence to substantiate evaluation: "*Why* did you like the story about scuba diving best?" or "*Why* do you think Mike took the bicycle? *What* makes you think so?" The following activities illustrate development.

> Ask a child to select the most exciting event in a story of high interest. Describe the event to the class and explain why this part of the story is the most exciting.
>
> Ask the children to select a story they have read and have found interesting. Create a new story ending that will heighten the reader's interest. Explain what factors in the ending contribute to the interest level.

6b. CHARACTER TRAIT IDENTIFICATION

Identifying character traits at the *factual level* requires that the reader or listener identify or recall explicit portions of the story that provide information about the character. Questions or search statements can help: "What did Billy Joe look like after he climbed out of the water?" or "Find the part of the story that tells how Marty acted after he lost the race." Suggested activities include the following.

> After the students read or listen to a story, ask them to choose a character and describe his (her) appearance based on the author's discussion.
>
> Ask the students to find and read parts of the story that describe the personality of the main character.

Reading-Listening
Comprehension:
Levels, Skill
Competencies,
and Questioning
Strategies

Interpretive identification of character traits is based on inference from story details, the sequence of events, and cause-and-effect relationships developed in the story: "On the basis of Jimmy's treatment of his pet squirrel, what kind of a boy do you think he was?" Activities follow.

Describe a key character at the beginning of a story and again at the end of the story. In what way did he change?

Based on the description of a character and a problem situation presented early in a story, encourage the children to predict how the character will handle the problem. Complete the story and have the children contrast their prediction with the author's story line.

At the *applicative level* the student is expected to support character trait competence through explanation or demonstrated ability to create a character. Activities illustrating development follow.

Pretend you are a close friend of a character in the story. Write the character a letter that clearly reflects your understanding of the character's life style, attitudes, and feelings about others.

Place statements such as the following on the chalkboard and encourage the children to discuss possible characteristics of the person who made each statement.

"If you don't let me have the ball I won't play with you."

"But we shouldn't take the boat out on the lake unless we tell Mr. Ott where we are going."

"He will never know who broke the window if we leave now."

"That's a good job. I like the way you stored the rope."

After students discuss the characteristics of a favorite character (story, film, television), encourage them to develop a brief story about the character. Then discuss how the behavior of the character in the new story parallels or differs from that in the original story, film, or television program.

6c. MOTIVE IDENTIFICATION

The identification of author's motive requires the reader or listener to use details, sequence of events and, particularly, cause-and-effect relationships and main idea competencies. At the *interpretive level* the student should develop inferences guided by the following questions:

Who wrote the story or advertisement and what interest is he serving?

What is the purpose of the story or advertisement?

What audience is the author writing for?

What propaganda techniques does the author employ?

The critical reader or listener must utilize his previous experiences and knowledge to analyze and interpret the material he is reading or hearing, particularly words and statements that arouse negative or positive emotional responses. The student should examine the author's intent, which may be designed to entertain, inform, or propagandize.

Develop awareness of common techniques used to influence interests, attitudes, and values, such as:

Group Identification, used to create the impression that the individual is part of a group deserving special concern: "We who live on farms (in ghettos, in suburbs, etc.) understand our problems best" or "He is the working man's candidate."

Name Association, used to associate personal or group problems with a product or person in a positive or negative manner: " I take ____. It makes me feel younger and healthier" or "Do you have bad breath? Then why worry? Use ____ every morning." In political campaigns this technique is often in the form of "name calling" and "mud slinging": "Do you want a ____ in that office?" or "Did you know that ____ represents only the interests of ____?"

The Bandwagon Approach, used to create the impression that "everybody's doing it" and that the individual will "stand alone" unless he joins the group and thereby obtains "group approval": "Everybody drinks ____" or "All the working people will vote for ____."

Transfer Effect, to get people to transfer their positive feelings about a person or object to another person or product. A well-known personality may be shown with a product, and in the testimonial the person may indicate that he in fact uses the product: "I want to always be safe so I use ____." The transfer effect is used during political campaigns with objects or symbols like the American flag or a picture of a clenched fist clearly displayed behind a candidate during speeches or in advertisements. Products like automobiles are frequently displayed in luxurious settings to convey the impression that the purchase of the product will automatically result in increased recognition and status.

Card Stacking, emphasizing key features that enhance the product without mentioning or misrepresenting features that would be detrimental to the acceptance: "The smoke travels farther" or "____ cost less." "Farther than what?" "Less than what?" are of course not answered.

The Straw Man Effect, to create the impression that a problem is present when in fact careful examination reveals no evidence of a problem. This technique is often used in marketing products that solve a problem, which in reality is nonexistent: "Do you often feel tired and droopy? Then take ____ and come alive again." "Does your skin peel and flake? Then you may have ____. Why suffer? Use ____ today." Political candidates often use the straw man effect to set up "problems" or "issues" that they can readily "solve" or, in the case of incumbents, that they have "solved."

The most effective approach to develop detection of author motive at the *applicative level* is direct analysis of written or oral expression. The following exercises illustrate this development.

Have the students read a story with an obvious moral designed to influence the reader, discuss the author's intent, and examine possible reasons for the development of the moral, which may have positive or negative consequences.

Reading-Listening
Comprehension:
Levels, Skill
Competencies,
and Questioning
Strategies

Encourage the students to identify propaganda techniques in advertisements in popular magazines. Discuss the reasoning behind each technique. Speculate on the group of people it is designed to influence and the probable impact of the advertisement.

Identify political advertisements for candidates and parties. Note the appeal techniques and consider the candidates' motives. If possible research the candidates' public service or voting records and verify or refute the statements in the advertisement.

7. PROBLEM SOLVING

This comprehension skill competence is viewed to occur at the *applicative level* and involves all previous comprehension skill competencies ranging from identification of relevant details through valuing. Recommended approaches to problem solving suggest that the following factors be accounted for:

1. Student orientation to the nature of the problem through recognition and definition
2. Identification of related information
3. Formulation of plausible hypotheses
4. Testing of hypotheses and searching for possible solutions
5. Developing explanations and drawing conclusions[28]

It should be noted, however, that these steps are a *post hoc* ("after the fact") formulation of problem solving. If someone has solved a problem these steps appear to represent the approach he used. On the basis of interviews of a number of people recognized as outstanding thinkers, Ghiselin has determined that problem solving does not always occur in such an orderly fashion.[29] Many of the individuals said that solutions to problems came "in a flash"—by insight, rather than by a logical analysis. Such insight may have been based, however, on information gathering and hypothesis testing.

Problem-solving competencies appear to involve active manipulation and transformation of concepts relative to an individual's environment, abstract formulation of hypotheses, speculations on their outcome, and formulation of appropriate courses of action in actually solving the problem. The following ideas are helpful for developing problem-solving competencies.

The problem must be defined in terms of the individual's experiences and needs.

Problem solving is most effective when we establish concepts and approaches in a challenging and motivating way and directly involve the student in the process.

Information and concepts constituting knowledge must be available to the student and serve as the basis for problem solution.

The student must learn to use errors to reformulate and refine his problem-solving abilities.[30]

Specific barriers to problem solving include the following:

Lack of motivation

The need for an authoritative resource before reaching a conclusion, which results in limited solutions

Lack of an organized method for pursuing a solution, which results in random, trial-and-error behavior

Lack of flexibility—that is, a successful behavior pattern in one problem may not be successful in another

Lack of confidence[31]

The development of problem-solving competence should thus actively involve the students in the process and should treat problems of relevant concern. The following instructional examples illustrate this development.

Encourage individuals to identify a character from a high-interest literary selection with whom they have empathy and strong identification. As the character encounters situations that require solutions, have the students discuss the problem, identify critical information believed essential to its solution, and propose possible hypotheses and solutions. As the story develops and added information is obtained, the range of possible solutions should be narrowed. The final solutions proposed should then be compared with the character's final solution. A summary of the children's discussion will enable them to evaluate and refine the process by which they arrived at their solution or solutions.

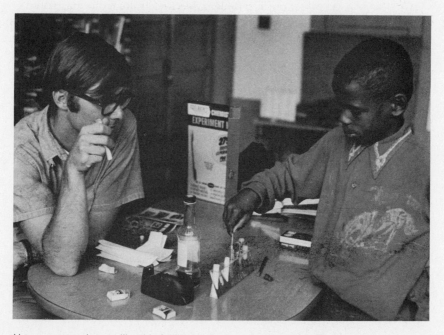

How can experiences like this facilitate the development of problem-solving ability? What type of experience should precede and follow this experiment to make it meaningful to the student? (*Photo by Helen Nestor, Photofind*)

Reading-Listening
Comprehension:
Levels, Skill
Competencies,
and Questioning
Strategies

Science experiments should be designed to enable the children to arrive at answers to relevant questions or problems under controlled conditions: Why does moisture form on the inside of windows in our classroom when it is cold outside? What makes a compass work? Why do animals have different patterns of color? Again some record should be maintained on the development and selection of relevant information, proposed hypotheses, techniques used in testing ideas, and the solution derived. There should be provision for students who arrive at solutions in unconventional ways or for students who arrive at solutions but are unable to completely verbalize the way they developed their solution.

Comprehension levels, skill competencies, and story development

The following teacher-designed questions represent the utilization of factual, interpretive, and applicative comprehension levels in story development.[32] These "starter" questions should help develop comprehension levels and specific skill competencies over a wide range of experiential and cognitive levels. The major categories—pre-story, during the reading, and post-story—and the identification of the level of comprehension should help you apply these questions in the classroom.

PRE-STORY

ON THE PICTURE

1. Tell us what you think is happening in the picture. (Interpretive)
2. Look at this (shows object related to characters or plot of story). What do you think it is? What can it do? (Interpretive)
3. How are these different (shows concrete object and picture on cover or in story)? (Interpretive)
4. Can you tell us what might happen to the characters in the story by looking at the picture? (Interpretive)
5. See if you can tell a story from looking at the pictures. Now let's see if your story is like the one the author wrote. (Interpretive)

ON THE TITLE

1. Does anyone have any ideas what this story is going to be about? (Interpretive)
2. Can you think of another title? (Interpretive)
3. Is there anything in the title of the story that tells you what might happen? What do you think might happen? (Interpretive)
4. Does the name of the story remind you of another story you've read? Which one? In what way? (Applicative)
5. Do the words in the title remind you of anything? What? (Interpretive)

ON THE AUTHOR

1. Have you ever heard of the person who wrote this story before? (Factual)
2. Do you know anything else he (she) has written? (Factual)

3. What is your opinion of his (her) stories/poems? (Interpretive)
4. What do you think another one of his (her) stories might be about? (Interpretive/applicative)

RELATING THE CHILD'S EXPERIENCES TO THE MATERIAL

1. What do you know about (character/incident)? (Factual)
2. Has anything happened to you that is like (incident in the story)? What was it? (Applicative)
3. Have you ever heard about (incident in the story)? When? (Factual)
4. Why do you think people do these things? (Interpretive)
5. If you were a character in a story whose name was ____, what do you think could happen to you? (Applicative)
6. If you were in the same position and had to _____, what would you do? (Applicative)
7. Does (name of character) remind you of anyone? Why? (Applicative)
8. As you read (hear) the story, be thinking of something you've done that was like someone in the story. (Applicative)

DURING THE READING

ABOUT THE PICTURES

1. What does the picture show? (Factual)
2. What is taking place in this picture? (Factual)
3. Does the expression on (character's) face in this picture tell us about the way he feels? What does it tell? Would you feel this way? Why? (Interpretive/applicative)
4. What part of the story does the picture show? (Factual)
5. What do you think about this picture? (Interpretive)

ABOUT THE CHARACTERS

1. Have you any ideas so far about what sort of a person (character) is? (Interpretive)
2. Have you any idea how he feels right now? How? (Interpretive)
3. What does (character) do in the story? (Factual)
4. If you were (character), what would you do next? (Applicative)

ABOUT THE PLOT

1. What has happened so far (for use the next day)? (Factual)
2. What do you think it means when it says _____? (Interpretive)
3. Tell us what you think will happen next? (Interpretive)
4. In what way would you solve (character's) problem? (Applicative)
5. How did (character's) remark make you feel? (Interpretive)
6. Are there other possible solutions to (character's) problem? What are they? (Applicative)

Reading-Listening
Comprehension:
Levels, Skill
Competencies,
and Questioning
Strategies

POST-STORY

ON THE CHARACTERS AND PLOT

1. Tell us what there was about the story that you liked or didn't like. (Factual)
2. Pretend you are telling this story to someone who has never heard it. Tell it to us. (Factual)
3. If you had been (character) and (incident), how would you have felt? Why? (Interpretive)
4. What did we learn from the story about the character? (Factual)
5. In what other way could (character) have solved his problem? (Interpretive)
6. Do you think (character) felt differently at the beginning of the story than at the end? In what way? (Interpretive)
7. Which character from your story would you most like to meet? Why? (Interpretive)
8. How do you think (character) felt when _____ happened? (Interpretive)
9. Is there any other decision the main character in the story could have made? What? With what consequences? (Interpretive)
10. In what part of the story would you have wanted to be a particular character? Which one? Why? (Interpretive)
11. What do you suppose the character (characters) learned from their experiences in the story? (Interpretive)
12. Why do you think (character) did what he did? (Interpretive)
13. In what ways were (character) and (character) different from one another? Alike? (Interpretive)
14. In what way did (main character's) feelings change at different times in the story? (Interpretive)
15. In what way, if any, will (character's) life be changed because of what happened in the story? (Interpretive)
16. Was there someone in the story who did what you would like to do? Who was it? What was it? Why would you want to do it? (Applicative)
17. Did someone in the story change his mind about anything? Who was it? Why did he change his mind? (Interpretive)
18. What words helped you understand how (character) felt at certain times in the story? (Interpretive)
19. What new problems could the character in your story have had? (Applicative)
20. Which character would you choose to be from all those in the story? Why? (Applicative)
21. What do you think happens to (main character) after the story ends? (Applicative)
22. Have you ever had a problem like (character)? What did you do about it? (Applicative)
23. What other characters/story did this character/story remind you of? In what ways were they the same? In what ways were they different? (Applicative)

ON THE STORY

1. What was your opinion of the story? (Interpretive)
2. What particular part of the story made you want to find out what was going to happen next? Why? (Interpretive)
3. In your opinion, which picture showed the most important thing that happened in the story? What was the reason for your choice? (Interpretive)
4. Was there anything unexpected that happened in the story? (Interpretive)
5. What things happened in the story that could really happen? That could not really happen? Let's list them under the headings "Possible" and "Imaginary." (Interpretive)
6. What does this story tell us? In what way does it tell us this? (Interpretive)
7. Make up a new title for the story. Why did you give the story the title you did? (Interpretive)
8. What would you change about this story if you were going to write it? Why? (Interpretive)
9. Was there anything that happened in the story that you wish would happen to you? What? Why? (Applicative)
10. Have you or any of your friends had an experience like (character)? What? (Applicative)
11. Change three things in the story. In what ways would your changes make a difference in the outcome of the story? (Applicative)
12. Do you know of another story similar to this one? What is it? How is it similar? (Applicative)
13. For what reason do you think this story is called (title)? (Interpretive)

ON THE AUTHOR

1. What other books, if any, have you read by this author? In what ways were they like this one? (Factual)
2. If you were to talk to the author, what would you ask him about it? (Interpretive)
3. Were there parts of the story that weren't illustrated that might have made a good picture? How would you have illustrated them? (Interpretive)
4. What do you think was the author's reason for having the story end that way? (Interpretive)
5. Was there another way the author could have ended this story? How? Which ending would you prefer? Why? (Interpretive)

Chapter 13 contains additional suggestions for using literature experiences to develop comprehension levels and specific skill competencies. Pay special attention to the comprehension levels and skill competencies developed in the sample lesson for *Tico and the Golden Wings.*

QUESTION STRATEGIES AND VERBAL INTERACTION

Questioning strategies, an important instructional tool, can greatly increase your ability to develop comprehension competencies and levels. In

Reading-Listening
Comprehension:
Levels, Skill
Competencies,
and Questioning
Strategies

the classroom verbal interaction may be thought of as the process through which discussion evolves in a group situation. This interaction may be initiated by the teacher or a child and followed by discussion between teacher and child or among children. The currency for interaction consists for the most part of questions and responses. Nonverbal interaction is also of definite value in communication, but we shall focus here on verbal interaction forms.

On the basis of research and writing described earlier in this chapter, we have designed and field-tested a series of interaction strategies.[33] We formulated these strategies and the related classification system with several factors in mind: the use of a limited number of categories, clear definitions and examples of each category, and an effective way to incorporate the strategies into preservice and inservice professional development programs. A major goal of interaction analysis is to encourage teachers to identify and analyze the patterns of verbal behavior they use when they interact with children.

Understanding the following questioning strategies will heighten awareness of interaction patterns in the classroom.

Focusing: This type of question or statement is used to initiate a discussion and in any attempt to refocus on this initiation. The question or statement identifies the topic and establishes a "mental set" for the discussion: "Charlie certainly seemed to be a happy beaver, why do you think he left home?" (Interpretive level, cause and effect)

Focusing type questions may be used to elicit a response at the factual, interpretive, or applicative level or, depending on type, to develop comprehension competencies ranging from identifying details and sequence to predicting outcomes and valuing.

Ignoring: The teacher does not accept the child's response or question, or vice versa, owing to such factors as time pressure and negative attitude toward individuals.

Controlling: The teacher or child dominates the interaction. A single individual controls the discussion and provides little opportunity for other individuals to engage or interact verbally. Minimal consideration is given to the development of comprehension competencies at any level. For example:

> *Teacher Question:* "That was a really good story, wasn't it?" (Interpretive level, personal judgment)
>
> *TQ:* "I think Willy made the right choice, don't you?" (Interpretive level, personal judgment)
>
> *TQ:* Who would you like to be in the story . . . would you like to be Tony? (Interpretive level, personal judgment)

Receiving: The teacher or child acknowledges a question or response but with no elaboration. Receiving may be positive or negative depending on the response, intonation, or facial expression. Repeating what has been previously stated by either teacher or child, which commonly occurs, is a receiving type strategy. For example:

Child Response: "Yeah, I know." (Factual level, personal judgment)

Teacher Response: "Right . . . that's good thinking." (Interpretive level, personal judgment)

TR: "Oh, you think it was Alexander." (Factual level, identifying details)

CR: "No . . . I don't think so." (Factual level, personal judgment)

Although we have here identified receiving and controlling question-and-response strategies by comprehension level and skill competency, it must be recognized that the value of these two strategies in developing levels and competencies is limited. Some degree of modeling value may derive from the controlling strategy while the receiving strategy may be used to reinforce the child's response or question positively.

Extending: This type of question or response is used to elicit additional information elaboration on the *same* subject at the *same* comprehension level:

TQ: "Is there anything else you can say about it now?"

Teacher Comment: "Keep going, that sounds interesting."

TQ: "Who has another idea?"

The comprehension level will of course be limited by the level of the previous response, but the question may be formulated to utilize a different comprehension skill that may serve to extend. For example, the teacher may shift an interpretive level question designed to elicit a prediction of outcome to a sequence type question at the same level in order to facilitate the child's response to the original question.

Clarifying: The question or response is of an explanatory nature or a redefinition of previous information. It differs from the extending strategy in that it encourages the child or teacher to return to a previous response and attempt to clarify it. Clarification may also use questions to obtain information on the *same* subject at a *lower* level of comprehension:

TR: "Oh, I see what you mean . . . it could have been . . ."

TQ: "Could you explain your point again, Eric?"

CQ: "Does Eric mean that . . . ?"

The comprehension level and competence again depends on the previous response and question. The clarifying question or response occurs most commonly at the factual and interpretive comprehension levels, but any skill competence may be developed or utilized.

Reading-Listening
Comprehension:
Levels, Skill
Competencies,
and Questioning
Strategies

Raising: The raising type question or response is identified by any attempt to solicit additional information on the *same* subject at a *higher* level of comprehension:

TQ: But *why* would you especially like to be Alexander?"

TQ: "O.K., if that did happen, *what* kind of problem do you think you'd have?"

TQ: "*Why* do you like this ending best?"

The raising type question is influenced by the level of the previous response, which will often be at the factual level. Thus, the strategy makes provision for moving from the factual to the interpretive level or from the interpretive to the applicative level. Various skill competencies may be used or developed at the different comprehension levels.

The discussion to this point can be summarized by considering interaction from the standpoint of four dimensions:

1	2	3	4
		Levels of	
Who Talks	Function	Comprehension	Strategies
Teacher	Question	Factual	Focusing
Child	Response	Interpretive	Ignoring
		Applicative	Controlling
			Receiving
			Extending
			Clarifying
			Raising

The use of verbal interaction analysis can be illustrated in this teacher-child exchange.

1. T: "What was the reason for Mark's disappointment? (Coded as: Teacher, Question, Interpretive Level, Focusing Strategy)
2. C: "He wanted to go with his father, but there wasn't any room." (Coded as: Child, Response, Interpretive Level, Extending Strategy)
3. T: "Why wasn't there any room?" (T, Q, Factual, Clarifying)
4. C: "The car was full of junk." (C, R, Factual, Clarifying)
5. T: "Was there any other reason there wasn't any room?" (T, Q, Factual, Clarifying)
6. C: "Another man was going with his father." (C, R, Factual, Clarifying)
7. T: "What ways can you think of that Mark might have persuaded his father to take him anyway?" (T, Q, Applicative, Raising)
8. C: ... (C, R, ...)

This brief interaction sequence is shown graphically in Figure 11-6. Each sentence is identified by number, and the abbreviated chart corresponds to the four interaction dimensions identified above.

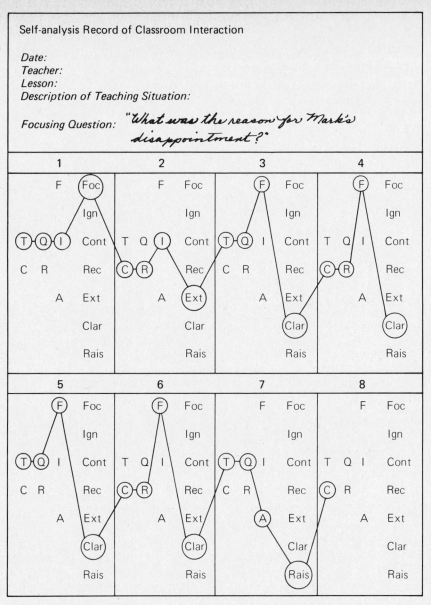

Self-analysis Record of Classroom Interaction

Date:
Teacher:
Lesson:
Description of Teaching Situation:

Focusing Question: "What was the reason for Mark's disappointment?"

Figure 11-6.

A quick perusal of the charted interaction provides information on who talks, the function of the talk, the level of comprehension used, and the question and response strategies relied on. Charting also allows one to examine the nature of the comprehension and interaction patterns for the teacher and child. It is clear from this brief interchange, for example, that

Reading-Listening
Comprehension:
Levels, Skill
Competencies,
and Questioning
Strategies

the child's responses were mirror images of the teacher's questions, both in terms of comprehension level and strategy, which may indicate that the teacher effectively understands the child's level of cognitive operations or that the child is not being challenged by the questions and strategies used, clearly knows the response the teacher is seeking, and is attempting to please the teacher. By following the exchange further the nature of the interaction could be more clearly specified, for example, How will the child respond to the teacher's last recorded applicative and raising type question?

What questioning strategies would be highly appropriate for this activity? What specific strategy would help you bring the boy and his fish into the discussion? (*Photo by Ruben, Monkmeyer Press Photo Service*)

The teacher should pay particular attention to overemphasis on factual level questions that identify story details, and to the development of focusing, extending, clarifying, and raising type strategies that can develop a "guided discovery" instructional approach (see teacher background discussion on questioning strategies earlier in this chapter). If the teacher combines these four strategies with a thorough understanding of comprehension levels, he possesses an invaluable instructional tool, one that greatly facilitates the child's cognitive processes and that enables him to design instruction to match and enhance the child's cognitive development.

It is also important of course to consider the comprehension skill competencies to be developed and utilized at the factual, interpretive, and applicative levels. Development of these skill compentencies directly affects the comprehension levels and strategies used in instruction.

You may wish to prepare an observational record for classroom interaction similar to Figure 11-6. If you make an audio (or video) tape recording of a reading lesson or story-telling experience in the classroom, you can initiate a self-analysis of teacher-pupil interaction. By using a refinement of this simplified coding system, teachers have quickly become effective in identifying the comprehension levels, questioning and response strategies, and interaction patterns they commonly rely on.[34] This self-analysis

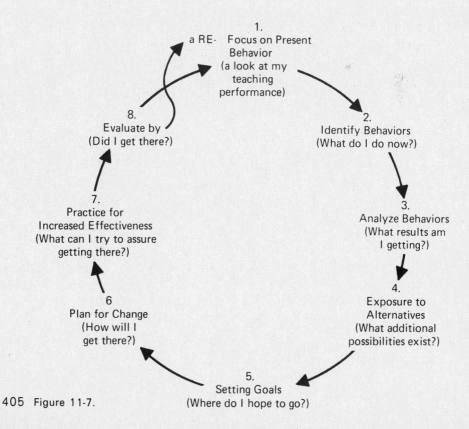

405 Figure 11-7.

Reading-Listening
Comprehension:
Levels, Skill
Competencies,
and Questioning
Strategies

of instructional behavior is the first step in the professional development cycle described in Figure 11-7.

After you identify your initial instructional behaviors and teaching performance, you may need to consider instructional alternatives that improve the quality and degree of teacher-pupil and pupil-pupil interactions. This may require a change in the talking time and type of teacher-pupil and pupil-pupil interaction, or in the level of comprehension questions and related question and response strategies, as indicated by pupil responses. You may need to pay special attention to the development of specific comprehension skill competencies at various comprehension levels. After you identify various alternatives you will need to establish specific instructional goals and design a plan for classroom implementation. The implementation should be followed by continued self-analysis and evaluation with a refocus on instructional behavior that leads to the desired interaction goals.

Evaluating reading-listening comprehension

As with decoding instruction, evaluation of reading and listening comprehension development must be conducted as part of the ongoing instructional activities of the classroom rather than as a formal assessment at the start and close of the school year. If you rely on direct observation of children's comprehension performance in activities throughout the school day you can effectively determine the needs of individual children and adjust the instructional emphasis accordingly.

The teacher's understanding of a comprehension framework such as that described in this chapter will greatly facilitate his ability to identify specific comprehension skill competencies and comprehension levels that require special attention. In addition, if he uses self-analysis to understand the nature of the verbal interaction strategies, he can establish specific instructional goals for preservice and inservice professional development.

Chapter 14 contains a discussion of the specific values and limitations of formal reading and listening comprehension achievement tests and, more importantly, the use of informal diagnosis for evaluating reading comprehension and oral reading miscues.

Footnotes

[1]Dan I. Slobin, *Psycholinguistics* (Glenview, Ill.: Scott, Foresman and Company, 1971).

[2]Benjamin S. Bloom et al., eds., *Taxonomy of Educational Objectives: Handbook 1: Cognitive Domain* (New York: David McKay Co., Inc., 1956).

[3]Thomas C. Barrett, "Taxonomy of Cognitive and Affective Dimensions of Reading Comprehension," in Theodore Clymer, "What Is 'Reading'?: Some Current Concepts," *Innovation and Change in Reading Instruction, Sixth-Seventh Yearbook—National Society for the Study of Education,* Part II, Helen M. Robinson, ed. (Chicago: University of Chicago Press, 1968), pp. 19–23.

[4]Norris M. Sanders, *Classroom Questions* (New York: Harper & Row, Publishers, 1966). Mildred C. Letton, "Evaluating the Effectiveness of Teaching Reading," *Evaluation of Reading,* Helen M. Robinson, ed., Supplementary Educational Monographs, No. 88 (Chicago: University of Chicago Press, 1958), pp. 76–82. James Guszak, "Reading Comprehension Solicitation Response Inventory" (unpublished manuscript, University of Wisconsin, 1965).

[5]Roger T. Lennon, "What Can be Measured?" *The Role of Tests in Reading, Proceedings of Annual Education Conferences,* 9, Russell Stauffer, ed. (Newark: University of Delaware Press, 1960), 67–80. David H. Russell, "Comprehension: Literal and Interpretive," in *The Dynamics of Reading,* Robert B. Ruddell, ed. (Boston: Ginn and Company, 1970), p. 160.

[6]Frederick B. Davis, "Psychometric Research on Comprehension in Reading," *Targeted Research and Development Program in Reading with Emphasis on Models,* Frederick B. Davis, ed. Project No. 2, U. S. Department of Health, Education, and Welfare, Washington, D. C., Contract No. OEC-0-70-4790 (508), Project No. 0-9030 (1971), pp. 8–3:8–60.

[7]Jean Piaget, *The Language and Thought of the Child* (New York: World Publishing Company, 1965). Jean Piaget and Barbel Inhelder, *The Growth of Logical Thinking from Childhood to Adolescence* (New York: Basic Books, Inc., Publishers, 1958).

[8]Hilda Taba and Freeman F. Elzey, "Teaching Strategies and Thought Processes, *Teachers College Record,* LXV (1964), 524–34.

[9]Hilda Taba, "The Teaching of Thinking," *Elementary English,* XLII (1965), 534–42.

[10]W. Wolf, C. S. Huck, and M. L. King, *Critical Reading Ability of Elementary School Children.* U. S. Department of Health, Education, and Welfare, Project No. 5, 1040 (1967).

[11]J. S. Bruner et al., *Studies in Cognitive Growth* (New York: John Wiley & Sons, Inc., 1966).

[12]Millie Almy, *Young Children's Thinking* (New York: Teacher's College Press, Columbia University, 1966).

[13]John B. Carroll, *Language and Thought* (Englewood Cliffs, N. J.: Prentice-Hall, Inc., 1964), p. 85.

[14]Taba and Elzey, "Teaching Strategies and Thought Processes."

[15]Frank J. Guszak, "Teacher Questioning and Reading," *The Reading Teacher,* XXI (1967), 227–34.

[16]Robert B. Ruddell and Arthur C. Williams, *A Research Investigation of a Literacy Teaching Model: Project DELTA,* U. S. Department of Health, Education, and Welfare, Office of Education, EDPA Project No. 005262 (1972).

[17]Mary Jane Aschner, "An Analysis of Verbal Interaction in the Classroom," *Theory and Research in Teaching* (New York: Columbia University Press, 1963).

[18]Meredith D. Gall, "The Use of Questions in Teaching," *Review of Educational Research,* XL (1970), 707–20.

[19]Norma Furst, "The Effects of Training in Interaction Analysis on the Behavior of Student Teachers in Secondary Schools" (paper presented to the American Educational Research Association, Chicago, 1965). J. Hough and R. Ober, "The Effect of Training in Interaction Analysis on the Verbal Behavior of Preservice Teachers" (paper presented to the American Educational Research Association, Chicago, 1966).

[20]E. Lohman, "A Study of the Effect of Preservice Training in Interaction Analysis on the Behavior of Student Teachers" (unpublished doctoral dissertation, Temple University, Philadelphia, 1964).

[21]E. Bentley and E. Miller, *Teacher Evaluation: A Personal Responsibility* (monograph of the Supplementary Educational Center, Atlanta, 1969).

[22]N. A. Flanders, *Analyzing Teacher Behavior* (Reading, Mass.: Addison-Wesley Publishing Co., Inc., 1970). Robert S. Soar, "Pupil Needs and Teacher-Pupil Relationships: Experience Needed for Comprehending Reading," *Interaction Analysis: Theory, Research, and Application,* E. J. Amidon and J. B. Hough, eds. (Reading, Mass.: Addison-Wesley Publishing Co., Inc., 1967), pp. 243–50. J. R. Campbell and C. W. Barnes, "Interaction Analysis: A Breakthrough?" *Phi Delta Kappan,* II (1969), 587-90.

Reading-Listening
Comprehension:
Levels, Skill
Competencies
and Questioning
Strategies

[23]Richard L. Ober, Ernest L. Bentley, and Edith Miller, *Systematic Observation of Teaching: An Interaction Analysis-Instructional Strategy Approach* (Englewood Cliffs, N. J.: Prentice-Hall, Inc., 1971), p. 36.

[24]We discussed the use of literary devices to develop comprehension in Chapter 6, and we shall discuss it again in Chapter 13.

[25]Ruth Krauss's *A Hole Is to Dig* is a collection of such association type meanings.

[26]Ernest R. Baele, "The Effects of Primary Reading Programs Emphasizing Language Structure as Related to Meaning upon Children's Written Language Achievement at Third Grade Level" (unpublished doctoral dissertation, University of California, Berkeley, 1968). Robert B. Ruddell, "Reading Instruction in First Grade with Varying Emphasis on the Regularity of Grapheme-Phoneme Correspondences and the Relation of Language Structure to Meaning," *The Reading Teacher,* XIX (1966), 653–60.

[27]Theodore Clymer and Robert B. Ruddell, *All Sorts of Things,* teacher's ed. (Boston: Ginn and Company, 1969), p. 199.

[28]Morris L. Bigge and Maurice P. Hunt, *Psychological Foundations of Education* (Harper & Row, Publishers, 1962). John Dewey, *How We Think* (Boston: D. C. Heath & Company, 1910). Karl C. Garrison, Albert J. Kingston, and Arthur S. McDonald, *Educational Psychology,* 2nd ed. (New York: Appleton-Century-Crofts, 1964).

[29]Brewster Ghiselin, ed., *The Creative Process* (New York: The New American Library, Inc., 1955).

[30]John F. Travers, *Learning: Analysis and Application* (New York: David McKay Co., Inc., 1964).

[31]Garrison et al., *Educational Psychology.*

[32]Robert B. Ruddell, *Developing Excellence in Literacy Teaching Ability: Project DELTA.* "In Search of Comprehension" (unpublished manuscript developed by teachers at Washington Elementary School, Berkeley, Calif., Barbara Schmidt, ed.).

[33]Ruddell and Williams, *Project DELTA.* Barbara Schmidt, "The Relationship Between Questioning Levels and Strategies and Listening Comprehension in K–3 Children" (unpublished dissertation proposal, University of California, Berkeley, 1972).

[34]Ober et al., *Systematic Observation of Teaching.*

12

Independent Reading Growth in the Content Areas: Research and Study Skills

Focusing Questions

1. When and how can the development of research and study skills be effectively initiated?
2. What instructional techniques can introduce and develop information location skills? Specialized reading skills? Information organization skills? Interpretation of graphic and pictorial information?
3. What reading competencies require special attention in content areas such as social studies, science, and mathematics? How can these competencies be developed?
4. How can the development of children's research and study skills be evaluated?

The reading skills we have discussed in previous chapters are taught with one purpose in mind—that the reading process is to be used, for independent learning or for pleasure, or both. If the child learns to read but fails to do so, our efforts and those of the child will have been wasted.

In this chapter we shall discuss the teaching of research and study skills for independent learning. Such instruction should be viewed from a developmental perspective. We do not teach children at a given grade level how to outline and then forget the subject if we really want them to use outlining effectively. Instead we must begin with the preliminary skills involved in learning to outline and aid the student in the development of effective organization.

If we expect our students to use the research and study skills, we must teach them in a meaningful context. For example, they are not going to be encouraged to use the dictionary just because they are handed a list of unrelated words to define. There must be a purpose for dictionary usage, one that is relevant to the student's learning needs.

You need not postpone teaching research and study skills necessary for reading in the content areas until the fourth grade level, as was widely believed in the past. You can introduce these skills as early as kindergarten with sequencing games and activities, learning the letters of the alphabet, interpreting pictures, and following directions. The primary grade teacher should be alert to the importance of content area reading in the primary grades. It must be kept in mind that teaching the general reading skills does not guarantee success in content reading. Neither can it be assumed that a skill developed for one content area will automatically be applied to another content area. Skill transfer must be accounted for in the instructional program.

Research and study skills the independent learner will need to master include: location of information, reading for information, organization of information, interpretation of information, and reading skills unique to the various content areas. Accomplishment in each of these areas depends upon development of a number of subskills. For example, the student who can read for information must be able to skim, scan, read intensively, evaluate information, and adjust his reading rate depending on purpose.

LOCATION OF INFORMATION

To be an independent learner a student must know how to find the information he needs to further his learning. This requires that he be familiar with and know how to use the various sources of information in the library and in the classroom, and how to locate information in the telephone directory, a newspaper, or other common information sources.

Book parts

In initial reading instruction we should help children understand the value of using organizational aids in their books. They will be exposed early to story titles as they prepare experience charts or give names to pictures. Later, as they learn to read, the teacher can encourage youngsters to use the title to predict what a story is going to be about.

After the children have developed some degree of basic skill in reading, give them the name of a story in their text and ask them to identify the page where it begins using the table of contents. Then discuss the organization of the table of contents and the information found there.

During the primary grades students should learn that if they consult the table of contents they can determine which chapter or chapters are most likely to contain stories or information that will be interesting or helpful or both. This aids the child in focusing on his purpose for reading.

Students soon discover that other sections of the book can be of value, sections like the glossary. (We shall discuss glossaries more fully under general references in conjunction with dictionaries.)

When a student meets a new book, he should first examine the title page, and speculate on the 'why?' of the title. He should also attend to the name of the author and to any background information that will provide some insight into the author's writing, style, and interests. This information is often helpful in understanding the intent of the writing and in detecting author bias.

Students should learn the purpose of the preface or foreword, that the preface usually provides an overview of the book and sets forth the author's reasons for writing it.

As children advance into third or fourth grade they should be made aware of the date of publication so that they can determine whether the book is recent. This is not so important in fictional materials, but when children are researching facts and information they should know how to obtain some indication of the currency of the book to which they are referring.

By the fourth grade children should begin to learn how to use the index. At this level text materials in areas such as science and social studies require use of the index for reference purposes. The children will need to know that items in the index are arranged alphabetically and that sometimes a topic is cross-indexed under several headings. They should also learn about the paging system used in indexes: that 300-305 means that a topic extends from page 300 to page 305; that 200, 206 indicates that the topic is discussed on pages 200 and 206; and so on. To use the index to best advantage, children will need to be able to classify information.

Using an index is a rather complex skill, and some children will need considerable assistance with it. This is best given when they have direct need for using specific information in the index. The following exercise (see Figure 12-1) illustrates a possible procedure.

1. On what page can we find information about papermaking in industry?
2. On what pages can we find out about the Inca Indians?
3. On what pages can we find out something about assembly lines?
4. Where can we find out what people in various places and at various times used for money?

As their books include such parts, children should be introduced to appendices, lists of illustrations, bibliographies, and lists of maps.

General references

Understanding alphabetical ordering of information is one of the first locational skills students need. The student may not learn the letters in alphabetical order at first but eventually it will be necessary for him to do so if he is to locate information rapidly in most informational resources.

Indians,
    Aztec, 46, 214; *p* 46
    in California, 16; *p* 16
    in early Colorado, 47
    of the forests, 73; *p* 73
    Inca, 44, 216
    Iroquois, 17, 216-217; *p* 17
    Plains, 72; *p* 72
Industrial Revolution, 176-
    179; *p* 177-179
industry,
    assembly line, 160-161; *p* 160-
    161
    automobile, 160-161, 180; *p*
    160-161, 180
    development of, 176-179
    iron and steel, 159-161, 164; *p*
    159-161
    papermaking, 180; *p* 181
    raw materials for, 164, 166,
    167, 168; *p* 164, 166-168; *m*
    165
    space, 65-67; *p* 64, 66, 67
    transportation, 160-161, 178,
    180; *p* 160-161, 178, 180
Ivory Coast, 135; *p* 135

government, *see* **great ideas
    of man,** rules and govern-
    ment
great ideas of man,
    cooperation, 20, 27, 35, 36, 63,
    65-82; *p* 21, 26-27, 34, 64, 66,
    67, 69-82, 190, 191
    definition, 63
    division of labor, 27, 32, 39,
    63, 184-194, 196, 197; *p* 16,
    17, 22, 26-27, 39, 184-194,
    195-197
    education, 63, 80, 132-149; *p*
    80, 89, 132-149
    exchange, 35, 39, 56, 63, 195-
    208; *p* 34, 39, 195-208
    language, 35-36, 63, 116-131;
    p 116-122, 124, 125, 128-131
    loyalty, 36, 42, 63, 101-115; *p*
    101, 103-115
    rules and government, 32, 40-
    42, 63, 76-77, 78, 83-100; *p*
    41, 76-79, 83-93, 95-100
    See also **natural resources,
    using** *and* **tools**

Figure 12-1. *From Jerry E. Jennings,* Great Ideas of Man. *Reprinted by permission of The Fideler Company.*

DICTIONARIES

An early lesson to assist children in understanding alphabetical order as it applies to dictionaries might involve the use of picture dictionary pages similar to those that follow. First ask the children to identify the letters in sequential order. This can be followed by naming a letter and having it located, along with the letters that immediately precede and follow. Letter order can also be developed by distributing letter cards and having the children arrange them in alphabetical order on their desks or in a card holder. They can then check their own arrangements referring to the alphabetical order in the dictionary.

Figure 12-2. *From* My Sound and Word Book, *by Theodore Clymer and Thomas C. Barrett, of the Reading 360 series,* © *Copyright, 1969, by Ginn and Company. Used with permission.*

Other activities to develop alphabetical order include the following.

1. Ask children to arrange pictures of various items under appropriate letters.
2. Have children make their own picture dictionaries by cutting a reference picture for each letter from a magazine, using a page for each letter. New pictures and words can be added to the collection as they are discovered.
3. Using alphabet cards, have children arrange sections of the alphabet in order.
4. Have children find all the words in a list that start with a given letter, then a second letter, and so on.
5. A child says, "I am a letter of the alphabet between *o* and *q*. Which letter am I?" Other children identify the letter.
6. Write the alphabet in groups of halves or quarters. Ask the children to specify in which half or quarter of the alphabet the letters in an exercise belong.

As the skill of using alphabetical order is developed, the children will transfer the skills learned in using their own and commercial picture dictionaries to the glossaries in their reading materials. Here they will need to learn to use the pronunciation key and guide words, both of which will be helpful to them when they begin to use the regular dictionary. They will observe that many words have more than the one meaning given in the early limited glossary.

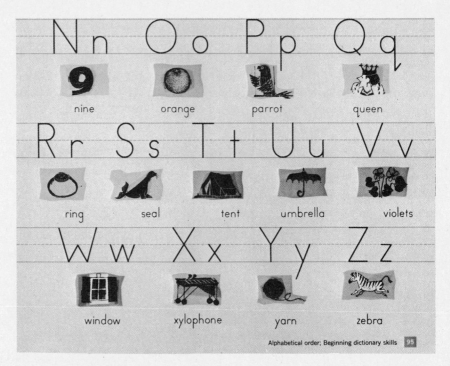

nine   orange   parrot   queen

ring   seal   tent   umbrella   violets

window   xylophone   yarn   zebra

Alphabetical order; Beginning dictionary skills   95

Figure 12-3. *From* My Sound and Word Book, *by Theodore Clymer and Thomas C. Barrett, of the Reading 360 series,* © *Copyright, 1969, by Ginn and Company. Used with permission.*

Introductory lessons in the use of the glossary should first involve a brief review of the concept of alphabetical order to be sure it is understood. Then ask the children to turn to the glossary, explain that a glossary is like a small dictionary, and guide them to realize that the glossary helps them by giving the meanings of words and that the pronunciation key helps them pronounce new words. Focus their attention on the alphabetical order of the words on a given page. The words printed in heavy black type are called *entry words,* followed by a respelling in parentheses to indicate pronunciation, and one or more definitions.

The children should note that two words are printed at the top of each page. These two words, called *guide words,* are the first and last words on the page and are useful in locating a word quickly.

A

ad·just (ə-jŭst′) 1. Change so as to be correct or workable. 2. Become suited and used to where one lives.

ad·mi·ral (ăd′mər-əl) High officer in the Navy.

ad·ven·ture (ăd-věn′chər) 1. Unusual happening. 2. Exciting, perhaps dangerous, deed.

air·shaft (âr′shăft) Walled-in open space down through the middle of a building to let in air.

a·muse (ə-myōōz′) 1. Keep someone from getting bored or restless. 2. Cause to laugh or smile.

an·guish (ăng′gwĭsh) Grief; torment; great pain.

an·noy (ə-noi′) Bother; disturb; vex.

ap·plause (ə-plôz′) Clapping of hands to show enjoyment.

ap·point·ment (ə-point′mənt) 1. Arrangement to meet at a certain time and place. 2. Naming of someone to fill a certain office or position: *He received an appointment from the President.*

ap·prove (ə-prōōv′) 1. Agree to. 2. Think well of.

aq·ua·naut (ăk′wə-nôt) Person trained to explore underwater for scientific purposes.

arch (ärch) 1. Part of a bridge or building that is curved at the top. 2. Bend into a curve.

as·sis·tant (ə-sĭs′tənt) Helper.

at·tract (ə-trăkt′) 1. Cause to come or look toward oneself. 2. Be pleasing to.

a·ware (ə-wâr′) Knowing about: *He's aware of his mistake.*

awk·ward (ôk′wərd) 1. Clumsy; not graceful in movement. 2. Uneasy: *an awkward feeling around strangers.*

B

bab·ble (băb′əl) 1. Continuing speechlike sounds that the hearer cannot understand. 2. Make such sounds.

ă pat / ā pay / âr care / ä father / ĕ pet / ē be / ĭ pit / ī pie / îr fierce / ŏ pot /
ō toe / ô paw, for / oi noise / ou out / ŏŏ took / ōō boot / th thin / *th* this / ŭ cut /
ûr turn / yōō use / ə about / zh pleasure

Figure 12-4. *From William K. Durr, Jean M. Lepere, and Ruth Brown,* Fiesta. *Reprinted by permission of Houghton Mifflin Company.*

An activity such as the following may be used in developing an understanding of the use of guide words. Give children sets of guide words and the dictionary page for each set, for example

p. 123 **hatch** **hinder**
p. 232 **saddle** **syrup**

Then provide a list of several words and have the children identify the page where each word would be expected to appear.

ship   _____

hefty   _____

help   _____

summer   _____

Follow this activity by direct experience in using guide words with real dictionaries.

Specific instruction should be designed to develop understanding of the pronunciation key, with emphasis on the sound representation system used and its value in pronouncing unknown words.

Full Pronunciation Key

Consonant Sounds

/b/	bib	/k/	kick	/sh/	ship, dish
/ch/	church	/l/	lid, needle	/t/	tight
/d/	did	/m/	man, am	/th/	thin, path
/f/	fast, off	/n/	no, sudden	/th/	this, bathe
/g/	gag	/ng/	thing	/v/	vine, cave
/h/	hat	/p/	pop	/w/	with
/hw/	which	/r/	roar	/y/	yes
/j/	judge	/s/	see, miss	/z/	zebra, size
		/zh/	pleasure		

Vowel Sounds

/ă/	pat	/ĭ/	pit	/oi/	noise
/ā/	pay	/ī/	pie	/ou/	out
/àr/	care	/ir/	fierce	/o͝o/	took
/ä/	father	/ŏ/	pot	/o͞o/	boot
/ĕ/	pet	/ō/	toe	/ŭ/	cut
/ē/	be	/ò/	paw, for	/ùr/	turn
		/yo͞o/	use		

/ə/   about, silent, pencil, lemon, circus

Figure 12-5. *From William K. Durr, Jean M. LePere, and Ruth Brown,* Fiesta. *Reprinted by permission of Houghton Mifflin Company.*

It is a natural step to transfer the understanding gained in using the glossary to a regular beginning dictionary. By this stage the children should have learned to use the second and third letters of a word in alphabetizing it.

We cannot assume, even as late as grades seven and eight, that all students

Pronunciation Key

The symbols and key words listed below will help you tell which sounds to use in reading the words in the glossary.

a	hat	e	let	o	hot	u	cup
ā	age	ē	be	ō	go	ù	put
ã	care	ėr	term	ô	order	ü	rule
ä	far	i	it	oi	oil	ū	use
		ī	ice	ou	out		

ch in child	th in thin	ə *represents:*	a in about		i in April
ng in long	ŦH in then		e in taken		o in lemon
sh in she	zh in measure			u in circus	

Abbreviations

n. noun   *v.* verb   *adj.* adjective   *adv.* adverb   *interj.* interjection

Figure 12-6. *From* Thorndike-Barnhart Junior Dictionary *by E. L. Thorndike and Clarence L. Barnhart. Copyright © 1968 by Scott, Foresman and Company. Reprinted by permission of the publisher.*

know how to use the dictionary proficiently. We must check each child at all levels to be sure that he has appropriate dictionary reference skills.

Dictionary definitions use several terms children should be helped to understand and use. For example in this definition

> **be • grudge** (bĭ grŭj), *v.t.,* **-grudged, -grudging.**
> 1. to be discontented at seeing (a person) have (something): *to begrudge a man his good fortune.*
>
> 2. to be reluctant to give, grant, or allow: *to begrudge him the money he earned.*
> —Syn. 1. See **envy.**[1]

the division of the word indicates the syllables; the respelling in parentheses with syllable division, the pronunciation; *v.t.,* that it is a transitive verb; *-grudged* and *-grudging,* the past tense and the past participle forms of the verb respectively. Two definitions are given, with examples and one synonym. This entry contains no explanation of etymological origin, but you should explain carefully to the children what it means when it is part of the entry.

The game which follows can be played by students of any level who have learned how to use the dictionary.

Dictionary Race

The purpose of this game is to increase speed and proficiency in using the dictionary. (Note: children should be grouped on the basis of proficiency.)

417

A dictionary should be provided for each child.

The teacher or another student holds up a card with a word on it or pronounces a word. The first student to find the word, read it, and give its meaning is the winner. The game can be played as a team game also.

What dictionary skills are needed for the effective use of this unabridged dictionary? What is the value of teaming youngsters for this type of activity?

ENCYCLOPEDIAS

Children in the primary grades don't use encyclopedias very much, but there are picture encyclopedias and junior encyclopedias available to help them get started using and understanding this valuable tool, and sometimes teachers use more advanced encyclopedias to furnish information on a particular subject. Excerpts can be read or explained to the students and pictures examined.

When children begin to use encyclopedias they will need to know that they are also arranged alphabetically, and that in some there is an index in the back of each volume, while in others there is a separate index volume, that identifies main articles and related articles and tells the locations of maps, charts, tables, graphs, and pictures.

Children should know about the guide letters on the spine of each encyclopedia, that when two letters, for example A – D, appear, it means that that volume contains topics that begin with the letters A, B, C, and D. Children should have encyclopedias available while you are discussing them. Explain to the children that the guide words on each page serve the same locational function as the guide words in dictionaries. Also, students will need to discover that name places like New Hampshire and New York are located under the first name, while the names of people are found under the last name.

There are several encyclopedias that can be used in the elementary grades. The *Golden Book Encyclopedia* can be used at the upper primary grade levels by children who have mastered basic reading skills. Other encyclopedias for use in the elementary grades are *The World Book, Britannica Junior,* and *Compton's Pictured Encyclopedia. The Book of Knowledge* and *Our Wonderful World* can also be used, but they use a topical instead of an alphabetical arrangement.

Encyclopedia use may be facilitated by guide questions related to a class activity. For example, when children are studying about hummingbirds, volunteers can consult an animal book or a junior encyclopedia to find additional information. Questions such as the following can guide organizing the information.

HUMMING BIRDS

1. What are some of the special characteristics of hummingbirds?
2. What kinds of food do they eat?
3. Are they common throughout the United States?
4. What are some of the other birds that are related to them?
5. Are they helpful to man?
6. Who are their enemies?

ATLASES

Once children have learned how to read maps, they enjoy using atlases to locate places the class may be discussing in textbooks or stories. They will also find that an atlas contains a wide range of information on physical and demographic characteristics. A school library should have at least one or two atlases. If your classroom has good wall maps and your textbooks contain clear maps, it is probably unnecessary to have an atlas in the classroom.

ALMANACS AND YEARBOOKS

For most children at the primary level these reference materials are of limited value, but they are a valuable resource for children in intermediate grades. From the *World Almanac* they can gain factual information about a wide range of topics including countries, business, trade, education, conservation, sports, and political parties. Other similar reference books include the *Information Please Almanac* (similar to the *World Almanac*), the

Statesman's Yearbook (facts on countries throughout the world), and *The*

Economic Almanac (information about labor, business, and government). These resources are of particular value in the social studies.

THE TELEPHONE DIRECTORY

Children should be introduced to the telephone directory as soon as they can read the items and classifications in it. A first, highly motivating task is locating their own phone numbers and the phone numbers of friends. Their attention should be called to the alphabetical arrangement by last names. Help students discover how the school telephone is listed in their area. Discuss the special pages and the index in the front of the directory, especially emergency numbers for fire, police, and medical aid. Then have students carefully examine the yellow pages to determine its arrangement. Refer them to the index that accompanies the yellow pages to note how to find various services.

An exercise like the following will reinforce skills in using the telephone directory.

1. If you need help in putting out a fire what number will you call?
2. On what page would you find the names of plumbing shops?
3. How would you call _____ School?
4. On what two pages would you find the number for the _____ Bicycle Shop?
5. What number would you call to get the local police or the county sheriff's office?

THE CLASSIFIED SECTION OF THE NEWSPAPER

Each child should have a copy of the newspaper, and if possible, there should be more than one newspaper publisher represented. Begin by examining the index on the front page. After the students have found the classified section, examine its index for classifications of high personal interest. For example, the children may wish to locate such items as used bicycles or transistor radios and to note information relative to their sale.

The library

The school library is basic to a good educational program. Many elementary schools now contain a library with a trained librarian, so that the children have the opportunity to learn to use a library from their very early school experience. If you do not have access to a school library, you should maintain a classroom library and make full use of the local public library. This is essential to the development of independent learners. Many children's first experiences with the library occur when they go there to hear stories told or read.

Before children visit the library for reference use, some aspects of the
library field trip should be discussed. Some teachers find it useful, for

example, to develop a list of rules from student-oriented discussion that will apply to behavior in the library and will be meaningful to the students. The most effective learning takes place when the children have a real reason for going to the library, which may range from interest in picture or story books about animals (kindergarten or primary grade children) to an interest in books on man in space (intermediate grade children).

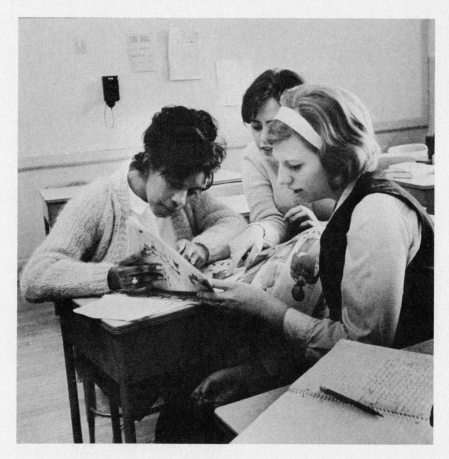

How can activities such as this motivate use of the newspaper index and later the classified section? (*Photo by Sybil Shelton, Monkmeyer Press Photo Service*)

Introduce the children to the librarian, who can take them for a tour and explain where to find various types of books and information. With upper primary and intermediate grades she may call attention to the way the card catalogue is arranged and explain how to locate a book using it. You or she should explain that there are three types of index cards in a card catalogue: the author card, the title card, and the subject card. Children should also be aware that when *a, an,* or *the* is the first word of a title, these words are always disregarded when the titles are alphabetized in the card catalogue. The children should then have an opportunity to search in the catalogue for a book that is of high personal interest to them.

After their initial visit to the library, small groups of children may go to the library to draw diagrams indicating the location of various books and resource materials. These can be discussed and a large diagram constructed for the classroom.

Using knowledge acquired about the arrangement of books in a library, students may be encouraged to classify the books which are kept in their classroom. They need not memorize the Dewey Decimal System or other library codes, because they may be confusing at this level, but it is valuable for them to understand how these codes work. The following list shows the ten major categories of the Dewey Decimal System.

000-099	General Works
100-199	Philosophy, Psychology
200-299	Religion
300-399	Social Science
400-499	Language
500-599	Science, Mathematics
600-699	Useful Arts
700-799	Fine Arts
800-899	Literature
900-999	History

For many their first library books are fiction, so they should be aware that fiction is not numbered according to this same system, but instead the books are listed in the card catalogue and arranged on the shelves according to the system indicated in the card catalog.

The periodical section is another source of information children should be introduced to at an early stage. Initially they will look at magazines and newspapers with the help of the teacher or librarian, but in the upper elementary grades they should learn to use the *Reader's Guide to Periodical Literature.* This information source is also organized alphabetically by subject, author, and title of the article.

An exercise similar to the following but tailored to student interest can be used to reinforce learning in the use of library reference materials.

Directions. In what library source would you find the following? Some may be found in more than one source.

1. A discussion of space
2. Who Ernest O. Lawrence was
3. A map of China
4. The work of Martin Luther King, Jr.
5. How many students are enrolled at Indiana University

6. An antonym for *rugged*
7. Information on the Civil War
8. The scores for the major league ball games for 1972
9. The qualifications for elective office in Indiana; California
10. An up-to-date article about the United Nations
11. The author of *Charlotte's Web; Little House on the Prairie;* what else these authors wrote

What classification skills are critical for efficient use of the card catalogue? How can such knowledge improve independent research ability? (*Photo by Carole Graham, BBM Associates*)

An inventory similar to the one in Figure 12-7 is a useful checklist for the teacher on library reference skills. Parts of the inventory could be adapted for use at the intermediate grade level.

The following list contains common reference sources, and students should be aware of their availability and informational value.

1. Anthologies
2. Atlases
3. Books of quotations
4. *Book Review Digest*
5. *Catholic Periodical Index*

LIBRARY SKILLS
INVENTORY

PART I—Fill in the blanks with the correct word or phrase.

1. The key to finding what books a library owns is the _____

2. The main key to finding a nonfiction book on the library shelves is its _____

3. The reference key to information about words is the _____

4. The reference key to general background information on many topics is the _____

5. The reference key to relatively current information on a wide variety of topics is the _____

6. The key to finding magazine articles on a specific subject is the _____

7. The key to determining what chapter in a book you may need to read is the _____

8. The key to locating specific facts or items of information in a book is the _____

9. The key to additional sources of information—a key which many authors include in their books—is the _____

10. The key to locating pictorial material in a book is the _____

PART II—Check the word or phrase which correctly completes each statement.

1. Instead of a call number, a novel is marked with the letter:
____ N
____ F
____ S

2. Instead of a call number, a book on the life of Mozart might be marked with the letter:
____ B
____ M
____ C

3. In consulting the card catalogue to find a book on U.S. prison reform, you should look first in the:
____ U drawer
____ P drawer
____ R drawer

4. The card you would find by looking up U.S. prison reform is called:
____ author card
____ subject card
____ title card

5. The book classification and numbering system used in most libraries was developed by a man named:
____ Dooley
____ Dennis
____ Dewey

6. *Spine* is a term librarians use for:
____ library floor plan
____ section of shelves
____ back of a book

7. It is best for you to:
____ use various encyclopedias
____ ask your teacher which encyclopedia to use
____ use the encyclopedia with which you are familiar

8. A glossary is a:
____ special dictionary
____ section card in a card catalogue
____ shelf sign in library stacks

9. You are most likely to find cross references in the:
____ table of contents
____ *Readers' Guide to Periodical Literature*
____ preface

10. To use the card catalogue, you have to know:
____ authors' names
____ titles of books
____ the alphabet

PART III—Using numbers 1 through 8—and remembering that articles are ignored—show correct shelf arrangement of these novels:

a. ____ *Northanger Abbey*, by Jane Austen
b. ____ *The Way of All Flesh*, by Samuel Butler
c. ____ *Emma*, by Jane Austen
d. ____ *The Good Earth*, by Pearl Buck
e. ____ *Lorna Doone*, by Richard D. Blackmore
f. ____ *The Tower of London*, by W. Harrison Ainsworth
g. ____ *Persuasion*, by Jane Austen
h. ____ *The Old Wives' Tale* by Arnold Bennett

PART IV—Check the phrase which correctly completes each of the following statements.

1. The card catalogue will tell you:
____ who published a book
____ how many chapters a book has
____ whether a book is—or was—a best seller

2. The card catalogue will tell you:
____ what edition of a book the library has
____ whether the type used in a book is large or small
____ what color of binding a book has

3. The card catalogue may tell you:
____ who has borrowed a book
____ who reviewed a book for newspapers and magazines
____ who illustrated a book

4. The card catalogue will tell you:
____ how many pictures a book has
____ how completely a book is indexed
____ how many pages a book has

5. The card catalogue will tell you:
____ how to use a book
____ where to find a book
____ whether the book is currently out on loan

PART V—For information on each item listed below, circle the abbreviation for the reference most likely to meet your needs. (A = almanac; D = dictionary; E = encyclopedia; RG = *Readers' Guide*.) NOTE: In some cases, you might indicate more than one reference.

a. A D E RG—Viennese waltzes
b. A D E RG—month-by-month review of last year's major news events
c. A D E RG—how the word *cipher* can be used as a verb
d. A D E RG—information about the newest models of automobiles
e. A D E RG—an important speech made before the U.N. last month
f. A D E RG—the first telescopes
g. A D E RG—how to pronounce *Laos*
h. A D E RG—what the U.S. Government is spending on space exploration
i. A D E RG—Queen Elizabeth I
j. A D E RG—Queen Elizabeth II

60   61

Figure 12-7. Special permission granted by How-to-Study Workshop, published by Xerox Education Publications, Inc.. © Xerox Corp. 1965.

6. Dictionaries
7. *Dictionary of American Biography*
8. *Dictionary of National Biography*
9. *Education Index*
10. Encyclopedias
11. *Goode's School Atlas*
12. *Information Please*
13. *Junior Book of Authors*
14. *National Geographic Magazine*
15. Newspapers
16. *Poole's Index to Periodical Literature*
17. *Reader's Guide to Periodical Literature*
18. Road maps
19. *Roberts' Rules of Order*
20. *Roget's Thesaurus*
21. *Subject Index to Poetry*
22. *The New York Times Index*
23. *United States Catalogue*
24. *Who's Who*
25. *Who's Who in America*
26. *Who's Who in American Education*
27. *World Almanac*

Even if your school has a library, take your students on field trips to the local public library and arrange for them to obtain library cards that will permit them to use the library resources.

READING FOR INFORMATION

As the student becomes more independent in his reading, he will need to use his reading skills for various purposes. Some materials he uses require careful and intensive reading; others may be skimmed or scanned. This requires that the student be able to adjust his rate and technique according to the purpose. We cannot assume that children will learn on their own to be flexible in their use of reading skills. Some few of them will, but research has indicated that many children have little understanding of flexibility as it relates to reading unless they have direct instruction.

Skimming

Skimming is a procedure for overviewing or previewing materials to determine content, to review material already read, or to determine whether the information is pertinent to the need at hand. By skimming a student can choose information he wants and discard that which is irrelevant. It allows him to cover a large amount of material rapidly to obtain some idea of the content.

Skimming techniques are as follows:

1. Read the title of the article, chapter, or book. What does it tell you about the contents of the selection? (A title can tell you what is not included as well as what is.)

2. Read the major headings and subheadings to determine what the author considers the main ideas of the selection.

3. Read the first and last paragraphs of a selection: the first will often indicate the direction the material is to take, while the last is often a summary.

4. Look closely at the illustrations and read the captions accompanying them, because they will often indicate what to expect in the selection.

5. If there are questions at the beginning or the end read them carefully, because they can indicate what the author considers to be important in the selection.

6. If you cannot obtain a clear understanding of the main ideas using these techniques, read the first sentence of each paragraph. In most topical material the first sentence provides the main idea of the paragraph.

7. Skim for review, that is, get an overview of something you have already read, to refresh your mind concerning the material in preparation for a discussion or an examination.

Here are several activities to reinforce the skill of skimming.

1. Try to guess what the story is about from the title.

2. Look at illustrations and pictures to tell what the story is about.

3. Skim a newspaper item for the main idea.

4. Skim tables, graphs, and charts to determine whether they provide needed information.

5. Skim a book with an interesting title to decide whether it would be interesting to read.

Scanning

Scanning is a technique for finding numbers, names, dates, and answers to specific questions. We are scanning when we look up a word in the dictionary or a telephone number in the directory.

To obtain the best results from scanning, we should keep the following procedures in mind:

1. Be sure you have the question you wish to answer clearly in mind.

2. Know the *kind* of answer you are looking for—a date, a word, a name, or a number.

3. Decide what clues will help you recognize the correct answer when you come to it.

4. Allow your eyes to scan quickly but methodically over the material until you find the information you are looking for. When you think you have located it, read more carefully to be sure it is the material which will answer your question.

These activities should reinforce the skill of scanning.

1. Find the names of characters in a story in preparation for dramatization.
2. Prove or disprove a statement by locating the appropriate sentence in the story.
3. Locate a certain character's brief response in a story.
4. Look for a new word in a story that was previously presented on the chalkboard.
5. Look for a picture about a particular subject.
6. Look through an index to find an entry pertinent to a certain topic.
7. Quickly review a graph, chart, or table to find certain information.
8. Find the portions of a story that characterize a person in it.
9. Look for the most interesting part of a story to read orally.
10. Scan to find the most exciting part of a story.

Intensive reading

The type of reading necessary to understand and synthesize new or difficult concepts may be classified as intensive reading. The reader must cover the material carefully because to fail to do so will result in faulty interpretation or inadequate understanding. Such reading may involve frequent regression to check an impression or clarify a question. This type of reading occurs most commonly in science and mathematics, and frequently in social science.

Such intensive reading will be more fruitful if it is done with a purpose. Activities to reinforce the skills involved in intensive reading are constantly available in the classroom. For example, when students are asked to follow directions to carry out an experiment or build a model, intensive reading is involved, just as it is in solving story problems in mathematics. Specific suggestions for developing intensive reading skills occur later in this chapter, under "Reading Competencies in the Content Areas."

Rate of reading

When we see the phrase "reading rate," we have a tendency to think in terms of how fast a child can read, without relating this speed to other factors inherent in the reading situation. It is not unusual at the fifth or sixth grade level for a child to ask the teacher, "How fast should I be able to read?" He has heard that is is important to read rapidly, but he is usually unaware of other factors that must be accounted for.

There are many factors in reading rate, among them

1. The developmental levels of the basic reading skills—word attack, use of context, and comprehension skills—directly affect rate.
2. The motivation that brings the individual to the reading task is significant. Most individuals have a tendency to let their minds wander if no definite purpose has been established for a reading task.
3. The reader's background knowledge is a critical factor. If a student is reading technical material on rockets, he is going to read it much more slowly than he will a sports article. The difficulty of the vocabulary has a direct influence on reading speed. If the words represent concepts he is unfamiliar with, his rate will be slower, to facilitate comprehension, even though he can decode the vocabulary in question.
4. Sentence structure, sentence length, and writing style also have an effect on rate. Complex sentence structures, unfamiliar writing style, and long, involved sentences will adversely affect the rate if comprehension is to result.
5. Size of print, length of line, number of illustrations, footnotes, and similar items influence the reader's processing of information. Any variable which intervenes in the reading material will require attention of the reader if he is to comprehend the selection.
6. The physical well-being of the reader is important. Is he tired or ill? It is more difficult to concentrate on any task when fatigue or illness interferes.

It is obvious that with so many factors exerting an influence on the reading act, the mature reader will of necessity adjust his reading rate to the task. He may read an interesting story rapidly, or check a fact by scanning, but he will read a mathematical formula slowly and carefully.

As with other reading skills, students need practice and guidance to develop flexibility in their reading rates. Children who are word-by-word readers need help in the effective use of context. Those who read all material at the same rate will have to be taught how to establish reading purpose and adjust their rate accordingly.

ORGANIZATION OF INFORMATION

The ability to organize information is of great importance to the independent learner. Once a student discovers that a confusing mass of details can be handled successfully when it is organized, much of the complexity of the learning process is dispelled.

Specific skills involved in organizing information include taking notes, classifying and ordering information, designating main ideas and supporting details, outlining, and summarizing. Several of these skills were discussed in Chapter 11; in this chapter we shall treat them from the
viewpoint of organizing information to aid learning.

Taking notes

We take notes for the purpose of recording information to use in reports, directions, discussions, problems, or special projects. The form a note takes varies with the purpose for which it is taken. If it is in answer to a specific question, it will be a brief response keyed to the question. If it is for a more general purpose, the information will be noted in detail and organized under a general outline. Be sure that students are aware of the purpose for taking notes. If this is not clear, the resulting notes may be only a confused selection of irrelevant information.

Most students' introduction to note taking occurs when a primary class or group is planning a project or an excursion and the teacher records the ideas and plans the children offer in a logical order on the chalkboard. Once students have learned to write, we can ask them to make notes on questions posed before they begin to read a selection. This may be no more than a simple listing of points, items, or ideas they are to look for in their reading material.

At a later stage students should be encouraged to begin notes with information about the source (author, title, page number, or speaker, title, and location) and to number their notes from the source in consecutive order. Notes from a single selection or chapter should probably be written in a notebook in outline form, with key ideas as the main headings followed by facts and supporting details.

Before they begin taking notes, students should learn to skim the material to identify the main idea. This will make outlining easier.

In most instances students should be urged to take notes in their own words, being careful not to change the meaning. In the process they should eliminate unnecessary words and information so that the notes will be brief yet convey the ideas the material contained. Occasionally, when the source presents the information in a particularly interesting way, the student will wish to take it down verbatim, with quotes. The student should learn to focus on the main idea and on the details which support that idea. He should also be aware of such verbal cues as "The principal point is . . .".

Michaelis has suggested the following points for note taking:[2]

Take Notes

To answer questions
To prove points
To get directions for making things
To summarize ideas
To get ideas for reports, charts, discussions, murals, and scrapbooks

Listening to Take Notes

Watch the speaker.
Note the main topic during the introduction.
List each main point.
Put specific ideas under each main point.
Ask about ideas that are not clear.

Taking Notes as We Read

Read the entire selection before beginning to
  take notes.
Find the main ideas in each paragraph, but select
  only those related to your subject.
Use your own words but do not change the
  meaning.
Write enough so that each idea can be recalled.
Number the notes in order.

Notes for Book Reviews

Write the author and title.
Note the main points about what happened.
Select a part you like very much and note what
  happened.
List the page numbers of two or three pictures
  to show.
List the page number of a good part to read
  to the group.
Note two or three reasons you think others
  should read it.

Notes from Interviews

List each question to be asked on a half-sheet
  of paper.
Arrange the papers in order.
Jot down main points as each question is answered.
Ask questions about points that are not clear.
Take notes on new ideas that are mentioned.

Notes from Films

Write the title of the film.
Note the main reasons given for seeing the film.
Get the main ideas as presented in the introductory
  part of the film.
Note main points as the film is shown.
Check to see if you have notes related to each
  reason for seeing the film.

Classification and ordering

In Chapter 11 we discussed classification as a comprehension skill. Now
430 we shall look at this skill from the perspective of formulating an organiza-

tion for classifying information. Information ordering involves classifying items or events into a logical order for a specific purpose.

In science and social science we are often confronted with the necessity of classifying objects and ideas. A young child may be asked to place various animals under the appropriate headings, depending on whether they have fur or feathers. An intermediate grade student may be given the task of creating and classifying problems unique to urban, suburban, and rural living. In science he may be expected to sort scientific terms or facts according to certain predetermined criteria.

Information ordering is needed to construct time lines in social science and to indicate the chronology of steps in a scientific experiment. It also takes place when children arrange their reports or plan a culmination activity. Alphabetizing is another form of ordering.

Activities to reinforce the skills of classification and ordering include the following:

1. Ask children to arrange sentences on a wall chart in the order in which events during a field trip took place.
2. Draw pictures that show the order of a series of events.
3. Have children classify ideas related to content area study. For example, if they have been studying the causes and effects of pollution in urban areas, have them place the labels for concepts on the board, then ask them to classify the words under the headings "Pollution Causes" and "Pollution Effects."
4. After a science experiment, have the children create a classification system for identifying the materials used and the order of the procedure.
5. Ask students to arrange recent civil rights events in chronological order and to identify their causes and effects.

Designation of main ideas and supporting details

If our students are to understand what they read in the content areas they must be able to determine main ideas. This topic was discussed briefly in Chapter 11 under the factual, interpretive, and applicative levels of comprehension. We shall now view it from the perspective of study skills.

In most content material each paragraph contains a main idea. If we go through the selection and choose the main idea of each paragraph, we should have a list of the author's major points.

To develop the concept of *main idea* with students, help them understand that if the main idea is removed from the paragraph, the supporting details no longer have a clear meaning or focus, but that if the supporting details are omitted the central idea is still present.

Here are activities in addition to those suggested in Chapter 11.

1. Ask the students to read a short selection and give it a title.
2. Have students read the summary of a chapter and tell the main idea in one simple sentence.

In the content areas, details usually support a main idea, answer a specific question, develop categories, or formulate specific directions for carrying out a process. Skill in selecting supporting details is particularly important in science, social science, and mathematics, but it is also relevant to such activities as art, music, and athletics.

Activities to promote reading for details:

1. Ask students to identify statements in a paragraph that support the main idea.
2. Request that students describe related details in a photograph.
3. Ask students to provide specific directions for carrying out an activity, such as a game.

Outlining

An outline is a method of organizing material in a logical order. Outlines help to organize ideas in relation to a topic and to understand the relationship between main ideas. The skills of classifying, ordering, and selecting main ideas and supporting details are all basic to outlining. For many students, it is a relatively difficult process.

Sequential steps in teaching outlining might follow these examples.

A SEQUENTIAL LISTING OF ACTIVITIES ON A FIELD TRIP

OUR VISIT TO THE FIRE STATION

1. We visited the firehouse.
2. We saw the firemen.
3. We saw the fire engines.
4. We saw the fire alarm bell.
5. We talked to the firemen about putting out fires.

COLUMN CLASSIFICATION OF ITEMS UNDER MAJOR HEADINGS

TREES	SHRUBS
1. Pines	1. Lilacs
2. Fir	2. Camellias
3. Apple	3. Roses
4. Magnolia	4. Oleander
5. Orange	5. Cotoneaster

Here are the basic levels of an outline form.

I. Main topic
   A. First Subtopic
      1. Supporting detail
      2. Supporting detail
   B. Second subtopic
      1. Supporting detail
      2. Supporting detail
II. Second Main Topic, etc.

The following examples illustrate the model.

KINDS OF WORKERS

I. Professional people
   A. Doctors
   B. Lawyers
   C. Teachers
   D. Accountants
II. Business people
   A. Grocerystore owners
   B. Barbers
   C. Insurance men

USE OF HELICOPTERS

I. Transportation
   A. People
   B. Products
   C. Mail
II. War
   A. Reconnaissance
   B. Bombing
   C. Transporting men
III. Peace
   A. Air rescue
   B. Fire control in remote areas
   C. Construction work

When you teach children to outline, use material that is a part of their classroom work. After they have had practice in selection and classification of main ideas and supporting details, place the outline of a selection on the chalkboard for them to read before they read the selection and to use as an organization aid. After students have read the selection, discuss the outline with them. When they have used this procedure several times and are familiar with it, place only the main ideas from an article on the

433

chalkboard and ask them to supply the supporting details after reading the
selection. After that you may wish to place only the form for the outline
on the chalkboard. Have students read a selection, then outline it in small
groups or individually. At first it is probably wise to encourage the use of
sentences in outlining. Gradually, however, students should learn to delete
certain words and thus abbreviate the outline without affecting the information in it.

Summarizing

This skill is so much a part of communication that many of us are not even
aware we are using it. For example, when we discuss an event with another
person we usually summarize (unless we bore him with myriad details).
Students who retell stories usually summarize, even in the first grade,
unless they have memorized them.

The process of summarizing in reading may begin much like that of outlining. First we should skim the passage to get a general idea of its content.
Then we should read the passage carefully to select the main ideas and the
most important or interesting supporting details. The next step involves
note taking on main points and supporting details. Following this we may
write a summary of the selection.

When students first learn to summarize, they should be provided with
selections they can read in their entirety and then in summary form. The
first summaries that students do should be in small-group situations, because these provide opportunities to understand and develop summarizing
skill. The material should be well organized and have a structure that is
easy to determine. First summaries may be one-sentence summaries.

The following is an activity by which to teach summarizing in the primary
grades.

> Read this story carefully. On the other side of this paper retell the story in six
> or fewer short sentences. Make sure you tell the most important parts of the
> story.
>
> Each summer a large group of boys attended the Wildwood Boys' Camp for two
> weeks at a time. They took part in hiking, boating, fishing, and many other
> activities.
>
> This summer Joe finally had been allowed to go. All of his friends had told him
> about camp so he was very excited.
>
> When he arrived he found that he was to share a cabin with four boys his age
> and an older boy. He was assigned a cot and told to report to the dining room
> when he had finished putting his things away.
>
> When he arrived at the dining room, he found it packed with boys all talking
> at the same time. His group leader called to him to join him at the same table.
> Joe was almost too excited to eat, but everything tasted good.
>
> After dinner everyone went down to the campfire circle for singing and stories.
> Already Joe had found a friend—quiet, smiling Rick.

After the campfire was put out, the two boys followed the others back to the cabin. There was a wild pillow fight for a short time and then everyone climbed into bed and was soon fast asleep.

Possible summary statements:

1. There were a lot of activities to do in two weeks at Wildwood Boys' Camp.
2. Joe was happy to be going.
3. He shared a cabin with five boys.
4. The dining room was noisy but the food was good.
5. Joe and Rick went to the campfire circle.
6. The boys in Joe's cabin had a pillow fight and went to bed.[3]

Activities such as the following will help to reinforce the skill of summarizing.

1. After reading a selection, ask students to select the best summary of a paragraph or poem from a series of three or four choices.
2. Have students practice condensing a letter to a friend to telegram form.
3. Ask students to summarize a favorite story in several brief paragraphs. They may wish to develop an accompanying illustration for each paragraph.

Combining information from several sources

For many students it is difficult to synthesize information from several sources. There needs to be instruction in the synthesis procedure to encourage students to rely on several research sources; otherwise we can expect to receive reports taken verbatim from a single source, such as an encyclopedia.

The first attempt to combine information should be done in a small-group situation to provide opportunity to work directly with individual children. After they identify their topic and formulate a brief outline, the students should locate information on the topic in one source, turn to a second source for additional information, then move to a third or fourth source to verify the main ideas and search for other supporting details.

It is good for a student to become familiar with several sources to be researched, because then he can skim various sources to find information whatever the topic. After he develops specific notes he should synthesize the range of informational content.

One good activity for reinforcing the skill of combining information from more than one source is to provide the students with two different accounts of an event and to have them synthesize the main ideas from both selections.

Again we must remind ourselves that this and all the other reading-study skills are developmental in nature, that we cannot assume that children at any level have mastered the skills and need no further help with them.

Graphic and pictorial materials present concise information that would otherwise require lengthy explanation. Each content area has its characteristic graphic materials, but some are common to several areas. Maps, charts, diagrams, graphs, tables, pictures, and time lines are used in most content areas, whereas globes and political cartoons are characteristic of social studies.

An abundance of excellent films, filmstrips, transparencies, models, charts, maps, posters, and other materials is available to aid in teaching the interpretation of graphic information. In addition, most texts and supplementary materials contain numerous examples to use in the instructional process.

Pictures

Interpretation of pictures is one of the first graphic interpretation skills children learn. When the kindergarten teacher reads a story to children, for example, she may use a picture to get children to predict the content of the story. Pictures can be used to clarify concepts, raise questions, provide vicarious experiences, stimulate discussion, and generate interest in a topic.

Through the use of pictures children can visualize comparisons and contrasts as well as cause and effect. They can compare family life styles in one area of the world to those in another, compare the moon's surface to that of the earth, and contrast farming practices in the United States with those in India. The effect of technology on the environment can be graphically portrayed through photographs. Herber terms this use of inferential reading of pictures "reaction to a pattern." He suggests that by contrasting the components of a concept students can understand the concept better.[4]

Pictures are one of the most effective means of making the past come alive for children. Describing a Conestoga wagon would be an exercise in futility unless the children have some way to visualize it. When children are making reports in any content area, the use of pictures will assist them with their presentation and provide a valuable aid for the development of observational and interpreting skills.

Here are some possible activities using pictures at the primary level.

1. Have children enumerate objects in pictures.
2. Have them make interpretive descriptions of pictures, either orally or in written form.
3. Have children predict what will happen next on the basis of information in a picture.
4. Use pictures to re-create ideas, thoughts, and hopes from other lands and to portray and contrast the lives of the people with life in this country.

5. Have children use their own illustrations to aid in telling a story they have read.

6. Ask students to verify a series of statements they believe tells about a picture and to add other statements they can support from inference based on the picture.

Political cartoons

The cartoons used should be related to discussions in the classroom or to current events that are being studied. Many children's newspapers contain easily interpreted cartoons that can be used effectively.

To understand a cartoon, children must know what its symbols represent. For example, in order to understand a cartoon depicting a large, round, sun-like oriental face in the background, and a teapot labeled *Two Chinas* with a question mark in steam coming from the spout, sitting on the slab-shaped UN building, the reader would have to know something about the problem of the admission of the two Chinas to the United Nations.

TEAHOUSE OF THE AUGUST MOON

437   Figure 12-8. *Reprinted by permission of Lou Grant.*

Activities to reinforce the ability to interpret cartoons might be similar to the following:

1. Ask children to find political cartoons in newspapers or magazines related to topics under study in the class. Provide time for the children to share their interpretation of the selection.
2. Encourage children to draw their own cartoons to illustrate the topics under study or political issues in the local community.
3. Prepare a cartoon bulletin board to aid in interpretation of current events and problems.
4. Locate cartoons that present different points of view on the same question and use them for class discussion and debate.
5. Encourage students to analyze cartoons for clues to the local newspaper's political philosophy.

Time charts and time lines

This type of graphic display is an important way of developing the relationship between time intervals and events for children. The earliest contacts children have with time charts may be in the form of daily or weekly logs that directly involve them. As historical events and changes are studied, an illustrated time sequence chart will be of value.

A time line gives a more graphic picture of time relationships than the time chart, and it can be introduced comparatively early in the primary grades. The most common time line has time intervals with the events to be depicted placed within these intervals. A time line can also be used to compare events taking place in more than one area of the world at approximately the same time. In country *A,* for example, the farmers may use a lot of power machinery; in country *B* oxen may be the basic farm power source; in country *C* the people may be nomads who require little or no power for their meager bit of farming.

This exercise illustrates one way to use a time line at the third grade level. It is based on the story of *The Dragon in the Clock Box,* by M. Jean Craig. This story is about Joshua, who carries a clock box with him everywhere, claiming it contains first a dragon's egg and then a baby dragon. The time interval covered in the story is eight days.

First have the children draw a line on a chart and mark it off in eight sections, as in the following diagram. The day the story started on should be identified and recorded above the line. The important events that took place on Tuesday and on each of the following days should be discussed briefly and summarized below the line. One option to the group activity might consist of duplicating the time line and having children complete the activity independently.

Tuesday	Thursday	Saturday	Monday
Wednesday	Friday	Sunday	Tuesday

This list contains some possible responses.

Tuesday: Joshua gets the box.

Wednesday: Joshua seals the box.

Thursday: The egg hatches late at night.

Friday: Joshua makes a hole in the box.

Saturday: Joshua sees the dragon.

Sunday: Joshua says the dragon's name is Emmeline.

Monday: The dragon flies away late at night.

Tuesday: Joshua puts marbles in the box.[5]

Tables

A table is a concise, comprehensive way of displaying related facts and information. Its format provides for easy and fast comparisons. When children are learning to use tables, their attention should be directed first to the information in the title, then to the headings and subheadings of the columns, and finally to the detailed information in the table.

A simple introductory table can be prepared by the children based on direct observation of outdoor temperatures:

Our Temperature Table

Day	Time	Temperature
Monday	9:00 A.M.	65°
Monday	1:30 P.M.	75°
Tuesday	9:30 P.M.	58°
Tuesday	2:00 P.M.	70°

A practical way to teach how to interpret tables is to present a table related to the direct experiences of the children and classroom topics being studied. Questions leading to interpretation should be designed to accompany each table.

Our Pets

Pets	Number
Dogs	15
Cats	10
Birds	3
Fish	16
Other	4

QUESTIONS

1. How many pet birds do the children in our class have?
2. Which animal do we have most of?
3. How many more dogs than cats do the children have?
4. How many special kinds of pets do we have?

High Temperatures in California
Wednesday

City	Temperature
Redding	98°
Sacramento	102°
Salinas	72°
San Jose	80°
San Francisco	60°

QUESTIONS

1. Which city had the highest temperature?
2. How many of the places had very hot weather?
3. Which places would be the most comfortable?
4. Why do you think San Francisco had the lowest temperature?

Classroom charts

In this discussion we use the term *classroom charts* in a broad sense to refer to a record of information that is valuable for frequent reference. Charts have a wide variety of uses: records of experiences, plans, questions to be answered, directions, class standards, poetry and songs, records of progress, new vocabulary, information of various kinds, classification of items, sequence or flow of events, and organization of committees or ideas.

1. *Experience charts* are prepared cooperatively by teacher and children to record information obtained as a result of excursions, experiments, or other first-hand experiences. The teacher or children may record various statements as dictated by the class. For example:

We went to the zoo.
The monkey was funny.
We gave him peanuts.
The lion roared at us.
We petted the baby elephant.
It was fun.

2. *Planning charts* are used to record suggestions for materials for construction projects; plans for an excursion; daily, weekly, or yearly activity

planning; and other projects that require cooperative planning. For example:

Make a list of countries.
Bring in pieces of cloth.
Look for pictures of costumes.
Cut out figures of people.

3. *Question charts* serve as a record of questions the children have decided they want or need to answer about a topic through research. Such a chart can also contain questions the children intend to ask a classroom visitor. For example:

Why did the Indians travel?
What did the Indians use for food?
Where did the Indians camp?
How did Indian children learn to do things?
Where do most Indians live today? Why?

4. *Direction charts* contain information the children and teacher have concluded is necessary to carry out some activity. For example:

MAKING AN ORAL REPORT

1. Have your report well planned.
2. Speak directly to the class.
3. Use clear expression.
4. Avoid run-on sentences.
5. Allow time and opportunity for questions.

5. *Class standard charts* are used to record mutually agreed-upon standards of behavior the children are to follow in tasks ranging from independently directed activities and small-group committee work to class reports and discussions. For example:

Work together.
Help other children.
Listen carefully and courteously.
Finish your work promptly.
Clean up quickly.

6. *Poetry and song charts* may be used to record outstanding creative efforts that the class as a whole or individual children have completed. For example:

MY THOUGHT

My thought was that a star fell out of the sky.
It was beautiful.
It was big.
I played with it all day.
I liked it, too.*

(Janice, Grade 2)

7. *Progress charts* may take the form of a diary to record the progress of a science experiment or of a social studies unit. For example:

October 3: We planned our project—constructing a model town in the Old West.

October 4: We brought our materials and supplies.

October 5: We began to build our town, following our plan.

8. *Vocabulary charts* may list new words encountered in a social studies unit or those necessary to understand a new concept in science or arithmetic. For example:

OUR NEW WORDS

meridian
longitude
hemisphere
latitude
equator

9. *Information charts* are lists of information about such social studies concepts as manufactured products, natural resources, and other similar items. They may also be items in science that are important to remember over a period of time. For example:

THE ORDER OF OUR PLANETS
    FROM THE SUN

Mercury	Saturn
Venus	Uranus
Earth	Neptune
Mars	Pluto
Jupiter	

*"My Thought" is reprinted from *Easy in English* by Mauree Applegate, Copyright © 1960 Row, Peterson & Company (now Harper & Row, Publishers, Inc.).

442

10. *Classification charts* can be used to tabulate information according to categories. In science a classification chart might be used to categorize amphibians and reptiles, while in social studies countries and types of government might be categorized. For example:

KINDS OF PLANTS

Evergreen	*Deciduous*
firs	apples
pines	plums
camellias	lilacs

11. *Flow charts* provide information on the process or way in which something is accomplished. In science such a chart might illustrate the way erosion changes the land; in social studies it could describe a manufacturing or distribution process. For example:

HOW OUR VEGETABLES TRAVEL TO US

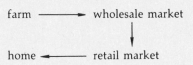

farm ——→ wholesale market

home ←—— retail market

12. *Organization charts* record things like committee membership in the classroom or the organization of a civilization, a government, or, in science, an atom. For example:

Chairman, Project Committee: Ann

Research	*Art Work*	*Reporting*
Joe	Marge	Mike
Mary	Jim	Phil
Ed	Bill	Rose

Charts posted in the classroom should be attactive, lettering should be legible and neat, meaningful phrasing should be observed, and the contrast between letter and paper should be sharp.

The experience children get from developing and constructing charts in the classroom will greatly facilitate their ability to interpret charts in texts and other reference books.

Graphs

Graphs present information in visual form, and can clarify an otherwise confusing mass of data. There are four basic types of graphs: the *circle*

443

graph, which shows relationships among parts and the whole; the *line graph,* which pictures the progress of some trend; the *bar graph,* which compares quantities; and the *pictorial graph,* which expresses comparisons in pictorial form.

1. *Circle graphs.* To understand circle graphs, children must understand the use of fractional parts. In the upper grades, when they have mastered the concepts of percent and degrees, these units can also be used in graphs. Before students understand these more abstract mathematical concepts, however, they can learn that the size of the part of the graph devoted to a particular item indicates that item's relationship to the whole, which is represented by the circle. This relationship may indicate the way family income is spent, the ethnic proportions of the school population, or other types of part-whole relational information. For example:

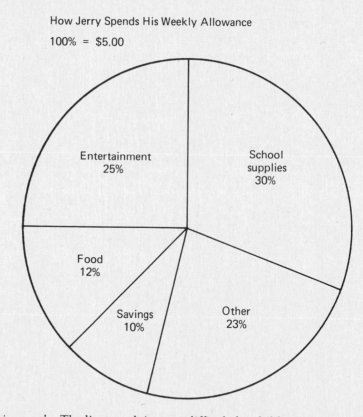

How Jerry Spends His Weekly Allowance

100% = $5.00

2. *Line graphs.* The line graph is more difficult for children to interpret than the circle graph, because the line graph has two dimensions. It is thus most useful in the upper elementary grades. When you teach the interpretation of line graphs, use examples from the children's experiences or from class-room reading materials that are easily interpreted. The children should understand that it is important to check both the vertical and horizontal

scales to interpret the graph, and that they must also attend to variations in the interval sizes of the scales, since the steepness of the line's slope will be altered when the interval is changed. When students are constructing their first line graphs, manila graph paper with one-fourth inch grids should be used. For example:

AMY'S GROWTH RECORD

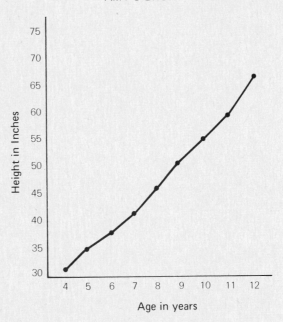

How tall was Amy when she was five years old?

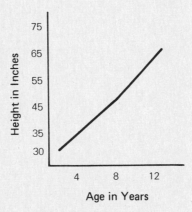

How does the change in age interval affect the impression created by the
445   first graph even though the data are identical?

3. *Bar graphs.* Because bar graphs are very easy to construct and interpret they are more widely used in the intermediate grades than either the circle or line graph. When they interpret bar graphs, children should be taught to read the title carefully and check the scale to determine the quantity represented by the height of each bar. Since a bar graph may be either horizontal or vertical, students constructing such graphs will need to decide which type they wish to use. They will also need to decide the scale, whether their bar arrangement is easy to read, and whether the title clearly indicates the content of the graph. For example:

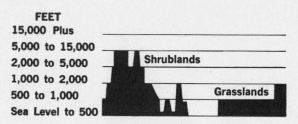

Figure 12-9. Vegetation at the Thirtieth Parallel South, in South America. *Reprinted from Teacher's Guide and Resource Manual, The Forest, by permission of Prentice-Hall, Inc.*

4. *Pictorial graphs.* This type of graph is used more in the elementary grades than any other. Be careful that the meaning of the symbols and the amounts they represent are clear to the students when they interpret or construct pictorial graphs. Each symbol should represent one unit in the early construction of pictorial graphs. When the student has more experience with such graphs, each symbol can represent multiple units of larger quantity. For example:

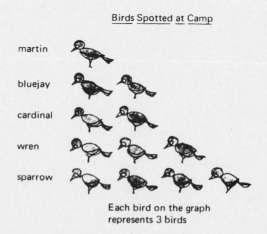

Figure 12-10. Picture Graph. *From Study Skills for Information Retrieval, 1 by Donald L. Barnes and Arlene B. Burgdorf. © Copyright 1970 by Allyn & Bacon, Inc. Reprinted by permission of Allyn & Bacon, Inc.*

The activities listed below may be used to teach how to interpret and construct various types of graphs.

1. Ask the students to construct a circle graph showing what part of the total group in the classroom has no brothers or sisters, what part has one or two, and what part has three or more.
2. Have each student draw a line graph showing the number of problems he worked correctly on his arithmetic papers each day for a week.
3. Have the students draw a bar graph showing the comparative sizes of classes in the school.
4. Request that the students construct a pictorial graph showing the number of boys and the number of girls in the school, using the scale of one symbol equals ten children.

What is the value of combining a picture and bar graph such as that illustrated here?

In addition to these activities, encourage students to construct graphs that relate to their experiences and to interpret their visual representations in small groups. Take time also to analyze the graphs in high-interest materials such as children's newspapers, magazines, and other reading materials.

Maps and globes

Many skills are involved in reading maps and globes. Probably the first concept to be learned is that of direction—east, west, north, and south—followed by the notion of distance beyond one's immediate environment. The child must then be able to relate this concept of distance to a scale for interpretation purposes. As he progresses in map reading skill, he must learn to recognize land and water forms and their representation on maps. Other map symbols deserving attention include identification of mountains, rivers, forests, and deserts. He will also need to recognize political boundaries, longitude and latitude markings, and numerous other details.

The following list represents a variety of uses for maps and globes in the elementary grades.

1. Making maps of the school, neighborhood, and community
2. Making maps of class trips; identification of explorers' routes in recent and ancient times
3. Using maps to find distances between places; comparing early travel routes with present highways; demonstrating how technological discoveries have changed travel patterns
4. Finding places on maps: states, cities, countries, parks, mountain ranges, oceans, lakes, rivers, historical sites, and capitals
5. Using maps in conjunction with oral reports to clarify points and answer questions
6. Finding locations of current events when they are reported: space recovery areas, floods, and the like
7. Using pictorial maps to find out about many things: resources, farming, historical events, and products
8. Using maps to make inferences concerning reasons for climatic conditions in certain areas, location of population centers, travel routes, and kinds of industries in an area
9. Using maps to indicate the location of the north magnetic pole and the true North Pole
10. Using maps to present a comprehensive picture of weather all over the country
11. Using overlay maps to interpret the weather fronts shown by satellite photographs
12. Using maps to show the limits of the glaciers of the last ice age and to indicate tornado and earthquake belts

Maps and globes in the elementary grades should be simple and clear, with limited detail. It is often wise to use both maps and globes at the same time in order to avoid the distortion that can result from map use alone.

The first maps that children construct will be of their school and neighborhood, followed by maps of larger geographical areas in the intermediate grades.

In the primary grades children can be introduced to map reading by having them locate their homes on a map of their town, city, or rural area. They can also locate their town or home area on a map of the state they live in, and their home state on a map of the United States.

With a globe you can help children locate the sites of stories they read or listen to in the classroom. You can also use it to show routes that one would take to go to some other country of the world.

What basic concepts are needed for understanding the representational nature of maps? How is the map being used here in connection with the San Francisco Bay Area Rapid Transit (BART)?

Activities like the following can be used to teach map and globe skills.

1. To reinforce understanding of basic directions, ask the children questions about the direction their houses face, the direction they walk to get to school, the direction from their house they walk to go to the store. A compass will help in this activity.
2. On short walks and study trips point out different surface features and then discuss how the same features are depicted on a map.
3. Use local, state, national, and world maps to show that the larger the space represented the less detail the map reveals.
4. Use pictorial maps to help the children find out about products, resources, and manufacturing. Construct maps showing these aspects of your local area.
5. Use maps to compare physical features, climate, distances, and other information concerning places being studied.
6. Encourage students to use maps in conjunction with oral and written reports.

READING COMPETENCIES IN THE CONTENT AREAS

Some reading-study skills are common to most content areas, many of which we have already discussed. These common skills should be taught and reinforced in relation to specific content areas as the need is encountered, even though they have been introduced in the reading program. You

449

cannot assume that automatic transfer to every content area will occur, because of differences among concepts in various content areas, differences in content, and differences in attitudes and interests.

In addition to these common study skills, every area has its own body of knowledge, and the skills relating to it demand instructional consideration. For example, the student must develop a reading vocabulary related to each subject area if he is to understand the material. He must also realize that some words have one meaning in one area and quite another in a second area. For example, *group* in social studies may refer to people with particular social characteristics, but in arithmetic it refers to the process of clustering numbers based on a specific quantity. The student must develop the ability to relate new concepts in a content area to previously learned concepts if his experiential background is to be utilized.

Understandings differ in different content areas. One area emphasizes the social concepts of our culture, while another gives priority to the scientific aspects. Each area has information peculiar to it, and the content can be approached in different ways. In English we may be concerned with the emotional impact of a literary selection, for example, while in science we are concerned with the development of new concepts and with the nature of the scientific process.

Literature

Reading in literature may be done for a variety of purposes, including the development of basic literacy skills, appreciation of literature in this and other cultures, and development of an awareness of human potential. Factors the teacher must account for in the literature program include conceptual development, vocabulary and label expansion, awareness of syntactical patterns, flexibility of style and usage, awareness of the symbolic function of language, decoding skills, and comprehension skills. These topics are treated in detail in Chapters 10, 11, and 13. Suffice to state here that the major reasons for reading literature in the elementary school are appreciation, self-understanding, and enjoyment.

Literature requires more interpretation of figurative language than social studies, science, or mathematics. Comprehension of supporting details is important to the extent that they contribute to the feeling portrayed by the author. Although complexity of sentence structure influences comprehension, context clues within sentence and across sentences greatly facilitate this task. Some conceptualization problems arise in reading literature because children lack the experiential background which parallels that of the author rather than because they lack content-related concepts. For this reason literature is an extremely important opportunity for gaining insight into the human experience captured in the author's work. We shall say

more about the literature experience in the next chapter.

Social studies

The nature of content in the social science area requires special instructional provision. Russell offers four guides for designing a program in the social studies:[6]

1. Reading materials should be related to the other activities of the classroom.

If children are working on a unit on Japan, for example, they should have available books on raising silk worms, pearl diving, haiku poetry, Japanese folktales, and books like *Sigemi, a Japanese Village Girl,*[7] which illustrates the changing customs of modern Japan.

2. Reading a rich variety of materials is a partial substitute for and the best supplement to firsthand experiences.

Not every child can visit the Indians as they live today, nor can anyone go back to the past to study their culture. But children can read such books as *Indians* and *Home of the Red Man.* In *The Chippewa Indians, The Cherokee Indians,* and similar volumes Sonia Bleeker gives an anthropologist's view of Indian life. *Getting to Know American Indians Today* is an accurate report of present-day conditions of the Navajo.[8]

3. Pupils in elementary and secondary schools need special help in reading social studies materials.

Social studies requires much use of the locational and interpretive skills discussed earlier, of general reference materials, and of maps, graphs, charts, and tables. Organizational skills are also used to a greater extent in social studies than in the other content areas. Note taking, summarizing, and choosing main ideas and supporting details for outlines are skills vital to the social studies area.

4. Pupils of the intermediate and senior grades need guidance in reading newspapers and magazines.

Newspapers and magazines can be of great value to children engaged in the problem-solving process. Periodicals can provide excellent resource material for learning to distinguish between fact and opinion, to determine cause-and-effect relationships, to evaluate different points of view, and to analyze propaganda.

Comparison is used much more in social studies than in other content areas. We compare a wide range of topics—eras, customs, people, ideas, and countries.

Sequencing of events in the social studies area involves social, economic, and political events to a greater degree than physical events. Usually associated with these events are dates and geographical locations that have less relevance in other subject matter.

Problem solving in social studies differs to some degree from problem solving in science and mathematics, because in social studies personal, social, and economic problems do not lend themselves to exact and single solutions. Students should be encouraged to search continuously and creatively for options and alternative solutions to social issues and problems.

Science

Scientific material is often the explanation of a technical process, and the student has to deal with more details than in any other area except mathematics. Students should be encouraged to read carefully and exactly. The ability to locate information and comprehend the generalized meaning of a passage by synthesizing a wealth of detail is extremely important.

The process of experimentation is uniquely scientific. The scientist states the problem, enumerates the facts, formulates a hypothesis, tests it, reaches a conclusion, and verifies it. Problem solving and the experimental process apply to other content areas, but in science they are much more specific and utilize information that can often be verified through direct observation.

There are numerous situations in science that require classification based on a wide range of criteria. In science sequences of events are controlled and observed over time. We plant the seed, water and fertilize it, and it sprouts and grows. Such experiences offer excellent opportunities for developing cause-and-effect relationships.

Mathematics

Mathematics content is more compact than that found in other content areas, particulary in problem-solving situations. Problem solving in mathematics is more specific and patterned than in other areas. An arithmetic problem must first be broken down. The student must ask himself, "What am I asked?" "What information do I use?" and "What process or processes will provide the solution?" When he arrives at an answer, he must ask, "Is the answer reasonable?"

The comprehension of specific information is critical to problem solving in mathematics. Mathematics concepts are abstract; concepts are represented by special symbols that must have meaning to the child before he can manipulate them. Children also need help with terms like *acre, rod, quart,* and *foot,* and concepts and labels related to the metric system.

Successful reading in mathematics requires that the student be analytical and able to note detail. He needs to be able to spot irrelevant sentences in the math problem. He needs to learn to read mathematics problems more than once in order to clarify the nature of the problem, assimilate details, and establish relationships that approach a solution. He needs to learn to conceptualize the approach to solution with questions that contain no numbers, for example, "Jim wants to use his allowance to buy presents for his parents. How will he find out how much money he needs to buy the things he wants?"

In mathematics one concept is built upon another; new learning depends on previous learning. If the child has not learned to add and subtract, he will be unable to multiply and divide beyond the most elementary level. Thus the evaluation of individual progress and the identification of learning needs are two of the teacher's most important areas of concern.

Materials on the history and development of mathematics should be included in this content area because they can create positive attitudes and generate interest in mathematics study.

EVALUATION OF RESEARCH AND STUDY SKILLS

The most effective way of evaluating the development of a child's research and study skills is through direct observation of his performance. To what degree can the child independently locate information, read for information, organize information, and interpret information? Can he utilize reading skills unique to the content areas and effectively read content area materials? The checklist that follows serves to summarize key parts of this discussion and to provide an evaluation overview to use in assessing student performance over a wide range of research and study skills.

Evaluation Checklist

Location of Information	*1	2	3	Reading for Information	*1	2	3
Use of				Use of			
Book parts				Skimming			
Title page	—	—	—	Previewing	—	—	—
Preface	—	—	—	Overviewing	—	—	—
Table of contents	—	—	—	Reviewing	—	—	—
Index	—	—	—	Scanning			
Glossary	—	—	—	Answering questions	—	—	—
Appendices	—	—	—	Intensive reading	—	—	—
				Flexibility of rate	—	—	—
General references							
Dictionaries	—	—	—				
Encyclopedias	—	—	—				
Atlases	—	—	—				
Almanacs	—	—	—				
Telephone directory	—	—	—				
Classified section	—	—	—				
Library card							
catalogue	—	—	—				
Reader's Guide							
to Periodical							
Literature	—	—	—				

*Levels of competence: 1 = low; 2 = average; 3 = high. All study skills are developmental. The grade level of your group must be taken into consideration.

Organization of Information				*Interpretation of Graphic and Pictorial Information*			
Use of	*1	2	3	Use of	*1	2	3
Note taking	___	___	___	Pictures	___	___	___
Classification	___	___	___	Political cartoons	___	___	___
Main ideas	___	___	___	Tables	___	___	___
Supporting details	___	___	___	Charts	___	___	___
Outlining	___	___	___	Graphs	___	___	___
Summarizing	___	___	___	Maps	___	___	___
Combining information from several sources	___	___	___	Globes	___	___	___

Content Area Reading

	1	2	3
Literature	___	___	___
Social studies	___	___	___
Science	___	___	___
Mathematics	___	___	___

*Levels of competence: 1 = low; 2 = average; 3 = high. All study skills are developmental. The grade level of your group must be taken into consideration.

Footnotes

[1] Reprinted by permission from *The American College Dictionary,* copyright 1970 by Random House, Inc.

[2] John U. Michaelis, *Social Studies for Children in a Democracy: Recent Trends and Developments* © 1972, pp. 350–51. Reprinted by permission of Prentice-Hall, Inc., Englewood Cliffs, New Jersey.

[3] Theodore Clymer and Robert B. Ruddel, *All Sorts of Things,* Level 10 Teachers' Edition, Reading 360 (Boston: Ginn and Company, 1969), p. 45.

[4] Harold L. Herber, *Teaching Reading in Content Areas* (Englewood Cliffs, N.J.: Prentice-Hall, Inc., 1970), pp. 40–42.

[5] From *Teachers' Edition of All Sorts of Things,* by Theodore Clymer and Robert B. Ruddell, of the Reading 360 series, © Copyright, 1969, by Ginn and Company. Used with permission.

[6] David H. Russell, *Children Learn to Read* (Boston: Ginn and Company, 1961), pp. 340–41.

[7] Ruth Kirk, *Sigemi, A Japanese Village Girl* (New York: Harcourt Brace Jovanovich, Inc., 1965).

[8] Edwin Tunis, *Indians* (Cleveland, Ohio: World Publishing Company, 1959); Robert Silverberg, *Home of the Red Man, Indian North America Before Columbus* (illus. Judith Ann Lawrence) (New York: New York Graphic, 1963); Sonia Bleeker, *The Chippewa Indians, Rice Gatherers of the Great Lakes* (illus. Patricia Boodell) (New York: William Morrow & Company, Inc., 1955), and *The Cherokee, Indians of the Mountains* (illus. Althea Karr) (New York: William Morrow & Company, Inc., 1952); Hildegard Thompson, *Getting to Know American Indians Today* (illus. Channon Stirnweiss) (New York: Coward, McCann & Geoghegan, Inc., 1965).

13

Developing Mature Readers: Literature Plus Response

Focusing Questions

1. What are the major goals of a literature program for children?
2. How can experiences with literature lead to conscious insight and increased self-understanding?
3. How can various fiction, nonfiction, and poetic forms of children's literature provide pleasure and knowledge for the young reader? What specific activities can be used?
4. What does the phrase "literature plus response" suggest about literature experiences for children?
5. Of what value is an understanding of comprehension levels and question strategies in developing literature experiences for children? (See also the discussion in Chapter 11.)
6. How can children's literature develop or reinforce decoding and comprehension skill competencies?
7. What critical factors must be considered in evaluating literature experiences in your classroom?

Literature represents life via language and in doing so offers the reader a range of experiences that not only equals but surpasses his base of experience. To define literature, however, merely as "a written record of life experience" is to disregard the essence of the literary experience. Literature can elucidate the unexpressed, and point to the not yet experienced; this capability awards it a unique role in the education and maturation of man. Literature speaks of man; literature speaks to man. Individuals contribute to literature as well as receive from it. The words are nothing more than print on paper until the reader brings to bear his experiences and emotions leading to responsive interaction.

Persons aware of the great potential of literature must help to perpetuate its full use. Albert Grande emphasizes this in describing the interaction process:

Literature, as an expression of human strife, conflict, feelings, and ideas, must engage the students' active response, evoking his fund of intellectual and emotional experience. . . . This response cannot be only cognitive in nature, simply because literature is not only cognitive in nature. The student, like literature itself, is a composite of noncognitive and cognitive elements, both of which must find expression in any authentic study of literature, otherwise . . . literature remains outside the genuine participation of the subjective individual. It would be unfortunate not to relate the individual student's personal experience to his interpretation of literature.[1]

Several educators have examined the relationship between literature and the reader. Isabel Lewis also made a thorough study of previous research, combined her own research with the work of Russell, Loban, Squire, and others, and developed an interaction model of reader response:[2]

The Reader	The Literature	The Process	Concept Development
Perception	Character	Identification	Model
Interaction	Plot Development	Catharsis	Interpretation
Creation	Solutions	Insight	Generalization

On the horizontal level one can observe the relationships among the level of reader input, the type of literary input, and the experience and learning that result. Lewis uses the terms "identification," "catharsis," and "insight" as they are now commonly used to designate psychological mechanisms.

Identification: Seeing similarities to one's self in others
Catharsis: Venting emotions, which reduces tension
Insight: Perceiving one's inner nature

For the young reader many experiences probably occur at the identification and catharsis levels rather than at the level of conscious insight. As the reader gains in age, maturity, and life experience, he becomes more able to experience literature at the level of conscious insight.

If the great potential of literature is to be realized, an extensive variety of life experiences must be available in symbolic form, ranging on a continuum from the formal classics to the child's own stories that create imagery and emotional effect. The "classics" end of the spectrum helps the child as reader or listener to relate to the world and his unique place in it through the life experiences of others. He also uses traditional folk rhymes and stories to express his own emotions and needs. The most informal literature is his own written expression.

The child should be exposed to the full scope of this spectrum if the full potential of a reading-language program is to be realized. A major part of the reading-language program is to realize literacy goals as well as literary

456

goals. Literature provides both a major purpose and a vehicle for learning to read.

←—————————————————————————————————————→

| Children's own stories in symbolic form | Children's oral tradition | Modern prose and poetry for children | Children's classics |

One goal of literature programs is to help children learn to decode, encode, and comprehend the native tongue. Another is to help them know and appreciate the literature of this and other cultures. Finally, there is a highly significant personal goal: to aid the individual in his awareness and realization of human potential. This last goal provides an instructional perspective for developing literary appreciation and literacy skills as means to a larger goal, that of human development.

Given these specific needs and offerings, the following purposes for literature emerge:

1. Affective level: To provide pleasure, through
   a. The *joy of language,* by entertaining, stimulating, and lulling with persuasive combinations of words
   b. An *appreciation of beauty,* by isolating, magnifying, or contrasting "pieces of life" for aesthetic observation
2. Cognitive level: To provide knowledge, through
   a. *Insight into man's behavior,* through contact with a broad range of human behavior and explanations of possible causes
   b. An *awareness of people* (and other living things), *events, and ideas not present in the reader's own life space,* by expanding the world he has experienced and suggesting worlds he has not experienced
   c. An *awareness of man as an integral part of a changing world,* by building in an expectation for change and promoting adaptation and growth
   d. An *awareness of the potential of language as a powerful means of human expression,* by demonstrating the skillful use of imagery, drama, humor, and pathos

The purpose of this chapter is to introduce you to types and samples of children's literature and to recommend more detailed resources for future use, so that you can realize these purposes in your reading-language program.

Various classification systems have been used for children's literature, depending upon the need or focus: reading levels, subject areas, and social themes, to mention a few. The most general system is similar to the one used for adult literature, with minor additions. The major distinction is between prose and poetry. Prose is further divided into fiction and nonfiction. All of children's literature might be handled adequately within the dual framework, but most librarians and teachers prefer to treat picture books and easy-to-read books at the introductory reading level as a separate entity. These books are found under all classifications of prose—folk tales, realistic fiction, and the like. If picture books and easy-to-read books were catalogued under the usual prose classifications, readers who could most benefit from them would have difficulty locating them. Therefore, book lists and libraries usually assign these two forms to separate sections, with the exception of nonfiction. These are usually not separated from the other prose offerings.

Libraries and book lists generally make some distinction between realism and fantasy in fiction, and subdivide nonfiction into informational and biographical (including autobiographical) materials. Poetry is similarly subdivided, generally into narrative and lyric. Other special forms are either singled out or simply grouped as special poetry.

The classification system looks like this:

Prose		Poetry
1. *Fiction*	2. *Non-fiction*	1. Narrative
a. Realism	a. Biography[*][†]	2. Lyric
Historical	b. Information[*][†]	3. Free verse
Modern[*][†]		4. Special Forms
b. Fantasy		
Modern[*][†]		
Traditional[*]		

[*] Picture books and easy-to-read books are a special form of this category.

[†] Easy-to-read books are a special form of this category.

Next we shall discuss children's books according to this classification, beginning with the unique features of picture books and easy-to-read books (we shall also discuss these in their appropriate classifications). We include in this discussion classroom activities that are especially well suited to a given type of prose or poetry. Following this discussion we shall provide a range of specific suggestions for the development of a literature program in the classroom.

Picture books

All picture books by definition feature pictures as the means of transmitting a message, but most contain written text as well. These books are primarily for young children (up to about age eight), but they are also of interest to older children, both for the pleasure of returning to "old friends" and for the experience of encountering something new. Take a look at Joan Walsh Anglund's diminutive books, or *Little Blue and Little Yellow* by Leo Lionni, and you will see that older children might enjoy delving again into many picture books, those with depth below the surface charm.

Since picture books are discussed under all of the classifications of prose, we shall talk here only of fiction and nonfiction, with representative examples.

Fiction picture books are usually referred to as *picture story books.* Whether pictures alone tell the story, or pictures and text combine to tell the story, the plot would be incomplete without the pictures. The text might state simply, "He waited," while the picture portrays the excitement, fear, or loneliness intended by the author.

Everybody had to cry—

not a single eye was dry.

In *Swimmy,* by Leo Lionni, the pictures are necessary to illustrate Swimmy's master plan for defense against the large, threatening fish of the sea. In *Where the Wild Things Are* (Maurice Sendak), a small boy's fantasy becomes vivid for the reader through color and the distortion of size.

How is this teacher using the illustrations in Leo Lionni's *Fish Is Fish* to enhance this story-reading experience for the children? *(Photo by Carole Graham, BBM Associates)*

Nonfiction picture books usually offer information via pictures and a small proportion of text. Alphabet books and counting books are included here, as are books like *Is It Hard, Is It Easy?,* which offer basic information.

For more examples of the way pictures plus simple text can present information, examine the alphabet books of Edward Lear and Brian Wildsmith and *Over in the Meadow,* a counting book by John Langstaff. The pictures

offer visual associations that many children continue to recall as the clues
to those particular concepts.

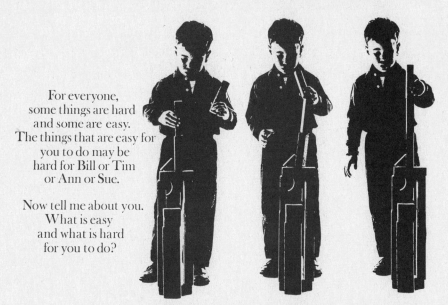

For everyone,
some things are hard
and some are easy.
The things that are easy for
you to do may be
hard for Bill or Tim
or Ann or Sue.

Now tell me about you.
What is easy
and what is hard
for you to do?

Reprinted from Is It Hard, Is It Easy?, *text © MCMLX, by Mary McBurney Green,
illustrated by Len Gittelman, a Young Scott Book, by permission of Addison-
Wesley Publishing Company.*

Easy-to-read books

This special form of prose has been a welcome innovation for children in
the early stages of mastering reading skills and for children who have been
slower than age-mates in acquiring decoding skills. Because of their restricted vocabulary, many of these books will not fulfill the aesthetic and
language goals of literature, but because of their other contributions they
deserve a place in the recommended range of offerings. For some children
these books provide the necessary bridge between being a listener and
being a reader.

These books usually have large manuscript print, amply spaced. They can
be identified easily by a designation on the cover, such as "An-I-Can
Read-Book," or "I Can Read It All by Myself." Several authors, such as
Dr. Seuss, make clever use of a very limited vocabulary. They expand the
language in special ways, such as rhyming or using nonsense. An example
of this is *Hop on Pop,* the Simplest Seuss for Youngest Use, wherein the
concept of size comparison is conveyed in colorful, humorous fashion.
Many of the easy readers are aimed especially at boys (Olaf Reads, Joan
Lexau), and many others deal with childhood frustrations (*Hurry, Hurry!,*
Edith Hurd; *I Should Have Stayed in Bed,* Syd Hoff).

461

ALL
TALL

We all are tall.

ALL
SMALL

We all are small.

From Hop on Pop, *by Dr. Seuss. Copyright © 1963 by Dr. Seuss. Reprinted by permission of Random House, Inc.*

PROSE

The bulk of children's literature is found under the prose heading. Many of these books contain pictures, but here they are termed illustrations because they add to the imagery portrayed through words but are not necessary to the story plot. The text is capable of standing by itself. In keeping with the previous discussion, picture book and easy-to-read examples will be cited under the appropriate categories.

Fiction

REALISM

Fiction is by definition free from the bonds of fact, but many works of fiction appeal to their audience by mirroring reality. This credibility strengthens reader identification and appeals to the child who feels he has grown beyond stories such as those where animals are personified.

Realism occurs in both historical and modern fiction. An example of *historical* fiction is *Ishi, Last of His Tribe,* by Theodora Kroeber, in which the lone survivor of an Indian tribe allows his own capture and proceeds to tell his story to the white man. In *Island of the Blue Dolphins,* by Scott O'Dell, a twelve-year-old Indian girl finds herself stranded alone, and must cope with the daily demands of survival. Many books about young people during America's colonial and frontier days are fictionalized history (*Tituba of Salem*, by Ann Petry; *A Head on Her Shoulders*, by Gladys Baker Bond). Examples of picture books and easy-to-read books that are works of historical fiction are virtually nonexistent because the content does not lend itself to that reading level.

A large quantity of writing for children falls into the category of *modern realistic fiction*. This mode of writing is especially appropriate for content designed to contribute to the reader's self-knowledge, through stories that display the frustrations of being the middle child (*And Now Miguel*, by Joseph Krumgold) or the feelings of Wanda Petronsky, who was ashamed of having only one dress (*The Hundred Dresses*, by Eleanor Estes). In a picture book, *A Pair of Red Clogs*, Masako Matsuno describes Mako, who becomes very unhappy attempting to hide the fact that she has cracked one of her new clogs. *The Boy Who Wouldn't Say His Name*, by Elizabeth Vreeken, an easy-to-read example of such fiction, portrays the events that ensue when Bobby Brown continues his fanciful play-acting even when he is lost in a department store.

Reprinted by permission of The World Publishing Company from A Pair of Red Clogs *by Masako Matsuno. Copyright © 1960 by Masako Matsuno. Illustrations copyright © 1960 by Kazue Mizumura.*

Most of the books in this category are for children beyond the easy-to-read phase, or for listening. They lend themselves to helping children deal with life situations relevant to the age involved. Books about sibling relationships, for instance, are often appropriate for children above age five. With six- to eight-year-olds, a teacher might choose to read such books as *Chie and the Sports Day,* by Masako Matsuno; *Willie Is My Brother,* by Peggy Parish; and *My Sister and I,* by Helen Buckley, in conjunction with discussions that help to legitimize feelings of jealousy, resentment, and hurt. A small group of older children might read a number of selections on their own for discussion purposes, or each might read a different book to bring a point of view to the other students.

Role playing and creative dramatics offer both age groups opportunities to re-enact situations and to create their own solutions to the conflicts.

FANTASY

Fantasy can be divided into modern and traditional. Fantasy suffers few of the bounds ordinarily imposed on existence. This freedom is appreciated more by children beyond the primary school level, as a greater awareness of reality is essential to fully enjoy its violations. To the young child, erasing drawings from the chalkboard, a caterpillar's metamorphosis into a butterfly and making jello may be as magical as the antics of Curious George or Charlotte.

Modern fantasy is represented by such well-known classics as A. A. Milne's *Winnie the Pooh* and E. B. White's *Charlotte's Web.* Most readers find greater depth in both of these books as they mature. Milne's "tiddely pom" should not mislead the parent or teacher into offering Pooh Bear only to the young child. If he does enjoy those stories at five or six, share them with him, but with eight or nine (even ten or twelve) years of life experience he is even more apt to appreciate "If you walk up and down with your umbrella saying, 'Tut-tut, it looks like rain,' I shall do what I can by singing a little Cloud Song, such as a cloud might sing."[3]

From the book Winnie-the-Pooh *by A. A. Milne. Decorations by E. H. Shepard. Copyright, 1926 by E. P. Dutton & Co., Inc. Renewal, 1954, by A. A. Milne. Published by E. P. Dutton & Co., Inc. and used with their permission and with permission of The Canadian Publishers, McClelland and Stewart Limited, Toronto.*

The Borrowers, Mary Norton's account of the adventures of a miniature family, is another fantasy that draws the reader into the logic of a world with entirely new dimensions. *The Phantom Toll Booth,* by Norton Juster, a fantasy on location in Dictionopolis, capitalizes on the power and play of words.

The results of Max's anger at his mother are described in Maurice Sendak's *Where the Wild Things Are,* a picture book of fantasy. Many easy-to-read books have simple, humorous plots of fantasy, like Syd Hoff's *Danny and the Dinosaur,* wherein a boy and his prehistoric animal friend spend an adventurous day together.

Fantasy appeals to children of all ages. Favorite stories include *Many Moons,* by James Thurber, and *The Troll Music,* by Anita Lobel (for younger children); *Charlotte's Web,* by E. B. White, and *Charlie and the Chocolate Factory,* by Roald Dahl (for intermediate age children); *The Wind in the Willows,* by Kenneth Grahame, *The Little Prince,* by Antoine de Saint-Exupery, and *The Hobbitt,* by J. R. R. Tolkien (for older children).

By about age seven, children begin to enjoy hearing a chapter a day of the longer books. Because of its descriptive detail, fantasy also lends itself to being illustrated, both by individuals and by groups (sketches, paint or chalk drawings, dioramas, murals). A small group can construct the setting and dramatize characters of a favorite chapter to introduce others to that book.

Traditional fantasy takes several different forms including folk tales, fairy tales, fables, myths, and legends.

Folk Tales

The oral traditions of a culture are perpetuated in folklore. This literature is a unique offering to children because it transmits their own culture and provides information about other cultures. Inner feelings and attitudes that are ordinarily disguised or denied are freely expressed in folklore. Sibling rivalry and sexual and role identifications are but a few of the aspects of human relationships permitted in oral traditions.

There are many collections of folk tales. Two of the better-known ones are *The Life Treasury of American Folklore,* by Herbert Brean, and Walter de la Mare's *Tales Told Again.*

Fairy Tales

The imaginative fairy tale is another kind of literature kept alive by tradition. Both oral and written, these tales embody the themes related to human experience, such as "beauty is only skin deep" or "good overcomes evil." When Cinderella becomes the prince's choice for a bride, or when the Ugly Duckling turns out to be a lovely swan, the reader is reinforced in the idea that virtue is rewarded.

Two famous fairy-tale collections are *Grimm's Fairy Tales* and *Fairy Tales of Hans Christian Andersen.* Many fairy tales are also available individually, such as *The Emperor's New Clothes,* a modern fairy tale by Andersen, or *Puss in Boots,* by Charles Perrault.

From The Ugly Duckling *by Hans Christian Andersen. Used by permission.*

Fables

A fable is a brief story wherein animals or inanimate objects speak and act to convey a moral lesson. The brevity of fables and the presence of outstanding pictures should not mislead you into offering them only to young children. The concepts, stated in condensed form, often challenge the intermediate reader.

The name most often associated with this genre is Aesop, who is believed to have been a Greek slave. If he indeed existed, he was proably only one of many recorders of these stories. There are numerous editions of Aesop's Fables, and there are other collections, such as the *Jatakas* tales, used by Buddhists in their early teaching. A useful resource in this area is *The Age of Fables,* by Thomas Bulfinch.

There are also many individual treatments, such as Brian Wildsmith's *North Wind and the Sun,* wherein the gentle sun is shown to be more powerful than the blustering wind. *Andy and the Lion,* by James Daugherty, is a modern version of the well-known story of Androcles and the lion.

Myths

Myths are ancient attempts to explain the mysterious and the unknown. They depict the deeds of the gods and the legendary heroes. The Greek, Roman, Eastern, and Nordic myths are the results of early searches for answers about the natural and human aspects of the universe.

Because of its content, this literature is best suited for children with enough life experience to begin to ask some of the larger questions about existence, children old enough to be ready to share primitive man's queries and to compare the quests of different cultures. As May Hill Arbuthnot has pointed out, myths "may help to prevent the older children of this generation from settling into a too tight literalness too young."[4]

Of what value is the children's development of "My Retold Greek Myths"? How can this experience be shared with other children?

Several collections contain myths from a variety of ethnic backgrounds, such as *Myths of the World,* collected by Padraic Colum, and Thomas B. Aldrich's *A Book of Famous Myths and Legends.* Other collections, such as *Greek Myths,* told by Olivia E. Coolidge, and *The White Archer,* told and illustrated by James Houston, are confined to one cultural group.

Legends

Societies often seek heroes, fellow humans who possess superior qualities of leadership and accomplishment. Legends provide heroes in two ways. One way is to take the life of a real person and to embellish his positive characteristics and his reactions to challenges, even to invent additonal ones. An example of this type is Daniel Boone, whose actual experiences have been built upon by story tellers. The second way is to create a character with superhuman abilities. An American hero of the latter type is Paul Bunyan, the logger who churned the earth with his walk and caused wind currents with his breath. The many stories of this legendary hero are told by various authors: Glen Round, Esther Shephard, and Maria Leach, to name a few.

Maria Leach's *The Rainbow Book of American Folk Tales and Legends* and *Heroes in American Folklore,* by Irwin Shapiro, are good collections of American legends.

These tales are often good for story telling, and because of their simplicity of plot and setting they are also quite adaptable to dramatization. Children can make their own costumes and assume the roles, or they can construct puppets (finger, sack, hand puppets) to depict the characters. As they manipulate the puppets they can either speak spontaneously or follow a script or sound track they have prerecorded. Some folk tales and legends, such as Pecos Bill, have musical versions that add another dimension.

Traditional literature offers opportunities for various contrasts. Older children can examine the themes and plots of several folk tales and write their own tales using a theme they have seen repeatedly.

Different versions of a plot, found either within a cultural group or across cultures, can help children begin to see that there are *different* ways of looking at things, not right and wrong ways. A discussion of this idea could develop from a comparison of *Stone Soup* and *Nail Soup,* for example. How are the versions different? What reasons might there be for preferring each version? Can you think of yet another version of the same tale? Endings to fairy tales can lead into similar kinds of discussions. Why might some people prefer not to have the villain killed? Which way do you like to have the story end? Could you write another possible ending? Another type of comparison involves identifying and examining themes common to several cultural groups. Versions of the Jack tale, for example, show how various groups seem to need to poke fun at a less intelligent member.

Nonfiction

BIOGRAPHY

A direct avenue for identifying with characters in books is the biography
(and autobiography). The child can vicariously undergo the experiences of

a person he admires by examining his life style, successes, and confrontations with discouragement and defeat. In such treatments teachers and students rely heavily on authors and publishers for accuracy of information.

At one time biographies were not included in children's literature collections, but now they even exist on the easy-to-read level. Just because publishers make them available does not mean that all six- to eight-year-olds want to read biographies, or that such simple versions do justice to the purpose of the biography. Certain famous persons may be of interest to the young child, but it is usually the older elementary school child who seeks biographies.

For the beginning reader who does want to learn about famous persons, publishers such as Follett and Putnam have produced biographies that limit and control vocabulary (*Beginning-To-Read Series,* for one). There are few picture book examples of biography, but the d'Aulaires have written and illustrated some. Some biographies of greater difficulty and detail stress the childhood of the person, others consider the entire life span. The *Landmark Series, American Heritage,* and *Breakthrough Books* are well-known biography series for the older reader. You can also obtain lists of biographies by referring to authors known to have written several biographies for children: James Daugherty, Genevieve Foster, Clara Ingram Judson, Reba Paeff Mirsky, Elizabeth Ripley, and others.

Children usually read biographies for themselves, but there might be occasions for reading at least parts of biographies to a group of children. Different biographies of the same individual can be compared for style or content, depending upon the ages and needs of students. A favorite biographer's style could be used as a model in biographies and autobiographies written by students.

INFORMATIONAL NONFICTION

Every children's library should contain a large number of books that supply information of varying sorts and at a variety of concept and reading levels. Informational books cover all areas of interest to children learning about their world.

When literacy and literary awareness and appreciation are the goals of a literature program, a distinction must be made among types of informational books. Many informational books are written solely to supply straightforward facts in a given area. This purpose is worthwhile and many authors achieve it well, but these books are offered to students in the context of the subject matter and are not expected to serve as a part of the literature program. Other informational books, which offer specific information in a literary style, are appropriate for a literature program. Facts in
469   these books are not exaggerated or modified (that would make them

fiction), but are brought alive in a meaningful context so that the reader can experience emotional as well as intellectual response. Gladys Conklin's *I Like Caterpillars,* for example, creates positive feelings about members of this insect stage.

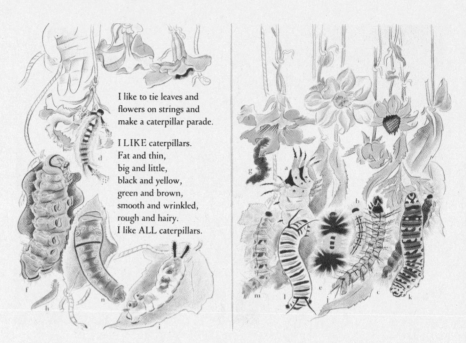

I like to tie leaves and
flowers on strings and
make a caterpillar parade.

I LIKE caterpillars.
Fat and thin,
big and little,
black and yellow,
green and brown,
smooth and wrinkled,
rough and hairy.
I like ALL caterpillars.

Reprinted from Gladys Conklin, I Like Caterpillars, *by permission of Holiday House.*

Any presentation of information for young children can be enhanced by large illustrations and photographs, so most informational books at this level are picture books. Smaller illustrations, sketches, diagrams, maps, and photographs are relied upon for clarification in many of the books for older children.

There are even informational books for the most basic cognitive level—the "sensory-motor stage," as Piaget terms it—but most school-age children have reached the preoperational level. At this stage, where the child can deal with objects in two dimensions, books dealing with simple identification and classification are appropriate. At the concrete level of operation (seven to eleven years), when the child can manipulate variables to make some judgments about cause and effect, informational books such as those suggesting opportunities for scientific experimentation are appropriate.

Some children will penetrate the level of formal operations before they leave elementary school. By this period they are beginning to function at the abstract level to deal with phenomena not present. A much broader world is now open to them, and they will be able to enjoy fairly technical

presentations in fields of great interest to them, such as rocketry, naviga-
tion, and agriculture.

WEIGHING AIR

It may seem strange to weigh something invisible. But you
really can weigh air.

Air is so light that you will need a good scale. Perhaps the
butcher or grocer will let you use his scale. You also will need
something that holds a lot of air—and something that the air comes
out of easily.

A football or basketball will do. Squeeze as much air out of the
ball as you can. Then weigh the ball. Write down its weight so
that you won't forget it. Blow up the ball and weigh it again.

If you use a standard football that is ready to use in a game,
the air inside will weigh a few ounces.

The air in a blown-up toy balloon, the size of a football, weighs
much less than this. The balloon can't hold as much air as the
football can, for it's made of thin rubber that breaks more easily
than the tough rubber lining of the football. To weigh the air in
a toy balloon, you need a delicate scale.

Reprinted from Rose Wyler, The First Book of Science Experiments, *by permission
of Franklin Watts, Inc.*

Informational books are usually read aloud to younger children, while
older children read for themselves. An informational book is often used in
471 conjunction with a unit of study, to add another dimension to a study

otherwise based solely on straight factual books. Series such as *The First Book of . . .* or the *True Book of . . .* can be enriched by presentations such as those of Gladys Conklin *(We Like Bugs, I Like Caterpillars, I Like Butterflies)* and Alice E. Goudey *(Houses by the Sea)* for younger children, or, for older children, those like *The Sense of Wonder* by Rachel Carson. Poetry can also add to information gathering. In a study of the rodent family, elementary school children of all ages have been delighted by "Mice."

MICE

I think mice
Are rather nice.
   Their tails are long,
   Their faces small,
   They haven't any
   Chins at all.
   Their ears are pink,
   Their teeth are white,
   They run about
   The house at night.
   They nibble things
   They shouldn't touch
   And no one seems
   To like them much.
But / think mice
Are nice.*

Another poem on the same topic has quite a different style.

THE HOUSE OF THE MOUSE

The house of the mouse
is a wee little house,
a green little house in the grass,
which big clumsy folk
may hunt and may poke
and still never see as they pass
this sweet little, neat little,
wee little, green little,
cuddle-down hide-away
house in the grass.†

*From *Fifty-One New Nursery Rhymes* by Rose Fyleman. Copyright 1972 by Rose Fyleman. Reprinted by permission of Doubleday & Company, Inc., and the Society of Authors as the literary representative of the Estate of Rose Fyleman.

†From the book *Another Here and Now Story Book* by Lucy Sprague Mitchell and co-authors. Copyright, 1937, by E. P. Dutton & Co., Inc. Renewal, ©, 1965 by Lucy Sprague Mitchell. Published by E. P. Dutton & Co., Inc. and used with their permission.

Fantasy throws off the constraints of realism. Poetry reveals another dimension. A poet, says Constantine Georgiou, is "one who sees with the eye of imagination; he hears with the ear of sensitivity; he touches the intangible, and he holds fast the fleeting intensity of experience."[5]

Poetry is not confined to grammatical conventions such as the complete sentence, logical development of idea, topic sentence, and summary. Poetry allows ideas just to *be*. Thoughts, images, and feelings can be presented as elaborately, briefly, simply, or abstractly as desired. Eve Merriam is often quoted on the nature of poetry, since she expresses it so well:

WHERE IS A POEM?

Where is a poem?
As far away
As a rainbow span,
Ancient Cathay,
Or Afghanistan;

Or it can be near
As where you stand
This very day
On Main Street here
With a poem
In your hand.

What makes a poem?
Whatever you feel:
The secrets of rain
On a window pane,
The smell of a rose
Or of cowboy clothes,
The sound of a flute
Or a foghorn hoot,
The taste of cake
Or a freshwater lake,
The touch of grass
Or an icy glass,
The shout of noon
Or the silent moon,
A standstill leaf
Or a rolling wheel
Laughter and grief
Whatever you feel.*

Through content, imagery, and rhythm, poetry can satisfy every taste.

In *content,* poetry can reach out to all interests and ages. Young children enjoy humor and animal adventures, but perhaps their most vital interest is *me.* Since establishing positive self-concepts of themselves as individuals and as members of their present group is of utmost importance, a poem like John Ciardi's about the preference for one's own name is very meaningful to young children.

AND OFF HE WENT JUST AS PROUD
AS YOU PLEASE

Said Billy to Willy,
"You have a silly name!"
Said Willy to Billy,
"Our names are much the same."

Said Billy to Willy,
"That is not true.
Your name is silly,
Just like you.

"Your name's a silly shame.
My name is fine.
For my name, my name,
My name is *mine!*"*

The following poem by Dorothy Aldis suggests another way a child can look at himself as an individual.

EVERYBODY SAYS

Everybody says
I look just like my mother.

Everybody says
I'm the image of Aunt Bee.

Everybody says
My nose is like my father's
But I want to look like me.†

To the older child, identification with strong character traits can be an important avenue to growth and understanding. "Charles," by Leonard Clark, holds such potential.[6] *Imagery* is a second gift of poetry. While prose

*From the book *You Know Who* by John Ciardi. Copyright, ©, 1964 by John Ciardi. Reprinted by permission of J. B. Lippincott Company.

†Reprinted by permission of G. P. Putnam's Sons from *Everything and Anything* by Dorothy Aldis. Copyright © 1925, 1926, 1927 by Dorothy Aldis; renewed 1953, 1954, 1955.

Poetry can also create imagery for the reader, poetry can sometimes do it more powerfully, because of its condensation. A classic example is Carl Sandburg's "Fog."

> The fog comes
> on little cat feet.
>
> It sits looking
> over harbor and city
> on silent haunches
> and then moves on.*

Illustration, © 1958, by Irene Haas. Reproduced from Something Special *by Beatrice Schenk de Regniers, by permission of Harcourt Brace Jovanovich, Inc.*

In another instance, children's imaginations can be easily aroused with a question like "What color do you think of for the day Monday?" or "What color do you think of when you picture a fierce wind blowing?" Mary O'Neill frees many more such images in the poem "Hailstones and Halibut Bones."

*From *Chicago Poems* by Carl Sandburg, copyright, 1916, by Holt, Rinehart and Winston; copyright, 1944, by Carl Sandburg. Reprinted by permission of Harcourt Brace Jovanovich, Inc.

The Colors live
Between black and white
In a land that we
Know best by sight.
But knowing best
Isn't everything,
For colors dance
And colors sing,
And colors laugh
And colors die,
And they make you feel
Every feeling there is
From the grumpiest grump
To the fizziest fizz.
And you and I
Know well
Each has a taste
And each has a smell
And each has a wonderful
Story to tell . . .*

One example of the many colors she paints for the reader is brown.

WHAT IS BROWN?

Brown is the color of a country road
Back of a turtle
Back of a toad.
Brown is cinnamon
And morning toast
And the good smell of
The Sunday roast.
Brown is the color of work
And the sound of a river,
Brown is bronze and a bow
And a quiver.
Brown is the house
On the edge of town
Where wind is tearing
The shingles down.

Brown is a freckle
Brown is a mole
Brown is the earth

When you dig a hole.
Brown is the hair
On many a head
Brown is chocolate
And gingerbread.
Brown is a feeling you get inside
When wondering makes
Your mind grow wide.
Brown is a leather shoe
And a good glove—
Brown is as comfortable
As love.*

Young children enjoy the topic of color, but Mary O'Neill's poetry is especially rich for older children, who can find great depth in such descriptive phrases.

Rhythm also plays an important role in poetry's contribution to children. All ages enjoy and respond to a pulsating beat. Very young children, because of the topic, enjoy the rhythm of "Happiness," by A. A. Milne:

John had
Great Big
Waterproof
Boots on;

John had a
Great Big
Waterproof
Hat;

John had a
Great Big
Waterproof
Mackintosh—

And that
(Said John)
Is
That.†

In "Disobedience" the child exerts a certain amount of control over Mother. Again the rhythm is very satisfying.

*From *Hailstones and Halibut Bones* by Mary O'Neill. Copyright © 1961 by Mary Le Duc O'Neill. Reprinted by permission of Doubleday & Company, Inc.

†From the book *When We Were Very Young* by A. A. Milne. Decorations by E. H. Shepard. Copyright, 1924, by E. P. Dutton & Co., Inc. Renewal, 1952, by A. A. Milne. Published by E. P. Dutton & Co., Inc. and used with their permission and with permission of The Canadian Publishers, McClelland and Stewart Limited, Toronto.

James James
Morrison Morrison
Weatherby George Dupree
Took great
Care of his mother,
Though he was only three.

James James
Morrison Morrison
Weatherby George Dupree
Said to his mother,
"Mother," he said, said he:
"You must never go down to the end of town,
if you don't go down with me."*

Slightly older children respond to the rhythm in this humorous "King's Breakfast" by Milne.

THE KING'S BREAKFAST

The King asked
The Queen, and
The Queen asked
The Dairymaid:
"Could we have some butter for
The Royal slice of bread?"
The Queen asked
The Dairymaid,
The Dairymaid
Said, "Certainly,
I'll go and tell
The cow
Now
Before she goes to bed."

The Dairymaid
She curtsied,
And went and told
The Alderney:
"Don't forget the butter for
The Royal slice of bread."
The Alderney
Said sleepily:

"You'd better tell
His Majesty
That many people nowadays
Like marmalade
Instead."*

This is not to say that content, imagery, and rhythm are mutually exclusive or do not occur together in one piece of work. The attributes were isolated here for discussion purposes only.

There are many ways to categorize children's poetry. In other books for teachers or poetry anthologies classifications vary in specificity, and some emphasize form while others emphasize content. We shall use a general classification related to form. The terms narrative, lyric, and free verse cover most children's poetry, and the heading special poetry will be used to include other. Rhyme and verse is also an important classification.

Narrative poetry

One form of poetry that usually relies on a regular rhyming pattern is narrative poetry. The difference between narrative and lyric poetry lies in the content. The narrative tells a story. The stories might be of various types, such as epic or ballad, but they are characterized by a plot of some kind. Many poems in American collections describe frontier or Civil War life, or historical events in Europe prior to the settling of the United States. An example of the latter can be seen in two stanzas from a narrative poem by Robert Browning.

HOW THEY BROUGHT THE GOOD NEWS
FROM GHENT TO AIX

I sprang to the stirrup, and Joris, and he;
I galloped, Dirck galloped, we galloped all three;
"Good speed!" cried the watch, as the gate bolts undrew,
"Speed!" echoed the wall to us galloping through;
Behind shut the postern, the lights sank to rest,
And into the midnight we galloped abreast.

Not a word to each other; we kept the great pace
Neck by neck, stride by stride, never changing our place,
I turned in my saddle and made its girths tight,
Then shortened each stirrup, and set the pique right,
Rebuckled the cheek-strap, chained slacker the bit,
Nor galloped less steadily Roland a whit.[7]

*From the book *When We Were Very Young* by A. A. Milne. Decorations by E. H. Shepard. Copyright, 1924, by E. P. Dutton & Co., Inc. Renewal, 1952, by A. A. Milne. Published by E. P. Dutton & Co., Inc. and used with their permission and with permission of The Canadian Publishers, McClelland and Stewart Limited, Toronto.

This kind of content, which can be found in most narrative poetry, is appealing to older readers. Younger children delight in simpler stories, many of which have a humorous theme, like the one below by Florence Page Jacques.

THERE ONCE WAS A PUFFIN

Oh, there once was a Puffin
Just the shape of a muffin,
And he lived on an island
In the
     bright
        blue
           sea!

He ate little fishes,
That were most delicious,
And he had them for supper
And he
     had
        them
           for tea.

But this poor little Puffin.
He couldn't play nothin',
For he hadn't anybody
To
     play
        with
           at all.

So he sat on his island,
And he cried for awhile, and
He felt very lonely,
And he
     felt
        very
           small.

Then along came the fishes,
And they said, "If you wishes,
You can have us for playmates,
Instead
     of
        for
           tea!"

So they now play together,
In all sorts of weather,

> And the Puffin eats pancakes,
>   Like you
>   and
>   like
>   me.[8]

Other examples of narrative poetry are *The Owl and the Pussy Cat,* by Edward Lear, and *The Pied Piper of Hamelin,* by Robert Browning.

Since this type of poem tells a story, some children may wish to illustrate the events, perhaps placing them in sequence to produce a visual display. Such illustrations can also be joined in strip form to be rolled past an opening resembling a film or TV screen.

Lyric poetry

As the term indicates, this form of poetry is written in a rhythmic style, like a song. It is usually composed of stanzas, and expresses the poet's feelings and impressions rather than merely events. "Fireflies," by Carolyn Hall, is such a poem.

> Little lamps of the dusk,
>   You fly low and gold
> When the summer evening
>   Starts to unfold
> So that all the insects,
>   Now, before you pass,
> Will have light to see by
>   Undressing in the grass.
>
> But when the night has flowered,
>   Little lamps agleam,
> You fly over treetops
>   Following a dream.
> Men wonder from their windows
>   That a firefly goes so far—
> They do not know your longing
>   To be a shooting star.[9]

Most of the poetry children read is of this type. Topics are as varied as the possible rhyme and rhythm patterns.

Humor plays such a large role in children's poetry that some put it in a category by itself. "Galoshes" is an example of a humorous lyric poem.

> Suzie's galoshes
> Make splishes and sploshes,
> And slooshes and sloshes,

As Suzie steps slowly
Along in the slush.

They stamp and they tramp
On the ice and concrete,
They get stuck in the muck and the mud;
But Suzie likes much best to hear
The slippery slush
As it slooshes and sloshes,
And splishes and sploshes,
All round her galoshes!*

It should be apparent in these two examples how the lyric form can appeal to children of all ages, since length and vocabulary correspond to the concepts involved, thus adapting to a specific maturity level.

Some poetry of this type is especially effective for choral reading. When a particular poem appeals to a group of students, they can divide the stanzas appropriately and learn the pacing and accenting necessary for unison recitation. Sometimes the very nature of the content or treatment dictates changes of speakers. "The Wonderful Meadow," for example, is a poem where a conversation is obvious.

Over in the meadow, in the sand, in the sun,
Lived an old Mother-Toad and her little toady one.
"Leap," said the mamma. "I'll leap," said the one,
And she leaped with her mamma in the sand, in the sun.

Over in the meadow, where the water runs blue,
Lived an old Mother-Fish and her little fishes two.
"Swim," said the mamma. "We'll swim," said the two,
And they swam and they danced in the water so blue.[10]

Free verse

Free verse is not governed by rules of rhyme or rhythm. Stanzas (if they are used at all) and lines may vary to any degree to meet the needs of the poet's thought or emotion. This form lends itself to strong imagery, as in the following selection.

When the moon has colored half the house,
With the North Star at its height and the South Star setting,

I can feel the first motions of the warm air of spring
        In the singing of an insect at my green-silk window.*

Choosing words solely for their ability to express the desired idea adequately can result in a much more condensed writing than using words with certain phonemes or particular numbers of syllables. E. E. Cummings is widely regarded as a master of the art of free verse. An example follows.

why

do the
fingers

of the lit
tle once beau
tiful la

dy(sitting sew
ing at an o
pen window this
fine morning)fly

instead of dancing
are they possibly
afraid that life is
running away from
them(i wonder)or

isn't she a
ware that life(who
never grows old)
is always beau

tiful and
that nobod
y beauti

ful ev
er hur

ries†

The creative possibilities are infinite in free verse. Again, vocabulary, concepts, and length vary to suit different maturity and interest levels.

*From *Jade Mountain: A Chinese Anthology,* translated by Witter Bynner from the texts of Kiang Kang-Hu. Copyright 1929, renewed 1957 by Alfred A. Knopf, Inc. Reprinted by permission of the publisher.

†From *95 Poems,* © 1958, by E. E. Cummings. Reprinted by permission of Harcourt Brace
Jovanovich, Inc.

Free verse is especially good for helping children expand their vocabulary for purposes of effective, colorful description. On a rainy day, for example, a teacher might turn to *Miracles*, poems by children collected by Richard Lewis,* and read:

RAIN

The rain screws up its face
and falls to bits.
Then it makes itself again.
Only the rain can make itself again.

Adrian Keith Smith, age four, New Zealand

RAINDROPS

Raindrops shimmer down dirty glass
And measle the window pane.
The raindrops glide—leaving a motionless road.
Raindrops fall breaking themselves to tiney china and run away like
blood.

Ken Dickinson, age ten, New Zealand

PEARLS ON THE GRASS

After the beautiful rain,
The rocks shine under the sun,
Like the droplets on the cobweb
Amongst the green, green grass.

Greeta Mohanty, age thirteen, India

Then the teacher might ask the children what thoughts come to their minds on a rainy day. She can record the spontaneous thoughts of all participating members in such a way that they, too, have created their own rain poetry:

Rain is
   wet windows
   wobbly umbrellas
   running for papers in the wind;

   cold raincoats
   yellow street lights
   a *special* time for a fireplace.

484 *Copyright © 1966, by Richard Lewis. Reprinted by permission of Simon and Schuster.

Several other forms of poetry appear less frequently. We shall offer a few examples here that illustrate characteristics different from the types we have already discussed.

Japanese haiku is a special form without the rhyme or rhythm found in traditional Western poetry. It is guided by very strict rules. A haiku contains only seventeen syllables written in three lines of five, seven, and five syllables respectively. Every haiku should include a reference to a season of the year. Here are some examples from a collection translated by Peter Beilenson.

> A short summer night . . .
>   But in this solemn
>   Darkness
> One peony bloomed.
>
>   Buson

> Long the summer day . . .
>   Patterns on
>   The ocean sand . . .
> Our idle footprints.[11]
>
>   Shiki

Haiku is now very popular in many elementary schools, and this popularization has sometimes resulted in considerable deviation from the structure of the genuine form. Many collections include haiku poetry, but there are also complete books of this form, such as Harry Behn's *Cricket Songs* and *In a Spring Garden,* edited by Richard Lewis.

The limerick is a special form devoted exclusively to nonsense humor. It usually consists of five lines; the first, second, and fifth lines rhyme, and the third line rhymes with the fourth. Edward Lear, who wrote many limericks, helped to establish its popularity.

> There was an Old Man of Dumbree
> Who taught little owls to drink tea;
>   For he said, "To eat mice
>   Is not proper or nice,"
> That amiable Man of Dumbree.[12]

The following example is typical of the large number of limericks that have been published anonymously.

A housewife called out with a frown
When surprised by some callers from town,
  "In a minute or less
  I'll slip on a dress"—
But she slipped on the stairs and came down.[13]

Limericks have long had a place in the classroom, because they lead to the world of nonsense and fantasy and because children like to try their own versions. The rhythm pattern is easy to establish and the rhyme is apparent, even to the eye.

These forms of poetry, with their special structural features, offer practical ways for some teachers to help students get a "hold" on poetry. Some find it easier to begin with a precise form as a model; others find the structure too inhibiting, and feel more comfortable with free verse or lyric stanzas. Perhaps the content is more important than the form in the reaching out to some students. In these cases the teacher might offer collections based on content, such as those compiled by William Cole *(Rough Men, Tough Men: Poems of Action and Adventure* and *The Sea, Ships and Sailors, Poems, Songs, and Chanties),* which appeal especially to boys.

Whatever the emphasis, a vast array of poetry is available for children. Several collections, such as May Hill Arbuthnot's *Time for Poetry,* cut across age levels. Others are collected for a particular age. One collection of short poems for younger children is *Hello Day,* by Dorothy Aldis. Another for this age, but in narrative poetry form, is Aileen Fisher's *Listen, Rabbit.* A collection of contemporary poetry for older children is *Reflections on a Gift of Watermelon Pickle,* compiled by Stephen Dunning, Edward Lueders, and Hugh Smith. Several collections are specialized: haiku, nonsense, ballads, and the like. Richard Lewis collected an array of children's poetry in *Miracles: Poems by Children of the English-Speaking World.*

Once they have been introduced to some of the special types, many children attempt to create their own selections. The specific rules of the limerick, for example, are easily understood by older children, and some enjoy the challenge of organizing fun and nonsensical thoughts within those guidelines.

Rhyme and verse

Separate from poetry in the formal literary sense are rhymes and jingles. Many rhymes represent another part of folklore. The most obvious examples are the Mother Goose rhymes.

  Hickory, dickory, dock!
  The mouse ran up the clock;
    The clock struck one,

> And down he run,
> Hickory, dickory, dock!

Humorous nonsense rhymes also belong in this section. A favorite of the young who are just beginning to separate reality from the impossible is Gelett Burgess's "Purple Cow."

> I never saw a Purple Cow,
>   I never hope to see one;
> But I can tell you, anyhow,
>   I'd rather see than be one.[14]

Once the child begins to read for himself, both the auditory and the visual aspects of Eletelephone can be delightful.

> Once there was a elephant,
> Who tried to use the telephant—
> No! Now I mean an elephone
> Who tried to use the telephone—
> (Dear me! I am not certain quite
> That even now I've got it right.)
>
> Howe'er it was, he got his trunk
> Entangled in the telephunk;
> The more he tried to get it free,
> The louder buzzed the telephee—
> (I fear I'd better drop the song
> Of elephop and telephong!)*

The slightly older reader is challenged by this excerpt from "The Modern Hiawatha," by George A. Strong:

> . . . With his skin he made the mittens,
> Made them with the fur-side inside,
> Made them with the skin-side outside;
> He, to keep the warm side inside,
> Put the cold side, skin-side, outside; . . .[15]

Many other rhymes and verses have tongue-twister nonsense qualities like this.

We have treated rhymes and jingles here as separate from the main body of poetry, but rarely does this happen in poetry collections. The question of classification is not a serious one. It is more important that a smorgasbord of poetry be presented to children frequently enough that they are able to find offerings to their taste. When poetry becomes a part of their daily life, we may see them "Take Sky."

TAKE SKY

Now think of words. Take sky
And ask yourself just why—
Like sun, moon, star and cloud—
It sounds so well out loud,
And pleases so the sight
When printed black on white.
Take syllable and thimble:
The sound of them is nimble.
Take balsam, fir, and pine:
Your woodland smell and mine.
Take kindle, blaze and flicker—
What lights the hearth fire quicker?
Take bucket, spring and dip
Cold water to your lip.
Three words we fear but form:
Gale, twister, thunderstorm;
Others that simply shake
Are tremble, temblor, quake.
But granite, stone and rock;
Too solid, they, to shock.
Put honey, bee, and flower
With sunny shade and shower;
Put wild with bird and wing,
Put bird with song and sing.
Aren't paddle, trail and camp
The cabin and the lamp?
Now look at words of rest—
Sleep, quiet, calm, and blest;
At words we learn in youth—
Grace, skill, ambition, truth;
At words of lifelong need—
Faith, courage, strength, and deed;
Deep rooted words that say
Love, hope, dream, yearn, and pray;
Light-hearted words—girl, boy,
Live, laugh, play, share, enjoy.
October, April, June—
Come late and gone too soon.
Remember words are life;
Child, husband, mother, wife;
Remember, and I'm done;
Words taken one by one
Are poems as they stand—

Shore, beacon, harbor, land;
Brook, river, mountain, vale,
Crow, rabbit, otter, quail;
Oak, apple, water, snow,
Wind, weather, flood and floe.
Like light across the lawn
Are morning, sea and dawn;
Words of the green earth growing—
Seed, soil and farmer sowing.
Like wind upon the mouth
Sad, summer, rain, and south.
Amen. Put not asunder
Man's first word: wonder . . . wonder . . .*

Like folk tales, many rhymes and jingles reflect the culture from which they come. Helping children to record some of their jump-rope and game rhymes can serve several purposes. It legitimizes and gives recognition to a "poetry" they already know. It offers opportunities for comparison of different versions of the same rhyme, and it permits visual examination of the rhyme pattern, which can be used as a model, if desired, for new rhymes created by the children.

DEVELOPING THE LITERATURE PROGRAM—CLASSROOM APPLICATION

Up to this point we have described children's literature in reasonably functional classifications, but it is still on the shelves. How does it reach the children? Leland Jacobs speaks of "giving children literature."[16] How can it be done in a way that inspires children to open the doors wide for themselves? Having literature available and making adult appreciation of it known is necessary, but not sufficient. Says William Iverson,

> You do not simply love literature, you teach it. You know the kind of joy you exemplify comes from learning. You know a child can't appreciate what he never learned to know. So you work hard to teach him the basic skills of word identification and sentence patterning. But you notice that increasingly these basic language skills are not enough. So, wisely, you add early to basic skill training the sustaining rewards of literary content. You do not believe that enjoyment of literature just naturally issues out of the basic skill training. You plan for literature. You work toward it. You have a program. You do not believe for a moment that appreciation of literature can ever grow out of the same materials you use in your basic skills program. The outcomes desired in basic reading skills and in literary appreciation are different. The materials must be different. You know that you cannot adapt material to serve for exercises in basic skill building and provide for solid growth in the enjoyment of literature at the same time. You know that you need stories, poems, plays, biographies chosen because they are literature, not adapted for linguistic calisthenics.[17]

*Copyright 1961, 1962 by David McCord. From *Take Sky* by David McCord, by permission
489 of Little, Brown and Company.

At this point a review of the purposes for literature may help to direct our working knowledge of children's literature into a full, vital, balanced literature program with the thrust that Iverson describes, yet with the student as the central concern. How do we plan for the two major purposes?

1. Provide pleasure, by offering experiences of
   a. The joy of language
   b. An appreciation of beauty
2. Provide knowledge, by developing
   a. Insight into man's behavior
   b. An awareness of people (and other living things), events, and ideas not present in one's own life space
   c. An awareness of man as an integral part of a changing world
   d. An awareness of the potential of language as a powerful means of human expression

To achieve these two purposes, pleasure and knowledge, one must ask what this literature program would look like in the daily classroom. What would the children and the teacher be doing if they were meeting these ends?

To discuss either goal, it is necessary to sketch briefly a (far from exhaustive) range of classroom activities for an elementary school literature experience. On any given day

A TEACHER MIGHT BE

1. Telling a story or reciting a poem to all or a part of the class
2. Reading a story or poem
3. Playing a record or audiotape of a story or poem
4. Showing slides, a film, or filmstrip of a story or poem while the children watch, listen, and participate

THE CHILDREN MIGHT BE

1. Role playing, manipulating puppets, or in some other way dramatizing a story or poem
2. Illustrating a story or poem with arts and crafts
3. Retelling a story to peers who have not heard it
4. Reading in chorus or reciting prose or poetry
5. Reading to each other
6. Reading independently
7. Writing responses to literature or original compositions
8. Discussing responses to literature (published or self-made)

This range provides a frame of reference for discussing the stated goals.

Provide pleasure (affective domain)

This is both an immediate and a long-term goal of literature. The teacher hopes that by building a backlog of pleasant encounters with literature, she is helping a student toward long-lived enjoyment and appreciation of prose and poetry. It is easier to begin by describing what such a program is not. A literature program that keeps this affective goal as a high priority is *not* characterized by

1. Children competing to see who has read the "most" books (with visual evidence of who is "ahead")
2. A large number of assigned factual book reports
3. Assigned memorization of poetry
4. A requirement that a certain number of books, which represent a variety of literature chosen by the teacher, must be read
5. Mandatory activities, such as making dioramas, puppets, illustrations, and the like for the entire class
6. Forced attendance for story time with a sitting upright posture required
7. Disapproval of children who subvocalize or move lips while reading independently
8. Teacher talk occupying over 50 percent of class time
9. Mandatory reporting of private thoughts and feelings about every book read

Such a program *is* characterized by

1. A considerable amount of free choice selecting literature to read, listen to, or illustrate
2. Simultaneous alternatives for forms of response to literature (drama, art, discussion, etc.)
3. A wide variety of reading levels and interests represented in a more than sufficient number of books for the class size
4. Discussions around open-ended questions or statements about a literature selection
5. Children listening, reading, talking spontaneously in postures that feel natural and comfortable
6. Frequent options for individual and small group projects
7. Adults who listen sincerely to a child's ideas, opinions, and descriptions indicating respect and regard for the child
8. Language models representing a variety of dialects, styles, and degrees of formality (via other persons, records, tapes, etc.)
9. A higher percentage of student talk than student listening (individual days vary according to immediate goals, but this should represent an average over time)
10. A higher percentage of active projects than passive receiving

Enjoyable experiences with literature are promoted by a classroom program that is, first, student centered. Literature needs no carefully structured selling job; the task is to make a good match of "person and print." A teacher can raise and extend a child's literature fare *after* he has discovered that stories and poems unlock an exciting universe of thought and feeling to share or to hold inside.

491

Provide knowledge (cognitive domain)

It is impossible to transmit all available knowledge to students. A more effective approach is to help students acquire basic competencies that man uses to deal with knowledge.

Communication competencies have already been dealt with elsewhere in this book. Literature provides fertile means of developing these competencies, but that is not the subject of this discussion. The concern here is to help the student learn how to learn.

The literature of a society can play an important role in educating for thinking because it provides a common orientation. Since one cannot think without something to think *about,* content is necessary for the process of thinking. What content will be likely to be most useful in the individual's education?

To answer this question, we turn to the disciplines that contribute to thinking and language development. We are aware (from Chapters 2 and 4) that the direct experiences of children should be drawn upon to help them move toward generalizations. According to Piaget, children in the five-to-twelve-year-old range fall primarily in the preoperational and the concrete operations stages, with the more mature children entering the formal operations stage. The intellectual demands we make of these children should be related to actual experience, whether past or present, direct or vicarious. "Hearing about" does not necessarily result in "knowing," because words have limited meaning without experience. Using this criterion as a guideline, we should begin with content that has been part of every member's ordinary life experience, such as eating and playing.

Psychoanalytic theory, a second source of guidance, tells us that to operate effectively as human beings we must first "know and accept ourselves," a principle that is easily compatible with the principle that knowledge should be built on a base of experience. It suggests the value of discovering a variety of acceptable ways of dealing with everyday life situations.

Anthropology, sociology, and psychology have helped us become aware of certain common denominators in human behavior. If men do have like needs, and there are similarities in the ways they cope with problems, this indicates the content relevant to all, for the present and in the future. Literature is composed of reflections of human behavior and is one of the most abundant sources of content fitting the purpose of understanding self and others.

This should help the teacher considerably in his planning. Instead of narrower purposes, such as being sure children read both nonfiction and fiction, he has a broader goal: to help children gain self-knowledge and discover ways of functioning in their environment. If balancing fiction with nonfiction seems important to that end, that will be included, but such a balance should not be an end in itself.

A literature program operating to fulfill the goals of providing knowledge is characterized by

1. A considerable freedom of selection for students, with guidance through individual conferences whenever possible
2. Daily opportunities for various kinds of responses to literature (discussion, art, drama, etc.)
3. Concrete experiences in conjunction with literature selections, to give meaning to the experiences of others in order to relate them to our own
4. Considerable effort by the teacher to get to know the students well, so that his program planning is based on knowledge of the students' experiential background, not "what they *should* know"
5. A high degree of active participation rather than passive receiving

Now that we have translated the purposes of literature into classroom behaviors for both students and teachers, we need to discuss in more detail the parts of the program. The two basic components of the program are the environment and the activities. It is difficult to separate the two, even for discussion purposes, but certain environmental aspects apply to the total program and merit special attention.

Environment

The right environment for literature and response is an important part of any program. The atmosphere and the physical setting can offer support and comfort or can inhibit and restrict.

The atmosphere should communicate an attitude that children's interests and means of expression as they presently exist are accepted and acceptable. To be a confident language user and explorer of literature, the child must feel approval of his choices and of his present level of accomplishment. If adults convey the impression of understanding the child's verbal expression and provide daily opportunities for real decision making, the child is more likely to gain an image of adequacy relative to these skills. The underlying principle here is that childhood behavior is acceptable, not substandard. Rather than "It's getting better, pretty soon you'll be able to do it perfectly," adults should offer a "now-acceptance" response: "This is a good job."

After this feeling of adequacy is established, the adults can attend to modeling language for expanded vocabulary and appropriate grammatical patterns as discussed in Chapters 6 through 9. Children's choices can be guided toward unexplored areas using their strengths to aid in reducing areas of weakness. The known thus becomes the path to the unknown.

Another aspect of this atmosphere is modeling behavior. The teacher, other adults, and older peers in the classroom who seek books for pleasure and information may be "telling" the children more about the purposes of literature than any words can.

Physical setting is important. Adults can create an inviting, comfortable atmosphere for a wide range of interests and stages of maturity. The reading area can be set up with a combination of couches, rocking chairs, mattresses, pillows, and rugs. Reading and writing need not be confined to stereotyped sitting postures. In an informal setting these activities will seem natural to children.

What is suggested by this reading environment and the children in it about the nature of their teacher's literature program?

The very location of the reading area can affect its use. To maximize its importance and function, establish a reading *center* rather than a reading *corner*. (Some teachers prefer to locate the center away from the traffic pattern, to provide quiet and privacy.)

The children can help to develop and vary the physical environment. For example, making a quilt for the mattress or couch is one way for children to make the reading center their own. They can also help select books from the main library source, arrange displays of the newer selections, and make illustrations to highlight certain favorites.

Activities

This discussion of activities is not exhaustive. Other specialized resources will be recommended for such purposes. Here we simply intend to describe how to match the purposes of literature with specific child-centered activities.

e thinks about how children are most often "given
a picture of the teacher reading to the class. This is
m for offering literature to elementary children, but
ues to literature must not be forgotten. The most
ns of conveying a story is simply to tell it. Story
e teacher to give of herself and convey a personal
ure through a story she especially likes. Moreover,
leasant hours for children, and add an important
orld of books. Consult resources such as Ruth
he Storyteller for help on choice of story and story-

Return this card for
your free listing of
inservice training
materials:

name

institution

address

ZIP

SELECTED TITLES AND AUTHORS AVAILABLE

PIAGET AND READING/Gilbert Voyat,
Loren Weybright & Ruth Adams
CREATING AN OPEN CLASSROOM/
Lillian Weber
WITHIN SCHOOLS-WITHOUT SCHOOLS/
John Holt
THE CONSPIRACY TO LEARN/Neil Postman
THE TEACHER AND THE OPEN CLASSROOM/
Gloria Channon
ON ACCOUNTABILITY/Leon Lessinger
TRAVELING FIRST CLASS ON THE TITANIC/
Jonathan Kozol
TOWARDS A HUMANISTIC EDUCATION/
Robert Pollock
INNER CITY BLUES/Nat Hentoff

e is being developed by a community resource person,
urce personnel in your school community could pro-

The luxury of sitting back and listening to a story (told or read) should not be for young children only. Children who do not yet sail with ease through books that interest them especially need the pleasant experience of enjoying literature without having to struggle to decode it.

495

Story reading. The literature medium used most in the primary classroom is story reading. Most texts on children's literature discuss techniques for reading to groups; one valuable source of information is *Children's Literature in the Elementary School.*[19] It will suffice here merely to remind you to be aware of your audience at all times. The children themselves are the most accurate barometer as to how long the story should be and what types of literature are appropriate for their age level.

If a story-reading session is to be compatible with principles of learning discussed at the beginning of this section, a certain amount of time should be spent establishing a mental set before the story is read. The particular children, the book, and any specific purposes will dictate the direction, duration, and depth of this preface. In some instances it is effective to ask the same major question posed in the book, to stimulate thought in that direction. In other cases it is useful to clarify definitions or to determine the backgrounds the children bring to this story (if you do not already know this).

The advisability of leading or allowing discussion during the reading is a matter of controversy. Some teachers feel that any discussion distracts from the continuity of the plot and from the flow of the language. Others feel that any attempts by children to make the story their own through verbalization will enhance the overall learning experience. There are probably occasions appropriate to each approach and to insist on one exclusively is very likely to disregard the varying needs of the children. One moment children may be silently entranced by Milne's

> The more it
> SNOWS-tiddely-pom,
> The more it
> GOES-tiddely-pom
> The more it
> GOES-tiddely-pom
> On
> Snowing.
>
> And nobody
> KNOWS-tiddely-pom,
> How cold my
> TOES-tiddely-pom
> How cold my
> TOES-tiddely-pom
> Are
> Growing.*

*From the book *The House at Pooh Corner* by A. A. Milne. Copyright, 1928 by E. P. Dutton & Co., Inc. Renewal, ©, 1956 by A. A. Milne. Published by E. P. Dutton & Co., Inc. and used with their permission and with permission of The Canadian Publishers, McClelland and Stewart Limited, Toronto.

Later in the day they may demand their separate turns to discover "Where's Wallace?" (Hilary Knight) and to guess where he will be next.

If you find that insufficient time is your reason for not allowing individual participation during story sharing it may be a clue that you should re-evaluate the size of the story group. Some teachers arrange to have assistants or parents help with the literature program, in order to offer small-group story sessions, where more choices are available and more personalized attention may be given. Literature is a very personal experience. If you serve it only as a banquet for thirty, you may dull some appetites.

Story reading need not be solely the responsibility of adults. Children who can read independently and volunteer to do so can read to small groups of other children. An ungraded or cross-age-grouped classroom lends itself well to this.

Picture reading is also a form of story reading. Since it usually involves the youngest children, very small groups are desirable, to allow for personalized attention and spontaneous participation.

Poetry reading. Although it has sometimes been treated as the frosting, poetry reading is an essential part of a child's encounter with literature, and deserves its equal status in the phrase "prose and poetry." Traditionally, however, it is the form of literature that has experienced the greatest rejection. To avoid this occurrence, we must look at possible reasons. Adults frequently impose inappropriate poetry upon children. Leland Jacobs speaks of the unfortunate use of poetry *about* children, but not *for* children. Not only does such poetry not speak to their interests and needs, it often preaches moral sermons. Seek poetry that interests and delights *children,* not poetry you think they should like or know.

Forced memorization has often been a part of children's encounter with poetry. Memorization of a poem of personal choice or spontaneous memorization caused by the impact of a particular stanza or poem can produce much pleasure, but forced memorization often results only in resentment and dislike for poetry. Mouthing words not one's own, which have no personal meaning, can be a very distasteful, even an embarrassing, experience. On the other hand, the infectious rhythm in a poem such as Milne's "Hoppity" can result in spontaneous memorization by some of its listeners, and can be very exciting.

> Christopher Robin goes
> Hoppity, hoppity,
> Hoppity, hoppity, hop.
> Whenever I tell him
> Politely to stop it, he
> Says he can't possibly stop.
>
> If he stopped hopping, he couldn't go anywhere,
> Poor little Christopher

Couldn't go anywhere . . .
That's why he *always* goes
Hoppity, hoppity,
Hoppity,
Hoppity,
Hop.*

The more bits of poetry you carry in your head, the better prepared you are for those moments when an expression of humor, beauty, humanness, or rhythm would improve, change, or complete a given situation. Equally important are those at-the-fingertips references containing poetry about various groups, situations, and relationships.

Literature through other media. As mentioned earlier, literature experiences should not be confined to the prose and poetry read by teachers and students. Children can discover literature through a variety of other media.

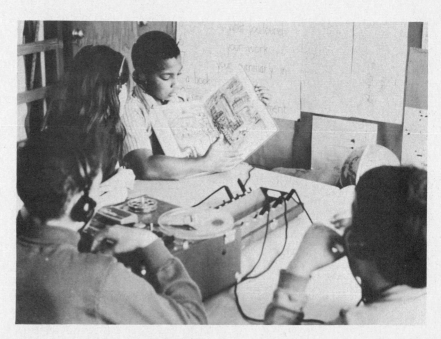

How are media being used to enhance the children's literature experience? What aspect of this experience might have been developed by the children?

This broader concept is being applied to school libraries today, with the result that many have been renamed media centers. In such a center a child may not only browse through a wide variety of books, he may also be

*From the book *When We Were Very Young* by A. A. Milne. Decorations by E. H. Shepard. Copyright, 1924, by E. P. Dutton & Co., Inc. Renewal, 1952, by A. A. Milne. Published by E. P. Dutton & Co., Inc. and used with their permission and with permission of The Canadian Publishers, McClelland and Stewart Limited, Toronto.

introduced to or be reminded of certain pieces of literature through films, filmstrips, film loops, 35 mm. slides, tapes, records, or large photographs. Many of the small machines can be operated by the children themselves, so individual and small-group listening or watching is easily managed. Children, in turn, can use one of the media forms to introduce literature selections to other children. Listening posts can accommodate several children enjoying a story simultaneously.

Receiver response. We have referred to this literature program several times as "literature plus response," because the program depends on the receiver (reader or listener). The teacher has an important role in providing many opportunities, spontaneous and planned, for receiver response. This role does not include prying or forcing children to reveal private thoughts, but it does include suggesting ideas, asking open-ended questions, and providing opportunities for varied modes of response.

Activities that encourage response can also be termed *surrounding activities,* since they occur "around" the story (before, after, and during), not just after. Such activities include open-ended questions, drama (role playing, puppets, etc.), art activities, and creative writing. Most of these activities are self-explanatory or are clarified in the following section, but questioning skills need special mention. The open-ended question has no single correct answer. Instead, it calls for a problem-solving approach on the part of the children. Strictly factual recall of the story has limited value; facts should be called forth only when they are related to the solution of a new problem. The goal of open-ended questioning is to transfer the principles involved, not the specific facts in one instance. In real life it is necessary to solve today's problems on the basis of yesterday's experience. You can offer children a great deal of this type of experience if you are alert to the opportunities.

Instead of asking who was in the story and what the main character did to solve his problem, pose interpretive and applicative type questions such as:

How do you think _____ felt when he _____?
What else might _____ have done when _____?
What would you have done when _____?
If you were _____, how would your story have ended?

Study Chapter 11 for further discussion of questioning strategies and comprehension levels to use with literature selections.

In the following discussion we present sample program ideas based on one literature selection, to illustrate application of the preceding principles. There are a number of plans, to show the kinds and levels of participation possible in a program designed to accomplish the purposes of literature. It should be understood, however, that you should not try to combine all these practices at once; instead, use only those that are relevant to the literature goals at the time and that are compatible with your literature program. The specific suggestions might serve best as initial ideas to modify in relation to your own needs.

The sample program plans are based on *Tico and the Golden Wings* by Leo Lionni.*

(¶ 1) Many years ago I knew a little bird whose name was Tico. He would sit on my shoulder and tell me all about the flowers, the ferns, and the tall trees. Once Tico told me this story about himself.

(¶ 2) I don't know how it happened, but when I was young I had no wings. I sang like the other birds and I hopped like them, but I couldn't fly.

(¶ 3) Luckily my friends loved me. They flew from tree to tree and in the evening they brought me berries and tender fruits gathered from the highest branches.

(¶ 4) Often I asked myself, "Why can't I fly like the other birds? Why can't I, too, soar through the big blue sky over villages and treetops?"

(¶ 5) And I dreamt that I had golden wings, strong enough to carry me over the snowcapped mountains far away.

(¶ 6) One summer night I was awakened by a noise near by. A strange bird, pale as a pearl, was standing behind me. "I am the wishingbird," he said. "Make a wish and it will come true."

(¶ 7) I remembered my dreams and with all my might I wished I had a pair of golden wings. Suddenly there was a flash of light and on my back there were wings, golden wings, shimmering in the moonlight. The wishingbird had vanished.

(¶ 8) Cautiously I flapped my wings. And then I flew. I flew higher than the tallest tree. The flower patches below looked like stamps scattered over the countryside and the river like a silver necklace lying in the meadows. I was happy and I flew well into the day.

(¶ 9) But when my friends saw me swoop down from the sky, they frowned on me and said, "You think you are better than we are, don't you, with those golden wings. You wanted to be *different.*" And off they flew without saying another word.

(¶ 10) Why had they gone? Why were they angry? Was it *bad* to be different? I could fly as high as the eagle. Mine were the most beautiful wings in the world. But my friends had left me and I was very lonely.

(¶ 11) One day I saw a man sitting in front of a hut. He was a basketmaker and there were baskets all around him. There were tears in his eyes. I flew onto a branch from where I could speak to him.

(¶ 12) "Why are you sad?" I asked. "Oh, little bird, my child is sick and I am poor. I cannot buy the medicines that would make him well." "How can I help him?" I thought. And suddenly I knew. "I will give him one of my feathers."

(¶ 13) "How can I thank you!" said the poor man happily. "You have saved my child. But look! Your wing!" Where the golden feather had been there was a real black feather, as soft as silk.

(¶ 14) From that day, little by little, I gave my golden feathers away and black feathers appeared in their place. I bought many presents: three new puppets for a poor puppeteer . . . a spinning wheel to spin the yarn for an old woman's shawl . . . a compass for a fisherman who got lost at sea . . . and when I gave my last golden feathers to a beautiful bride, my wings were as black as India ink.

(¶ 15) I flew to the big tree where my friends gathered for the night. Would they welcome me?

(¶ 16) They chirped with joy. "Now you are just like us," they said. We all huddled close together. But I was so happy and excited I couldn't sleep. I remembered the basketmaker's son, the old woman, the puppeteer, and all the others I had helped with my feathers. "Now my wings are black," I thought, "and yet I am not like my friends. We are *all* different. Each for his own memories, and his own invisible golden dreams."

SAMPLE LESSON

Suggestions for the Literature Plus Response Program.

I. Before reading the story
   A. Discussion questions (on or before the day of the story)
      1. "Sometimes people feel bad if they are not like their friends. What is one way you would change yourself to be like others, if you could?"
      2. "Have you ever wanted something very much and then gotten it, and found that it didn't turn out to be as wonderful as you thought it would be? Tell us about it."
   B. Role playing: "If you had a gang of friends (designate group) and you (designate *one*) were different because of _____, how would you feel when you noticed the difference? When they teased you?"
      1. Set up an ugly duckling situation. Several members similar in appearance gang up on the one who is different. Rotate several times, so that each of the "gang" also plays the duckling. "How did _____ act differently when he was in the gang from the way he acted when he was the duckling?" Re-enact the situation to develop coping behavior for such a situation.
II. During the story
   following ¶ 2
      1. "If he could not fly, what things would Tico not be able to do that other birds can do?" (Probe this idea for as many detailed responses as the group can manage, considering food, shelter, safety from enemies, and the like.)
      2. "How could he get food?" (If not already discussed.)
   following ¶ 6
      1. "What will his wish be?"

following ¶ 7

1. "What will Tico do, now that he is able to fly?"

following ¶ 8

1. "How will his friends feel about his getting wings?"

following ¶ 9

1. "How did his friends feel when they said that?"

2. "Why would they feel that way?"

following ¶ 10

1. "What could he do so he wouldn't be sad and lonely?" (Probe for many alternatives.)

following ¶ 12

1. "How will a gold feather help this man?"

2. "Will the bird still be able to fly?"

following ¶ 13

1. "What has happened each time he gave away a gold feather?"

following ¶ 14

1. "What is happening to Tico?"

2. "How do you think he feels now that all of his feathers are black?"

3. "If he can't help any more people with gold feathers, what will he do now?"

following ¶ 15

1. "How do you think his friends will feel?"

following ¶ 16

1. "Now they all have black wings, but he said, 'We are all different.' What did he mean?"

III. Follow-up discussion. If the questions are not used during the reading of the stories, many of them could be used for a discussion after the story. The discussion questions under the heading "Before reading the story" can also be used in a follow-up discussion.

A. Questions dependent upon knowing the story

1. "Now that you know what happened, if you were Tico at the beginning of the story and could have one wish, what would it be?"

2. "Tico's friends were all angry that he had such beautiful wings. If they had been happy for him instead, how might the story have ended?"

3. "If Tico had not thought to give his feathers as presents, what else could he have done?"

4. "How might the story have ended if Tico's friends had not welcomed him back?"

B. Drama

1. Children create and roleplay situations where the subjects would have a need and be the recipients of Tico's feathers.

2. Children create and roleplay different reactions to Tico's gain of golden wings.

C. Art

   1. Some children might enjoy illustrating one or more situations in the story. The availability of "gold" in various forms (such as gold paint, gold gum-backed paper, gold foil) could increase motivation and interest in such a project.

   2. Illustrations can be used for individual enjoyment or for a group project. With young children, several different illustrations can be made and used for recalling the sequence of the story. Older children could connect several illustrations into a long strip to be rolled through a TV screen box while students retell the story. A tape recording could be made for a soundtrack, to replace "live" voices.

D. Creative writing

   1. Some of the discussion questions could be used as starters for students to write alternative endings.

   2. A group could be guided through the components of the plot, in order to create a parallel story.
      a. Who was the main character?
      b. What other animal could the story be about? (camel)
      c. What was the problem?
      d. What problem would a (camel) have? (no hump)
      e. How was the problem solved?
      f. How could the (camel) solve his problem?
      g. What new problem was created by the solution?
      h. How did Tico solve it?
      i. How could (camel) solve a similar problem?
      j. How would your new story end?

CONTRIBUTIONS OF LITERATURE TO THE READING-LANGUAGE PROGRAM COMPONENTS

Earlier in this chapter we made a distinction between literacy and literary goals. Iverson reminded us that the materials needed for building skills in the reading process are different from those needed for reading for information, pleasure, and personal development. In the independent reader's school program, the place of literature is obvious: he can use literature to open doors commensurate with his interests, maturity, and pace. Literature also has much to offer the child who has not yet reached the "reading-to-learn" stage. Several important areas of a complete reading and language program receive direct support from literature experiences:

Conceptual development
Vocabulary and labels expansion
Awareness of a variety of syntactical patterns and flexibility of style
Awareness of the symbolic function of language

Flexibility of style and usage
Decoding and encoding skills

Most good literature selections serve many purposes. That is, a book selected to expand a child's vocabulary would probably also add to or reinforce certain concepts, employ a variety of syntactical patterns, and provide possibilities for building comprehension. Some selections, however, seem to have special capabilities in certain areas. We shall discuss each area in detail and categorize selections on the basis of their contributions to the reading-language program. Skills of comprehension have been discussed in detail in Chapter 11 and in the discussion about questions designed to develop reader response.

Concept development

It could be said that all books enhance concept development for the right child at the right time, but certain books have a sequential development for a clarity of presentation that make them helpful teaching tools. *The Storm Book,* by Charlotte Zolotow, is such a tool.

Another reason for using literature selections to develop concepts is that they provide opportunities to deal with issues that otherwise might not surface. With any age at the elementary level, a teacher might feel a need to direct children's thoughts to the subject of the similarities existing among men regardless of superficial differences. *People Are Important,* by Eva Knox Evans, would supply a base for a number of discussions or projects. Several other books on different levels of critical thinking could follow the introductory selection, to any degree or depth the children desired.

Literature selections can also serve to increase children's understanding of concepts by directing experience or through purely factual books, as previously described under "Informational Books." Opportunities to contrast realistic attributes with those confined to the world of fantasy are offered by Dr. Seuss in *If I Ran the Zoo,* which is a delightful accompaniment to a zoo trip and to a factual study of its animals. *The Zoo for Mister Muster,* by A. Lobel, can provide another kind of supplemental information.

The choice of book(s) for concept development is extremely important, since the book may not be effective by itself. If the child has not had sufficient experience to give meaning to the material, or if the material only repeats what he already knows, it cannot serve the desired purpose.

Vocabulary expansion

Every literature selection can expand vocabulary at some level of language development, even picture books. Some selections offer models of rich descriptive language, while others contain vocabulary of a specialized area.

Wingfrin and Topple, by Evans G. Valens, Jr., is in the former category. Finger-painted illustrations reinforce the imagery of sections like

> "They made your fins too long," they said.
>
> Indeed they were, twelve times as long as ordinary fins; when Topple spread them they caught hold like anchors, tripped him, rolled him belly up.[20]

A focus on description itself exists in *The Blind Men and the Elephant* by Lillian Quigley, which enables readers or listeners to begin to appreciate that a particular description stems from a particular point of view. To continue consideration of this idea, an interesting object could be brought into the classroom for children to describe "from their own point of view." It must not be forgotten that vocabulary expansion occurs individually from child to child as well as from teacher to child. Models for sentence stretching, for adding detailed description to basic information, are offered in books such as *Hit or Myth,* by J. Riddell.

Books on specialized areas can be found for just about any subject area. The Walter Farley books develop terminology related to horses; other subjects of interest might be science fiction, medicine, or baseball. Biographies are frequently useful for acquainting readers with specialized fields. Poetry, of course, provides a universe of descriptive vocabulary ranging from "The fog comes on little cat feet" to very abstract imagery for the older reader.

Variety in syntactical patterns

The literature the child is currently encountering can be used to demonstrate models of syntactical patterns. Whether the teacher is working with an individual around the book he is reading or has just finished or with a group around a book known to all, he can find examples of principles that enhance expression in language, especially in written form. There should be no implication that any one form is correct or incorrect; the goal is communication effectiveness.

There are several ways teachers can help students examine and vary the syntax of a given sentence, increase their understanding of the functions of language, and work toward maximum personal effectiveness in the use of language. The University of Nebraska's *Curriculum for English* outlines specific lessons for this purpose in considerable depth.[21]

A number of approaches are available for developing sentence patterns. Transforming sentences from one form to another can be done very simply and is appropriate for the primary grade level. In Ruth Krauss's *Is This You?* questions could be changed to both declarative and negative statements throughout the book, for example.[22] Shifting phrases to new positions within the sentence could be attempted on extracts from works like *Beezus and Ramona,* by Beverly Cleary:

If Ramona drank lemonade through a straw, she blew into the straw as hard as she could to see what would happen.

Children should experiment to see what sounds right and what doesn't. Substitution of phrases is especially appropriate for use with younger children, since "finding another way to say it" does not require a particular level of language maturity. A sentence such as this one from *The Saturdays,* by Elizabeth Enright, can be presented to children for paraphrasing:

> When they had eaten all they could . . . they began to wonder what they should do next.

The class should discuss whether suggested substitutions contain all the essential components of the sentence. Variations of this sentence might range from "After they ate, they wondered what to do" to much more complex versions, but the meaning must be retained.

Another form of variation is to condense the sentence by eliminating redundancies. Older children's writing might resemble the following: "A lady and a chauffeur in a large shiny black car stopped in front of the lunchroom and the chauffeur helped the lady out of the rear door." Robert McCloskey's line from *Homer Price* could be offered in contrast:

> Just then a large shiny black car stopped in front of the lunchroom and a chauffeur helped a lady out of the rear door.

There are several ways to vary a sentence by expansion. One obvious method is modification. By answering the How, What, Where kinds of questions, children can expand a statement like "He could see the peach" to a version more like Roald Dahl's:

> Not far away, in the middle of the garden, he could see the giant peach towering over everything else. *(James and the Giant Peach)*

Adding conditions is a second means of expansion. Sentences like the following can be used to illustrate how important a conditional phrase can be to complete understanding of a thought.

> Now that Mr. Gruber mentioned it, he did remember his Aunt Lucy taking him to a firework display. (Michael Bond, *More About Paddington*)

Expansion can also be accomplished by combining simple sentences into a complex sentence. A sentence from Louise Fitzhugh's *Harriet the Spy* can be separated for purposes of demonstration:

> The bell rang.
> Pinky Whitehead jumped up.
> He ran down the aisle.

After making their own combined version of these thoughts, children might refer to the author's version:

When the bell rang Pinky Whitehead jumped up and ran down the aisle.

These methods of varying syntactic patterns must be adapted to fit the particular language maturity level of the children involved. The important point is that in addition to classroom models of speech and written language, literature provides ready-made models for language development. Children can examine the alternatives that were available to an author to convey a particular idea, examine the choice he made, and explore the reasons for that choice. Perhaps they will agree that was the most effective choice, perhaps they will not; but this kind of evaluation is one way learning takes place. In other instances students might follow the reverse process; that is, they might examine literature for illustrations of certain principles in language. At any rate, the world of literature offers a panoramic mirror of the language of the society, and so its potential approaches that of the language itself.

Symbolic function

Throughout the K–6 educational experience, teachers should watch and plan for opportunities to discover and rediscover the symbolic representation of experience called language. In his early development a child may recall a story as the one about "the ducks who walked down the street behind their mother" *(Make Way for Ducklings)*. Just as he does with cereal boxes and record jackets, he begins with the content material, using only external clues. Later, however, as the child begins the primary grades, he will associate certain names, phrases, or sections of a story, as a result of any number of possible visual or auditory cues. The context of the story may trigger "Rain makes applesauce" after the first few introductions of that line, for instance. Children will come to recognize additional cues to meaning when they see words spaced far apart denoting loneliness, tiredness, or a slowed pace, in contrast to bold print and color designating excitement, loudness, or accelerated pace.

In a more advanced stage they examine the origin and makeup of words, so that a word such as recreation, which has been read many times, suddenly becomes re-creation. At that time a child may begin to appreciate the power of language through symbols, from detailed, mysterious descriptions to highly emotional scenes. The understanding of the symbolic function is established in an early period and continues to grow to a well-defined bridge between abstract symbols and the objects and feelings they represent.

Flexibility of style and usage

Since English usage undergoes continual changes (as discussed in Chapter 3), emphasis must be placed on language appropriateness relative to social settings. Such an increase in latitude produces a greater need for a broad knowledge of language at both the formal and informal levels. In addition an increasing amount of dialect-related speech is now finding its way into written language, so more alternatives for expression are now available for use. It is thus essential that students be aware of a variety of language forms beyond their own. Literature is one avenue through which this can be accomplished. The younger children can receive this exposure by being read to or by hearing the spoken word via tape or records. Older children can listen to or read literature for themselves, but they also benefit from having contrasting versions of one message pointed out to them. For example, upper grade children might be asked for their translations of these phrases from Zachary Ball's *Bristle Face:*

"You recollect how he listen up there when you blew your horn?"

"A young dog will allus want to pry. . . ."

"I tried to feel heartened up when he said that."

Children can also compare formal and informal usage. One way to do this is to write an informal translation of a formal passage. This occurs naturally by recording (written or taped) a child's retelling of a story.

Decoding and encoding skills

All these areas in the reading-language program feed into the process of breaking and reconstructing the code of language. Again, children's literature can contribute directly to all aspects of development, from auditory perception to oral intonation. A few contributions will be mentioned here.

First, children can gain some *general knowledge* about books through repeated exposure to literature. As a listener a child can come to know which side of a book is the front, which direction pages are turned, and the left-to-right direction of eye movement as he notices the function of printed symbols. He can also learn the importance of pictures (especially in picture books) in providing additional information to the story.

For the preschool listener or the child at the reading readiness stage, literature can provide experience in *auditory perception,* such as discrimination of initial consonants and rhyming. One way to provide practice in rhyming in a meaningful context is to let children supply the rhyming word in a story such as "Drummer Hoff," by Barbara Emberley, or a folk song such as "A Fox Went Out on a Chilly Night." "One Misty Moisty Morning" can serve as an alliteration model for children, either for identification of other phrases like it, or for construction of their own. One collection designed for this very purpose is Louise Binder Scott's *Talking Time,* which uses poetry and short stories to emphasize particular phonemes in meaningful ways.

Since young children always want "to see the pictures" as they listen to the story, they are also being given opportunities for *visual discrimination.*
508 In the case of alphabet books and others with oversized print, some chil-

dren begin independently to relate sounds and symbols. A book like *Roar and More,* by Karla Kuskin, offers this opportunity, as do many of the Seuss books, such as *Sam and the Firefly,* in which significant messages are written in the sky by the firefly. The many books written in large print, like Ruth Krauss's *Carrot Seed* and Crockett Johnson's *The Little Fish That Got Away,* also aid visual discrimination for those who are able to deal with letter and word configurations.

The child's *sight vocabulary,* to which road signs and food cartons contribute informally, can also be built up by literature. Oversized print, repetition, and significant meaning also aid in the acquisition of sight vocabulary. Edith Hurd's *Stop! Stop!* and *Hurry! Hurry!* can fulfill these requirements nicely. The imaginative presentation and dramatic pictures of *Four Fur Feet,* by Margaret Wise Brown, contribute to both auditory and visual discrimination for beginning readers.

When students begin to examine *phonic elements* in words, stories written in rhyme and poetry containing rhymed couplets can be introduced. P. Cameron's *I Can't Said the Ant* offers numerous possibilities, along with other stories and poems using alliteration. When the size of print or other distracting details inhibit examination of the book page itself, a usable portion of the text can be recopied in chart form or an overhead projector can be used to project those portions useful for the designated purpose.

At yet a later stage, attention can be called to *structural elements,* such as inflectional endings, in a variety of ways. One might take a character known to the children, like Curious George, have them list characteristics he had that are similar to their own, then have them compare singular and plural inflections.

> Curious George rides a bike.
> I ride a bike.
> We ride bikes.

Different characters and verbs can be repeated to work toward the necessary generalizations.

Decoding on the basis of *contextual clues* applies to nearly all literature. The only literature selections that would not be helpful to the less-than-independent reader in this regard are special form presentations without plots. Free verse and forms of poetry that concentrate on vivid imagery through metaphors provide limited contextual clues.

The contributions of literature to the reading-language program are not isolated, as these segmented descriptions might imply. It may be helpful, however, to examine them in this way, to show the barrenness of a reading program that does not include literature.

If the primary vehicle in a child's reading program is his own language, familiar literature provides opportunities for *group* language experiences. A rhyme, poem, or story line familiar to several children can provide the reading content, which is enriched and enjoyed by being shared.

This section has a dual purpose: It is a summary of the chapter, and it presents a system for evaluating the literature portion of the elementary reading and language program. Its summary role will be served by including the major components of such a program, and its evaluative role will be filled by the question-like nature of the items. The chapter implies three basic questions and related subquestions by which to assess a program:

I. Are you fulfilling the literary objectives of the literature program?

    A. By assessing your students' literary background prior to planning a program

        1. Does someone read to your children (nonreaders or beginning readers) regularly at home?

        2. Do your children (readers) read books outside school regularly?

        3. What are their favorite poems?

        4. What are their favorite books?

        5. Do they have library cards?

        6. Do they own books personally or as a family?

        7. Do they *enjoy* listening? Reading?

        8. Are they acquainted with literary characters up to their own age level? (See the section entitled "Literary Assessment," end of this section.)

    B. By offering a balance between prose and poetry, fiction and nonfiction, realism and fantasy

    C. By providing an inviting environment for exploring literature

        1. Do you provide time each day for free choice activity? Do students browse through books during leisure time?

        2. Do students ask for certain books to be "read again"?

        3. Do students ask to take home a book that has been read to the class?

        4. Do students look forward to a story hour and remind you if you forget?

        5. Do students frequently exchange information about story plots informally?

        6. Are assignments based and evaluated on motivation to read for personal gain and enjoyment rather than on speed and quantity?

        7. Do students read independently at their own pace rather than compete with others, or do they read merely to fulfill assignments?

        8. Do students initiate comparisons between books, authors, and plots?

        9. Do students initiate response activities relating to literature read individually and in group situations?

      10. Are assignments open-ended rather than specific to allow for different interest and ability levels so that all might make worthy contributions? Do your questions and tasks elicit problem-solving and creative thinking rather than factual recall?

D. By continuing to add to your own familiarity with and knowledge of children's literature

1. Are you acquainted with the authors listed below? Could you supply the titles of their best-known books, or the types of literature or stories they are known for?

Joan Aiken	Robert Lawson
Dorothy Aldis	Munro Leaf
Lloyd Alexander	Madeleine L'Engle
Hans Christian Andersen	Leo Lionni
Joan Walsh Anglund	Robert McCloskey
Harry Behn	Masako Matsuno
Natalia Belting	A. A. Milne
Claire H. Bishop	Mary Norton
Marcia Brown	Scott O'Dell
Margaret Wise Brown	Mary O'Neill
Lewis Carroll	Charles Perrault
Rebecca Caudill	Beatrix Potter
Beverly Cleary	Margaret Rey
Elizabeth Coatsworth	J. Rojankovsky
Alice Dalgliesh	Carl Sandburg
James Daugherty	Ruth Sawyer
Edgar and Ingri d'Aulaire	Maurice Sendak
Beatrice de Regniers	Dr. Seuss
Elizabeth Enright	Louis Slobodkin
Eleanor Estes	Dorothy Sterling
Walter Farley	Mary Stolz
Aileen Fisher	J. R. R. Tolkien
Genevieve Foster	Janice Udry
Don Freeman	Tomi Ungerer
Robert Frost	Kurt Weise
Kenneth Grahame	Leonard Weisgard
The Brothers Grimm	E. B. White
Russell Hoban	Laura Ingalls Wilder
Syd Hoff	Brian Wildsmith
Langston Hughes	Taro Yashima
Ezra Jack Keats	Charlotte Zolotow
Ruth Krauss	

2. Could you direct a student to specific authors and titles for exploration if he asked you for a subject of interest? Can you relate such interest to the following "Who is?" questions?

a. Preschool

Red Riding Hood	Mike Mulligan
Gingerbread Boy	Jack and Jill

Three Little Pigs | Ping
The Cat and the Fiddle | Little Toot
Little Miss Muffet | Peter
Humpty Dumpty

b. Primary
(K, 1, 2)

Curious George | Madeline
Max | Cat in the Hat
Swimmy | Ferdinand
Betsy | Harry
Bartholomew Cubbins | Crow Boy
Cinderella | Flip
Sal | Muley-Ears
Lyle | Blaze
Stevie

c. Middle grades
(3, 4)

Winnie the Pooh | Pippi
Paddington | Henry Huggins
Wanda Petronski | Harriet
Homer Price | James
Charlotte | King of the Wind
Stuart Little | Zeee
Lassie | Beezus and Ramona
Borrowers | Charlie
Red Balloon | Mafatu
Thumbelina | Ugly Duckling
Dr. Doolittle | Christopher Robin
Chitty Chitty Bang Bang | Mary Poppins

d. Upper grades
(5, 6)

Ishi | Dorothy
Paul Bunyan | Hobbit
Anne Frank | Moby Dick
Mary Jane | Pecos Bill
The Wild Stallion | Alice
Little | Tom Sawyer
Dobry | White Fang
Little Prince | Gulliver
Peter Pan | Mrs. Whatsit,
Johnny Tremain | Mrs. Who and
Tituba | Mrs. Which

Miguel | Buck

II. Are you fulfilling the broad literacy and literary objectives of a literature program?

   A. By assessing students' present literacy levels, oral and written language levels, decoding levels, and reading-listening comprehension levels

   B. By providing for "response" to literature

      1. A simultaneous variety to accommodate different styles, interests, abilities

      2. Acceptance of varieties of language and other means of expression

      3. Plan "response" as an everyday experience for those who wish to participate

   C. By providing for *use* of the students' literacy abilities, whatever the levels of competence

      1. Relying on a wide variety of materials with no status based on length or difficulty

      2. Ready access as part of an efficient clerical system

      3. Emphasis on understanding and enjoyment, not on quantity

   D. By providing instruction and experience in use of the library

      1. Do the students check out library materials regularly?

      2. Do the students make use of other media and A-V equipment?

      3. Do the students possess basic library skills?
        Retrieval (Dewey Decimal)?
        Responsibility for materials and equipment?
        Use of reference materials?

   E. By providing opportunities for students to experience the potential and importance of language (oral and written)

III. Are you fulfilling objectives that contribute toward total development of self through literature experiences?

   A. By providing suggestions through informal conferencing about literature selections that offer insight into man's behavior

   B. By providing suggestions about literature selections that offer knowledge about other living things and aspects of the world that would build upon the child's present experience base

Matrix for suggesting literature selections

The age group labels shown in the following matrix reflect a traditional approach to children's reading material but are included here to provide a common base from which to work. Any child might read material in any of the age categories. As a teacher, locate the age level you teach and try to complete that column for each subject area. Then try to add selections in each subject area for children slightly younger, then for children slightly older.

As you evaluate your literature program, what information have you identified about its strengths and weaknesses? From a personal standpoint what areas reflect your greatest instructional strength? Your weakest? What plan of action can you design that retains your strong points and

improves your weak areas?

Subject	Primary	Middle	Upper
ANIMALS			
Personified			
Domestic			
dogs			
horses			
others			
Wild			
PEOPLE			
Everyday family life			
Humorous predicaments			
Problems in growing up			
Fantasizing the ideal			
and the improbable			
Adventure and mystery			
Living in a changing world			
Different life styles,			
habits, values			
Heroes			
real persons			
fictionalized stereotypes			
Activities and functions			
occupations			
sports			
avocations			
Appreciation of beauty			
and nature			
INFORMATION OF ALL KINDS			
Natural science			
Physical science			
Social science			

Footnotes

[1] Albert Grande, "Authentic Existence and the Teaching of Literature" (unpublished doctoral dissertation, University of Pittsburgh, 1965), 12.

[2] Isabel Lewis, "Psychoanalytic Points of View," in *The Dynamics of Reading,* Robert B. Ruddell, ed. (Waltham, Mass.: Ginn-Blaisdell, 1970), 44–89.

[3] A. A. Milne, *Winnie the Pooh* (New York: E. P. Dutton & Co., Inc., 1926), p. 16.

[4] May Hill Arbuthnot, *Children and Books,* 3rd ed. (Chicago: Scott, Foresman and Company, 1964).

[5] Constantine Georgiou, *Children and Their Literature* (Englewood Cliffs, N. J.: Prentice-Hall, Inc., 1969), p. 110.

[6] "Charles," in *A Flock of Words,* coll. David Mackay (New York: Harcourt Brace Jovanovich, Inc., 1969), p. 180.

[7] Robert Browning, "How They Brought the Good News from Ghent to Aix," *The Golden Treasury of Poetry,* ed. Louis Untermeyer (New York: Golden Press, 1959), pp. 149–51.

[8] From *Child Life Magazine,* Copyright 1930, 1958 by Rand McNally & Company. Reprinted by permission of Florence Page Jacques and Rand McNally & Company.

[9] Carolyn Hall, "Fireflies," *Favorite Poems Old and New,* ed. Helen Ferris (Garden City, N.Y.: Doubleday & Company, Inc., 1957).

[10]Olive A. Wadsworth, "The Wonderful Meadow," *A Small Child's Book of Verse,* ed. Pelagie Doane (New York: Oxford University Press, 1948), p. 74.

[11]*Japanese Haiku,* trans. Peter Beilenson (Mt. Vernon, N. Y.: Peter Pauper Press, 1955), p. 56. Reprinted by permission of Peter Pauper Press.

[12]From Edward Lear, *Complete Nonsense Book.* Reprinted by permission of Dodd, Mead & Company, Inc. and the Administrators of Constance S. Ester Rosa Cipelletti Lady Strachey deceased.

[13]Ibid.

[14]From *The Burgess Nonsense Book* by Gelett Burgess. Copyright, 1901, Renewed, 1929, by Gelett Burgess. Reprinted by courtesy of J. B. Lippincott Company.

[15]George A. Strong, "The Modern Hiawatha," *American Literature in Parody,* ed. R. P. Falk (New York: Twayne Publishers, Inc., 1955), p. 59.

[16]Leland B. Jacobs, "Give Children Literature," *Education Today* (Columbus, Ohio: Charles E. Merrill Publishing Co., 1961).

[17]William Iverson, "Reading and Literature" (unpublished manuscript presented to California Reading Association, March 1971, Fresno, Calif.), p. 5.

[18]Ruth Sawyer, *The Way of the Storyteller* (New York: The Viking Press, Inc., 1962).

[19]Charlotte S. Huck and Doris Young Kuhn, *Children's Literature in the Elementary School,* 2d ed. (New York: Holt, Rinehart and Winston, Inc., 1968).

[20]Evans G. Valens, Jr., *Wingfrin and Topple* (New York: World Publishing Company, 1962), pp. 4–5.

[21]*A Curriculum for English: Language Explorations for the Elementary Grades* (Lincoln: University of Nebraska Press, 1966).

[22]Ruth Krauss, *Is This You?* (illus. Crockett Johnson) (New York: William R. Scott, Inc., 1955).

Additional References

ANDERSON, MARIAN POSEY, *Books to Grow On: Helping the Very Young Explore Their World and Its People.* New York: The American Jewish Committee, Institute of Human Relations, 1961.

BETZNER, JEAN, *Exploring Literature with Children in the Elementary School.* New York: Teachers College, Columbia University Press, 1943.

GILLESPIE, JOHN, and DIANA LEMBO, *Introducing Books: A Guide for the Middle Grades.* New York: R. R. Bowker Co., 1970.

HIGGINS, JAMES E., *Beyond Words: Mystical Fancy in Children's Literature.* New York: Teachers College, Columbia University Press, 1970.

HUCK, CHARLOTTE S., *Get Children Excited about Books.* Glenview, Ill.: Scott, Foresman and Company, 1971.

KUBLITZ, MINNIE W., *The Negro in Schoolroom Literature: Resource Materials for the Teacher of Kindergarten Through Sixth Grade.* New York: Center for Urban Education, 1966.

LARRICK, NANCY, *A Teacher's Guide to Children's Books.* Columbus, Ohio: Charles E. Merrill Publishing Co., 1963.

REID, VIRGINIA M., ed., *Reading Ladders for Human Relations.* Champaign, Ill.: National Council of Teachers of English, 1972.

Developing Mature
Readers: Literature
Plus Response

ROBINSON, EVELYN ROSE, *Readings about Children's Literature.* New York: David McKay Co., Inc., 1966.

ROLLINS, CHARLEMAE, *We Build Together.* Champaign, Ill.: National Council of Teachers of English, 1967.

SUNDERLIN, SYLVIA, ed., *Bibliography of Books for Children.* Washington, D. C.: Association for Childhood Education International, 1971.

14

Diagnostic Instruction: Screening and Informal Diagnosis of Reading-Language Miscues

Focusing Questions

1. What factors may interfere with children's reading-language progress?
2. How can the communication framework be used as a basis for diagnostic instruction?
3. What are the limitations and values of group achievement tests? What specific factors may handicap the performance of minority group children on achievement tests?
4. What is a "reading miscue"? How can reading miscues be recorded and interpreted to meet the instructional needs of individual youngsters more effectively?
5. How is dialectal variation related to interpretation of reading miscues?
6. How can reader interest and motivation be assessed?
7. What key diagnostic principles can increase teaching effectiveness and instructional sensitivity?

Diagnostic instruction is essential to avoid chronic remedial problems. You must identify reading and language difficulties early in the school year through frequent evaluation of individual progress, and develop appropriate instructional experiences to account for individual needs. Thus a major goal of diagnostic teaching is to prevent serious remedial problems. When severe remedial problems are present, however, the teacher must be able to identify the nature of the difficulty in order to initiate remediation or to refer the child to the reading specialist for in-depth diagnostic and remedial work.

Estimates of the number of children who have significant difficulty learning to read vary. It has been estimated, for example, that one of every four students experiences reading retardation, and that about 50 percent of the pupils in large urban school systems read below age-grade norms. As we have previously noted, about 15 percent of American adults read at the fourth grade level or below, and an additional 25 percent fail to reach sixth grade standards. In other words, approximately 40 percent of American adults cannot function above the reading level we expect of the average twelve-year-old student.

517

Diagnostic
Instruction:
Screening and
Informal Diagnosis
of
Reading-Language
Miscues

Rarely can reading difficulty be attributed to a single cause; for this reason the teacher must be aware of a number of factors that may contribute to difficulties in reading and language learning. Early identification of these factors and immediate adjustment of the curriculum can in many cases prevent a cumulative learning problem that otherwise would result in severe reading retardation. In this discussion we identify causes of reading-language retardation, develop specific suggestions for diagnostic instruction, and present a range of instructional recommendations related to the difficulties identified.

CAUSES OF READING-LANGUAGE PROBLEMS

Instructional difficulties can be largely attributed to one or a combination of the following factors: a physical handicap or interference, emotional difficulties, intellectual development, environmental problems, and instruction. The teacher who is aware of the nature of these problem sources should be able to deal more adequately with the individual's learning needs. For example, a physical handicap such as visual acuity will require parent cooperation and medical attention for correction, while inferior past instruction will demand careful assessment and curriculum adjustment of a remedial nature.

Physical handicap or interference

Although many physical impairments will have already received attention by the time children enter school, the teacher must be alert to "obvious" difficulties that may inhibit learning. Specifically he should be concerned with vision, hearing, and speech problems.

A near vision problem is evident if the child holds reading material very close or far away in the attempt to focus vision. The child who squints at writing on the chalkboard, rubs his eyes, and has a short attention span may have a distance vision difficulty. The commonly used Snellen vision test will identify students who have difficulty with distance vision, but not those who have difficulty with close vision, nor will it detect fusion difficulties. Strabismus, the muscular imbalance of one or both eyes, may result in fusion difficulty, while aniseikonia presents fusion problems because of the unequal size or shape of the ocular images in each eye. Rapid eye fatigue, frequent rubbing of the eyes, headaches, and a limited attention span in dealing with symbols at close range can be symptoms of visual-related problems and may dictate referral for a detailed visual examination.

A hearing loss is, of course, a serious impediment to reading and language development. The child who requires that you constantly repeat simple directions and who fails to respond to questions or comments when you are out of his visual field exhibits characteristics of a hearing loss. Auditory discrimination is essential to progress in word recognition. Hearing loss, particularly for sounds in high frequency ranges, can make it difficult to perceive sound differences and establish sound-letter correspondences. For example, the consonants /c, b, k, p, s, th, and v/ are produced with a relatively high frequency and may require special attention in the instructional program.[1]

You should also look out for speech difficulties, but be careful not to confuse a speech problem with the highly regular nature of nonstandard dialect forms used by minority group speakers. It has been estimated that approximately 10 percent of children have a speech defect that will interfere to some degree with communication.[2] About half these youngsters have problems with simple sound substitution, such as f /f/ for th /θ/ or th /θ/ for s /s/. Many of the less serious problems can be treated in the classroom with help and suggestions from the district speech therapist, but problems of a more serious nature will require specific therapy and medical attention. For example "cleft palate," a pathological problem in which the roof of the mouth has failed to fuse before birth, can be corrected by surgery, but if this is not completed early in the child's language development, it is more difficult for the child to develop clear enunciation after correction. The special therapy required for the later correction will need to be effected by the speech therapist.

You must also consider differences in physical maturation. For example, attention span will differ greatly between the kindergarten and intermediate grade levels. Younger children are relatively unable to sit for a long time in listening situations.

For many children the hand-eye motor coordination necessary for handwriting presents a formidable task. Handwriting involves small muscle coordination and control that take time to develop in young children. Individual variation in muscular control must be expected and accounted for. Manuscript printing, for example, requires less fine muscular coordination than does cursive writing, and some children should be encouraged to use manuscript forms even after many youngsters have been introduced to cursive writing.

General health is an important factor in the child's ability to learn. Fatigue, undernourishment, or a chronic disability such as asthma can result in a low energy level and a lack of persistence, and can gradually affect the child's progress in a cumulative manner. Excessive absences from school are commonly associated with such physical problems, and correction requires close cooperation between home and school. Some minimal provision can be made in the school setting for such children by providing a hot lunch program and creating an area in the classroom for brief rest periods. Establish close cooperation with the school nurse for diagnosis and referral of health problems.

In recent years there has been a tendency to overemphasize the role of brain injury in learning difficulties. Reading retardation has for some teachers become synonymous with dyslexia, now a common catch-all for

Diagnostic
Instruction:
Screening and
Informal Diagnosis
of
Reading-Language
Miscues

various reading problems. Many hyperactive children, for example, have been identified as dyslexic without adequate diagnosis, and so have other youngsters exhibiting behavior associated with emotional disturbances. A child's inability to deal with printed symbols requires careful diagnostic attention and in severe instances an in-depth diagnosis by a neurologist.

Emotional problems

It is difficult to determine whether a child's emotional instability is the source of his reading disability or if the disability has contributed to his emotional state. There are children with emotional problems who read without difficulty and even use reading as an escape from their problems. Conversely, there are children who show no sign of emotional difficulty outside the instructional setting but evidence considerable adjustment problems when confronted with reading and language-related tasks. Frequently these children have come to school anxious to learn, but repeated failure in the classroom and inadequate provision of instructional needs have produced frustration and emotional instability. Such children can profit greatly from diagnostic teaching and individualized remediation programs.

Some children are indeed severely disturbed emotionally when they enter school, and they will experience great difficulty attending to instructional tasks in reading. This does not mean, however, that they cannot learn to read, provided the teacher can work with them with understanding and patience. In severe cases specialized help may be required from the reading specialist and the school psychologist. For such youngsters the frustration that accompanies failure to learn to read will only magnify the emotional disturbance.

Although negative parental attitude toward the school can contribute to a child's learning difficulty, such attitudes are seldom the sole causal factor in a reading disability. Be alert to evidence suggesting that the child may be subjected to excessive pressure from the home to achieve, continuous quarreling between parents, overprotection, or other emotionally disturbing home influences. Such a home environment can contribute heavily to a child's anxieties and uncertainties, interfere with his concept of self in relation to parents and school, and thus impede optimum achievement.

One psychologically based problem that can be produced or aggravated by parental pressure and reinforced by school difficulties is stuttering. This occurs more frequently with boys than with girls and may result from pressure exerted by overly anxious and concerned parents or teachers who misinterpret the child's hesitation in producing words at certain peak speech development periods as evidence that he is becoming a stutterer. The adult often insists that the child stop and start over again, which causes self-consciousness and lack of confidence and directly affects fluent language production.

Dislike of the physical act of writing as well as the inability to express one's self fluently in writing can produce negative emotional reaction toward writing tasks. It is important that the teacher understand the child's level of physical development and avoid pressuring him into tasks such as precise letter formation that may be beyond his performance potential. Careful planning and creative instruction based on an understanding of the child's developmental growth can provide positive emotional response to initial writing experiences.

There are additional factors, such as inadequate social adjustment and personality conflict between teacher and child, that can interfere with the child's emotional stability and retard the development of his reading and language skills. Some children use classroom failure as a way of getting special attention from the teacher, which may reflect lack of emotional support at home, at school, or both. Many of these factors can be mitigated to a degree by developing a sympathetic and supporting atmosphere in the classroom.

Intellectual development

Intellectual development in children varies, and it is important to take this into account in the instructional program. A child whose learning rate is very fast may be completely frustrated in a classroom that provides only for average rates. On the other hand, the slower learner will be constantly discouraged and soon experience motivation and achievement difficulties if his limitations are not understood by the teacher, even though he may be working at full capacity. Use caution, however, in categorizing children as slow learners or as having limited mental potential on the basis of group intelligence tests that are based on reading skills or that place the child with limited experiential background at a disadvantage. Evaluation of intellectual potential should be based on individually administered tests where the examiner can establish rapport with the child and observe performance directly.

Among children of average intellectual ability, it is not unusual to find one who does not perform at his level of ability. At the early levels a disproportionately large number of such children will be boys. The reason for this sex difference is not completely clear, but a probable cause in this country is cultural expectation, which in the past has differed for boys and girls. Girls are encouraged to play games that are more verbally oriented, but boys, being "rough and tumble," are supposed to be more physically oriented. Another factor deserving consideration is that girls are more apt to develop more rapidly in such physiological areas as fine motor control.

As you might expect, intellectual development is positively related to reading achievement; but some students who are well above the normal range on tests of mental maturity experience difficulty in learning to read. Such difficulty may be at least in part a consequence of inappropriate

Diagnostic
Instruction:
Screening and
Informal Diagnosis
of
Reading-Language
Miscues

instruction or the absence of diagnostic teaching. It is important, however, to distinguish between the mentally retarded reader and the remedial reader. In the former case the child may be working at full capacity and yet performing at a relatively low level because of his slower intellectual development. The remedial reader, however, may be performing at a level below that of his mental age peer group not because of intellectual difference but because of physical, emotional, environmental, or educational factors.

Environmental problems

We have already identified such factors in the home and school environments that can interfere with the child's learning as excessive parental and school pressure, parent's attitude toward the school, and teacher-pupil relationships. There are other problems, however, that stem from environmental factors. For example, children coming from a home culture that differs markedly from that of the school frequently experience a high degree of reading retardation, especially children from ghetto and low socioeconomic bilingual or bidialectal home environments.

The ghetto child does not have communication difficulty within his community; the problem arises when he encounters the language of the classroom: unfamiliar labels for directions, new concepts related to instruction and content areas, and standard English forms that differ markedly from the nonstandard or first language he is familiar with. In addition, the child's motivation to learn to read may be at a minimal level because nobody at home treats reading as if it is very important.

To account for variations between school and home, the teacher must carefully assess new labels and concepts to determine which ones are unfamiliar to the child, and must provide many opportunities for using labels and concepts in meaningful situations in the classroom and in the community. The use of reading, which may range from reading labels on cans in the "classroom store" to reading store signs, street signs, and traffic signs on the downtown walking field trip, should be emphasized. In this manner the need and motivation for one dimension of reading becomes clear to the child.

As we discussed in Chapter 9, the teacher must clearly understand the highly regular nature of nonstandard and second language forms, to establish a classroom atmosphere that encourages the child to use his oral and written communication skills. If the child gets the idea that his oral language is undesirable and that his language use is inferior, he will feel rejected by the teacher, and as a result he may reject the teacher as well as the school and use language as little as possible in the instructional setting. The teacher's attitude toward the child and his language is the crux

of a positive language environment.

Instructional provision

An instructional environment that meets the wide achievement range in a classroom is the most significant factor in preventing reading and language achievement problems. The teacher's knowledge of child development, of the learning process, and of reading and language methodology, and his sensitivity to individual child needs are other key factors in optimum reading and language growth for the child.

Often the teacher who feels intense pressure to cover a specified amount of material within a certain time period forgets that he must account for individual variation over varied time periods. Instruction in some instances has overemphasized isolated drill on skills and has sacrificed child interest, and thus resulted in negative attitudes toward reading. On the other hand, failure to develop reading skills systematically can also result in frustrating and negative learning experiences for the children.

Many approaches to reading instruction can be successful if you systematically plan how to evaluate progress and to adjust skill development instruction as needs are indicated. Attention must also be given to the relationship between reading and language development and other classroom activities throughout the day. Communication skill development should not be set apart as a separate entity but should be integrated into various activities.

The classroom atmosphere that favors communication does not occur by chance. The child who encounters the classroom setting where idea sharing is frowned upon, where his ideas are constantly ridiculed or rejected, and where the teacher does most of the talking will soon be discouraged in reacting to the printed page and in projecting his ideas before the class. Conversely, the completely "free" classroom that has no criteria for sharing in discussions, taking turns in contributing ideas to the group, and respecting the communication rights of others can result in a type of "communication anarchy" with minimum provision for language growth.

Instructional provision for each child must account for diagnostic teaching through evaluation and adjustment of the instructional program to meet his needs. This text contains specific suggestions designed to develop an instructional program based on individual learner needs. We shall now explore a range of suggestions designed to help the teacher identify specific reading-language difficulties more effectively.

DIAGNOSTIC INSTRUCTION

Evaluation of instruction should be basically concerned with the degree to which instructional objectives are being achieved. The communication framework in Chapter 2 revealed specific competencies and related performances essential to progress in reading and language development.

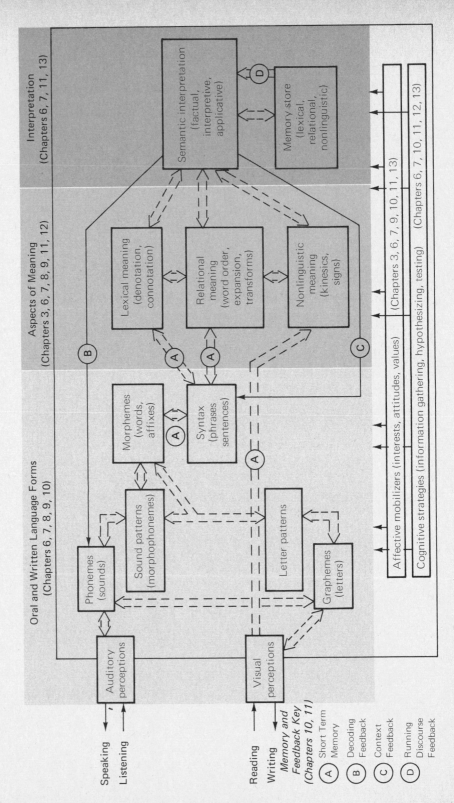

Figure 14-1. Communication Framework.

These include the five general areas of oral and written language forms, aspects of meaning, interpretation, memory and feedback, and affective and cognitive dimensions. Objectives of the instructional program should be related to these areas and to the specific reading performances identified. It is essential that the teacher clearly understand which reading objectives are of high priority if he is to effect diagnostic instruction. For example interpretation, the third area of the model, includes evaluation of the child's ability to comprehend material at the factual, interpretive, and applicative levels. Once he has evaluated progress in these areas, the teacher can adjust the program to account for individual strengths and weaknesses.

In diagnostic instruction several basic principles should be kept clearly in mind. The following principles, identified by William Sheldon, will serve to orient the teacher's effort:

1. Diagnosis is an essential aspect of teaching and is a preliminary step to sound instruction.
2. Diagnosis should be continuous because child growth in reading depends upon the sequential development of skills, which is promoted through the teacher's knowledge of each child's progress.
3. Diagnosis is an individual task and reflects the fact that each child is different.
4. Diagnosis of reading status demands far more than an assessment of reading because reading difficulties are symptomatic of many causative factors.
5. Because reading is but one aspect of language, teachers must understand the listening, speaking, and writing status of children to fully understand their reading abilities.
6. Because the instruments of diagnosis have not been perfected the limitation of each instrument must be thoroughly understood.[3]

Instructional diagnosis is clearly a formidable task. It may appear impossible for the teacher with thirty-plus youngsters. For this reason, in the discussion that follows we are mainly concerned with evaluation via group assessment instruments and informal reading and language inventories. We identify instructional techniques for adjusting the program on the basis of classroom evaluation, but for greater detail refer to the communication model and the chapters that are keyed to it.

Group assessment and screening procedures

The press of accountability at the state and local levels has led to the widespread use of achievement tests, often with little consideration of the specific objectives in a given classroom. If group assessment is to be meaningful, the criteria for selecting test instruments must be based on the objectives of the reading program, and even then the teacher must become aware of limitations by carefully examining the manuals and information related to the formulation and standardization of a specific instrument.

Diagnostic
Instruction:
Screening and
Informal Diagnosis
of
Reading-Language
Miscues

Many of the test limitations are often stipulated but receive little attention in the selection and interpretation of a given test. Here are six cautions to observe using group achievement tests.

1. Standardized reading achievement tests are designed to measure highly generalized skills. They do not measure specific objectives.

2. Achievement tests should not be the basis for planning a complete instructional program, because only a few of the complex skills of reading can be sampled in any one measurement instrument.

3. Standardized reading achievement tests include tasks closely related to those used to measure intelligence, so they reflect many factors other than the effectiveness of classroom instruction.

4. Because the "objective" scores for standardized reading achievement tests are based on norm groups, these tests tell little about student achievement unless the norm groups are completely and accurately defined. Boards of education, the community, parents, and even professional educators often misinterpret achievement test scores for this reason.

5. Pressure for high test scores can corrupt standardized tests. Each test can only sample specific areas of student achievement. Emphasis on these areas in an instructional program can make test results an invalid measure of total student achievement.

6. Reliability measures for group achievement tests, provided they are not corrupted by such special preparation, assure the comparability of results if tests are administered in the same manner and at the same time to a group equivalent to the norm group, but the test score of any one individual student is subject to a significant error of measurement. Group tests can measure group achievement accurately, but not necessarily the achievement of any individual. In spite of this the results of group achievement tests are frequently used to assess and place individuals.[4]

If achievement test evaluation in reading is even to assess groups meaningfully, several dimensions of the reading process must be accounted for in order to obtain an improved understanding of the nature of reading progress. For example, information based on reading comprehension, word analysis skills, and listening comprehension tests enables one to identify the relative strengths and weaknesses of a specific group of students. An analysis based on the Cooperative Primary Test battery[5] of the achievement patterns of twenty-four classrooms in a West Coast school district revealed six exclusive patterns, as shown in Figure 14-2.[6]

The achievement variation in reading comprehension, word analysis, and listening comprehension for each pattern reveals a number of implications for instruction. The six patterns do not simulate grade-level achievement because the purpose is to display relative strengths and weaknesses in each of the three areas irrespective of age-grade norms. In other words, instruction must relate to children's needs rather than to the age-grade norm, which for the most part will be obvious to the teacher. The following discussion on instructional implications is keyed to each pattern.

526

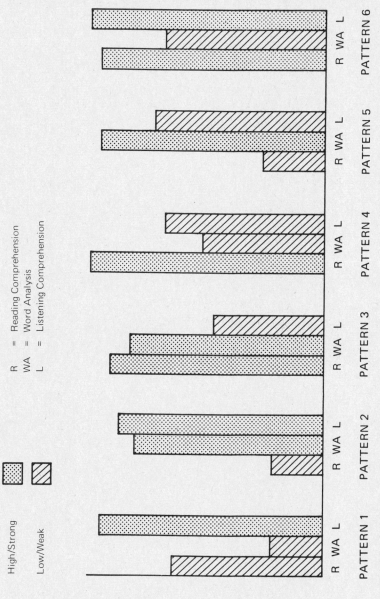

High/Strong

Low/Weak

R = Reading Comprehension
WA = Word Analysis
L = Listening Comprehension

R WA L	R WA L	R WA L	R WA L	R WA L	R WA L
PATTERN 1	PATTERN 2	PATTERN 3	PATTERN 4	PATTERN 5	PATTERN 6

Figure 14-2. ETS Reading Comprehension, Word Analysis, and Listening Comprehension, Six Representative Patterns.

Diagnostic
Instruction:
Screening and
Informal Diagnosis
of
Reading-Language
Miscues

Pattern 1: Listening comprehension relatively strong; reading comprehension and word analysis relatively weak. This means that the children are relatively effective in comprehending what they heard but can't transfer this language skill to comprehend written language. Perhaps this is because they can't decode written words for comprehension purposes. The teacher should concentrate on the weakest area or areas (reading comprehension and word analysis) to elevate the reading comprehension or word analysis ability to the level of listening comprehension ability.

Pattern 2: Listening comprehension and word analysis relatively strong; reading comprehension relatively weak. In this case the children seem incapable of *processing* written language, of reading and comprehending word groups clustered into sentences. This pattern illustrates the value of using a set of related instructional tests. Without a word analysis assessment, the teacher might continue to drill children on decoding small segments because he does not realize that the problem is their inability to *process* written language using context and graphic intonation clues.

Pattern 3: Reading comprehension and word analysis relatively strong; listening comprehension relatively weak. This pattern emphasizes that the graphic and oral presentations reflect a comparison of the *relationship* of one skill to another. In other words, these children are *relatively* strong in reading comprehension and word analysis and *relatively* weak in listening comprehension. These children will benefit from increased oral language practice and experience (oral attending, identifying key meaning elements rather than many details) to enhance comprehension of a functional variety of language at the formal oral level.

Pattern 4: Reading comprehension relatively strong; word analysis and listening comprehension relatively weak. This is a common pattern, even though it seems contradictory, since we typically assume that strong listening comprehension and word analysis skills *lead* to relatively strong reading comprehension performance. Such a pattern may result from introverted children who read well by relying heavily on *context clues;* the children may at the same time exhibit characteristics described in Pattern 3, daydreaming during listening comprehension tests (low oral attending) and performing poorly without context clues (word analysis).

Pattern 5: Word analysis relatively strong; listening comprehension and reading comprehension relatively weak. In this case the children seem unable to apply word analysis skills to sentences or clusters of sentences, and the pattern indicates need for help in developing the broad skill of comprehension rather than the more narrow skill of word analysis.

Pattern 6: Reading comprehension and listening comprehension relatively strong; word analysis relatively weak. This pattern describes children who possess a high degree of oral attending and who derive much information from context in both listening and reading. It appears that these individuals habitually make lucky guesses, but the pattern is too consistent to be based solely on guesswork. Without context clues word analysis performance is at a relatively low level.

The identification of such achievement patterns is of significant practical value to a teacher. He can obtain information about an individual student by completing a content analysis of individual test items, provided of course he observes the cautions identified above.

The group achievement test can also provide screening information for the teacher early in the school year. Although this use also suffers from the limitations described earlier, the information will alert the teacher to the achievement range in the classroom and should lead to informal diagnostic observation of the reading performance of children who score relatively low on the instrument.

A number of recently developed group diagnostic instruments provide achievement profiles similar to those just discussed. With selective use and careful interpretation they can be of value to the teacher early in the school year. Representative tests include the following:

Stanford Diagnostic Reading Test. Harcourt Brace Jovanovich, Inc., New York. Includes diagnosis of comprehension, vocabulary, syllabication, sound discrimination, and blending.

Diagnostic Reading Test: Pupil Progress Series. Scholastic Testing Service, Inc., Chicago. Includes diagnosis of word recognition, rate, comprehension, vocabulary, and study skills.

Diagnostic Reading Tests. Committee on Diagnostic Reading Tests, Inc., Mountain Home, North Carolina. Includes diagnosis of vocabulary, comprehension, rate, and word attack skills.

When a basal reading system is one aspect of an instructional program, the accompanying achievement test series should be carefully examined, because often it reflects the objectives of the program more closely than do other achievement test batteries. When this is the case the evaluation results can be related to the instructional program more effectively as screening devices. Even so diagnostic information on individual pupils will need to be based on direct observation of reading performance.

In addition to the standardized group diagnostic tests, a variety of individual diagnostic tests are also available. These instruments require considerable time and specialization to administer and interpret, and are often used in clinical situations by the reading specialist. Most of these contain an oral reading test and a silent reading test, each consisting of a series of paragraphs graduated in difficulty. Each paragraph is usually accompanied by a series of questions to evaluate the child's comprehension of the selection. The test also often includes a list of words for recognition and analysis and sometimes diagnostic sections to evaluate letter memory, visual memory of words, and related variables.

Diagnostic
Instruction:
Screening and
Informal Diagnosis
of
Reading-Language
Miscues

Representative of the more widely used tests are the following:

Durrell Analysis of Reading Difficulty. Harcourt Brace Jovanovich, Inc., New York. Evaluates a limited range of reading and listening comprehension skills, visual recognition of letters and words, sounds of letters and blends, and spelling. Grades one through six.

Gilmore Oral Reading Test. Harcourt Brace Jovanovich, Inc., New York. Evaluates comprehension, rate, and accuracy of oral reading. Grades one through eight.

Silent Reading Diagnostic Tests. Lyons & Carnahan, Chicago. Evaluates recognition of words in isolation and in context, recognition of reversible words in context, locating elements, syllabication, locating root words, beginning sounds, rhyming sounds, letter sounds, and word synthesis.

The Botel Reading Inventory. Follett Educational Corporation, Chicago. Evaluates phonics mastery, word recognition, word comprehension, and reading and listening comprehension.

The Gates-McKillop Reading Diagnostic Tests. Teachers College, Columbia University Press, New York. Evaluates oral reading, rapid and untimed word recognition, blending, spelling, recognition of word parts, and meaning vocabulary. Grades two through six.

The sampling of reading skills to construct these tests has the same problem the group-administered tests have—namely, the lack of fit between the skills evaluated and the skill objectives of the classroom program. The primary value of individually administered tests lies in the direct observation of the child's reading performance and the interpretation of these observations by the reading specialist.

The teacher who uses assessment and screening procedures in the classroom must be aware of factors that can influence performance, such as

1. Inability to respond because of unfamiliarity with the labels or the concepts that explain the nature of the test task.
2. Unfamiliarity with the labels and concepts the instrument evaluates.
3. Difficulty in attending to and processing oral stimuli in standard English.
4. Difficulty in correctly interpreting picture test items in response to oral stimuli.
5. Little understanding of test-taking behavior, like eliminating obvious detractor items to enhance the possibility of selecting correct responses.[7]

When the teacher and reading specialist interpret test results, they should give careful attention to these dimensions. For example, factors 1, 3, 4, and 5 could partially explain the relatively low performances by minority children in test situations. They should also view reading test items that present unknown words and phrases in isolation with caution, because such items deprive the child of familiar grammatical clues and a normal language context. Additionally, they should carefully examine test instruments for penalties that result from value-based "right answers"—a situation where the child's experience, concepts, and labeling system fail to match that of the test maker. Evaluation of children's reading performance must go beyond simply counting errors to a careful analysis of performance, in order to relate the instructional program to development of the student's reading competence.

Informal diagnosis and reading miscue analysis

The basis for diagnostic instruction is a thorough and continual understanding of the child's reading progress obtained through informal observation techniques designed to evaluate the child's oral and silent reading performance in a variety of reading settings. These techniques include

1. Oral and silent evaluative reading of a prepared informal inventory with a range of difficulty levels
2. Oral and silent instructional reading using instructional programs available or developed in the classroom
3. Oral and silent recreational reading using literature selected by the child
4. Oral and silent informational reading using content area material from the classroom

The teacher should use his observations of the child's reading performance to make a series of inferences about

1. Decoding ability
2. Lexical, relational, and nonlinguistic (picture or graphic) meanings
3. Interpretation or comprehension ability
4. Interests and attitudes toward reading instruction or specific content areas or both
5. Strategies for decoding words and comprehending content

These areas relate directly to the major components of the communication framework in Figure 14-2.

Most of the teacher's evaluation inferences will be based on three types of observation: (1) the child's success in reading and comprehending the printed page; (2) the nature of his oral reading and comprehension miscues (commonly thought of as reading errors); and (3) observations that reflect his attitude and persistence in dealing with the reading task and content. The reader who demonstrates fluent oral reading or silent reading with high comprehension on various question levels presents few problems for the teacher. This type of reader often demonstrates a high degree of interest and a positive attitude toward the reading task, and may reflect a wide range of reading interests. Often he will also use several strategies to decode new words and comprehend content as he efficiently relates new information to his well-established background of concepts. Obviously this child is succeeding in the instructional program and offers positive evidence of successful reading instruction.

531

Diagnostic
Instruction:
Screening and
Informal Diagnosis
of
Reading-Language
Miscues

What diagnostic information could the teacher obtain from this experience?
(Photo by Helen Nestor, Photofind)

Oral reading miscues are important indications of the nature of a child's reading problem and sometimes of shortcomings in the instructional program. Yetta Goodman offers three questions to use in approaching the reading process through qualitative miscue analysis:

1. Why do readers make miscues?
2. What categories or patterns do the miscues make?
3. What is the significance of the miscues?[8]

Miscues can occur at any point in the processing of written language to meaning. The type of miscue suggests the nature of the conflict point and the reason it was made, but it should be emphasized that some miscues do not interfere with meaning and therefore are of minimum consequence. For example, there is no meaning problem here:

Text: The girls are drawing a picture.
Response: The girls is drawing a picture.

The response suggests that the child may be a nonstandard speaker using his decoding ability to move the printed text to meaning. The same is true of the following response:

Text: Every day the boy is going fishing.
Response: Every day the boy be going fishing.

Some miscue responses, however, reflect a meaning interference problem of a severe nature. The inability to accurately produce the oral equivalents of key nouns or verbs in a reading passage suggests that the child is unable to use either letter-sound and letter pattern–sound pattern relationships or relational meaning or context clues. Such an inability will obviously produce meaning interference. Another type of meaning interference can result from written language forms (surface structure) that can be interpreted (deep structure) in two different ways: *"They* are *eating apples,"* or "They are *eating apples."* If the child's lexical and relational meaning store is extremely limited because his background experiences differ markedly from those re-created on the printed page he will be unable to process the information for interpretation.[9]

Yetta Goodman and Carolyn Burke have suggested a series of questions useful in identifying types of miscues.[10] The possible significance of the miscue is indicated in the righthand column.

QUESTION	POSSIBLE SIGNIFICANCE
1. Is a dialect variation involved in the miscue?	A "yes" answer may indicate that the child has gained enough proficiency in reading that he is able to use his oral language competency.
2. Is a shift in intonation involved in the miscue?	A "yes" answer may suggest that the child has anticipated a different structure or is unfamiliar with the author's language structure.
3. How much does the miscue look like what was expected?	A high degree of similarity may indicate inaccurate decoding in addition to lack of familiarity with the word or material.
4. How much does the miscue sound like what was expected?	High similarity may indicate both faulty decoding and lack of familiarity with the word used.
5. Is the grammatical function of the miscue the same as the grammatical function of the word in the text (e.g. noun substituted for noun)?	A "yes" answer may indicate that the child probably is reading with comprehension but may not know the word given or may have perceived it incorrectly.
6. Is the miscue corrected?	Self-correction probably indicates that the child comprehends what he is reading but perceived the word or punctuation inadequately the first time.
7. Does the miscue occur in a structure which is grammatically acceptable?	A "yes" answer suggests that the child is sufficiently proficient in reading that he can use his oral language communication competency.

Diagnostic
Instruction:
Screening and
Informal Diagnosis
of
Reading-Language
Miscues

8. Does the miscue occur in a structure which is semantically acceptable?

A "yes" answer suggests the same possibility as 7.

9. Does the miscue result in a change of meaning?

A "yes" answer may indicate that the child is trying to read language structures that are unfamiliar even though he can decode part of the sentence in word-by-word reading.

These questions and possible interpretations are initial considerations for developing an understanding of the nature of oral reading miscues.

The informal inventory is concerned with the child's comprehension ability as it is reflected in meaning miscues. Interpretation ability and strategies for comprehending content must also be assessed in a story retelling situation or by questions designed by the teacher. Story retelling provides direct evidence of the child's ability to recall factual and interpretive type content, whereas question formulation by the teacher can permit evaluation of the child's factual, interpretive, and applicative responses (see Chapter 11). Often there is not enough time for story retelling by each child, though this does help to identify the nature of oral reading and comprehension miscues. Questions and question strategies which involve various comprehension levels, however, can stimulate discussion between child and teacher in individual and group conferences to shed light on the nature of comprehension miscues.

The child's attitude toward reading will be reflected in his enthusiasm and persistence. Be alert to special interests the child shows in activities throughout the school day. High-priority interests can be especially important for the reluctant reader, because the teacher can match interest with reading content and reading level. There is a sample interest inventory later in this chapter to assist in identifying and evaluating high-interest areas.

RECORDING AND INTERPRETING MISCUES

The teacher will need some system for recording oral reading miscues during individual informal reading inventories. The following notational system is relatively easy to use and will be of value in recording miscues for interpretation.

ORAL MISCUE	NOTATION
1. Pronunciation	Underline the word and write a pronunciation above the word that shows the child's miscue as closely as possible.

Ex.: pretend

ORAL MISCUE	NOTATION
2. Substitution	Draw a line through the word and write substitution above word.

Ex.: Soon he was ~~asleep.~~ **sleeping**

3. Insertion — Place a caret at the point of insertion and write the word or words above the line.

Ex.: Miguel ^is^ my son, let me look at you.

4. Omission — Circle the word or punctuation omitted.

Ex.: He (placed) the box (under) the chair.

5. Correction of miscue — Circle the word and the recorded miscue. Place a *C* above the circle.

Ex.: He (kicked)^threw^ ^C^ the ball with his new hard toed shoe.

6. Repetition — Underline the word or words repeated using a reverse arrow.

Ex.: <u>He is still</u> breathing hard.

7. Word-by-word reading — Place a diagonal mark between the words.

Ex.: She/threw/the purse into/the open/window.

8. Hesitations of more than two seconds — Place a check where the hesitation occurs.

Ex.: He ✓scrambled over the fence.

9. Word supplied by teacher after five-second pause* — Ex.: She jumped ^T^ into the cold water.

*For diagnostic purposes there is some value in not providing pronunciations for the child in order to note the decoding, meaning, and interpretation strategies he may use. For example, context clues may enable him to identify a word he initially mispronounced or for which he used a substitution. But when the child becomes discouraged and is unable to pronounce several words in close proximity the teacher may elect to provide the pronunciation.

Diagnostic
Instruction:
Screening and
Informal Diagnosis
of
Reading-Language
Miscues

The following passage illustrates the use of the miscue notational system. (The original passage was presented in primer-sized type for easy reading.)

Bill and Jimmy ~~were~~ [was] on ~~their~~ [they] way to the store.

Jimmy said, "That dog (is) looking out the window."

"Yes," said Bill. "He is the ~~worst~~ [more worser] one in town. I am glad he (is) inside ^[the house] today."

The boys went to the (IN) [new] door. [C]

Swoosh!

The door ~~opened~~ [open] all by itself!

"Wow," said Jimmy. "Look at that! A magic ~~door~~ [dow]!"

"You (are) silly!" said Bill.

"The new doors work by ˅[electric] electricity."

"What(s) ~~electricity~~ [electric]?" asked Jimmy.

"I(ll) tell you later," said Bill.

"Come on, let's get the bread."

The boys' mother need(ed) bread for ˅[sanwiches] sandwiches.

Bill look(ed) for a long time. The bread had been moved to a new place in the store.

Then he spott(ed) it.

But where ~~was~~ [were] Jimmy?

The miscue notations suggest that this child has a severe reading problem, as revealed by pronunciation, substitution, insertion, and omission miscues. But if you look closer you will see that the miscues are mostly dialect related; that is, they are highly consistent with the child's dialect, which may indicate that the content was meaningful to him (see Chapter 9). The two repetitions and hesitations indicate minor difficulty in decoding the words *electricity* and *sandwiches,* but the miscue responses for these words closely approximate the text. The insertion of the words *the house* in the sequence *inside the house today* offers evidence of the child's inference about the location of the dog. The child used context clues effectively to correct the miscue substitution of *new* for *IN* in *the IN door.* On the basis of these responses the child's oral reading performance appears to be of good quality. It should be clear from this example that the teacher's understanding of variant dialects (see Chapter 9) is vital to understanding oral reading miscues. It is important to develop comprehension questions to help you better understand the child's information-processing ability, especially when the reading passage is of short length (100–200 words). These questions should represent factual, interpretative, and applicative levels as we discussed in Chapter 11. The following questions were designed for the above passage.

CHILD'S RESPONSE

1. What did the boys' mother need from the store? (factual)

   bread

2. What made the door work? (factual)

   electric

3. Why did Bill have trouble finding the bread? (factual)

   it was moved from the old place

4. Do you think Bill was older or younger than Jimmy? (interpretive)

   older

5. Why do you think so? (interpretive)

   don't know

6. Why did Bill think the dog was the worst one in town? (interpretive)

   the dog bite him one time

7. Where would you have looked for Jimmy after finding the bread? (applicative)

   at the electric door

8. What would you do if you did not find Jimmy there (the location the child suggests in response to question 7)? (applicative)

   keep looking

The child's responses indicate that his factual recall is excellent. The interpretive responses reflect his experiential background, perhaps with an older brother or sister, even though he has some difficulty verbalizing the reason he thinks Bill is older than Jimmy. The applicative responses provide evidence that the child is able to recall and integrate information in directing his search for Jimmy. The options for the search, however, appear to be limited to self and may reflect his experiential background and his cognitive strategy in offering solutions at his stage of intellectual development. It is clear from the responses that the child's comprehension of the text is of high quality, and his reactions to the interpretive question (5) and the applicative question (8) provide grounds for better understanding his cognitive development and problem-solving strategies.

The most important aspect of the informal reading inventory stems from the direct observation of the child's decoding and comprehension performance. There will of course be many instances where you use the inventory with silent reading followed by discussion of comprehension questions. You may wish to note evidence of lip movement, finger pointing, head movement, and requests for assistance that indicate the child is

Diagnostic
Instruction:
Screening and
Informal Diagnosis
of
Reading-Language
Miscues

having some difficulty with the material. These factors, however, are only suggestive and should be used in combination with oral miscue and comprehension analysis to identify specific problem areas. For example, lip movement at the initial stages of instruction may suggest that the child is effectively decoding the printed page and utilizing his familiar oral language system to aid in comprehension.

A rough index for determining the child's functional reading level in decoding is suggested at the 80 to 90 percent criterion level. This means that the child should be able to read 80 to 90 percent of the words orally with no miscues or help. This level, however, must be qualified from the standpoint of dialectal variation and meaning miscues. If pronunciation, substitution, insertion, and omission miscues are dialect related and do not interfere with meaning, the miscues should not be counted. For example, the child's miscues on the 120-word passage above were almost all dialect related. The few errors, such as *electric* for *electricity*, place him well above the 90 percent criterion.

From the standpoint of comprehension the successful functional level may be considered generally to be above the 70 to 80 percent level. The child's comprehension responses to the questions following the passage placed him above the 80 percent level, which indicates highly functional comprehension. The same criterion level can be considered sufficient should the teacher elect to use the story-retelling procedure rather than relying on comprehension questions. Again, however, it should be emphasized that the major value for instructional purposes derives from direct observation of the child's oral reading and comprehension performance rather than from a quantitative estimate.

The following summary charts will help you analyze and interpret the nature of the child's miscues.

Name_____ Teacher_____

Grade_____ Date _____

Text _____ No. of Words in Passage_____

Oral Reading Miscues

Type of Miscue	Dialect related		Meaning Miscue Examples	Meaning Miscue Frequency
A. Decoding	Yes	No		
1. Pronunciation				
2. Substitution				
3. Insertion				
4. Omission				

Type of Miscue	Dialect related		Meaning Miscue Examples	Meaning Miscue Frequency
	Yes	No		
Criterion of Success (%)				
Miscue-related Performance				
5. Correction of miscue				
6. Repetition				
7. Word by word reading				
8. Hesitations				
9. Teacher supplied word				
B. Comprehension				
1. Factual				
2. Interpretive				
3. Applicative				
Criterion of Success (%)				

C. Interpretation and Instructional Recommendations:

_____

Silent Reading Miscues

	Dialect related		Meaning Miscue Examples	Meaning Miscue Frequency
	Yes	No		
A. Comprehension				
1. Factual				
2. Interpretive				
3. Applicative				
Criterion of Success (%)				

Diagnostic
Instruction:
Screening and
Informal Diagnosis
of
Reading-Language
Miscues

B. Miscue-related
   Performance
   Comments

4. Lip movement _____

   _____

5. Finger pointing _____

   _____

6. Head movement _____

7. Requests for assistance _____

   _____

C. Interpretation and Instructional Recommendations:

   _____

The following is a useful summary checklist for identifying the nature of decoding miscues from the oral reading miscue analysis.

Decoding Miscue Checklist

Skill	Miscue Frequency	Example	Strategy
A. Perception 1. Auditory discrim.			Recognizes phonemes
2. Visual discrim.			Recognizes graphemes
B. Sound-symbol and Pattern Relationships 1. Consonants (initial, medial, final) 2. Consonant clusters 3. Consonant digraphs			Relates phonemes and graphemes and letter-sound patterns; substitutes consonants by position
4. Vowels (initial, medial, final) 5. Vowel clusters 6. Vowel digraphs			Relates phonemes and graphemes and letter-sound patterns
C. Structural Analysis 1. Graphemic bases			Recognizes and pronounces parts of words
2. Compound words 3. Root words			Analyzes word bases
4. Prefixes 5. Suffixes 6. Inflections 7. Syllables			Recognizes affixes Uses generalizations for visual location of word parts for analysis

8. Contractions			Recognizes contractions
9. Stress			Uses in determining sound-symbol correspondences
10. Environment 11. Position			
D. Context Clues 1. Picture clues 2. Grammatical clues 3. Meaning clues 4. Organizational clues			Uses as meaning aid to decoding

E. Interpretation and Instructional Recommendations:

Interpretations of the information obtained from the miscue analysis are valuable for accounting for skill needs for individualized or small-group instruction.

DEVELOPING AN INFORMAL INVENTORY

A functional informal inventory must account for several factors. The teacher must first consider the inventory from the standpoint of diagnostic teaching and placement of children in the instructional program. If he uses a reading system, he can draw the content in the inventory directly from the basal program by sampling key pages from various levels of the program. The content of the selections should be of high interest and as complete a context as possible given the sampling procedure. The length of each selection will vary according to level; at the first grade level a selection should be at least 100 words and preferably longer. Selections for the upper grades should be at least 200 words and much longer if possible.

The primary grade samples for the inventory should be typed on a large print typewriter, but the size of type may be reduced for later grade levels. Also consider the possibility of xeroxing the samples from the reading material, though publisher permission will often be required in this case. The obvious value in using samples from the classroom reading program is that vocabulary and story content approximate the vocabulary and content in the program.

A second option is to construct an inventory based on the vocabulary in the reading system, or derived from the instructional program the teacher has developed.

A third possibility is to use the vocabulary in word lists—the Dolch or the Kucera-Francis word lists (see Chapter 10)—as the basis for the inventory

Diagnostic
Instruction:
Screening and
Informal Diagnosis
of
Reading-Language
Miscues

passages.[11] Check the word lists you use against the introduction of vocabulary in the classroom reading program in order to design passages that approximate the difficulty levels of the instructional program. The following three passages were designed for the most part by utilizing words from the more recent Kucera-Francis list. The word placement for vocabulary was determined by matching vocabulary with that in the grade one, grade two, and grade three books of three widely used basal reading systems. Comprehension questions at the factual, interpretive, and applicative levels were designed for use with each passage.

The New Dog (Level One)

A new dog was playing with the children at school.

He had fun running after the ball.

After recess the teacher said the dog could come into the school room.

"Who would like to get him some water?" said the teacher.

"He likes milk, too," said Rosa, as she gave the dog a drink.

Soon it was time to go home.

"Here, little dog!" said Tony. "You can ride home with me."

"But that is not your dog," said Ken.

"Where did he come from?" asked Pete.

"He could have run away," said one of the boys.

"He may live near here," said Carmen.

"But how can we find his home?" asked Rosa.

QUESTIONS

1. What did the dog like to run after? (factual)
2. Who gave the dog a drink of water? (factual)
3. How do you think Rosa knew the dog liked milk? (interpretive)
4. How was Tony going home? How do you know? (interpretive)
5. Would it be right for Tony to take the dog home? Why, or why not? (applicative)
6. How would you help find the dog's home? (applicative)

Danny's Trip Home (Level Two)

Danny's home was on a farm very far away.

It was the first time Danny had been away from home.

He was waiting for a bus.

He thought, "How long will I have to sit here and wait at the bus stop?"

Just then Martin and his mother stopped near Danny at the corner.

They were going to ride on the same bus.

Martin said, "Where are you going?"

Danny smiled at him. "I am going on the bus to my home. I live on a farm."

"I have never been on a farm," said Martin. "Are there animals on your farm?"

"Yes," said Danny. "I have a big red horse and she eats sugar from my hand."

When the bus came they got on.

Danny put his bag under the seat.

The other boy had a small toy horse in his hand.

The boys played with it as they rode through the night.

At last they fell asleep.

QUESTIONS

1. What was Danny waiting for on the corner? (factual)
2. Who was with Martin? (factual)
3. Do you think Danny was a friendly boy? What makes you think so? (interpretive)
4. Do you think Danny is happy to ride the bus home? What makes you think that? (interpretive)
5. Where do you think Martin and his mother were going? Why? (applicative)
6. Do you think Danny will wake up in time to get off the bus at the right place? Why do you think so? (applicative)

The Game (Level Three)

Bob was not listening to the story his teacher was reading. It was always hard to do school work before the big game. His thoughts kept flying to the team. Bob and Andy thought they had the best team ever. Most of the boys on the Blue team were either too small to bat or they couldn't catch the ball.

When Bob's team had played against them the first time Bob's team had won. All the boys hoped this would happen again. They had been playing better this year.

The bell rang and the children left the classroom. Bob found his friend Andy outside the door. Both boys ran part of the way to the playfield.

They thought they had left most of the other boys behind. But they found that almost all of the boys on both teams were already there. The boys on the other team wore blue shirts.

Bob and Andy pulled on their red shirts and threw the ball to each other before play began. They were glad the field was dry.

"What is the number of players on your team?" a little girl asked.

"We have seven players," said Andy. "If we had only about two more we could play much better."

"You should ask those older boys to play. They might help you," said the little girl.

"Yes, that would be great," said Bob, "but you see we have enough players to beat this team."

Diagnostic
Instruction:
Screening and
Informal Diagnosis
of
Reading-Language
Miscues

QUESTIONS

1. Where was Bob at the beginning of the story? (factual)
2. Why couldn't he do his work? (factual)
3. What kind of ball game do you think the boys were going to play? (interpretive)
4. Why do you think the team members had arrived so early? What makes you think so? (interpretive)
5. Can you think of other ways the boys might have gotten two more players for their team? (applicative)
6. Who do you think won the game? Why do you think so? (applicative)

One aspect of informal inventory development may deal with the evaluation of rapid recognition vocabulary. Such vocabulary may be derived from the classroom instructional program and can be of value in providing information on the child's decoding ability. It is extremely important, however, that the vocabulary meanings be present in the child's oral language use, and that such evaluation be used only to supplement the oral reading miscue analysis wherein there is meaningful natural language context for unknown words.

Meaningful rapid recognition vocabulary can be effectively presented in tachistoscopic fashion for a brief duration of time and then re-exposed if the child does not recognize a given word during the first exposure. Use flash cards or a teacher-made tachistoscope. A tachistoscope permits a faster, more uniform speed, with some practice. Figure 14–3 shows how to build a tachistoscope.

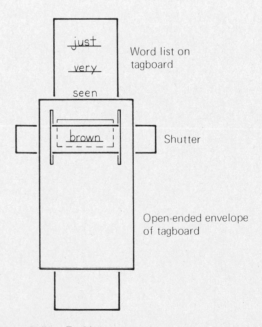

Word list on tagboard

Shutter

Open-ended envelope of tagboard

544 **Figure 14-3.** How to Build a Tachistoscope

Use a simple miscue record sheet to record each child's rapid recognition
performance.

Miscue Record: Rapid Recognition Vocabulary

Word	Flashed	Exposed for Analysis	Comment
just	jet	✓	
very	there	T	
seen	sin	✓	
brown	✓		
tree	three	✓	
under	✓		

Use a check (✓) to indicate the word was read correctly, and a *T* to indicate
that the teacher helped. The child's response for both flashed and exposed
vocabulary should be recorded to note the nature of the miscues.

A tape recorder can be useful here because it will enable you to study a
child's reading miscues more carefully. With older children a recording can
help identify the specific areas that require special attention. A periodical
recorded sample of a child's oral reading is also one way to demonstrate
reading progress to parents.

How can this experience contribute to an understanding of the child's decoding
strategies and abilities? *(Photo by Mimi Forsyth, Monkmeyer Press Photo Service)*

Diagnostic
Instruction:
Screening and
Informal Diagnosis
of
Reading-Language
Miscues

The informal inventory can help evaluate reading progress through decoding and comprehension miscues, but the teacher must establish a close rapport with the child if optimal performance is to occur. It is important to understand the limitations of evaluation procedures whether formal or informal in nature. Look at the evaluation of a child's reading performance in a developmental context, for purposes of designing a more effective reading program.

Identifying reader interests

In diagnostic instruction you must be acutely aware of your children's interests and the factors related to them. Through daily observation of individuals you can get a general idea of the range of interests, though these are often classroom oriented: conversations with children on the playground and in the lunchroom can reveal an entirely different set of interests.

How does child interest affect reading ability? What clues to reader interest can be obtained from informal observation of children during the school day? *(Photo © 1972 Susan Ylvisaker/Jeroboam)*

The interest inventory is another excellent way of identifying important information. On the bases of the child's responses to inventory questions and of the teacher's understanding of the child literature experiences can be more effectively personalized. This will especially help to meet the interest and motivational needs of the "slow-starting" child and the reluctant reader.

For younger children administration of the inventory must be on an individual basis; older children can complete the inventory independently, but even at the upper grades you will obtain much more direct information if you can administer the inventory to the individual child. Tutors and teaching assistants can administer the inventory, provided they have established close rapport with individual students.

The primary and intermediate grade inventories that follow contain questions that suggest important areas to include in your discussion with each child. The primary inventory has been completed with the responses of a third grade boy.

Inventory for Primary Grades

Name __Christopher__   Age __8__

Grade __3__   (Boy) - Girl   Date __September 8__

1. What do you like to do when you can do anything you want to?
   Play in the water with boats
2. What are your three favorite games?
   1. _Monopoly_
   2. _Checkers_
   3. _Bingo_
3. When you go home from school, what do you do?
   Watch TV. Play baseball.
4. What do you do on weekends?
   Go to Grandmother's
5. Do you like to make things? _yes_
   If so, what kinds of things do you like to make?
   Models of boats and cars
6. Of all your toys and other belongings at home, what things do you like best?
   Baseball mitt, souvenir hat
7. Do you collect anything? _No_ If so, what?
   _____
8. Do you take music or dancing lessons? _No_
   If so, do you like them? _____
9. Do you have any pets? _No_ If so, what are they? _____

Diagnostic
Instruction:
Screening and
Informal Diagnosis
of
Reading-Language
Miscues

10. Are you afraid of some things? __No__
    If so, what are they? _____

11. Suppose you could have three wishes, what would they be?
    1. _I wish I had a thousand dollars._
    2. _I wish there was no bills to pay._
    3. _I wish there was no war._

12. Do you watch TV? __yes__ If so, how much time do you spend watching it?
    several hours a day
    What is your favorite program?
    Lost in Space

13. Do you listen to the radio? __No__ If so, what programs do you like? ___
    _____

14. How often do you go to the movies? _I don't go._
    What kind of movies do you like best?
    _____

15. Does someone read to you? __No__ If so, what is your favorite story? __

16. Do you like to look at magazines? __Yes__ If so, what are your favorite
    magazines? _Jack and Jill_____

(For children who have had reading instruction)

17. Do you like to read? __Yes__ If you do, what kinds of stories or books have
    you read? _Adventures of Mr. Toad_____
    _____

18. Which book or story did you like best?
    Adventures of Mr. Toad

19. Do you have any books of your own? __Yes__

20. Do you have a library card? __No__ If so, how often do you go to the library?
    _____

21. Which of these activities do you like best?
    a. Reading books. _____
    b. Listening to stories. _____
    c. Going to the movies. _____
    d. Listening to the radio. _____
    e. Watching TV. __✓__
    f. Playing outside. _____
    g. Playing with my friends. _____
    h. Playing with my older brother (sister). _____
    i. Playing with my younger brother (sister). _____
    j. Playing with or helping my mother or father at home. __✓__
    k. Other _Listen to music. Play Monopoly with Uncle._

Miscellaneous information
    Father's occupation _Accountant_____
    Mother's occupation _Housewife_____
    Older brothers or sisters _none_____
    Younger brothers or sisters _none_____
    Other _An uncle lives in the home._

Inventory for Intermediate Grades

Name_____   Age_____

Grade_____   Boy - Girl   Date_____

1. What do you like to do when you can do anything you want to?
   _____

2. What are your three favorite games?
   1._____
   2._____
   3._____

3. When you go home from school, what do you do?
   _____

4. What do you do on weekends?
   _____

5. Do you like to make things? _____ If so, what kinds of things do you like
   to make? _____

6. Of all your belongings at home, what things do you like best? _____

7. Do you collect anything? _____ If so, what? _____
   _____

8. Have you any hobbies? _____ If so, what? _____

9. Do you take music or dancing lessons? _____ If so, do you enjoy them?
   _____ What are they? _____

10. Do you have any pets? _____ If so, what are they?
    _____

11. Is there anything of which you are afraid? _____
    If so, what? _____

12. Suppose you could have one wish, what would it be?
    _____

13. Do you watch TV? _____ If so, how much time do you spend watching it?
    _____
    What is your favorite program? _____

14. What magazines, if any, do you read? _____
    _____

15. Do you read comic books? _____ If so, which ones?
    _____

16. Which of these activities do you like best?

    _____ Reading books
    _____ Listening to stories
    _____ Going to the movies
    _____ Listening to the radio
    _____ Watching TV
    _____ Playing outside
    _____ Playing with my friends
    _____ Playing with my older brother (sister)

Diagnostic
Instruction:
Screening and
Informal Diagnosis
of
Reading-Language
Miscues

_____ Playing with my younger brother (sister)
_____ Playing with or helping my mother or father at home
_____ Other

17. Do you read newspapers? _____ If so, which parts?
_____

18. What kinds of books do you like best? (sports, animals, etc.) _____
_____

19. Do you like school? _____ Why, or why not? _____
_____

20. What is your favorite subject in school? _____
Which one do you like least? _____

Miscellaneous information
Father's occupation _____
Mother's occupation_____
Older brothers or sisters _____
Younger brothers or sisters_____
Other _____

The interests of the third grade boy, Christopher, appear to be centered about indoor activities such as games, model building, watching TV, and listening to music, though he does mention baseball as an after school activity. Christopher also appears to enjoy the companionship of older persons more than that of his own age group (see response to question 21). This may be attributed in part to his relationship with the uncle who lives with the family. His wish responses suggest that there may be financial problems in the home.

Christopher's responses suggest that areas of interest reside in informational content related to model building, space, and games. He may also enjoy selections about sports heroes and easy reading material of a science fiction nature. His favorite book, *Adventures of Mr. Toad,* would suggest other books of this type. The information obtained from such an inventory should be compared to the interests Christopher displays in school to determine high-interest reading areas and appropriate material.

Additional suggestions for creating interest in reading include reading and dramatizing plays, creating and sharing classroom experience books, piquing interest by reading a small portion of an exciting literature selection appropriate to the child's interest, and helping children identify literature that deals with problems they have encountered or may be encountering. Chapter 13 contains numerous suggestions for stimulating reading interests and responses.

DIAGNOSTIC TEACHING AND INSTRUCTIONAL SENSITIVITY

Your sensitivity to diagnostic teaching will develop through experience in utilizing the information you get from observing reading-language miscues. If you look at the reading-language performance and interests of each child from a developmental perspective, you will understand the role of individualizing instruction better. Arthur Heilman has identified six points essential to diagnostic teaching and individualization of instruction.

1. Go back to the child's present reading level.
2. Do not expect the child to read material which forces him to experience failure, i.e., he must have developed readiness for the task.
3. Help the child build self-confidence—use abundant praise. Undue pressure in the learning situation may interfere with learning.
4. Use a variety of approaches.
5. Base information on a thorough diagnosis.
6. Build interest in reading—have a large stock of supplementary reading materials.[12]

These factors apply directly to instruction in all communication skills.

What instructional factors do you consider critical to effective diagnostic teaching? Are any of them evident here?

After you have informally diagnosed the child's learning needs in the classroom, establish an instructional program to meet them. Instructional recommendations and suggestions for a wide range of individual needs have been presented throughout this text. The next chapter contains suggestions for organizing and individualizing instruction, and the last chapter provides a framework for developing a tutor, teacher assistant, and parent education program for the purposes of meeting individual needs and enhancing individual pupil growth.

Diagnostic
Instruction:
Screening and
Informal Diagnosis
of
Reading-Language
Miscues

Footnotes

[1]George D. Spache, *Toward Better Reading* (Champaign, Ill.: Garrard Press, 1963), p. 113.

[2]Paul S. Anderson, *Language Skills in Elementary Education* (New York: The Macmillan Company, 1972), p. 91.

[3]William D. Sheldon, "Specific Principles Essential to Classroom Diagnosis," *The Reading Teacher*, XIV, No. 1 (September 1960), 2–8.

[4]Rodney Skager, "The System for Objectives-Based Evaluation—Reading," *UCLA Evaluation Comment*, III, No. 1 (September 1971), 6–11. Kenneth S. Goodman, "Testing in Reading: A General Critique," an unpublished position paper for the Commission on Reading, National Council of Teachers of English, 1971. Robert B. Ruddell, "Achievement Test Evaluation: Limitations and Values," a position paper prepared for the School Psychologist Conference on Testing, University of California, Berkeley, December 1971.

[5]*Cooperative Primary Tests* (Princeton, N.J.: Educational Testing Service, 1967).

[6]Robert B. Ruddell and Arthur C. Williams, *A Research Investigation of a Literacy Teaching Model: Project DELTA,* University of California, Berkeley; U. S. Department of Health, Education, and Welfare, Office of Education, EPDA Project No. 005262 (1972), p. 106.

[7]Ruddell, "Achievement Test Evaluation: Limitations and Values."

[8]Yetta M. Goodman, "Qualitative Reading Miscue Analysis for Teacher Training," *Language and Learning to Read: What Teachers Should Know about Language,* eds. Richard E. Hodges and E. Hugh Rudorf (Boston: Houghton Mifflin Company, 1972), pp. 160–66.

[9]Robert B. Ruddell and Helen G. Bacon, "The Nature of Reading: Language and Meaning," *Language and Learning to Read,* eds. Hodges and Rudorf, pp. 169–88. Kenneth S. Goodman, "The Reading Process: Theory and Practice," *Language and Learning to Read,* eds. Hodges and Rudorf, pp. 143–59.

[10]From *Reading Miscue Inventory, Manual, and Procedure for Diagnosis and Evaluation* by Yetta M. Goodman and Carolyn L. Burke. © Copyright 1972 The Macmillan Company. Used by permission.

[11]E. W. Dolch, *Teaching Primary Reading* (Champaign, Ill.: Garrard Publishing Co., 1941), pp. 196–215. Dale D. Johnson, "The Dolch List Reexamined," *The Reading Teacher,* XXIV, No. 5 (February 1971), 449–57. H. Kucera and W. N. Francis, *Computational Analysis of Present-Day American English* (Providence, R.I.: Brown University Press, 1967).

[12]Arthur W. Heilman, *Principles and Practices of Teaching Reading* (Columbus, Ohio: Charles E. Merrill Publishing Co., 1972), p. 555.

15

Organizing and Individualizing Instruction: The Reading-Language Program

Focusing Questions

1. What are the basic differences between administrative grouping and classroom organization?
2. How do the ability grouping plan, the individualized instruction plan, and the flexible ability grouping plan differ? In what ways are they similar?
3. What are the strengths and limitations of an individualized reading-language program? A flexible ability grouping program? How can the strengths of both approaches be used effectively in classroom organization?
4. How can special need groups and interest centers be developed in the classroom?
5. How can the physical arrangement of the classroom be adjusted to provide for greater individualization of instruction?
6. How can learning packets and contracts meet special learning needs and individual interests?

The elementary classroom teacher needs to know how to organize the classroom for instruction in reading and language development. The wide range of ability, achievement, and interest in a typical classroom, grade level, or school makes this a difficult task. In a third grade classroom in a low-middle socioeconomic area of Northern California, for example, IQs ranged from 81 to 144, and reading performances ranged from a low second grade level to a high fifth grade level. This variation is not unusual; many classrooms, especially those organized on a nongraded or cross-aged grouping basis, have even wider differences, and the range usually increases at the intermediate levels.

Not only must you account for the ability and achievement levels of the child, you must also meet his special instructional needs and interests. Is he having problems with decoding or comprehension skill development? Is lack of oral or written language fluency a barrier to his progress? Are there other language-related difficulties that require special assistance?

553

And what are his interests and how can you use them in the instructional program? These are only a few of the vital factors to consider in developing an organizational pattern that can effectively meet individual needs.

In this section we shall first develop a brief background of instructional grouping procedures, then we shall examine several popular administrative organizational plans, discuss plans for classroom organization that account for individual variation, and finally consider the organization of groups and interest centers. Try to relate the discussion to your own classroom experience, so that you can evaluate, relate, and transfer ideas to your program.

A BRIEF BACKGROUND ON GROUPING FOR INSTRUCTION

When mass public education began in this country, children were placed in the same classroom regardless of age or ability. The size of such a group might be as many as fifty or as few as five. Often the more able students were used to teach the younger ones, the primary function of the more advanced being to hear the children recite their lessons.

In 1848 the graded school system, based on age categories, came into being with the opening of the Quincy Grammar School.[1] This system was an improvement in that it made some degree of provision for individual differences.

Some educators soon became aware that the graded system was only a partial answer to meeting children's needs and, as conceived, was unfair and frustrating to certain students. The concept, however, had been so well accepted by parents and teachers that any change was met with strong resistance, so attempts were made to provide for individual differences within the graded classroom structure. One was the multiple reading group plan. In most instances three groups were established in the primary grades and two or three groups in the intermediate and upper grades. This grouping plan was widely accepted by teachers as a way of providing at least to some degree for a wide range of achievement variation.

In both the graded system and the multiple reading groups, the primary aim was an organizational pattern to educate masses of children; the needs of the individual child were not the primary focus. Many teachers viewed children to be highly similar, and the inability of some children to learn was thought to be because of laziness or lack of effort.

Significant changes in organizational patterns for reading-language instruction have been slow to develop. Most organizational practices have been initiated in comparatively small numbers of schools and have depended heavily on a few innovative educators. As a result new organizational plans have had a limited potential for transfer beyond a few school systems. It is not uncommon, however, to find an administrative organizational plan that had been unsuccessfully implemented in an earlier period to be resurrected with a new name or other slight change at a later time. In the next section we shall examine several practices, recurring and new, that may be termed administrative (so termed because the focus is on the entire administrative structure rather than on the individual classroom).

ADMINISTRATIVE ORGANIZATION

Homogeneous grouping plans

Homogeneous grouping takes many forms. Students may be grouped on the basis of intelligence, reading achievement, average achievement, teacher judgment, or some combination of these.

The Joplin Plan. The plan instituted at Joplin, Missouri, was a cross-grade plan.[2] At a designated time all the children at a given grade placement in reading went to the same teacher for instruction without regard for their regular grade level. For example, children placed in the second, third, fourth, fifth, and sixth grades but reading at a third grade level would report to the third grade teacher or the teacher designated to teach reading at that level. Some studies of this plan have shown favorable results; others have not.[3]

Some of those who have used the plan feel that it has unfavorable psychological effects on the older children who must work in the same room on the same type of material with the younger children. It has often been assumed that children whose achievement test scores reflect, for example, a third grade achievement level must have similar reading strengths and weaknesses. Further, the departmentalized organizational nature of the plan separates reading instruction from the other classroom activities.

XYZ Grouping. A plan still used in some schools, particularly in the upper grades, was to group children on the basis of achievement or intelligence level in three categories at each grade level.[4] The high-achieving or high-IQ children, the X group, constituted approximately 20 percent of the total group. The average students, or the Y group, made up about 60 percent, and the slow learners, or Z group, comprised the remaining 20 percent. In some systems the classes the slower students were placed in were smaller. Different curricula were adopted for the groups. Although the range of differences was somewhat reduced, it was found that such grouping did not produce the homogeneity expected and presented problems from a social and psychological standpoint.

Heterogeneous grouping plans

Heterogeneous grouping is the assignment of children to classes or groups by some random method. This plan has also taken various forms.

Nongraded plans. The *Cambridge Plan,* which came into being in the late 1800s, allowed fast learners to study one-third more work than slow learners and thus finish the elementary grades in six years instead of eight.[5]

Under the *Winnetka Plan* (established by Carleton Washburne during the first quarter of the twentieth century) instruction was individualized and work done on a contract-type basis.[6] A pupil started working on a basic skill or body of knowledge at a very simple level and progressed to higher levels on the basis of test results. Academic instruction filled half the school day; the rest was devoted to creative and social activities. The children were assigned to classrooms in a heterogeneous manner.

Another individualized approach was the *Dalton Laboratory Plan,* designed in 1920.[7] Children from several grade levels moved from subject laboratory to subject laboratory working on a "contract" or "job" system in a way that permitted individual progress in different school subjects. The period for a contract was twenty days, except for very slow children who were allowed more time. A student might do his work one subject at a time, subject by subject, or work on all subjects every day. The curriculum was the same for everyone even though it allowed for individual progress.

In 1935 an ungraded plan was proposed for the Los Angeles schools and later put into practice at the primary level.[8] As first proposed, it consisted of a "junior school," with students classified only as Group One, Group Two, and so forth. Reading was to be the major emphasis, and the children were promoted once—to the "upper school." Each child remained in the junior school for as long as it took him to reach the level necessary for promotion to the upper school. The junior school might take two, three, or four years.

Only recently has this plan for ungraded schools been adopted elsewhere. In most instances it involves only the primary level, but in some areas it has been continued into the intermediate and upper elementary levels.[9] The problems in implementing the ungraded school have been (1) administrative and (2) making adequate provision for individualized instruction.

In theory the nongraded primary is an organizational pattern designed to provide for all individual differences in the instructional setting without reference to grade level, but in reality many of the present programs fall short of these goals. In too many instances children are grouped by ability, by reading age, or by some other criterion that fails to provide for individual learning needs.

The nongraded primary, as conceived today, randomly assigns kindergarten, first, second, and third graders to primary classrooms. Each child remains in the primary unit for the length of time necessary to meet his instructional needs; this may be as few as two or as many as five years. Some school systems have successfully offered a choice of graded or nongraded classrooms within the same school. Such a plan requires cooperation and support from parents.

A nongraded primary organization plan can also offer team teaching and pupil teams (children of different maturity levels assisting each other on reading skills under teacher direction).

Multi-age grouping is a concept somewhat similar to the nongraded plan. This plan groups children of various ages and grades in the same classroom. For example, an equal number of kindergarten, first, and second grade students may be placed in a single classroom and allowed to work together in subgroups based on individual needs. Each multi-age group may remain with the same teacher until the more advanced children go to the third or fourth grade and new kindergarten or first grade children take their places.

The most common approach to administrative organization is still the grade level, heterogeneous classroom containing children with a wide range of ability but of approximately the same chronological age. This is the easiest form of organization to administer and is readily accepted by parents. Many teachers also favor this organizational approach over nongraded plans.

CLASSROOM ORGANIZATION

Interest in classroom organization stems directly from the need teachers feel to make the classroom easier to administer by providing more adequately for individual differences. Effective and creative organization of the classroom can enable the teacher to help the student develop his abilities to the fullest extent.

Ability grouping

The first approach to ability grouping and probably still the most popular is the three-group plan. Under this arrangement children are divided into three groups according to achievement or performance, particularly in reading. This practice is to be found in both homogeneous and heterogeneous classrooms. High-achieving students are put in one group, the average in another, and the slow in a third. The disadvantages of a grouping plan based on this premise alone are obvious: The child in the top group feels superior, while the student in the low group often comes to consider himself as stupid. Much of the motivation for learning is removed. Even though attempts are made to disguise the groups with euphemisms, children are soon aware of the differences. Too many times such grouping, if rigidly practiced, means that an underachiever is grouped with learners who require more time in developing reading abilities. The underachieving child is expected to follow the pace and instruction of the slower children, and so, because one of his reasons for underachieving in the first place was probably partly lack of motivation, he will only fall further behind.

Another major problem with ability or performance grouping is that when
557 a child has been assigned to a group he may not have the opportunity to

change to a higher achieving group because he is not exposed to the skills being taught the more advanced group or because he is stereotyped as a low achiever and as a result "frozen" into a particular group.

Individualized instruction

The Winnetka and Dalton Plans were attempts to individualize instruction, but they were primarily examples of administrative organization. Individualized instruction, viewed here as a procedure for meeting individual differences in the classroom, takes many forms. In its ideal form it involves the principles of (1) *seeking,* which supposes that the child has a compelling desire to read; (2) *self-selection,* which allows the child to select a book he wishes to read and can read; and (3) *pacing,* which allows the child to read the book at his own rate with no time limit.[10]

To conduct a successful individualized reading program, particularly at the primary level, it is recommended that the class not exceed twenty-five students. It is difficult for one teacher to provide for the learning needs of even that number.[11]

The teacher should be able to work with individual students from one to two hours daily (preferably two at the primary grade level), divided about equally between morning and afternoon. This much time is needed for the pupil-teacher conferences that enable the teacher to assess the child's needs and provide opportunity for skill development.

Most teachers find that it is best to spend about ten minutes with each child in these individual conferences, which are so central to the entire individualized program. They schedule the conferences on a regular basis, twice a week with each child if possible. The teacher may also meet with small groups to work on common problems or to provide opportunity for children to discuss their reading with one another.

An individualized program requires a large number of books at various levels of difficulty to meet different child interests. At a minimum the classroom library should contain three times as many books as there are students in the room, and classroom materials must be exchanged throughout the school year for books from the school library, with child interest and achievement level as key criteria.

The teacher must understand the procedures used to facilitate an individualized program if he wants to begin such a program, especially the concepts of seeking, self-selection, and pacing. He must also have a thorough knowledge of reading skills and how to teach them because the program is teacher-child created and a handy teacher's manual will not be present to provide the necessary information as the child progresses. The following areas of reading instruction must be accounted for: child interest and a wide range of literature selections, comprehension and study skills, word recognition and analysis, oral reading, flexibility of rate, appropriate reinforcement procedures for various skills, and evaluation of progress. The teacher must also understand that children need different amounts of guidance in selecting books to read. Both teacher and child should keep records of the books the child has read, and the teacher should carefully evalute the child's reading on a continuous basis so that the child progresses in developing reading skills and interests. The teacher should note any special needs of the child.

Because a developmental program of reading skills is an important component of an individualized reading program, basal readers are often used during the week as a systematic program of skill development. Otherwise it is easy to overlook important areas because they do not become apparent during individual conferences. Efforts to combine an individualized program and a basal reading system should be carefully coordinated so that the two approaches complement rather than contradict one another. Vocabulary in an individualized program such as described here is not so carefully controlled as in the basal reader program, so the teacher must determine whether the child is acquiring phonic analysis skills and a rapid recognition vocabulary at a reasonable rate.

During individual conferences the teacher must keep five factors in mind. First, can the child use the necessary word attack skills to analyze words? Second, is he able to read and critically evaluate the selection he has chosen? Third, is he aware of his personal interest in what he has selected? Fourth, is he able to read the material aloud in an interesting way? And fifth, what is the nature of the oral reading miscues he makes during oral reading?

In the first grade the teacher usually sits with the children who are reading their own books to help with any difficulties. This practice is gradually reduced as the children become more independent.

Since the teacher spends considerable time with individuals, it is important to have available a large variety of self-directing reading and nonreading activities for students who are working independently or in small groups. These should consist of creative and enjoyable activities that will contribute to the learning process rather than simply routine workbook and worksheet activities, although such workbook and worksheet activities have a place when used wisely. A more advanced reader may be appointed on a rotating basis to help other children with words during independent story reading. This function can also be filled by teacher assistants and volunteer resource persons.

At times the teacher can encourage several students who have read the same story to come together as a small group and discuss it, to exchange story ideas and reactions, and to develop group discussion processes. The teacher may also wish to invite students to form an interest group with their friends to read and discuss a story in which everyone is interested. Multiple copies of single stories should be obtained in paperback form for 559 these purposes.

Flexible ability grouping

A third approach to classroom organization is flexible grouping. Opportunity must be provided to move a child from one group to another when it appears advisable. For example, the child who finds himself in difficulty in one group may be spurred on to greater achievement when he is moved to a group in which greater challenge is offered. Provision must also be present for regrouping according to a variety of needs and interests. This approach allows the teacher to avoid rigid grouping procedures around good and poor readers. The following chart provides ideas for possible groupings.

TYPES OF GROUPING

Special Interest

Varieties possible: Science, social science, story writing, drama, reading
Development: Student-initiated ideas with teacher guidance
Preplanning by students and teacher, followed by student/teacher evaluation
Composition: Individual student, small group (2-5), large group (7-15), whole class. (Whether the teacher is a participant in any group depends on the circumstances.)

Need

Varieties possible: Word attack skills, study skills, comprehension skills, oral language development, oral reading (partners-audience), or any other grouping for which children demonstrate or voice a need
Development: Student or teacher initiated
Fulfills a predetermined student need
Composition: Same as for special interest groups

The advantages and disadvantages of individualized programs and ability grouped programs are summarized in the following sections.[12]

Advantages of the individualized program

1. Because the child chooses the material himself, he finds it more interesting. There are great differences among children in any classroom, in interests as well as in ability. The individualized program allows each child to explore his own interests to a greater depth. Also, the reading material covers a wide range of literature rather than the limited range in a basal reading text.

2. The child's motivation and drive are self-initiated. Because he is interested, he is more likely to persist in reading the materials he selects. Often the child will read more difficult materials than previous performance has indicated because of the interest factor.

What type of special interest grouping is suggested here? What special provision has the teacher made for this interest? *(Photo by Hays, Monkmeyer Press Photo Service)*

3. The child reads more material, which can lead to positive reading attitudes. There is some research to indicate that children in individualized programs read more and are more interested in what they read than are children in conventional programs. If the child can locate several books on a topic of special interest, he will read to satisfy this interest. Such reading is important in developing positive attitudes toward reading and in developing fluency.

4. The child reads at his own rate. He does not have to keep up with other children, nor does he have to wait for others to finish before he continues. The slow reader thus avoids pressure and embarrassment and the fast reader can work at his own pace. Different children learn in different ways, and the individualized approach can provide for such differences.

5. Because each child is taught the skills he needs at the time he needs them, he is more likely to realize their usefulness. The teacher is continually diagnosing each child's needs as they meet in conference. The child understands why he is working on a particular reading skill because it has

been discussed with him. With enough conferences, the skills program can be tailored to fit the child's needs.

6. Reading can be integrated more closely with the other language arts. Because most individualized programs that are initiated in the first grade begin with experience charts and dictated stories, an immediate relationship between oral and written language is established. As children discuss their stories with the teacher and, in some instances, with the other children, they learn to express themselves orally. For many children, reading stories related to their interests opens avenues to creativity in writing.

7. Individual conferences encourage closer relationships between teacher and pupil. The teacher has an opportunity to get better acquainted with the child, and the child feels more confident because he has the undivided attention of the teacher. The child has an opportunity to express his ideas and reactions concerning the material he has read. The conference also offers an opportunity for the development of human values that are fostered by such personal interaction.

8. The individualized program has a salutary psychological effect on the child. Because he plays a major role in selecting his own reading material and because the teacher works with him as an individual, the child feels more competent. He also tends to develop more independence and greater responsibility in the learning process.

Disadvantages of the individualized program

1. Many elementary schools don't have the quantities of materials an individualized program requires. When the range in variety, quality, and quantity of books and support materials is limited, many of the advantages of the program are lost.

2. Some children have difficulty choosing appropriate books. Either they select books that are too difficult and waste time trying to read them or they select books that are so easy they contribute little to reading growth. If not appropriately guided, some children expend too much time in the selection process.

3. Primary grade children are rarely able to attend to a single task for long periods of time. Some studies have indicated that many slow learners profit least from individualized reading because they can't work independently, especially for extended periods of time, between conferences.

4. In the primary grades new vocabulary and concepts often need to be developed before a story is read. Techniques for attacking new vocabulary may not be developed. Most teachers find that materials that control the introduction of vocabulary provide more opportunity for reinforcement of that vocabulary in the areas of both recognition and concept load. A major problem for slow learners is the lack of vocabulary growth.[13]

5. Few teachers are sufficiently versed in developmental reading skills or have the time to develop these skills with each individual, and many teachers are not adequately prepared to employ the opportunities for teaching word recognition and comprehension skills offered by individualized reading.

6. If the class is large it is difficult to provide each child with enough attention. The teacher may be able to hold individual conferences no oftener than once a week and sometimes less frequently. The teacher must use time with great efficiency and possess a high energy level to develop an individualized reading program.

7. It is difficult for a teacher to consistently provide an entire class with meaningful tasks at the same time as he is working with individual children, with the result that children spend too much time on "busywork" assignments. The slower children often become restless when they are expected to pursue a task on their own, and some children require more structure in the learning process than others.

8. In a highly individualized program the values of group dynamics may be lost. For example, the process of thought interaction within the group will require special attention. Frequently a group needs to read the same selection, analyze it, and discuss it to discover its meaning. The teacher must assume a major responsibility in developing the higher levels of comprehension in an individualized program.

Advantages of flexible ability grouped program

The flexible ability grouped program is conceived of here as being used with the support of a basal reading system. The following discussion thus identifies key advantages and limitations within this framework.[14]

1. A flexible ability program allows the systematic introduction of story background, vocabulary, and concepts. Because vocabulary is introduced developmentally in basic texts, the teacher knows the words to present and discuss. He can assess the background the children have for reading a story and develop the concepts they need before they read the story.

2. Ability grouping presents sufficient opportunity to develop a thorough comprehension program of higher comprehension skill levels. The teacher can give more attention to comprehension because he will usually meet with the group at least once every day.

3. A program using ability grouping provides a carefully developed sequence of word recognition. The teacher is more likely to know which skills have been taught and which have not, can diagnose students' needs on that basis, and can reinforce those skills that need it.

4. Small-group instruction can make provision for an interchange of ideas. Students in the group use a common background of knowledge furnished

by the story to develop further understanding of the ideas presented. Discussing ideas and feelings of others in relation to a common literature experience allows children to understand their own behavior and that of others. Group discussion provides an opportunity to challenge and be challenged.

5. The teacher can provide a more effective balance of reading skills instruction, and more thorough instruction in each skill area by assisting children with a common problem at the same time.

6. The teacher can diagnose children's needs daily through observance of reading performances in a variety of skill areas. If each child in the group receives attention, his needs and problems can be dealt with as they arise.

7. A highly effective atmosphere for critical and interpretive reading is provided by the group situation. Children learn to question and respond to one another's ideas.

Disadvantages of an ability grouped program

1. There is a danger that teachers will administer a uniform program to all children. When a teacher assigns the same reinforcement activities to all members of a group, it may mean that fast learners will have to spend time on unnecessary types of activities, or that some children will not receive help with skills in which they are deficient.

2. Unless care is taken, a stigma can attach to certain groups. Children soon learn that the "redbirds" are the slow readers and the "bluebirds" are the fast readers. Because their placement is supposedly disguised by such a labeling system some children may come to feel that it is a disgrace to be a slow reader, that they are inferior to the other children.

3. The teacher may not provide for reading experiences beyond the basic text, may make no effort to provide opportunities to select books and stories of high interest and to read them independently. This can have the negative effect of producing children who will not read even though they have the skills to do so.

4. Teachers may not deviate from the manual to provide for the special needs of children. When the teacher's manual makes little provision for individual differences, this can mean that the child who has difficulty with comprehension but not with decoding must complete the same exercises as the child whose problems are principally in the area of decoding.

5. The teacher may rely too heavily on workbooks, may require every child to complete every page in the workbook, even those who have already mastered the skills in question. Some teachers who feel it is necessary to keep children occupied at their seats when they are not in a reading

or discussion group sometimes assign workbooks without considering their appropriateness. For children at all levels of proficiency, this process is devoid of motivation and interest and is an ineffective use of the child's time.

6. Some children are usually too advanced or too retarded in their reading-language skills to fit into any given group. When children are grouped according to ability for reading instruction, there is no way to provide groups appropriate for all children. The range of ability within any group will still be very great. This may lead to boredom for the very advanced child and frustration and confusion for the slow child.

There is nothing inherent in either an individualized program or a flexible grouping approach which precludes using the best features of both in organizing your program. A comparison of procedures can help to show how one approach can supplement the other.

INDIVIDUALIZED PROGRAM	FLEXIBLE GROUPING PROGRAM
Basis	*Basis*
Individual interests and needs serve as basis of instructional program	Child and group needs serve as basis of instruction
Criteria for Adequacy	*Criteria for Adequacy*
Preplanning—teacher-pupil	Three or more groups, depending on size and composition of class
Adequate and appropriate books available	Each group using a basal series for skill development
Time for individual conferences allotted	Flexibility of grouping
Careful individual records kept on each child	Regrouping for special needs and interests
Groups formed for common needs and interests	Opportunity for individual reading
Sharing and discussion periods, either classwide or in groups	Continual skills diagnosis
Continuing evaluation during the individual conferences of comprehension skills, attitudes, decoding skills, study skills, vocabulary development, oral reading ability, and silent reading ability	Individual conferences as needed
	Group size varied according to purpose
	Children learning from each other
	Judicious use of workbooks

If we combine the two programs we find that they have much in common and we are left with a program that eliminates most of the disadvantages of each. The following individual, small group, and total class activities illustrate the potential offered by drawing on both methods of organization.

Individual activities

1. Selecting and reading trade books of high personal interest. The student selects his book and reads at his own rate and may discuss it with the teacher in conference or report that he has completed it.

2. Practicing word attack skills and other reading skills through games and exercises. Practice is achieved during the conference and through following activities selected on the basis of the conference.

3. Oral reading and conferencing with the teacher. The child discusses his story with the teacher and reads portions of it aloud to support key ideas or to answer questions.

4. Working at interest centers. During planning periods the child decides which interest centers (see discussion later in the chapter) he would like to participate in after he completes his reading conference, silent reading, or skill reinforcement activities.

5. Writing experience stories. At early instructional levels the child can dictate his story; the more advanced child can develop his written ideas independently. After he has developed the experience story, he can share it with a small group, the entire class, or add the story to the class storybook collection.

Small-group activities

1. Discussing stories. Children who have read the same story in a basal text or by using multiple copies of a literature selection come together to discuss it.

2. Introducing reading skills. New reading skills are introduced and taught inductively to a group. Those in the group who need additional skill reinforcement form a new group to work together.

3. Research or committee work. Children who have a common research interest work together after a planning period with the teacher.

4. Writing experience stories. When they have shared a common experience, like a field trip, children work together to discuss and write about the experience.

5. Dramatizing stories. After a group has read a story, children select parts and dramatize it.

6. Choral reading of poetry. Opportunity is provided for children who need expressive oral reading practice to participate in small-group choral reading with the teacher.

7. Sharing stories. Children who have similar reading interests share favorite stories related to that interest.

8. Pupil-partner groups. Two-pupil teams are organized for oral reading and discussion activities.

9. Introducing new vocabulary. Words representing new concepts in a story are presented by the teacher and discussed with the group. Purposes for reading are set to provide motivation for reading the story.

Whole class activities

1. Dictionary skills activities. Use of the dictionary is introduced to the whole class. Activities and games that reinforce these skills are provided for small groups in follow-up activities.

2. Reading of stories by the teacher. There should be a time in every day during which the teacher reads a story or part of a story to the class. Stories should be chosen on the basis of appeal to the class.

3. Planning activities, field trips, and other group learning experiences. Children should share in planning activities and have a part in formulating the standards to be maintained by participants.

4. Viewing films or filmstrips. Films may be shown to the entire class and then discussed in small groups with students as discussion leaders. The teacher can assist by furnishing leading questions to initiate the discussion.

When teachers are developing a plan of organization for the classroom careful preparation is essential. The following are suggestions that should prove helpful in this effort.

1. If inexperienced in small group teaching, begin gradually. Establish rapport and good work habits with the class as a whole before starting a two-group system. When two groups are running smoothly, start the third. For any kind of new organizational practice, start gradually. Make a careful study of the research findings on the plan.

2. Discuss the arrangement of furniture with the class and routinize the mechanics of moving furniture early in the year. Have a "reading center" of chairs near a chalkboard. Sit with the pupils and be a member of their group or reading club.

3. Make the "low" group feel as important as the "high" group. Help to promote an atmosphere of warmth, friendliness, pride, and willingness in each group. (Do not use such terms as low or top or high.) If names are chosen for the reading groups, be sure there is no association between the name and the group ability. A popular practice is to name the group after the chairman or any group member. Rotate the office of chairman periodically.

4. Have flexible grouping because of the varying rates at which some pupils progress and because of irregular attendance.

5. Be sure that directions concerning assignments are given clearly and understood by the pupils. Provide a variety of challenging and helpful seatwork activities. Check the work faithfully.

6. Confer with parents regularly by letter, report, or interview. Also, have regular conferences with teachers of your own grade and with your whole staff.

7. Draft daily and weekly plans for group activities. Give a fair proportion of time to each group and pupil.

8. Do not become discouraged. Let your reading periods be enjoyable for both you and your pupils.[15]

Individualization can be gradually started from such an initial program. One way is to begin with the children who have shown greater independence in their work habits. Let them choose books and meet in conference to discuss the books and to develop specific reading skills. Another way is to begin with those pupils who need the most help and who do not fit into any of the groups that have been formed.

ORGANIZATION OF GROUPS AND INTEREST CENTERS

The mechanics of grouping, of establishing learning or interest centers, and of placing furniture are certainly not the most important aspect of classroom organization, but you must consider all these factors if the classroom is to function effectively.

Organization of groups

Special-need groups are groups organized to deal with two or more children who demonstrate a need for help on the same skill. They may meet with the teacher initially, but gradually they begin to work together without direct supervision. As members of the group master the skill, the group can be gradually disbanded. It is helpful to have such a group meet where a chalkboard is available. Tape recorders may be used to provide directions and special exercises, or to record parts of the lesson for playback.

When children are grouped for developmental reading instruction, a small group can read the same story in a basal reader. The group members can work around a small table or move their desks into a small circle to have backrests. After the teacher introduces the story and the vocabulary, she can set the purpose for reading. After silent reading, the children can often discuss the story and answer comprehension questions about it. They may be asked to read portions of the story orally to support responses. Discussion can be followed or preceded by a dramatization, puppet show, or other related special activity. Activities of this nature may necessitate regrouping on the basis of child interest.

A special interest group is often preceded or accompanied by a planning session to determine procedure. The planning research can use many of the research and study skills discussed in Chapter 12. A group planning to dramatize a story should meet in an area where they are free to talk quietly and move about. Those working on a puppet show should first plan their project in a planning area and then use the art center to construct the puppets. When they have finished, they will need to develop dialogue and practice before they present the show to the class.

Other children who have read the same selection may wish to come together for discussion. At the primary level the discussion may be guided by the teacher, though even here some groups, after experience with the procedure, can manage their own discussion. These children may decide to present a panel discussion of their story or to formulate a "TV show" —perhaps a question-and-answer program—that relates to it.

Interest centers

The learning or interest center has been a successful organizational supplement to classroom instruction. Such centers provide meaningful learning experiences that support and enrich instruction on an independent or a small-group basis. Children can be actively engaged in one of the centers while the teacher is working with individuals or other small groups.

Materials and activities in the centers should require a minimum of carefully constructed written directions. The activities should rely heavily on manipulative and concrete experiences as well as on a wide range of reading and browsing material. Activities should encourage children to explore and investigate, they should be easy to use, and they should relate to the curriculum.

How can this interest center experience contribute to reading-language growth? What instructional preparation and materials would be necessary to establish this experience? *(Photo by Carole Graham, BBM Associates)*

Here is an overview of various types of centers and materials that closely relate to reading and language instruction.

THE READING CENTER

This is a place where children can explore and read materials of their own choice. It should contain trade books, books of poetry, children's magazines, newspapers, and a collection of stories and poetry written by the children. It should contain tables, chairs, pillows, carpeting, and, if possible, an old sofa, to create an informal atmosphere conducive to reading. The center can be in a central part of the room to demonstrate the importance of reading, or in a quiet corner where children can read with a minimum of interruption. See Chapter 13 for additional ideas related to the reading center.

THE REFERENCE SHELVES

Here are kept all the reference materials—reference books, encyclopedias, magazines, dictionaries, maps, globes, and atlases—children might need in connection with literature units, social studies, and science to research an interest, complete an assignment, or develop a reference skill.

THE AUDIO-VISUAL AND LISTENING CENTER

A center of this type offers opportunities for self-directed listening lessons, comprehension exercises, and work in decoding skills for individuals and small groups. The teacher is free to work elsewhere with individual students and small groups, because direct teacher involvement is not essential. This center also enables children to tape small group discussions, dramatizations, and oral reading. In order to use the center, children should be carefully instructed in use of the various machines there. A side benefit from this experience is the development of responsibility and self-direction as a learner.

The center should contain equipment of the following nature: a tape recorder, record player, set of six or eight earphones, slide and filmstrip projector, tapes, records, filmstrips, and a television set. There should be instructions available on how to use all the equipment in the center. Teacher- or pupil-constructed materials for structured listening lessons and sets of books and accompanying records may also be present. There should be at least one table, six to eight chairs, and a storage cupboard for storing machines when they are not in use.

THE ART CENTER

Children can use the art center individually or in small groups to prepare illustrations of various kinds for story sharing, to make puppets for dramatizing stories, to make scenery for plays, and for regular art activities.

Activities stemming from the center can also serve to motivate creative written expression and to improve the ability to follow directions.

Among the desirable items for an art center are a work table, storage cabinets, and available water; paints, both water and tempera, crayons, and colored chalk; paper for cutting, drawing, and construction; library paste, glue, and wheat paste; scissors, yarn, pieces of cloth, burlap, and needles; a folder of directions for making a variety of things such as mobiles, bookmarks, bulletins, bulletin board displays, puppets, scenery, collages, posters, etc.; clay and papier-mâché materials for making masks and models; paper bags for construction of masks; and saws, hammers, nails, pieces of wood, and wire for constructing dioramas, models, and similar objects. Some of these materials can be contributed by parents.

As with the other centers, there should be explicit directions for using the art center and for cleaning afterward.

THE COMMUNICATION CENTER

In this area children find inspiration to do creative writing, develop vocabulary, and share with others the things they have written. They can expand their vocabularies by using new words in games and creative writing projects. There also should be times when small groups meet here to discuss ideas and plan projects.

Furniture, materials, and supplies here should consist of a table, chairs, shelves, reading and language games, a file of pictures, paper, pencils, folders of class stories, samples of child-produced newspapers, a word box containing descriptive and often-used words compiled by the children, a dictionary, a thesaurus, and a file of story starters. There should be flannel boards, alphabet letters, small blackboards, and chalk for use by children in the early grades. There should be a bulletin board nearby to display children's stories and illustrations.

THE ROLE-PLAYING CENTER

This center provides for individual and small-group development of story dramatization, role playing of problem-solving situations, and creating and presenting puppet shows of various types. If possible, partially screen this area from the rest of the classroom.

A puppet stage made from a refrigerator or moving carton or some other large container and sheets for shadow plays should be available, together with space for children to act out roles. To make a puppet stage from a refrigerator or moving carton, follow the directions in Figure 15-1.

Physical organization of the classroom

Always take into account the physical arrangement of the classroom when
571 you organize for instruction in reading and the language arts. Consider not

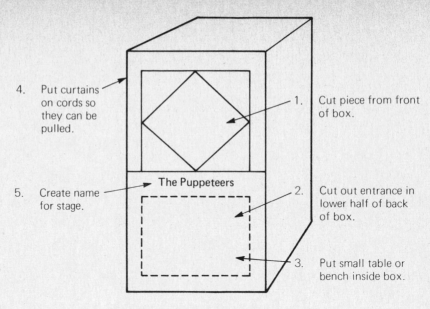

4. Put curtains on cords so they can be pulled.

1. Cut piece from front of box.

The Puppeteers

5. Create name for stage.

2. Cut out entrance in lower half of back of box.

3. Put small table or bench inside box.

Figure 15-1. Puppet Stage Front

only the size, type, and number of desks, chairs, tables, and other furniture, but also the permanent facilities. The presence and the location of a source of water must be considered in planning science and art activities and thus, indirectly, reading activities. The location of the coat closet, the windows, and the door (or doors) is similarly important. The desks and chairs should lend themselves to mobility, as should the other furniture that is not of necessity stationary.

Figure 15-2 pictures the arrangement of various centers and furniture in a classroom that is fairly typical in shape.

OTHER STRATEGIES FOR INDIVIDUALIZING INSTRUCTION IN READING AND THE LANGUAGE ARTS

Two approaches to individualization, both of which are used more often in the upper primary and intermediate grades, are individual learning packets and contracts. Both require careful planning and are more successful with students who function well independently.

In learning packets materials are organized to allow the child to progress at his own rate. He can be evaluated by a pretest in a certain skill area; if he completes the test satisfactorily, he proceeds to the next skill. If he needs additional reinforcement, he is referred to a variety of activities that will give him such practice. Once he completes the evaluation posttest satisfactorily he proceeds to the next skill.

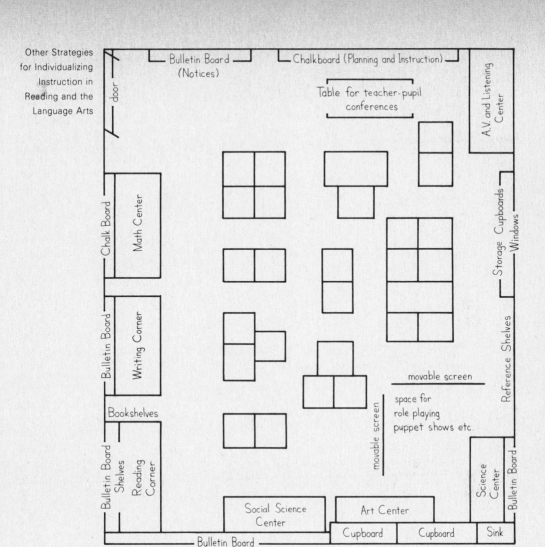

Figure 15-2. Diagram of a Classroom with Interest Centers

The student evaluates his practice work and his pretest and posttest results in cooperation with the teacher. He should also record his progress and growth in a particular skill.

Contracts, usually formed in a conference with the teacher, can be used in conjunction with the learning packet. As the student confers with the teacher he decides what and how much he hopes to accomplish in the area or areas under contract. At the end of the contract period the student meets with the teacher to evaluate what he has accomplished. Teacher and student then organize a new contract.

Learning packets and contracts can be incorporated into any type of classroom organization and are particularly useful for offering enrichment for 573 the more mature student.

What evidence suggests provision for individualized instruction? How does the physical organization and plan of the classroom help? *(Photo by Monkmeyer Press Photo Service)*

What is the value of individualizing instruction through teacher-student contracts?
What achievement and attitude factors are necessary for an effective contract?

It is important to the success of any reading program that the teacher create a positive and supportive atmosphere for the individual child. For this reason he should encourage the student to participate as much as possible in planning classroom organization so that he feels the classroom is really his own.

In his search for instructional alternatives, the teacher will be interested in a number of recent approaches to organization and individualization of instruction.[16] These references are practical volumes that offer suggestions, ideas, and methods for implementation which are in harmony with many of the suggestions made in this chapter.

In previous chapters we have consistently emphasized the importance of identifying individual needs and making provision for them in the instructional program. Creative organization of the classroom can greatly facilitate instruction, but the teacher's sensitivity to the needs of individual children is the key to individualization. Administrative and classroom organizational patterns may reflect great ingenuity and careful planning, but the classroom teacher must assume the direct responsibility for individualizing the program. In the final analysis it is the classroom teacher who must organize and individualize the program on site to account for achievement and learning differences and the variety of background experiences that children bring to the classroom.

575

Footnotes

[1]George I. Thomas and Joseph Crescimbeni, *Individualizing Instruction in the Elementary School* (New York: Random House, Inc., 1967), pp. 23–24.

[2]Cecil Floyd, "Meeting Children's Reading Needs in the Intermediate Grades: A Preliminary Report," *Elementary School Journal,* 55 (October 1954), 99–103.

[3]Wallace Ramsey, "An Evaluation of a Joplin Plan of Grouping for Reading Instruction," *The Journal of Educational Research,* 55 (August 1962), 567–72. Pauline L. Williams, "Some Group Reading Results," *Chicago School Journal,* 31 (1949), 90–94.

[4]Charles S. Berry, "The Introduction of Homogeneous Grouping," *The Grouping of Pupils, Thirty-Fifth Yearbook, NSSE, Part I* (Bloomington, Ill.: National Society for the Study of Education, 1936), pp. 37–38.

[5]Nila Banton Smith, *American Reading Instruction* (Newark, Del.: International Reading Association, 1965).

[6]Carleton Washburne, "Burke's Individualized System as Developed in Winnetka," *Adapting the Schools to Individual Differences, Twenty-Fourth Yearbook, NSSE, Part II* (Bloomington, Ill.: Public School Publishing, 1925).

[7]Helen Parkhurst, "The Dalton Plan," *Adapting the School to Individual Differences, Twenty-Fourth Yearbook, NSSE, Part II* (Bloomington, Ill.: Public School Publishing, 1925).

[8]Robert Hill Lane, "The Junior School: Its Plan and Purpose," *Addresses and Proceedings of the NEA* (Washington, D. C.: NEA, 1935), pp. 381–82.

[9]John I. Goodlad and Robert H. Anderson, *The Nongraded Elementary School* (New York: Harcourt Brace Jovanovich, Inc., 1963).

[10]Willard C. Olson, "Seeking, Self-Selection, and Pacing in the Use of Books by Children," *The Packet* (Boston: D. C. Heath & Company, 1952), pp. 3–10.

[11]Some advocates of the individualized approach maintain that much larger numbers of children can be instructed.

[12]Harry W. Sartain, "Advantages and Disadvantages of Individualized Reading," *Current Issues in Reading,* 13, 2, ed. Nila Banton Smith (Newark, Del.: International Reading Association, 1969), 328–43.

[13]Harry W. Sartain, "The Roseville Experiment with Individualized Reading," *The Reading Teacher,* 13 (April 1960), 277–81.

[14]See Nila Banton Smith, *Reading Instruction for Today's Children* (Englewood Cliffs, N.J.: Prentice-Hall, Inc., 1963).

[15]Margaret A. Robinson, "Differentiating Instruction to Provide for the Needs of Learners Through Organizational Practices," *Readings on Reading,* eds. Alfred R. Binter, John J. Dalbal, Jr., and Leonard K. Kise (New York: Intext Educational Publishers, 1969). Used by permission.

[16]Lillian Weber, *The English Infant School and Informal Education* (Englewood Cliffs, N.J.: Prentice-Hall, Inc., 1971); Joseph D. Hassett and Arline Weisberg, *Open Education: Alternatives Within Our Tradition* (Englewood Cliffs, N.J.: Prentice-Hall, Inc., 1972); Maurie Hillson and Joseph Bongo, *Continuous-Progress Education: A Practical Approach* (Palo Alto, Calif.: Science Research Associates, Inc., 1971); Anne Bremer and John Bremer, *Open Education: A Beginning* (New York: Holt, Rinehart and Winston, Inc., 1972); Maurie Hillson and Ronald T. Hyman, *Change and Innovation in Elementary and Secondary Organization,* 2nd ed. (New York: Holt, Rinehart and Winston, Inc., 1971); Thorwald Esbensen, *Working with Individualized Instruction: The Duluth Experience* (Belmont, Calif.: Fearon Publishers, 1968); Robert A. Weisgerber, *Perspectives in Individualized Learning* (Itasca, Ill.: F. E. Peacock Publishers, Inc., 1971), and *Developmental Efforts in Individualized Learning* (Itasca, Ill.: F. E. Peacock, Publishers, Inc., 1971).

16

Tutors, Teaching Assistants, and Parent Education: A Program of Involvement

Focusing Questions

1. How can the services of tutors, teaching assistants, and parents help provide for children's individual learning needs?
2. What are the values of expanding staffing for the student? The teacher? The tutor or teaching assistant? The community at large?
3. How can you assess your attitude toward the involvement of tutors and teaching assistants in the instructional program? What instructional planning will be required to prepare for the effective use of tutors and teaching assistants?
4. How can tutors and teacher assistants be recruited from the community for classroom participation? What tutorial and instructional competencies will the tutor and teaching assistant need? How can these instructional competencies be developed?
5. What approaches can you use to interpret the instructional program to the community effectively?
6. How can you develop parents' understanding and support of and active participation in the instructional program?
7. How can the effectiveness of the tutor, teaching assistant, and parent participation program be evaluated?

The nuclear age has magnified the problem of educating youth for survival, self-realization, and participation in our society. The educator's task has changed from one of transmitting great masses of information to one of facilitating learning through inquiry, discovery, and creative thinking. As Kahlil Gibran puts it in *The Prophet,*

> If he is indeed wise he does not bid you enter the house of his wisdom, but rather leads you to the threshold of your own mind. . . .
>
> The musician may sing to you of the rhythm which is in all space, but he cannot give you the ear which arrests the rhythm nor the voice that echoes it. . . .
>
> For the vision of one man lends not its wings to another man.*

*Reprinted from *The Prophet,* by Kahlil Gibran, with permission of the publisher, Alfred A. Knopf, Inc. Copyright 1923 by Kahlil Gibran; renewal copyright 1951 by Administrators C.T.A. of Kahlil Gibran Estate, and Mary C. Gibran.

This is not to imply this new role is easier; indeed, it requires more individualization and personalization than does the role of purveyor of facts. "Children do not learn when the adult does the doing."[1] We may seriously question whether the daily needs of thirty children can be met by one adult alone in the classroom. The person who organizes the learning environment and facilitates the learning process must have the time and energy available for that purpose, and not be burdened with other tasks that keep him from direct contact with students. The knowledge explosion demands that many persons with varied skills be included in today's school, so students can be helped and guided as individuals to develop their abilities and realize their potential.

A second reason for an expanded specialized staff is recognition that school is only part of the child's learning milieu. An expanded staff makes possible educational programs that involve the child's whole life experience. A child probably spends about 15 percent of his time in school during his elementary school years, the remainder at home and in the wider community. The concept of learning described above recognizes that learning takes place throughout the waking hours. When home and school cooperate, time and energy can be more efficiently spent. Only when a team concept such as this implies is achieved can student needs be dealt with directly, rather than working through the hidden agenda of either side. As Bowman and Klopf have emphasized:

> The goals of such a team concept are: first to establish rapport and mutual trust between school, home, and child; then to create a learning environment in the school which is rich, varied, and alive; next, to analyze each pupil's behavior within the environment so as to identify his needs, his interests, his anxieties, his goals—conscious and unconscious—his learning style, his modes of attacking a problem, and his apparent feelings toward self and others. The final step in the process is to restructure the environment, while providing the medley of supportive services that are needed, as the learner meshes his strivings to an educational task which is consonant with his own goals, and at the same time replete with opportunity for his growth and development. This process, to be maximally effective, must be repeated ad infinitum, with continuous feedback from analysis and incessant restructuring of the environment as new needs and new potentials are identified.[2]

THE DEVELOPMENT OF EXPANDED STAFFING

The need for expanded staffing is related to two significant innovations in American education in the '60s. It would be difficult and perhaps inaccurate to say that these developments caused this need; instead, the need for an expanded staff for individualized educational programs that recognize the life of the whole child *contributes to* and *benefits from* these two innovations.

The first was a trend toward beginning formal education earlier than five. This trend is evident in the development of private and cooperative nursery schools, programs and books on teaching the toddler age to read, early reader book clubs, and educational television. Publication of Wann, Dorn, and Little's *The Intellectual Development of the Young Child* and of Jerome Bruner's theory of the possibility of teaching difficult concepts at any level also contributed to the trend. Educators began to emphasize cognitive learning for the preschool child, and parental awareness and the search for educational programs for young children were elevated in importance.

The second major development was the advent of federal funding in education. Opposition to federal entrance into what had been a domain of the states and local school districts was finally overcome in light of the dire needs in many sections of this country. Three congressional acts passed between 1962 and 1965 provided state, county, and local school districts with funds for training and using teaching assistants in public schools. The Manpower Development and Training Act of 1962 provided assistance to persons desiring but financially unable to acquire teacher training.

The two other acts, the Economic Opportunity Act of 1964 and the Elementary and Secondary Education Act of 1965, had even greater direct effect upon bringing community persons into the schools. The first created the Head Start Program, to provide learning experiences and health care for low-income preschool children. Its intent is to be a catalyst rather than a permanent structure, to encourage communities to expand educational services related to preschool programs. Among other Head Start requirements, parents must be directly involved in every program. Where this aspect of the program is emphasized and developed, a parent is an assistant in her own child's classroom, attends parent meetings, and, through representation on the Parent Advisory Councils, helps to choose program contents. Council functions vary from community to community; they may assist in establishing guidelines on personnel, facilities, and equipment.

Through this involvement parents are becoming aware of the influence they can have on the immediate educational experiences of their children, and not solely during the preschool years. These same parents may have older children, and their preschoolers soon enter public school. Parent participation can then contribute to the larger educational system.

When the first Head Start children entered kindergarten it was evident that revisions were necessary to maintain this "head start." To meet this need, Follow Through was created by the Office of Education in 1967. It was designed for kindergarten programs following Head Start programs, but has been expanded to include first, second, and third grade. Until this time few schools in low-income areas had many children enter with formal preschool backgrounds. Head Start (and state-funded equivalent programs) and Follow Through benefited parents and children. In 1968 the National Consultants for Follow Through met in Atlanta to find ways of reinforcing and making workable parent Follow Through programs. They recommended that Follow Through sponsors offer guidance to school districts on how to involve parents in their programs in a meaningful way.

579 Follow Through now continues through grade three, so those parents can

play a vital role in their child's schooling at the classroom level throughout the primary grades.

Title I of the Elementary and Secondary Education Act of 1965 (ESEA) provided funds for "helping children whose educational achievement is below the norm, including those with physical, mental, or emotional handicaps."[3] This allows a concentrated effort on reading instruction where it is needed, since it includes

Mobile libraries

Development of instructional materials

Tutoring programs

Involvement of parents and other community residents[4]

Other pressure was exerted in this area by the *Report of the National Advisory Commission on Civil Disorders* (1968). The Commission made nine recommendations for quality integrated education, one of which was "enlarged opportunities for parent and community participation in public schools."[5] These changes broaden educational experiences of a greater portion of a child's daily life and personal contacts than was covered in more traditional schooling. If parents are aware, for example, that number concepts can be reinforced by dinner table conversation and grocery store errands, the child's education on number concepts does not occur just between 10:00 and 10:20, Monday through Friday. And if schools are aware of differences in life styles, classroom activities can be made more relevant to the experiences of the child. When there are parent and student volunteers to listen and respond to individual kindergarteners, language development is not limited to teacher-directed reading and language instruction.

This broader view demands that the total community share the responsibility for educating the young, and brings many changes to the existing school system:

Parents and other adults are volunteering to help in classrooms.

Older students are volunteering to help younger children.

Adults are assisting part-time in schools, as part of their own education as credentialed teachers.

Classroom assistants are paid to help regularly with responsibility to children and teachers.

Parents are more aware of the school's educational goals, and can be more supportive with home activities and dialogue.

Schools are revising curricula in light of insight gained from closer contacts with families.

The teacher's role can now extend to diagnosing, counseling, and facilitating learning for individuals instead of the frustrating role of teaching only in groups.

It takes a wide variety of willing, knowledgeable, caring persons to share in this twenty-four-hour-a-day endeavor, and it demands the best possible communication between home, school, and community. The parts of this triad have numerous resources to share with each other, if they can become aware of their combined potential.

It is not enough to know about the development of assistance programs, based on needs and changing views in education. One must ask whether such programs actually yield the desired positive results. This was a concern, of course, from the outset. There is evidence from Head Start and Follow Through programs that parent participation and staff awareness of different life styles have affected the children in the following ways:

1. Better attendance figures
2. A more supportive relationship between home and school
3. Bond issue support
4. Revitalization of the curriculum
5. Reassessments of objectives
6. New challenges to teacher and administration for clarity[6]

The elementary school district in Fairfield, Connecticut conducted research on their Teacher Assistant program and concluded that assistants helped in overcrowded classrooms by freeing teachers to spend more time on the professional aspects of teaching.[7]

In a large-scale project for youth of low-income background, assistants were used to increase individualization and the overall effectiveness of education. Positive results were reported from all fifteen programs included, which were representative of the major geographical sections of the United States.[8] It is important to note that there were gains for all parties involved: students, teachers, new professionals, tutors and assistants, administrators, families, and the community at large. The positive effects can be magnified throughout an entire community.

Since classroom assistance comes from many sources, it is important to set forth several basic descriptions of support personnel. The different titles in the literature for the variety of community support can be classified into two major categories, the *tutor* and the *teaching assistant*. Examples will be given with reference to a reading-language program.

1. Tutor: An adult or student (any age) working with an individual student on a paid or volunteer basis
    A. Instructional tutor: Gives tutorial help in specific reading and language skills on a regular basis for a designated period of time
    B. Support tutor: Gives tutorial help in reading and language on an informal basis for a flexible period, as often as needed or convenient
2. Teaching assistant: Usually an adult from the local community or a college student on a paid or volunteer basis

A. Instructional Assistant: Performs an instructional role under direction of the teacher by instructing the whole class or a group in a particular academic or skill area

B. Organizational and Clerical Assistant: Assists the teacher by setting up supplies, checking paper work, preparing materials, and so forth

Tutors are very often other members of the student body or older students from a nearby junior high school, high school, college, or university; they can also be parents who have the time and interest to work in the classroom. Most tutors now are volunteers, but there are tutorial programs wherein parents are paid to tutor students regularly in reading. A few programs have trained and paid older students to tutor younger students in late afternoons or early evenings.

Instructional tutors usually require a certain amount of specialized training and monitoring to be effective. We shall discuss training later in the chapter. Instructional and support tutors should be offered guidance in developing positive relationships with students.

Teacher assistants are usually adults from the community or college students. Many parents volunteer for such a position, but sometimes parents, other adults, or college students are hired as part of a career development program. Such people simultaneously receive teacher training on the site or at a nearby campus. Volunteer assistants may perform an instructional role, a clerical role, or both. Paid assistants preparing for educational careers usually serve as instructional rather than as clerical assistants, but often they perform in both roles throughout a day or session. Adults not necessarily interested in educational careers may be hired with special funding, such as ESEA monies, in the instructional role, the clerical role, or both.

Most regular classroom assistance is rendered by tutors or assistants as described here, but there can be other kinds of special help from the community, such as special one-time events or demonstrations, and for things such as the library or audio-visual materials.

GOALS AND GAINS STEMMING FROM SCHOOL-COMMUNITY COOPERATION

The most obvious goals of a cooperative school-community effort are student centered: more individualized planning and instruction, more personal attention, and an enriched variety of activities designed to meet the needs of individual youngsters. Accomplishing these goals can result in gains for all involved, as described here in terms of an elementary reading-language program.

The student gains by

1. Increasing his reading and language knowledge and skills
2. Improving his self-image as a reader, a language user, and a learner, through success that can be attributed to

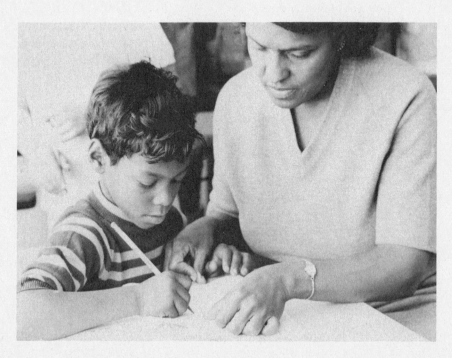

How can teachers and teaching assistants help individualize instruction? What teacher attitudes and tutor and assistant competencies are necessary for effective individualization?

A. Instruction and guidance in terms of his specific needs
B. Being in control of his own pace rather than having to hurry or wait to maintain an average
C. Emphasis on what he *can* do rather than on the very areas he shows greatest weakness in

The teacher gains

1. Time and energy—both physical and psychological—for developing relationships with his students
2. Additional views and insights regarding relationships and learning experiences in the classroom, because of
   A. A more relaxed classroom experience through working with fewer children at one time
   B. Peer support and sharing opportunities

The assistant or tutor gains

1. In self-image as a teacher and helper of others
2. Reinforcement of his own learning habits and academic skills
3. Experiences that contribute to consideration of a future career through
   A. Maintaining a success orientation with the students
   B. Discovering new insights about reading and language development through working to teach others
   C. Learning what children are really like as individuals

The community at large gains

1. Knowledge about children and effective educational programs
2. A program for youth adapted to local needs, values, and strengths
3. Compatibility between the children's home and school experiences, with complementary and consistent expectations and standards
4. The students' appreciation and respect for their own community's resources, strengths, and unique qualities, through
   A. Direct contacts with parents and other assistants from the community
   B. Seeing available talents and skills taking responsibility for education outside the school

A school may choose from among these gains those most relevant to its needs. We assume here that tutoring in the classroom is primarily for the elementary child who receives the help, but in some programs, the tutors themselves make equal or greater gains. In view of this, students in the intermediate grades who are not succeeding in the reading-language area might profitably be used to provide tutorial help (to beginning readers, for example) rather than solely as the receivers of tutorial help from successful students. Anyone planning or evaluating classroom assistance programs should keep such alternatives in mind.

TEACHER ATTITUDES AND ORGANIZATION FOR CLASSROOM ASSISTANCE

Traditionally the school classroom has been conceptualized as a learning
setting where all activities and experiences pivot around the central figure,

the teacher. In the past teachers have even felt guilty when they were not in complete control of classroom activities. A more realistic view of the teacher's role is that of learning facilitator helping students design and carry out experiences related to their needs and interests. A facilitator is supportive and directly available with guidance, but works toward the goal of helping the student assume greater responsibility for behavior and expenditure of time. This instructional viewpoint is more appropriate in light of the information explosion now occurring and because it tends to emphasize the importance of individual strengths and needs. The facilitator role, however, requires additional assistance in the self-contained classroom.

Any community help must be within the context of the teacher's views. If a teacher views other persons in the classroom negatively, as time consuming or threatening, he is not apt to look upon tutors or assistants favorably. But if a teacher welcomes additional help, then recruiting, training, and evaluating will seem to him to be profitable uses of time.

A teacher must carefully examine his attitude toward tutors and assistants by asking himself

1. Do I feel comfortable with other people in the classroom?
2. Am I able to express my goals and my program clearly enough that others might apply them in concrete ways?
3. Am I able to share with other people the roles of helper, leader, parent-substitute, authority figure—the many functions I perform with children every day?
4. Am I willing to be questioned about my educational program, defend certain practices, and perhaps change others for alternatives that are more effective or more consistent with my educational philosophy?
5. Am I willing to admit my weaknesses, inconsistencies, lack of information (in other words, my humanness) in order to enlist the help of others in the attempt to offer students a richer, more caring, more individualized school program?
6. Do I consider the increase of individual attention a great enough payoff, given the time and effort required for organization and planning?

In addition to a positive attitude toward help within the classroom, the teacher must possess or develop the ability to organize for assistance. The most effective means of facilitating reading and language development must be identified, and the how and why of instruction must be explained to others. Further, instructional tasks must be organized in such a way that assistants can clearly identify their contributions to the program. And finally, the teacher must determine the assistant or tutorial role best suited to each individual.

In order to make decisions about assistance for a given task, information about the results of existing programs might be helpful. Earlier we pointed out the reported mutual benefits of expanded staffing. In tutorial programs

where older students tutored younger students, both groups benefitted, but the greatest gains were made by those who served as tutors. The rationale behind this is referred to as *LTT, Learning Through Teaching.*[9] In a Mobilization for Youth project where older children tutored younger children for five months, the younger group gained 6.0 months of reading ability while the tutors gained 3.4 years! Another application of LTT was a project of Ronald and Peggy Lippitt in Michigan, where older children made good progress in the role of tutor. At Boston University Donald Durrell has reported that students helping each other were more effective than when instruction was by one teacher who was being pulled in many directions simultaneously. On a project in Portland, Oregon, older students kept written logs of their tutoring experiences. Quotes from two of these demonstrate the opportunities for self-insight and learnings about human behavior.

> *November 29.* Sherry was stubborn and wouldn't work today. We are working on division. She doesn't try any more.
>
> *December 5.* I don't know what to do about Sherry. She still won't try.
>
> *December 9.* All of a sudden Sherry understands division. She was pleasant and cooperative today. She was like she used to be. I guess I was wrong about her trying. She didn't understand and lost confidence. I am sorry I didn't understand the situation. She is a real good kid. I am never going to accuse her again.
>
> *October 25.* Kim still reads too fast.
>
> *October 29.* Today I devised a way to slow Kim down. If he reads aloud too fast, I give him a red strip of paper for a speeding ticket. If he reads with expression, I give him a green strip. We are going to make a graph of the strips and try to have it all green.
>
> *November 25.* Kim does better all the time. I swear he is smarter than me.*

In another project an evaluator wrote these comments about a tutorial program:

> I asked everyone I interviewed what changes they had seen in the children who are tutors. From the parents came the response that they had noticed that they no longer were having trouble with their grades. From the tutors themselves, they nearly all said that they now understand how a teacher feels, they understand how a student feels, and that they are more understanding of the teaching/learning process. One curious thing that came up again and again, from the tutors, was that they said that one of the gains was that the things they had missed in kindergarten or first grade came up and they had to learn them for the first time. Such things as alphabetical order, number concepts, reading, singing, memorizing, etc., and particularly the rules of behavior and how much of a problem is created when the learner is not attending. Nearly all the tutors

*From p. 47 in *Children Teach Children* by Alan Gartner, Mary Conway Kohler, and Frank Riessman. Copyright © 1971 by Alan Gartner, Mary Conway Kohler, and Frank Riessman. By permission of Harper & Row, Publishers, Inc.

learned this from being teachers for a while. When I asked if they thought the classes could get along without them, they said, no, that they needed them now, that there were things that they couldn't do in class when they were without tutors being present and this gives them a feeling of being needed, being important and this is verified by the teachers that I interviewed.*

These authors continue to point out in their research reports and anecdotal records of LTT that the "key to learning is individualization, and the use of the student or pupil as a teacher is one way to increase this individualization."[10]

It is obvious from these statements that teachers must carefully consider their goals for each tutoring situation from the perspective of both the tutor and the tutee. This information will be valuable in selecting individuals for instructional assistance and in determining their role in the program.

Here is one way one might go about the organization for classroom assistance. A teacher should begin with questions such as the following: In describing my reading comprehension program, what do I consider to be

The major goals
The specific objectives for students
The essential materials for achieving the goals
The student experiences that lead to goal achievement
An efficient record-keeping procedure
An adequate instructional evaluation approach

Once he has the answers, the teacher can consider the value of proposed instructional assistance in the forms of

1. Instructional tutoring
2. Support tutoring
3. Instructional assistance
4. Clerical assistance

and at home as

1. Direct experiences with students
2. Clerical or organizational tasks

A teacher would then repeat this process for other aspects of the reading-language program.

From Table 16-1 the teacher can estimate the variety of instructional skills to be developed and the instructional assistance and time requirements of

*From pp. 58–59 in *Children Teach Children* by Alan Gartner, Mary Conway Kohler, and Frank Riessman. Copyright © 1971 by Alan Gartner, Mary Conway Kohler, and Frank Riessman. By permission of Harper & Row, Publishers, Inc.

the program. Such estimates help to establish instructional priorities and to determine options for utilizing assistance in the instructional program. Now the teacher is in a position to submit requests for assistance to a staff coordinator (if one exists) or to instigate recruiting procedures of his own.

Table 16-1. Proposed Assistance to This Program

	Reading Comprehension/ Decoding	Writing	Speaking	Listening
At school				
Instructional tutoring				
Support tutoring				
Instructional assistance (group)				
Clerical assistance				
At home				
Direct experiences with students				
Clerical or organizational tasks				

RECRUITMENT AND SELECTION OF TEACHER ASSISTANTS

In schools where classroom assistance is a relatively new concept, some form of education for parents and teachers will be necessary, preceding or coinciding with the instigation of a teacher-assistant program. This may require informal discussions and written invitations for community help or formal, regular exchanges of information and feelings between school and community. In schools where classroom assistance already exists to any degree, the next step is to expand or refine present practices. In either phase it is desirable to establish specific goals and guidelines for the program.

The question is not "Does the community have any resources to offer its school program?" Any community has a wide variety of people to meet many school needs. The main question is how to recruit and use assistance

in a planned manner.

Depending upon the types of assistance requested, recruitment can coincide with informing the community. For example, if a school is requesting elementary, junior high school, high school, and college students as tutors, the parents would be less involved than in the case of a school asking parents to tutor or assist.

The recruitment procedure itself must be planned carefully to attract the available resources. Existing tutorial and assistant programs have found that the following two criteria provide a more fruitful approach in the search for resource people than searching for skills already developed in specific academic areas: (1) interest in helping others to learn, and (2) motivation to accept the challenge of this new experience personally and intellectually. Give some thought about the persons that would be most suitable. There may be some balances or gaps to consider. For example, if there are no teachers in the school from a particular minority group or life style of the community, it may be extremely helpful to have someone from that group assist at school. Such a person may help provide the missing link, identification of the needs of certain children who have "tuned out."

In the past, many of our schools have been staffed by a homogeneous group of people with a limited range of values and behaviors. If we select only volunteers who perpetuate this image of American culture, we merely repeat old patterns and do not take full advantage of a multicultural opportunity. Hayden has suggested that assistants be selected "who will bring a whole new set of life experiences into the school and become a real communication link between the school and the community with information flowing in both directions."[11]

Each local school staff must decide which form of communication to use in the recruiting. Selection at the local level is more likely to be effective than is a district-wide policy, which may not be sensitive to individual neighborhood needs and characteristics.

The teaching staff, whether it is one teacher, several, or an entire school, should identify the list of possible tasks. An attempt should be made to match the interests and motivations of the people offering to help with the tasks identified. As more people volunteer, more of the instructional tasks will be chosen, but a volunteer for each is an unrealistic expectation. In the case of paid assistance, specific skills or interests are the criteria, so the best people for the jobs are actually selected through interviews. Where both types of assistance are available, an overall plan can best determine how to make optimum use of available resources.

There should be someone to coordinate community assistance in a school. Where organization and scheduling have been left to chance, most programs have remained haphazard, irregular, and with unknown (or at least undocumented) results. Whether for a single room or a whole school, someone must assume responsibility for recruitment, selection, training, 589 scheduling, and evaluating the program. If no one has time to encourage volunteers and to notice their positive contributions, school personnel will soon find that the first volunteers no longer have time to work at school. A resource person such as the reading specialist or vice-principal effectively coordinates this effort in many schools.

Identifying tutorial and instructional competencies

The development program for tutors and classroom assistants will take as many forms as there are schools implementing such programs. Training given exclusively to paid assistants or primarily to volunteers will be different from training given to a combination of both types. The specific competencies being developed will demand that content vary considerably. The training program described here provides for a wide variety of options in personnel and in desired skills but it is not all-inclusive. The competencies cited in Table 16-2 represent a general range of skills that teachers may wish to consider for development with individuals assisting in the classroom. In the last section we stress the importance of identifying the precise tasks a tutor or assistant would be expected to perform. These competencies show how various skills pertain to the different tutor and assistant roles. Any comparable list, developed for a given tutor or teacher assistant program, will of course determine the direction and type of training. The pace, depth, and extent of training should be adjusted according to the interests and skills of the volunteers and paid assistants.

A brief discussion of the four sets of tutor and teacher-assistant competencies follows.

The children

1. Awareness of the developmental characteristics of children

Children have particular unique characteristics; they are not miniature adults. Knowing these characteristics helps classroom assistants to plan and act in a manner compatible with children as they find them.

2. Application of techniques that enhance and maintain a positive self-image

Instruction should emphasize a child's positive growth rather than his weaknesses and failures, what they can do rather than what they cannot do. A child is not constantly called upon to perform in areas that are threatening to him until he builds skill and confidence in such areas.

3. Ability to convey a friendly, supportive attitude to children

If children are to become effective individuals with positive self-concepts, they must live with people who are that way. They need to find acceptance as individuals. Tutors and assistants who work with children must realize the importance of their interest, friendliness, and trust.

> 4. Ability to relate to children and offer leadership and guidance to them in a learning situation

A person aiding a child should be able to speak to him in vocabulary he can understand, but not below his maturity level.

In most situations when a child is treated in a matter-of-fact, respectful manner rather than as an inferior person, he will strive to live up to the expectation.

Equally important is the ability to offer a child freedom of choice in appropriate areas and leadership and guidance when he needs it. Training for teacher assistants that stresses the characteristics of children helps develop a realistic balance between freedom and structure.

The instruction

> 1. Ability to apply knowledge about conditions conducive to children's learning

Basic information about concepts such as motivation, mental set, practice, and transfer of learning is helpful to assistants, as is understanding the meaning of "telling is not teaching." Such understanding encompasses other instructional aspects, such as pacing, degree of abstraction, and attention span.

> 2. Ability to work with individuals and small groups in a learning situation.

Factors important to individual learning include appropriate vocabulary, providing opportunities for decision making on the part of the child, and recognizing his need for guidance. The group situation introduces new instructional considerations, such as comfortable pacing, different expectation levels, and the ability to handle dominant and aggressive group members. The dynamics of a group produce a very different situation than is found in a one-to-one teacher-child relationship. Many experiences are needed to develop an understanding of individual and group needs.

One training program for assistants in the area of reading recommends that tutors

> Be consistent
> Follow through on promises
> Hear the child's ideas about the sessions
> Don't pry or betray confidences
> Give praise, but not undeserved

Table 16-2.

Competencies	Tutors			Assistants		
	Support		Instructional adult	Clerical		Instructional adult
	child	adult		child	adult	
The Children						
1. Awareness of the developmental characteristics of children	x*	x	x			x
2. Application of techniques that enhance and maintain a positive self-image (emphasizing and using capabilities rather than isolating and drilling on weaknesses)	x*	x	x			x
3. Ability to convey a friendly, supportive attitude to children	x	x	x			x
4. Ability to relate to children and offer leadership and guidance to them in a learning situation			x			x
The Instruction						
1. Ability to apply knowledge about conditions conducive to children's learning			x			x
2. Ability to work with individuals and small groups in a learning situation			x			x
3. Ability to work with large groups in a learning situation						x

	C1	C2	C3	C4	C5	C6
4. Development of special instructional skills (use of the library, use of art materials in a reading-language program, use of drama in a reading-language program, listening to children read or speak, taking dictation, reading or telling a story, and others)	x			x		
The Organization of Instruction						
1. Development of specific skills (preparation of class materials, record-keeping, checking paper work, lettering in manuscript print, etc.)	x	x	x			
2. Ability to initiate necessary tasks, to perform assigned tasks, and to follow through to completion	x	x				
The Agreement to Do a Job						
1. Performing the responsibility on a regular basis, with the obligation to notify in case of absence	x	x	x	x	x	x
2. Acceptance of the necessity to receive training and guidance to perform the job, and the desire to improve	x	x		x	x	
3. Skill in communicating with and relating to other personnel, especially the classroom teacher	x	x	x	x	x	x

*To a limited degree.

Do tasks, chores *with* him or her

Be alert to cues; respond to them, use them in the session

3. Ability to work with large groups in a learning situation

The comments about small groups also apply to large groups, with an emphasis upon the balance between individual and group needs. The primary value of assistants, though, is their potential for giving much-needed individual attention. They must be helped to realize this and to assign a high priority to individual needs of children.

4. Development of specific instructional skills

We have discussed several examples of teaching skills in the elementary reading-language program. Since it is not our purpose here to dictate content for a program, other references need to be sought that are compatible with the reading program. Refer first to the discussion in Chapters 6 through 15 on developing a wide range of reading and language skills. Two additional resources are Sliesenger's *Guidebook for the Volunteer Reading Teacher* and the IRA *Handbook for the Volunteer Tutor.*[12] Both discuss specific materials, methods, activities, and diagnostic measures, and the latter gives detailed descriptions of decoding and comprehension lessons.

Since the single greatest contribution of assistants in the classroom is giving individual attention, a guiding principle for selecting activities would be helpful: *Reading is one important part of the total language development.* Functional application of any of the language skills works to improve reading. Aiding a child with his reading is not limited to decoding or reading comprehension activities. "Creating a social setting in which language can be used as a necessary force in the sharing and shaping of ideas"[13] is as important as providing the right book at the right time. This total program demands the use of the children's spontaneous experiences and expressions as well as planned situations.

The organization of instruction

1. Development of special instructional skills

Each teacher must determine the range of special instructional skills. For example, preparing classroom materials for the reading program involves awareness of such considerations as the size and clarity of visual symbols. In addition, the ability to use the specific method of manuscript printing is necessary for developing experience charts. It is also important, however, that reasons for the task and the principles behind their use be identified for the tutor and assistant. If persons helping in the classroom understand the reasons for a particular practice or routine, they are more likely to follow the practice and be able to succeed in transferring it to new situations.

2. Ability to initiate necessary tasks, to perform assigned tasks, and to follow
   through to completion

Once an assistant gains confidence in his ability to perform a task and the
teacher displays trust and approval in the quality of performance, he often
begins to act spontaneously as needs arise. Teacher expectations play an
important role in the process of initiation, performance, and completion of
instructional tasks.

The agreement to do a job

1. Performing the responsibility on a regular basis, with the obligation to
   notify in the case of absence

If there is a need for assistants, these individuals must see the importance
of regular participation. If assistants develop independence in performing
instructional tasks, the true importance of their regular attendance will
become clear.

2. Acceptance of the necessity to receive training and guidance to perform the
   job, and the desire to improve

These are important requirements for a paid position, but they are also
very desirable with volunteers. Teachers must convey acceptance of the
assistant's present behavior and clarify that teachers, too, must continue
to learn and improve their performance. Assistants will respond positively
to praise and appreciation of their strong qualities.

3. Skill in communicating with and relating to other personnel, especially the
   classroom teacher

To develop this competence persons in direct contact with the assistant
should be open and friendly in accepting an additional person on the
"educational team." If the teacher finds listening to assistants' concerns an
important use of time, he is apt to be listened to in return. The teacher
should set the tone for this kind of professional exchange and encourage
the assistant to share successful experiences as well as problem areas.

Developing tutorial and instructional competencies

Some beginning assistants may already possess many of the skills they
need for clerical work. For people who type and have knowledge of duplicating machines, for example, training per se requires assessing their initial
competencies and then planning a program to help them acquire the additional ones important to their assignment.

Selection criteria vary according to the nature of the tutor or assistant
assignment. Experience is the first variable to consider. As one might

conclude from the competencies chart, certain abilities are desirable, but it would be unrealistic to assume mastery in all areas from, say, eleven- or twelve-year-olds in those positions. Second, the degree of structure in the task is another variable. The role of support tutor is generally rather informal, and a warm, receptive attitude toward children is more important than any specific skill. Third, whether the assistant is paid or volunteer also has a bearing on standards. A volunteer can work in areas of his present strengths without being expected to learn more, but a paid assistant is expected to fit a particular job description that probably includes a certain number of tasks unfamiliar to him. Finally, relevance of this position to the assistant's total daily life at this point is a factor to consider. For pre-teen and teen-age student tutors, these experiences do not necessarily feed into a particular career plan, but they offer a direct means of learning to relate to people effectively, and they provide some idea of what teaching might be like. For college students, feedback on teaching and communication skills may contribute to career decisions. For adults within the community, being an assistant may be part of a career development plan, or it may be a position they enjoy because it allows them to be involved in their own elementary children's school experience, and to gain appreciation for the teaching role.

An important consideration in initial contacts with all out-of-school assistants is the possibility that these people may themselves have a background of school failure or dislike much of what school represented for them. It is imperative, then, first to build a positive, pleasant image of school. Their presence may indicate that they have a more positive attitude, but they still lack confidence in a school environment, confidence that will be important to their success in their roles.

The preparation program itself can take different forms. Four different approaches for developing knowledge, attitudes, and competencies related to instruction include observation, discussion, simulation, and direct experience. In most instances a combination of these will be used, but at certain times one is more valuable than another, or one is meaningless without the accompaniment of another.

Observation means being present while someone else performs the task in question. It is preferable that discussion accompany an observation session, but an observer can also be guided by pre-observational discussions that identify key factors to look for within a session, followed by discussion. Observation is appropriate for all ages of assistants and for all tasks asked of them. Where there are a variety of acceptable ways to teach rhyming sounds, for example, the trainee might observe several methods before he decides one that is comfortable for him. Discussion should thus focus on optional routes to a common goal. Audio and video tape recordings can be valuable tools for examining certain instructional behaviors. Repeated viewings of a video tape can be very useful for emphasizing a limited number of key points designated at the outset.

Observational experience is valuable in two major ways in training: (1) to provide an overview and orientation to school environment and operation, and (2) to provide models of instruction and support for specific skills and attitudes. In the former case the experiences offered will depend upon the information needed for future use and the interests of the trainees. For individuals planning to work with students in a classroom, an orientation observation might put most emphasis on students, teachers, or room design.

Observation usually means being present in the classroom; it can also mean using audio-visual media. Films, video tapes, slides, and audio tapes are extremely helpful for teaching purposes because they can be stopped or repeated for optimum instruction. Attending a live session being video taped for discussion to follow can be an effective means of learning. There are films available on, for example, characteristics of various ages of children or room organization that capsulize what would take at least a full semester's time to see through live observation. As with the other aspects of a training program, it is important for teachers to remain open to many methods of conveying information and attitudes, so the most effective ones are not omitted by virtue of tradition or habit. Specific components for observational experiences include the following.

1. Room design related to the reading-language program
   A. Furniture arrangement (desks, tables, materials, work and quiet areas, conversation areas, traffic patterns, teacher's base)
   B. Bulletin boards and walls (decoration, displays, announcements)
   C. Location and accessibility of books, paper, and other reading and writing supplies
   D. Location and accessibility of audio-visual equipment (projectors, phonograph, listening posts, records, language master, slide viewer)
2. How students learn reading and language skills
   A. Participation of each student in total group, small-group, and individual instruction
   B. Community background, home life, and family speech patterns reflected in student responses
   C. Display of the language development skills (decoding, writing, listening, and speaking)
      1. Emphasizing each separately
      2. Examining the interrelationship among skills
3. How reading and language skills are taught
   A. Type of lesson being taught (phonics, creative writing)
   B. Type of introduction to lesson, motivation techniques, using children's background experiences, involvement of students directly
   C. Aids and materials used in the presentation
   D. Grouping of students, differences in the activities or work of the various groups
   E. Evaluation procedures used by the teacher, involvement of the students in this process

4. The library or media center and the application of reading-language skills
   A. Atmosphere created by the environment (arrangement of furniture, displays, etc.)
   B. Frequency of use of printed and audio-visual materials
   C. Percentage of the total enrollment using the facility
   D. Kind and frequency of instruction in the skills of using a library or media center
   E. Checkout system and availability of adult assistance for various needs

Adults interested in becoming better informed about the school or planning careers in education might find an additional type of observation helpful.

5. Use of the reading and language development skills in the total school
   A. Verbal interaction between adults and children (principal, secretary, teachers, custodians, all supporting staff)
   B. Evidence in the school environment of the use of communication skills (displays, announcements, and student participation in various aspects of organization, decision making, and presentation of announcements)
   C. School communication with home and community

Any of these items could be expanded with key questions to guide an observer followed by discussion. For example, under component 1, Room Design, consider specific observational questions related to item C, location and accessibility of books, paper, and other reading and writing supplies:

Are there enough books to provide a wide range of choice for each member of the class?

Is there a wide range of reading levels represented, so that every student can find a book he can read successfully?

Are there children's literature books available and supplementary readers and a variety of literature (prose, poetry, fiction, nonfiction)?

Does the classroom library area invite relaxed reading and browsing?

Are there opportunities for student discussion and exchange?

Is there a readily available supply of writing materials (lined and unlined paper of different dimensions and spacing, pens, pencils, felt pens)?

The questions would vary with the age of the observer, his interest, and his past experience. Written comments by the observer may be helpful for discussion purposes.

The second major area for observation involves all persons working directly with children in a support or instructional role. Experiences might include observation of the following aspects of a reading-language program in operation.

Children listening to a story or poem

A child reading orally

A child dictating a description for an adult or other assistant to record

An adult helping a child to do his own writing

Children taking directions for an assignment or project

A lesson in decoding

Children choosing and using library materials

A child (children) taking a spelling test

A child telling about an event or demonstrating an item he would like to share with class members

A lesson in critical listening

A lesson in manuscript or cursive writing, letter formation

Children working on follow-up aspects of a lesson (answering questions, drawing pictures, role playing, constructing puppets)

Depending upon the needs of the trainee, the focus in such observations can be the adult in the situation (usually a teacher), the student, or the interaction between teacher and student. Observations can be repeated as necessary or coupled with simulation or actual experience.

The impact of unplanned, natural observation occurring every day must not be underestimated. Even though there may be verbal descriptions of recommended methods or techniques, daily contact with a classroom teacher in action is a major influence on the development of an assistant's competencies. The power of a model is demonstrated in Arline Hobson's record of a classroom assistant's comment to a teacher: "I see you talk to children with the same kind of voice and in the same kind of words you talk to me."[14] She went on to report that her girls had been afraid of her and her husband, but they tried the teacher's approach of talking with them like other human beings, and it was effective.

Discussion is an obvious means of teaching new tasks, but the power of "telling" should not be overestimated. A most desirable plan is to accompany the means of demonstration (observation, simulation) and actual experience with discussion. This is even important with adults, since activities, routines, and learning tools common to the experienced teacher may be unknown to an assistant. Depending upon needs and numbers, discussion may consist of individual conferences or seminar sessions, or modifications of either. The term *discussion* is chosen deliberately, instead of *lecture,* to indicate a sharing of the talking time. There may be times, however, when a presentation, even a lecture, is appropriate for the content involved, but the important point to remember is the need to provide opportunity for the receivers (trainees) to respond, each in his own way, to the information in order to apply it more effectively.

Discussion cannot be confined to particular topics of the reading-language program. Of the four forms of training, it is the most informal, personal, and spontaneous mode of information exchange. One of its most important contributions is its support to the other three forms.

Simulation, a middle ground between observation and classroom experience, gives the trainee practice in a given task without experiencing the actual consequences of his acts. This technique is appropriate for all age and experience levels, and is especially valuable in situations involving human interaction (as opposed to clerical tasks). Depending upon the desire of the trainee, the simulated experience can be observed by the instructor or peers or both via observation or an audio or video tape recording. Like observations, simulation must be planned around specific goals, in order to evaluate its effectiveness. It can be repeated and modified as many times as desired to achieve the predetermined goals effectively. Once the technique has been introduced and found to be helpful, trainees may begin to ask for simulated experiences in areas they recognize as unknown, threatening, or where they need practice.

Suggestions for specific application of this mode to the reading-language program may parallel those itemized and discussed under observation.

Actual experience is, of course, the real test of the trainee's understanding and ability to tutor and assist in the classroom. Experience can be gained in a variety of ways. With clerical work, sample tasks may be assigned. The trainee and instructor can evaluate the work and determine the assistant's strengths and identify areas that need special attention. With classroom instruction or support, the process is less clear, because it is impossible to determine in one session whether an assistant or tutor helped to improve the child's self-esteem or his language or reading skills. A long-term perspective is needed. The best that can be done in evaluating a single session is to examine the assistant's performance and the student's short-term accomplishments—for example whether student appears to know initial consonants—and attitudes present—whether student was relaxed and motivated to attempt the task.

Regardless of the group size the assistant will eventually be assigned to, it is advisable to begin with an individual. This provides him with an opportunity to become sensitive to the instructional needs of one child before he deals with the special techniques of group management. Then he can proceed to a small-group setting, followed by a large-group situation. Specific experiences can include reading or telling a story, playing a word game, giving a spelling test, or taking a short walk, to name a few.

Discussion and tape recording (audio or video) can also be used with the experiences, which are most valuable if the trainee is helped to evaluate his performance in some way, to see how to improve his behavior for future situations. Suggestions for specific application of experience to the reading-language program can also be similar to those identified under observation.

As with most learning, the more individualized the instruction, the more effective the training is likely to be. If the trainees are allowed frequent

opportunities to question and to help mold their own training, morale and
actual performance will be at a relatively high level.

Trainees themselves have requested prime consideration for the following
topics during training:

> Social backgrounds of students
> Understanding of various grouping patterns
> New legislation and programs
> New trends in curriculum planning[15]

Time has proved a key factor in the success of assistance programs—time
for planning and conferring with individuals and groups of tutors and
assistants, time for developing teacher understanding in using assistants,
time to initiate, develop, and maintain a program smoothly at the local
level. It requires creative thinking to find teacher time during school hours,
but adding tasks at the end of the day is not realistic and will result in
minimal support from many teachers.

SCHOOL-COMMUNITY COMMUNICATION

Of great importance to the effectiveness of a school program is a favorable
image communicated to parents and other community members. Even
when there is an active paid or volunteer assistance program, many parents
will not be able to be part of it and will miss the firsthand opportunity to
be involved directly and learn about the philosophy and practices of the
school staff.

The absence of a well-planned, open communication system produces an
unfriendly, aloof image, which can result in disinterest, lack of cooperation, alienation, and even hostility on the part of parents. An extreme
version of this situation resulted in the step-by-step plan of Marie Lurie
in her book *How to Change the Schools.* The ways of reaching out to the
community suggested in this chapter are intended to prevent a total break-
down in relations such as must have occurred in Lurie's New York situation.

It should not be assumed that teacher and school administrators are automatically effective in the area of human relations. Considerable thought,
effort, and experience are needed to build school-community interaction.
"Teachers need and should have preparatory training in the dynamics of
parent-teacher communication, but the more basic requirements are competence, quiet self-confidence, empathy, and acceptance."[16]

All participants can benefit from an honest, open, fully functioning com-
601 munication system. Two goals are basic:

1. Bringing about better understanding between teacher and parents of what children are like
2. Bringing about a better understanding between teacher and parents of what constitutes a worthwhile, fulfilling education

The schools need the parents' knowledge about children as seen in continuous patterns of growth, and the parents can gain from knowing about teachers' experiences with children in situations involving peers and learning challenges. For school and home to remain separate implies basic differences in their goals. Mutual listening with respect, not just hearing, will often reveal that "no fundamental conflict exists between the wishes of parents and those of teachers."[17] Acknowledgment of this and subsequent cooperation can bring about more consistent guidance and a richer, fuller, more nourishing life for students, both in school and out.

Where a traditional "hands-off" or "closed-door" policy still exists, it is up to the school to take the initiative in communicating with the community. This effort can consist of two complementary components:

1. Interpreting the existing school program
2. Developing the understanding and abilities of parents to give home educational support

How can parent-teacher conferences improve home-school communication and thus the child's educational program? How can the assistant teacher help in such discussions?

Interpreting the existing school program

There are several established procedures for interpreting the existing school program to parents, but they may need re-evaluation to determine whether they are working as well as they might. For most elementary schools the vehicles include parent-teacher conferences, parent visits to the school in session, parent-teacher organization meetings, informal social functions, and special visits. The following questions should help evaluate the effectiveness of each.

1. Parent-teacher conferences
   A. Have you developed a discussion format and sufficient conference time that you and parents are comfortable with and that enables you to accomplish satisfactory discussion closure?
   B. For reluctant parents, working parents, families with several children, or for other special situations, do you offer child care, evening conferences, additional telephone calls, or home visits to show your sincere concern for this type of communication?
   C. Do you include the child in the conference (intermediate grade children) or hold an individual child-teacher conference *prior* to the adult conference (primary children)?
2. Parent visits to school in session
   A. Do you make an obvious attempt to help parents feel welcome when they respond to a general invitation to visit classes? Do you have adult-sized chairs available, allow for a brief discussion or question period, extend an invitation for another day or a special period that may be of particular interest to them?
   B. Do you have sufficient confidence in your ability as a teacher to feel comfortable demonstrating before visitors?
3. Parent-teacher organization meetings
   A. Do both parents and teachers have a voice in choosing the topics and business to be discussed?
   B. Are the topics relevant to today's children, and are optional avenues provided in developing goals of the educational program?
4. Informal social functions
   A. Do the functions reflect the life styles and culture of the community?
   B. Do parents and teachers work together as people (not as members of two groups) and accept joint responsibility for an enjoyable, successful function?
5. Special visits (open house, back-to-school nights, scheduled home visitations)
   A. Is there visible evidence of positive accomplishment by each child in the room?
   B. Are the children given real responsibility during those functions they are allowed to attend?
   C. Are the children the primary conveyors of the invitations and messages concerning the functions?

603 Regarding all these activities, school staffs need to ask themselves:

1. Are parents and other community people made to feel that the school is a public place where all persons interested in the education of youth are welcome?
2. Are instructional concerns for children viewed as *our* concerns (teacher and parents), not *theirs* (parents) or *mine* (teacher)?
3. Are informal contacts with parents considered important to the total school program?
4. Is the present system of reporting or conferences (or both) the best means of sharing information of a student's educational progress with parents?

The above discussion covers most common means of communication, but many others can be added to fill gaps and to improve relationships. For example, some teachers find home visits to be an invaluable means of reaching out to parents in the community. With some groups it has been found that personal contacts are necessary to help parents understand the importance of their participation. One half-hour in the home can

Show a mother you are considerate of her responsibility to her other children

Possibly include both parents, instead of only one

Make you visible as a person in the community, not just a "teacher up at the school"

Offer you a wealth of information about the child which cannot be obtained elsewhere

Another idea employed by some schools is *open office hours* held by the principal at a scheduled time each week. Parents and other community people are welcome to stop by to express concerns and make suggestions or comments over coffee and doughnuts.[18] Other ideas can be tried in the attempt to bring all persons closer together in this educational effort.

Probably the most important carrier of information providing an image of the school is the *child himself*. His daily reports about what he did and how he feels about the school situation should not be underestimated. Whether he is consciously aware of it or not, the teacher plays an active role in this daily message. If a child feels satisfied after a day that included more successes than failure, he conveys one message to his family, through words, mood, and other means of expression. If he concludes a day feeling frustrated and without real accomplishment or worth, he delivers another message to his home that day.

Besides planning for the needs of individual children, a teacher can also show respect for parents' concerns about curriculum by sending brief notes when new subjects or expectations are introduced. The brevity of a note enables the child to supply details, but parents learn through repetition of this practice that the teacher considers their awareness of the current program important to their children's schooling. The self-fulfilling prophecy is employed here: positive expectations bring positive results, but failure to inform parents of new school activities and then not expecting them to care are self-fulfilling.

Developing the understanding and abilities of parents to provide educational support

The preschool years hold potential for a vast amount of learning. The school-age child spends more time at home than in school and often has a different teacher each year, so it is very important that school personnel develop a parent education program to benefit the younger siblings still at home and to provide some degree of consistency between home and school. This can be accomplished through a wide variety of direct and indirect ways, depending on the particular community and culture. Ideas to help parents become active participants in their children's learning experiences include the following.

ADULT EDUCATION OR EXTENSION COURSE WORK

Courses for parents, parents and teachers, or parents and children can add to parents' knowledge and experience in areas such as children's literature, child development, story telling, and alternatives for teaching reading, language development, and creative writing. One version of this is a Saturday workshop of experiences for parents and their children.[21]

PARENT-TEACHER INFORMAL, SPONTANEOUS DISCUSSIONS

Talks between parents and teachers can help parents understand the importance of using daily happenings to enrich the child's total development. By reading regularly to a child, listening to his descriptions of the day's events, becoming involved in his home projects, praising him for accomplishments more often than reprimanding him for faults, and providing a quiet time entirely his just before bedtime, a parent can offer considerable support to his child's educational development. This message needs to be conveyed strongly to parents, and is best accomplished individually during brief conversations.

If there is sufficient interest, a teacher can hold regular discussion sessions about daily living with children. A book group might evolve out of such concern. The school professional library should be made available to interested parents to help them understand educational practices and innovations. School specialists (nurse, speech therapist, guidance counselor) can also help the flow of information to parents, and can demonstrate the value of a team approach in meeting a wide range of student needs.

USE OF THE ROOM MOTHER ORGANIZATION

Traditionally room mothers have only been used for such tasks as collecting money, serving refreshments at class parties, and chaperoning field trips. The role can be a much more active one, if the teacher desires. A room mother can organize several kinds of parent participation for the classroom (including suggestions in this discussion). A teacher who is willing to share such responsibility merely needs to make that known, and volunteers for room mother will begin with these new role expectations. These individuals often have the time, talent, and perseverance to encourage reluctant parents who would remain home otherwise, unaware of their possible contribution to their children's education and the self-satisfaction such work can provide.

TEACHER-INITIATED PARENT EDUCATION

In addition to giving requested information and views, the teacher or other staff members can identify issues that should be brought to the attention of parents, through informal discussions, letters, courses, or scheduled meetings. As a part of the reading-language program, a teacher might wish to pose questions about

Television viewing (specials, "Sesame Street," "The Electric Company," "Misterogers")

Movies and live theater

Reading materials from libraries, bookstores, supermarkets (books, comics, children's magazines, records or tapes and text)

Birthday and holiday presents (appropriate to age level, possibilities for creating, learning)

Plans for rainy days, times of illness (bedtime stories—importance, choice, repetition, child participation)

DIRECT REQUESTS FOR INVOLVEMENT OF PARENTS

Parent participation can be developed by sending letters to all parents early in each school year enlisting their participation in special activities and asking them to identify any special hobby or skill they would be willing to demonstrate or share. Since a number of these activities are not a regular commitment, many busy parents can be enlisted to go on a field trip, assist in a neighborhood walk, or demonstrate a special skill. Here is a model letter for this purpose.

Dear [Parent]

[Express source of request: total school, group of classes, single class, specialist, librarian, etc.]

[Relevance at this time: initiating new program, continuing old one, starting new year, entering busy season]

As we begin our new school year, we would again like to invite the cooperation of our total community to offer the best possible educational program for our children. To do this, we need to know any specific ways you would be willing to offer time and effort to school activities.

If you are new to the school or wish to change or add to your responses from previous years, please fill out the following form and return it with your child. We need the assistance of all who enjoy and are willing to help in this kind of activity. Mothers, fathers, grandparents, and relatives are welcome.

--(tear here)--

I. I wish to participate at school
    (Designate preferred days and hours)

    M   T   W   Th   F   any

    a.m.   p.m.   _____
                                 certain hours

Comments:

Name(s) _____

Phone _____

Children at this school:

1. _____   _____
        (name)   (teacher)

2. _____   _____

I (we) would like to help at school performing:

1. Clerical tasks

    ____ typing

    ____ operating duplicating machines

    ____ making phone calls

    ____ collating, stapling, addressing

    ____ other

    ____ preparing materials, supplies

    ____ checking work

    ____ record-keeping

    ____ making games and puzzles

2. Classroom task, working directly with students

    ____ listening to children read

    ____ taking dictation of children's stories, poems, captions

    ____ going on short walks with children

    ____ going on field trips

    ____ assisting children as they do assigned work

    a. assisting a small group or individuals with a special project in:

        ____ arts or crafts

        ____ drama (plays, choral reading, puppets)

        ____ creative writing

____ music

____ literature

____ film-making or photography

____ sewing

____ cooking

____ special hobby, collection, or skill

____ other:

3. Other school tasks

____library assistance

____office assistance

    a. assistance to specialists

      ___nurse

      ___speech teacher

      ___reading specialist

      ___resource teacher

      ___welfare and attendance counselor

      ___guidance consultant

    b. assistance with large school projects

      ___fund raising

      ___carnival, fiesta (or similar event)

      ___student council

      ___student tutoring program

      ___school newspaper

    ____other:

II. I (we) would like to assist the school by helping at home to:

____ do clerical tasks

____ run errands for supplies and scrap materials

____ make phone calls

____ make games, puzzles, aids

____ collect home scrap materials

____ make things—puppets, bean bags, pillows, etc.

____ other:

_____ will be contacting you regarding the kind of assistance you have described. Thank you for your cooperation and support.

[Signed]

Responses to the letter can be recorded in a master card file or looseleaf
608   notebook called "Community Resources," and all teachers can refer to it

as specific needs arise. As mentioned in another section, such a program needs coordination to assure efficient use of volunteer resources and to benefit all involved.

INVOLVEMENT OF PARENTS FOR TASKS AT HOME

Many parents unable to participate during school hours are willing to perform supportive jobs at home. A teacher's beginning reading program can be enhanced by home-constructed word games and cards, sound-symbol picture cards, story cassette tapes, stapled paper booklets for written or picture stories, mounted photos ready for captions, sandpaper letters for tracing, characters cut of felt for flannel story boards, puppet characters for dramatization, songs and poetry printed or typed on dittoes or chart paper, and many other learning aids.

These materials can be made in the home at the parent's convenience. Parents frequently complete such a job within twenty-four hours, even if the teacher indicates no specific deadline or completion date. Most parents welcome the chance for the whole family to do something to help in tangible ways. When a child has a working mother and feels left out because other children get to experience this "sharing," such home involvement is an effective way to allow the family to make a contribution.

Another form of "out-of-school" task for parents is running errands to obtain supplies. If they are notified in advance, several mothers can, for instance, regularly collect and bring to school scrap supplies such as ice cream cartons, wood scraps from a cabinet maker, wall paper catalogues, carpet samples, and telephone wire. This frees a teacher's time for program planning and organizing for better instruction, and allows volunteers to make real contributions to the daily program. This option can be included in the parent letter already discussed. Parents who volunteer for errands should be listed in the master card file.

SPECIAL LIAISON PROGRAMS

Depending upon needs and interests, special activities can strengthen home-school cooperation. Three illustrations follow.

Photo Project

The child checks out a camera from school (perhaps an instamatic) and is instructed to enlist his family's help to take pictures according to criteria like: pictures to show some of your family activities, pictures to show what your neighborhood looks like to you, pictures to show your walk to school. Once developed the pictures are used as the core of a vital reading-language lesson such as: captions indicated or written by the child, a story with a sequence, part of a year-long scrapbook, a bulletin board display, an "It's About Me" reader.

"What Happens If" Projects

For readers beginning to gain independence, brief experiments can be written up (with rebus insertions if necessary) and taken home to be performed. Instructions to parents ask them to be active participants, with suggestions offered in reading or setting up the experiment. Experiments vary with age level, but might include such experiences as these.

What happens if:

Colored construction paper is left in direct sunlight for three days

One teaspoon of sugar mixed in three teaspoons of water is left in a shallow pan for five days

Radish seeds are placed in a dish on a paper towel that is kept very wet for seven days

Directions can be as detailed as desired or appropriate. Children return to school with the final materials and recorded results to share with others. There are many opportunities for reading-language development through written accounts, tape recordings of results, charts with pictures and labels to describe the sequence of events, and demonstrations and discussions by repeating the experiment for the class.

Story-Sharing Kits

A selection of three or four paperback books is packaged in a kit for children to check out for home use. The materials may be related, or they may instead offer a variety in reading or listening pleasure (fiction, poetry, factual material). They can be read by the student to the parents, by the parent to the student, by the parent to the student and other children in the family, or a combination of these. The kit can also contain suggested activities or experiences for optional use by the family while sharing these particular literature selections. For example, a kit containing *Curious George* by Rey, *Bread & Jam for Frances* by Hoban, and *Crictor the Boa Constrictor* by Tomi Ungerer might include the following suggestions.

1. Take a trip to a nearby zoo or museum, being sure to visit and observe the animals included in these stories. Discuss the actions and habits, and compare them to those of George, Frances, and Crictor.

2. Discuss or draw what you think George would do if he found a large box on the sidewalk. Why do you think he would do that? What would *you* do?

3. Carefully observe one animal several times (a pet in your home, a pet belonging to a neighbor, or an animal or bird that frequents your yard). In what ways did your animal behave like the story animals? In what ways were they different? Draw, write, or tell about it.

The suggestions, written separately on five-by-eight-inch cards, can be instructions to adults (as above), or worded for the child to read himself.

Both kinds might be advisable, to give the parent some independence, but also to give the parent certain responsibility as a teacher.

A regular procedure for feedback can be used (written comments by parents, verbal comments by children), or reaction can be left at an informal, spontaneous level, depending upon the children and parents involved.

How can this type of experience actively involve parents in their children's education? *(Photo by Fujihira, Monkmeyer Press Photo Service)*

DIRECT REQUEST FOR ASSESSMENT OR ASSISTANCE IN
EDUCATION PLANNING

The formulation of new programs often provides a natural opportunity for parent participation. Such topics as family life education and drug abuse are obvious examples, but the reading-language curriculum also offers opportunities for parent and teacher input to develop new programs or evaluate well-established ones. When parents and others from the community are involved, they develop appreciation for the effort and instructional conditions essential for a successful program.

An assessment technique recently developed by Robert Reasoner for use with parents, teachers, and administrators involves all persons in educa-

611

tional programming.[19] The system ranks thirty school activities (each on a separate three-by-five-inch card) in two categories, most important, and least important. Such an assessment can lead to (1) comparison of the stated value system with the existing school program, (2) reinforcement of certain present practices or programs and elimination of others, and (3) a search for models or innovations to fulfill unmet needs.

There are many innovative ways in which parents and other community members can be directly informed and involved in the educational program. These various avenues plus imaginative modifications and additions by teachers can provide means for all interested community members to contribute. The key factor is the communication effort and involvement program initiated by school personnel. The following questions designed by James Hymes will help the school staff assess its communication effort.

1. Is home-school relations in your school a two-way, give-and-take process?
   A. Are your various efforts balanced so that parents have as much opportunity to influence your thinking and action as you have to influence their behavior?
   B. Are you trying to sell parents some bill of goods: a way of living with children, your school's program, some facts you think they ought to know?
   C. Are you using home-school relations as a technique to put over to parents some pet ideas you have up your sleeve about children or education?
2. Does your school truly regard working with parents as important, or are home-school relations an incidental concern tacked on for appearances' sake? Has your school recognized the importance of this new area, for example, through any of the following:
   A. Providing time for home visits?
   B. Providing comfortable adult chairs in classrooms for parents?
   C. Providing you with more secretarial services so you can keep a record of your work with parents?
   D. Providing a conference room where teachers and parents can talk together?
3. Do you and your colleagues enjoy parents? Do you like working with them and feel comfortable doing it? Are you sympathetic with parents?
   A. Do you confine your relationships to the more or less "official" times—your group meetings, conferences, and so forth—or do you call parents up on the telephone, look forward to seeing them unexpectedly, chat freely with them?
   B. Do you have approximately the same number of relationships with all your parents, or do you find it easier to get along with certain types—the wealthier parents, the better educated ones?
   C. Do many parents make you feel impatient? Do you want to squelch those who dominate meetings, or give those a good shove who won't change their ways, or turn a deaf ear to those who always have a complaint?
4. Does your work with parents square with what you know about all good education?

612

A. Do you realize that there are causes that make parents act the way they do, just as there are causes that underlie the difficult behavior with which some children confront you?

B. Are you aware that parents are learning through all that happens to them, just as you know that children are continuously being educated not only by what you say but by what you do?

C. Do you try to search out and begin with the problems parents most keenly feel, whether or not these check with your notions of a good program?

D. Are you sensitive to individual differences in parents as much as you are to the spread of differences in children? Do you have variety in content and in ways of learning to take these differences into account?

E. Are your various programs for parents planned so that parents can study their problems until they work their way through to satisfying solutions?

F. Are your parents active in the solution of their own problems, or are pat answers handed to them on a silver platter?

5. Are you clear in your own mind that home-school relations ought to lead to continuously improving conditions for children, and not become a device whereby adults "gang up" on youngsters or a means for the preservation of the status quo?

A. Can you spot instances where you have further individualized your program because of information that has come through your work with parents?

B. Are you aware of ways in which your program has changed because parents have helped you to see new goals?

C. Has your classroom program for children become richer, more varied, and more extensive as a result of your relationship with parents?[20]

MATERIALS FOR TUTORS AND TEACHER ASSISTANTS

Besides the many publications and resources that teachers can offer and suggest to participating community persons, some authors have compiled special lists for tutors and teacher assistants.

SIDNEY J. RAUCH. *Handbook for the Volunteer Tutor* (Newark, Del.: International Reading Association, 1969).

Materials for volunteer tutors

Materials emphasizing word analysis skills, vocabulary development, spelling, listed by reading and interest levels

Materials emphasizing comprehension, pleasure, and interest, listed by reading and interest levels

Periodicals with suggestions for reading-language instruction

Published games and aids

Background reading in the field of teaching reading-language

Directory of publishers
Materials for adult basic education (pp. 86–106)

LENORE SLEISENGER, *Guidebook for the Volunteer Reading Teacher* (New York: Teachers College Press, 1965).

Controlled vocabulary series, titles, publishers, age levels, and content
Bibliographies helpful to the volunteer (pp. 46–47)

ALAN GARTNER, MARY KOHLER, and FRANK RIESSMAN, *Children Teach Children* (New York: Harper & Row, Publishers, 1971).

Extensive bibliography of books and articles on tutoring projects, materials, and research on the tutoring relationship
Films

BETTY ATWELL WRIGHT, *Teacher Aides to the Rescue* (New York: The John Day Co., 1969).

Discussion on selection of curriculum materials
List of basic books as adult resources for study and discussion

MARY LOU BROTHERSON and MARY ANN JOHNSON, *Teacher Aide Handbook* (Danville, Ill.: The Interstate Printers and Publishers, Inc., 1971).

Recommended reading list for teaching assistants on art, child development, education and our nation, language arts, mathematics training, and utilization of aides
Resources for pamphlets, periodicals, organizations, and addresses for informational materials
Sources and funds for the utilization and training of teacher aides
State administered programs (federal funds)
Nonstate administered programs (federal funds) (pp. 163–70, 183–84)

These publications identify materials for direct use by school assistants as well as materials for use by school personnel for purposes of inservice development. Educational organizations and local school districts are excellent sources for special treatment of many of the topics discussed in this chapter, such as parent conferences and home visits. The many projects, such as those listed in *Children Teach Children,* also list reports on the knowledge and experience gained from such projects.

SUMMARY

The advent of federal funding for educational programs and emphasis on the need for individualization in education have helped bring about the use of a variety of persons in the classroom. Acknowledgment of the impossibility of teaching children *all* important knowledge necessitates sorting out
614 that which is universally important—the ability to learn itself. All avail-

able resources must be tapped for this purpose. This is a deviation from the traditional image of education in this country. Involving the broader community can result in these changes:

> Parents and other adults work in the classrooms as volunteers.
>
> Older students tutor younger students as volunteers.
>
> Adults assist in the school as part of becoming credentialed teachers.
>
> Some classroom assistants who work regularly according to a job description are paid for their work.
>
> Parents more aware of the local school program can support it with home activities.
>
> Schools are revising curriculum commensurate with information about the community.
>
> Teachers turn to individualizing and personalizing students' programs, away from a major emphasis upon large-group instruction.

This new conception demands and builds upon effective home-school communication and involvement. Positive teacher attitude toward the presence of other people in the classroom is of central importance to the success of an extended staffing program. Before the installation of such a program, some teachers will need time to explore the implications of additional help. They should begin by examining their feelings about having other people in the room and acknowledging the advantages of extra hands and minds in providing for individual student needs on a daily basis. They must clearly identify long-term goals so they can plan and organize classroom activities for effective analysis of instructional needs. Then they can determine the resource help that will be of greatest value and develop a recruiting and training plan.

Since mutual benefits are possible from an expanded staffing program, it is important to plan and watch for opportunities where the giver and the receiver both profit from the experience as much as possible. If only the student (as receiver) is considered in planning and evaluating a program, much of the potential for self-insight, career development, and community relations and understandings will be missed.

In seeking personnel and designing the training program, it is necessary to define the desired competencies for various types of tutors and assistants. There will undoubtedly be certain competencies common to all personnel, such as those related to taking the responsibility for the job itself, and establishing rapport with students and other personnel. Whatever the general or specific competencies, the training plan must describe the means of achieving them. Four major development modes are suggested here: observation, discussion, simulation, and direct experience. The goal, the trainee, and time will help determine the mode or modes to employ in developing a specific competence.

How can community-school cooperation be established to enhance children's educational experiences? For such cooperation to be effective, what responsibility must be assumed by you, the teacher? By the tutor or teaching assistant? By the principal? By the parent?

A school with limited community involvement in the daily classroom program still needs effective school-home communication. Where a community involvement effort exists, communication is extremely important, since good communication provides the basis for establishing positive human relationships—the heart of the instructional and the school-community program. It is this communication system that interprets the existing school program to parents. Its components vary from school to school, but often include parent conferences, parent club meetings, open house, and special events.

A vitally important function of this system is development of a home support program, to team home and school to accomplish major instructional objectives. Additional means of communication may be designed especially to demonstrate the school's educational goals in terms of daily life, from informal discussions with parents to carefully detailed projects that require home-school participation.

Table 16-3 will be of value in estimating the degree to which a tutor and teaching assistant program is operating in your school. In addition to this kind of assessment, a staff might ask itself some of the following questions.

616

Table 16-3.

Assistance from the Community

1	2	3	4	5	6	7
Parents come to school *only* at scheduled structured times (meetings, etc.)	Occasional specific help in special areas or programs of the school: library, nurse, office, cafeteria, playground	Regular assistance in special areas of school: library, nurse, office, cafeteria, playground	Use of limited assistants in classroom for specific tasks or occasions	Use of regular assistants in classrooms for specific assistance and tutoring tasks	Use of regular assistants as tutors in specific areas and limited use of classroom assistants in general areas	Full-time program using trained classroom assistants and tutors, with a full-time employee as coordinator

Assistance from Within the School

1	2	3	4	5	6	7
No tutorial or clerical help	Occasional specific help (clerical, mechanical) office, library, a-v help	Regular assistance in clerical and mechanical tasks	Limited use of tutors for special activities or classes	Frequent use of tutors	Regular use of tutors	Full-time scheduled tutor program with coordinator

Has a need for community assistance been defined?

Has teacher attitude toward such a program been assessed?

Has the need been discussed in terms of the many alternative approaches possible with available personnel?

Has a training program been designed with a school staff person serving as coordinator?

Does that training program include

Training for the principal and all other personnel who wish to be included in the assistant program?

Recruiting and selecting procedure?

Specific training for each job description?

Feedback mechanisms for *all* involved?

Evaluation procedures?

There must be a time in the near future when the total community sees itself as an active and vital part of the local school. The instructional responsibility, however, must still reside with the teacher aided by coordinated support from many different community resource persons who possess a wide range of instructional abilities. The potential of such a school for meeting individual learning needs is vastly greater than a school operating on the one teacher/one class concept. An instructional program wherein the teacher is the key learning facilitator can more effectively identify individual learning needs and use tutors and teaching assistants to design an individualized curriculum based on these needs.

Footnotes

[1]Mary Lou Brotherson and Mary Ann Johnson, *Teacher Aide Handbook* (Danville, Ill.: The Interstate Printers and Publishers, Inc., 1971).

[2]Carda W. Bowman and Gordon V. Klopf, *New Careers and Roles in the American School* (New York: Bank Street College of Education, 1968), p. 219.

[3]U. S. Department of Health, Education, and Welfare, *Profile of ESEA, The Elementary and Secondary Education Act of 1965,* Titles I, II, III, IV, and V (Washington, D. C.: U. S. Government Printing Office, 1967), p. 3.

[4]Ibid.

[5]National Advisory Commission on Civil Disorders, *Report of the National Advisory Commission on Civil Disorders* (New York: Bantam Books, Inc., 1968).

[6]New Jersey Department of Education, *Planning Parent-Implemented Programs* (Trenton: New Jersey Department of Education, 1970).

[7]Brotherson and Johnson, *Teacher Aide Handbook,* p. 46.

[8]Ibid.

[9]Alan Gartner, Mary Kohler, and Frank Riessman, *Children Teach Children* (New York: Harper & Row, Publishers, 1971).

[10]Ibid., p. 2.

[11]Sylvia Sunderlin, *Aides to Teachers and Children* (Washington, D. C.: Association for Child Education International, 1968), p. 8.

618 [12]Lenore Sleisenger, *Guidebook for the Volunteer Reading Teacher* (New York: Columbia Uni-

versity Press, 1965). Sidney J. Rauch, ed., *Handbook for the Volunteer Tutor* (Newark, Del.: International Reading Association, 1969).

[13]Sunderlin, *Aides to Teachers and Children,* p. 40.

[14]Betty Atwell Wright, *Teacher Aides to the Rescue* (New York: The John Day Co., 1969), p. 54.

[15]*Parents-Children-Teachers: Communication,* Association for Childhood Education International Bulletin No. 28-A (Washington, D. C.: Association for Childhood Education International, 1969), p. 46.

[16]James L. Hymes, Jr., *Effective Home-School Relations* © 1953, p. 60. Reprinted by permission of Prentice-Hall, Inc., Englewood Cliffs, New Jersey.

[17]Ibid.

[18]Sunderlin, *Aides to Teachers and Children.*

[19]Robert Reasoner, *Instructional Goal Cards* (Concord, Calif.: RWR Educational Publishers, 1971).

[20]Hymes, *Effective Home-School Relations,* pp. 229–31. Reprinted by permission of Prentice-Hall, Inc., Englewood Cliffs, New Jersey.

Additional References

BADGER, EARLADEEN D., "A Mother's Training Program: The Road to a Purposeful Existence," *Children* (September–October 1971), pp. 168–73.

CHAMPAGNE, DAVID W., and RICHARD M. GOLDMAN, *Teaching Parents Teaching* (unpublished manuscript from Urban Education Series, 1970).

Conference Time for Teachers and Parents. Washington, D. C.: National School Public Relations Association, NEA, 1961.

FUSCO, DR. GENE C., *Improving Your School–Community Relations Program.* Englewood Cliffs, N.J.: Prentice-Hall, Inc., 1967.

GALLUP, GEORGE, *Guidebook for Parents.* Dayton, Ohio: Institute for the Development of Educational Activities, Inc., 1970.

GARTNER, ALAN, MARY KOHLER, and FRANK RIESSMAN, "Every Child a Teacher," *Childhood Education* (October 1971), pp. 12–16.

HARRISON, RAYMOND, *The Selection, Orientation, and Use of Teacher Aides.* Fresno, Calif.: GW School Supply, 1967.

LURIE, ELLEN, *How to Change the Schools: A Parents' Action Handbook on How to Fight the System.* New York: Random House, Inc., 1970.

MALLERY, DAVID, *Beyond All Those Books.* Boston: National Association of Independent Schools, 1965.

NATIONAL ADVISORY COMMISSION ON CIVIL DISORDERS, *Report of the National Advisory Commission on Civil Disorders.* New York: Bantam Books, Inc., 1968.

Parents Are Needed, Project Head Start. Washington, D. C.: Office of Economic Opportunity, 1966.

Parents-Children-Teachers: Communication, Association for Childhood Education International Bulletin No. 28-A. Washington, D. C.: Association for Childhood Education International, 1969.

Parent Involvement: A Workbook of Training Tips for Head Start Staff. Washington, D. C.: Department of Health, Education and Welfare, 1969.

PERKINS, DR. BRYCE, *Getting Better Results from Substitutes, Teacher Aides, and Volunteers.* Englewood Cliffs, N.J.: Prentice-Hall, Inc., 1966.

Planning Parent-Implemented Programs. Trenton, N.J.: New Jersey Department of Education, 1969.

"A Question of Relationships." New York: National School Volunteer Program, Inc. (a pamphlet, 1970).

SMITH MILDRED B., *The Parent's Role in Children's Success.* Glenview, Ill.: Scott, Foresman and Company, 1971.

U. S. DEPARTMENT OF HEALTH, EDUCATION AND WELFARE, *Staffing for Better Schools.* Washington, D. C.: U. S. Government Printing Office, 1967.

VAN WESSEM, KATHERINE, *A Tutoring Program: The Second Year.* St. Ann, Mo.: Central Midwestern Regional Educational Laboratory, Inc., 1968.

Volunteer ABC's: A Handbook for School Volunteer Programs, an adaptation of National School Volunteer Program, Inc., material. Washington, D. C.: Department of Health, Education and Welfare, Office of Education, 1969.

Working with Parents. Washington, D. C.: National School Public Relations Association, NEA, 1968.

Criteria for Evaluating Reading Systems

The following criteria represent a wide range of critical factors in an instructional reading system. These criteria should be applied to the child's materials, the teacher's instructional materials, the supplementary instructional aids, the inservice professional development program, and the parent participation program. Space is also provided for your reaction to each major area. Where possible provide page references for the child's text, the teacher's materials, the supplementary aids, the inservice training program, and the parent participation program as you illustrate significant evaluation points. You should complete an evaluation page for each level of the reading system (vertical) and make an overall reaction to the entire system. Be sure to examine all dimensions of the evaluation criteria before you initiate the analysis. This will facilitate reaction, because several criteria overlap.

Name of System _____

Publisher _____

Address _____

Copyright date _____

Senior Author _____

Author of this level _____

Title of this level: Child's text _____

                Skill book _____

Level (circle appropriate level):   1. Early Childhood (Age 3, 4)

                                 Kindergarten (Age 5)

2. Grade 1, Grade 2, Grade 3

3. Grade 4, Grade 5, Grade 6

I. Skill Development and Content

	Poor				Excellent
A. Language-based approach	1	2	3	4	5

    1. Use of oral language

        a. Concept development

        b. Story development

        c. Oral expression

    2. Development of entering behavior

        a. Ability to follow directions, etc.

        b. Attention span

        c. Classroom labels and concepts

    3. Language experiences and reading

        a. Language as a symbol system

        b. Writing representing oral language

        c. Social class dialects

        d. Functional nature of language

        e. Power of language

    4. General reaction to language-based approach

	Poor				Excellent
B. Decoding skills	1	2	3	4	5

    1. Auditory perception

        a. Sounds (rhyme, nonrhyme, initial consonants, medial consonants, final consonants)

        b. Sound patterns (same as above)

        c. Words in context of sentence or story (same as above)

    2. Visual discrimination

        a. Letters (minimal pairs, initial, medial, final)

        b. Letter patterns (same)

        c. Words (same)

    3. Sound-symbol correspondences

        a. Vowels (which, where introduced)

        b. Consonants (which, where introduced)

        c. Blends

        d. Digraphs

    4. Letter patterns

        a. CVC (which, where introduced)

        b. CVCe (same)

        c. Other

    5. Words (structural analysis)

        a. Base (isolated, context)

        b. Prefixes

        c. Suffixes

        d. Compounds

6. Picture and sentence context

    a. Content words

    b. Function words

    c. Discourse beyond sentence

7. Logic of sequence of decoding program

    a. Obvious—research base

    b. Obvious—internal logic of sequence

    c. Not obvious

8. Strategy of presentation

    a. Inductive

    b. Deductive

    c. Combination (if so how oriented)

9. General reaction to decoding program

	Poor				Excellent
C. Comprehension and problem solving	1	2	3	4	5

1. Emphasis on levels: Factual % _____, Interpretive % _____, Applicative % _____

2. Factual level

    a. Estimate percentage of following

    % subskill—details _____, sequence _____, cause and effect _____, main idea _____, predicting outcome _____, valuing _____, problem solving _____

    b. General reaction

3. Interpretive level

    a. Estimate percentage of following

    % subskill—details _____, sequence _____, cause and effect _____, main idea _____, predicting outcome _____, valuing _____, problem solving _____

    b. General reaction

4. Applicative level

    a. Estimate percentage of following

    % subskill—details _____, sequence _____, cause and effect _____, main idea _____, predicting outcome _____, valuing _____, problem solving _____

    b. General reaction

5. Questioning strategies

    a. Estimate percentage of following

    % type—focusing _____, controlling _____, extending _____, clarifying _____, raising _____

    b. General reaction

6. General reaction to comprehension

	Poor				Excellent
D. Study and research skills	1	2	3	4	5

1. Location of information

    a. Book parts (title, table of contents, etc.)

    b. General reference (use of dictionary, encyclopedia, card catalog, directories, classified newspaper, etc.)

2. Reading for information
    a. Skimming (main idea)
    b. Scanning (particular source)
    c. Intensive reading (difficult concepts, style differences)
3. Organization of information (classification, outlining, summarizing information, synthesizing information)
4. Interpretation of information (maps, charts, diagrams, pictures, time lines, cartoons, photographs)
5. Reading in content areas
    a. Math
    b. Science
    c. Social studies
6. General reaction to study and research skills

E. Literature as response—attitudes   Poor   Excellent
    toward reading, self, and others   1   2   3   4   5

1. Selections make provision for
    a. Affective dimensions
        (1) Joy of language (selections entertain, excite, persuade, stressing combinations of words)
        (2) Appreciation of beauty (selections isolate, magnify, contrast "pieces of life" and nature for observation)
    b. Cognitive dimensions
        (1) Insight into behavior of self (explanation and causes)
        (2) Awareness of people, events, and ideas not available to our own environment (social variation, cultural variation—new experiences)
        (3) Awareness of man and self as part of changing world (expectation for change)
        (4) Awareness of potential of language as means of human expression (skillful use of imagery, drama, humor, pathos)
    c. General reaction

2. Provision for range of literary   Poor   Excellent
    experiences   1   2   3   4   5
    a. Prose
        (1) Fiction
            (a) Realism
                [1] Historical (*Island of Blue Dolphins, Ishi—Last of His Tribe*)
                [2] Modern (*And Now Miguel, The Hundred Dresses*)
            (b) Fantasy
                [1] Traditional (folk tales, fairy tales, fables, myths, legends)
                [2] Modern (*Winnie the Pooh, Charlotte's Web*)

624

(2) Nonfiction

    (a) Biography (*American Heritage, Breakthrough Books*)

    (b) Informational (*I Like Caterpillars*)

b. Poetry (range of content, imagery, rhyme)

    (1) Lyric ("Fireflies," rhythmic style, like that to be sung)

    (2) Narrative ("There Once Was a Puffin," tells a story)

    (3) Free verse ("A Moonlight Night," strong imagery and expresses emotion, not governed by rules of rhyme or rhythm)

c. Rhyme and verse (not considered literature in the parallel to information books; part of folklore, however, e.g., "Hickory, Dickory, Dock," "Eletelephony")

d. General reaction

3. Provision for complete literary selections (versus part of selection)

          Poor   Excellent
          1   2   3   4   5

a. Fiction

b. Nonfiction

c. Poetry

4. To what extent are the following questioning strategies used in achieving the previously identified *affective* dimensions (E, 1, a.)

a. Clarifying

b. Extending

c. Raising

5. To what extent are the following questioning strategies used in achieving the previously identified *cognitive* dimensions (E, 1, b.)

a. Extending

b. Clarifying

c. Raising

6. Are supplementary literature selections recommended

a. Range

b. Quality

7. Does the system have supplementary paperback books available to accompany this level

8. To what extent do the literary selections reflect various socio-ethnic groups (black, Oriental, white, Chicano, for example)

9. To what extent do the literary selections reflect other nationalities and other countries

10. General reaction to Literature Selections and Instructional Treatment

          Poor   Excellent

F. The author's craft   1   2   3   4   5

1. To what extent are the following dimensions of the writer's craft reflected in the instructional program

a. Character development (indirectly, dialogue, first-person, third-person narrative)

b. Author's style (description, symbolism, contrast, dialogue, flashback, foreshadowing, humor, language)

c. Plot development (introduction, action develops, climax, action falls, ending; problem, plans for solution, outcome)

d. Mood, setting

2. To what extent is provision made for understanding similarities and differences between realistic fiction, modern fiction; traditional fantasy, modern fantasy; fiction and fantasy; fiction and nonfiction; poetic forms—lyric, narrative, free verse

3. What provision is made for the pupil to participate in creating literary forms

4. General reaction to author's craft

	Poor			Excellent	
G. Evaluation	1	2	3	4	5

1. To what extent are criterion reference tests or some variation of such tests used to determine pupil progress on a frequent basis (at least weekly)

2. What instructional provision is present after problem has been identified

a. Word recognition
b. Comprehension
c. Study skills
d. Other

3. Are placement (informal reading) inventories provided with the program

a. What form are these in (taken from child's literary selection? other?)
b. What range of skills is covered (see B, C, and D)

4. Are achievement tests provided with the program

a. Can these be used in a diagnostic fashion
b. What range of skills is covered (see B, C, and D)

5. What provision is made for grouping and individual differences in the system

6. General reaction to evaluation

II. Describe the major components of the reading system (identified A through F below) in terms of

Organization and format

Use of illustrations and type

Levels of interest and variety

Ease of use from an instructional viewpoint

	Poor			Excellent	
A. Child's Anthology	1	2	3	4	5

	Poor			Excellent	
B. Child's Skill Booklet	1	2	3	4	5

	Poor			Excellent	
C. Teacher's Manual	1	2	3	4	5

	Poor			Excellent	
D. Instructional Aids	1	2	3	4	5

1. Basic
2. Supplementary

	Poor			Excellent	
E. Inservice Training Materials	1	2	3	4	5

	Poor			Excellent	
F. Parent Participation Program	1	2	3	4	5

III. Instructional approach: Describe the instructional approach (inductive, deductive, combination) which is present in the following materials

	Poor			Excellent	
A. Child's Anthology	1	2	3	4	5

	Poor			Excellent	
B. Child's Skill Booklet	1	2	3	4	5

	Poor			Excellent	
C. Teacher's Manual	1	2	3	4	5

	Poor			Excellent	
D. Supplementary Instructional Aids	1	2	3	4	5

	Poor			Excellent	
E. Inservice Training Program	1	2	3	4	5

	Poor			Excellent	
F. Parent Participation Program	1	2	3	4	5

IV. Identify the outstanding characteristics of the total reading system based on the previous analysis information

A. Child's Anthology

B. Child's Skill Booklet

C. Teacher's Manual

D. Supplementary Instructional Aids

E. Inservice Training Program

F. Parent Participation Program

V. Identify the weaknesses of the total system based on the previous analysis information

A. Child's Anthology

B. Child's Skill Booklet

C. Teacher's Manual

D. Supplementary Instructional Aids

E. Inservice Training Program

F. Parent Participation Program

Author Index

Subject Index

Achievement testing, 525–31
Acting out, 176–81
Activities, 566–68
Administrative plans, 113, 555–58
Affective development
  and communication, 36–37
  and environment, 160–62
  through literature programs, 455–503, *cf.*
    489–91
  mobilizers in, 36, 100
  and reading readiness, 308–9
  and skill adequacy, 493
Affective learning, instruction for, 364–69
Affective responses, and cultural frame of
  reference, 264–65
Almanacs and yearbooks, 419–20
Alphabet
  history of, 62–64
  Initial Teaching Alphabet (I/T/A), 120
  manuscript, 257–61
Alphabet books, 460
Alphabetical ordering, 411–14
Announcements, preparation of, 244,
  254–55
Applicative level, 364, 379–99
Art forms, expression through, 212–21
Atlases, 419–20
Attitudes, 36
  and positive interest development,
    132–36
Audience awareness, 169–71, 200–201
Auditory discrimination. *See also* Hearing
  and reading readiness, 313–18
Auditory perception, 508
Austin-Morrison study, 10
Author's craft, evaluation criteria of,
  625–26

Biography, 468–69
Body signals, 31–33

"Body talk," 310
Book parts, 410–11
Books, children's. *See* Literature, children's

Cambridge Plan, 556
Cartoons, 437–38
Catharsis, 456
Characters, describing, 185–88
Charts, classroom, 440–43
Chinese, as second language, 264, 276–78,
  279
*Civil Disorders, Report of National
  Commission on* (1968), 580
Classification and ordering, 361–408
  passim, 430–31
Classroom, physical organization of,
  571–75
Classroom assistants. *See* Teacher aides
Clymer-Barrett Prereading Battery, 318
"Cognitive commerce," 365–66
Cognitive development
  language-influenced, 366–67
  through literature, 457
  through literature programs, 492–93
  and question strategies, 366–69
  and reading readiness, 308–9
Cognitive strategy, 35–37, 295–96, 308–9
Communication
  and affective environment, 36–37
  competence and performance essentials,
    83–85
  dialect and second language instruction
    priorities, 266–67
  functional variety levels, 100–102
  and instructional environment, 523
  instructional goals in, 148
  interests, attitudes, values, 149
  listening and speaking rights, 242–44
  school–community, 11, 601–13
  speech interaction routines, 239–50

634